Physical Education

Foundations
Practices
Principles

The Joy of Effort—One of the most famous of the many sculptural masterpieces of R. Tait McKenzie, a physician, artist, scientist, author, and physical educator who held important positions at McGill University and the University of Pennsylvania. His many masterpieces are found in several institutions in Canada and the United States. The one pictured above now hangs in the Carlisle Foyer of Alumni Hall, Springfield College. (Courtesy of Springfield College.)

Physical Education

Foundations

Practices

Principles

Reuben B. Frost
Buxton Professor, Emeritus
Springfield College

Addison-Wesley
Publishing Company
Reading, Massachusetts
Menlo Park, California
London • Amsterdam
Don Mills, Ontario • Sydney

This book is in the
ADDISON-WESLEY SERIES IN PHYSICAL EDUCATION

Copyright © 1975 by Addison-Wesley Publishing Company, Inc.
Philippines copyright 1975 by Addison-Wesley Publishing Company, Inc.

Library of Congress Catalog Card No. 74–10351.

ISBN 0-201-02107-2
ABCDEFGHIJ-HA-798765

To all my
former and present students,
who have taught me so much,
and who have made
my life's work
worthwhile.

Preface

The author, after nearly half a century coaching, teaching, and administering physical education programs, is eager to continue sharing with students past and present ideas and theories both old and new. It is essential that those who are young and those who are older learn from each other and temper each other's thinking. As John Silber said,

> The old, with their wisdom and earthbound experience, are necessary correctives to the soaring fantasy, untested idealism, and despair of youth. But the intensity, idealism, and despair of youth are equally needed correctives to the pragmatism, cynicism, and pallor of age. It is important, desperately important, that we accept our youth for their idealism and that they accept us for our experience.*

This book, dedicated to former and present students throughout the world, was planned and written as a textbook and as a reference book. It is intended to serve those who are looking forward to careers in physical education and related areas, those who are helping to prepare teachers for these fields, and those who are already at work coaching, teaching, and conducting programs.

With societal changes appearing one after another on the horizon, with the constantly increasing speed of the technological revolution, and with the foundations of our value systems and our very existence shaken to the roots, it is important that we in the physical education profession contribute as best we can to the adaptability and copeability which are so needed, to the strength and endurance which are becoming increasingly essential, and to the quality of life which will help make all our endeavors worthwhile. To accomplish this is the larger purpose of this book.

Readers will find here the theoretical and the factual, the philosophical and the pragmatic, the ideal and the real. The past and the future, the how and the why,

---

*John R. Silber, "The Pollution of Time," *Bostonia,* September 1971, p. 14.

and the prosaic and the imaginative are included. Discussion of the high drama of athletics, the serenity of mountain climbing, and the objectivity of body mechanics are all to be found here.

The book begins with a modest review of some philosophical foundations for education and for life. Meanings and purposes of physical education and related fields are next explored. Historical foundations set the stage for what the future may hold.

Pertinent scientific facts and principles, drawn from the disciplines of philosophy, biology, physics, psychology, and sociology comprise the middle portion of the book. Anatomical and physiological bases for movement and exercise, biomechanical principles governing physical activity, theories of motivation and personality, and the relationships of society and sports are included in this section.

The second half of the book deals with practical matters. Programs of physical education, recreation, and athletics are described and explained. Health education, the development of fitness, the building of value systems, and community dynamics are examined. Teaching methods and practices, careers in physical education, and the vagaries of administration are explored.

Here under one cover is a cross-section of the concepts and subject-matter areas which form the theoretical framework for physical education. It is hoped that it will serve as a source of information, insight, and inspiration to those who contemplate physical education as a career.

The author wishes to acknowledge with sincere appreciation those individuals, institutions, and publishers who furnished and gave permission for the use of photographs and written materials. Gratitude is also expressed to the many persons with whom the author discussed various aspects of the book and who willingly gave their insights and experiences. Special mention must be made of my many Doctoral Seminars and other professional classes where we discussed these topics so freely and fully.

To my wife, Jean, I express my love and thanks. She typed the manuscript and shared with me its editing and preparation for the publishers.

Springfield, Massachusetts   R.B.F.
November 1974

Contents

Education
for a
Better World

Chapter 1

1.1 THE SUBSTRUCTURE

Good foundations make good buildings. Footings which are deep and durable prevent the foundations from buckling and furnish the strength which enables the structure to withstand the ravages of time and the pressures of destructive forces from within and without.

The stability, resilience, permanence, and vitality of our democracy depends in a large measure on the quality, relevance, and significance of our educational programs. Education and its offshoot, physical education, are *for* life, are *part of* life, and are *lifelong.* They permeate and influence our actions, our thoughts, and our experiences. If they are to enhance the quality and increase the quantity of life for all people, education and physical education must rest on a firm and solid foundation.

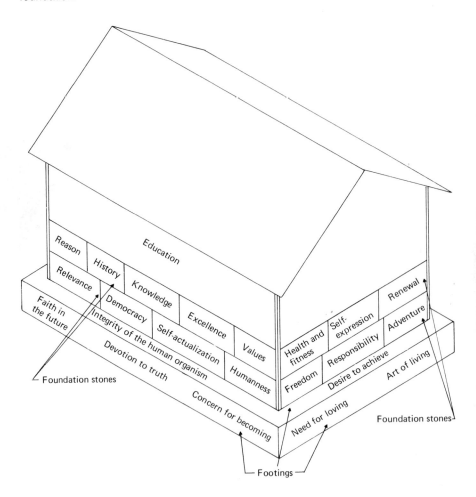

Undergirding education's foundation must be carefully designed footings containing the right mixture of essential ingredients painstakingly forged by master workmen. See Figure 1.1. Each foundation stone must be fitted into its proper position, adjusted to support and be supported by its counterparts, and integrated into the whole, culminating in a complete and functional structural pattern. To be secure, this structure must be joined to a solid base. Footings reaching deep into the wisdom of the past and tested in the fires of experience provide this solidarity.

1.2 EDUCATIONAL FOOTINGS

If our educational system is to achieve its goals and maintain a positive influence on the quality of life in our society, there are certain basic elements which must undergird our planning and our programs. For purposes of analogy let us call these *footings.* The seven footings presented are (1) faith in the future, (2) devotion to truth, (3) concern for becoming, (4) desire to achieve, (5) need for loving, (6) integrity of the human organism, and (7) the art of living.

✳ Faith in the future (*1*)

The entire concept of education is based on the premise that it is possible for people to teach and learn certain basic truths, fundamental skills, and modes of behavior which will lead to a better world. Essential to a conviction in the worthwhileness of education are the beliefs that good can conquer evil, behavior can be modified so as to produce better citizens, coming generations can learn from the events and lessons of the past, and individuals in the future can be stronger and better than they are today.

If truly great things are to be accomplished, a person must believe in himself, his fellow man, the future, and the strength of a Supporting Power. Without faith one does not have the courage to attempt new and challenging tasks or to embark on dangerous journeys. As has been said, "Education is a journey, not a destination." It becomes obvious, then, that *faith* is one of the essential ingredients of education. Faith on the part of administrators, parents, teachers and pupils must be nurtured if schools are to fulfill their important role in the world of today and tomorrow.

✳ Devotion to truth (*2*)

A deep concern for truth should pervade the thoughts and actions of those guiding our educational efforts. Present knowledge must be carefully scrutinized while the search for new discoveries continues. Errors in current thinking and present prac-

◀ **Figure 1.1 Foundations and footings.** Education, to be worthwhile, must be undergirded by a sound foundation based on strong and lasting footings.

4

"Men seek to discover truth in many different ways." (*Top left:* courtesy of Springfield College; *others:* courtesy of South Dakota State University.)

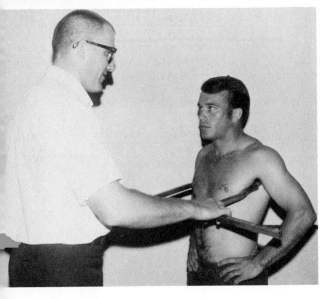

tices should be noted and eliminated and newly found truths disseminated with the least possible delay. Principles guiding our lives are self-defeating if they are not based on truth. Research findings and conclusions are invalid if the evidence is false. An attitude of trust between people is impossible without a solid foundation of truthful communication. A high regard for truth is our obligation as the search for new discoveries continues and as the wisdom of the past is inherited by future generations.

Men seek to discover truth in many different ways. Some are rational in nature, some are experiential, and others combine various methods and techniques. Many disciplines become involved in serious search for what is true and what is false. In a pamphlet published by the Educational Policies Commission, the following statement appears:

> In his efforts to understand the world and to control it for his benefit, man has used many methods. He has accepted as truth—or at least as a basis sufficient for action—the insights of seers, prophets, artists, scientists, and men of practical experience. Some truths have been taken to be revealed; some have been gleaned through common sense; some have been created by intuitive processes; some have been discovered by rational inquiry. Education has traditionally given credit to all these approaches. [15, p. 1]

The discovery of new truths is a tedious and often painful task. The sorting of truth from falsehood is equally difficult. As scientists and educators continue to discover and piece together bits of truth, we can hope that everyone involved will continue to employ integrity in their interpretations, utilize all available resources in the quest, and do everything in their power to shorten the time between the discovery of new facts and concepts and their application. All who aspire to the high calling of teaching must indeed be devoted to truth.

Concern for becoming (3)

As children attend school, as young people go to class, as adolescents interact with their parents, and as all men learn from life itself, education is taking place. During all such processes the individual is *becoming.* He is becoming older, wiser, bigger, more skillful, stronger or weaker, more rigid or more understanding, more anxious or more serene. As each day passes, every person changes in subtle and imperceptible ways. Except for those who are extremely handicapped, people are constantly growing, maturing, learning, and developing. Each is, in his own way, *becoming.*

When all teachers perceive as their goal the assisting of individuals in their efforts to become that which they are capable of becoming and that which they were intended to become, and when these teachers see the subject matter and their own efforts as a means to that end, education will have taken a giant step toward maturity. *Physical education,* then, must be considered as one aspect of becoming.

* Desire to achieve (4)

Unless students *desire* to learn and achieve, there is little probability that any substantial progress toward becoming will be made. Motivation is required to initiate and energize action. The satisfaction of needs reinforces behavior and influences future acts. Overcoming obstacles strengthens the individual for future tasks and engenders feelings of satisfaction which follow success. The intensity with which one aspires determines the amount of energy an individual will give to accomplishing a task.

"As education proceeds, each person changes in subtle and imperceptible ways—each is, in his own way, *becoming*." (Courtesy of the *Journal of Health, Physical Education, and Recreation*.)

Within the hearts of most people there exists a deep desire for self-fulfill-ment. Each person possesses to a greater or lesser degree a need to realize his potential, reach upward, become that which he was destined to be, and achieve the goals he has set for himself. Whether we call it ambition, a yearning for knowledge, a need for self-realization, or nostalgia for the future, there must be a deep desire to learn and improve on the part of both those being taught and those doing the teaching if education, as we know it, is to accomplish its mission.

Need for loving (5)

"My grandfather is a kind man who lives in a house where I get an old-time feeling and gladness all around me." [39] This answer, given by little Anita in response to the question, "What is a grandfather?" contains the core of what loving is all about and why it is so important in education. When one person feels "gladness all around" because he is with another, the probability is great that real love is present. The atmosphere described so delightfully in Anita's answer portrays quite accurately the spirit which should pervade classrooms, especially those where physical education is being taught. The answer also suggests an attitude of mutual trust which is urgently needed in our schools as well as in all facets of our society. Where this trust is present, there is no fear to ask questions, no hesitation to voice doubtful answers, no anxiety of being laughed at, and no trepidation at the pros-pect of possible failure. There is a feeling of partnership and "we-ness" that indicates both the student and the teacher are engaged in a mutually happy and beneficial enterprise.

"There is a feeling of partnership and 'we-ness' that indicates both the student and the teacher are engaged in a mutually happy and beneficial enterprise." (Courtesy of Springfield College.)

Love implies respect and esteem for the other person. Where this exists there will be no vindictiveness, no desire for revenge, no attempt to humiliate an opponent, and no intentional injury to another person. There will be respect for the dignity of each individual, an attitude of helpfulness and good sportsmanship, and an honest attempt to see things through another's eyes. There will be fairness, impartiality, and a serious effort to accept a person for what he is and what he can do. There will be an absence of bigotry and prejudice and, as much as possible, an avoidance of stereotyping. With an honest effort to achieve such goals, the quality and effectiveness of education cannot help but improve. Truly, man has a deep need to love and be loved.

Integrity of the human organism (6)

Integrity implies wholeness, soundness, completeness, entirety, and perfection. The integrity of the human organism refers to the reciprocal interrelationships between all its components as each affects and is affected by the others. The unity of all parts and the perfection of the whole is also acknowledged.

In education we must realize that the individual is affected as a totality by all experiences. The student is a whole person and as such is affected by the teacher's methods, mannerisms, and attitudes as well as by the course content and total environment. The whole person is taught and the whole person learns. The behavior of the student can only be observed as the total organism moves and acts. (This concept will be developed in greater detail in Chapter 8.)

The art of living (7)

> Man struggles to find life outside of himself, unaware that the life he is seeking is within him.
>
> —Kahlil Gibran

How futile are all the other facets of education if one knows too little about the full and satisfying life! The search for such a life is an all-encompassing, never-ending quest which demands constant attention, time, and dedication. The recipe is never perfect and successes are sprinkled with failures. What appears to be an excellent prescription for one person may not be so for another. Education which does not attempt to achieve the full and satisfying life is sterile and doomed to ultimate failure. Physical education and recreation can make vital contributions to the art of living.

Stuart Chase, in an article entitled "Are You Alive," describes an ascending scale of values containing a line below which man merely *exists* and above which he *lives*. He then goes on to list states of being in which he feels he is alive:

"I seem to live when I am creating something."
"Art vitalizes me."
"The mountains and the sea and the stars . . . renew
  life in me."
"Love is life, vital and intense."
"I live when I am stimulated by good conversation."

"I live when I am in the presence of danger—rock climbing, for example."—Stuart Chase
(Courtesy of the *Journal of Health, Physical Education, and Recreation.*)

"I live when I am in the presence of
   danger—rock climbing, for example."
"I feel very much alive in the presence
   of genuine sorrow."
"I live when I play—preferably out of doors."
"One lives when one takes food after
   genuine hunger, or when burying one's
   lips in a cool mountain spring after a long climb."
"One lives when one sleeps."
"I live when I laugh—spontaneously and heartily." [6, pp. 5–7]

We could all make out similar lists. There are those who feel completely alive when arriving at the top of a mountain. The exhilaration of achievement and the glorious view from the top are memories which linger. Some feel very much alive when in the throes of intense competition in basketball, tennis, badminton, or baseball. Skiing down a snowy slope, skating on a glassy lake, canoeing in the quiet of the evening, or landing a fighting game fish make others feel as if they are truly alive.

Living includes sharing. The pleasures of traveling and reviewing one's adventures are greatly enhanced when the experiences are shared. The comradeship engendered when two people take a canoe trip into the wilderness does not soon wear off. The experience of shared achievement on the part of team members when they win a meaningful victory may never be forgotten. The friendships that are formed when people share adventure, danger, sorrow, or joy often last a lifetime.

The art of living must include the adherence to sound principles of healthful living. Those who have experienced true "fitness" know the joy of just being alive. For this there is also a price. Self-discipline, hard work, and a good deal of perseverance are necessary if one is to know the zest and vitality that accompany "high-level wellness."

There are many expressions of a philosophy of life which lead to self-realization and self-fulfillment. Each person needs to work out his own. It becomes clear that one of the tasks of a complete education is to develop a life pattern which is satisfying and meaningful. The following paragraph, written by Robert Louis Stevenson, is suggestive:

That man is a success who has lived well, laughed often, and loved much; who has gained the respect of intelligent men and the love of children; who has filled his niche and accomplished his task; who leaves the world better than he found it, whether by an improved puppy, a perfect poem or a rescued soul; who never lacked appreciation of earth's beauty or failed to express it; who looked for the best in others and gave the best he had. [53, p. 94]

Man has a need to discover the meaningful life and learn where he fits into the scheme of things. He needs to know what is true and significant for him as an individual. The search for identity, the search for meaning, and the discovery and acceptance of one's role in life are important aspects of education. Physical education experiences can be helpful in this quest.

1.3 FOUNDATION STONES

On the firm and lasting base provided by the footings described above, there are foundation stones upon which the structure of education must rest. Learning and knowledge alone will not suffice. Wisdom is the goal. Knowing the sources and the right use of knowledge, possessing the ability to see things in proper perspective, having the good judgment to know the real value of things both tangible and intangible—these are elements of true wisdom. That person is both educated and wise who recognizes his limitations, who finds happiness within himself, who is concerned about and appreciates people of all walks of life, who is conscious of the continuing need to learn, and who is searching for quality rather than mere quantity of life. Education has many foundation stones, some of which are listed and briefly described below.

Reverence for history /.3/

Not to know what has been transacted in former times is to be always a child. —If no use is made of the labors of the past ages, the world must remain always in the infancy of knowledge.

—Cicero

These words written centuries ago are equally applicable today. It would be a pity if every generation needed to start again from the beginning and learn everything in the same painstaking and elementary way that was necessary in the dim, distant past. This applies not only to scientific and technological knowhow but also to the things we should know to get along with people and live the good life.

We learn from the past in order to interpret the present and plan for the future. For if there is a key to the future, it must be found in the records of the past and the occurrences of the present. As H. G. Wells said, "A sense of history as the common adventure of all mankind is as necessary for peace within as it is for peace between the nations." [56, p. vi] Truly, reverence for history is important in education.

Concern for relevance /.32

While a knowledge and appreciation of history is important, education has little significance if it does not take on meaning for the present and the future. If we listen to the voices of those in our schools and give some heed to what they are saying, certainly the most obvious and consistent complaint is the lack of relevance of many experiences which have, through tradition, become part of so many educational programs. While some of the discontent is thoughtless and invalid, a considerable number of protests and dissatisfactions prove, upon examination, to be both reasonable and justifiable. This is as applicable to physical education as it is to other aspects of education.

When analyzing educational programs and individual subjects for relevance, one must examine them from every viewpoint and ask pertinent questions about possible changes. Relevant for whom? Relevant for when? Relevant for what? These three questions must be answered before any decisions can be reached and changes made.

1.32 a

Relevance for whom? A given educational experience will not be equally mean-ingful for a prospective bricklayer and a prospective lawyer. Those preparing to be music teachers will not find a course in statistics as significant as will those planning to conduct research. Coaches will find courses in athletic training and care of injuries more practical than will those who are teaching movement educa-tion in the elementary school. A course in Greek will be more practical for a clergyman than for a farmer. One can go on and on. However, it becomes obvious that one must consider a person's background, intellectual and motor capacities, and future plans before passing judgment on the relevance of any educational experience.

1.32 b.

Relevance for when? There is a tendency for college graduates, during the first year or two earning a living, to be critical of the college courses which do not seem to have immediate practical value or do not relate specifically to the work in which they are engaged. This is particularly true of courses in art, literature, philosophy, physical education, history, and the like. They are so engrossed in the immediate problems facing them and so concerned with the specific details of how to perform their tasks that they see no further. In later years, however, they begin to realize the value of being able to communicate readily and meaningfully, to apply lessons of the past to the present, to create solutions to new problems, and to think, speak, and interact with understanding in the intellectual community. They find it is impor-tant to be recognized as educated persons and look back on some of their general education courses as having special benefit and value. They also become much more concerned about their health and ability to sustain demands placed upon their bodies in the competitive and hectic environment of today's society.

1.32 c

Relevance for what? The purpose for which education is undertaken must also be considered. Goals and purposes which have often been presented for the various programs of education include learning a trade, earning a livelihood, dis-covering the truth, controlling technology, and setting free the mind of modern man. Some educational philosophers also speak of raising the level of intelligence of a society, of affording every child the opportunity to realize his potential, and of the pursuit of knowledge as ends in themselves.

To be relevant, education must be meaningful for specific individuals, must serve the future as well as the present, and must contribute to the achievement of the objectives and purposes for which it is intended. Relevance is a serious and worthy challenge.

Thirst for knowledge *1.33*

Wanting, wishing, desiring, and striving are precursors to accomplishment. Teach-ing students who are eager to learn is satisfying; instructing a class whose mem-bers are enthusiastic is rewarding; observing the progress of students who are thirsty for knowledge is inspiring. Those who wish intensely, desire deeply, and are committed to the task of learning will, regardless of the subject, exert themselves to the utmost to achieve their goal. They possess a moving, driving, and energizing force which arouses and sustains them. Those who have a zeal for learning generally accomplish their objectives. This applies equally whether one is learning to move, read, dance, speak, compute, or play basketball.

The role of reason *1.34*

To develop the ability to think is one of the most universally accepted purposes of education. The educated person should be able to learn something from one situation and apply it intelligently to another. He should be able to relate facts and events and integrate what he already knows with new knowledge. He should be able to organize concepts and draw conclusions from a set of findings. He should be familiar with the processes of induction and deduction and be able to utilize the steps in the scientific method. In short, he should be able to reason in a logical manner and express himself articulately in summarizing evidence and presenting results.

    The person who has developed his rational powers to a high degree can free himself from the bondage of past rituals and can formulate his own value system. He can better understand himself and has the capacity to make desirable choices. He adjusts more readily to change and is adept at solving problems. He is better prepared to meet the future and deal with the unknown. The person who uses reason to solve problems is generally a stable and responsible person. The use of reason is reflected in his entire personality.

The actualization of capacities *1.35*

Thomas Carlyle epitomized this concept when he wrote:

> The great law of culture is: let each become that he was created capable of being: expand, if possible, to his full growth; and show himself at length in his own shape and stature, be these what they may.

To assist the painter to become an artist, the sprinter a champion, the athlete a good coach, the writer a poet, and the scientist an Einstein are the goals of a teacher. To help the carpenter build better homes, the architect design more beautiful buildings, the grocer sell food better, the farmer raise finer crops, and the clergyman preach more inspiring sermons are equally worthy objectives. To keep everyone healthier, happier, and more understanding of one another is also an important aim. To assist each person to approach, as nearly as possible, his full potential is one of the great purposes of education.

    Men are born with many different capacities. Some are destined to play a leading role, others a supporting role. Man has many dimensions—physical, intellectual, emotional, social, and spiritual. The ideal education should provide for growth and maturation in all dimensions with special opportunities to develop to their fullest those abilities with which a given person is especially endowed.

    The actualization of all latent talents and the development of a fully functioning supporting organism is the hope of every mother for her new-born child. Education can help. Physical education has a role.

Regard for excellence *1.36*

As one contemplates the effort and discipline that go into high standards of excellence, whether it be in academic achievement or athletic performance, one is led to ask, "Is it worth it?" The requirements include self-discipline, subjugation of selfish pleasures, and tedious hours of work and practice. There can, however, be only one answer. The satisfaction that comes from work well done and the feelings of dissatisfaction and even guilt which result when a person knows he could have done much better give testimony to the significance of high-quality performance.

"The desire to excel and to perform to the best of their ability was the deep and abiding motive that aroused and sustained them . . ." (Courtesy of Springfield College.)

Not long ago, the author interviewed a number of well-known athletes and inquired as to their motivation for peak performances in athletic contests. While there were numerous replies, the one that was mentioned the most frequently was *pride in performance.* The desire to excel and to perform to the best of their ability was the deep and abiding motive that aroused and sustained them when trying to do their very best.

John Gardner, in the concluding chapter of his book *Excellence* has this to say:

. . . excellence implies more than competence. It implies a striving for the highest standards in every phase of life. We need individual excellence in all its forms—in every kind of creative endeavor, in political life, in education, in industry—in short, universally. [19, p. 160]

Excellence or mediocrity, which do we choose? Most Americans have grown up with the motto, "What's worth doing at all is worth doing well." The theme for the National Convention of the American Association for Health, Physical Education, and Recreation in 1961 was *"the pursuit of excellence."* There is no reason why we should not hold fast to those ideals today, but we must be willing to pay the price. Excellence is an important foundation stone of a good education.

Understanding human fallibility *1.37*

When discussing education, there is a temptation to deal too exclusively with intellectual learning, scientific accomplishments, research, scholarship, and peak performance. We tend to forget that people are fallible, that some are handicapped, that there are those who are culturally or educationally deprived, that not all are equally gifted, and that individuals differ in their interests and their abilities. If we eliminate on one end of the scale the ten percent who are the most highly endowed with unusual capacities and abilities and at the other end of the scale the ten percent who have the greatest difficulty learning and performing, we are left with the vast majority who are rather ordinary. They have problems at school and at home, they are able to be reasonably successful if they put forth the effort, they do not enjoy spending too much time with drudgery, and they like to laugh, sing and play. They also have a real need for interaction with other people and would often benefit by more sympathy and understanding.

In an article entitled "Learning from Within," Robert Fleming proposes a new focus for elementary schools which applies the principle of humanism. This new focus, in his words,

> . . . has to do with relating and responding to people and renewing their faith in themselves. It calls for a kind of dedication that is both feasible and realistic. It converges from a conviction that each child has a right to be wanted, to be known, to be encouraged and to succeed. It diverges into opportunities for each child to look and to see, to listen and to hear, to touch and to feel. [18, p. 395]

Education must be for the mentally retarded, the victim of poliomyelitis, the slow learner, and the inept performer. It must also be for the potential artist and the prospective leader. The middle eighty percent must not be forgotten.

Teachers must seek to understand the problems of all their students and must share with them the responsibilities for solutions. Teachers who feel a sense of partnership with their students, who sincerely want them to succeed, and who give of themselves as well as of their time and effort can do the most to bring humanism into education. It is essential, of course, that they be supported by the appropriate administrative officers and the community which they serve.

Health and fitness *1.38*

Halbert Dunn, a physician in the United States Public Health Service, defined "high-level wellness" as "an integrated method of functioning which is oriented toward maximizing the potential of which the individual is capable, within the environment where he is functioning." [12, p. 447] This essentially defines health and fitness. It refers to total fitness, and the integration of the whole being. It coincides closely with the way in which the President's Council* defined fitness in 1959: "It is the capacity of the individual to live and function effectively, purposefully, and zestfully, here and now; and to meet confidently the problems and crises which are among life's expectations."

Physiologists today usually think of circulorespiratory capacity, muscular endurance, flexibility, and strength as measures of physical fitness. Coordination, explosive force, agility, balance, speed, and reaction time are considered performance factors. All are related to *fitness to perform*. Not all have the same relationship to health, which approaches more closely the concept of *fitness for living*.

The details of developing and maintaining health and fitness will be discussed in a later chapter. For the present, let us remind ourselves again of the meaningful words of President Kennedy in his presidential message to the schools:

> ✱ The strength of our democracy is no greater than the collective well-being of our people. The vigor of our country is no stronger than the vitality and will of all our countrymen. The level of physical, mental, moral and spiritual fitness of every American citizen must be our constant concern. [33]

Health and fitness provide energy, enthusiasm, courage, and zest. They assist in the development of a positive self-concept. They enhance self-confidence and move individuals in the direction of self-realization.

Release through expression /, 39

> ⚡ The flow of movement fills all our functions and actions; it discharges us of detrimental inner tensions; it is a means of communication between people, because all our forms of expression, such as speaking, writing, and singing are carried by the flow of movement.
>
> —Rudolph Laban

These words [37, p. 97] are indicative of the universal need to express oneself. Deprived of the release which comes through the expression of inner feelings, a personality may become stifled and never reach its full development. Creativity, spontaneity, and catharsis are all fostered by opportunities for self-expression. The sense of exultation and even ecstasy which result from achievement through creative endeavor and self-expression are both satisfying and developmental.

One of the ways in which physical education contributes to self-realization is in providing opportunities for self-expression. Sports, games, and dance all lend themselves to the communication of inner feelings through creative movement.

---

*"The President's Council on Youth Fitness," changed first to "The President's Council on *Physical* Fitness" and more recently to the "The President's Council on Physical Fitness and *Sports.*"

The gymnast performing a free-exercise routine, the dancer expressing a mood, the football player giving vent to a pent-up need for rough bodily contact, and the joyous and spontaneous play of children exploring ways to jump and climb and swing—are all examples of how self-expression can be one of the outcomes of physical education when it is rightly taught.

The problem, of course, is how to provide the maximum opportunities for creativity and self-expression in the schools without encouraging chaos and disorganization. It is also difficult in some instances to secure acceptance on the part of traditionalists in the school system and supporting communities. The answer probably lies in a moderate approach and careful orientation of everyone concerned. It may be that the focus and priorities need to be reevaluated. More involvement by children of all levels of creative experience and greater emphasis on exploration and self-expression are partial answers.

Chicagoland. "The flow of movement fills all our functions . . ."—Laban
(Courtesy of the *Journal of Health, Physical Education, and Recreation.*)

The spirit of adventure /. 39/

To share with teammates the dramatic moments of hard-fought games, to enjoy the camaraderie of a climb up a difficult mountain trail, to feel together the sense of achievement after shooting rapids in a canoe, to relive the dangers experienced together in combat—these and many more "tests of the spirit" reveal man's deep need for challenge and adventure. To run a risk, to pit one's skill against the elements of nature, and to face danger and overcome fear are experiences that test one's courage and breed self-confidence .

✳ Self-discovery through sports, however, does not involve merely the discovery of one's ability to perform athletic feats. The satisfaction that comes from achieving something for which one has paid a great price, the knowledge that you can face up to an opponent as a man, the understanding that, when you are both mentally and physically prepared, you can do great things, the recognition of what it feels like to help a teammate succeed—these and many other features are discovered about the self.*

It is becoming more and more obvious that if young people are to be guided into activities that are wholesome, the programs must have meaning for them. There must be opportunity to explore, to run the hazard, to excite the chance. Where there is no challenge, no excitement, and little action, the youth of our nation will charge us with irrelevance and dullness. Education must pay heed to the needs of young people and must constantly be alert to new and stimulating, challenging and exciting activities. Schools as well as community agencies are in a position not only to promote and conduct such programs, but also to give the necessary guidance and exercise the control which is essential if they are to have the value which is intended and meet the educational objectives which are contemplated.

In summarizing the Outward Bound programs which have gained recognition in many parts of the world, the Bishop of Portsmouth said:

> . . . there is in every boy the desire to prove himself, a desire to be tested and challenged, a latent urge which needs to be heroic and needs to be called upon. The means by which this can take place are amongst the most important and most formative influences in his character, for they are ways in which he is discovering himself and learning to master his fears. [31, p. 216]

There are sound reasons for believing that the inclusion of some adventure in the activities of educational programs will contribute to the prevention of juvenile delinquency, drug abuse, and alcoholism. It may also have a salutary effect on mental health. Physical education must make this a matter of concern.

---

*Frost, Reuben B., *Psychological Concepts Applied to Physical Education and Coaching*, Reading, Massachusetts: Addison-Wesley Publishing Company, Inc., 1971, pp. 83–84.

Freedom with responsibility /.392

The emphasis on human dignity and the importance attached to the enhancement of individual personality in our current educational philosophy is very worthwhile if seen in proper perspective. Individual freedom, if blended with self-discipline, can lead to spontaneity and encourage creativity. Unbridled freedom in the hands of immature and thoughtless persons may, however, result in chaos, disruption, and even anarchy. Education has an important role in informing, guiding, and leading young people as they leave their home environment to strike out for themselves. Teachers must respect the right of students to exercise individual initiative but at the same time must impress upon them their responsibility to promote the welfare of everyone.

Needless restrictions, repressive disciplinary measures, and meaningless and obsolete rules can, of course, stifle initiative and lead to apathetic performance. Artists and geniuses who are striking out in new and original directions certainly need the encouragement afforded by unhampered efforts and limitless horizons. *Freedom with responsibility*, with due consideration for the rights and feelings of others, must be the guide. Education's responsibility is to both the individual and the group—to the individuals composing the group and to the group composed of individuals.

Need for renewal /.393

The human organism has marvelous powers of rejuvenation, but there are limitations. Too long a period without relaxation, too prolonged a period of tedious work, and too strenuous an effort without frequent rest and diversion—these and similiar stresses will exceed even the capacity of the human body to restore itself. Tensions accumulate and become chronic, spirits become depressed and lose their vitality, nerves become strained and tempers flare, and the individual loses his ability to think sharply and work constructively. All of these ills can in many instances be avoided if provision is made for proper rest, relaxation and recreation.

There exists in living things a rhythmic pattern. The heart muscle contracts and relaxes, the lungs inhale and exhale, sleep and wakefulness alternate, and effort is followed by relaxation. The "stroke-glide principle" has been used by teachers of recreation and healthful living. During periods of rest, relaxation, and "gliding," the cells in the human organism are growing and developing and new cells are replacing those which are worn out. In this way, the body is truly being "re-created." The principle of balance between work, rest, relaxation, and recreation has been advocated and employed for many years. More tranquil and productive lives have been the result.

Understanding and appreciating the stroke-glide principle and providing for adequate recreational skills and knowledge of relaxation techniques are even more meaningful for future generations than they have been in the past. Education for the future must include both recreational skills, which will make for worthy use of leisure moments, and knowledge of the restoration and renewal of body, mind, and spirit.

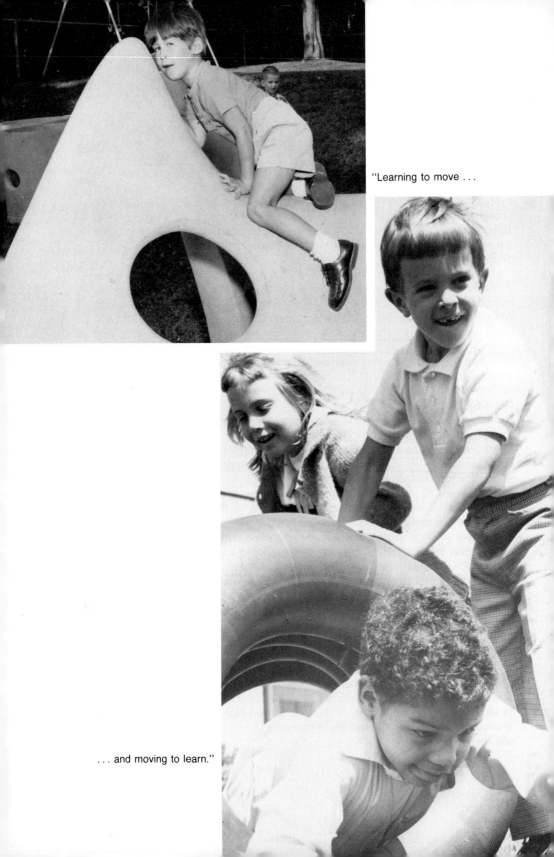

"Learning to move . . .

. . . and moving to learn."

Fun, joy, and laughter are necessary ingredients of the good life. The healthy glow that shines on the faces of children when they give themselves wholeheartedly to play, the friendly exchange of glances and the feeling of camaraderie that follow a well-played and hard-fought game, the emotional exhilaration after an evening of folk dancing, the elation that is felt as a pair of canoeists finish shooting the rapids—these and similiar experiences are not only enjoyable but healthful and therapeutic as well. Even the warmth and friendliness that exude when old friends reminisce about shared experiences are beneficial to both physical and mental health.

Technological advance, economic affluence, population growth, expanded leisure, the decreasing need for strenuous manual labor, a changing philosophy of life in our culture, and many other social changes predict an even greater and more significant role for recreation than in the past. It will include more than fun and pleasure. It will, in truth, be "re-creation." Education for the future must therefore include education for *renewal.*

The nurturing of values /,394

Character development is the great, if not the sole, aim of education.

—O'Shea

Robin Hood was acclaimed by some because he stole from the rich and gave to the poor. The buccaneers in Robert Louis Stevenson's *Treasure Island* had their code. Buddhists, Hindus, Moslems, and Christians have guidelines to govern their lives. Each person must eventually adopt a set of principles as his code of behavior. These are, in a sense, his values. In the life of every man, alternatives must be weighed and priorities established. This involves placing a value on different kinds of action. Behavior is controlled by the kinds of things upon which the individual places greatest value. For some it may be money; for a number it may be power; for many it is a set of guiding principles. Such guidelines may be derived from the Bible, the Koran, the Constitution, or some other written document, or from a combination of sources both written and oral. Parents, siblings, teachers, playmates, employers, and all others with whom a person has long and continuous contact have perhaps the greatest influence on values which develop and behavior which results. Each individual learns from experience. Some call it character development and others speak of moral education; for many it is "education in values." Regardless of what it is called, experience is a significant and important aspect of a person's life. And if education consists of learning from past experiences, this kind of education needs serious and committed attention. Ac-

◀"The healthy glow that shines on the faces of children when they give themselves wholeheartedly to play . . ." (Courtesy of the *Journal of Health, Physical Education, and Recreation.*)

cording to the evidence now available, the early years are the formative ones, and the home must carry a heavy responsibility. Nevertheless, changes are wrought as a result of school experiences and formal education must share in the task. And as Seth Arsenian said at the National Conference on Values in Sports:

> Physical education, including health and recreation, as part of education in general, and of college education in particular, shares in the responsibility for the development of student values. In many respects, physical education, if it centers on play as a basic characteristic of human behavior, is better situated that any other course in the school curriculum in influencing the development of values. [55, p. 59]

The nurturing of values is a many-faceted enterprise. The home, our leaders, churches, classrooms, social agencies, government, the news media, police departments, youth organizations, etc. have a role. John Gardner in his book, *Self-Renewal,* has this to say:

> In short, the nurturing of values that maintain society's moral tone—or allow that moral tone to slacken—is going on every day, for good or ill. It is not the dull exercise in ancestral piety that some adults make it seem. It goes on in the dust and clamor of the market place, the daily press, the classroom and the playground, the urban apartment and the suburban ranch house, and it communicates itself more vividly through what men do than through what they say. The moral order is not something static, it is not something enshrined in historic documents, or stowed away like the family silver, or lodged in the minds of pious and somewhat elderly moralists. It is an attribute of a functioning social system. As such it is a living, changing thing, liable to decay and disintegration as well as to revitalizing and reinforcement, and never any better than the generation that holds it in trust. [20, p. 126]

Education for the development of values must not be relegated to the list of secondary or unimportant objectives.

1.4 EDUCATION FOR AMERICAN DEMOCRACY
To describe education for American democracy is to depict, as best we can, the ideal education for all people. The first basic principle is *to assist each individual to become all that he is capable of becoming.* This should be the guiding star for education everywhere and for the future as well as the present. Other guidelines for education in our country are:

1. *To educate all people to govern themselves.* This is necessary if democracy is going to work. In a society as complex and cosmopolitan as ours, it is not a simple matter to govern people who know some of the principles of democracy but not all of them. The natural impulse is to select those guidelines which seem appropriate and advantageous to our own particular situation and use them to further our own interest. There can be conflict between self-government and personal freedom—the specific interests of one segment of the population are not

always the same as those of another group, the basic philosophy of one group may be quite different from that of another, and the ethnic backgrounds of the various groups often differ considerably. It becomes quite obvious, then, that participatory democracy and self-government do require an educated populace to make them work.

2. *To educate all people to be free.* It is necessary in a democracy not only to want freedom enough so that one is willing to fight for it, but also to learn what true freedom entails. Freedom must be distinguished from license and those who wish to be free must accept the restraints imposed by elected leaders and wise and empathetic authorities. Guidelines and regulations will always be necessary where many people live together in an organized society. There are also situations, usually of an emergency nature, where prompt obedience to commands is essential. A neurosurgeon and his staff performing a delicate operation, a fire chief and his firemen trying to save a burning building, a leader and his men in battle, a guide and his group searching for a lost child in a forest, a quarterback and his football team trying to win a hard-fought game—these are some fairly obvious instances. True freedom, then, means not only the right of each person to be himself and make decisions with regard to his actions, but also the acceptance of authority when rightly imposed.

3. *To believe in each individual as a person of infinite worth.* The education of a handicapped person and the education of a genius are equally important. Teaching those who are in the middle areas of ability and capacity is as significant as helping the exceptional pupils with their learning. Teaching the average person to swim may be as meaningful as coaching champions. In emergency situations a human life is far more valuable than any material consideration. Multimillion-dollar airplanes have been scuttled to save the lives of pilots and passengers. Hundreds of workers often leave their jobs to search for a lost child. In a democracy, the preservation of mind, spirit, and body becomes very important. Preventive and rehabilitative measures are considered worthwhile. In a democracy, individuals are not to be made means to the selfish ends of others . . . they are all to have an equal opportunity to learn to know themselves and to realize their potential.

4. *To teach by precept and practice the elements and techniques of cooperative action.* This will entail the methods of group work, the acceptance of majority rule, the protection of minority opinion, and cooperative planning and formulation of guidelines and policies. It will include respect for the opinions and rights of others, sharing the responsibilities for making things work, accepting blame for failures and credit for achievements, and the maintenance of positive attitudes toward democratic procedures. Teamwork is essential not only in athletics but in democratic processes.

5. *To teach the effectiveness of reason in solving problems and achieving self-realization.* Individuals who wish to be free must be able to think. The formulation of a set of values to serve as a guide to living can only occur through intelligent appraisal and thoughtful selection. Awareness of one's self and recognition of one's limitations and abilities comes about by reason. Deeper understanding of

both oneself and others requires the utilization of the rational process. Difficult decisions should be made only through the application of reason to all available information. This is the way of democracy.

Another thought is expressed by Edward Power in his book, *Education for American Democracy:*

> As these features of American education evolved, educational institutions were organized into a system which made all the schools available to all people, and finally a feature that had always been implicit in American educational ideals was made explicit: Artificial barriers to educational opportunity have no place in democratic education. [43, p. 56]

The "artificial barriers" about which he speaks could refer to admissions barriers, financial requirements, physical or mental handicaps, racism and other forms of prejudice, or other indications that educational opportunities are being denied through some form of discrimination or bigotry. As Power says, these "have no place in democratic education."

The traditional purposes of education, namely (1) the development of the individual in all his dimensions to the point that he approaches his potential as closely as possible, and (2) the contribution which education must make to the betterment of society, are still valid. The problem is that both are becoming more complex and more difficult to achieve. The individual living in this highly complex world has more things to learn and more personal problems, both psychological and physiological, than ever before. At the same time, attempting to contribute to the betterment of society seems many times to be both frustrating and hopeless. The difficulties encountered in solving problems related to racial imbalance, the poverty gap, individual differences, relevance, sudden fluctuations in population, and various vested interests are almost overwhelming.

There are, however, many compensations for those who are dedicated to education as a career. Teachers still observe and marvel at the almost phenomenal growth and development of students with whom they become deeply involved. Administrators can still take pride in the achievement of graduates and the performances of staff members. Geniuses evolve, artists develop, and great executives, doctors, and statesmen emerge. More important, perhaps, children still stare in starry-eyed wonder as they are exposed to new and interesting phenomena. The sense of achievement as children learn to swim, paint a picture, solve a problem, demonstrate a dance, give a speech, or complete a dissertation is compensation enough for those who have been privileged to share the successes and failures along the way. These are permanent values which make life worthwhile for many individuals and are worthy objectives in any society.

1.5 THE HUMANIZATION OF EDUCATION

There is a great deal of discussion in educational circles about "humanizing" education. This term is extremely difficult to define, as each person tends to attribute to it different shades of meaning. Generally speaking, it has to do with

"The sense of achievement, as children learn . . . is compensation enough." (Courtesy of the *Journal of Health, Physical Education, and Recreation.*)

concern for the *human being* attending school. Emphasis is on individualization, respect for each student's developing personality, and the attempt to minister to all types of needs—psychological, physiological, social, intellectual, and spiritual. It emphasizes the human as distinguished from the material; it deals with each person as an individual rather than as a cog in a machine or a component of a group. The affective domain is recognized as being of equal importance with the psychomotor and cognitive domains.

Charles Reich, in his book *The Greening of America,* speaks of the need for humanization in these words:

> ... today's emerging consciousness seeks a new knowledge of what it means to be human, in order that the machine, having been built, may now be turned to human ends; in order that man once more can be a creative force, renewing and creating his own life and thus giving life back to his society. [44, p. 4]

There are many who believe that our society and our educational system are suffering from a combination of materialism, conformity, and runaway technology. Where these symptoms are too pronounced, society becomes over-organized, families seem to dissolve in the selfish interests of children and parents, juvenile delinquency gains an easier foothold, mental illness thrives, and government and industry tend to become more corrupt. We also find, both in our schools and in other segments of society, many instances of discrimination on the basis of race, socioeconomic status, religion, and influence. Powerlessness, hypocrisy, corruption, and the destruction of environment have also been singled out as contributing factors to dehumanization. War and lawlessness are perhaps the most frustrating problems of all. These are some of the factors which cause young people to dissent and rebel. Depersonalization and dehumanization are caused in part by combinations of the above.

We in education must be careful not to overemphasize the role education can play in the alleviation of such conditions. If we were to accept the responsibility for preventing social problems and healing the ills of society, we would be forced to admit that we have failed miserably. Nevertheless, schools and colleges do have a role and can make a contribution. The first step is to determine where and how the present programs can be humanized.

The most obvious need in most schools is empathy. Empathy is participation in the feelings of another person. It is involving yourself so deeply that what hurts another person hurts you and what gives him joy makes you joyful also.

When a teacher is deeply involved, there is a sharing of problems. Solving the unsolvable problem or overcoming the difficult obstacle can be almost fixating when faced alone; it can be developmental, satisfying, and exhilarating when shared.

There are few things that contribute more to the humanization of education than fun, joy, and laughter. All teachers, especially physical education teachers and recreational leaders, must never forget that. Even formalized education need not become solemnized. Kenneth Eble has a word of advice for parents which may appropriately be applied to teachers as well:

> The willingness of parents to play, to listen, to answer questions, to direct investigations, to enter in when invited and to stay out when asked, are all education experiences that a child should not have to wait until school to find. What I am getting at is that play should be taken for what it's worth and it is worth a great deal. Robert Frost said that the figure a poem makes is the same as for love—each "begins in delight and ends in wisdom." The figure, it seems to me, fits learning as well. Parents need to laugh at their vexations, to respond more and reprimand less, and to enter fully into the spirit of play, which too much of their own learning and too much concern for their children's learning may have taken away from them. [13, pp. 16–17]

And George Leonard, writing in *Education and Ecstasy,* says:

> *Learning is sheer delight.* This doesn't mean it avoids tension or fears to look tragedy in the eye. But education devoid of the ecstatic moment is a mere shadow of education. We may assume that, when learners are apathetic, bored or just matter of fact, something is drastically wrong and that wrong can be remedied. [38, p. 216]

In schools where sincere efforts are being made to humanize education, there will be personal and empathetic attention to each individual, there will be more praise than blame, there will be counseling and guidance in the light of each person's limitations, capacities, and background, and opportunities for success will be provided for each individual. In such a school, competition will be controlled so that students may experience victory and defeat, comparison will, for the most part, be with one's own previous achievements rather than with those of others, and the student will be assisted to develop a realistic self-concept. Most important of all, every effort will be made to be fair and impartial and help the individual understand the reasons for regulations and controls.

It is acknowledged that the above description of humanizing education is idealistic and that no teacher or school situation will be perfect in all respects. It is also recognized that every individual must learn to face up courageously to failures and to bounce back after defeat. The goal should be to provide situations in which obstacles and hurdles are challenging but not impossible and where the difficulty of overcoming them is appropriate to the ability and the background of the student. Teachers and fellow students should assist those who falter, be judicious in criticism and praise, notice other students when they achieve and stand by them when they are in trouble. These precepts must apply to students of all ethnic backgrounds, to the handicapped regardless of the nature of their impairment, to the culturally and educationally deprived as well as to those who are overprotected or hampered by too many material possessions.

Those who are trying to humanize education must deal with the human and personal dimensions of man. While college entrance examinations, computers, teaching machines, and laboratories are important adjuncts in the educational process, they must not be allowed to substitute for personal attention, compassionate understanding, helpful counsel, and generous opportunities to interact with other human beings. Preoccupation with other aspects of teaching must not be allowed to replace personal involvement with the student.

Physical education has many opportunities to humanize its programs. Except for the more advanced and theoretical courses, such as most of those in professional preparation programs, much of the programs consist of dancing, games, sports, and challenging adventure. Excitement, fun, joy, and complete involvement are prevalent. Empathetic personal interaction is quite usual. Triumphs and disasters are often shared. Opportunities to make friends and exchange tales of exciting experiences abound. Physical education can, in a large percentage of cases, be very human.

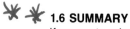 **1.6 SUMMARY**

If we are to educate for a better world, our programs must be undergirded with the soundest base and the firmest foundation conceivable. Footings comprising this base include faith in the future, devotion to truth, concern for becoming, desire to achieve, need for loving, integrity of the human organism, and the art of living. These are relatively permanent and there appears to be little likelihood that they will crumble.

The foundation stones of education are many and diverse. Nevertheless, it is with considerable confidence that these are enumerated and explained. Both teachers and students should have reverence for history, concern for relevance, thirst for knowledge, and respect for the rational process. Education must be committed to the actualization of capacities, have a high regard for excellence, demonstrate a concern for man's fallibility, and exhibit a dedication to the health and fitness of everyone.

Self-expression, a spirit of adventure, and the relationship of man to man are of deep concern in a good educational system. The need for renewal and the developing and nurturing of values cannot be neglected if our people are to be truly educated.

Our teachers and administrators have a responsibility to educate for a better democracy, for that is our commitment as a nation. The concepts of individual worth, self-government, freedom with responsibility, and cooperative action must be taught and demonstrated. The humanization of our schools and colleges is a matter of high priority and attention to equality of educational opportunity is a mandate. The personalization of educational practices and procedures cannot wait. Physical education must do its share.

SELECTED REFERENCES

1. Adler, Alfred, *The Education of the Individual,* New York: Philosophical Library, 1958.
2. Arnstine, Donald, *Philosophy of Education,* New York: Harper and Row, 1967.
3. Arsenian, Seth (ed.), *The Humanics Philosophy of Springfield College,* Springfield, Massachusetts, 1969.

4. Brameld, Theodore, *Patterns of Educational Philosophy,* New York: Holt, Rinehart, and Winston, 1971.
5. Brubacher, John S. *Modern Philosophies of Education,* New York: McGraw-Hill, 1969.
6. Chase, Stuart, "Are you alive? " Reprinted with permission from the September 1922 *Reader's Digest.* Copyright © 1922 from The Reader's Digest Association, Inc. Condensed from *The Nation* (July 19, 1922).
7. Commoner, Barry, *The Closing Circle,* New York: Alfred A. Knopf, 1971.
8. Crary, Ryland W., *Humanizing the School,* New York: Alfred A. Knopf, 1969.
9. *Decisions for Better America,* The Republican Committee on Program and Progress, Garden City, N.Y.: Doubleday and Company, 1960.
10. *Developing Democratic Human Relations,* First Yearbook, American Association for Health, Physical Education, and Recreation, Washington, D.C., 1951.
11. Dewey, John, *Philosophy of Education,* Totowa, N.J.: Littlefield, Adams and Company, 1966.
12. Dunn, Halbert L., "What high-level wellness means," *Canadian Journal of Public Health,* Vol. 50, No. 11, November 1959.
13. Eble, Kenneth E., *A Perfect Education.* Copyright © 1966 by The Macmillan Company, New York. Reprinted by permission.
14. Educational Policies Commission, *The Central Purpose of American Education,* National Education Association, Washington, D.C., 1961.
15. _____, *Education and the Spirit of Science,* National Education Association, Washington, D.C., 1966.
16. _____, *An Essay on Quality in Public Education,* National Education Association, Washington, D.C., 1959.
17. _____, *Moral and Spiritual Values in the Public Schools,* National Education Association, Washington, D.C., 1951.
18. Fleming, Robert S., "Learning from looking within," *Journal of the Association for Childhood Education International,* Vol. 48, No. 8, May 1972.
19. Gardner, John W., *Excellence,* New York: Harper and Row, 1961.
20. _____, *Self-Renewal,* New York: Harper and Row, 1964. By permission.
21. Glines, Don E., *Creating Humane Schools,* Mankato, Minn.: D. M. Printing Company, 1972.
22. Gordon, Chad, and Kenneth J. Gergen (eds.), *The Self in Social Interaction, Vol. 1: Classic and Contemporary Perspectives,* New York: John Wiley and Sons, 1968.
23. Gunther, John, *Death Be Not Proud,* New York: Harper and Row, 1949.
24. H'doubler, Margaret N., "Dance: A creative art experience," *Background Reading for Physical Education,* A. Paterson and E. C. Hallberg, (eds.), New York: Holt, Rinehart, and Winston, 1967.
25. Hein Fred, Dana L. Farnsworth, and Charles E. Richardson, *Living, Health, Behavior and Environment,* 5th edition, Glenview, Ill.: Scott, Foresman and Company, 1970.
26. Henderson, Stella V. P., *Introduction to Philosophy of Education,* Chicago: The University of Chicago Press, 1947.
27. *Higher Education for American Democracy,* Report of the President's Commission for American Democracy, Washington, D.C.: United States Printing Office, 1947.
28. Holt, John, *How Children Learn,* New York: Pitman Publishing Company, 1969.
29. Horton, Mildred M. and Robert C. Clothier, *Moral and Spiritual Values in Education,* Address to the Board of Regents of the University of the State of New York, Albany, 1951.

30. Hutchins, Robert M., *The Learning Society,* New York: Frederick A. Praeger, 1968.
31. James, David (ed.), *Outward Bound,* London: Routledge and Kegan Paul, 1964.
32. Johns, Edward B., Wilfred C. Sutton, and Lloyd E. Webster, *Health for Effective Living,* 3rd edition, New York: McGraw-Hill, 1962.
33. Kennedy, John F., "A presidential message to the schools on the physical fitness of youth," *Journal of Health, Physical Education and Recreation,* September 1961.
34. Kneller, George F., *Existentialism and Education,* New York: John Wiley and Sons, 1963.
35. _____, *Foundations of Education,* New York: John Wiley and Sons, 1963.
36. Kraus, Richard, *Recreation and Leisure in Modern Society,* New York: Appleton-Century-Crofts, 1971.
37. Laban, Rudolf, *Modern Educational Dance,* 2nd edition, London: MacDonald and Evans, 1963.
38. Leonard, George B., *Education and Ecstasy,* New York: Dell Publishing Company, 1968.
39. McGrath, Lee P. and Joan Scobey, *What is a grandfather?,* New York: Simon and Schuster, 1970.
40. Nolte, Chester M. (ed.), *An Introduction to School Administration,* New York: The Macmillan Company, 1966.
41. Oberteuffer, Delbert, *Physical Education,* New York: Harper and Row, 1956.
42. Paine, Thomas, preface to *Eyewitness to Space,* Hereward Cooke and James D. Dean, New York: Harry N. Abrams, 1971.
43. Power, Edward J., *Education for American Democracy,* New York: McGraw-Hill, 1965.
44. Reich, Charles A., *The Greening of America,* New York: Bantam Books, 1972.
45. *The Royal Bank of Canada, Monthly Letter of,* Vol. 39, No. 1, January 1958.
46. Steinhaus, Arthur, *"Common ground,"* Lecture presented at the annual convention of the Central District Association for Health, Physical Education, and Recreation, Minneapolis, Minn., April 1947.
47. Taylor, Harold, *On Education and Freedom,* Carbondale: Southern Illinois University Press, 1967.
48. _____, *The World as Teacher,* Garden City, N.Y.: Doubleday and Company, 1970.
49. Tead, Ordway, *The Art of Administration,* New York: McGraw-Hill, 1951.
50. Titus, Harold W., *Living Issues in Philosophy,* 2nd edition, New York: American Book Company, 1953.
51. Toffler, Alvin, "Can we cope with tomorrow?" *Redbook Magazine,* January 1966.
52. _____, *Future Shock,* New York: Random House, 1970.
53. Tussing, Lyle, *Psychology for Better Living,* New York: John Wiley and Sons, 1965.
54. Ullman, Albert D., *Sociocultural Foundations of Personality,* Boston: Houghton Mifflin Company, 1965.
55. *"Values in sports,"* Joint National Conference of the Division of Girl's and Women's Sports and the Division of Men's Athletics, American Association for Health, Physical Education, and Recreation, Washington, D.C., 1962.
56. Wells, H. G., *The Outline of History,* Garden City, N.Y.: Garden City Publishing Company, 1929.
57. Whitehead, Alfred N., *The Aims of Education,* New York: The Free Press, 1957.
58. Zeigler, Earl F., *Philosophical Foundations for Physical, Health, and Recreation Education,* Englewood Cliffs, N.J.: Prentice-Hall, 1964.

Meanings
and
Purposes

Chapter 2

2.1 INTRODUCTION

If one were to select at random a group of people and ask each of them "What is physical education?," the responses would vary widely. One person might indicate that physical education is synonymous with exercise; another would say it is the teaching of sport; there would be those who remember their military experience and relate it to calisthenics; a few would think of dance, others of play and games; a number would remember their own school experiences and associate them with many kinds of physical activity. Lay persons generally associate physical education with calisthenics, athletics. fitness, postural development, and games.

If teachers and professional leaders in the field were asked the same question, there would still be a good deal of disparity among the replies. The elementary teacher might associate physical education with movement education; the coach might think of it as preparation for a contest; the secondary teacher might see it as consisting of lifetime sports; the research professor might relate it to physiological experimentation. The teacher of professional preparation courses is apt to think of physical education in terms of supervision, curriculum planning, testing, and teaching of sociological, psychological, and physiological principles.

In a position paper entitled *Guidelines for Secondary School Physical Education* prepared by a carefully selected committee of professional physical educators, a statement appears summarizing the meaning of physical education and its objectives. Those who seek to comprehend its significance and the accomplishments which are sought will profit by a careful study of the following:

Physical education is that integral part of total education which contributes to the development of the individual through the natural medium of physical activity—human movement. It is a carefully planned sequence of learning experiences designed to fulfill the growth, development, and behavior needs of each student. It encourages and assists each student to:

Develop the skills of movement, the knowledge of how and why one moves, and the ways in which movement may be organized.

Learn to move skillfully and effectively through exercise, games, dance, and aquatics.

Enrich his understanding of the concepts of space, time, and force related to movement.

Express culturally approved patterns of personal behavior and interpersonal relationships in and through games, sports, and dance.

Condition the heart, lungs, muscles, and other organic systems of the body to meet daily and emergency demands.

Acquire an appreciation of and respect for good physical condition (fitness), a functional posture, and a sense of personal well-being.

Develop an interest and a desire to participate in lifetime recreational sports. [2]

If read thoughtfully, this statement should serve as a good foundation for the discussion of definitions and meanings which follows.

2.2 DEFINITIONS AND MEANINGS

In spite of many attempts by scholars in our profession to analyze meanings and sort out discrepancies, controversies and confusion with regard to terms used in the study of health, physical education, and recreation still persist. There will undoubtedly be many changes and new proposals in the future, as there have been in the past. Because a clear understanding of key words is basic to accurate communication, a number of selected terms will be defined as they are used in this book. The following, disputed by some but accepted by many, are presented as reasonably descriptive definitions.   # 1 Thru 22

1. *Education consists of the modifications and adjustments that occur in an individual as a result of his experiences.* Education results from activity of the human organism as it moves, perceives, reacts, thinks, and responds. The total organism is modified as a result of its interaction with the environment. The total person feels, perceives, responds, and becomes educated. Education is a cumulative process continuing throughout life . . . it occurs in a great variety of situations and through innumerable kinds of experiences.

2. *Physical education,* as used here, *consists of the modifications and adjustments that occur in an indivudual as he moves and as he learns about movement.* In this instance, movement includes creeping, crawling, walking, running, climbing, jumping, swinging, stretching, and twisting as well as all those movements which occur as people participate in games, sports, gymnastics, aquatics, and dance. Many other activities can also be part of physical education, such as canoeing, mountain climbing, orienteering, rappelling, and snowshoeing. Physical education also includes cognitive learning. Learning about movement as well as how to move occurs in an activity class, academic course, or science laboratory. Physical education takes place in many different settings and may affect any and all dimensions of human existence. Modifications of the feelings, emotions, and attitudes (affective domain) are of equal importance with changes in the cognitive and psychomotor domains. Physical education takes place both inside and outside the school. It is concerned with the ultimate improvement of both the individual and the society of which he is a part.

3. *Movement education is an approach to physical education which emphasizes the early teaching and learning of basic skills, the development of self-awareness through movement, and the appreciation of movement both as an end and as a means.* By basic skills is generally meant the old "racial activities"* such as crawling, climbing, walking, running, jumping, and hurling. These basic skills are studied in terms of shape, body action, position, spatial relationships, laterality, and quality of movement. Movement education encourages self-directed learning, movement analysis, and the individualization of learning.

---

*Term used by a number of physical educators to denote the basic activities of the human race. It has a slightly different connotation than "fundamental activities" in that it emphasizes those movements that are natural to all humans.

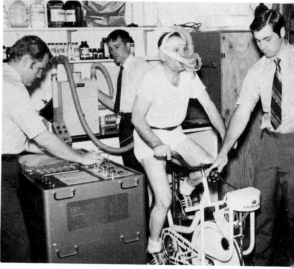

"Physical education takes place in many different settings . . ." (Courtesy of: page 34 *top and bottom,* the *Journal of Health, Physical Education, and Recreation; center,* Minnechaug Regional High School, Wilbraham, Massachusetts; page 35 *left,* the *Journal of Health, Physical Education, and Recreation; right,* South Dakota State University.)

4. *Movement exploration is related to movement education and is really an individualized method of teaching and learning motor skills. It emphasizes response to challenge, creativity, and self-discovery.* Children are challenged to accomplish a given act but permitted their own way of achieving the goals. As they keep trying to achieve their objectives and progress toward the accomplishment of their goals, they are instructed as to the best way of moving and, when necessary, assisted in the performance.

5. *Physical training consists of specific movements performed in a specific way for specific purposes.* Gymnasts can be trained to perform a giant swing; classes may be doing calisthenics as endurance training; a weightlifter trains himself to lift great weights; and a boxer prepares himself to react defensively to specific offensive moves. In some instances "training" is almost synonymous with "conditioning." Swimmers are trained for the 880-meter race, runners train for the marathon, and members of football teams train for their specific roles. Physical education has largely supplanted physical training in the schools of the United States at this time. Because physical training also provides experiences, education is also occurring as individuals train. The objectives, however, are not identical with those of physical education.

6. *Gymnastics* in this text will refer to the movements which are included in the *sport*. It will consist of *those activities which are used in gymnastic competitive meets or in gymnastic exhibitions.* It will include classroom teaching and learning of gymnastic movements. Only as used in historical commentary will the term be employed to describe the total physical education program (e.g., the *gymnastics* of the Greeks in Hellenic times.)

7. *Athletics* will be used to denote *organized, competitive, vigorous sports.* It will include intramural, extramural, interscholastic, intercollegiate and professional programs. (It should be noted that in many parts of the world "athletics" pertains to track-and-field activities only.)

8. *Recreation is renewal and refreshment; it is that which one does when one is not required to work; it consists of the positive, wholesome and re-creative things one does during leisure hours.* Recreation may be relaxation, it may be renewal of body and spirit by a change in occupation, and it should be enjoyable and satisfying.

9. *Health is the total well-being of the organism; it is a positive state and includes physical, mental, and emotional health.* Health is more than the mere absence of disease ... it includes optimal functioning of the whole organism; it implies progress toward self-realization; it eventuates in a satisfying and enriched life.

10. *Health education consists of the modifications and adjustments in health knowledge, health behavior, and health attitudes* which occur as a *result of all one's experiences.* Health education includes health instruction but is more than that. Much is learned about health through sound practices, through experience with sickness, injury, and therapy, and through everyday living. Although these experiences do not take place in the classroom, they too are health education.

"Recreation is renewal and refreshment . . ." (Courtesy of the *Journal of Health, Physical Education, and Recreation.*)

11. *Fitness*, in its broad context, is almost synonymous with health. *It consists of a state of "high-level wellness" and includes the absence of remediable handicaps and disease, optimal functioning of all body systems, and a zest and enthusiasm for work and play.* It includes physical, emotional, and spiritual fitness. It enables an individual to live a contributing, rewarding, and self-fulfilling life.

12. *Physical fitness is that aspect of total fitness which is concerned especially with organic vigor, strength, muscular endurance and, last but not least, cardiorespiratory endurance.* Agility, flexibility, and motor coordination also contribute to physical fitness and are usually included in the measurements when testing for this quality.

13. *A discipline is a branch of learning that is studied and taught for the sake of becoming more knowledgeable.* It consists of facts, principles, and theories which are known to be true or for which there is considerable substantiating evidence. Knowledge for the sake of knowing is the purpose of a discipline. For those concerned with a discipline, the practical application of the knowledge is of secondary importance.

14. *A profession is a calling or occupation requiring specialized knowledge, intensive specialized education, a philosophy of commitment and service, and high standards of conduct and achievement.* Professional education attempts to prepare, through the medium of its curriculum, individuals who are competent in the skills of their profession, imbued with the zest for continued study, and concerned more with the service they can render than with the material gain their work will bring.

15. *A body of knowledge consists of an organized set of statements about what is known, all relating in some way to a common phenomenon or interest and drawn from all disciplines which contribute to the central subject or theme.* A body of knowledge may form the core of a discipline but is usually concerned with more practical aspects and the pragmatic results of knowing. A body of knowledge is often related to a given vocation or profession.

16. *A concept is a generalized idea conceived on the basis of a number of particulars.* It is a thought, notion, or generalization which usually summarizes and synthesizes several smaller ideas into a more comprehensive and all-embracing one.

17. *A principle is a general truth or maxim which serves as a guide to further thinking or action.* It can flow out of general concepts, theories, or conclusions. It may be a maxim, a law, a tenet, or a rule of conduct. It may be an element of a larger truth or generalization.

18. *A purpose is that which a person intends or sets before himself to be accomplished.* It is generally a broad goal and indicates what a person proposes to do.

19. *A goal is the end toward which a person is moving and which he hopes to reach.* It is the point or the phase of an enterprise which is the object of this effort. It is more general than an aim and more specific than a purpose.

20. *An aim is that which a person is trying to achieve.* It is the point or stage of endeavor toward which his effort is directed. It is more specific than a goal but more general than an objective.

21. *An objective is the object of one's endeavor; the specific end of a planned action.* An objective, as used in this text, usually refers to a step toward the aim or goal. It should be both measurable and achievable. It is something to be accomplished, an outcome to be sought. It often refers to something to be achieved in a given lesson.

22. *Concomitant learnings are those which accompany the achievement of the aims or objectives of a lesson or program.* For example, a teacher may have as the objective for a lesson the learning of soccer. Accepting the decision of an official during play might be a concomitant learning.

2.3 PHYSICAL EDUCATION: DISCIPLINE OR PROFESSION? *Both p. 41*

Is physical education a "discipline"? Is it a "profession"? Does it have a true "body of knowledge"? These questions have been occupying the time of a number of theoreticians and plaguing the minds of many others who are eager to know the answers. While there are those who believe time could be better spent working on the more pragmatic aspects of physical education, certainly leaders in the field need to do some profound thinking in regard to these matters.

Some writers feel that a true discipline must have a body of knowledge. Physical educations's body of knowledge would be the many bits of knowledge drawn from many disciplines and interwoven into an integrated unit related to physical education. Such a body of knowledge would be derived from the disciplines of biology, anthropology, sociology, psychology, philosophy, physics, and others. Physical education must be concerned with all the components which belong to its body of knowledge. All the concepts, including those which are drawn from related fields, are significant to those who choose this career.

In the publication edited by Celeste Ulrich and John Nixon entitled *Tones of Theory,* the following paragraph appears:

A discipline which could be titled *Human Movement Phenomena* is the broad category under which the body of knowledge labeled *physical education* can best be subsumed. Other bodies of knowledge, such as human engineering, physical therapy, recreation, educational-athletics, dance, physical medicine, professional athletics, and human ecology also are integral parts of the context of disciplinary organization of the phenomena indentified as *human movement.* [7, p. 11]

This concept is illustrated graphically in Figure 2.1. It serves to clarify the relationships described above.

Physical Education is both a discipline and a profession. The discipline of physical education has been gradually emerging for many years but has recently, at least in some places, burst forth in full bloom. There *is* a body of knowledge that can be studied just for the sake of knowing. There *are* concepts which should be mastered by those who plan to enter the career of physical education. There *are* facts and statements drawn from many of the classic disciplines which have now been incorporated into the discipline of physical education. Physical education also has its subdisciplines—the sociology of sport, psychology of sport, physi-

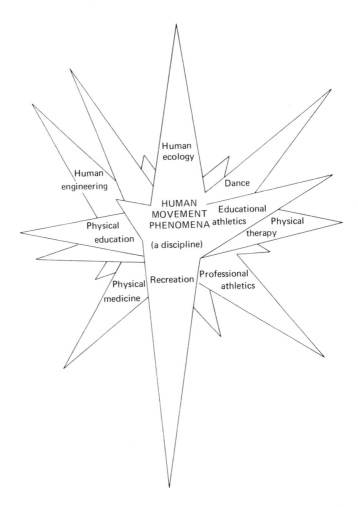

Figure 2.1 Human movement phenomena. "The model of the star need not be interpreted as indicating that the discipline dealing with human movement phenomena has only nine points. Stars have many points in a three-dimensional model. There is the opportunity and flexibility in the discipline pertaining to human movement for multifaceted design." [7, pp. 12–13] (Courtesy of the American Alliance for Health, Physical Education, and Recreation.)

ology of exercise, biomechanical analysis of movement, philosophy of physical education, and motor learning could be so classified. The study of these subjects is a necessary requisite to learning what needs to be known by a physical educator.

As a profession, physical education is designed to contribute to the development of individuals by teaching people what they need to know to make a better world. The professional person needs more than abstract knowledge; he needs to know how to do things, how to teach, how to motivate, how to inspire. The physical education teacher must be able to organize and manage classes, plan lessons, evaluate progress, and formulate curricula. He should know the basic principles of administration, supervision, budget making, and public relations. The professional person should have a sense of *vocation*, recognize his opportunities for service, and accept his responsibilities. As Leona Holbrook wrote:

> Our profession calls for those who will gain and maintain a full knowledge of the field so fully professional service can be maintained. Our profession calls for persons who will serve informedly, attentively, and thoughtfully through their instruction periods and who will bring something of their own worthwhile lives to the students.
>
> The professional must be educated for the assignment, dedicated to the rigors and demands of the work schedule, attentive to the needs of the students, thoughtful and evaluative of his working technique. There must be an ethical, moral, professional person for the call. [23, p. 174]

To summarize, physical education is both a discipline and a profession. It has a body of knowledge which can be mastered by the true professional. It involves the skills and abilities needed by teacher and coach.

2.4 PURPOSES, GOALS, AIMS, AND OBJECTIVES

> One whose *aims* are worthy, whose *aspirations* are high, and whose *designs* are wise, and whose *purposes* are steadfast, may surely hope to reach the *goal* of his ambition, and will surely win some *object* worthy of life's endeavor.*

The above quotation is found in Funk and Wagnall's New Standard Dictionary and is an attempt to clarify the distinction among the several terms employed to denote a person's *intention.* And yet, as one reviews dictionary definitions and sections of physical education textbooks dealing with these matters, one finds the words *purpose, goal, aim,* and *objective* used interchangeably and oftentimes even synonymously.

---

* *New Standard Dictionary of the English Language,* New York: Funk and Wagnall Company, 1939, p. 60.

For purposes of this book, we will think of all these terms as signifying the object of someone's ambition and the intention of his action. Nevertheless the term *purpose* will have the broadest connotation; the terms *goal* and *aim* will be used almost synonymously and will indicate a subdivision of a purpose. The term *objective* will denote a step in the achievement of the goal or aim.

A number of authors have reviewed comprehensively the purposes, aims, and objectives of physical education and we shall not repeat that process. Rather we shall enumerate what we believe to be the purposes, goals, and objectives in today's world and then discuss their formulation and interpretation.

Aims and objectives must be perceived from more than one viewpoint. If one asks a sixth grader why he likes "gym," he says without hesitation, "because it's fun." If one asks a high school student why he likes to be on the basketball squad even though he seldom plays in a game, he may reply, "because I like to be with the guys." If a grown lady is asked what motivates her to attend fitness classes, she wil probably answer, "They keep me trim and feeling good." Fun and joy, satisfaction of the need to belong, and the development of a good figure and zestful spirit are all legitimate goals under the right circumstances. Physical education *is* many different things to many different people and not "all things to all people." It is also one thing at a certain stage of life and another thing at a different stage. Even the same individual will participate in a church volleyball league for relaxation and fun, in handball for a vigorous workout and release from tension, in skiing for the exhilaration of exercise outdoors and the thrill of a daring run, and in dancing for emotional release and self-expression.

Purposes of physical education

As mentioned earlier, the purposes of education laid down by the Educational Policies Commission are:

a) "To foster that development of individual capacities which will enable each human being to become the best person he is capable of becoming," and

b) To serve society's needs. [13, p. 1]

These purposes can also serve as the purposes of physical education. The self-realization of the individual and his service to society are of course reciprocally interrelated. The development of a great society is only possible when it is essentially composed of fine and capable individuals, and productive individuals of high character are generated by a great society.

Physical education, as one phase of education, makes a contribution to the whole. The Commission on the Reorganization of Secondary Education published in 1918 its *Cardinal Principles of Secondary Education.* These were (1) health, (2) command of fundamental processes, (3) worthy home membership, (4) vocational competence, (5) good citizenship, (6) worthy use of leisure, (7) ethical character. Whether one accepts these, the four objectives of the Educational Policies Commission (self-realization, human relationship, economic efficiency, and civic responsibility), or some other statement of educational objectives as basic guidelines, physical education contributes to all of them. It does not contribute equally to all of them, but it shares its responsibility for the achievement of these outcomes with other elements of education. As the whole, integrated person is being educated, all dimensions are being affected. One subject or phase of education cannot and does not educate one part of a man while other subjects are educating other parts. Man is an indivisible entity and what happens to one part of the organism influences all the others.

Nevertheless, movement as a whole has certain kinds of influences on an individual's development which sedentary activities do not have. Specific kinds and intensities of movement will have specific effects on the human organism. This is the principle of *specificity*. To effectively assist in the guidance of the overall development of the individual, and to exert specific influences on certain aspects of his sociological, physiological, and psychological functioning, a physical education teacher must be able to identify those forms of development which are particularly amenable to the influence of physical education. He must know the specific objectives of a given element of the curriculum and the modifications and adjustments resulting from a given activity in a specific situation.

Jesse Feiring Williams presented in succinct form a diagram indicating the relationships of three kinds of objectives (technical, associated, concomitant) to the overall aim of physical education and to the outcomes (Figure 2.2). He goes on to say that the objectives are related to methods and that teachers should formulate their specific objectives with desired outcomes in mind. This diagram assists in clarifying objectives and outcomes in physical education as employed even today by traditional physical educational teachers.

Keeping in mind that objectives must be specific, that aims are more general, and that both teachers and curriculum experts must be keenly aware of where they are headed, let us now look at a list of aims as they might well be envisioned by a well educated and dedicated teacher of physical education.

Aims of physical education

1. To assist the individual to grow and mature as nature intended.

2. To provide a favorable environment and opportunities for a wide variety of physical activities which lead to optimal perceptual-motor development.

3. To provide the wise guidance, necessary control, and educational opportunities which lead to optimal health—physical, mental, and emotional.

4. To contribute to the learning of motor skills and movement patterns which are part of the normal life of most human beings (creeping, crawling, sitting, standing, walking, running, jumping, pushing, pulling, lifting, climbing, etc.).

5. To assist the individual to develop adequate strength, endurance, flexibility, and coordination.

6. To assist in the prevention and amelioration of handicaps and defects which are amenable to improvement through physical education.

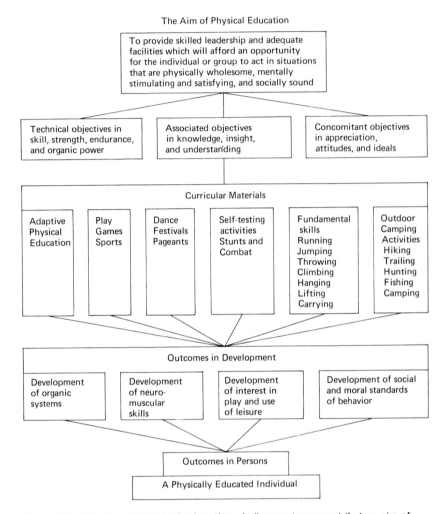

The Aim of Physical Education

To provide skilled leadership and adequate
facilities which will afford an opportunity
for the individual or group to act in situations
that are physically wholesome, mentally
stimulating and satisfying, and socially sound

Technical objectives in skill, strength, endurance, and organic power	Associated objectives in knowledge, insight, and understanding	Concomitant objectives in appreciation, attitudes, and ideals

Curricular Materials

Adaptive Physical Education	Play Games Sports	Dance Festivals Pageants	Self-testing activities Stunts and Combat	Fundamental skills Running Jumping Throwing Climbing Hanging Lifting Carrying	Outdoor Camping Activities Hiking Trailing Hunting Fishing Camping

Outcomes in Development

Development of organic systems	Development of neuro-muscular skills	Development of interest in play and use of leisure	Development of social and moral standards of behavior

Outcomes in Persons

A Physically Educated Individual

Figure 2.2 The aim of physical education. A diagram to suggest that an aim of
physical education in harmony with its objectives operates through the activities of a
program to secure certain outcomes that can eventuate in a physically educated
individual. [58, p. 331]

7. To assist in the learning of neuromuscular skills in a variety of physical
activities which will be developmental and rewarding. These will normally include
games, sports, aquatics, gymnastics, dance, and vigorous outdoor recreational
activities.

8. To teach and nurture appreciation for the role of movement, in all its forms,
as one means by which man can achieve pleasure, joy, and self-fulfillment.

9. To teach and foster understanding and appreciation of the body as a marvelous organism, through which the individual may express his thoughts and feelings and by means of which all his achievements are made possible.

10. To contribute to the satisfaction of the students' psychological needs. These include the needs for security, belonging, self-esteem, self-realization and self-transcendence.

11. To assist individuals in making the adjustments necessary for wholesome and satisfying social interaction.

12. To contribute to the satisfaction of the students' needs for fun, joy, and relaxation.

13. To provide opportunities for individuals to test their mettle, satisfy their spirit of adventure, and discover hidden resources through participation in challenging and hazardous activities.

14. To provide opportunities to compete and cooperate, to lead and follow, and to share defeats, triumphs, joys, and sorrows.

"... opportunities to compete ... and cooperate ..." (Courtesy of the *Journal of Health, Physical Education, and Recreation.*)

In summation, then, the ideal teacher would aid, wherever possible, in the development of good health, personal fitness, organic vigor, motor skills, social adjustment, and the appreciation of movement in all its forms. He would help the student satisfy his needs, be they biological, psychological, sociological, or spiritual. He would also assist in the formulation of value systems and the development of a philosophy of life which would make all other aspects of physical education meaningful, harmonious, and self-fulfilling.

Objectives of physical education

As has been indicated, objectives are more specific than goals or aims, their achievement is more readily assessed, and they denote outcomes which can serve as a guide to evaluation.

However, even objectives vary greatly in their specificity. In planning their work, some teachers will write a single objective indicating the expected outcome for an entire unit. Examples might be "to learn to play baseball," "to develop a strong body," "to learn how to square dance," or "to develop an appreciation for the outdoors."

Objectives may be written for a single individual or for a given grade. These are often termed "performance objectives." Lowell Klappholz explains and gives examples of performance objectives in his November 1972 *Physical Education Newsletter:*

> It (a performance objective) is the statement of what the learner is expected to do or know at a specified time in his educational career under specific conditions as evaluated by prescribed criteria which makes for accountability in education.
>
> Let's take a good hard look at what a performance objective is. In simplest terms a performance objective contains three basic elements. They are:
>
> Set out the conditions under which students will perform a specific task or activity.
>
> Describe the activity to be performed as accurately as possible.
>
> State the criteria for evaluation of successful performance.
>
> Performance objectives are usually written as single sentence statements. [27]

It is becoming increasingly common to talk about "behavioral objectives." These should also be specific and measurable but deal with changes in *behavior* which may accrue from educational experiences.

Ann Boehm writes meaningfully about both of the above-mentioned types of objectives:

> Most writers in the field would agree that a behavioral objective is a statement of an observable end—behaviors desired of the learner after the completion of an instructional unit. Objectives need to be stated both in terms of

performance and in terms of what is minimally acceptable behavior. With objectives so stated, it is possible for the instructor to evaluate the individual's performance in terms of defined goals. This, in fact, becomes the function of evaluation, for it is clearly unfair to include areas not covered in instructional units on classroom tests. [9, p. 117]

Student teachers are often required to write out lesson plans and to include specific objectives in some detail. One lesson form with which the author is familiar requires the statement of one or two general objectives and, under each of these, several specific objectives. The portion of the lesson plan dealing with objectives might appear as follows:

General objective: To learn to bat in softball.

Specific objectives:

1. To stand with the knees slightly flexed, feet parallel and 12 to 18 inches apart, with the frontal plane of the body parallel to a line leading to the pitcher.
2. To grip the bat a few inches from the small end and hold it correctly about shoulder high, ready for a quick swing.
3. To swing the bat parallel to the ground and in a path where it will meet the ball.
4. To shift the weight correctly from the rear foot to the front foot so as to get the most body weight into the swing.
5. To meet the ball just as it is crossing the plate and ahead of the body so as to increase the force imparted to the ball.
6. To follow through with adequate wrist action and correct timing to achieve speed and quickness in swinging.
7. To learn the mechanical principles of imparting force to an object, properly shifting one's weight, and applying the principle of summation of forces when batting.
8. To learn to keep the eye on the ball when hitting.
9. To learn the importance of proper practice when aquiring a motor skill.
10. To learn the importance of attention to the instructor or coach when in a teaching/learning situation.

Objectives may also be classified according to the level of learning. Some objectives are for beginners, some for intermediate performers, and some for those who are of championship caliber (see Figure 2.3). It must also be remembered that the physical educational teacher must know how to provide objectives for individual instruction as well as for classes or groups.

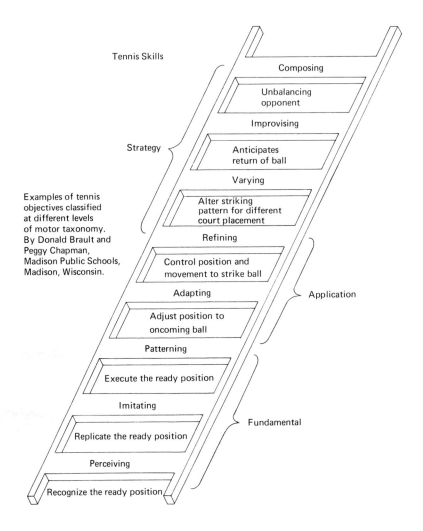

Tennis Skills

Composing

Unbalancing
opponent

Improvising

Strategy

Anticipates
return of ball

Varying

Examples of tennis
objectives classified
at different levels
of motor taxonomy.
By Donald Brault and
Peggy Chapman,
Madison Public Schools,
Madison, Wisconsin.

Alter striking
pattern for different
court placement

Refining

Control position and
movement to strike ball

Adapting

Application

Adjust position to
oncoming ball

Patterning

Execute the ready position

Imitating

Fundamental

Replicate the ready position

Perceiving

Recognize the ready position

Figure 2.3 Another example of objectives. [25, p. 51] (Courtesy of the
American Alliance for Health, Physical Education, and Recreation.)

Figure 2.4 Physical education thrusts. [7, p. 14] ▶
(Courtesy of the American Alliance for
Health, Physical Education, and Recreation.)

Thrusts

Figure 2.4 depicts, in form of an arrowhead, some of the potential beneficiaries of physical education as well as its varied "thrusts." The figure also portrays the breadth of influence and points out that, as services are extended to a broader segment of the population, the total thrust is increased. And as stated in *Tones of Theory:*

> It is obvious ... that the usual way of looking at physical education can diminish the thrust of the arrowhead. If physical education, as a body of knowledge, relates only to young skilled males, or young unskilled females, or any combination of discrete wedges, a portion of the arrowhead is missing and the thrust of the physical education interpretation of human movement phenomena is lessened. Additional wedges could be added to the arrowhead to hone the point to a finer, more precise end. Wedges representing morphological characteristics, psychic readiness, and social aptitude are all potential additions. Other arrows of the human movement phenomenon exist for other bodies of knowledge, each capable of making an impact on the personal and societal life experience. The human movement phenomenon has a quiver of arrows. [7, p. 15]

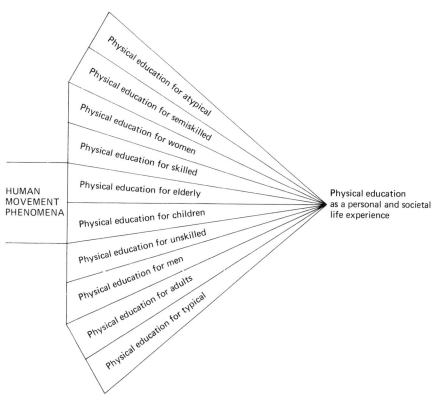

The teachable moment and concomitant learnings

Regardless of how earnestly a teacher tries to plan for the achievement of outcomes, there are always unexpected situations which occur spontaneously and in which the teacher's response and behavior can have a great influence on the student's learning. There may be a class in gymnastics where a student is careless in "spotting" and, as a result, the performer is injured. The manner in which the teacher deals with the careless spotter* as well as the injured person may be turning points in the lives of both of them. The amount of concern, the degree of understanding, the method of discipline, and the opportunity to demonstrate his interest in both students will reveal the quality and the effectiveness of the teacher.

The class may be one in wrestling. The instructor observes a fourteen-year-old boy using unfair tactics against his opponent. When the student referee remonstrates, the wrestler becomes angry and obdurate. The instructor has an opportunity to teach respect for authority, belief in fair play, and other values usually associated with good sportsmanship. He knows, however, that the offending wrestler has no father, lives in a slum, and has fought in the streets while growing up. He also knows him as a person who is always on the defensive and who lives with a feeling of inferiority. Again we see the teachable moment, and one for which advance planning is difficult.

Physical education classes can be planned for outcomes leading to physical fitness, strength, and endurance, or for providing opportunities for self-expression. For purposes of analysis, these may be thought of as *focal learnings.* It is relatively easy to plan for the achievement of such objectives. It is more difficult to plan specifically for experiences which lead to good sportsmanship or other forms of desirable character development. It is also difficult to plan specific lessons for the satisfaction of the need to belong, the development of a positive self-concept, or the self-actualization of the individual. Nevertheless physical education environments and situations abound with opportunities for such experiences. Let us call these *concomitant learnings* (Figure 2.5). Instructors must be prepared to deal with such opportunities intelligently and constructively.

While one must be careful not to subdivide education into its elements and assign to each segment responsibility for certain objectives, it is true that the general public and many administrators have certain expectations with regard to the outcomes of physical education. The unique responsibilities of physical education have to do with the development of organic vigor, neuromuscular facility, and some learnings concomitant to these. As Edward Voltmer and Arthur Esslinger have so aptly stated:

> The unique objectives of physical education are physical development, motor skills and knowledges and understandings about physical education and related activities. If these purposes are not accomplished in physical education, they will not be achieved elsewhere in the school. Consequently, they

*An individual who stands next to a trampoline, for example, and observes the performer to prevent accidents.

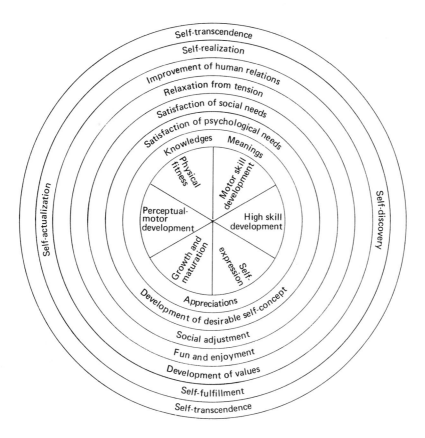

Figure 2.5 Focal and concomitant learnings. Center circle—focal learnings. Outside circles—concomitant learnings.

deserve a high priority insofar as the physical educator is concerned. To give these objectives a priority does not represent an attempt to set up an order of value, but rather an order of approach. [56, p. 45]

Figure 2.6 illustrates the concept that while one strives to achieve certain goals which belong more specifically to the realm of physical education, there are many other learnings taking place simultaneously, often unobtrusively, but sometimes in the full glare of the spotlight. Primary and shared responsibilities are suggested.

Physical education *is* education and the master teacher will strive to assist students in as many ways as possible, with the achievement of those goals and objectives which are both tangible and intangible in mind. Some aims and objectives are the principal and unique responsibility of physical education, while there are others where the responsibilities and the outcomes are shared with other disciplines. All are significant. All contribute to the development of the educated person.

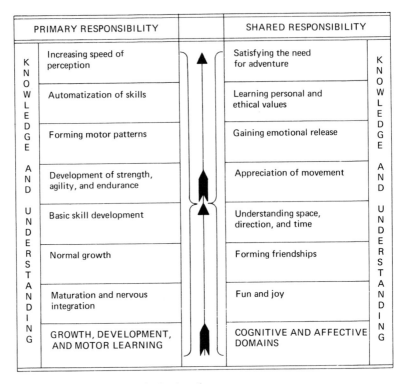

PRIMARY RESPONSIBILITY	SHARED RESPONSIBILITY
K N O W L E D G E — Increasing speed of perception	Satisfying the need for adventure — K N O W L E D G E
Automatization of skills	Learning personal and ethical values
Forming motor patterns	Gaining emotional release
A N D — Development of strength, agility, and endurance	Appreciation of movement — A N D
U N D E R S T A N D I N G — Basic skill development	Understanding space, direction, and time — U N D E R S T A N D I N G
Normal growth	Forming friendships
Maturation and nervous integration	Fun and joy
GROWTH, DEVELOPMENT, AND MOTOR LEARNING	COGNITIVE AND AFFECTIVE DOMAINS

Figure 2.6 Goals of physical education.

As stated in *Tones of Theory:*

Physical education shares its concern about human movement with other areas. The specific concerns of these areas are not mutually exclusive, but have a meaningful relationship with each other. Athletics and recreation are both sensitive to physical education and physical education shares a portion of their special focus on sports and leisure. [7, p. 13]

Just as physical education, athletics and recreation share their concerns and responsibilities, so also do the psychomotor, cognitive, and affective domains have interrelationships which render complete separation or isolation impossible. While focussing on objectives classified in one of these domains, the effect of any educational experience spills over into the other domains as well.

A contemporary view

Not all contemporary writers agree with the foregoing exposition of goals, aims, and objectives. Daryl Siedentop deals extensively and thoughtfully with these concepts in his recent book, *Physical Education: Introductory Analysis.* After discussing "Physical Education as a Means of Achieving the Goals of General Education," "Physical Education as Human Movement," and "The Role of Physical Education in the Last Quarter Century," he summarizes his thinking in the chapter entitled "The Aims and Objectives of the New Approach." [51, pp. 187–207] Siedentop's central thesis is that physical education should be perceived as a form of play education and that a person's play life is as important and significant as any other phase of his life. He then states that *"the aim of physical education is to increase human abilities to play competitive and expressive motor activities."* He emphasizes "increasing human abilities" and presents the following three objectives to support this emphasis.

1. A developmental objective: the goal of which is to bring about a state of readiness for playing the activities of physical education.

2. A counseling objective: the goal of which is to provide opportunities for players to match their interests and abilities to various activities with the help of the physical educator.

3. A skill objective: the goal of which is to develop competencies in the players' chosen activities. [51, p. 195]

A careful analysis of the above objectives will reveal a good deal of similarity between these and the traditional objectives as listed by Hetherington, Nash, and others: (a) organic development, (b) neuromuscular development, (c) interpretive-cortical development, and (d) emotional-impulsive development.

The above objectives also cover much the same ground as do those indicated by Williams (Figure 2.2). Siedentop recognizes the similarities but insists on a basic difference presented below:

It is important to recognize that whatever benefits might accrue, they occur because the participant has *played*, and because of this it seems that the wisest course to follow is to aim at increasing abilities to play, and to state objectives that rigorously adhere to the intrinsic nature of play activities.

The suggestion being made here is that it is time for physical education to take play seriously; to examine the depth and breadth of the implications of play; to recognize it as the source of the meaning that we all have found in the activities of physical education; and to develop theories and programs which are consistent with the overriding human importance of an active play life. If other desirable changes occur as a result of participation in physical education, then so much the better, but we must first recognize that if abilities to play are not increased, but instead are held still, stunted, or thwarted, then it is unlikely that desirable changes will occur; and that most importantly, students will be left on their own to discover this important source of meaning. If this occurs, then what has caused it can only be called physical mis-education. [51, p. 206]

It is hoped that the foregoing presentation will provide ample food for thought and that each professional student will try to systematically formulate his philosophy of physical education including what he sees as its purposes, goals, aims, and objectives. In the next chapter, a summary of some of the historical concepts and principles involved in formulating such a philosophy is presented.

2.5 CONCEPTS AND PRINCIPLES

As one contemplates the variety of meanings different individuals attach to terms and the many reasons people have for engaging in physical activity, certain concepts and principles emerge. These are presented here for the consideration of teachers, coaches, and those who may be contemplating entering the field of physical education. The following are suggestive but by no means all-inclusive:

1. Each person has a different expectation as he begins to play a game, move to music, lift a barbell, or participate in a sport. Instructors should be constantly aware of the many possibilities.

2. Most students are not aware of all the subtle modifications which are transpiring as they run, dance, throw, tackle, or climb. They need help to understand the physiological, sociological, and psychological phenomena which are related to movement and complete involvement in physical activity.

3. Words, sentences, and actions are perceived differently by different people. For this reason, terms need to be defined and concepts illustrated.

4. It is important that teachers try to understand students and that students try to understand teachers. The more they cooperate as they work toward common goals, the greater the probability of their achievement.

5. Many of the outcomes of physical education occur subtly as a result of both the activities and the total environment. Coaches and teachers are usually much more aware of this than are the students and athletes.

6. Many of the modifications which occur (e.g., increase in strength and size, development of sex characteristics, etc.) are the result of maturation and should not be attributed entirely to physical education. Nevertheless, the role which vigorous activity does play should not be ignored.

7. The formulation of aims and objectives is worthwhile for at least two reasons: (a) it gives direction to the activity, and (b) it affords an opportunity to evaluate the success of the effort by comparing outcomes with objectives.

8. A carefully formulated statement of purposes, aims, and objectives can be useful in assisting administrators, parents, and the general public to understand and appreciate the program.

9. The development of physical fitness is only one aspect of physical education, albeit an important one. Teachers and coaches must also be aware of the effects of their classes, programs, and practice regimens on the intellectual, psychological, and social dimensions of their students and athletes as well.

10. Physical education is more than physical training. Training refers to learning responses to commands, to forming habits of exercise, and to preparation for contests. Education also includes creativeness, decision making, freedom of choice, and self-expression.

11. Professional physical educators should appreciate the acquisition of knowledge for its own sake. They should also understand and appreciate the application of both old knowledge and new research findings to the practice of physical education.

12. Education and its branch, physical education, must be concerned with *both* the development of individuals and the improvement of society. The two are not divisible as one contributes to the other.

13. Planning is essential to the success of any enterprise. The formulation of goals, aims, and objectives based on a sound philosophy is vital to effective planning. Shared plans and shared goals are an important first step toward achievement.

14. As explained by Muriel Gerhard:

> Traditionally, teachers have operated within a framework of general goals. In recent years, we have recognized the need to broaden this approach, to spell out specific applications of general goals to fit individual students. For the teacher, the pupil, the parent, the community—the realities of education are best expressed as specific student objectives. [20, p. 1]

15. Those who write and interpret aims and objectives, those who formulate curricula and lesson plans, those who administer physical education programs, and those who teach or coach must be aware that society and the world we live in are continually changing. Objectives must be appropriate to the cultural milieu, societal demands, and the changing environment. While goals, aims and objectives must be student-centered, they must also be formulated in light of the environment in which students live, study, play, and work.

16. Because aims and objectives are related to philosophies of education and life, and because there are as many philosophies as there are persons who attempt to delineate and interpret such aims and objectives, it cannot be expected that there will be universal agreement on these matters. Nevertheless, it is important that the purposes, goals, aims, and objectives be continually scrutinized and reevaluated. As environments and societal requirements change, so must the purposes and the intentions of education be adjusted. Expectations, outcomes, and the methods to achieve them must be modified and adapted to serve the purposes of the time, the place, and the circumstance.

17. Physical education is not, and cannot be, all things to all people. *It is many different things to many different people.* One individual benefits from it in one way and another finds it valuable in another way. The same individual may develop perceptual motor skills one year, increase in strength and endurance at another time, learn the values of relaxation through a different experience, and appreciate the benefits of expression through movement on still another occasion. The various outcomes of physical education may occur simultaneously or one at a time; they may be similar for several members of a group and different for others; they may be easily discernible and very evident or they may be subtle and hardly noticeable. The outcomes may affect the physical, intellectual, social, psychological, and spiritual dimensions individually or they may exert an influence on all simultaneously. The important thing is that the teacher and coach shall not hinder but shall be prepared to assist in *whatever positive development* may accrue from the experiences.

SELECTED REFERENCES
1. American Association for Health, Physical Education, and Recreation, *Essentials of a Quality Elementary School Physical Education Program,* Washington, D.C.: National Education Association, 1970.
2. _____, *Guidelines for Secondary School Physical Education,* Washington, D.C.: National Education Association, 1970. Reprinted by permission.
3. _____, *Guide to Excellence for Physical Education in Colleges and Universities,* Washington, D.C.: National Education Association, 1970.
4. _____, *Knowledge and Understanding in Physical Education,* Washington, D.C.: National Education Association, 1969.
5. _____, *Physical Education '73,* Washington, D.C.: AAHPER, 1973.
6. _____, *"This is physical education,"* a statement prepared by the Physical Education Division of AAHPER, Washington, D.C.: AAHPER, 1965.
7. _____, *Tones of Theory,* Washington, D.C.: National Education Association, 1972. Reprinted by permission.
8. *The Body of Knowledge Unique to the Profession of Education,* Washington, D.C.: Pi Lambda Theta, 1966.
9. Boehm, Ann E., "Criterion-referenced assessment for the teacher," *Teachers College Record,* Vol. 75, No. 1, September 1973. Reprinted by permission.
10. Bookwalter, Karl W., and Harold J. VanderZwaag, *Foundations and Principles of Physical Education,* Philadelphia: W. B. Saunders Company, 1969.
11. Bucher, Charles A., *Foundations of Physical Education,* 4th edition, St. Louis: The C. V. Mosby Company, 1964.
12. Cowell, Charles C. and Wellman L. France, *Philosophy and Principles of Physical Education,* Englewood Cliffs, N.J.: Prentice-Hall, 1963.
13. Educational Policies Commission, *The Central Purpose of American Education,* Washington, D.C.: National Education Association, 1961.
14. _____, *Moral and Spiritual Values in the Public Schools,* Washington, D.C.: National Education Association, 1951.
15. Evaul, Tom, "Where are you going? What are you going to do?," in *Curriculum Improvement in Secondary School Physical Education,* Washington, D.C.: AAHPER, 1973.

16. Felshin, Janet, *Perspectives and Principles for Physical Education,* New York: John Wiley and Sons, 1967.
17. Frost, Reuben B., "Physical education for the 70's—the YMCA way," *World Communique,* September–October 1970.
18. "Futuristics," *Nation's Schools,* Vol. 89 No. 3, March 1972.
19. Frost, Reuben B., *Psychological Concepts Applied to Physical Education and Coaching,* Reading, Mass.: Addison-Wesley Publishing Company, 1971.
20. Gerhard, Muriel, "Behavioral objectives," *Professional Report,* New London, Ct.: Croft Educational Services, December 1971.
21. Havel, Richard C., and Emery W. Seymour, *Health, Physical Education, and Recreation,* New York: The Ronald Press Company, 1961.
22. Henry, Franklin M., "Physical education: an academic discipline," *Journal of Health, Physical Education, and Recreation,* Vol. 37, September 1964.
23. Holbrook, Leona, "Basic instructional program at the college level," in *Comtemporary Philosophies of Physical Education and Athletics,* Cobb, Robert A. and Paul M. Lepley (eds.), Columbus, Ohio: Charles E. Merrill Publishing Company, 1973. By permission.
24. Jenny, John H., *Physical Education, Health Education, and Recreation,* New York: The Macmillan Company, 1961.
25. Jewett, Ann E., "Physical education objectives out of curricular chaos," *Curriculum Improvement in Secondary School Physical Education,* Proceedings of the Regional Conference, AAHPER, Mt. Pocono, Penn., 1971.
26. Kenyon, Gerald S., "A sociology of sport: on becoming a sub-discipline," in *New Perspectives of Man in Action,* Brown, Roscoe C. and Bryant J. Cratty (eds.), Englewood Cliffs, N.J.: Prentice-Hall, 1969.
27. Klappholz, Lowell A., "Preparing and using performance objectives," *Physical Education Newsletter,* November 15, 1972, Physical Education Publications, Old Saybrook, Connecticut. Reprinted by permission.
28. Kneller, George F., *Foundations of Education,* New York: John Wiley and Sons, 1963.
29. Kohl, Herbert R., *The Open Classroom,* New York: Random House, 1969.
30. Kroll, Walter P., *Perspectives in Physical Education,* New York: Academic Press, 1971.
31. Larson, Leonard A., "Professional preparation for the activity sciences," in *Anthology of Comtemporary Readings,* Slusher, Howard S. and Aileene S. Lockhart, Dubuque, Iowa: Wm. C. Brown Company, 1966.
32. McCloy, Charles H., *Philosophical Bases for Physical Education,* New York: F. S. Crofts and Company, 1947.
33. Munrow, A. D., *Physical Education,* London: G. Bell and Son, 1972.
34. Nash, Jay B., *Physical Education: Interpretations and Objectives,* New York: A. S. Barnes and Company, 1948.
35. _____, Francis J. Moench, and Jeannette B. Saurborn, *Physical Education: Organization and Administration,* New York: A. S. Barnes and Company, 1951.
36. National Conference on Interpretation of Physical Education, Report, Chicago: The Athletic Institute, 1961.
37. National Education Association, "Education in a changing society," Washington, D.C.: NEA, 1963.
38. *New Horizon: The Becoming Journey,* Washington, D.C.: National Education Association, 1961.
39. "New students and new places," a report and recommendations by the Carnegie Commission on Higher Education, New York: McGraw-Hill, October 1971.

40. Nixon, John E., "The criteria of a discipline," *Quest,* Monograph IX, December 1967, pp. 42–48.
41. Nixon, John E., and Ann E. Jewett, *An Introduction to Physical Education,* 7th edition, Philadelphia: W. B. Saunders Company, 1969.
42. Oberteuffer, Delbert, *Physical Education, A Textbook of Principles for Professional Students,* revised edition, New York: Harper and Row, 1956.
43. "PEPI'S first year," *Journal of Health, Physical Education, Recreation,* Vol. 43, No. 6, June 1972.
44. Peterson, A. D. C., *The Future of Education,* London: The Cresset Press, 1968.
45. "Physical education '73," *Instructor,* January 1973.
46. Randall, M. W., and W. K. Waine, and M. J. Hickling, *Objectives in Physical Education,* London: G. Bell and Sons, 1966.
47. Rarick, G. Lawrence, "The domain of physical education as a discipine," *Quest,* Monograph IX, December 1967, pp. 49–52.
48. Reich, Charles A., *The Greening of America,* New York: Bantam Books, 1970.
49. Ridini, Leonard M., "Physical education for the inner city," *The Physical Educator,* Vol. 28, No. 4, December 1971.
50. Seidel, Beverly L., and Matthew C. Resick, *Physical Education: An Overview,* Reading, Mass.: Addison-Wesley Publishing Company, 1972.
51. Siedentop, Daryl, *Physical Education: Introductory Analysis,* Dubuque, Iowa: Wm. C. Brown Company, 1972. Reprinted by permission.
52. Smith, Michael A., Stanley Parker, and Cyril S. Smith, *Leisure and Society in Britain,* London: Allen Lane, 1973.
53. Turner, Edward T., "Physical education: a paradoxical phenomenon," *The Physical Educator,* December 1968.
54. *"Values in sports,"* Joint National Conference of the Division for Girls' and Women's Sports and the Division of Men's Athletics, American Association for Health, Physical Education, and Recreation, Washington, D.C., 1962.
55. VanderZwaag, Harold J., *Toward a Philosophy of Sport,* Reading, Mass.: Addison-Wesley Publishing Company, 1972.
56. Voltmer, Edward F., and Arthur A. Esslinger, *The Organization and Administration of Physical Education,* 4th edition, New York: Appleton-Century-Crofts, 1967.
57. Whitehead, Alfred N., *The Aims of Education,* New York: The Free Press, 1957.
58. Williams, Jesse F., *The Principles of Physical Education,* 8th edition, Philadelphia: W. B. Saunders Company, 1964. By permission.
59. Young, Michael, and Peter Willmott, *The Symmetrical Family,* London: Routledge and Kegan Paul, 1973.
60. Zeigler, Earle F., "Intramurals: profession, discipline, or part thereof?," Proceedings of 76th Meeting, National College Physical Education Association for Men, January 1973.

Historical Overview to 1950

Chapter 3

3.1 EARLY BEGINNINGS

As far back as the Neanderthal man and the Cro-Magnon man of the Paleolithic age, there are records testifying to the importance of movement to life. Those who inhabited the earth at that time climbed trees, ran, manufactured stone implements, carved, and scratched and engraved designs and pictures. One may surmise that their offspring were "educated" to do all the things which prepared them to survive and protect themselves. The records are, however, too sparse and too difficult to decipher to form any firm conclusions about their physical education.

The Neolithic age followed the Paleolithic and was characterized by primitive agriculture, domestication of animals, weaving, pottery making, and a continuation of hunting. Stone implements were more precise, varied and polished. In the latter part of this era, copper, iron, and tin were hammered and molded into useful implements for war and domestic use. With the Bronze Age, the first civilizations arose. Meanwhile, children were taught the crafts of their elders as well as hunting and fighting. Little more than this can be said with any certainty about the advent of physical education. It may be concluded, however, that education for effective movement is as old as the human race.

3.2 FIRST CIVILIZATIONS

Civilizations arose and historical records became clearer. The regions of the Euphrates and Tigris rivers became "the cradle of Western civilization." Many people settled down instead of continuing their nomadic life. They raised crops and tended their domestic animals. Milk and grain became principal sources of food.

Fighting broke out between the settlers and the nomads. Warlike tribes from the mountains united to conquer the settlers. Then the conquerors also settled down and eventually became part of the civilization they had captured. Thus fighting and training to fight continued to be an important aspect of Akkadian, Babylonian, Assyrian, Chaldean and Persian life. What evidence there is indicates that throughout the earliest civilizations, physical education was essentially militaristic. People were taught the use of weapons and were trained for strength, stamina, skill, and courage.

Other forms of physical activity were, however, part of the daily life of these early people. To search for food, hunt wild game, build homes, and keep warm required a considerable amount of strength, endurance, and physical skill. In any event, the daily regimen required enough vigorous movement to supply the fitness needs of most of the people. There is also every reason to believe that the play instinct and the competitive urge existed in those early civilizations, and that individuals were even then striving to run faster, lift more, throw farther, and wrestle more adroitly than their fellows.

3.3 THE NEAR EAST, MIDDLE EAST, AND FAR EAST

Egypt. Formal education received considerable attention in Egypt, especially after the flowering of early civilization, probably around 2000 B.C. Wrestling, weight lifting, ball games, aquatics, and gymnastics became part of the physical education of youth. Many of these activities were performed to honor gods and, in some other countries, had a religious significance. Music and dancing also played an important cultural role. The aristocrats favored religious dances, the common people engaged in folk dancing, and the professional dancers performed at festive occasions. All things considered, the Egyptians developed a fairly sound physical education program as their civilization took form.

India.   India is known as a land of religious mysticism. Since its beginnings, Buddhism, Hinduism, and Mohammedanism have played an important cultural role. While tolerant of some practical objectives, Indian educational philosophy emphasized ultimate "salvation" as the most important goal. But the children played games and many adults took part in boxing, riding, and hunting. Chariot racing, horsemanship, fencing, wrestling, and hurling contests are mentioned by some historians. The practice of Yoga has been identified with India since the earliest times.

India, like many other Eastern countries, has a long history of dance. Because of its intimate relationship with religion, dance became particularly significant to the people of early India. Dancers performed at religious ceremonies, marriages, and other festive occasions.

China.   Gunsun Hoh tells us that the earliest Chinese civilization was characterized by general intellectual and physical development. He states further that the "all-round educational system" began about 2000 B.C. and that the "higher branches of learning" consisted of rituals, music, archery, horsemanship, literature, and mathematics. [8, pp. 2–3] The education of youth at that time included attention to the aspects of moral, intellectual, military, and physical training.

Physical education for the masses did not prevail in China. Because the Chinese felt secure from outside attack, they did not feel it necessary to build and train great armies. With the military motive lacking and because they were quite isolated, their culture became static and peace-loving. There was no pressure on them to become universally physically fit. In their civilization the emphasis was on art, philosophy, and academic excellence. They encouraged music and dancing, but these were primarily for the wealthy. "Kong Fu," a form of medical gymnastics, was also developed and practiced. This was intended to be therapeutic in nature and consisted of special forms of bending, kneeling, lying, breathing, and standing. Archery, polo, fishing, swimming, hunting, and a form of football are also mentioned in Chinese historical records as an integral part of their culture.

According to George Tan, football and polo definitely originated in ancient China. Chinese scholars report that baseball, volleyball, basketball, tennis, and pingpong were also played in ancient times but may not have had their origin in China. A form of football was introduced by Emperor Huang about 2697 B.C. as the basic physical exercise for warriors training to overcome their opponents. Tan indicates that football was utilized in this fashion because it was believed to develop not only valor but also strategic planning and team action. [20, p. 26]

Tan also reports that at the end of the Han dynasty (221 A.D.), the Three Kingdoms who had been engaged in war for many years challenged one another in football, thus developing the game to where it became very popular and important in the life of the Chinese people. [20, p. 26]

According to Tan, polo also originated in China. It did not gain the popularity of football and was played principally by the elite. Emperor Ming Huang of the Tang Dynasty (713–756 A.D.) played polo with his empress and knights on the palace grounds. But maintaining horses for the game prevented it from becoming popular with the masses.

Because of the need to standardize the rules for these games, they gradually became more systematically and scientifically taught. Coaching, then, had its early beginnings in China. One of the early "coaches" in recorded history was General Huoh Chi-Ping of the Han Dynasty. He devised methods to effectively teach the games to the soldiers.

3.4 PHYSICAL EDUCATION IN GREECE

Clarence Forbes says that "physical education played a larger part in Greek life than it has in the life of any nation before or since." [6, p. 3] While this may seem like an exaggeration, a careful examination of Greek culture corroborates the statement.

It is not merely because they originated the Olympic, Isthmian, Delphic and Nemean games; it is not just because the Greeks developed many young men with fine physiques . . . rather it is because the Greeks held it in such high esteem that made physical education so significant a factor in their society. For them it was the center of life, the core of education, the essence of culture. The great philosophers, Plato, Aristotle, and Protagoras, thought and wrote copiously about physical education. The wealthy and the poor as well as the educated and the unschooled considered this aspect of life essential. Both as individuals and as communities, they "were willing to make heavy sacrifices in the cause of physical education." [5, p. 260]

The goal of education in Greece was the development of the individual as a man of action and of wisdom. Symmetry and beauty as well as strength, endurance, agility, and speed were admired. In the museums of Greece, there are statues of youth (*Kouros*) which depict the grace and strength of the ideal athlete. It is noteworthy, however, that when visitors come, the museum guides call attention not only to the bodily beauty of the figures but to the facial expressions as well. A slight smile illumines the face which depicts the serenity and contentment which should accompany beauty and strength. In other words, the Greeks feel that the spirit of man is equally important as his physique . . . that physical well-being, spiritual well-being, and wisdom all reside in the individual who has achieved perfect development. This is the ideal toward which the Greeks of the Hellenic period were striving. Those who conduct and support the International Olympic Academy in Olympia today also espouse this philosophy, which was so indicative of the civilization in Athens during the "Golden Age."

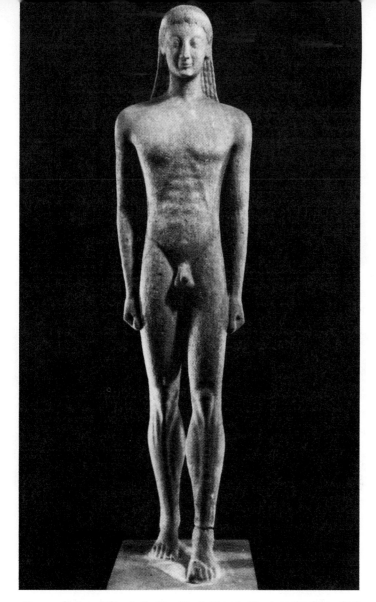

Kouros, Statue of Greek Youth—"A slight smile illumines the face which depicts the serenity and contentment which should accompany beauty and strength." (Courtesy of the International Olympic Academy, Athens, Greece.)

Early Greece was composed of several "city-states." One of these was Sparta, where the objective of physical education was militaristic. At the age of six, all strong and healthy boys were brought to a public barracks where they began training for the army. A strenuous conditioning program which included marching, running, jumping, and wrestling constituted the major part of this training. Throwing the javelin, hurling the discus, riding horseback, and using the sword and shield were also practiced.

Olympia, A Unifying Force—Olympia, the sanctuary, was the meeting place of the Hellenic world. Every four years Greeks from the city-states on the mainland and from the colonies bordering on the Mediterranean assembled here to worship Zeus, the supreme god, and thus pay tribute to the unity of Hellas. Within the Altis, the sacred grove bounded by a wall, near the earlier Temple of Hera (upper left) there was dedicated to Zeus in the fifth century a great Doric temple (center) which stood as a symbol of the devotion of all Greeks to the sky-god of the Hellenic race. The period of the festival was a time of peace. All wars ceased, and competitors from rival city-states took part side by side in religious ceremonies and athletic contests. The merchant from

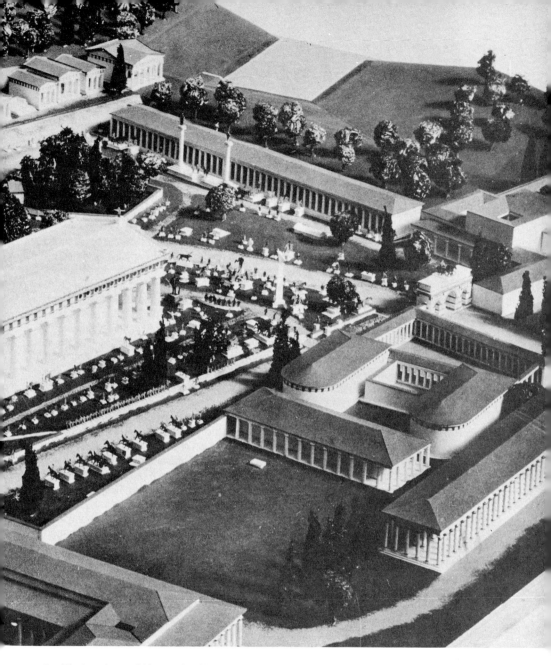

the West exchanged his goods with the trader from the East. Treaties between states were recorded on stone slabs set up in the Altis under the protection of Zeus. And in times of danger from outside aggression pleas were made for Panhellenism by leading spokesmen of Greece. The fact that the Olympic games were carried on until 393 A.D., and that many of the buildings and statues illustrated above were dedicated by city-states or individuals after the fifth century, indicates the hold which the Olympian religion had on the hearts of Greeks and Romans. (Courtesy of The Metropolitan Museum of Art, Dodge Fund, 1930.)

In the thousand years immediately preceding the birth of Christ, there were many festivals where athletic contests and games were conducted in honor of the gods. The most famous of these were the four Panhellenic festivals: the Olympic Games at Olympia, the Isthmian Games at Corinth, the Pythian Games at Delphi, and the Nemean Games at Argolis. Athletic contests were mingled with speeches and presentations of poetry with religious themes predominating. Art, music, and dance were also included in these great festivals, attracting participants from all over the Mediterranean world.

Competitors in the games were required to be free Hellenes and to take an oath to abide by the rules of the games. They trained for the games and considered it a great honor to win. Winners were crowned at Olympia with an olive wreath and at other games with other wreaths. As punishment for breaking the rules, contestants were required to build small statues (*Zanes*)—upon which a description of their violation was inscribed for all to see. Contestants competed in the nude and only men were admitted as spectators.

In later Greek times, emphasis on intellectual education was intensified and there was a corresponding diminution of interest in physical education. The great festivals were commercialized and professionalism made inroads on the high ideals of athletics. Athletes were glorified and paid well for a brief period but many soon deteriorated into parasitic and quite useless citizens. Physical education lost the respect and important place it once held in the entire educational scheme.

The decline of Greek physical education from this pinnacle, perhaps never reached before or since, was caused by (1) the philosophy of the Stoics who scorned the body, (2) the emphasis of Christians on the spiritual aspect of life to the detriment of all else, (3) the commercialism and professionalism which accompanied athletics, (4) the opposition of the Romans who were passive and unsympathetic to this phase of Greek life, and (5) the rise of the Roman Empire and the decline of Greece as a world power.

Nevertheless, educational philosophy and the role of physical education in Greece, particularly Athens, had more impact on later theories and practices than did the philosophies of any other early civilization. We still refer to the concept of the whole man, to the balanced and interdisciplinary educational curriculum, to the appreciation of the arts, and to the importance of the spiritual aspects of life found in the Greek educational scheme. It was when their priorities became distorted, their values selfish, and their developmental aims one-sided that their effectiveness and influence declined.

3.5 THE ROMAN EMPIRE

While the Romans learned much from the Greeks, and in part assimilated their culture, they contributed little toward the advancement of physical education. In fact, the term "physical training" better described their methods of preparing to move and perform. Roman citizens were essentially military in nature, their objective for captives and slaves being gladiatorial combat. The Greek ideal of harmonious development played a minor role in Roman education . . . instead, spectacle and professionalism were characteristic of their culture.

However, it is impossible to generalize about physical education in the Roman Empire. For as Peter McIntosh indicated, "this empire spanned many centuries in time and, in space, stretched from Scotland to the Sahara Desert and from the Atlantic Ocean to the Caspian Sea. It embraced the tribal societies of Gaul and Britain, the city-states of Greece and the ancient monarchy of Egypt." [11, p. 35]

The Romans were practical, disciplined, and militaristic. Roman citizens trained their sons to box, ride, swim, hurl javelins, and fight. Older boys were also required to labor in the fields and perform other menial tasks. They did not lack for physical activity. They had ample opportunity to play when young and spend time at the circus and amphitheater when older. Soldiers and professional athletes underwent elaborate practice and training, but there is little evidence of systematic physical *education* for the masses.

3.6 THE MEDIEVAL PERIOD

The decline and fall of the Roman Empire has been attributed, in part, to the moral and physical decay of its citizens. When a country has neither the strength nor the will to fight or resist, it is easy prey to more imperialistic nations. Barbarians from the East and North conquered and ravaged what had been the great Roman Empire . . . education, art, culture, and architecture ebbed to their lowest level.

During the Middle Ages, the Germans, Goths, Norsemen, and other barbarians invaded, conquered, and eventually mingled with the European populations. Because they were all warlike outdoorsmen and fierce hunters, they had a form of physical education, but it was not formalized. Nevertheless they brought hardiness, strength, endurance, and good health to the Europeans and infused the conquered lands with new blood and energy.

Christianity, which had been repressed by the Greeks and Romans, began to flourish. With it came the rise of *Asceticism,* a philosophy of austere self-denial, fasting, and in extreme cases, self-torture which had a disastrous effect on health and physical vigor. The physical needs of man were subjugated to the spiritual and physical education, as we know it, suffered greatly. Man was separated into body, mind, and soul, a division which has impeded the progress and understanding of physical education to the present day. Life for its own sake was not considered important. Christians were taught to be concerned about their souls and eternal salvation and not about the health and comfort of the body. The ancient Olympic Games were abolished because they were thought to be pagan. Chariot races and other "debasing" sports were terminated for much the same reason. The desires of the flesh were to be subdued. Early universities and monasteries where intellectual and spiritual education were fostered and where scholarship was the aim did not provide for athletics or physical education. The youth, therefore, turned to destructive rather than constructive pursuits. *Scholasticism* took its place beside asceticism as enemies of physical education.

3.7 THE RENAISSANCE

From the Dark Ages which followed the fall of Rome to the beginning of modern times was the period known as the Renaissance. This was an age of enlightenment and progress. There was renewed interest in the civilizations of Greece and Rome. The emphasis was on *Humanism,* investigation, discovery, and reason. It was a period of tremendous progress for education.

Physical education was fostered and nurtured during the Renaissance. Hygiene was emphasized and the role of physical education highlighted. Authoritarianism and rigidity gave way to liberalism and individual freedom. Unity and self-containment replaced the theories dividing man's being. Great men such as Da Feltra, Luther, Milton, Pope Pius II, and Comenius espoused the cause of health and fitness.

Jean Jaques Rousseau was a naturalist who said, "All is good as it comes from the hands of the Creator; all degenerates under the hands of man." In his book *Emile,* he describes the ideal education of a boy who lived in the country under simple conditions unhampered by man. He learned naturally and was given the opportunity to explore and learn at will. Physical exercise was natural and varied and occurred without any outside coercion. Emile jumped, scaled cliffs, leapt over obstacles, and grew into a sturdy agile youth. "Let him work and move about and run and shout and be continually in motion," said Rousseau. He talked about ball games, hygiene, and gymnastic exercises. He believed in the relationship of the mental, physical and emotional. His philosophy of physical education is in harmony with much of the best thought about physical education today.

3.8 THE GERMAN INFLUENCE
While there were a number of German physical educators who made substantial contributions to physical education during the period following the Renaissance, only a few will be mentioned here. Johann Bernhard Basedow, Johann Christian Frederich Guts Muth, Frederich Ludwig Jahn, and Adolph Speiss are four Germans whose contributions and influence have been worldwide. It is their work which had such impact both in their own country and in the United States.

Basedow founded Philanthropinum, an institution for physical education and games founded upon the philosophy and teachings of Rousseau. Basedow believed that sports, games, and other forms of physical education played a significant role in intellectual and moral development as well. Guts Muth taught at the Philanthropinum and through his leadership and writings earned the name of "Grandfather of German Gymnastics." Rope ladders, masts, and climbing ropes were important pieces of equipment at the Philanthropinum. Swimming, stunts and tumbling, hiking and camping were included as important activities. The two best books authored by Guts Muth were *Gymnastics for the Young* and *Games.* These plus the leadership Guts Muth exercised for half a century had a marked influence on physical education in the West.

There are many who would point to Jahn as the greatest of the physical educators in Germany during the first half of the nineteenth century. While his motives and methods have occasionally been challenged, his dedication and influence are seldom questioned. Jahn inaugurated the *Turnverein* (turning society) and its success and growth were phenomenal. The "Turner" movement, which began in the early part of the nineteenth century, grew rapidly and continued to expand until about 1920 when there were nearly 10,000 such societies, many of which still exist today.

The Turner Societies included in their activities excursions to the woods and mountains, games and exercises, and a great deal of running, jumping, leaping, climbing, and swinging. The real innovation for which Jahn was largely responsible, however, was the introduction of several pieces of gymnastic equipment which are still part of our programs today. The parallel bars, the horizontal bar, the rings, and the "horse" were the most important.

Jahn was a spirited and unconventional leader. He was an individualist in thought and deed. He was in trouble with authorities on more than one occasion. He was a loyal citizen and much of his zeal for physical education came from his commitment to the building of a strong nation. Nevertheless he brought variety to the field of education and his contributions to American physical education are significant.

Adolph Speiss continued the work of Jahn and the development of the Turner movement in Germany. He encouraged more authoritarian methods than did Jahn and gymnastic routines became more systematized. Speiss published *Turnbuch für Schulen,* a manual for teachers which became the guide for physical education in most German schools. He is known as the "Founder of School Gymnastics" in Germany and his major contribution was the influence he exerted in making physical education a part of the curriculum in Germany's public schools. He is one of the great leaders in the field of physical education.

3.9 THE SCANDINAVIAN COUNTRIES
Sweden has contributed much to physical education in the West. Per Henrik Ling was perhaps the greatest of the Swedish leaders, the "Lingiad"* taking its name from him. Among his contributions was the development of the scientific aspects of physical education. Anatomy, physiology, and kinesiology became important basic subjects in the area of physical education. Health and physical fitness became important objectives. The harmonious functioning of the human organism in all its dimensions was emphasized. Per Ling is also noted for the establishment of the Royal Central Institute of Gymnastics in Stockholm.

When Lars Gabriel Branting succeeded Ling as the Director of the Central Institute of Gymnastics, he continued Ling's scientific emphasis but directed it toward therapeutics and medical gymnastics. His work attracted attention in countries throughout Europe.

Hjalmar Fredrik Ling, a son of Per Henrik Ling, taught and wrote while at the Central Institute. He traveled extensively, exchanging ideas with leaders in other

---

*Periodic celebrations of physical education named in honor of Per Henrik Ling. Exhibitions of medical gymnastics, aesthetic gymnastics, standing free exercises, dances, and newer forms of physical education have featured these occasions. Thousands of people of all ages have participated.

European countries. He studied administrative problems and school life. He became an expert on growth and development and tried to establish a curriculum based on the child's needs. He, too, was one of the great Swedish leaders.

Denmark, located between Germany and Sweden, absorbed ideas from both of them. Elements of German gymnastics, the scientific emphasis from Sweden, and their own insistence on rhythmic and continuous swinging exercises became assimilated and integrated into Danish physical education.

Franz Nachtegall was himself an outstanding gymnast and wanted to teach his skill to others. He was influenced by the teachings of Basedow and Gutsmuth but was also a great organizer and leader. It has been said, "Denmark owes it to him that during the first third of the nineteenth century she held the leading place among European nations in the realm of physical education." [10, p. 183] Nachtegall was the first Director of Gymnastics and a pioneer in the field of physical education during the first half of the nineteenth century.

Niels Bukh was a Danish leader in physical education almost one hundred years after Nachtegall. He was the gymnastic leader of the Ollerup Gymnastic High School. Especially concerned with the problems of rural youth, he was interested in the physical fitness of the Danish people, both young and old. He placed great emphasis on suppleness, strength, and mobility as objectives of physical education. Niels Bukh contributed to physical education the concept and practice of what he termed "Primitive Gymnastics." He developed a specific routine of exercises which would systematically develop each part of the body as well as the joints. "The perfect physique" was one of his goals.

3.10 THE BRITISH EMPIRE

The heritage of sports, which has played such a significant role in American physical education has come in largest measure from England. During the development of the German, Danish, and Swedish gymnastic systems, sports and games were not only being developed in England but were being incorporated into the cultures of the many parts of the far-flung British Empire. The military objective was inappropriate due not only to British individualism and love of liberty, but also the protection from foreign assault afforded Britain by her isolated setting. During the nineteenth century, "English public schools evolved their own peculiar physical education which was no less comprehensive and just as highly organized as its continental counterparts. It took the form of games and sports . . . yet games and sports were rarely thought of as physical education." [11, p. 177]

Character development, sportsmanship, team play, and desirable social qualities were the objectives emphasized in British programs of games and sports. Both public and private schools gradually came to accept this philosophy of sports and the importance of their role in education. The participants generated most of the features of the sports and games and self-government was an essential element in the development and administration of the programs. This feature is considered very meaningful and explains the current philosophy of coaching and playing in England. It also explains why the history of physical education in England is replete with names of educators who assisted in developing sports but does not list one or two "giants" in the profession such as Jahn of Germany or Ling of Sweden.

Pride in personal fitness, a philosophy of life which included exercise and sport, and continuation of exercise programs throughout life marked, and still mark, British physical education. Indeed, these are commendable characteristics which are worthy of emulation.

The Dominion of Canada, a member of the British Commonwealth, conducts programs of physical education and recreation which, in many ways, resemble those of the United States but which have been influenced more strongly by the British and, in Quebec, the French. Control of these programs has been vested in the provincial departments of education, although there is also some stimulation and influence at the national level. The National Fitness Act of 1943, administered by the Physical Fitness Division of the Department of National Health and Welfare, has played an important role in improving physical, recreation, and health education programs in the last quarter century. The role of the Physical Fitness Division has been that of coordination, stimulation, and advising. McGill University has led the way in developing professional preparation programs. It began preparing physical education teachers in 1912 and awarded the first bachelor's degree in that field in 1945. Today, Canada's program for preparing teachers is among the best in the world. Even though Canada's schools have many of the same sports and physical education elements as the United States, they have more clubs and their emphasis on hockey, rugby, and cricket is much greater. The Province of Quebec, especially the French-speaking city of Quebec, has its own system of physical education which reflects the culture of France.

3.11 OTHER COUNTRIES

In *France,* the emphasis on education for leisure, aesthetic appreciation, dance, and grace of movement, as well as the mammoth contributions of Baron De Coubertin to sport deserve special mention. De Coubertin's devotion to amateur sport and his tireless effort to restore both the Olympic ideals and the Olympic Games must never be overlooked.

The early years of physical education in France were essentially militaristic in philosophy and scope. In recent years, more emphasis has been placed on leisure activities and on social, moral, and aesthetic objectives. The dash and color of many French sport programs and the variety of their interests resemble in some ways the physical education programs of the United States.

The emphasis on education to support communism, mass participation as a basic method, the objective of personal fitness, compulsory physical education in the schools, and the strenuous effort to prepare winners for the Olympic Games have characterized the physical education of the *Soviet Union.* Recreation programs, rest and rehabilitation centers, team sports, and Physical Culture Days are also noteworthy developments. Physical education to enhance Russian nationalism, good citizenship, and military service has also been a basic aim. Folk dancing by the many and varied ethnic and cultural groups has also enriched their physical education.

As in many other countries, nationalistic spirit and strong military forces were the early goals of Soviet physical education in the nineteenth and twentieth centuries. Physical fitness and gymnastics dominated the program until after World War II. There was also a strong interest in sports, camping, and rehabilitation. Olympic development, aquatics, exercise physiology, and riflery were among the activities receiving emphasis.

The Coubertin Stele in Olympia—The ancient Olympic games, which began in 1776 B.C. and were abolished by order of Theodosius I in 393 A.D., were revived in 1896 largely through the efforts of Baron Pierre de Coubertin. When he died his heart was buried in the above stele now located on the grounds of the International Olympic Academy in Olympia. (*Left to right:* Mr. Otto Szymiczek, Curator, International Olympic Academy; Mrs. Sara Jernigan, Director of Women's Physical Education, Stetson University; Mrs. and Mr. Reuben B. Frost.)

The *Sokol* organizations from *Czechoslovakia*, youth organizations in *Bulgaria*, sport schools of *Rumania*, and outstanding dance programs of *Yugoslavia* have made noteworthy contributions to physical education. *Finland's* enthusiasm for gymnastics and sport is worthy of emulation. The skating and swimming programs of *Holland*, the colorful dancing and "Jai Alai" from *Spain*, and the balanced and well-organized physical education programs of *Switzerland* must also be mentioned. Each country made contributions to the pool of knowledge from which ideas can be drawn and a physical education program formulated.

John Groth in his *World of Sport* describes forty-three exciting sports from all parts of the earth, only a few of which are familiar to the average American. He tells of the violent game of *buz kashi*, a version of polo, which he saw in Afghanistan; he describes a game of *kabaddi*, a fluid form of tag played by the Sikhs of India; he reviews the *basque* games, indigenous to the people of the Pyrenees, which include *stone-pulling, scything, boules*, and *pelota*. In this book are depicted the *highland games* of Scotland, *football* as played in Italy, *camel racing* across the Jordanian desert, and *elephant racing* in Kandy, Ceylon.

Other interesting games and contests described by Groth are *tilting the ring* in Holland, *road bowling* in Ireland, *whip ball* among the Eskimos, *tacraw* in Bangkok, *guks* in Ethiopia, and the *joust of the saracens* in Arezzo, Italy. Natives of Africa are pictured in *donkey races* and *pyramid climbing races*. The *kushti* wrestling matches in Pakistan are recorded as well as *curling, barrel rolling, ice canoe racing,* and the great *tug-o-war* in the Quebec Winter Carnival. [7, pp. 12-149]

All cultures of the world have their form of physical education, their ethnic dances, their own games and sports. Countries with mixed citizenry and heritage, such as the United States, are rich in resources from which to draw ideas and program elements. In addition to those countries discussed, the cultures of *Latin America, Africa, Australia,* and *Asia,* have contributed much to American programs. No doubt, much more will be extracted and assimilated as immigrants become citizens and as worldwide communications continue to become more effective.

3.12 PHYSICAL EDUCATION IN THE UNITED STATES

The early colonists brought with them both the instinctive urge to play and certain religious tenets which were a hindrance to the development of sport, recreation, and free play. There were times and circumstances in which one influence or the other would dominate. However, in the colonial period there was little formalized physical education in the schools.

In the eighteenth and nineteenth centuries when physical education was evolving in the United States, there were many forces influencing those concerned with the establishment of schools and the formulation of curricula. Immigrants were pouring in from many countries. The Puritans, with their strong religious guidelines, settled in the Massachusetts Bay Colony and other parts of New England. The Dutch brought their love of skating and sledding to the area that is now New York. The Germans brought with them their gymnastics and the *Turn-*

verein; the Swedes and the Danes continued to teach their version of gymnastics and the scientific aspects of physical education. The British colonists imported their sports traditions and the French their appreciation for the aesthetic, their rhythmic calisthenics, and their dances. In 1802 the United States Military Academy was founded, and sports and physical education were included as important elements in cadet training. Meanwhile, scholars were reminding school administrators of the Greek philosophies and the people from the Balkan countries were demonstrating their folk dances and establishing sports societies.

In the middle of the nineteenth century, educational institutions began to take physical education and athletic programs seriously. In 1837, Catherine Beecher included physical education in the curriculum at the Hartford Female Seminary. The first American turnverein was founded in Cincinnati in 1848. In 1852 Yale and Harvard held a rowing match which is said to be the earliest intercollegiate athletic contest on record.

From that time on, events relating to physical education and athletics were occurring so rapidly that they can be better comprehended and remembered if they are categorized by the decades in which they occurred. Let us begin with 1850 and briefly summarize the key events and trends which mark each decade.

1850–1859. Boston led the way requiring daily physical education classes for school children. Other cities soon followed suit. Williams and Amherst played the first intercollegiate baseball game. The growth of intercollegiate athletics had begun. Meanwhile, Charles Beck, Charles Follen, and others were teaching German gymnastics and encouraging the establishment of turnvereins in cities such as Cincinnati, Milwaukee, Kansas City, St. Louis, Boston, and New York.

1860–1869. Education by means of play was stressed in the Kindergarten School in Boston. Amherst College, under the leadership of Edward Hitchcock, required physical education for all students. Dio Lewis established the Normal Institute for Physical Education. He called his system "The New Gymnastics," which employed rhythmic exercises with wands, clubs, dumbbells, and rings. By 1862 over seventy physical education teachers had been trained in his school. With gymnasiums being built in this decade by Amherst, Oberlin, Bowdoin, Wesleyan, and others, a new era began. The Morrill Act creating land-grant colleges was passed in 1862 ... to receive a grant, an institution must agree to teach military tactics and conduct the standardized ROTC program. Thus began the continuing controversy over the substitution of reserve officers' training for physical education. In 1866 California passed the first state law requiring physical education in the public schools, triggering efforts in other states to secure similar regulations. But progress in this decade was impeded by the Civil War. Military objectives were again emphasized and most of the effort during the sixties was directed toward the war and recovery from its effects.

1870–1879.   Because the effects of the war were still being felt, this decade was characterized in part by controversy over physical training for military purposes versus a return to gymnastics. Dr. Dudley A. Sargent of Harvard led the battle for gymnastics. Immigration on a large scale continued and the German system, the Swedish system, and the Danish system of gymnastics all had their advocates. This was also a decade of building, and with new gymnasiums came new programs and new leaders, giving renewed impetus to physical education and athletics. The famous Hemenway Gymnasium at Harvard was built in the late seventies.

1880–1889.   This was a developmental period for physical education. The American Association for the Advancement of Physical Education (forerunner of the AAHPER) was founded, with Dr. Hitchcock as the first president. The School for

The First Intercollegiate Football Game—November 6th, 1869 was a memorable day in football history. On that day Rutgers and Princeton clashed at New Brunswick, New Jersey in what was to be the first intercollegiate football game in the world. The first intercollegiate game in England was played three years later between Oxford and Cambridge.

The game, with 25 players to a side, was a running, kicking, continuous one with no holding of the ball and played with compromised rules agreed upon before the start of the game. The team which scored six goals first would be declared the winner. With the score tied four all, Rutgers kicked two more goals, becoming the first college football team to defeat another.

The picture, which is an accurate representation of the first game, was painted in 1932 by W. M. Boyd. The artist interviewed a few elderly players who were then still alive to ensure accuracy of detail. (Courtesy of the *Journal of Health, Physical Education, and Recreation.*)

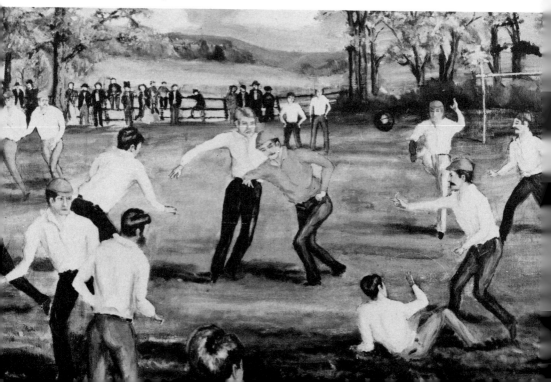

Christian Workers was founded in Springfield, Massachusetts in 1885. This was later to become The International YMCA College and then Springfield College, which is its designation today. It rapidly became one of the leading institutions, inaugurating its first professional education course for the preparation of physical education teachers in this decade. Great leaders such as Hartwell, Hitchcock, Sargent, Roberts, Gulick, McCurdy, and Wood were instrumental in gaining acceptance for physical education as an important part of the curriculum. In 1889 the first National Conference on Physical Education was held. Mrs. Hemenway and Amy Morris Homans founded the Normal School at Framingham and helped establish another in Boston. Sports and athletics had begun their period of rapid growth. Oberlin and the University of California at Berkeley established departments of physical education.

1890–1899. During this decade, the "Battle of the Systems" occurred. The German system, the Swedish system, the Danish system, and others vied with each other for recognition. Athletics and newer methods of physical education joined the fray. Calisthenics, formality, command-response, mass activity, drill, and marching were found in most programs where physical education had been formally recognized. Meanwhile, basketball was invented by James Naismith at Springfield College, the Amateur Athletic Union was founded, and the American Physical Education Review was first published with Dr. McCurdy as editor. Fourteen state universities established departments of physical education: Illinois (1894), Iowa (1896), Indiana (1890), Kansas (1893), Michigan (1894), Minnesota (1896), Missouri (1900), Nebraska (1894), Ohio State (1897), Oregon (1894), Utah (1894), Washington (1894), Washington State (1890), and Wisconsin (1899).

1900–1909. This was the period of athletic emphasis. Sports, interschool competition, and stress on winning took on such importance that it caused many institutions and people to lose sight of real values. Athletics for the highly gifted few received more attention than athletics for all. Educational outcomes were often obscured, and the values of traditional physical education programs were overlooked in too many places.

The Intercollegiate Athletic Association became the National Collegiate Athletic Association and assumed greater responsibility for the conduct of organized sport in colleges and universities. The Playground and Recreation Association was established with Dr. Gulick as president.

1910–1919. In contrast to the previous decade, mass participation and recreation became the emphasis. "A game for every boy and girl and every boy and girl in a game" became the slogan. Intramural and extramural athletics were fostered and nurtured. "Many teams in many sports" was the growing trend in athletics. Lifetime sports and activities for leisure were important program elements. Strength, endurance, and skill were deemphasized. At the same time, universal education at public expense was now generally accepted as a basic principle. Education was recognized as essential to a successful democracy and all scholastic subjects were scrutinized with this in view. The goals of physical education were broadening and the objectives increasing in both number and diversity.

It was also during this decade that The Athletic Research Society was organized. As members, this society included colleges, secondary schools, elementary schools, YMCA's, church leagues, turners, boys' clubs, social centers, and rural organizations. A committee of the society investigated athletics in 1912 and its report revealed an interesting resemblance to the athletic phenomena of today, with respect to both philosophy and problems. The following excerpt from that report is indicative:

> It seems clear from the work thus far accomplished that the real function and possibilities of properly conducted plays and games as agents in social and moral improvement as well as physical development, and as important factors in the educational system, are coming to be more generally appreciated; that the promotion of these activities among young people in schools and elsewhere should be conducted with less emphasis on the spectacular championship contests, with their tendencies toward recruiting and professionalism, and more regard for the effect on the mass of individuals that take part; that plays, games, and athletic competitions of all sorts should be freed from the commercial and professional influences that exploit them for money and as a basis for recruiting professional teams; and that a definite effort must be made to organize and conduct these activities in such a way as to encourage the spirit of "sport for sport's sake." [1, pp. 585–586]

1920–1929. By this time, physical education had become fairly eclectic. It included some of the rugged fitness activities of gymnastics, the military drills, some of the motivating and true-to-life situations found in sports, some of the grace and suppleness developed in dance and rhythmic gymnastics, and some of the free, pleasurable, and relaxing activities associated with the wise use of leisure. Nevertheless, educators felt that there was at least one important ingredient still lacking . . . health education. During the twenties this came with a vengeance. School teachers and officials were flooded with health literature, individual health needs were stressed, many health education agencies became involved, related programs (remedial, therapeutic, relaxation) were again emphasized, and, as had happened before, benefits from other traditional programs were overlooked.

1930–1939. The decade of the thirties was a period of assessing past trends, reviewing the traditional programs, examining practices in various ethnic groups, and trying to build a scientifically prepared program based on sound educational principles. Great stress was placed on analyzing goals, aims, and objectives. Educational outcomes were defined and sought, educational psychology was studied with renewed vigor, and the concept of "physical education as the medium" was emphasized and expounded. The thirties was also the period of the Great Depression and the beginning of economic recovery. While in many ways this was detrimental to the development of physical education programs, there were a few benefits. The recreational facilities constructed, repaired, or prepared by the WPA and PWA programs helped considerably to meet the needs of the increasing school population and those with available leisure on their hands. Valuable lessons were learned in trying to alleviate the sufferings of the unemployed and deprived. Many playgrounds and athletic fields came into being under the programs mentioned.

It was also in the thirties that the emphasis on progressive education really began. Self-directed education, individual freedom, the group process, problem solving, and participatory democracy were emphasized. The natural method, the student-centered class, learning by doing, and social efficiency were other aspects of this educational philosophy expounded by its greatest proponent, John Dewey.

Standards were raised, professional preparation improved, and the status of teachers and other school personnel enhanced. In general, education took great strides forward in the thirties. The number of institutions providing major offerings in physical education, health education, and recreation increased tremendously, and this area of education began to be accepted as a necessary and vital part of general education.

1940–1949. World War II: preparation—conflict—aftermath. These words most adequately depict the forties. The strides forward in both theory and practice came suddenly to a halt and physical education once again had one objective—to prepare the nation for war. Calisthenics, vigorous combative sports, competition, conditioning, correcting remedial defects—these constituted the program until 1946. Then came slowly a reversion to peacetime goals, the training of new leadership, the adjustment to new positions and different circumstances.

After 1950. Only a few remarks concerning the history of physical education since 1950 are appropriate at this time—events and developments of the immediate past will be treated as part of the present. A few introductory sentences, however, are in order.

The period from 1950 to the early 1960's was a period of expansion, growth, improvement of standards, and stabilization. Curricula and programs were organized and administered on a sounder educational basis than previously. Educational programs became more rigorous and certification standards more demanding. Professional preparation institutions were flooded with students, both undergraduate and graduate, who had selected physical education as their profession. Increased salaries and other benefits made this vocational choice more satisfying. Most important, better teachers were being prepared and better programs conducted. The best elements of the physical education of the varied cultural groups were finding their way into the curriculum. Conferences, workshops, and in-service training tended to integrate and homogenize the many disparate elements. As one leader put it, the profession was "growing up."

Physical education in the United States is definitely eclectic. The many ethnic groups, the diversity of professional preparatory institutions, the geographical and climatic differences, the socioeconomic disparities, the philosophical disagreements, and the innumerable experiences of our leaders and practitioners—these cannot help but produce an education that is rich, varied, and challenging. There is, however, a continual need for sifting and organizing information, honest appraisal, commitment to the optimal benefit of the child, and finally, the ultimate benefit to society.

We have suffered through and learned from the battle of the systems, we have heard the arguments concerning "education *of* the physical" versus "education *through* the physical," we have heard the discordant tones as the proponents and opponents of athletics presented their views, and we learned the differences of opinion with regard to fitness, perceptual-motor development, movement education, and recreation. Some consensus is gradually evolving with regard to our aims and objectives, desirable and undesirable practices, good and bad methodology, and effective versus noneffective practices.

We now come to what this book is all about—physical education programs for the present and the future. The chapters that follow will present philosophical, physiological, psychological, and sociological concepts and will contain discussions of current trends and developments as they affect physical education. Hypotheses and scientific evidence, current practices and methods, and administrative problems and their solutions will be examined. The effort in the remainder of the book will be to present current concepts, conclusions, and practices which will prove helpful to the teacher and the student.

SELECTED REFERENCES

1. "The Athletic Research Society—Resume of organization work and plans," *American Physical Education Review,* Vol. 18, No. 8, November 1912, pp. 585–598. Reprinted by permission.
2. Beck, Robert H., "The Greek tradition and today's physical education," *Journal of Health, Physical Education, and Recreation,* Vol. 34, No. 6, June 1963.
3. Bucher, Charles A., *Foundations of Physical Education,* 4th edition, St. Louis: The C. V. Mosby Company, 1964.
4. Contoumas, Solon S., *Olympic Games and Art in Greece,* Athens: PEAK, 1956.
5. Cowell, Charles C., and Wellman L. France, *Philosophy and Principles of Physical Education,* Englewood Cliffs, N.J.: Prentice-Hall, 1963.
6. Forbes, Clarence A., *Greek Physical Education,* New York: The Century Company, 1929.
7. Groth, John, *World of Sport,* New York: Winchester Press, 1970.
8. Hoh, Gunsun, "Past and future of physical education in China," *Thesis,* Young Men's Christian Association College of Springfield, Massachusetts, June 1923.
9. _____, *Physical Education in China,* Shanghai: The Commercial Press, 1926.
10. Leonard, Fred E. *A Guide to the History of Physical Education,* R. Tait McKenzie (ed.), Philadelphia: Lea and Febiger, 1923.
11. McIntosh, P. C., et al. *Landmarks in the History of Physical Education,* London: Routledge and Kegan Paul, 1957.
12. Rice, Emmet A., *A Brief History of Physical Education,* New York: A. S. Barnes and Company, 1932.

13. Rice, Emmet A., John L. Hutchinson, and Mabel Lee, *A Brief History of Physical Education,* 4th edition, New York: The Ronald Press Company, 1958.
14. Rogers, James E., "Trends in physical education," *Journal of Health, Physical Education and Recreation,* Vol. 2, No. 8, October 1931.
15. Savage, Howard J., et al., *American College Athletics,* New York: The Carnegie Foundation for the Advancement of Teaching, 1929.
16. Savage, Howard J., John T. McGovern, and Harold W. Bentley, *Current Developments in American College Sport,* New York: The Carnegie Foundation for the Advancement of Teaching, 1931.
17. Scott, Martha B., *The Artist and the Sportsman,* New York: Renaissance Editions, 1968.
18. Stevenson, John J., "College diversions," *Popular Science Monthly,* Vol. 76, No. 1, January 1910.
19. Strutt, Joseph, *The Sports and Pastimes of the People of England,* London: William Tegg, 1850.
20. Tan, George G., "Chinese origins of football and polo games," *Physical Education Today,* Vol. 19, Nos. 3–4, September–December 1972.
21. Van Dalen, Deobold B., and Bruce L. Bennett, *A World History of Physical Education,* Englewood Cliffs, N.J.: Prentice-Hall, 1971.
22. Vendien, C. Lynn, and John E. Nixon, *The World Today in Health, Physical Education, and Recreation,* Englewood Cliffs, N.J.: Prentice-Hall, 1968.
23. Wildt, Klemens C., "Historic phases of physical exercise," *Physical Education Today,* Vol. 19, Nos. 3–4, September–December 1972.

Physical Education for Future Generations

Chapter 4

Four billion years ago, the earth was formed. Four hundred million years ago, life moved to the land. Four million years ago, man appeared on earth. One hundred years ago, the technological revolution that led to this day began.
—George E. Mueller*

---

*"One Small Step—One Giant Leap, The Voyage of Apollo II," *Reader's Digest,* October 1969, pp. 251–298.

4.1 TOMORROW'S WORLD

In this century of technolgical revolution and the cybercultural society, machines have replaced man in many ways. Daily tasks in the home as well as much of the labor in factories and on the farm are now automated. Robots can duplicate much of man's physical movements. Pushbutton shopping and pushbutton cooking are a reality. We now have computers which can do much of the "thinking" and "remembering" which has always been the province of man.

Some technological developments are only in the minds of men and women; some are on the drawing board. Houses and factories at the bottom of the ocean, sea farms, and vacations in submarines may be commonplace within the foreseeable future. Satellites for improved communications, reconnaissance, controlling the weather, and concentrating the sun's rays are a reality. Rocket-type vehicles, ramjet engines, atomic powered bombers, and space platforms are beyond the experimental stage. Extraterrestrial travel and the exploration of Mars and other planets are real possibilities for the next generation. Even the recognition of unidentified flying objects (UFO's) is no longer considered impossible.

New forms of energy

Lasers and masers for sensing, cutting, illuminating, and operating are rapidly moving out of the experimental stage. The speed and range of aircraft are increasing far beyond our expectations. Before long, the electronic "chip" will make even smaller radios and pocket-sized television sets as well as invisible hearing aids possible. The sun, tide, and wind will soon be utilized as additional sources of energy.

Medicine and genetics

For medicine and related fields, new developments are equally dramatic. "Cyborg" techniques (combining parts of man with artificial or synthetic parts) hold much promise and are even now being used with considerable success. Artificial or synthetic hearts, aortas, pacemakers, heart valves, and blood vessels are already helping many with damaged circulatory apparatus. Developments in this field are just beginning. Artificial joints, bony structures, intestines, ears, and limbs are among the most successful of the newer experiments. Even supplying man with "gills," enabling him to breath both in and out of water, appears possible.

The field of genetics has moved so rapidly and so far that society is not prepared for many of the changes. Many hereditary and congenital defects are being repaired and even prevented. It also appears scientifically possible to breed a race of "super men" and "super women" or, in other instances, individuals who are superior in some special talent or ability. Control of sex, size, courage, intelligence, and other characteristics appears to be within the realm of possibility.

Computer technology

The computer has been recognized as the symbol of the neotechnological age. From fewer than 1000 in 1955, the number of computers in operation in the United States rose to about 80,000 in 1975, and it has been predicted that the total will double in the next ten years. In the opinion of many, it will bring about more significant changes in society than any technological advance in the history of man. Many of these changes have already taken shape.

The computer has joined together the processes of "thinking" and "remembering" and is fast becoming the principal foundation stone of future technological advance. The amount of information that can be sensed and stored is almost beyond comprehension. The ability of the computer to draw various bits of information from its memory bank and organize them for the purposes designated by scientists make the possibilities of its utilization almost infinite. The capability of instantaneous language translation presages for the future unimaginable facility for international communication.

Significance of technological development
The harnessing of atomic energy, the high-level development of electronics, and the perfecting of sophisticated computing machines have produced more change than all previous discoveries combined. Transportation, communications, research, business methods, farming, and warfare have changed to a degree that would have been incredible half a century ago. Almost twenty years ago, David Sarnoff wrote, "The last 100 years have been but a split second in human history. Yet they have compassed more technological achievement than all the millenia that preceded."* These words take on added significance with each passing day.

While the potential for the computer in industry, government, health and medical programs, education, and daily living is almost incredible, there are those who feel its use is a mixed blessing. Automation, which is generally regarded as a boon to society, has its accompanying problems. Particularly at the lower levels of the socioeconomic spectrum, there are many who, as a result of automation, lose their jobs and find themselves unable to fit into the posttechnological society.

However, we cannot accept the pessimistic statements condemning all technological advances and blaming them for all the ills of the world. Instead, we as intellectual and scientific leaders must take seriously the responsibility of making machines serve man instead of the reverse. Margaret Mead has called this the "challenge of automation to education for human values." She concludes her statement with the following:

> Making the post-automation world human will demand new educational measures: an immediate interpretation of the relationship between human instruction and machine execution; new programs which will prepare children for a world in which they will work, not under threat, but as part of their membership in their society; emphasis on human skills rather than upon routine machine tending skills; and greater attention to the development of individual interests and talents to use the greater leisure which everyone may expect to have. [46, p. 70]

---

*David Sarnoff, "Preview of the next 25 years," *Reader's Digest,* March 1955, p. 9.

Again we are reminded of the unlimited potential for the future. Again we are made aware of the possibilities for a better—and the possibilities for a worse—society. Again and again we should ponder the words of John MacIver:

> The potentials of man as a creator and artist are barely realized today. Technology, as his master, may well destroy much that is now innate and hidden, not yet in flower. Technology, as his servant, will bring him closer to the self-realization he has always sought. [42, p. 318]

Other societal developments

It appeared for a while as though population growth in the United States was out of control and would cause a serious sociological problem. While this nation has now gained control of her own population expansion, the solution in some other parts of the world appears to be more difficult. Starvation, poverty, and over-crowded conditions in other countries will, of course, affect all nations and will need attention on the international level. Education cannot avoid being involved in this problem, inasmuch as the number of students in school is the most important factor in school planning. Because family living and sex education are a very important part of the solution, educators, particularly health educators, must take cognizance of population trends.

Urbanization

If educational programs for all are to achieve their objectives, the general movement of people to cities is another trend which deserves attention. Reports indicate that over ninety percent of our population now lives in an essentially urban environment. This being the case, we must plan the educational experiences of students and prospective teachers so that maximum benefit may be derived. Attention must be given to the needs of those living in the inner city as well as in the suburbs and rural areas. Thought should also be given, especially by health educators, to finding ways of encouraging more people to live in the less densely populated areas.

Racial turmoil

The racial revolution has many facets. On occasion there have been violent out-breaks, but in recent years, the expression of discontent has been more peaceable and constructive. The racial revolution is deep and complex and it is difficult to unravel all the threads. Some of the factors which underlie this turmoil are fear, intolerance, injustice, violence, misunderstanding, racism, and lack of consideration for the rights of others. Frustration, humiliation, lust for revenge, feelings of inferiority, and plain desperation are also discerned by the sensitive and observant. In some instances the fanning of emotions leads to hatred and violence, but more important, the positive qualities of humility, love, understanding, and faith are too often lacking. Human frailties are the ultimate sources of most of the trouble. James Farmer indicates the need to feel respected and treated as equals. He speaks eloquently about racial problems in these words.

This does not mean that we will be loved, but it is not necessary that people be loved in order to be respected and dealt with as equals. Black people now would much prefer to be respected than to be loved if there is a choice. In fact many care little about being loved. They want to be respected as eyeball-to-eyeball equals and sit down and negotiate as others negotiate.

The first step toward sharing is to discover ourselves, and to understand that humanity transcends color. I will not give up, I will never give up the ultimate ideal of a colorblind society, where color is put in proper perspective as an irrelevancy and loses its power to divide and to intimidate. But that time is not now. That will come perhaps at the millenium or in the kingdom of God. In the meanwhile we must live in the real world, and the real world is not the world of universal love. Ultimately, we hope it will come.

Humanity, I say, transcends color, but remember, man cannot love humanity until he first learns to love himself. If one hates himself, how in the world can he love mankind of which he is a part? [17, pp. 200–201]

Farmer fingered the crux of the matter. Utopia will contain people of all ethnic backgrounds and the color of their skin will be entirely irrelevant as far as status, rights, privileges, and the judgment of behavior are concerned. Stereotyping will be passé. What a person is, what he can do, how he behaves, and how he interacts with others will be the criteria. These will transcend the happenstances of ethnic background, cultural environment, and other factors for which an individual cannot possibly be held accountable.

But Utopia is not a reality yet. Ethnic background or race has often relegated the individual to inferior status, leading in turn to poorer housing, unemployment, and a lower standard of living. Educational and cultural deprivation is the inevitable result, and only the especially gifted and determined can work their way out of the situation in which they find themselves. Their self-concept is damaged, their self-confidence is limited, and their view of their role in society is decidedly pessimistic. Race, in such situations, becomes an important factor in personality development.

To at last approach Utopia, society must continue emphasis on equal educational and employment opportunities for all and have the faith and courage necessary to continue the struggle. Minority group members must recognize that they too have a burden of responsibility for their behavior and that their role in building good interpersonal relationships is also essential. They must try to control their frustrations and their anger before irreparable damage is done. The elimination of prejudice and bigotry on the part of all people, to an extent humanly possible, must be the larger goal. The nurture and development of love, empathy, and understanding are essential first steps.

And Eric Lincoln's faith may be the final answer:

It is only my emotions that say run. My reason knows that man must live in this world until he knows some world that is better. And my faith insists that the heritage you pass on to your children will be less contingent and less tentative than the heritage you yourselves have already received. [41, p. 240]

Family instability

Divorces have become relatively more common than they were a generation or two ago and the trend shows little evidence of tapering off. Desertions and separations have increased many times over. In some segments of society, unmarrieds living together is no longer frowned upon to the degree that it once was. The fatherless child is becoming relatively more commonplace.

Because opportunities to travel and find employment away from home have markedly increased, children are more prone to leave the community in which they were born and raised. The love of freedom and the thrill of seeing and experiencing new things are enticing.

It is now common practice for industries to move their factories and plants from one place to another. Many of the employees and their families are also relocated. Suburbia is filled with people who move every few years. As a result, fewer young people than in the past remain on their father's farm after they reach adulthood.

All this leads not only to family disorientation but also to the casting aside of parental values and customs. New values emerge as old ones are discarded. The "generation gap" between parent and child has been the result.

Multirevolution

According to Toffler, industrial society itself is experiencing a crisis in the United States and this crisis has many components:

> We are simultaneously experiencing a youth revolution, a sexual revolution, a racial revolution, a colonial revolution, an economic revolution, and the most rapid and deep-going technological revolution in history. We are living through the general crisis of industrialism. In a word, we are in the midst of the super-industrial revolution. [63, p. 186]

If such a cataclysm is actually occurring, we are facing challenges and opportunities which exceed those of any previous period in history. Education and physical education must give careful heed to changes which are taking place and to the new demands which will be placed on teachers and leaders.

Youth and new life styles

The many diverse subcultures in existence today are definitely affecting our society. Educators must evaluate carefully the respective phenomena and try to meet the needs of both the individuals concerned and the society of which they are a part. To merely stereotype the younger generation as "beatniks" or "hippies" is not only harmful but inappropriate. A search for effective means of communicating and understanding is increasingly essential.

Donald McDonald identified some of the elements that help describe the "youth scene" of the late sixties and early seventies:

1. *The age of affluence.* Youths who themselves have experienced only affluence have difficulty understanding their parents' concern for economic security and their emphasis on jobs and material possessions.

2. *The atomic age.* The youth of today was born and raised under the shadow of the atomic bomb and the constant threat of world annihilation.

3. *The hot wars.* Korea, the Dominican Republic, Cuba, Guatemala, Vietnam, Cambodia . . . the conflict of values between what occurs in wars and many of the things they have been taught to believe make their personal decisions difficult.

4. *The inversion of national priorities.* Youths have difficulty accepting as right the disproportionate (in their view) expenditures for military purposes, education, the handicapped, and the general welfare of society.

5. *The technological revolution.* When youths themselves are motivated toward "people helping" and service professions, the lack of emphasis on humanization and personalization on the part of others is difficult for them to accept.

6. *Television.* Youths are motivated and united by what they see on television. The programs serve as a common center of interest. Youth movements seek to be dramatic enough to attract news media, for without massive publicity they know their cause will fail.

7. *Existentialism.* The importance of the individual and his immediate experience has caused many young people to accept existentialistic thought. They feel they can best explain their philosophy of life in terms of the concepts of individual freedom espoused by existentialism.

8. *The rigidity of basic social institutions.* Resistance to change and to the participation of youth in decision making has antagonized many young people. They have difficulty appreciating the deep-seated values which older people have developed through experience.

9. *Art and Technology.* Lifestyles are communicated and encouraged by art forms and creative expression. Youths have a natural tendency to unite in their admiration for contemporary art and to join in appreciation of contemporary music and dance.

10. *Literature.* There is a substantial body of literature which criticizes and satirizes the "establishment" and the past in general. Much of it also points out instances of dehumanization and depersonalization. This literature identifies with much of the thinking of young people and furnishes themes around which they can rally both figuratively and in fact. [44, pp. 25–28]

These principles should be studied carefully by all who are working with and teaching young people. At the same time the young people should be made aware of some obvious inconsistencies in their thinking. Lack of consideration for older people, little gratitude for what parents have done for them, and hypocrisy in their own lives and thinking should be called to their attention. The conformity of youth as they feel obligated to adopt the lifestyles of their peers and the selfish concern for their own opinions as they arbitrarily reject opposing views are also evident in some instances. These too should be thoughtfully, patiently, and tactfully pointed out.

Once again we find human frailties and human virtues intermingled in the personalities of both young and old, teacher and student. As the world becomes more crowded and people are forced to live in close proximity to one another, it becomes increasingly obvious that understanding and love are a large and significant part of the answer. Compassion and empathy combined with adequate and effective self-discipline must be the means to the ultimate answer.

There are many young people today who are establishing their own lifestyles and sets of values, improving on those developed by their parents and others of previous generations. Idealism and the urge to help people are characteristic of a large part of today's youth. The rejection of material values, even though temporary, may help them discover real values which will support and guide them in times of stress. The glorification of poverty practiced in some youth ghettos may be a relatively transient phenomenon. We can hope that drug experimentation will create revulsion and reaction which will eventually bring about its demise.

Youth groups who were so embroiled in campus demonstrations have now largely turned to other methods of bringing about change in both society and education. Many now realize that demonstrations, particularly violent ones, are not effective in the long run and that more can be accomplished by working within the system. Many now recognize the fact that a number of educational practices against which they were formerly protesting have now been corrected, and that the "establishment" is both cognizant of what needs to be done and is willing, within the limits of available resources, to do it.

The rather sudden and dramatic reversal of the financial condition of both educational institutions and individual families is also playing a role. As parents begin to feel the financial squeeze, they become more reluctant to spend money on an education they do not consider worthwhile. When colleges are in greater financial need, students accept with better grace the fiscal difficulties involved in hiring additional staff, erecting new buildings, and starting new and innovative programs.

It becomes more and more obvious that change and the acceleration of change are inevitable. It becomes imperative, therefore, that people learn to cope with change. This requires a careful study of the forces at work and an analysis of both the new and the old. To be able to discern that which is transient and that which has the qualities of permanence will be one of the objectives of the future. Educational programs must develop the quality of adaptability in young people. The study of the future must become a fully recognized part of the curriculum.

The young people of today will be the adults of tomorrow. The qualities which must be developed are patience, confidence, courage, adaptability, empathy, and faith. A world peopled by such individuals will not only survive but will be better than the present one. In speaking of what he terms "Consciousness III," Charles Reich summarizes his thoughts beautifully when he says:

... We have all been induced to give up our dreams of adventure and romance in favor of the escalator of success, but it says that the escalator is a sham and the dream is real. And these things, buried, hidden, and disowned in so many of us, are shouted out loud, believed in, affirmed by a

"The young people of today will be the adults of tomorrow."
(Courtesy of the *Journal of Health, Physical Education, and Recreation.*)

growing multitude of young people who seem too healthy, intelligent and alive to be wholly insane, who appear, in their collective strength, capable of making it happen. For one almost convinced that it was necessary . . . to be a miser of dreams, it is an invitation to cry or laugh. For one who thought the world was irretrievably encased in metal and plastic and sterile stone, it seems a veritable greening of America. [55, p. 429]

4.2 IMPLICATIONS FOR PHYSICAL EDUCATION

We have taken a quick look at "tomorrow's world." What meaning can such developments have for physical education? Let us consider some possible implications.

The influence of cybernetics

The machine has replaced man in many situations. Man continues to need physical activity for his optimum growth, maturation, and development. Because the essentials for survival no longer require physical activity, we must now plan and provide for organized physical education experiences. It is also important to somehow influence all people in such a way that their lives include a proper portion of exercise. Because these activities must be artificial in many cases, they must be learned and practiced.

Computers can now furnish information and analyze data with a degree of speed and accuracy unimagined a short while ago. Therefore, scholars in the area of physical education must learn a whole new set of concepts as they pursue their research and teach advanced students. Educational institutions must plan and budget for new and expensive equipment if they are to furnish programs appropriate for the graduate level. The whole process of research is changing so rapidly that many who were once considered scholars in their field are now finding it difficult to cope.

Materialism and values
Technology and the machine age have placed such emphasis on cybernetics, the hard sciences, competitive endeavors, success in attaining wealth, and materialism in general that it has been difficult to assign suitable priorities to human values, to intangible values, and to permanent as opposed to transient values. Physical education must reassess its role in improving the quality of life as it continues to foster activity programs, many of which are competitive in nature. Better interpersonal relationships, more consideration for others, impartiality in all our dealings, and sensitivity to the feelings of others must be among the values which are given high priority.

New forms of physical education
If people are to live in outer space, farm the bottom of the ocean, explore other planets, and travel for years on end, new forms of physical activity and kinds of nutrition will need to be discovered, researched, and practiced. The human organism is very adaptable, but new ways of maintaining health and fitness must be found.

As the lives and activities of individuals change, so must their physical education. More crowded conditions will require different kinds of facilities and possible new modes of transportation. As lifestyles become more individualized, so will educational needs. As racial integration continues, regulations and practices needed to iron out differences may become increasingly necessary. As philosophies undergo change the education of young people will be modified. As artists produce different kinds of paintings, new art forms, and a variety of new musical productions, all educational programs will be affected. As financial and natural resources oscillate between scarcity and plenty, so will schools need to adapt their methods and practices.

It is impossible to predict with any degree of accuracy or detail what may happen during the next century or even during the next decade. The best we can do is try to keep abreast of current developments.

Wisdom, stamina, adaptability, and copeability
In general, the man or woman of the future will need:

1. The *wisdom* that comes from a willingness to learn, the acquisition of knowledge, the ability to reason, and from deep and rich experiences.

2. The *strength* and *endurance* to withstand stress, to work without undue
   fatigue, and to persevere under the pressures imposed by life.
3. The *flexibility* and *intelligence* required to recognize change and to adjust to
   new situations, new events, new ways of living, and new philosophies.
4. The *ability to cope* with the acceleration of change, with needed physiological adaptations, with the need for new competencies, and with the harassments attending a crowded, fast-moving world.

   It is to satisfy the needs enumerated above that the education of tomorrow
must be designed. Physical education must assess not only its aims and objectives
but also its role, programs, and procedures.
   In the next section we will observe current trends and attempt to identify the
general direction physical education is taking.

4.3 FUTURE DIRECTIONS IN PHYSICAL EDUCATION
To design relevant plans for future physical education programs is certainly difficult. To provide a program that will contribute to the acquisition of wisdom, to the
development of strength, endurance and flexibility, and to the attainment of the
ability to cope is not an easy task. Nevertheless, it would be irresponsible to
neglect planning. The significance of studying trends and indications of future
trends becomes more pronounced as the rate of change accelerates. For there
is an element of truth in the statement of H. G. Wells when he said, "Human history
becomes more and more a race between education and catastrophe."

Current trends and future projections
In a changing universe where most things appear to have little stability, trends may
suddenly disappear only to reappear a short time later. What seems at first to be
a trend occasionally turns out to be only an unsuccessful experiment; what begins
as an innovative experiment may eventually be adopted as a practice. With this
instability in mind, let us delve into the past and present and sift out those developments which appear to have some significance for the coming years.
   Anthony Annarino's summary statement may be a good way to begin:

> We've run the gamut of preparedness for war. We've taken motor trips to
> Deweyland, Fitnessville and Sportsburg. We've outfitted scaling parties to
> Mt. Movement. We've formed safaris to penetrete the darkest jungles
> searching for Dr. Justification living among the underdeveloped, physical,
> motor, intellectual and social-emotional integrated tribes. We've joined the
> expeditions of Kephart and Delacato to explore the distorted world of percep-
> tion. We've sent scientists spelunking to investigate the rectal temperature
> of bats. We've reproduced Aladdin's genie to provide exercise for the busy
> executive, the super-athlete, and the cramped astronaut. We've stood alone
> at the battle of the little-bitty league warding off the attacks of a million
> fanatics crying for blood and competition. We've won victories. We've

suffered defeats. We've appeased. We've compromised. We've rationalized. We've generalized. We've learned from the past. But what is ahead? [1, p. 27]

The following paragraphs are an attempt to summarize what appears to be ahead —at least for the foreseeable future.

   1. *Flexibility.** The true goal, educators say, shall be the achievement of sufficient flexibility and individuality in programs so that it will not be necessary for any student, in order to avoid humiliation, to move ahead year by year, grade by grade, course by course, just as all the others do. This concept is called "breaking the lockstep" and has become a byword among many educators. Each person shall have as one of his personal rights the freedom to choose his own path and set his own pace. The words of Wilton Krogman state clearly the essence of this concept:

> *To grant the child the right to individuality.* Philosophically, this guarantees the integrity of the child's own growth progress: practically it relegates "averages" and similar arbitrary framework to the limbo which is long overdue. We now, in effect, no longer demand that the child tread the straight-and-narrow of a mean value (in height, or weight, or any measure); rather we regard the path of growth as a broad human highway, along which he may saunter as his own inner biological impulse to development sees fit; he may saunter to the left (shorter, shall we say), or to the right (taller); he may saunter to one side (slower grower) or to the other (faster). The important point is that in today's growth studies we follow one child at a time; the study marches along as he marches along; he is the one who, within reason, sets tempo, establishes timing, achieves synchrony and integration in the unfolding process. In very fact we are at an "individual-normal" level of operation. [36, p. 122]

Physical education, too, is concerned with this kind of individual freedom.

   2. *Copeability.* We are beginning to see, and will continue to see with increasing frequency, "copeability" listed as an important objective of education. Good programs of physical education will continue to aid men and women in their ability to cope. The development of stamina and zest, the ability to relax, and the energy and determination to overcome hazards and obstacles will be increasingly acknowledged as goals in education. The role of physical education in the development of these capacities will be recognized and programs will be developed to enhance them.

   3. *Broadening the program.* The emphasis on providing for individual differences, the stress on creativity and innovation, the need for relevance, the removal of requirements, and the desire to offer the best possible programs—these things

---

*Flexibility is also related to humanization, individualization, learning modules, increasing electives, and broadening the programs. These are discussed in subsequent paragraphs.

and more have led to a broadening of programs. The Lifetime Sports Program of the American Association for Health, Physical Education, and Recreation, the emphasis on physical fitness, the cultural influences of ethnic groups from many lands, the vast improvement in both indoor and outdoor facilities, and the many new and innovative types of equipment have all given support to increasing the number and kinds of program offerings.

4. *Humanization of programs.* Psychological and sociological as well as physio-logical bases have now been accepted as important foundation stones for physical education. Fun and joy, sensitivity to the feelings of others, and the development of compassionate and considerate individuals have taken their place as respected objectives. Methods helping teachers and coaches to lead and inspire rather than drive and coerce are being increasingly emphasized.

5. *Elective physical education.* It may be the unprecedented number of stu-dents flocking to colleges and universities, it could be the lack of financial re-sources, it could be the changes in educational philosophies—most likely a combination of all of these—that explains the continuing trend toward elimination of required physical education classes and the substitution of elective programs. Educational institutions have been unable to build enough facilities, employ enough personnel, and find the financial resources to enlarge their required pro-grams in keeping with the burgeoning enrollments. Students were unhappy about the kind of physical education being offered and began to complain. Campus unrest became rampant and one of the targets was physical education, particularly the required program. Institutions began dropping requirements right and left and physical education did not escape unaffected. Educational philosophy began to espouse more loudly than before the concept of individual freedom and existential-ism. Because the establishment was already under attack, it became difficult to resist the elimination of requirements. Many institutions found elective physical education more to their liking, and after a period of trial declared it to have many advantages. New and innovative programs more suitable to the times and more acceptable to the students were adopted. Lifetime sports and tension-relieving activities were introduced. Institutions which retained the requirement improved their programs. There were therefore a number of benefits which resulted. How-ever, those students needing physical education the most (the weak and the poorly coordinated) did not benefit by the deletion of physical education as a required subject.

It is difficult to predict where this trend will lead. Hopefully there will be good programs established for the "subpar" in physical fitness and programs will be made so enticing that almost all will participate. There are signs that the pendulum will swing back and that the benefits of certain basic requirements in education will be rediscovered.

6. *Learning modules.* Flexible time schedules and facilities emphasizing the "pod" lend support to the trend toward modular scheduling (see Figure 4.1). Schedules can include twenty-, thirty-, or even sixty-minute "modules" depending on the needs of a specific activity. Some activities may even require a full day or

two days. Others may require only ten minutes. Modular scheduling is not the answer to all problems and in some instances has been found too chaotic and unmanageable. It does, however, hold promise for the future and it may open up new vistas in physical education and recreation.

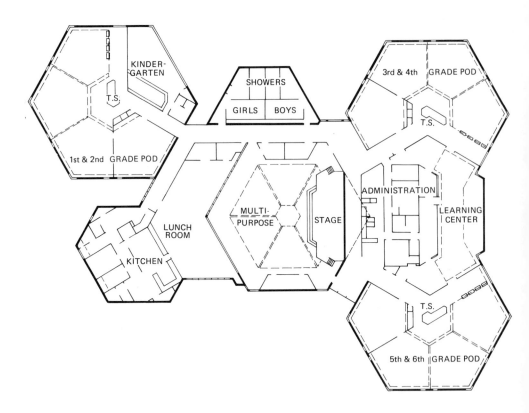

Figure 4.1 Flexible plan with pods. ". . . floor plan which symbolizes the changes in the instructional organization taking place in the American school. An open, carpeted area replaces the traditional schoolroom pattern. The core of the building is the central activity area, consisting of a multipurpose room and cafeteria. Around the core are so-called "pods" which house groups of varying sizes. With their movable walls, the pods allow for a variety of student relationships and student-teacher relationships. Appropriate spaces are provided for individual counseling and for the storing and use of various learning materials and media equipment." [27, cover]

7. *Demise of paternalistic attitudes.* Schools and social agencies are rapidly changing their philosophy from one of "helping people help themselves" to one of "sharing." The planning, work, resources, and manpower are shared as different groups cooperate toward solving their problems and accomplishing their tasks. There is an increasing number of problems in our present society and our shrinking world. Overpopulation, pollution, disease, poverty, and war are common problems that depress our society and other countries of the world. They can best be solved by a multifaceted attack, all appropriate agencies in every country sharing in the responsibility, planning, and implementation of remedial programs.

8. *The inner city.* Increasing attention is being given to physical education programs in the inner city. Selection and admission to college of inner-city students, efforts made to give prospective teachers more exposure to inner-city life, and improved in-service training for inner-city teachers cannot help but improve the quality of education in those areas. Physical education, especially athletics, has been a powerful force reaching and influencing children and youth of the inner city. Children who reside in these densely populated and disadvantaged areas urgently need the benefits derived from *good* physical education and athletic programs. If such opportunities are to be extended to them, more teachers must be recruited for the inner city, more attention must be given to preparing these teachers, more emphasis on developing true understanding and good interpersonal relationships is needed.

9. *Community involvement.* We have witnessed an era of considerable friction and conflict between communities and their schools. The trend is now toward more cooperation and interaction. Educational facilities are being opened to the community and community facilities are being utilized by schools. At the same time, community leaders from all walks of life are being employed as teachers and educational personnel are becoming more involved with parents and other members of the community.

Students are infiltrating their communities in large numbers working as recreation leaders, physical education teachers, coaches, and health educators. They tutor the slow learners, help the handicapped children, organize teams, and officiate contests. They clean up the environment and stir up enthusiasm. They involve themselves with the children, youth, and adults of the community. They do these things sometimes as part of their prescribed programs, sometimes on a volunteer basis, and sometimes for salary. This is one of the salutary trends in education today.

10. *Schools without walls.* Such schools are being established in a number of places throughout the nation. In these schools there are no buildings, classrooms, campus boundaries, or physical limits to the school environment. Factories, churches, libraries, stores, laboratories, streets, and parks are the "classrooms"; doctors, lawyers, businessmen, plumbers, executives, builders, and professors are the teachers. Physical education in such schools must rely on the mountains, lakes, YMCA's, and parks. Teachers will need to be versatile and work irregular hours. For those attending such schools, much remains to be discovered.

11. *Student involvement.* Another trend today is the dramatic increase in student involvement in curriculum planning, college government, and student life, and in making arrangements for affairs such as commencement, cultural programs, intramural athletics, and other activities. Some student groups are also involved in faculty and course evaluation, in administration of intercollegiate athletics, and in formulating policies for student life in the dormitories and other college housing.

Physical education, health education, and recreation are so intimately related to student life that administrators must heed this trend and exercise sound judgment with respect to the amount of control which should be placed in the hands of the students. While student opinion is important in formulating policies which affect them so directly, there are a number of functions which require considerable knowledge, sophistication, and experience and which should not be placed in the hands of novices. The most effective and workable solutions come with cooperative action, commensurate authority being in the hands of those who have the ultimate and long-range responsibility.

12. *"Stopouts."* There has been a significant increase in the number of students who, for one reason or another, drop out of school for a term, a year, or even more, and then return to complete their formal education. For those who interrupt their education because of undetermined goals or a sense of lack of relevance in their educational endeavors, this may be a salutary act. When they return to school, such students often demonstrate an increased sense of purpose, greater intrinsic motivation, and far more noteworthy achievement than before they left school.

13. *Role of teachers in political action.* Teachers, whether they wish it or not, have been increasingly drawn toward unionism and political action. Collective bargaining, united fronts on academic freedom, and renewed emphasis on their rights and privileges as citizens are bringing about a change in their "modus operandi." Where this will eventually lead is not clear. It does seem apparent, however, that they will continue to play a more active, visible, and verbal role in community and political life.

14. *Increasing leisure.* While the amount of leisure varies greatly and the ways in which free time is used differs even more, the vast majority of those who study and write in this area indicates an increasing portion of each person's time available for leisure activities. The need to do things which will "re-create" and renew, as well as relieve tension and provide fun and joy, becomes more evident every day. The technological revolution has provided the available time, brought on the need for relief from noise and other harassment, and furnished the equipment and transportation which make possible a steadily increasing number of recreational opportunities. Charles Brightbill added this thought:

> The leisure we encounter in the future, accompanied by a higher standard of living for more people, will have to be identified more with causes and services than activities and amusement; more with creativeness and adventure than with hollow vanities and shallow pastimes; more with involvement and fulfillment than with apathy and comfort. [3, p. 228]

Most signs point to a still further increase in available leisure and a fuller utilization of activities which will make it worthwhile. Lifetime sports, travel, and hobbies, together with restful and relaxing activities will be sought and utilized. It will be one of government's responsibilities to provide recreation for all. Education will need to do its part.

15. *Concern for the environment.* Pollution of rivers, oil on beaches, smog in cities, stacks and piles of waste paper, used cans, junked cars, and industrial sewage—these must be the concern of everyone, especially the professionals working in the fields of outdoor education, recreation, and health education. The control of pesticides, the development of "ecotactics," and the reduction of noise must receive greater attention from more citizens if this planet is to remain an ideal home for mankind. All human resources must be mobilized to conserve the limited natural resources of this earth. Physical educators and recreation leaders must accept a significant role.

16. *Outdoor education and recreation.* Increasing ecological awareness, together with some assistance from the federal government, has given outdoor education an impetus that will carry well into the future. Especially noteworthy are the programs which take inner-city children to the mountains, oceans, prairies, and forests. School camping trips, excursions to city parks, seminars at historical sites, outdoor educational travel, curricular units on conservation, and classes held in National Forests and on ocean shores are examples of recent developments.

"Especially noteworthy are the programs which take inner-city children to the mountains, oceans, prairies, and forests." (Courtesy of the *Journal of Health, Physical Education, and Recreation.*)

Field-work assignments and performance contracts for outdoor study and adventure are examples of feasible methods.

Lifetime sports of an educational nature are being emphasized as never before. Orienteering, mountaineering, pack trips on horseback, boating of all kinds, and hiking are among the offerings of many physical education departments. Such developments are only the beginning of what will be happening in the next decade.

17. *Physical education and recreation.* The trend in this relationship is difficult to determine. There are conflicting forces—some educators are intent on separating physical education and recreation completely and others accept the fact that they cannot be separated.

Because the purpose of physical education is, among other things, to help individuals prepare for the good life and at the same time to be a part of that life, recreation and physical education must become even more closely related. Activities which lead to broader and more flexible physical education programs are lifetime sports and outdoor activities which are clearly intended for leisure moments. Canoeing, hiking, mountain climbing, skiing, skating, and similar activities are legitimately physical education—yet they are also recreation. The two fields appear to be drawing closer together as more and more individuals are being trained in both recreation and physical education.

18. *Outward Bound.* Outward Bound is an educational program developed in Europe and is spreading rapidly in the United States. It is an experience in self-discovery where students are confronted with challenges and seemingly impossible tasks in natural, outdoor situations. The emphasis is on self-discovery, shared responsibility, and satisfying the need for adventure. Rock climbing, survival swimming, rapelling, and isolation hikes are among the activities which test a person's courage, endurance, and stamina, helping him discover his own hidden resources. Such activities can be presented as group projects, in which the sharing of accomplishments becomes an unforgettable experience. Experiencing the affection and support of peers and teachers as individuals struggle to conquer the environment is part of true education. Versions of Outward Bound programs have now been incorporated in the curricula of schools and colleges. Without doubt, we will see more of this type of education in the future.

19. *Recreation for the handicapped.* During the past decade, there has been a renewal of interest in therapeutic exercises for the perceptually handicapped, modified programs for the mentally retarded and those with associated disorders, and recreation for the handicapped. Special developmental programs for those who are physically below par and corrective exercises for those with poor body mechanics are now being stressed in some schools. Physical education for the disadvantaged and economically deprived has been examined and special programs devised. Strength, endurance, and positive health are the concerns, and these concerns must continue for a fit and healthy citizenry.

> Outward Bound—"Versions of Outward Bound programs ▶
> have now been incorporated in the curricula of schools
> and colleges." (Courtesy of the *Journal of Health, Physical
> Education, and Recreation.*)

20. *Improved programs of physical fitness.* Better assessment of physical condition, the recent emphasis on cardiorespiratory endurance, the involvement of physicians, and the scientific advances in the study of exercise are forward steps taken in recent years. Programs of aerobics, jogging, circuit training, cycling, and isometrics have broadened the opportunities for participation. The fitness programs of the YMCA's, boys' clubs, and similar social agencies are supplementing school physical education programs. The President's Council on Physical Fitness and Sports, together with private health clubs and "spas," are providing needed encouragement and support. These developments which are so necessary in today's society will continue to flourish and expand.

"Olympic fitness circuits," which are jogging tracks with exercise stations located at intervals along the way, have been established in parts of the United States. These are patterned after courses found in Europe and are on the increase in other parts of the world. Instructions posted at the exercise stations explain exactly what to do. These fitness circuits are almost certain to multiply rapidly and will make an increasingly important contribution to the fitness of our nation.

21. *Relaxation and tension control.* In the harassing and stimulating society in which we now live, the control of tension and the ability to relax become increasingly essential. Classes utilizing many different techniques are springing up in all parts of the nation. It is predicted that methods and content will be reexamined and that those which prove to be the most universally effective will become part of many physical education curricula.

22. *Health education plans.* The President's Committee on Health Education, established by President Nixon in 1971, has been instrumental in arranging regional hearings on health education, conducting the National Health Forum and holding several special conferences including the National Conference on Legislative Action for School Health. Future plans include long-term, comprehensive government support, a concentration on continuing education, in-service training programs, national, regional, and state training centers, efforts to involve the entire community, and a coordinated approach to health education. The continued interest of governmental agencies, better programs to inform the public, and the drive for better prepared health education teachers are efforts which should produce a far more effective health education program than in the past.*

23. *Health education and the behavioral sciences.* It is becoming increasingly obvious that the problems associated with drug abuse, sexual education, smoking, and alcoholism are too pervasive and deeply rooted to be solved by education alone. Sociologists, psychologists, clergymen, physicians, lawyers, and parents need to be involved if much progress is to be made. Public Health agencies, child welfare agencies, churches, social agencies, and law enforcement agencies must join forces with the schools to rid our society of the menaces of drugs, alcohol, and tobacco. Young people must find meaning in their lives through encourage-

---

*Joy G. Cauffman, "The President's Committee on Health Education," *School Health Review,* Vol. 3, No. 4, September–October 1972, pp. 2–3.

ment and assistance. Health educators have an important role to play but cannot make a significant impact if they try to accomplish these goals by themselves. The future must include far more cooperation among all individuals and responsible agencies to help solve these problems.

24. *Health aides.* A salutary trend which has been tested at the University of Nebraska and is being tried elsewhere is the use of health aides in the Health Education Program. Health aides are students trained by nurses, psychologists, and doctors to serve as communicative links between the Health Center and the students, to survey student health needs, to help identify health problems, and to provide first-aid services.

Health aides are carefully screened and selected, are required to take certain health courses, and are familiarized with health agencies with which they might be required to work. Because these pilot programs have been successful, the further-ance of this trend in the future is likely. [25, pp. 33–34]

25. *Aesthetic aspects.* Attention to beauty and flow of movement, increased interest in body mechanics, and renewed enthusiasm of both men and women for dance, gymnastics, and diving have caused far greater appreciation for the aesthetic aspects of physical education than existed a decade ago. The concept of "body image" in the development of the individual has also lent increased aware-ness to this facet of physical education. As more people recognize the relationship of art to sport and dance, and as the emphasis on grace and dexterity of movement continues, an even greater appreciation for this aspect of physical education will result.

26. *Early childhood education.* The significance of preschool experiences in the development of a child is being increasingly acknowledged by leaders in educa-tion. Perceptual-motor development during the first few years of a child's life plays an important role in his ability to function in later years. Many schools, both public and private, are providing education for three- to six-year-olds. Optimum develop-ment of all one's dimensions requires a broad and varied program of developmen-tal physical activities. While in many instances these may be provided in the home, it may be necessary in others for the schools to offer appropriate programs.

27. *Perceptual-motor development.* The resurgence of interest in perceptual-motor development and the recognition that this is also the domain of physical education is an important trend. Attention to a complete set of movement experi-ences for every child and special exercises for those who have perceptual-motor handicaps is a significant forward-looking step in physical education.

28. *The elementary level.* Concentration on perceptual-motor development, judi-cious use of movement education, and employment of problem-solving methods are noteworthy developments at the elementary level. The implementation of the "single salary schedule" and the improvement of teacher education for those who teach at the elementary level are contributing to the improvement of physical education in the lower grades. More specialists are being employed to teach physical education in the elementary schools and more men are finding that

teaching at this level is especially rewarding. The idea has now been generally accepted that, of all levels of education, the lower grades have the most urgent need for physical education programs which are both appropriate and excellent.

29. *Movement exploration and problem solving.* The extensive utilization of problem solving and movement exploration in physical education is a comparatively recent trend. The child learns through his own efforts and thus develops independence and self-reliance. Because different ways of solving problems can be found, creativity is encouraged. Throughout infancy and childhood the young child explores and learns through movement. The body's capacity for movement, the relationship of movement to emotion, and the abilities to leap, throw, swing, hang, and run can all be learned through solving challenging problems. Exploring locomotion, discovering how to relax, and expressing oneself through movement is the trend. Problem solving and movement exploration have made a significant contribution to physical education and their increased use in the future is predicted.

30. *Individualization of physical education.* Each person has different inherited characteristics, needs and interests, and capabilities. It is acknowledged that educational programs should be, to the extent feasible, individualized. Good advisors and counselors coupled with varied and increased numbers of activities will make further individualization of programs possible. It must also be recognized that mass education on an individual basis poses some very difficult administrative problems and is not entirely compatible with the long-held principle of "education for all." Nevertheless there are many situations in which "group-paced instruction" can be replaced by individualized instruction and where an individual's progress can be measured in terms of his own previous achievements rather than in terms of the accomplishments of his peers. Large group activities may, in some instances, be replaced by individual and dual activities, thus avoiding too much comparing. In making such program changes, however, care must be taken that room remains for personal interaction and social adjustment.

31. *Independent study.* The trend toward more independent study is also a form of individualization but with broader objectives. This method of education has been in use for some time but has not been employed to any great extent in physical education (except in theory courses). The newer trend is to permit credit requirements to be satisfied by independent study. A student may go backpacking for two or three weekends and, per previous agreement with the instructor, write a report covering such things as his observations, feelings, state of fatigue, diet, and his ability to negotiate obstacles. He may make a map of the trip and measure the distance with a pedometer. He may combine it with geological or nature studies. Such trips are preceded by a conference with the instructor and the individual agrees to certain requirements before he sets out. The trip may include several persons, in which case observations of interpersonal reactions may also be included in the report. The study may become interdisciplinary involving not only physiology but also psychology, sociology, and some phases of ecology.

32. *Performance contracting.* A related method of individualizing physical education is performance contracting. One or more individuals can work out a plan whereby they will do a certain amount of work or achieve a certain performance

"Physical education today has something for everybody." (Courtesy of West Springfield High School, West Springfield, Massachusetts.)

record and thus receive credit for physical education. A person may agree to improve to a specific level in a physical fitness test; he may agree to achieve a specific height in the pole vault, a certain time in the mile run, or a prescribed distance in the shotput. The decathlon and pentathlon lend themselves nicely to such arrangements. Plans may include reading, preliminary training, and the final performance. The instructor assists with preliminary testing and guides the student in the establishment of goals which are challenging, yet realistic. Performance contracts might also be designed for white-water canoeing, mountaineering, or sailboating. Tasks would be agreed upon, reports written, and credit awarded.

33. *Audiovisual aids.* Closed-circuit television, videotapes, filmstrips, and other forms of audiovisual aids have done much to improve teaching. Tasks can more readily be perceived and objectives understood when perfect demonstrations are seen. Seeing oneself perform provides effective feedback. Electronic technology and audiovisual devices will continue to support and improve teaching in the areas of health, physical education, and recreation.

34. *Microteaching.* Microteaching is a scaled-down version of teaching with smaller classes and shorter periods. It is normally videotaped or recorded on closed-circuit television. Criticisms and comments of the supervising and cooperating teachers may be recorded as the class proceeds. The student teacher (or regular teacher) should review the record of the class period as soon after its completion as possible. This provides an excellent form of feedback and an accurate means of evaluation. It can be employed either as a form of in-service training or a means of educating student teachers.

"... audiovisual aids have done much to improve teaching." (Courtesy of the *Journal of Health, Physical Education, and Recreation.*)

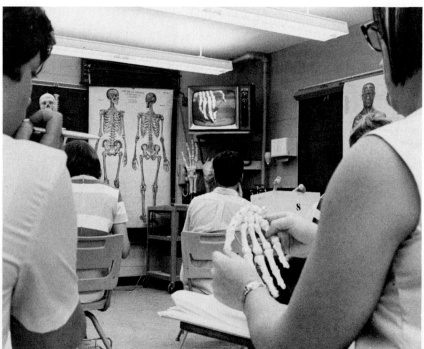

35. *Subspecializations.* Students are permitted to choose the area of physical education in which they wish to specialize. While this is especially true in teacher education programs, the trend is making its presence felt in general education and even in the secondary schools. Instead of electing a subject known as "physical education" or "gym," they now take dance, sociology of sport, gymnastics, aquatics, skiing, or team sports. In many teacher education programs, they no longer major in general physical education but in elementary school physical education, physical education for the handicapped, or coaching. In all probability, there will continue to be a call for generalists and many broad programs will remain, but there will also be opportunities for more specialization.

36. *Team teaching.* The purposes of team teaching are to teach more effectively and to use personnel more efficiently. Every teacher cannot be expected to know and to possess expertise in all the diverse physical education activities being taught today; almost every teacher is expert in only one or two aspects. A highly qualified Judo instructor, for example, explains and demonstrates a particular maneuver. Other members of the teaching team then move around the gymnasium assisting and correcting wherever necessary. The poorer students are taken aside by one of the team teachers and given special help without affecting the rest of the class. As another method, three or more elementary teachers may have different abilities. One of them may teach physical education, one music, and another art, each teaching his specialty to all the students.

A "master teacher" may use senior physical education majors to help him teach. He may hold special sessions with them, allowing them to do most of the teaching while he takes responsibility for planning, supervision, and evaluation.

There are many ways teams of teachers can work together. The important thing to remember is that team teaching is for the purpose of enhancing instruction and providing for more individualization and not for removing the master teacher from the actual teaching scene.

37. *Paraprofessionals.* The utilization of paraprofessionals to relieve highly qualified teachers of routine tasks related to physical education and to provide help in situations where a small teacher/student ratio is desirable is another salutary trend. The use of paraprofessionals must, however, be carefully planned and well organized. If paraprofessionals are to teach, there must be careful selection, a thorough orientation of all involved, and a good in-service training program. Parents, former teachers, recreation and community workers, and upperclassmen can be effective in this capacity. They can prepare equipment and facilities for class, check objective-type examinations, look up library references, perform secretarial work if qualified, and assist in the actual teaching. When well conducted, such a program can be invaluable.

38. *Innovative efforts in public relations.* The establishment of the Physical Education Public Information Project (PEPI) represents a significant positive trend. It exemplifies an organized effort on a scale never before attempted to acquaint the public with what physical education and related areas are really designed to achieve. Fay Biles, who was instrumental in launching the project, indicated the path to be followed.

PEPI is a national project that has to be implemented at the grass roots level. . . . And now, with 600 PEPI coordinators off and running, nothing can stop us. But we've got to learn to talk to the public—every single one of us. We've got to talk in the language they understand. And we've got to speak with one voice for physical education. [53, p. 11]

If these thoughts are implemented at both the local and the national level, we will soon see throughout the nation a growing recognition of the values of physical education.

39. *Changes in certification.* Many changes are appearing on the horizon in the area of teacher certification. Certification on the basis of "performance competencies" instead of on the basis of course completion is now being tested in a number of states. There is talk of eliminating teacher certification altogether. Individual institutions rather than state departments of education are being given increasing responsibility for the quality of education which prospective teachers are receiving and for the standards by which they will be judged.

Advances are being made toward the establishment of some form of coach certification. It is felt that the teaching of sports, particularly those in which bodily injury is frequent, should never be placed in the hands of unqualified or untrained persons. Coaching minors are being established in some institutions, coaching subconcentrations are being offered at others, and regulations pertaining to "minimum essentials for coaching" are being established in a number of states particularly interested in this problem. Certification of athletic trainers also appears to be imminent, especially in the larger schools.

40. *Community colleges.* The community college movement is not a new trend. Junior and community colleges have expanded in number and scope until they now serve a substantial number of freshmen and sophomores who wish to attend college. The significance for physical education lies in the fact that (a) it is during the first two years of college that the most emphasis is placed on basic instruction in physical education, and (b) the community colleges are increasing their efforts to provide students with the first two years of their professional preparation program in physical education. Of course, program planners wish to coordinate the first two years of their curriculum with the last two years of senior college work. This, in turn, requires some adjustment on the part of senior colleges that are interested in cooperating with the community colleges.

Games and sports in Hong Kong. ". . . the trend of the ▶
future in physical education will be international
cooperation for the benefit of all." (Courtesy of Frank Fu,
Hong Kong.)

41. *International cooperation.* Such problems as pollution, poverty, racism, drug abuse, smoking, and ignorance are found throughout the world today. As we strive to improve the quality of life, we must recognize the challenge of this worldwide struggle. All nations must unite against poverty, disease, war, and pestilence, and technological advances have given us the means to fight side by side to eradicate many of these problems. It appears now as if the trend of the future in physical education will be international cooperation for the benefit of all. The common purpose of all nations must transcend the selfish interests of individuals and nations. The role of sport in accomplishing this unity of purpose is generally accepted as being significant. In sport it is the deed that counts. Among sportsmen creed, color, citizenship, and status fade in the light of performance and behavior. International sports events will continue to expand. There will, however, be a more critical reexamination and reevaluation of the conduct of such competitions as well as of the values and other outcomes sought.

42. *Girls and women in athletics.* One of the most striking developments during the last decade is the participation of girls and women in full-scale interscholastic and intercollegiate athletic competition. Programs have grown so rapidly that it has put a real strain on the need for facilities, since they were constructed with essentially boys' and men's interscholastic and intercollegiate programs in mind. Leagues have been formed and programs organized on both local and national levels. In some instances girls are competing on boys' teams and in many institutions there are coeducational varsity teams in some sports. It is predicted that, while girls' and women's programs will continue to expand, and equal opportunities for both sexes will be mandated, the common practice will be to have separate teams for the two sexes except in certain sports where differences in strength, size, and stamina will not be an important factor in capability and competence.

43. *Club sports.* As interests are becoming ever broader in sports, college and university athletic departments are finding it impossible, with their limited resources, to promote and conduct programs in all the sports which the students want. Students themselves are therefore organizing and forming clubs in a variety of different sports. Because it is necessary to exercise some control and because most athletic departments do not feel it is their responsibility to promote these sports, most of them are sponsored by the physical education departments. Here they receive official sanction and usually some use of facilities. Occasionally, the physical education department furnishes some equipment. Other than the above, students finance the activity themselves. They also engage the officials, schedule the games, and do whatever promoting is necessary. In some institutions the club sports are under the jurisdiction of the intramural department. Club sports may include skating, skiing, boxing, riding, bowling, judo, mountaineering, lacrosse, bicycling, rowing, canoeing, soccer, and rugby, for example.

44. *Facility innovations.* Air-supported structures, movable partitions, synthetic surfaces, and portable equipment are part of many modern physical education facilities. Portable swimming pools, artificial surfing pools, plastic ice, and covered soccer and football fields are on the drawing boards and even in actual experimen-

tal use. Gymnasiums are now being built according to innumerable functional plans. Where space is a premium concern they may be many stories high; where there is plenty of room they may sprawl over several acres. Covered physical education facilities that are twenty to fifty acres in size are projected.

"Artificial surfing pools and carefully planned swimming facilities enhance programs and increase opportunities." (Courtesy of the *Journal of Health, Physical Education, and Recreation.*)

45. *New and better equipment.* To supplement traditional equipment and to serve the needs of new methods of physical education, many new and innovative kinds of apparatus have been devised and placed on the market. Jungle gyms and Swedish windows of every imaginable description, homemade equipment improvised from barrels, hoops, culverts, trees, and junkyard scraps, equipment for crawling, squirming, climbing, stretching, twisting, balancing, and climbing, equipment to develop awareness, spatial judgment, agility, strength, coordination, and grace—these and many others are being manufactured and implemented. There appears to be no limit to what man may devise to challenge and encourage children to move.

4.4 CONCEPTS AND PRINCIPLES FOR FUTURE GENERATIONS

1. Change is real. Change is a part of life. It is a part of being born, of growing, of maturing. No amount of wishing can eliminate the processes of change. Change is as certain as the passage of time.

2. Change is relative. It may occur faster or slower; it may be more dramatic or less dramatic; it may be languid and flowing or it may be rapid and violent.

3. The social and technological processes of change are accelerating. New ideas and new inventions burst upon us with ever-increasing suddenness. Change is self-sustaining. Each new invention and each new bit of knowledge produces food for more technological and scientific advances. This, in turn, increases the speed and enlarges the scope of change. Change, therefore, increases exponentially.

4. One change inevitably leads to another. A change in purpose leads to a change in content, methods, and criteria for evaluation. These lead to changes in individuals. Changes in individuals result in a changed society. Societal changes yield a different environment. A new environment requires new objectives. Change is therefore cyclic.

5. Improvement and change go hand-in-hand. To remain static is to stagnate. Possible changes must therefore not be ignored. They must be examined, evaluated, and if deemed worthy, implemented.

6. Change for the sake of change is not the answer. There must be direction, purpose, analysis, and evaluation before a change can be implemented. Only then can there be a reasonable expectation of something that is better than it was before.

7. It is more difficult to evaluate the new and different than the old and tried. Therefore if progress is going to occur, the new must be examined and evaluated. Each new endeavor involves a calculated risk.

8. Before something which has been found effective and good is discarded, there should be reasonable assurance that its replacement will be better. The road back should always be kept open.

9. Some things change more slowly than others. Granite erodes very slowly. Individual species take eons to change appreciably. Man as a biological organism is not very different from what he was two thousand years ago. As Toffler said,

". . . despite all his heroism and stamina, man remains a biological organism, a 'biosystem,' and all such systems operate within inexorable limits." [63, p. 325]

10. Education must not only prepare individuals for the foreseeable future, but must assist them to become more adaptable and copeable. The increasing rate of change makes it necessary to prepare for a future which is becoming more and more unpredictable.

11. The needs of today in our physical education programs include more and better ways of motivating students, more effective methods of teaching, more recognition of each individual's needs, interests, and capacities, and more empathetic understanding of each student and his/her problems.

12. If innovation and change are to be based on a sound foundation, there must be not only an increased amount of good basic and applied research but also adequate dissemination of the findings and actual application to teaching and coaching.

13. Physical educators of the future must be prepared to make an ever-increasing number of decisions. They must be able to adjust to more rapid change than was formerly necessary. They must be able to anticipate and react quickly. Education for tomorrow must consider these needs in planning.

14. Physical education for the future must be more completely interwoven with the life of the community. The barriers between the schools and the communities are being slowly but steadily broken down.

15. Because education will, for many people, become more spasmodic and *lifelong,* physical education must be oriented more toward service to those who are no longer in school—the young employed, the middle aged, the part-time workers, and the elderly.

16. Curricula, at all levels and in all areas, need to become more and more future oriented. The acceleration of change will necessitate continuous projections into the future.

17. Curricular changes must be simplified and expedited. A necessary curricular innovation should not be delayed by the traditional processing procedures before it can be implemented. The system must be accelerated.

18. Students of all ages should now be receiving education for travel on the bottom of the ocean and among the planets. Physical educators must join forces with others who are investigating such possibilities and plan their programs for this environment.

19. If team sports and other physical education activities are going to positively influence the lives of people in the next few decades, there must be increased emphasis on the development of friendship, the fostering of trust, and the reduction of loneliness. Programs and lessons should be planned with such outcomes in mind.

20. If physical education is to keep pace, courses such as "Futurism and Physical Education" must be offered, and a variety of ways to adapt and cope must be employed.

21. While futurism and change are concepts which need to be studied and considered, there must also be contact with the past. What Toffler calls "stability zones" or "enduring relationships" [63, p. 378] must be maintained if the bombardment is not going to be more than people can bear. Permanence must be considered in the light of transience and transience in the light of permanence. And it may be that we will rediscover "eternal verities."

22. Stability zones may well be the mountains, the seashore, or other places in nature where man can find solitude. Trips and expeditions to places where the environment appears more permanent than man and where the pace is slower than in industrial regions usually have a stabilizing influence.

23. Solid family relationships, playing games, fishing with old friends, vacations in old haunts, visits to ancient monuments, listening to familiar music, and the retention of old familiar rituals and customs may provide stability zones for many. Physical education and recreation can play an important role in all of these.

24. Flexibility is the key concept in coping with change. Flexibility in research, planning, scheduling, organizing, pacing, grouping, and building are all needed. Flexible individuals, flexible facilities, flexible parents, and flexible administrators are essential if the pace of change is not to result in physical educators losing the race.

25. Progress can only proceed in a climate that is congenial to change. A receptive administration and a responsive faculty are the two most important ingredients in productive change. Differentiated staffing, team teaching, and variable student grouping are organizational details that will also help.

26. If innovation and change are to occur at the practical level, there must be a sincere effort to involve teachers and coaches in planning. If staff members are to cooperate in implementing new ideas and practices, they must be included in the initial dreams and plans. A leader without followers is no longer a leader.

27. Subconcepts which support the larger concept of innovation and progress in physical education are:

a) Free experimentation
b) Individualization
c) Setting priorities
d) Human interaction
e) Behavioral objectives
f) Multimedia learning
g) Relevance
h) Interdisciplinary study
i) Creative planning
j) Self-instruction
k) Problem solving
l) Team teaching
m) Differential staffing
n) Pods and mods
o) Computerized learning
p) Systems analysis
q) Immediate feedback
r) Microteaching
s) Community involvement
t) Public relations
u) Independent study
v) Performance contracting
w) Performance-based evaluation
x) Conceptual approach
y) Cybercultural society

28. Finally, in Toffler's words:

This, then, is the ultimate objective of social futurism, not merely the transcendence of democracy and the substitution of more humane, more far-sighted, more democratic planning, but the subjection of the process of evolution itself to conscious human guidance. For this is the supreme instant, the turning point in history at which man either vanquishes the processes of change or vanishes, at which, from being the unconscious puppet of evolution he becomes either its victim or its master. [63, pp. 485–486]

SELECTED REFERENCES
1. Annarino, Anthony, "The quest for physical education," *Journal of Health, Physical Education, Recreation,* Vol. 42, pp. 27–28, May 1971. Reprinted by permission.
2. Andrews, Gladys, Jeannette Saurborn, and Elsa Schneider, *Physical Education for Today's Boys and Girls,* Boston: Allyn and Bacon, 1960.
3. Brightbill, Charles K., *Educating for Leisure Centered Living,* Harrisburg, Penn.: The Stackpole Company, 1966.
4. Caffrey, John (ed.), *The Future Academic Community,* Washington: The American Council on Education, 1969.
5. Carnegie Commission on Higher Education, *Less Time, More Options: Education Beyond High School,* Hightstown, N.J.: McGraw-Hill, 1971.
6. Cobb, Robert A., and Paul M. Lepley, *Contemporary Philosophies of Physical Education and Athletics,* Columbus, Ohio: Charles E. Merrill Publishing Company, 1973.
7. Cogan, Max, "Creative approaches to physical education," Paper presented at the 73rd Annual Meeting of the National Physical Education Association for Men, Chicago, Ill., December 30, 1969.
8. Diem, Liselott, *Who can . . .?,* Germany: Wilhelm Lippert, 1964.
9. Donaldson, George W., and Alan D. Donaldson, "Outdoor education: its promising future," *Journal of Health, Physical Education, Recreation,* Vol. 43, No. 4, April 1972.
10. Dupuis, Adrian M., and Robert B. Nordberg, *Philosophy and Education,* Milwaukee: The Bruce Publishing Company, 1964.
11. Eble, Kenneth E., *A Perfect Education,* New York: The Macmillan Company, 1966.
12. Educational Policies Commission, *The Contemporary Challenge to American Education,* Washington, D.C.: National Education Association, 1958.
13. _____, *Public Education and the Future of America,* Washington, D.C.: National Education Association, 1955.
14. Ehrlich, Paul R., *The Population Bomb,* New York: Ballentine Books, 1968.
15. Eurich, Alvin C. (ed.), *Campus 1980,* New York: Delacorte Press, 1968.
16. Fait, Hollis F., *Physical Education for the Elementary School Child: Experiences in Movement,* 2nd edition, Philadelphia: W. B. Saunders Company, 1971.
17. Farmer, James, "To be black and American," in *The Future Academic Community,* John Caffrey (ed.), Washington, D.C.: The American Council on Education, 1969. Reprinted by permission.
18. Frost, Reuben B., "Trends for the '70's," Paper presented to the South Dakota Association for Health, Physical Education, and Recreation, October 9, 1969.
19. _____, "What will physical education be like in 1977?," *Journal of Health, Physical Education, and Recreation,* March 1968.
20. "Futuristics," *Nation's Schools,* Vol. 89, No. 3, March 1972.

21. Gartmann, Heinz, *Man Unlimited,* New York: Pantheon Books, 1957.
22. Glines, Don E., *Creating Humane Schools,* Mankato, Minn.: Campus Publishers, 1972.
23. Grobstein, Clifford, *The Strategy of Life,* San Francisco: W. H. Freeman and Company, 1964.
24. Havel, Richard C., and Emery W. Seymour, *Health, Physical Education, and Recreation,* New York: The Ronald Press Company, 1961.
25. Helm, Carl J., Celeste Knipmeyer, and Mary Martin, "University students as health aides," *School Health Review,* Vol. 3, No. 4, September–October 1972.
26. Hutchins, Robert M. *The Learning Society,* New York: Frederick A. Praeger, 1968.
27. *Innovation in Education: New Directions for the American School,* Statement on National Policy by the Research and Policy Committee of the Committee for Economic Development, New York, 1968.
28. James, David (ed.), *Outward Bound,* London: Routledge and Kegan Paul, 1964.
29. James, Preston E., *One World Perspective,* New York: Blaisdell Publishing Company, 1965.
30. Jewett, Ann E., "Would you believe public schools 1975," *Journal of Health, Physical Education, and Recreation,* Vol. 42, No. 3, March 1971.
31. Kahn, Herman, and B. Bruce-Briggs, *Things to Come,* New York: The Macmillan Company, 1972.
32. Kirchner, Glenn, *Physical Education for Elementary School Children,* 2nd edition, Dubuque, Iowa: Wm. C. Brown Company, 1970.
33. Kirchner, Glenn, Jean Cunningham, and Eileen Warrell, *Introduction to Movement Education,* Dubuque, Iowa: Wm. C. Brown Company, 1970.
34. Kneller, George F., *Existentialism and Education,* New York: John Wiley and Sons, 1958.
35. Kraus, Richard, *Recreation and Leisure in Modern Society,* New York: Appleton-Century-Crofts, 1971.
36. Krogman, Wilton M., "Factors in physical growth of children as they may apply to physical education," *Professional Contributions No. 3,* American Academy of Physical Education, November 1954. Reprinted by permission.
37. Kustermann, Howard H., "Changes to match the times," *The YMCA World Service Reporter,* Fall 1972.
38. Laughlin, Neil, "Physical education—2000 A.D.," *The Physical Educator,* Vol. 29, No. 3, October 1972.
39. LeBato, Loretta T., "Should tension control classes be included in the curriculum," *The Physical Educator,* Vol. 28, No. 2, May 1971.
40. Leonard, George B., *Education and Ecstasy,* New York: Dell Publishing Company, 1968.
41. Lincoln, C. Eric, *Sounds of the Struggle,* New York: William Morrow and Company, 1968.
42. MacIver, John, "Technological change and health," in *Automation, Education, and Human Values,* William W. Brickman and Stanley Lehrer (eds.), New York: School and Society Books, 1966.
43. Mackenzie, Marlin M., *Towards New Curriculum in Physical Education,* New York: McGraw-Hill, 1969.
44. McDonald, Donald, "Youth," *The Center Magazine,* Vol. 3, No. 4, July 1970. Reprinted by permission.
45. McLuhan, Marshall, *Understanding Media: The Extensions of Man,* New York: The New American Library, 1964.

46. Mead, Margaret, "The challenge of automation to education for human values," in *Automation, Education and Human Values,* William W. Brickman and Stanley Lehrer (eds.), New York: School and Society Books, 1966.
47. Morphet, Edgar L., and Charles O. Ryan (eds.), *Implications for Education of Prospective Changes in Society,* New York: Citation Press, 1967.
48. Munroe, A. D., *Physical Education,* London: G. Bell and Son, 1972.
49. National Education Association, "Education in a changing society," Washington, D.C.: NEA, 1963.
50. *New Horizon: The Becoming Journey,* Washington, D.C.: National Education Association, 1961.
51. "New students and new places," a report and recommendations by the Carnegie Commission on Higher Education, New York: McGraw-Hill, October 1971.
52. Owen, J. Wyn, "New and old in p. e.," *Trends in Education,* Vol. 23, pp. 48–50, July 1971.
53. "PEPI'S first year," *Journal of Health, Physical Education, Recreation,* Vol. 43, No. 6, June 1972.
54. Peterson, A. D. C., *The Future of Education,* London: The Cresset Press, 1968.
55. Reich, Charles A., *The Greening of America.* Copyright © 1970 by Random House, Inc., New York. Reprinted by permission.
56. Ridini, Leonard M., "Physical education for the inner city," *The Physical Educator,* Vol. 28, No. 4, December 1971.
57. Sage, George H. (ed.), *Sport and American Society: Readings,* Reading, Mass.: Addison-Wesley Publishing Company, 1970.
58. Scarnati, Richard A., "Special Olympics," *Journal of Health, Physical Education and Recreation,* Vol. 43, No. 2, February 1972.
59. Seidentop, Daryl, *Physical Education—Introductory Analysis,* Dubuque, Iowa: Wm. C. Brown Company, 1972.
60. Shearer, Lloyd, "What will the laser do next?," *Parade, Springfield Republican,* October 22, 1972.
61. Smith, Michael, Stanley Parker, and Cyril Smith, *Leisure and Society in Britain,* London: Allen Lane, 1973.
62. Toffler, Alvin, "Can we cope with tomorrow?," *Redbook Magazine,* January 1966.
63. _____, *Future Shock,* New York: Random House, 1970.
64. Walker, June, et al., *Modern Methods in Secondary School Physical Education,* Boston: Allyn and Bacon, 1973.
65. Wall Street Journal, Staff of the, *Here Comes Tomorrow,* Princeton, N.J.: Dow Jones and Company, 1966.
66. Young, Michael, and Peter Willmott, *The Symmetrical Family,* London: Routledge and Kegan Paul, 1973.

Philosophical Considerations

Chapter 5

5.1 THE PHILOSOPHICAL APPROACH

If we accept the premise that philosophy is the search for the *real,* the *true,* and the *good,* and if we believe that a sound and satisfying basic philosophy is needed for consistency of behavior, good mental health, and harmonious personal and social relationships, then a unit dealing with the philosophy of physical education is essential to a book of this nature. Actually, we philosophize whenever we analyze and express what we believe about various aspects of our lives. Philosophy cannot, and should not, be separated from human experience. We must have an underlying basic belief about our profession, about what we are trying to do in physical education, sport, dance, and our daily lives. If a coach or teacher does not have a firm foundation of beliefs about his profession and his life as a basis for action, he will soon find the pressures and stresses more than he can bear. It is important, then, that we continue to search for what is true, what is real, and what is good and seek to harmonize our findings with our daily lifestyles and actions. To do this, we must apply the processes and methods of philosophy.

Metaphysics, epistemology, logic, and axiology are the four divisions of philosophy. Metaphysics is the study of the ultimate reality, epistemology the study of perception and the acquisition of knowledge, logic the study of the best methods of thinking and research, and axiology the study of values. All these branches of philosophy are found in the discipline and profession of physical education. As we seek the body of knowledge of physical education and as we learn the basic facts and principles of physiology, psychology, sociology, and philosophy, we are involved in epistemology. As we apply these facts and principles to practical situations and search for what is real and what is not, we are dealing with metaphysics. As we conduct investigations, analyze data, and draw conclusions from evidence, we are utilizing logic. And as we seek the key to the development of value systems and ethical behavior in sport, we are involved in axiology. The application of formal philosophy to any aspect of education is termed *educational philosophy.*

It is the observation of the author that very few physical educators confine themselves to any one of the branches of philosophy identified above. Some use logic and rational methods in their thinking and everyday living more consciously than do others. Most of those who teach and coach are concerned about what is genuine and what is fraudulent, about the facts, principles, and knowledges which form the foundation for theory courses and skilled performance, about the quest for truth through the scientific method, and about the development of desirable character traits and value systems through physical education experiences. The philosophies of most physical educators and coaches are eclectic in nature.

It is obvious that only a brief orientation to the philosophy of physical education can be presented in this book. Seven basic schools of philosophical thought are presented for review and analysis with respect to goals and practices in physical education. These shall be described and explained, after which their relationship and application to physical education will be discussed.

The seven schools of thought are (1) naturalism, (2) realism, (3) idealism, (4) pragmatism, (5) progressivism, (6) reconstructionism, and (7) existentialism. Each of these has a significant and pervasive influence on physical education and sport.

The first four of these philosophical areas are major classical philosophies and can be broadly applied to almost any facet of life. The last three (progressivism, reconstructionism, and existentialism) have more recently entered the stream of philosophical thought. Progressivism and reconstructionism are basically educational philosophies which have far less general application than the others. Because most all philosophical thought as expressed by physical education teachers consists of a combination of elements found in these general areas, more detailed discussion of these schools is pertinent.

5.2 NATURALISM

When a physical educator hears the word "naturalism," thoughts of Jean Jacques Rousseau and his discussion of Emile's education come to mind (see Chapter 3). Rousseau criticized the practice of sending children to the academy at an early age. He emphasized the development of health and strength from outdoor living and cited instances of lessons learned from nature. He discussed the value of exercising unhampered by excessive clothing and advocated eating and drinking as dictated by natural instincts. He was a champion of reasonable permissiveness and the simple self-regulated life. Rousseau indicated that nature was, in fact, his god.

The philosophy of naturalism in education holds that a child should proceed in his learning at the pace intended by nature. Each individual should develop according to the dictates of his inborn characteristics. The goal of man should be his adaptation to the natural scheme. Naturalism finds truth and reality in material things and the results of scientific discovery. Man should be free from artificial bondage but should be educated both in body and mind. Religious truths are derived from nature, which is the ultimate reality for the naturalists.

Many of the notions of Rousseau and other disciples of naturalism became important principles of education. Charles Brightbill is one of those who accepted many of Rousseau's earlier teachings:

> Wherever plants grow, the wind blows, animals live, the sun, moon, and stars shine, and the snow and rain fall, we find, along with the chance for adventure, the opportunity for learning. [5, p. 148]

Physical education benefits even today from Rousseau's insistence that a variety of natural movements is necessary for optimal development. The integration and unity of man's many dimensions are fundamental teachings of the early naturalists. Rousseau's ideas with regard to the importance of the individual are not unlike those of modern existentialists. Spontaneity and creativity as goals were also suggested by Rousseau and his followers. Throughout his *Emile,* we find reference to the development of desirable character traits. [21]

The current emphasis on outdoor recreation, the Outward Bound movement, and education in the mountains and forests can be traced back to similar efforts on the part of Rousseau, Basedow, and others who believed in being guided by the laws of nature. As we tackle the problems of pollution and study the broad aspects of ecology, we find ourselves constantly confronting these inexorable laws. As we deal with the delicate balance between plant and animal life, the pollution of the streams, and the health of man and other forms of life, we find ourselves asking, "What will happen if we disturb nature's way of functioning?" Naturalism has and will continue to exert a significant influence on the areas of health, recreation, and education.

5.3 REALISM

Realists believe in solving problems through scientific inquiry. They recognize that "real" things can exist regardless of whether or not man knows anything about them. They believe that education consists of learning about things as they are and then adjusting to the situation. Realists advocate freedom of thought and action rather than reliance on "authority." They generally think of an orderly world in which scientific observation and formal logic are the basic ingredients of education. Great dependence is placed on the scientific method as a way of solving problems.

Realists resemble naturalists in their reverence for natural law. They feel that the laws of nature and environmental factors often determine what behavior will be and that individuals have the responsibility for recognizing what occurs in nature and adapting to it. Realists feel in general that environmental factors rather than social determinants have the greatest influence on their actions.

Those who espouse the philosophy of realism generally support the emphasis on personal fitness and the development of neuromuscular skill as objectives of physical education. Organic development and the improvement of performance are "real" in their opinion. The distinctions between these objectives and more intangible ones are more significant to the realist than to the idealist. Military objectives would also be likely to receive more acceptance by realists, especially if attack from another nation appeared imminent.

Realism emphasizes objectivity and the reality of things tangible. Realists rely on observation and research for answers to philosophical problems. They support curricular offerings which are relevant here and now. Objects and events are *real* even though they are *not perceived.* However, it is important for understanding and living to perceive as many of these objects and events as possible. For this, realists rely on stimuli received through their senses and subsequent organization and interpretation of these sensory impulses. If, however, objects and events are not perceived, it does not affect their reality.

It is largely to the early realists that we owe our gratitude for the beginning of laboratory work, audiovisual aids, field trips, and other forms of experience through which the "real" can be observed. The use of cadavers in teaching anatomy, mechanical apparatus in teaching kinesiology, and demonstration classes in preparing professionals were undoubtedly the innovations of realists.

Characteristics of the realist's program in education would be a logically and sequentially arranged curriculum, a relatively high percentage of required courses, carefully outlined aims and objectives, and a systematic means of evaluating progress. There would be emphasis on scientific research, adequate discipline, and carefully planned motivational techniques.

The realist physical educator meticulously teaches the mechanical principles of skills. He utilizes step-by-step progressions in his planning and exact techniques of performance in his teaching. He explains, demonstrates, teaches, and evaluates according to carefully prepared lesson plans.

Elements of realism pervade almost all other philosophies. In fact, a program seldom exists which can be identified simply as realistic, idealistic, pragmatic, or naturalistic. The concepts of the various schools of thought overlap, and individual philosophies are generally a combination of several philosophical schools of thought. Unique to realism, however, is the idea that "real" objects exist in a specific form regardless of whether they are perceived or not, irrespective of how they are viewed by any individual. It is the student's responsibility to seek and discover "real" truths and to test them in the crucible of practical life. What actually is good for personal health, what actually leads to a winning performance, what actually leads to self-realization must be sought and found.

5.4 IDEALISM

Traditional idealists believe that the *idea* of a thing is the reality, not the thing itself. The perfect chair, or the ideal chair, *is* the real chair. Likewise the idea of a perfect man, the ideal man, is the real man—a "mental reality," as Oberteuffer pointed out. [10, p. 17] To an idealist, all one can know about something is his own idea of what it is. The idea, as he perceives it, is the only reality.

Idealists place a high value on the mental and intellectual. They are also concerned about the spiritual dimensions of man and are interested in his total, integrated, and unified development. Social and moral values belong in their scheme of education. The development of the ideal man is one of their notions, the ultimate end of education therefore being to assist the student to become what he is destined to be.

There have been many forms of idealism. One can find idealistic theories referred to as Platonism, Hegelianism, or Cartesianism. There is monistic, pluralistic, subjective, and transcendental idealism. Idealism in America has been classified as personal or absolute. These classifications are only meaningful for philosophical analysis and will not be discussed individually here. More significant are the meaning and implications idealism has for physical education. Idealists are concerned about mental and spiritual values and oppose materialism and hedonism. They believe in reason and seek a rational basis for morality and religion. Important things are not found in matter or mechanical processes but in intellectual, spiritual, and philosophical pursuits.

Idealism has given to education a pervading concern for the whole man in all his aspects. The idealist will teach moral and spiritual as well as biophysical values of physical education. Both self-realization and concern for others will be included as objectives of the idealist. Interest in the aesthetic and concern for perfection and excellence for their own sake are characteristic of the idealist physical educator. It is because ideals are the goals that the idealist physical educator is constantly challenged to improve his teaching and coaching. It is the discovery of a cause worthy of his best effort that keeps him striving. His concern for the self-actualization of his students gives his work meaning.

5.5 PRAGMATISM

The pragmatist asks the question, "Will it work?" He tests a proposition by attempting to assess the consequences. He examines an idea by mentally applying it to a practical situation.

Pragmatism is the basis for much of the emphasis on *learning by doing.* Pragmatists obviously are very concerned about measurement and evaluation. Coaches are pragmatists when it comes to selecting players for a team. As Roger Burke said, "Experience is the master criterion, the source of truth, the only reality; all else is unknown and unknowable." [10, p. 7]

Burke goes on to list and define seven tenets of pragmatism:

1. *Experience*—gained through a process of dynamic and reciprocal changes inside and outside the organism.
2. *Interactive adjustment*—adjustment to the reconstructed medium.
3. *Instrumentalism*—the use of man's thoughts, ideas, and theories in resolving needs.
4. *Experimentalism*—testing theory and action by problem solving.
5. *Relativity*—the inevitability of change and the relationship of action and theory to the new conditions.
6. *Social experiment*—truth is established, not only according to the criterion of individual experiment, but social experiment as well.
7. *Democracy*—social experiment leads inevitably to democratic interaction. [10, pp. 7–9]

Pragmatists support change and experiment. They want to test new practices and trends to see if they work. On the other hand, if some practice is fruitful and productive, they would not discard it merely because it was traditional.

Where pragmatism is the guiding philosophy, the physical education student is given the opportunity to try many activities, determine the most meaningful ones to him, and continue in those. Social adjustment, cooperation, and education for democratic living are also their concerns. Relevance to living is the essence of their philosophy.

Several aspects of movement and problem solving techniques belong in the pragmatist's educational scheme. Characteristic of this scheme are challenging activities which require ingenuity to accomplish, opportunity for teamwork in their solution, competition with other teams and with nature, problems of one's own making, and opportunity to discover one's own hidden inner resources.

Whether we call it experimentalism or pragmatism, this school of educational thought has made great contributions to physical education. It has elements in common with both realism and idealism. It may be destined to play an even larger role in the future than in the past. It should be studied by all those who make physical education an important part of their life.

5.6 PROGRESSIVISM

Progressivism is a modern-day version of pragmatism integrated with some newer elements to make it more encompassing and relevant. Progressivism includes most of the tenets of instrumentalism and experimentalism. In these philosophies man is seen as "an evolving, struggling organism interacting with his environment . . . a behaving, thinking animal, subject, no less than other animals, to experimental understanding." [4, p. 94] He is seen as one who has proven his capacity to compete in and with his environment.

The social, economic, and political conditions of our times have been responsible to a large extent for the growth and spread of progressivism. It is characterized by a tolerant, flexible, open-minded attitude and an enthusiasm for exploration and experiment. It represents the philosophy of a large segment of the population that is leaving behind traditional patterns of living and shifting in favor of a new American culture.

Experience and *evolution* are key words in progressive thought. Theodore Brameld, when he wrote about the pragmatist/progressivist philosophy, expressed it thus:

> Ontological beliefs founded on experience may be said to possess also a strong evolutionary quality. Experience is struggle. Life is action and change. Chance, the unexpected, the novel, and unforeseen always play a major role. Men, like other animals, survive and advance as they, too, change and struggle, explore and dare, probe and act. [4, p. 101]

Progressivists believe that the whole child is involved in learning, that learning is a natural experience, that man is infinitely more complex and capable than other animals, and that he learns from all his experiences at home, in school, in the community, and in the world. The child is modified in response to quarreling at home, achieving in school, losing a basketball game, fighting in the alley, wading in a stream, or going to church. Progressivists believe that if the child's behavior and actions are to be influenced in a major way, all learning situations must be examined and directed. The child will then be modified by a multitude of experiences. The question is whether the learning will be positive, enriching, and growth-producing or whether it will be weakening and destructive.

Progressivists emphasize the uncertainty of the future, the continuous growth of the individual, the changing environment, the uniqueness of each new situation, and the unpredictability of life. Individual differences, freedom of choice, intelligent self-direction, and the unfolding of childrens' personalities are other points of emphasis in their educational philosophy.

Generally speaking, progressivists are more interested in the future and less interested in the past than are the proponents of the philosophies discussed earlier. They tend to feel that change is not only inevitable but necessary. They have less reverence for history than do those who espouse idealism, realism, and naturalism, perhaps because of the relative age of these philosophies. They believe that educational institutions should be agents of social change and leaders of cultural change. Therefore, they want students to be involved in social action.

As a result of the basic beliefs enumerated above, progressivists have considerable influence on the administration and conduct of our educational institutions. Traditional curricula and practices are under scrutiny. Counting credit hours, requiring courses, specifying criteria for certification, and standardizing educational programs are practices now being questioned. Students are becoming involved in decisions regarding curriculum, practices in grading, dormitory rules and regulations, as well as in the solution of administrative problems and policy formulation.

In physical education, the progressivists suggest a more varied menu of courses, "pass-fail" grades or no grades, fewer requirements and more electives, more communication among administrative officials, faculty, and students, and more freedom for the student to choose his own approach to learning. Diversity and flexibility are their bywords. They oppose distinctions between curricular and extracurricular activities, what they consider overemphasis on winning, and the disproportionate attention paid to the highly endowed athletes. Progressivists tend to be more "antiestablishment" than the essentialists. They have less regard for what has already been established and occasionally an unreasoned eagerness for change.

5.7 RECONSTRUCTIONISM
Theodore Brameld says about reconstructionism:

> It is this function—the envisioning of radical, innovative projections—that suggests the spirit of the theory we have chosen to call reconstructionism. More explicitly than any other contemporary philosophy of education, it directs its attention to the goals needed equally by a period of fearful danger and breathtaking promise. In the sense that its thinking extends well beyond the ways of living to which we are accustomed, it strives for the imaginative audacity that Montague lauds. The vision differs, however, from the almost purely speculative vision of a Plato or a Democritus: this philosophy seeks to design cultural patterns for the future upon the solid foundation of burgeoning knowledge about nature and man, and to develop viable means of establishing them. [4, pp. 346–347]

Obviously, reconstructionism is future-oriented. The concern for the future is generated to a large degree by dissatisfaction with the present. The basic thesis is that although great tangible and intangible edifices have been built in recent generations, they are no longer capable of meeting the exigencies of the present and the future.

Reconstructionists are especially concerned about relevance, about experience, and about culture. Social, moral, political, and economic problems are of utmost importance in reconstructionist thinking. Leaders in the reconstructionist movement would like to supplant many current educational practices with new ones of their own making. *Cultural renewal* is one of the mandates which they espouse. *Social self-realization* is another.

Preliminary designs for reconstructionism as outlined by Brameld include: (1) an *economy* which assures full employment and guarantees a minimum income for all; (2) a *political system* which is responsible for anti-pollution measures, for public control of transportation, communication and utilities, and for a balance between federal and state governmental responsibilities; (3) a *scientific order* committed to subsidizing research, assuring experimental freedom, and utilizing trained behavioral scientists in government leadership roles; (4) an *esthetic pattern* that will regard cultural transformation as a worthwhile creative achievement, provide direction in renewal of homes and cities, encourage artistic talent and creative achievement, and offer uncensored access to works of fine and applied art; (5) an *educational system* which is supported proportionately by federal, state, and local taxes, which provides free and universal education from nursery school through college, which is geared to reconstructionist goals, and which works cooperatively with media for mass communication; (6) a *humane order* which regards erotic expression as having affirmative value of power and delight, encourages liberalized family and cultural patterns, provides security and meaning in the lives of the aged, and guarantees full participation in all phases of culture by minority groups; and (7) a *world order* dedicated to the international application of all reconstructionist principles, an international governing force with power to keep the peace and prevent aggression, technological, educational, and medical assistance to underdeveloped regions, and maximum interrelationships of all kinds among nations. [4, pp. 437–439]

Curriculum designs based on reconstructionist beliefs exhibit the idea of *general education* in grades 11 through 14, a core or *central theme* for each year, and related studies and experiences supporting the core. Flexibility is encouraged so that the unique and the dramatic will not be hampered or limited. New schedules, school calendars, vacation provisions, and recreation plans are all given fair trial. An unlimited variety of methods is encouraged. Teachers move from group to group and serve as integrators and guides. Individuality and independent study is encouraged, as are activities traditionally extracurricular. As Brameld says, "In the area of physical education, little time is devoted to competitive interscholastic sports; emphasis is, rather, on intramural games, the dance as both a recreation and art form, and other shared activities." [4, p. 480] Adult education is encouraged. Parent involvement is stimulated in all possible ways. Education is planned to harmonize with and support the basic principles of reconstructionism.

Social self-realization is the all-embracing goal sought in the reconstructionist scheme. This includes maximum satisfaction of wants and needs of both individuals and groups. This shall apply to physical education as well as other aspects of education.

5.8 EXISTENTIALISM

There are almost as many versions of existentialism as there are people who claim to be existentialists. This is not really paradoxical inasmuch as existentialism proclaims the right of each person to develop his own philosophy of life. Many existentialists repudiate all "systems" of philosophy when they ask, "How can an existentialist be an authentic individual if he adopts another person's philosophy?" Existentialism is a quest for authenticity. The right of an individual to be "his own person" is certainly the crux of existentialism.

Selfhood, including self-responsibility, is another principle of existentialism. The individual's responsibility for what he becomes and his personal acceptance of the consequences of his own acts are also part of existentialistic tenets. Three basic threads which permeate the existentialist credo are *individual freedom, self-responsibility,* and *personal authenticity.* These are at the heart of existentialism and it is belief in these that has brought many to the point of rebellion against those social structures and establishments that thwart their efforts to be themselves and do as they please. It is also these tenets that have caused them to be disinterested in group activity.

It should not be concluded, however, that existentialists have no regard for their fellow man. They are not only looking inwardly but also at their own "selves" in relation to other "selves." They do not intend, however, to let their concern for the masses or social structures interfere with what they see as their own rights as individuals. As Elwood Davis puts it:

> Nevertheless, says the follower of Existentialism, if and when man "takes charge" of the inner self, he begins to *exist* as *homo sapiens.* He begins to understand himself. He "takes charge," in the existentialist sense, as he makes the effort, takes the initiative, and forces himself to make decisions, to select preferences, to choose the sort of person he is to be, what he shall think, feel and do, how he shall live, what his goals and values shall be—*all without guidance from anyone or anything* outside himself. Then he "takes charge" in accepting responsibility for the consequences. [10, p. 112]

Choice, ambiguity, and *authenticity* are important concepts in existentialism. Of necessity, they are also related. Each situation and every set of circumstances, is fraught with many possibilities for action. Because each individual is an authentic person with the privilege of choosing his course of action and with the responsibility of accepting the consequences, each situation, each hour, each day is uncertain, or ambiguous, with respect to the ensuing action. There are no permanent guidelines covering every situation which a person will encounter. He makes one choice, acts, and soon faces another choice. Therefore life is ambiguous.

It becomes obvious very quickly that there are many kinds of existentialism. It is therefore not feasible to enumerate them in this chapter. However, George Kneller in *Existentialism and Education* has summarized some weaknesses and strengths which seem particularly pertinent to this discussion:

1. In a freedom-loving society, the preachings of existentialists are less poignant. "Their criticism is leveled at fundamentally stagnant or repressive societies."

2. Existentialists are unduly harsh toward scientific inquiry. Their claim that science treats man as an object, therefore destroying man's essential dignity, hardly stands up under scrutiny. There are innumerable discoveries made in the laboratory that contribute to the improvement of the "human condition."

3. Existentialist insistence on individual freedom is hardly compatible with the commonly accepted theories of group dynamics and the desirable interrelationships of communities and their individual members. Acts which consider only the individual can be damaging if they are, by common consent, injurious to the body politic. Existentialism which exhibits little concern for others cannot be said to improve the human condition.

4. "Introspection and self-analysis cannot take place in a vacuum, else it becomes solipsistic, self-flagellating, abortive." Our actions must be determined by our relation with the real world. Without a system of values, chaos would reign. Man must be able to measure the results of his actions against the norms of social progress. If meaning is to be derived from man's existence, it must be through projects which are part of the world in which he exists. [26, pp. 153–155]

Positive contributions of existentialists listed by Kneller are:

1. "Individuals need to find their place in the crowd and not be swallowed by it." Their cry against complacency and their demand for intensive personal commitment is justified. People should come forward and stand up for what they believe. Protests against sham and hypocrisy are valid.

2. The substitution of the concrete and the individual for sterile abstractions and objective absolutes is justifiable. The individual *is* a striving, aspiring, responsible being. This is the strength of existentialism.

3. The exaltation of the value of the individual human personality is another contribution of existentialism. Each man should be able to be himself, to live his own life, and to become what he is capable of becoming.

4. "Especially in an age which strives to understand the whole man, a doctrine stressing emotional and creative growth and the affective states of man takes on immeasurable importance." The existentialist emphasis on the emotional life of man is an important contribution to education.

5. Existentialism has forced a reexamination of neat hierarchies of absolutes, of traditional structures and practices, of a rigid intellectual approach to education. "Mood and feeling are capable of understanding and even interpreting the nature and destiny of man at points where the intellectual approach no longer serves." [26, pp. 156–158]

Elwood Davis has summarized his discussion of existentialism with some "possible implications for physical education." He points out that the physical education experience enhances the individual's sense of self-responsibility, an existentialist tenet. He mentions the existentialist concern for the development of the student's personality and its indifference toward objective measurements. He explains the existentialist view that students cannot be held responsible for obeying rules which were formulated without student participation.

According to Davis, a student can be encouraged to exercise his individual freedom in several ways. He can formulate his own system of values. He can be given a voice in student government, he can choose some of his own courses, and he can make progress toward the life goals he has chosen. [10, pp. 113–121]

Harold VanderZwaag points out that "sport for sport's sake" is an existentialist point of view. "There are no values other than sport itself when the individual makes the decision to engage in sport." [49, p. 212]

VanderZwaag also believes that the concept of authenticity is difficult to reconcile with the idea of sport. He declares that one is playing a role as soon as he enters a game, causing him to yield to the essence of the sport which in turn acts as a handicap to his own existence. [49, p. 213]

The articulation of any kind of universal is contrary to the basic concept of existentialism, for it does away with choice and eliminates the possibility of each individual "doing his own thing" for his own reason. The listing of objectives, aims, goals and outcomes for any activity is therefore antiexistential. Existentialists would eliminate these from physical education and simply say, "I chose soccer because I wanted to; I participate in sport for the sake of sport; I climbed the mountain because it was there."

5.9 IMPLICATIONS OF PHILOSOPHICAL CONCEPTS FOR PHYSICAL EDUCATION

It is difficult for a physical educator to identify with any one philosophical school of thought, or even two or three. Such attempts are too confining, too prescriptive. The freedom to select from among all philosophical concepts—individual freedom to choose and to find the authentic self—is more common and more to be preferred. There are gems of wisdom to be found in the writings of many different philosophers, thousands of combinations of circumstances calling for individual responses, and quite a number of individuals searching for a different key to unlock the door to their potential.

The following philosophical concepts and their implications have been drawn from a wide range of sources, written and unwritten. It is hoped that they may be helpful, or at least interesting:

1. *Philosophy.* The search for the true, the real, and the good will generally reveal only partial answers. Truth can be gleaned from living close to nature as espoused by the naturalists, from careful adherence to the scientific method as

Aspen Middle School eighth level students rappeling during ▶ their Fall, 1969 Outdoor Education Program at Marble, Colorado. (Courtesy of the *Journal of Health, Physical Education, and Recreation.*)

described by the realists, from intellectual and spiritual pursuits as practiced by many idealists, through testing the consequences in accordance with the tenets of pragmatism, from experiences encountered in the struggle to prepare for the future, as in progressivism, from planning cultural patterns for the next generation as propounded by reconstructionists, and from the march toward self-realization and individual freedom as defined by existentialists.

Truth may also be glimpsed through the eyes of the prophets of Israel, the seers of India, the scientists of Germany, the artists of Italy, and the religious leaders of the Moslems, Hindus, Buddhists, Christians, and all others who search sincerely and intently. Truth may also be discovered spontaneously and accidentally when living, feeling, observing, and experiencing. There are no fences around the discovery of truth.

2. *Excellence.* All athletes desire to be excellent. Excellence in sport is self-fulfilling. Most people admire excellence ... some are awed by it, others are challenged. Excellence can be a matter of superb performance. It may also be reflected in a warm personality. Striving for perfection in one's own way and according to one's own capabilities is progress toward authenticity and self-realization. Existentialism supports this.

3. *Values through physical education.* Those teachers and coaches who are indifferent toward the teaching of values as they conduct classes and practice sessions or deal with athletes during contests are ignoring the opportunities to make their contributions toward a better world. Physical education is replete with intense and dramatic situations where valuable lessons of life can be taught. Generalization is the clue. Idealistic leaders are needed.

4. *The best of the past.* Before discarding past practices to make room for the new, both should be carefully evaluated. All the evaluative tools of science and technology should be utilized to make the assessment. The disciplines of biology, psychology, and sociology should be applied to the problem and data should be carefully analyzed and interpreted. The findings should also be interpreted subjectively in order to arrive at the best possible conclusions. Things are not necessarily better merely because they are new ... neither are things to be preferred just because they are old. The best of the past should be retained and combined with the most promising of the new. Realism is illustrated here.

5. *The broadening curriculum.* The trend toward a greater variety of physical education activities and more choices for the student is being met with enthusiastic response from the pragmatists because of the increased motivation which is engendered. Existentialists like it because of the choice.

"All athletes desire to be excellent.... Striving for ▶ perfection in one's own way and according to one's own capabilities is progress toward authenticity and self-realization." (Courtesy of: *top left,* the *Journal of Health, Physical Education, and Recreation; top right,* University of Wisconsin–LaCrosse; *bottom,* Springfield College.)

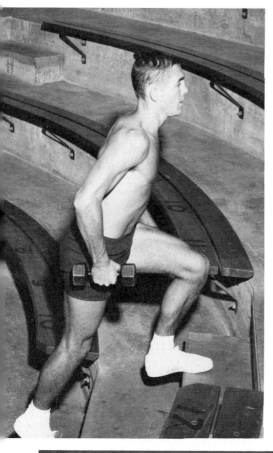

6. *Personal involvement.* When the physical education teacher and/or coach become deeply involved with the lives and personal problems of the students, the response is usually positive and enthusiastic. When the teacher gives of himself because he sees his job as a vocation and because of a deep affection for the students, his influence is usually great. Such moral and spiritual involvement is characteristic of idealism.

7. *Personal fitness.* Amidst revolutions of all descriptions, man as a biological organism has changed very little. Vigorous exercise leading to sound organic development is one of the central aims of physical education, and justifiably so. Evidence abounds as to the biophysical values accruing from such demanding activity. Therefore, every child should be guided through a program of basic vigorous physical education activities. This is an approach to teaching characteristic of realism.

8. *Innovative programs.* There are many places in the United States where physical education courses, or syllabi, differ very little from those of ten or twenty years ago. There is an urgent need to supplant such programs with new, stimulating, and challenging ones. This is a reconstructionist approach.

9. *Perceptual motor development.* Nervous integration is completed only as the organism responds to movement. To ensure preschool children opportunity to realize all their innate capabilities, they should be given a program of movement with careful attention paid to a balance of motor patterns. They must all be given the experience of moving in many different ways and helped to master the basic, fundamental movements needed for living. Existentialists, realists, idealists, and progressivists all subscribe to this principle.

10. *Skills for the future.* There is general enthusiastic support for the teaching of lifetime sports in college, high school and even in the elementary school. Golf, tennis, archery, canoeing, badminton, and swimming are among such lifetime sports. Fun and joy, fitness for life, and relief from stress are among the objectives. Idealists, reconstructionists and existentialists favor such objectives.

11. *The affective domain.* The traditional objectives of physical education have centered around organic and neuromuscular development. More recently, attention is turning toward emotional outcomes, psychological needs, and spiritual implications. Idealists, pragmatists, progressivists, and existentialists support such trends.

12. *Sport and meaning.* Howard Slusher, in his postscript to *Man, Sport and Existence,* said:

> Sport was intimate, profound and even spiritual. It reached the root of human existence and, as such, provided an arena for the discovery of personal truths. Neither man alone, nor sport alone provided the completeness of existence. Sport and man revealed to each other the opportunity of determining meaning. In this way, once again, man located a realm of value formation. It was *a* source of worth and meaning. [43, p. 215]

The above paragraph contains elements of both idealism and existentialism.

13. *System and standards.* For many years physical education leaders and teachers have been concerned with the development of a systematic curriculum in which elements to be learned are carefully organized and arranged, thereby providing logical progression and complete coverage of subject matter. This has led to more efficient use of resources, more effective teaching, and raised standards. This is a contribution of realists.

14 *Mind and body.* Today there is a great emphasis on psychosomatic relationships and mental health. Anxieties and mental stresses have a great effect on organic development. Good mental health is essential to good organic health. A serene, contented frame of mind emanating from a positive and sound philosophy of life can do much to enhance both mental and physical health. Emphasis on this principle is basically idealistic.

15. Social adjustment has long been listed as one of the important aims of physical education. The increasing importance of interpersonal relationships, the recognition of the influence of social determinants on behavior, and the emphasis on community are more recent developments. Physical education leaders of today are concerned about these elements, particularly idealists and reconstructionists.

16. *Exploration and problem solving.* Movement exploration and problem solving techniques are receiving far more emphasis than they did in the past. These methods appear to motivate the student and help him to learn by doing. Physical educators who support the schools of pragmatism, progressivism and reconstructionism are advocates of these methods.

17. *High-level motor learning.* Automatism and individuation in motor learning at the high-skill level are theoretical concepts important in physical education. The process of making unconscious those movement patterns which began by being conscious is also part of learning at that level. Scientific inquiry is at the base of such theorizing, and realists will teach these concepts.

18. *Teamwork.* Paul Weiss, in *Sport, A Philosophic Inquiry,* says:

> Alone, a man usually makes his activities turn in a circle about himself. When he plays on a team he carries out a role in relation to the roles others assume. As a consequence, he functions on behalf of all the members of his team. Not until he actually plays with others as part of a team, however, does he face up to what they can do, what they are doing, and what they will do. The response and even the presence of others involves contingencies no one can entirely anticipate. [52, p. 160]

Since *existentialists* object to role playing, they would not subscribe to being members of such teams.

19. *Dance.* Rhythmic activities contribute to a student's well-being by providing vigorous activities of a social nature performed to the rhythm of music. Dance provides the opportunity for self-expression and creativity. When dancers communicate with an audience through movement, they have particularly satisfying expe-

riences. Joyous, creative, expressive, rhythmic movement can be especially self-fulfilling. Idealists, progressivists, and existentialists would be quick to recognize the contributions of dance to the full and abundant life.

20. *Certification and standardization.* Teachers in the United States are still being certified on the basis of courses taken and credits received. Reciprocal certification practices, whereby a number of states accept teachers certified in other states, has done much to standardize the criteria which serve as the basis for certification. There is currently an effort to use the "performance assessment" concept in evaluating those who wish to become certified. To date, certification has been essentially a realistic concept. Changing to "performance based certification" would be reconstructionist in nature.

21. *Flexibility and modules.* The breaking down of traditionally rigid schedules to permit varying lengths of class periods and the new designs of educational build-

"The response and even the presence of others involves contingencies no one can entirely anticipate."—Paul Weiss (Courtesy of Luther College.)

ings to provide flexibility in classroom size and teaching stations are both pragmatic and reconstructionist in nature.

22. *The child as the central focus.* The basic purpose of education is the development of the individual. Regardless of the educational philosophy, every educator
worthy of the name will agree that the final judgment of any practice, any policy,
any decision, must rest on the answer to the question, "What is best for the child,
for the pupil, for the student, for the athlete?" A second question is, "What will
provide the greatest good for the greatest number?" On the sigificance of these
questions in physical education, there is general agreement among all the schools
of philosophy discussed.

We see then that a philosophy of physical education can be built around
elements from the various philosophical schools of thought. Each educator must
develop his own sound philosophy which will serve as a guide in his teaching and
coaching as well as his living. It must be his individual and well thought-out philosophy—it cannot be merely a combination of elements plucked from the philosophies
of others. It will, however, be influenced to a great extent by the thoughts of others.
It will be tinged with the learnings of each individual's personal experiences. As
Zeigler has told us, "Keep in mind that the philosophic quest is a never-ending one.
You won't suddenly, at some advanced stage of your development, find all the
answers to the problems which have been perplexing you. But you will be leading
a greatly enriched life that may truly be an 'adventure of ideas.' " [56, p. 294] And
we have been told by Adrian Dupuis and Robert Nordberg that,

> To become conscious of one's assumptions about the ultimate principles
> and causes of things, to evaluate these assumptions for clarity and consis-
> tency, to restructure them in that light, to apply the consequences where they
> fit, this is the philosophic enterprise. [15, p. 325]

SELECTED REFERENCES

1. Arsenian, Seth (ed.), *The Humanics Philosophy of Springfield College,* Springfield,
   Mass.: Springfield College, 1969.
2. Bair, Donn E., "An identification of some philosophical beliefs held by influential
   professional leaders in American physical education," unpublished Ph.D. dissertation,
   University of Southern California, 1956.
3. Bookwalter, Karl W., and Harold J. VanderZwaag, *Foundations and Principles of Physical Education,* Philadelphia: W. B. Saunders Company, 1969.
4. Brameld, Theodore, *Patterns of Educational Philosophy,* New York: Holt, Rinehart,
   and Winston, 1971. Reprinted by permission.
5. Brightbill, Charles K., "What comes naturally," *Background Readings for Physical
   Education,* Paterson, Ann, and Edmond C. Hallberg, New York: Holt, Rinehart, and
   Winston, 1967.
6. Brownell, Clifford Lee, and E. Patricia Hagman, *Physical Education—Foundations and
   Principles,* New York: McGraw-Hill, 1951.
7. Brubacher, John S., *Modern Philosophies of Education,* New York: McGraw-Hill, 1969.

8. Bucher, Charles A., *Foundations of Physical Education,* 4th edition, St. Louis: The C. V. Mosby Company, 1964.
9. Bucher, Charles A., and Myra Goldman (eds.), *Dimensions of Physical Education,* St. Louis: the C. V. Mosby Company, 1969.
10. Davis, Elwood C. (ed.), *Philosophies Fashion Physical Education,* Delbert Oberteuffer, "Idealism and Its Meaning to Physical Education," Chapter 3, and Roger K. Burke, "Physical Education and the Philosophy of Pragmatism," Chapter 2, Dubuque, Iowa: Wm. C. Brown Company, 1963. Reprinted by permission.
11. Davis, Elwood C. and Donna M. Miller, *The Philosophic Process in Physical Education,* Philadelphia: Lea and Febiger, 1967.
12. *Developing Democratic Human Relations,* First Yearbook, Washington, D.C.: American Association for Health, Physical Education, and Recreation, 1951.
13. Dewey, John, *Philosophy of Education,* Totowa, N.J.: Littlefield, Adams and Company, 1966.
14. Downey, Robert J., et al., *Exploring Physical Education,* Belmont, Calif.: Wadsworth Publishing Company, 1962.
15. Dupuis, Adrian M., and Robert B. Nordberg, *Philosophy and Education,* Milwaukee: The Bruce Publishing Company, 1964.
16. Durant, Will, *The Story of Philosophy,* Garden City, N.Y.: Garden City Publishing Company, 1927.
17. Educational Policies Commission, *Quality in Education,* Washington, D.C.: National Education Association, 1959.
18. Fadiman, Clifton (ed.), *I Believe,* New York: Simon and Schuster, 1939.
19. Fairs, John R., "The influence of Plato and Platonism on the development of physical education in western culture," *Quest,* Monograph XI, December 1968.
20. Frankl, Viktor E., *Man's Search for Meaning,* New York: Washington Square Press, 1968.
21. Frederick, Mary M., "Naturalism: the philosophy of Jean Jacques Rousseau and its implications for American physical education," unpublished doctoral dissertation, Springfield College, Springfield, Massachusetts, 1961.
22. Halsey, Elizabeth, *Inquiry and Invention in Physical Education,* Philadelphia: Lea and Febiger, 1964.
23. Harper, Ralph, *Existentialism,* Cambridge, Mass.: Harvard University Press, 1965.
24. Henderson, Stella V. P., *Introduction to Philosophy of Education,* Chicago: The University of Chicago Press, 1947.
25. *Higher Education for American Democracy,* Report of the President's Commission for American Democracy, Washington, D.C.: The United States Printing Office, 1947.
26. Kneller, George F., *Existentialism and Education,* New York: John Wiley and Sons, 1958.
27. _____ (ed.), *Foundations of Education,* 3rd edition, New York: John Wiley and Sons, 1971.
28. Kroll, Walter P., *Perspectives in Physical Education,* New York: The Academic Press, 1971.
29. Lincoln, C. Eric, *Sounds of the Struggle,* New York: William Morrow and Company, 1968.
30. McCloy, Charles H., *Philosophical Bases for Physical Education,* New York: F. S. Crofts and Company, 1947.
31. McIntosh, P. C., *Sport in Society,* London: C. A. Watts and Company, 1963.

32. Morland, Richard B., "A philosophical interpretation of the educational views held by seven leaders in American physical education," unpublished doctoral dissertation, New York University School of Education, 1958.
33. Murrow, Edward R., *This I Believe,* New York: Simon and Schuster, 1952.
34. Oberteuffer, Delbert, *Physical Education,* New York: Harper and Row, 1956.
35. Paterson, Ann, and Edmond C. Hallberg, *Background Readings for Physical Education,* New York: Holt, Rinehart, and Winston, 1967.
36. Patka, Frederick, *Existentialist Thinkers and Thought,* New York: The Citadel Press, 1964.
37. Piaget, Jean, and Bärbel Inhelder, *The Psychology of the Child,* New York: Basic Books, 1969.
38. Power, Edward J., *Education for American Democracy,* New York: McGraw-Hill, 1965.
39. Reich, Charles A., *The Greening of America,* New York: Bantam Books, 1970.
40. Reinhart, Kurt F., *The Existentialist Revolt,* New York: Frederick Ungar Publishing Company, 1960.
41. Reisman, David, *Constraint and Variety in American Education,* Garden City, N.Y.: Doubleday and Company, 1958.
42. Siedentop, Daryl, *Physical Education,* Dubuque, Iowa: Wm. C. Brown Company, 1972.
43. Slusher, Howard S., *Man, Sport and Existence,* Philadelphia: Lea and Febiger, 1967.
44. Slusher, Howard S., and Aileen S. Lockhart, *Anthology of Contemporary Readings,* Dubuque, Iowa: Wm. C. Brown Company, 1966.
45. Taylor, Harold, *On Education and Freedom,* Carbondale: Southern Illinois University Press, 1967.
46. _____, *The World as Teacher,* Garden City, N.Y.: Doubleday and Company, 1970.
47. Titus, Harold H., *Living Issues in Philosophy,* 2nd edition, New York: American Book Company, 1953.
48. Van Dalen, Deobold B., and Bruce L. Bennett, *A World History of Physical Education,* 2nd edition, Englewood Cliffs, N.J.: Prentice-Hall, 1971.
49. VanderZwaag, Harold J., *Toward a Philosophy of Sport,* Reading, Mass.: Addison-Wesley Publishing Company, 1972.
50. Wayman, Agnes, *A Modern Philosophy of Physical Education,* Philadelphia: W. B. Saunders Company, 1938.
51. Weber, Alfred, *History of Philosophy,* New York: Charles Scribner's Sons, 1925.
52. Weiss, Paul, *Sport, A Philosophic Inquiry,* Carbondale: Southern Illinois University Press, 1969. Reprinted by permission.
53. Whitehead, Alfred N., *The Aims of Education,* New York: The Free Press, 1967.
54. Williams, Jesse F., *The Principles of Physical Education,* 6th edition, Philadelphia: W. B. Saunders Company, 1954.
55. Young, Michael, and Peter Willmott, *The Symmetrical Family,* London: Routledge and Kegan Paul, 1973.
56. Zeigler, Earle F., *Philosophical Foundations for Physical, Health, and Recreation Education,* Englewood Cliffs, N.J.: Prentice-Hall, 1964.

Anatomical and Physiological Bases

Chapter 6

6.1 INTRODUCTION
The human organism is indeed a unique and wondrous creature. It grows, develops, and learns. It can reason as well as run. It has the capacity to feel emotions and to become angry. It is composed of many intricately constructed and smoothly functioning organs which perform their specific tasks in close harmony with each other. The specialized cells of these organs act in an integrated and coordinated fashion to move the various body segments either automatically or on command, to manufacture the different kinds of blood cells needed at a specific place at a certain time, to rid our body of impurities and waste products, to transport oxygen from the lungs to the tissues, to flash messages from one part of the body to another, and to manufacture and transport chemicals which are used for many specific purposes.

Our body, when functioning as it should, can heal its own wounds, restore itself through sleep, prepare itself for greater stress, and adjust to a multitude of different environmental factors. The human being reproduces its kind and thus provides for survival of the race. Within most individuals, there exists the desire to improve, the instinctive ambition to move upward toward a better life at a higher level. Man can experience joy and sorrow, exhilaration and apathy, love and hate. Man can also run, jump, hurl, and lift. Together with others he can play football, tennis, golf, or soccer. By himself he can swim, ski, soar, hunt, or dance.

If man is to achieve his potential, all activities of the human body must be coordinated, all aspects must be integrated. What is done by or happens to one part of the organism affects and is affected by every other part. Any educational procedure, physical activity, or exercise regimen must be considered with respect to its effect on the total individual. Every change in environment shall be considered with respect to its influence on *all* the many dimensions of the person, all dimensions being interrelated and interdependent, all parts together forming a unified and integrated whole.

Man is an active animal. He possess the capacity and desire for physical movement, one of the ways in which man responds to his environment. During movement, he is dependent upon his skeletal muscles, his circulatory system, his nervous system, and many other parts of the body. All components of his body are in turn dependent upon movement for their continued vigor, health, and development. Physical activity is a biological necessity. It is with physiological processes and principles as they relate to movement that this chapter is concerned.

6.2 STRUCTURE AND FUNCTION
While the body is a unified and integrated whole, it is analyzed system by system for purposes of study. Each system has its own specific kinds of cells, and each is responsible for specific functions. The systems of the human organism are:

1. *The skeletal system,* consisting of bones, ligaments, and connective tissue. Its function is to provide support for the body, furnish anchorages for muscles and tendons, protect delicate parts of the body, assist in formation of blood cells, and facilitate movement of the body parts.

2. *The muscular system,* comprising the striated, nonstriated and cardiac muscle fibers bundled together to form muscles. Muscular tissue is contractile, extensible, and elastic, Muscles contract to move bones, digest food, control blood flow, and regulate breathing. Cardiac muscle is responsible for maintaining the heart beat and pumping blood to all parts of the body.

3. *The nervous system,* made up of the brain, spinal cord, nerves, and ganglia. Nervous tissue possesses the properties of irritability and conductivity and functions to transmit impulses, stimulate muscles and other organs to act, coordinate movement, perceive, think, express, and remember. It is incredibly intricate, complex, versatile, and capable.

4. *The circulatory system,* composed of the heart, arteries, veins, arterioles, venules, capillaries, and lymphatic vessels. It also includes the blood and the lymph themselves. This system transports blood and oxygen, supplies the tissues with nutrients, removes waste products, carries internal secretions, helps regulate body temperature, and assists with the organism's fight against disease.

5. *The respiratory system,* consisting of the bronchi, lungs, trachea, throat, and nose. It functions to move carbon dioxide (CO_2) from the blood to the atmosphere and oxygen (O_2) from the atmosphere to the blood. It is concerned with inspiration, expiration, and related processes.

6. *The digestive system,* including the mouth (with teeth and tongue), esophagus, stomach, small and large intestines, liver, gall bladder, pancreas, salivary glands, and the rectum. It contains many cells, each differentiated for a specific function. It ingests and digests food, selects and assimilates needed nutrients, discharges wastes, assists in the manufacture of blood sugar (glucose), and in general, tends to the dietary needs of the organism.

7. *The excretory system,* made up of the kidneys, ureters, bladder, and urethra. In a broader sense it also includes the skin, lungs, and intestines. The function of this system is to purify air and liquid intake and to eliminate the unused portions in the form of carbon dioxide, water, and nitrogenous waste.

8. *The reproductive system,* comprising (in the female) the ovaries, uterine tubes, uterus, vagina, and mammary glands, and (in the male) the testes, vas deferens, prostate gland, penis, and urethra. The function is the production of germ cells and sex hormones and (in the female) the prenatal and postnatal nurture of offspring.

9. *The endocrine system,* including the islet cells of the pancreas, the pituitary gland, thyroid gland, parathyroid glands, adrenal glands, and gonads. These glands, when stimulated, secrete hormones into the blood stream and thus drastically affect the emotions, the growth, behavior, and general health of the organism.

10. *The tegumentary system,* consisting of the *epithelium* (epidermis), the *corium,* and the *tela subcutanea*. It protects the body, houses nerve endings and blood vessels, contains hair follicles and sweat glands, and includes a layer of subcutaneous fat for insulation.

These are the systems which together constitute the human organism. Their harmonious, synchronized, and integrated functioning enables man to move, talk, think, act, sense, and respond. They provide for the vital functions necessary to complete living.

6.3 BONES AND JOINTS

The 206 bones of the human body may be divided into those comprising the *axial* skeleton and those comprising the *appendicular* skeleton. The axial skeleton contains the 29 bones of the skull and the 51 bones of the trunk. They include the cranial and facial bones, the vertebrae, the ribs, and the sternum. The other 126 bones comprise the appendicular skeleton containing the clavicles (collar bones), the scapulae (shoulder blades), the left and right arms (humerus, ulna, radius, carpals, metacarpals, and phalanges), and the left and right legs (femur, patella, tibia, fibula, tarsals, metatarsals, and phalanges). The pelvic girdle is also part of the appendicular skeleton (see Figure 6.1).

The bones are joined together by ligaments. Cartilage (a softer, more pliable tissure than bone) is found in most joints. At birth there is a great deal of cartilaginous tissue in the skeleton, but these cartilages ossify rapidly as the child matures. The skeletal maturity of the individual is termed the *physiological age* or, occasionally, the "bone age." As some individuals mature earlier than others, the chronological is not always the same as the physiological age. Other indications of maturation (puberty, etc.) correspond quite closely to the bone age.

It is important for physical educators to be aware that children in the lower grades have much more cartilaginous tissue in the joints and in the epiphyses (broad rounded ends) of the long bones than they do at a more advanced age. Care must be taken to see that those activities which put a strain on such developing joints are avoided.

Joints are classified as *synarthroses* (immovable), *amphiarthroses* (slightly movable), and *diarthroses* (freely movable). The synarthrodial or fixed joints are either *sutures,* in which the bones are interlocked, or *synchondroses,* in which the bones are originally joined by a strip of cartilage, eventually to be replaced by bone. Cranial bones are generally joined by sutures and the epiphyses of long bones by synchrondroses. The *symphysis pubis* and the articulation between the lower ends of the tibia and fibula are examples of amphiarthroses.

It is with the diarthrodial joints that the physical educator must be most concerned. These are the joints which are freely movable, whose flexibility can be increased by appropriate exercise, and which are most subject to serious injury and strain. The ends of the bones comprising such joints are covered with *articular*

Figure 6.1   The human skeleton. (From *(left and center)* W. P. Bowen ▶ and H. A. Stone, *Applied Anatomy and Kinesiology,* Philadelphia: Lea and Febiger, 1953, p. 64; and *(right)* Katharine F. Wells, *Kinesiology,* 5th edition, Philadelphia: W. B. Saunders Company, 1971, p. 375. By permission.)

143

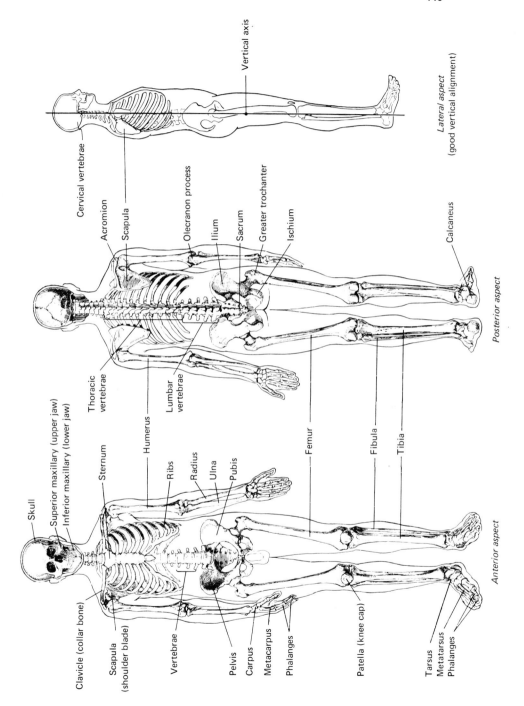

Vertical axis

Lateral aspect
(good vertical alignment)

Cervical vertebrae

Acromion

Scapula

Olecranon process

Ilium

Sacrum

Greater trochanter

Ischium

Calcaneus

Posterior aspect

Thoracic vertebrae

Lumbar vertebrae

Humerus

Femur

Fibula

Tibia

Skull

Superior maxillary (upper jaw)

Inferior maxillary (lower jaw)

Sternum

Ribs

Radius

Ulna

Pubis

Clavicle (collar bone)

Scapula (shoulder blade)

Vertebrae

Pelvis

Carpus

Metacarpus

Phalanges

Patella (knee cap)

Tarsus

Metatarsus

Phalanges

Anterior aspect

144

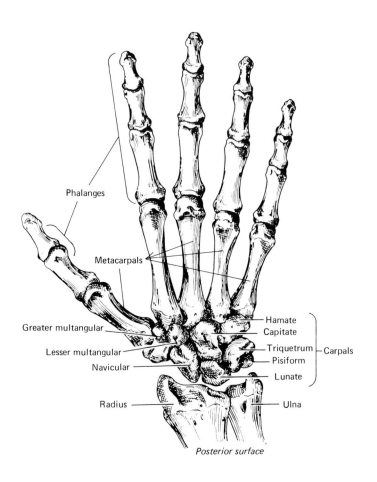

Phalanges

Metacarpals

Greater multangular
Lesser multangular
Navicular

Hamate
Capitate
Triquetrum
Pisiform
Lunate

Carpals

Radius

Ulna

Posterior surface

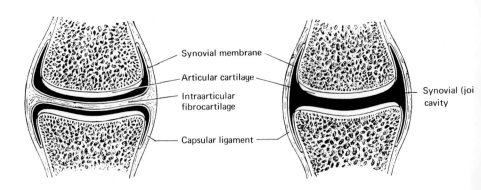

Synovial membrane

Articular cartilage

Intraarticular
fibrocartilage

Capsular ligament

Synovial (joi
cavity

Figure 6.2 Bones of the hand and foot. (From C. P. Anthony, *Textbook of Anatomy and Physiology*, p. 115, and Wells, *Kinesiology*, pp. 297, 304.)

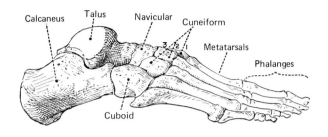

Calcaneus Talus Navicular Cuneiform Metatarsals Phalanges

Cuboid

Lateral aspect

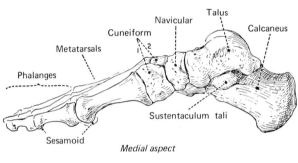

Talus
Navicular
Cuneiform
Calcaneus
Metatarsals
Phalanges
Sustentaculum tali
Sesamoid

Medial aspect

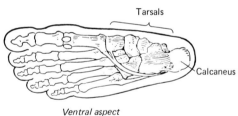

Tarsals

Calcaneus

Ventral aspect

cartilage and the joint enclosed in a ligamentous *articular capsule* (see Figure 6.4). This capsule is lined by a *synovial membrane* and the joint cavity is filled with thick viscous, synovial fluid. Such a joint can move in two or more directions, can support the body in many positions, and is lubricated so that motion can continue almost indefinitely. The ball-and-socket joints of the shoulder and hip are examples of diarthroses.

◀**Figure 6.3 Typical synovial joint.** (From Bowen and Stone, *Applied Anatomy and Kinesiology*, p. 65. By permission.)

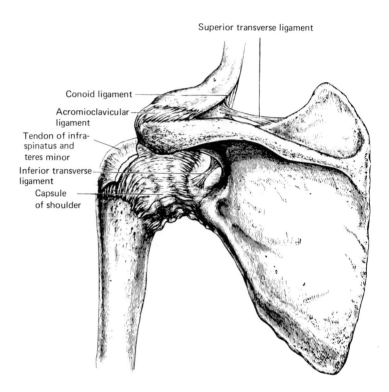

Superior transverse ligament

Conoid ligament

Acromioclavicular
ligament

Tendon of infra-
spinatus and
teres minor

Inferior transverse
ligament

Capsule
of shoulder

Dorsal aspect of shoulder

Figure 6.4 A diarthrodial joint. Note how the shoulder
joint is encased in a ligamentous capsule which is
extensible and flexible. Note also the articular cartilages
which are lubricated by synovial fluid as this ingeniously
constructed joint permits movement of the head of the
humerus in many different directions. (From Edwards,
Anatomy for Physical Education, pp. 188, 193. By
permission.)

It should be remembered that bone is living tissue, that both the bones
themselves and the origins and insertions of muscles are strengthened in response to exercise, and that a balanced diet which contains all the essential
nutrients and vitamins is necessary for normal growth. It should also be kept in
mind that nutritional deficiencies are often the cause of rickets, "bowlegs," abnormal spinal curvatures, and other bone malformations.

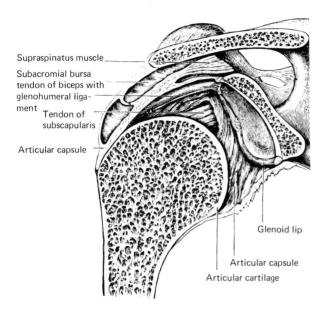

Supraspinatus muscle

Subacromial bursa
tendon of biceps with
glenohumeral liga-
ment
    Tendon of
    subscapularis

Articular capsule

Glenoid lip

Articular capsule
Articular cartilage

Shoulder-joint cavity
(cross-section)

6.4 MUSCLE AND MOVEMENT

Whether in work or play, man's tasks are accomplished by muscles acting on bony levers. Muscles can only pull, they cannot push. The point at which a muscle is attached to the fixed bone, usually the proximal end, is called the *origin*. The end of the muscle which is attached to the movable bone, usually the distal end, is termed the *insertion*. (see Figure 6.5.) The origin and insertion may be reversed, depending on the direction of the motion.

The growth and development of muscle and nerve are stimulated by movement. As the sensory nervous mechanisms respond to fundamental movements, nervous integration proceeds and the ability to perceive increases. The development of the muscular system also stimulates the development of the internal organs of the vegetative (involuntary) system.

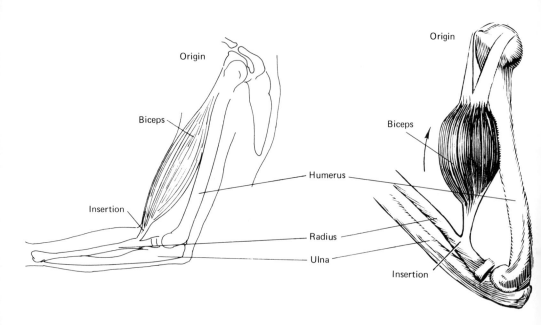

Figure 6.5 Biceps, showing origin and insertion. As the biceps contracts (shortens), the point of origin is held stationary and there is a powerful pull on the radius at the point of insertion. The joint formed by the distal end of the humerus with the socket of the ulna and the proximal end of the radius becomes the axis. As the distal end of the humerus slides in the socket of the ulna, the radius moves around the distal end of the humerus. The pull on the radius lifts the forearm and hand. (From Wells, *Kinesiology*, p. 107, and A. Ravielli, *Wonders of the Human Body*, New York: The Viking Press, 1961, p. 59. By permission.)

Muscles perform work by contracting. This may take the form of static or isotonic contractions which are involved in maintaining a given posture or in locomotor or manipulatory movements such as running or throwing. A working muscle is composed of many *motor units,* each of which contains many contractile fibers innervated by a single nerve. The force generated by a muscle consists of the summation of the contractions of many such motor units. The frequency of the contraction of each motor unit can be increased (to a point) or decreased, depending on the force the individual wishes to exert. The strength and frequency of the electrical stimuli and the corresponding activation of motor units will determine the power mobilized and the work done.

The strength of muscles can be increased by exercising them against progressively greater resistance. Muscular endurance can be developed by increasing the length of time the muscle is exercised. In weight training classes, it is recognized that the ability to lift great weights can be developed by using heavy resistance and few repetitions, while conditioning exercises generally consist of less resistance and a greater number of repetitions. Muscles increase in size as a result of a program of strong, powerful contractions. Since the number of fibers does not increase, it follows that the individual muscle fibers and the tissues between them must become larger following such a continued program.

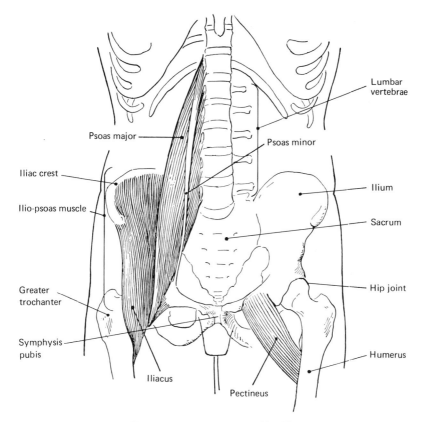

Figure 6.6 Flexor of the body at the hip. The ilio-psoas muscle group (anterior aspect). The iliacus and the psoas muscles combine to form the ilio-psoas muscle group. This group provides much of the force used in performing situps or when lying on the back and raising both legs while keeping them straight at the knees. It is contended by many that this latter exercise, because of the stress it puts on the ilio-psoas muscle group, should not be performed unless the muscles of the trunk are well-conditioned. (From Wells, *Kinesiology*, p. 256. By permission.)

Muscular endurance can be increased phenomenally by programs of exercise in which work is carried on to the point of fatigue and in which moderate resistance is overcome a great many times. In such exercises, muscles do not increase correspondingly in size.

Muscle tonus (tone) is the product of the elasticity of a muscle and/or the constant partial contraction of motor units in the muscle. This constant contraction is the result of a continuous discharge of nerve impulses stimulating many motor units at once. A muscle deprived of its nerve supply becomes flabby and loses its firmness (atrophy). A muscle with good tone responds readily to stimulation and contracts with vigor.

The *all-or-none principle* applies to a single muscle fiber or a single motor unit. According to this principle, a fiber or motor unit responds maximally to any stimulus that is strong enough to excite it. The force of contraction of a given muscle can, in some instances, be increased by raising the intensity or the frequency of the stimulus. Either of these may bring more motor units into action at a given time, thus increasing the force the muscle exerts.

6.5 COORDINATION OF MOTION

The nervous system is divided, for purposes of analysis, into the *central nervous system* and the *peripheral nervous system.* While the peripheral nervous system is made up of the craniospinal nerves and the autonomic nerves, the central nervous system contains the cerebral hemispheres of the brain, the midbrain, the pons, the cerebellum, the medulla oblongata, and the spinal cord as it passes through the cervical, thoracic, and lumbar vertebrae, and finally the sacrum and the coccyx.

The 15 pairs of cranial nerves and the 31 pairs of spinal nerves connect the central nervous system with the periphery. Nervous impulses traveling from the periphery to the central nervous system are *afferent,* while those from the central nervous system to the peripheral parts of the body are *efferent.*

The autonomic (sometimes called the visceral) portion of the nervous system consists of (1) the fibers which arise from the cranial and sacral regions of the central nervous system forming the *parasympathetic* division, and (2) the fibers which arise from the thoracic and lumbar regions forming the *sympathetic* division. The autonomic system controls the activities of the digestive, cardiovascular, endocrine, respiratory, and reproductive systems. Most of the control exercised by the autonomic system is involuntary and regulates the vital processes. The regulation of voluntary movements is, for the most part, controlled by the central nervous system.

Coordination and control of motion is in the corticospinal system and occurs by levels as follows:

1. Antigravity reflexes controlling erect posture and reflexes maintaining muscle tone are at the spinal level.
2. Cardiovascular and respiratory adjustments to exercise are largely controlled at the bulbar (medullary) level.

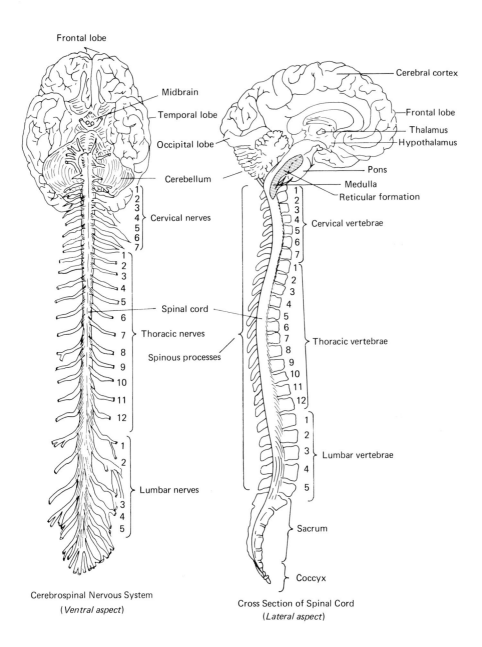

Frontal lobe

Midbrain

Temporal lobe

Occipital lobe

Cerebellum

1
2
3
4 } Cervical nerves
5
6
7

1
2
3
4
5
6
7 } Thoracic nerves
8
9
10
11
12

Spinal cord

Spinous processes

1
2
3 } Lumbar nerves
4
5

Cerebrospinal Nervous System
(*Ventral aspect*)

Cerebral cortex

Frontal lobe

Thalamus

Hypothalamus

Pons

Medulla

Reticular formation

1
2
3
4 } Cervical vertebrae
5
6
7

1
2
3
4
5
6
7 } Thoracic vertebrae
8
9
10
11
12

1
2
3 } Lumbar vertebrae
4
5

Sacrum

Coccyx

Cross Section of Spinal Cord
(*Lateral aspect*)

Figure 6.7 Central nervous system—brain and spinal cord. (From Edwards, *Anatomy for Physical Education,* pp. 55, 58. By permission.)

3. Body-righting and postural reflexes originating in the labyrinth controlling the position of the head and neck are centered in the medulla.

4. In the cerebellum are located nervous mechanisms for strengthening, inhibiting, steadying, and coordinating intricate body movements.

5. The reticular formation, consisting of a system of interlacing neurons, interprets incoming messages and assigns priorities to them, assists with the selection of responses, and screens out the least significant impulses.

6. The red nucleus and the corpus striatum are among other bodies which assist in postural control and inhibit extraneous and wasteful movement. They are located in the midbrain.

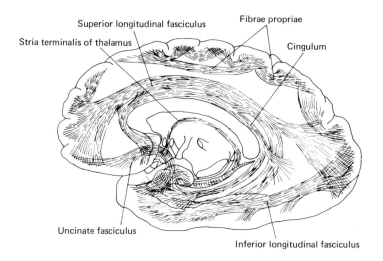

**Figure 6.8 Schematic representation of association
fibers of cerebral hemisphere.** (From Edwards, *Anatomy
for Physical Education,* p. 75. By permission.)

7. The cortex is the outer layer of gray matter of the cerebral hemispheres. The cortex contains sensory areas for receiving stimuli, motor areas for sending outgoing messages, and an infinite number of internuncial or association fibers for thinking, remembering, combining, interpreting, organizing, and deciding. Voluntary movements are initiated in the cortex, motor patterns are established, sensory impulses are received and combined with previously stored patterns to form new ones, cues are sorted out and stored for future recall, and thousands of learned facts and principles are tucked away for recall when the right stimulus is received. Sensory areas and motor areas in the brain are located side by side, on either side of the central sulcus, so that the greatest possible efficiency can be effected (Figure 6.9).

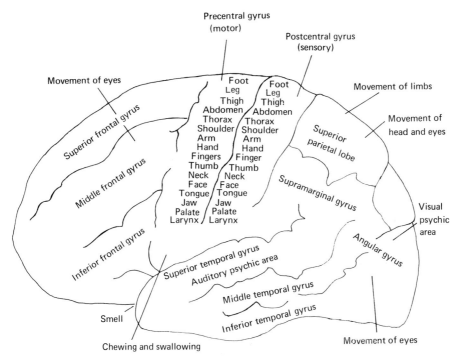

Figure 6.9   Sensory and motor areas of the cortex.

6.6 REFLEXES

There are many reflexes in the human body important to movement, performance, and motor learning. A simple reflex arc consists of a receptor organ, an afferent neuron, an internuncial neuron, and an efferent neuron (see Figure 6.10). A few reflexes, important to physical educators are:

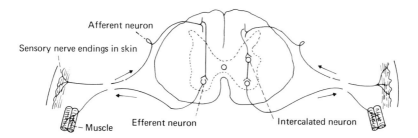

Figure 6.10   A simple reflex arc. Diagrammatic representation of simple spinal reflex arc. Arrows indicate direction of conduction. (From Bowen and Stone, *Applied Anatomy and Kinesiology*, p. 108. By permission.)

1. *Stretch reflex.* The muscle spindle (receptor) is stimulated by a stretch on the muscle, nerve impulses are transmitted to the spinal cord, the impulse travels out again through an efferent neuron causing a reflex contraction of the same muscle. This reflex is useful in maintaining upright posture and is therefore also called an *antigravity reflex.* When the extensors of the hip, knee, or back begin to relax with a resultant sag of the body, they (the extensors) are stretched. Reflex action keeps stimulating these extensors to contract and thus maintain erect posture.

2. *Postural reflex.* Not only is erect posture maintained by reflexes, but balance and stance are maintained through automatic or reflex compensatory movements. Athletes automatically regain their balance when pushed or hit. Several internuncial neurons and coordinating elements of the nervous system are involved in these instances.

3. *Righting reflex.* This reflex enables animals (or in some instances humans) to right themselves (Figure 6.11) when in upside down positions in midair. Messages from the eyes, the inner ear, and the proprioceptors are relayed to the central nervous system, informing it of the problem. Reflexes in the head, neck, shoulders, back, and limbs enable the animal (rooster, rabbit, cat, etc.) to right itself in midair and land on its feet.

4. *Nociceptive reflex.* Sometimes termed the *withdrawal* reflex, it provides for instant removal of an affected body part from a dangerous or painful stimulus. A child withdrawing his hand from a hot pan or the thigh contracting at the hip when the hamstrings are pricked with a pin are examples. While the withdrawal is instantaneous and reflexive, the sensation is perceived and recorded in the cortex.

5. *Conditioned reflex.* Movements which are originally volitional and unlearned can, in the case of a highly skilled athlete, become conditioned reflexes. The trained athlete reacts automatically to cues, whereas thought processes were once necessary. Some of these cues are internal stimuli which come from the sensory organs in muscles and tendons (proprioceptors). Others are visual or auditory cues which come from outside the body (exteroceptors). Reactions and motor patterns which originally required thought and volitional action become automatic.

6. *Reciprocal innervation.* If an agonist (e.g., the biceps) contracts to flex the arm, the antagonist (e.g., the triceps) will receive a message or stimulus causing a simultaneous controlled relaxation. This coordination keeps muscles from tearing and produces smooth movements. This reflex occurs constantly in many body segments as intricate movements take place.

7. *Crossed extensor reflex.* This reflex is sometimes discussed as a form of reciprocal innervation. However, it is a bit more complex in that the contralateral limb is involved. As a dog steps on a bramble and the nociceptive reflex brings about withdrawal, the extensors of the opposite limb are stimulated to provide needed support for the body.

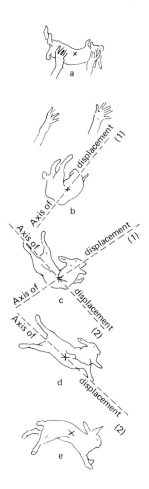

Figure 6.11 A rabbit righting itself. A cat or rabbit, dropped from an upsidedown position, will land in a normal upright position. Body-righting reflexes become operative and, while not always exactly the same, follow the following general pattern. Due to the action of the optical or the labyrinthine righting reflexes, the head orients itself. The neck-righting reflex causes the neck to return to the upright position. This triggers the righting reflexes of the thorax, lumbar region, and pelvis and they right themselves in turn. The animal "pikes" during the first stage of its fall, then twists the fore part of its body, and finally the hind part, being then entirely free from any deformation and ready for landing. (From G. H. G. Dyson, *The Mechanics of Athletics,* 5th edition, London: The University of London Press Ltd., 1962. By permission.)

Reflexes exist in innumerable forms and combinations and serve the human organism well. The nervous system functions in complex and often mysterious ways. To better understand some of the mechanisms, let us look briefly at the smallest unit of tissue, the cell.

6.7 THE NEURON

The *neuron* and the *glia* constitute the cells of the nervous system. The functions of the glia are not well understood. The structure and function of the neuron, however, should be understood by students of physical education.

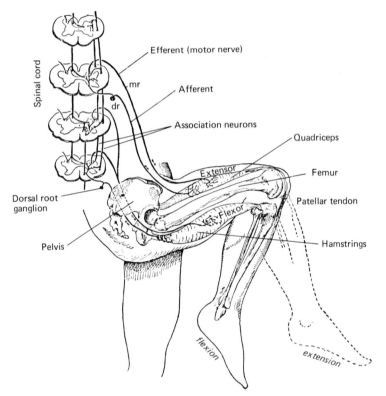

Figure 6.12 Reciprocal innervation. Schema of the reciprocal innervation of the flexor and extensor muscles of the leg. Cord has been rotated 90 degrees to the left. Afferent nerves enter the dorsal root of the spinal cord, bringing messages from muscles and joints. Internuncial, or association, neurons connect the afferent nerve to the efferent, or motor, nerves which carry messages to motor units and stimulate muscles to contract and move the body. In the above figure, both the quadriceps (extensor of the lower leg) and the hamstrings (flexors of the leg) have afferent and efferent nerves going to and from the spinal cord. As the quadriceps contract, the hamstrings are stimulated to relax; as the hamstrings contract, the quadriceps are stimulated to relax. (From Bowen and Stone, *Applied Anatomy and Kinesiology,* p. 111. By permission.)

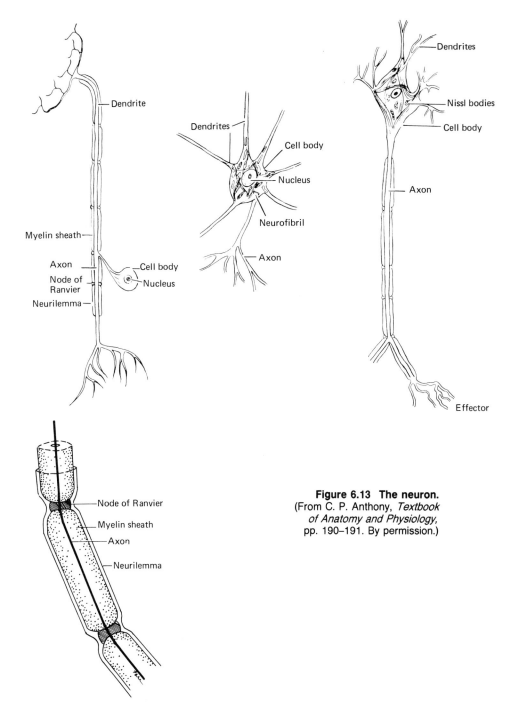

Figure 6.13 The neuron.
(From C. P. Anthony, *Textbook of Anatomy and Physiology*, pp. 190–191. By permission.)

Diagram of an axon and its coverings.

The neuron has a cell body containing the nucleus and two types of branching processes extending from the cell body (see Figure 6.13). The dendrites receive nerve impulses and the axon transmits them to the synapse or motor endplate. Then they either move along to the dendrites of another neuron or terminate in the muscle or glandular organ, stimulating it to respond. Impulses may originate in an organ of the viscera, cause a decision to be made in a ganglion or the spinal cord itself, or travel immediately out to an effector cord to bring about action (see Section 6.6, Reflexes). Most nervous impulses travel a much more involved route. A stimulus originating in the patellar tendon may go to the spinal cord, move along a nervous tract to the medulla, be modified as it passes through the reticular formation, pick up further information in the cerebellum, travel to the red nucleus, and finally terminate in the sensory area of the cortex where perception and decision making will occur. The impulse carrying the message to act will originate in the motor area of the cortex, start on its journey to the quadriceps muscle, pick up further impulses in the cerebellum, medulla, and spine, and finally end at a motor endplate of the vastus medius muscle stimulating it to carry out the command of the brain. If decisions made in the cortex are complicated and require the organization of facts previously stored, many more neurons in the cerebra will be involved and the original impulse, along with all the others that have caused its modification, will bounce around the brain on association fibers and among memory cells until the appropriate message is ready. This message will then travel via efferent neurons to the effector organ for action.

6.8 CARDIOVASCULAR AND RESPIRATORY FUNCTION
Nothing can be more significant to the living and working human organism than the functions of the heart, the blood vessels, the lungs, and the respiratory tract. Arthur Steinhaus sums this up dramatically when he says:

> Five to six quarts of blood, distributed through some 5 billion tiny tubular vessels or capillaries with a total length of 1500 miles, bring oxygen and food to all body parts and carry off their wastes. In rest, the blood makes between one and two trips a minute from heart to lungs, back to the heart, then to all body parts and back to the heart. During strenuous exercise it may make nine such trips in a minute. To pump the blood is the work of the heart. Even at rest, the heart handles about 11 tons of blood a day, pushing it out under a pressure of about 3 pounds per square inch.*

The heart is a muscular organ containing four chambers, the right and left ventricles and the right and left auricles (see Figure 6.14). Blood is pumped out of the left ventricle into the aorta, then to several large arteries supplying major parts of the body. From these it goes to smaller branching arteries, next to the still smaller arterioles, and finally to the tiny interlacing capillaries where oxygen and nutrients carried by the blood are fed to the tissues and where impurities and

---

*Steinhaus, Arthur H., "Fitness beyond muscle," *The Physical Educator,* Vol. 23, No. 3, October 1966. Reprinted by permission.

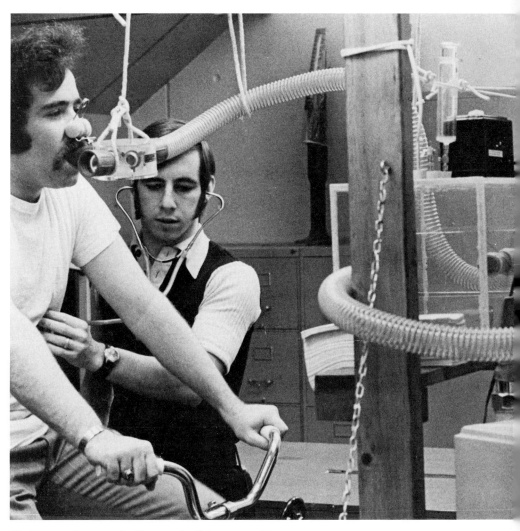

"Nothing can be more significant to the living and working human organism than the functions of the heart, the blood vessels, the lungs, and the respiratory tract." (Courtesy of Eastern Kentucky University.)

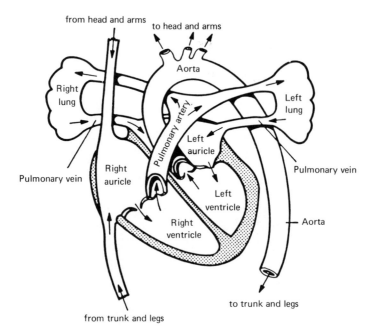

Figure 6.14 Circulation of blood through heart and lungs. (From *Health Observation of School Children,* G. M. Wheatley and G. T. Hallock. Copyright 1961, McGraw-Hill Book Company. By permission.)

carbon dioxide are picked up by the blood for the return trip to the heart and lungs. After exchange of nutrients and wastes, the blood goes to the venules, then to the veins, next to the upper and lower venae cavae, and back into the right auricle of the heart. It passes next into the right ventricle which pumps it through the lungs for purification. From the lungs it returns to the left auricle and goes from there into the left ventricle for another trip through the body (Figure 6.15).

The cardiac cycle consists of auricular systole (about 0.1 second), ventricular systole (about 0.3 second), and diastole (about 0.4 second). In all, the average heartbeat takes a little less than one second. When the heart rate is increased, diastole is shortened more than systole.

An understanding of the mechanisms involved in the circulation of blood is of particular significance to the physical educator. Heart rates during rest, exercise, and recovery are meaningful when dealing with conditioning and when measuring fitness. Systolic, diastolic, and pulse pressures are indicative of the condition and health of the organism.

Cardiac output, which is the product of the heart rate times the stroke volume, is about five liters per minute for the average person in the supine position and one or two liters per minute in the standing position. During exercise, trained

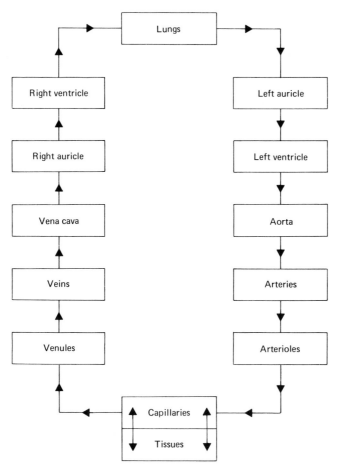

Figure 6.15. Circulatory pathways (schematic).

athletes have attained a cardiac output as high as 30 liters per minute, the untrained person 20 liters per minute. Both the heart rate and the stroke volume increase during strenuous exercise.

Heart rate is influenced by temperature, emotional state, posture, and exercise. The heart rate for adults varies widely from individual to individual with the average rate under resting conditions being 78 beats per minute for men and 84 for women. It is greater in children, diminishing until adolescence. Heart rate generally increases again as an individual becomes older. The measurement of heart rate preceding, during, and after exercise serves as the basis for many physical fitness tests and is therefore important to physical education teachers.

Recovery occurs more rapidly when subjects are in good condition. Likewise, the heart rate for a given work load will be lower in those who are the most physically fit.

The lungs are located in the thorax, one on each side of the heart. The diaphragm, which has a vital role in breathing, lies immediately below the lungs. The volume of the chest cavity can be decreased or increased by moving the ribs and contracting the diaphragm (see Figure 6.16).

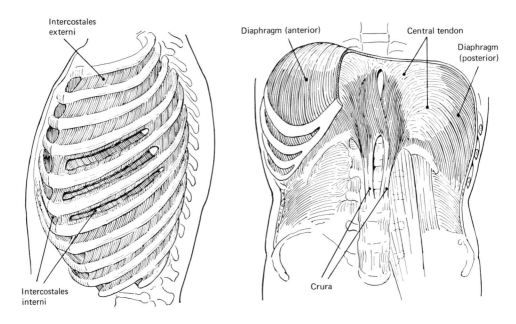

Figure 6.16 Intercostal muscles and diaphragm. (From Wells, *Kinesiology*, p. 357. By permission.)

Increasing the size of the chest cavity in *inspiration* causes air to be forced into the lungs by atmospheric pressure. The elasticity of the thoracic walls, the weight of the rib cage, and the relaxation of the diaphragm in *expiration* permit the elastic lungs to recoil, thus expelling most of the air. Breathing is under both reflex and voluntary control. Reflexes protect the lungs by inhibiting breathing during swallowing or when irritating gases enter the pharynx.

Both the heart and the lungs are under chemical and nervous control. Excess CO_2 and lactic acid in tissues will cause vasodilation with a resulting increase in blood and metabolites in that area. Excess CO_2 in the lungs causes an acceleration of respiration. Excess CO_2 in the blood in the aorta or in the carotid artery increases the heartbeat and causes vasodilation. The secretion of adrenalin also increases pulse rate, causes muscular contractions to be more powerful, and causes respiration to accelerate. Other metabolic changes have similar effects.

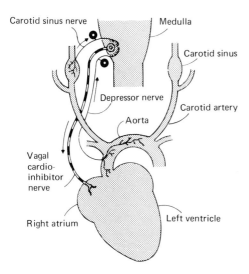

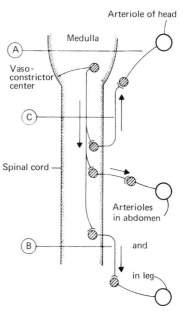

Figure 6.17   Nervous centers controlling heart rate and circulation. Acceleration of the heart rate causes more blood to be injected into the aorta and carotid arteries. The carotid sinus nerve and the depressor nerve are stimulated by this increased blood pressure. The cardioinhibitory center is in turn stimulated and the heart slows down. Meanwhile, the pressure in the blood vessels is being controlled by impulses going to and from the vasoconstrictor and vasodilator centers also located in the medulla. The importance of the role of these centers in the regulation of the flow of blood in the body is obvious. (from A. J. Carlson, V. Johnson, and H. Mead Cavert, *The Machinery of the Body,* 5th edition, Chicago: University of Chicago Press, 1961, pp. 188, 221.)

A number of reflexes bring about changes in respiratory and circulatory action. In the medulla oblongata are found cardioaccelerator and cardioinhibitory centers, vasodilator and vasoconstrictor centers, and respiratory centers. To summarize:

Increased muscular activity
and
Increased emotional arousal

↓

Increased CO_2 production.
Increased adrenalin secretion.
Increased heat production.
Stimulation of nervous centers.

↓

Increased pulmonary ventilation.
Increased pulse rate.
Increased stroke volume.
Vasodilation in active skeletal muscles.
Vasoconstriction in splanchnic region.
Increased volume of circulating blood.
Increased CO_2 where needed.
Increased removal of waste products.

Pulmonary ventilation is dependent upon the rate and amplitude of respiration and upon the alveolar gas exchange. The alveolar gas exchange is a function of the pressure gradient between the air in the alveoli and the gases in the blood. During exercise the oxygen supply to the tissues is greatly increased due to a steepening of the pressure gradient, the increase in the alveolar surface, and an increase in the amount of blood carried to the lungs. Training increases the pulmonary ventilation, decreases the oxygen requirement, and increases the oxygen reserve.

6.9 CONCEPTS AND PRINCIPLES OF EXERCISE PHYSIOLOGY

It is obviously impossible and inappropriate in a volume such as this to present a complete course in exercise physiology. Only the barest rudiments of important biological mechanisms have been described. It is important, however, for those who teach physical education, coach, or deal with physical handicaps and injuries to be familiar with key concepts and significant scientific principles which pertain to their profession. The following additional principles have been selected for relevance and practical usefulness.

1. *People as biological organisms have a persistent need for activity.* Strength, stamina, and physiological efficiency are the results of demanding and vigorous physical activity (assuming no disease or remediable handicaps). Weakness, atrophy of muscles, and vulnerability to degeneration are the effects of inactivity.

2. *The living organism differs from the nonliving in that it does not wear out with use, but instead renews, restores, and even repairs itself.* Cells are restored,

wounds are healed, metabolites replaced, and catabolic effects of activity are balanced with anabolic effects.

3. *There is in the human organism a constant tendency toward homeostasis.* This results from interaction between a constantly changing environment and an adjusting organism. Upset of homeostasis is a stimulus to action.

4. *The growth and development of skeletal muscles stimulates the growth and development of internal visceral organs.* While the activities of these organs are involuntary, their use and movement are necessary for complete development.

5. *Muscles are responsive to the demands made upon them.* Demands for strength at specific angles of motion develop the muscles used at that angle; demands for long continued work produce a gain in endurance; demands for explosive power develop this ability; and demands for single bouts of sheer strength develop the ability to overcome great resistance.

6. *An increase in muscle mass occurs during the growing period of the human organism; it is greatest during the "adolescent growth spurt."* Not all increases in muscle size can be attributed to training.

7. *Skeletal growth passes successively through three stages: connective tissue, cartilage, and bone.* These stages of calcification are indicative of the "physiological age" or state of maturation of the individual. They can be assessed by taking X-rays of the bones of the hand or the joints of long bones.

8. *Perceptual motor development proceeds most rapidly during infancy and early childhood.* Full opportunity for all forms of normal locomotor and manipulative movements are important at this time. Development of the nervous system is partially a response to movement.

9. *Excitement and emotional arousal can augment the strength of an individual to an unusual degree.* History is replete with instances of unusual feats of strength, speed, and endurance performed under conditions of strong emotional arousal.

10. *Exercise is one of the factors that inhibit cardiovascular degeneration, coronary disease, and related conditions.* Exercise helps to keep the blood vessels elastic and the capillaries open. Exercise counteracts the effects of anxieties and tensions which stimulate vasoconstriction.

11. *Exercise, by means of a squeezing and "milking" action, assists in forcing venous blood to move upward against the pull of gravity during its return trip to the heart.* This assists in total ventilation and in the maintenance of tonus in the veins.

12. *Exercise exerts a beneficial effect on the circulatory system* by increasing (a) the numbers of red cells, (b) the "toughness" of red cells, (c) muscle hemoglobin, (d) oxygen utilization, (e) capillarization, (f) the potential minute-volume, and (g) the size, strength, efficiency, and endurance of the heart and circulatory system.

13. *Some of the reflexes present at birth disappear and new and more useful ones appear.* This is an indication of the integrity of the nervous system.

14. *Many of the beneficial effects of exercise are transient.* One cannot store strength, endurance, health, or fitness.

15. *Improved efficiency in skilled performance results in part from the elimination of extraneous and unnecessary movements.* The more automatic and flawless motor patterns become, the less oxygen will be required.

16. *The energy needed to support exercise is derived from the oxidation of carbohydrates, fats, and other foods.* Appropriate exercise improves appetite and elimination and, in children, stimulates the growth process.

17. *A high cholesterol content has been found to correlate with the incidence of atherosclerosis.* While a causal relationship has not yet been firmly established, and while heredity, diet, and stress factors may also be involved, evidence points to the salutary effect of appropriate vigorous exercise in reducing the incidence of "hardening of the arteries."

18. *A rise in environmental temperature increases the pulse rate, respiratory rate, and body temperature; at the same time, work capacity is decreased and the capacity for optimal performance reduced.* Initial athletic practices, before the body has had a chance to adapt, should be governed accordingly.

19. *The hypoxia of higher altitudes affects performances which cannot be completed anaerobically.* The organism acclimatizes in a relatively short time, adjusting to a higher altitude in approximately two weeks. Coaches and trainers should familiarize themselves with all aspects of this phenomenon.

20. *Physiological and anatomical sex differences which should be considered in physical education are:* (a) the heart is larger in the male, (b) the heart rate of the male is lower, (c) the amount of hemoglobin per unit of blood is greater in the male, (d) the number of red cells per cubic centimeter of blood is greater in the male, (e) the basal metabolic rate of the male is higher than that of the female, (f) the female tends to have narrower shoulders and proportionately wider hips, (g) the femur of the female is positioned at a more oblique angle, (h) the female tends to have a lower center of gravity, (i) the arms and upper body of the male are more muscular, (j) the carrying angle of the arm is greater in the female (due to narrower shoulders and wider hips).

It should be emphasized that these are averages. Both males and females tend to distribute themselves on a continuum (normal curve) with respect to each of these factors. Many females exceed many males in strength, speed, athletic ability, etc. The normal curve for females overlaps that of males in all of these characteristics.

21. *The alkali reserve in trained athletes is roughly ten percent higher than in untrained individuals.* Since the akali reserves serve to lower the amount of lactic acid (a fatigue product) in the blood, training increases endurance.

22. *During strenuous bouts of exercise, a great deal of sugar is consumed by athletes.* Eating carbohydrates and sugar before a contest leaves the athlete in better physical condition after the contest is over.

23. *The heart has a high oxygen-utilization quotient.* It can utilize oxygen more readily than can other tissues and operates on a "pay-as-you-go" basis. It therefore does not develop an oxygen debt. This is to protect the heart in situations where there is an oxygen shortage.

24. *"Second wind" is a phenomenon whereby, in a long race or other demanding contest, a condition of distress and breathlessness is followed by a sense of relief and renewed ability to continue.* All of the physiological mechanisms are not known, but it can be assumed that the body responds to the increased oxygen supply and the removal of fatigue products and that the total organism is then mobilized to meet the demands of the activity.

25. *A combination of exercise and dietary control is the most effective method of preventing obesity.* The exercise must be sufficient to use up a substantial number of calories. Psychological aspects of a reducing program must not be overlooked.

26. *The ability to relax is an important aspect of an individual's health and fitness.* The "stroke-glide" principle applies equally to systole and diastole, exertion and rest, work and recreation, duty time and vacation.

27. *Compulsiveness is an enemy of fitness and health.* Driving oneself, or being driven beyond reasonable limits, is damaging. Activity due to a "guilt complex," working to satisfy a demanding spouse, or exerting oneself beyond reasonable limits for other reasons can be destructive instead of constructive.

28. *Fatigue can be mental, physical, or both.* Mental attitude can cause or prevent physical fatigue and vice versa. Stress and hypertension can be temporarily stimulating but eventually cause emotional and mental fatigue. Many factors including emotional mood, personal relationships, health, and environment may be involved.

29. *Fatigue reduces the number of fibers that respond to stimuli, the power of contractions, and the excitability of motor units.* Tired muscles do not relax and extend as efficiently as do rested muscles. Good condition for peak performance is obvious.

30. *Dehydration of athletes may be caused intentionally or accidentally. In either case, it can lead to impaired performance, illness, and even death.* It behooves coaches and athletes to exercise care and good judgment in witholding water in order to "make weight" or in practicing with heavy uniforms during extremely hot weather.

31. *The ingestion of food prior to exercise generally has the following results:* (a) vigorous and exhausting exercise inhibits digestion and peristaltic action during exercise and for a short time thereafter, (b) mild exercise increases gastric motility, (c) the motility of the stomach and the secretion of digestive juices are increased above normal shortly after exercise is completed.

32. *Conditioning, skill development, and psychological preparation should proceed simultaneously.* They are interrelated and interdependent. Good condition

and a thorough overlearning of skills create confidence and a desirable self-concept. Proper mental attitude will lead to motivation for practice and performance. The building of confidence, the self-discovery that leads to faith in one's ability, and a positive self-concept are both enhanced by, and contribute to, excellent performance and high-level achievements.

33. *Vigorous exercise increases aerobic capacity or maximum oxygen intake.* This is the most meaningful measure of a person's fitness.

34. *Other things being equal, the heart of the trained athlete is larger than that of the untrained person.* This adaptation to exercise is normal and natural. The heart of the athlete, however, tends to become smaller after exercise while the "overcompensated" heart becomes larger after exercise.

35. *Exercises of endurance lead to hypertrophy of the heart* while skeletal muscles show little change in size. *Exercises of strength, speed, and power lead to hypertrophy of the skeletal muscles* and little change in heart mass.

36. *The resting pulse rate of athletes trained for endurance tends to be low.* (For athletes of Olympic caliber, the average rate is about 50 beats per minute.)

37. *The "trained" or "athletic" person generally has a higher-than-average minute-volume* of circulating blood in proportion to his size and weight.

38. *In the conditioned individual,* (a) *the systolic pressure generally rises more rapidly* and to a greater extent than in the untrained individual, (b) *the diastolic pressure returns to normal more quickly,* and (c) *there is a large increase in pulse pressure.*

39. *The reciprocal interrelationships which exist among all the organic systems of the body must be continually emphasized.* As physical educators focus on developing strength, teaching skills, and conditioning, they must be constantly aware of the effects on emotions, confidence, attitudes, and the stress tolerance of the individuals concerned.

6.10 SUMMARY
Certainly one of the foundations on which our knowledge of movement and teaching rests is that of physiology. The functions of the human organism, the mechanisms which control these functions, and the biological principles which govern motor learning, conditioning, and the development of excellent performers form part of the bases on which we must build our body of knowledge. The information contained in this chapter provides a small introduction.

SELECTED REFERENCES
1. Anthony, Catherine P., *Textbook of Anatomy and Physiology,* 6th edition, St. Louis: The C. V. Mosby Company, 1963.
2. Arsenian, Seth (ed.) *The Humanics Philosophy of Springfield College,* Springfield, Mass.: Springfield College, 1969.
3. Astrand, Per-Olaf, and Kaare Rodahl, *A Textbook of Work Physiology,* New York: McGraw-Hill, 1970.
4. Best, Charles Herbert, and Norman Burke Taylor, *The Physiological Basis of Medical Practice,* Baltimore: The Williams and Wilkins Company, 1945.

5. Bookwalter, Karl W., and Harold J. VanderZwaag, *Foundations and Principles of Physical Education,* Philadelphia: W. B. Saunders Company, 1969.
6. Carlson, Anton J., et al., *The Machinery of the Body,* 5th edition, Chicago: University of Chicago Press, 1961.
7. Cureton, Thomas K., *The Physiological Effects of Exercise Programs on Adults,* Springfield, Illinois: Charles C Thomas, 1969.
8. Daniels, Arthur S., and Evelyn Davies, *Adapted Physical Education,* New York: Harper and Row, 1965.
9. Davis, Elwood C. and Gene A. Logan, *Biophysical Values of Muscular Activity,* Dubuque, Iowa: W. C. Brown Company, 1961.
10. Edwards, Linden F., *Anatomy for Physical Education,* Philadelphia: P. Blakiston's Son and Company, 1934.
11. Falls, Harold B., *Exercise Physiology,* New York: The Academic Press, 1973.
12. Franks, B. Don (ed.), *Exercise and Fitness,* Chicago: The Athletic Institute, 1969.
13. Frost, Reuben B., *Psychological Concepts Applied to Physical Education and Coaching,* Reading, Mass.: Addison-Wesley Publishing Company, 1971.
14. Greisheimer, Esther M., *Physiology and Anatomy,* Philadelphia: J. B. Lippincott Company, 1936.
15. Jewett, Ann E., and Clyde Knapp (eds.), *The Growing Years,* Washington, D.C.: American Association for Health, Physical Education, and Recreation, 1962.
16. Jokl, Ernst, *The Clinical Physiology of Physical Fitness and Rehabilitation,* Springfield, Ill.: Charles C Thomas, 1971.
17. Karpovich, Peter V., and Wayne E. Sinning, *Physiology of Muscular Activity,* Philadelphia: W. B. Saunders Company, 1971.
18. Lee, Mabel, and Miriam M. Wagner, *Fundamentals of Body Mechanics and Conditioning,* Philadelphia: W. B. Saunders Company, 1949.
19. Matthews, Donald K., and Edward L. Fox, *The Physiological Basis of Physical Education and Athletics,* Philadelphia: W. B. Saunders Company, 1971.
20. Morehouse, Laurence E., and Augustus T. Miller, Jr., *Physiology of Exercise,* St. Louis: The C. V. Mosby Company, 1971.
21. Morgan, William P., *Ergogenic Aids and Muscular Performance,* New York: The Academic Press, 1973.
22. Ricci, Benjamin, *Physical and Physiological Conditioning for Man,* Dubuque, Iowa: W. C. Brown Company, 1966.
23. Riedman, Sarah R., *The Physiology of Work and Play,* New York: The Dryden Press, 1950.
24. Sage, George H., *Introduction to Motor Behavior,* Reading, Mass.: Addison-Wesley Publishing Company, 1971.
25. Seidel, Beverly L., and Matthew C. Resick, *Physical Education: An Overview,* Reading, Mass.: Addison-Wesley Publishing Company, 1972.
26. Sills, Frank D., Laurence E. Morehouse, and Thomas L. DeLorme (eds.), *Weight Training in Sports and Physical Education,* Washington, D.C.: American Association for Health, Physical Education, and Recreation, 1962.
27. Simonson, Ernst, *Physiology of Work Capacity and Fatigue,* Springfield, Illinois: Charles C Thomas, 1971.
28. Van Huss, Wayne, et al., *Physical Activity in Modern Living,* Englewood Cliffs, N.J.: Prentice-Hall, 1960.
29. Watson, Ernest H., and George H. Lowrey, *Growth and Development of Children,* Chicago: The Year Book Publishers, 1958.
30. Williams, Jesse F., *The Principles of Physical Education,* Philadelphia: W. B. Saunders Company, 1954.

Basic Biomechanical Concepts

Chapter 7

7.1 INTRODUCTION
The term *biomechanics* refers to the application of biological and mechanical principles to movement. If a teacher, coach, therapist, trainer, or researcher is to understand what he is doing and why, he should be familiar with the rudiments of biomechanics. As Katharine Wells said:

> Any teacher of physical education who has a good knowledge of motor skills can probably teach them to his students. If, in addition, he has a good understanding of kinesiology* he will be in a better position to select effective techniques and methods and to diagnose and remedy individual difficulties. He will thus be improving his method of teaching his students how to learn new skills and how to improve their performance. This is desirable but it does not go far enough. Some students may be satisfied with it but the more intelligent student wants to know the *why* of the directions given by the instructor or coach. He wants to understand the reasons for what he does and why one approach is more effective than another. [21, p. 479]

Whether it be a wrestling coach demonstrating how to obtain maximum leverage, a track-and-field coach teaching the mechanics of the hammer throw, a teacher assisting a pupil with a headstand, or a diver controlling his twists, scientific laws apply. It will be the purpose of this chapter to acquaint the reader with a few basic scientific concepts which apply to human motion and present examples of their application.

7.2 TERMINOLOGY
Every physical education student should become familiar with the terms describing movement or motion of the human body. An understanding of the following will be helpful:

Abduction.   Motion away from the midline of the body (e.g., toes and fingers) or away from the median line of the foot or hand.

Acceleration.   Increase in velocity.

Adduction.   Motion toward the midline of the body or toward the median line of the hand or foot (opposite of abduction).

Anatomical position.   An erect standing position with feet parallel, arms hanging down at sides, and palms facing frontward.

Angular motion.   Rotary motion; movement of a segment of the body around an axis and in a plane which is at right angles to the axis.

---

*Kinesiology, while sometimes used interchangeably with biomechanics, is technically a broader term meaning "the scientific study of movement."

Articulation.   The connection between two bones; a joint.

Concentric contraction.   A muscular contraction in which the muscle shortens.

Caudad.   Toward the feet.

Cephalad.   Toward the head.

Circumduction.   Moving the arm, leg, or other segment in such a way that the whole limb forms a cone. The medial end of the segment remains almost stationary while the distal end describes a circle.

Depression.   Downward movement of a part of the body.

Distal.   Away from the midline.

"If a teacher, coach, therapist, trainer, or researcher is to understand what he is doing and why, he should be familiar with the rudiments of biomechanics." (Courtesy of Eastern Kentucky University.)

Dorsal. Posterior aspect (on humans).

Dorsiflexion. Flexion of the foot in a dorsal direction; movement of the top part of the foot upward (when in a standing position).

Eccentric contraction. Lengthening contraction; a movement in which the muscle moves gradually from its shortened condition to its normal resting length.

Elevation. Movement in the upward direction.

Evertion. Movement of the foot causing the plantar (sole) surface to face outward.

Extension. Movement of two body segments away from each other forming a "straighter line."

Flexion. Movement of two body segments toward each other forming a smaller angle.

Hyperabduction. Moving the arms or legs "sideoutward" beyond the horizontal.

Hyperadduction. Moving the arms or legs toward and across the midline.

Hyperextension. The extending of a limb or other part of the body beyond 180 degrees.

Inversion. Movement of the foot causing the plantar surface to face inward.

Isometric contraction. Muscle contraction in which the length of the muscle does not change.

Isotonic contraction. Dynamic contraction; a contraction in which the muscle shortens.

Lateral flexion. Bending sideward.

Linear motion. Translatory motion in a straight line during which the object and its parts all move in the same direction.

Pendular. As a pendulum; swinging with the upper end attached.

Pronation. Turning the palm of the hand inward and downward.

Protraction. Forward movement of the shoulders.

Proximal.   Toward the midline.

Retraction.   Backward movement of the shoulders.

Rotary motion.   (See *angular motion.*)

Supination.   Movement of the thumb of the hand outward so that the palm faces upward.

Translatory motion.   Motion in which a body moves as a whole, all parts moving the same distance.

Ventral.   Anterior aspect (on humans).

7.3 MUSCLES AND BONES AS LEVERS

It is not difficult to find examples of levers among our everyday implements and tools. The nutcracker, bottle opener, pliers, crowbar, wheelbarrow, nail puller, spade, teeter-totter, and car jack are common examples. Levers are equally common in the human "machine." Every movement of the human body or one of its parts involves levers, sometimes many, each applying force in a particular direction and in its own special way. The use of electrogoniometry, cinematography, and electromyography has clarified much of our former vagueness about the work of muscles to accomplish specific tasks. We know now that the number of motor units involved may be many or few, that they may be from one or several muscle groups, and that they can apply force in more than one direction in order to accomplish their purpose. Now we are also able to identify with considerable accuracy the specific muscles involved in a given movement.

It is common to classify levers in terms of the way in which the force is applied. Levers have three important points: (1) the point at which the force or effort is applied, (2) the point about which the lever turns or rotates, called the axis or fulcrum, and (3) the point at which the *resistance* is concentrated, sometimes called the load. In discussing leverage, we will use the terms force (F), axis (A), and resistance (R).

Levers are classified as follows:

1. *First class levers* are those in which the axis is located between the force and the resistance.

2. *Second class levers* are those in which the resistance is between the axis and the fulcrum.

3. *Third class levers* are those in which the force is between the axis and the resistance.

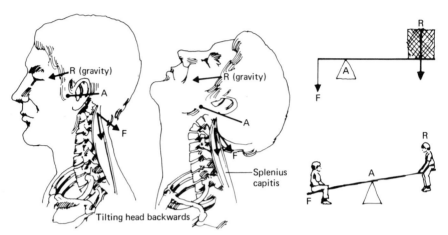

Figure 7.1   First class levers.

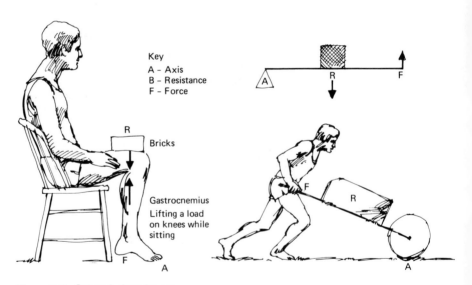

Key
A – Axis
B – Resistance
F – Force

Figure 7.2   Second class levers.

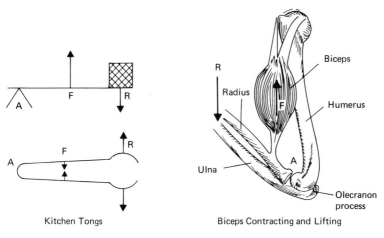

Figure 7.3   Third class levers.

The distance from the axis to the point where the force is applied is termed the lever arm. The longer the lever arm, the greater the effectiveness in overcoming resistance. In developing velocity, however, a short lever arm and a long resistance arm are more effective. This latter combination is advantageous in hurling, throwing, and the like.

First class levers in the human body include the muscles used to tilt the head forward and backward when standing erect, and the triceps used to push something away from the body. The first example is a clear-cut case of a "seesaw" arrangement (see Figure 7.1). In the second example, the triceps exert force on the end of the olecranon process, the middle of the elbow joint serves as the axis, and the object pushed away from the body with the hand and arm constitutes the resistance.

There are few good examples of second class levers (Figure 7.2) in the human body. However, if one lies on his back on the floor with legs straight and feet flat against the wall and then pushes his body away from the wall, movement will be accomplished by the pull of the gastrocnemius and the soleus muscles on the end of the calcaneus. This provides the force. The resistance will come through the tibia, while the axis will be the place where the ball of the foot pushes against the wall.

There are hundreds of third class levers in the human body. The most common example is flexion of the forearm while holding a weight in the hand. The contraction of the biceps provides the force, the elbow joint is the axis, and the weight lifted in the hand provides the resistance (see Figure 7.3).

Many combinations of muscles and bones act as more than one kind of lever. As body position changes and as muscles move the body, origins of muscles become insertions and insertions become origins. Likewise, force and resistance can exchange functions. The way a lever functions is determined largely by the location of the lever axis.

Depending on whether it is important to increase force at the sacrifice of distance and speed or to gain speed and distance at the sacrifice of strength, different arrangements of muscles and lever arms will be utilized. Function is dependent on structure and nature has provided in a miraculous way the abilities to run, throw, lift, and swing. The long lever arms used in hurling the javelin or the discus, the power developed by the extensors of the back and legs, and the speed and accuracy of movement of the fingers and eyes all speak eloquently for the effective and efficient arrangement of muscles, bones, and nerves.

7.4 PLANES OF REFERENCE

There are three reference planes which are customarily used to describe positions and movements of the body. These are:

1. The *saggital* plane. This is the vertical plane which is often described as the anterior-posterior plane. The *cardinal* saggital plane divides the body equally into right and left halves. The *parasaggital* plane is any plane parallel to the saggital plane.
2. The *frontal* plane. This is sometimes called the coronal plane and divides the body into posterior and anterior halves. It is perpendicular to the saggital plane.
3. The *transverse* or horizontal plane. This divides the body at the center of gravity into the upper portion and the lower portion (see Figure 7.4).

The three planes will intersect at the center of gravity when the body is erect and the arms are in anatomical position. Any extension of a limb or movement of the head from the erect position will change the center of gravity. Carrying a load under one arm or a pack on the back will likewise affect the location of the center of gravity.

Rotary movements of body segments occur in one of the planes mentioned above and around an axis. The axes in the human organism are (1) the *vertical (longitudinal)* axis, which runs up and down perpendicular to the ground, (2) the lateral-horizontal *(transverse)* axis, which runs horizontally from side to side, and (3) the anterior-posterior horizontal *(saggital)* axis, which passes horizontally from front to back. Movement takes place around an axis which is at right angles to the plane in which the movement occurs.

7.5 PRINCIPLES OF EQUILIBRIUM

If the body (or any other object) is to rest in a state of stable equilibrium, the *gravital line* must fall within the base of support. Stability may be increased by lowering the center of gravity or by widening the base of support.

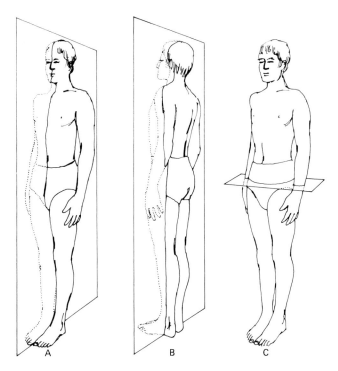

Figure 7.4 The planes of reference. A, sagittal or
anteroposterior plane; B, frontal or lateral plane; C, horizontal or
transverse plane. These three planes intersect at the center of
gravity. Parasagittal, parafrontal, and parahorizontal planes are
those which are parallel to their counterparts but do not pass
through the center of gravity. (From Wells, *Kinesiology,* p. 10. By
permission.)

It may be seen (Figure 7.5) that, other things being equal, the nearer the
gravital line is to the center of the base of support, the more stable the object will
be.

A person in erect position is not very stable. The feet which serve as the base
do not provide a very large area of support. This base can be increased in size
by standing with the feet apart and one slightly ahead of the other. One can
increase his stability significantly by placing one or both hands on the ground. In
this way, one not only increases the area of support but also lowers the center of
gravity.

The maintenance of equilibrium during physical activity consists of controlling
the center of gravity of the body and its parts by continually adjusting it with respect
to the location of the base of support. A kneeling position on the floor of a canoe,
is more stable than a sitting position on the seat because the center of gravity is

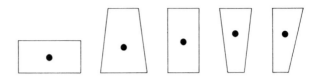

Figure 7.5 Examples of stable and unstable objects.
Stability is directly proportional to the area of the base, the
distance of the gravital line from the edge of the base, and
the weight of the object. It is indirectly proportional to the
distance of the center of gravity above the base. (● = center
of gravity.)

lower. Wrestlers keep their feet apart when trying to maintain the "top position"
because it provides a wider base of support. When building pyramids it is wise for
beginners to position the "bottom man" on all fours, providing the greatest possible area in the base of support.

7.6 PRINCIPLES GOVERNING MOTION
Principles governing motion include the following:

1. *To put a body in motion, it must be acted upon by a force.* The greater the
   mass of the object, the greater the force required to move it.
2. *In order to stop or change the direction of a moving object, it must be acted
   upon by a force greater than the existing force of the moving object.* Batting
   a baseball, kicking a soccer ball, blocking a punch, tackling a runner, or
   returning a tennis serve illustrate this principle.
3. *In order to apply effective force with the body or any part of it, there must
   be an equal and opposite counterforce.* Progression will not occur if the
   ground or floor does not present a firm resistant base. In swimming, the water
   supplies the necessary counterforce.

   These principles are based on Newton's three laws of motion:

1. An object at rest or in motion remains in that state unless acted upon by a
   sufficient force (the law of inertia).
2. When an object is acted upon by a force, the resulting acceleration is proportional to the force and inversely proportional to the mass of the object.
3. To every action there is an equal and opposite reaction.

   A pitched baseball is affected by these laws in many ways. As the pitcher
begins his windup, the ball moves with his hand in several directions (affected by
forces in several directions), then accelerates in a straight line toward the plate
until it is released. The resistance of the air, the spin of the ball, and the force of
gravity then act upon it to slow it down, to make it change direction, or to cause

it to drop. When it reaches the plate, it may be met by the bat and the change in direction and the acceleration will then be related to the weight and speed of the bat, the direction it is pointed at the time of the impact, and the total force behind the swing. As the ball sails through the air, it is affected again by the resistance of the air and the pull of gravity acting to pull it toward the ground. If caught, it is stopped by the resistance of the fielder's glove and a whole new cycle of forces acts upon it.

Forces acting upon one's muscles in physical education are of many kinds: the mass of the body itself, the pull of gravity, the push of another human body, the force of wind or water, the explosiveness and elasticity of the springboard or the trampoline, etc. Forces may consist of bats or hockey sticks in motion, thrown hammers, hurled javelins, or a combination of many of the above. An understanding of the laws of motion is essential to the scientific analyses of movement.

Principles governing the delivery of impetus to an external object are the following:

1. *In order to move an external object, the force must be great enough to overcome the object's inertia.* Since force is a function of mass and acceleration, and since acceleration is a function of velocity and time ($F = m\, v/t$), it follows that in hitting a baseball, for example, the weight of the striking implement and the speed with which it is moving are key factors in the result.

2. *An object to which sufficient force is applied will move in the direction of the resultant of the forces affecting it.* Gravity, the force exerted by the throwing arm, and the wind all affect a baseball as a player throws it.

3. *If the force applied is in line with the center of gravity of an object, the motion will be linear* (e.g., pitching a fast ball). *If the force applied is not in line with the center of gravity, the motion will be partially rotary* (e.g., batting a high foul).

4. *The angle at which a ball is met by an implement will equal that at which it will leave the implement* (other forces being negligible). When a batter bunts in baseball, this becomes an important principle and an understanding of it will assist the batter in placing his bunts.

Momentum may be defined as *the force possessed by a body in motion.* It is the impetus or the potential which a body has to remain in motion. The linear momentum of a body is the product of its mass and linear velocity.

Teachers of sports must be concerned with ways of increasing momentum. In sports where striking implements are utilized, it is important to know the weight of each implement. A light bat may be swung faster than a heavy one. A good baseball coach will know whether the ball, when struck by a bat, will go farther if the weight of the bat were increased or if the weight were decreased and the speed of the swing increased. The optimal combination of the speed of the swing and the weight of the bat should be determined for each player and employed.

When two football players collide, it is usually the one who is moving faster who is hurt the least. Assuming their weights are the same, the momentum of the faster player will be greater. If they are running at right angles when they collide, the direction of the one who is moving more slowly will be changed more than will the path of the faster one.*

If two balls of exactly the same size, weight and material roll directly toward each other at the same speed, they will stop as they collide. If they are of different weight and the velocity is not the same, the one which has the greater momentum (mv) will reverse the path of the smaller one. It will, however, lose some of its own momentum and slow down. Therefore, the momentum of one body may be transferred to another.

7.7 ELASTICITY AND COEFFICIENT OF RESTITUTION

Most substances are elastic to a greater or lesser degree. This simply means that most materials, when they are acted upon by certain forces, can be forced out of their original form or shape but will also regain that form or shape. In physical education we find many examples. When a golf ball, baseball, tennis ball, football or soccer ball is struck by the appropriate instrument, its shape as well as that of the instrument is changed (see Figure 7.6). When a gymnast jumps on the minitramp, a squash ball hits the racket, or a ball bounces against a rebounding surface, the elasticity of the minitramp, the racket, and the rebounding surface will increase the force imparted to the object to which impetus is given.

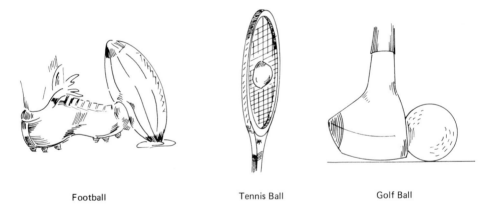

Football   Tennis Ball   Golf Ball

Figure 7.6 Shape of balls being struck. The difference in the degree to which balls are flattened is due to the coefficient of restitution, the mass, and the velocity of both the object struck and the striking instrument. Obviously, neither the football nor the golf ball have any velocity at the moment of impact. (Adapted from Bunn, *Scientific Principles of Coaching.*)

The *coefficient of restitution* is the measure of elasticity of the object struck, the striking object, or the rebounding surface. We can now add to the principles governing motion articulated in the preceding section (7.6).

---

*Refer also to Section 7.9, ''Moving One's Body.''

1. *The greater the coefficient of restitution of the object acted upon, the greater will be the velocity and distance* (other forces being equal).

2. *The greater the coefficient of restitution of the implement or the rebounding surface acting upon the object, the greater will be the velocity and distance of the object.*

3. *The speed and distance of a struck object is a function of the mass and striking force of both the object and the striking implement and is dependent on the coefficients of restitution of the two.* An elastic and resilient ball struck by an elastic and resilient implement will produce a high velocity in the object being projected.

4. The five factors which influence the direction taken by a struck ball are (a) the direction of the force applied in relation to the center of gravity of the ball, (b) the position of the striking implement at the moment of impact, (c) the angle of rebound, (d) the coefficient of restitution of the ball, and (e) the firmness and stability of the arm and wrist holding the striking implement.

Many of the principles listed for striking a ball also apply to catching it. The momentum of the ball (or other object) should be stopped gradually. Using more technical terms, we might say that the resistance to the moving object should be applied over a period of time. Good baseball players catch a ball with a slight "give" motion of the hand and glove at the moment of impact in the direction the ball is moving.

7.8 THROWING AND HURLING

In events where the intention is to throw or hurl an object as far as possible, the controlling factors are speed and the angle of release. Beyond these are several aerodynamic factors which are specific for each event.

Some principles which apply to the development of maximum speed are the following:

1. The "thrower" should exert the forces of his body over the greatest possible range (time and distance). The longer a force can be exerted upon an object (other things being equal), the greater will be the release speed and the distance thrown.

2. Insofar as possible, *the forces employed in projecting the missile should be exerted in the direction of the optimum angle of release.* Forces which are released in the wrong direction, or in movements extraneous to the objective, are wasted and may actually be a hindrance to the achievement of distance.

3. *The principle of summation of forces is particularly important in events where an object is thrown for distance.* In summation of forces, all parts of the body involved must make their maximum contribution toward the objective. The sequence of involvement will generally be the legs, hips, trunk, shoulder, arm, and hand. As each segment is involved, it must be able to move faster than the implement to be thrown and the forces must accumulate and flow smoothly from one segment to another. The arms and hands at first transmit forces from the more

Figure 7.7. Shotputter controlling the shot as long as possible. As soon as the shotputter has completed his preliminary movement, the glide, the rear (right) leg is extended forcibly and the "putting" of the shot is begun. The center of gravity continues to be moved forward and upward without diminishing the speed built up during the glide. The rotation and extension of the body begins with the larger and stronger muscles, moves downward through the ankles and toes and upward through the shoulder, elbows, wrists, and fingers, and ends with the shot being released just before the body leaves the ground for its reversal and followthrough.

powerful trunk and leg muscles but finally add their strength and force in order to apply the sum total of all the forces at the moment of release.

4. *The ground must provide adequate resistance throughout the throw.* Maximum force is limited by the counterthrust of the surface against which the thrower

pushes at the moment of release. It also becomes clear that there must be contact with the surface at the moment of release, for there can be no force or speed generated (except for very light objects) when the body is no longer able to push against a counterthrust.

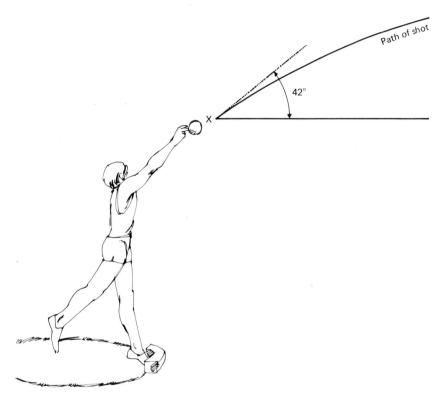

Figure 7.8   Optimal angle of release when an object is above the ground.
Theoretically, if an object such as the shotput were projected from ground level, the optimal angle of release would be 45 degrees. However, because it is released approximately six to eight feet above the ground, it has been determined that the optimal angle of release for most shotputters is about 42 degrees. The path of the shot will form a parabola. The positive vertical velocity component will gradually diminish up to the halfway point, while the negative vertical velocity component will increase until the shot lands.

5. In the four field events (shotput, discus, hammer, and javelin), the implements are released at various distances above the ground. Therefore, although the ideal angle of release is 45 degrees when points of release and landing are at the same height above the ground, the actual optimum angle of release will be slightly

less than that. Aerodynamic factors also affect the flight of the discus and the javelin. The discussion of these is quite technical and beyond the scope of this text.

Different factors are brought into play when throwing or hitting light objects such as baseballs, footballs, tennis balls and pingpong balls. In such instances the counterthrust of the ground is often relatively unimportant. Balls can be thrown with the mass of the body, while in the air, furnishing the counterthrust. Speed can be developed by the use of the long resistance arm in the levers of the forearm and upper arm. Accuracy and quickness of delivery may be more important than distance or speed. Throws of this kind need to be made from many different positions. A number of additional kinesiological principles become involved. The elbow, wrist, and fingers become much more important. Rotation, spin, and aerodynamics play an even greater part.

7.9 MOVING ONE'S BODY
In general, the laws and principles so far discussed are applicable to the movement of one's own body as well as to the movement of objects. Nevertheless the application of these laws to specific movements of the body needs some additional explanation. Some general principles which govern moving one's body are:

1. The body may be supported (a) by the ground, floor, or other support on which one can stand, walk, or run, (b) by water, or (c) by a bar, branch, or parachute on which it is suspended.

2. Propulsion of the body while walking, dodging, running, or jumping is accomplished by diagonal pressure of the foot against a resistant, supporting surface. This surface supplies the counterpressure and friction (grip) necessary for movement.

3. During translatory motion of the body, accomplished largely by the alternate movement of the legs, there is a vertical component and a horizontal component

◀ "Propulsion of the body while walking, dodging, running, or jumping is ▲ accomplished by diagonal pressure of the foot against a resistant, supporting surface." (Courtesy of the *Journal of Health, Physical Education, and Recreation*.)

in the propulsive stage. This alternates with the restraining phase. All of these must be coordinated to effect smooth, efficient locomotion. The most economical gait is one which permits a pendular motion of the legs.

4. The linear velocity of any point on a turning body is proportional to its distance from the axis. The longer the arms of a discus thrower, the greater will be the speed of the discus in proportion to the velocity of the turning body.

5. The moment of inertia of an object rotating about its axis is equal to the mass of the object times the square of the distance from the center of rotation.

6. Angular momentum is the product of the moment of inertia and the angular velocity. A turning body, without being acted upon by any external forces, will have a constant angular momentum. In spite of this, however, a person standing on a "frictionless" turntable can speed up or slow down the rate of his turn by retracting or extending his arms and hands. In this case he changes the moment of inertia while the angular momentum remains the same. Divers, trampoliners, figure skaters and gymnasts are well aware of this principle.

7. Centripetal and centrifugal forces also play a role in moving one's body. Centripetal force is the inward pull exerted to keep an object which is moving in a circle from flying outward. The equal and opposite force, centrifugal force, is that which pulls such an object away from the center of the circle. These forces play an important role in hurling the discus, throwing the hammer, racing around a curve in track, cutting sharply in football, performing the giant swing, and a number of other athletic events. The centrifugal and the centripetal forces are proportional to the mass of the moving object, the square of the velocity, and the radius of the circular motion.

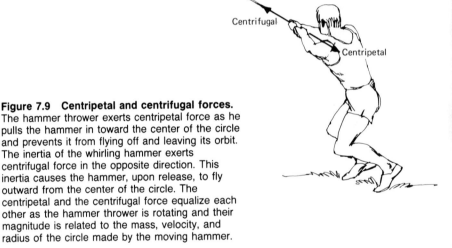

Centrifugal

Centripetal

Figure 7.9   Centripetal and centrifugal forces.
The hammer thrower exerts centripetal force as he pulls the hammer in toward the center of the circle and prevents it from flying off and leaving its orbit. The inertia of the whirling hammer exerts centrifugal force in the opposite direction. This inertia causes the hammer, upon release, to fly outward from the center of the circle. The centripetal and the centrifugal force equalize each other as the hammer thrower is rotating and their magnitude is related to the mass, velocity, and radius of the circle made by the moving hammer.

Walking, running, and jumping have been part of human activity since the erect posture was first assumed. They are also considered quite efficient as human movements go. Reflexes act to coordinate extension and flexion of limbs in propulsive acts. Other automatic movement patterns come into play during weight bearing and landing. The principles of continuity of motion and transfer of momentum apply in moving the body as well as in other motor patterns.

7.10 BIOMECHANICAL CONCEPTS AND PRINCIPLES
It is evident that volumes could be written analyzing human movement. That is not the purpose here. It is rather the intention to give examples of principles and concepts which can be applied to human movement as it is studied and practiced in physical education. In concluding this chapter, some additional miscellaneous concepts and principles are briefly reviewed.

1. The human body derives its facility for complex movements from its segmentally arranged skeletal structure. A large number of combinations of muscular contractions give this skeletal structure great potential for a variety of movements. These are all subject to analysis through physiological, mechanical, and other scientific principles. The movements of the human body are, however, restricted to those actions permitted by the structure of the skeleton (particularly the joints).

2. The many external forces such as inertia, air resistance, gravity, friction, momentum, and acceleration may act singly or in combination as a person moves during the numerous and varied physical education activities. Combined with the physiological complexity of movement, the intricacies of mechanical forces make the analysis of motor learning and performance challenging indeed.

3. Because gravity exerts its force vertically in a downward direction, the body is most stable when (a) the center of gravity is directly over the supporting base, (b) the individual body segments are centered over each other, and (c) the feet are placed so as to present a broad base of support.

4. When the body is employed to move heavy objects, the strongest muscles and the most efficient leverages should be utilized. Carefully aligning body segments, establishing a firm and resistant base, and relating the center of gravity to the task at hand should receive attention. As an example, a person lifting a heavy object should squat rather than bend at the hips, move so as to lift as straight up as possible, carry the weight close to the body, lift by extension of the powerful leg muscles, and use a slow, steady pace.

5. Unless an object is acted upon by an outside force, friction is normally necessary for movement to begin. Friction is needed between the supporting surface and the foot in walking or running and between the wheels and the supporting surface in self-propelled vehicles.

6. In pushing or pulling an object or load, the greatest efficiency and effectiveness is obtained if (a) the force is exerted through the center of gravity, (b) the force is exerted in the exact direction of the desired movement, and (c) the body segments are aligned, insofar as possible, in the direction of the movement.

7. When in contact with a supporting surface, the momentum of any part of the body will be transferred to the rest of the body (e.g., flinging the hands, kicking the feet, or tossing the head).

8. When an object is acted upon by two or more forces, the movement will be in the direction of the resultant* of those forces. The resultant is a function of both the magnitude and direction of each individual force. The more nearly a force is applied in the direction of the desired motion, the more effect it will have. The effective *force arm* is the perpendicular distance from the axis to the point where the force is applied.

---

*The force resulting from a combination of two or more forces acting on a body.

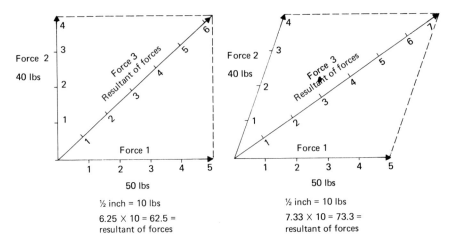

Figure 7.10(a) The resultant of forces. It is possible to determine the resultant of two forces acting in the same plane by constructing a parallelogram. Each force is represented by a line indicating its direction and magnitude. A parallelogram is then constructed and a line drawn from the point where the forces are applied to the opposite corner. This line represents the composite effect of the two forces. If each line is drawn to scale and represents the magnitude and direction of the force, the diagonal can be measured and the resultant force calculated.

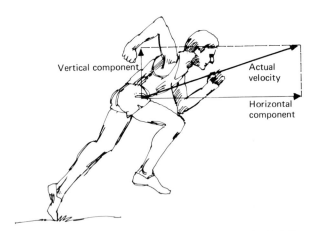

Figure 7.10(b) The parallelogram of forces, depicting the resultant of the vertical component and the horizontal component of a sprinter as he leaves the starting blocks.

9. When the body is unsupported (flying freely in air), nothing a person can do will alter his or her center of gravity. Rotatory motion in any direction (around the center of gravity) can be initiated, but not translatory motion.

10. When the body rotates, the velocity is accelerated by shortening the radius and decelerated by lengthening the radius.

11. In swinging exercises (e.g., giant swing), shortening the radius on the up-swing accelerates the movement while lengthening the radius on the downswing increases the velocity of rotation. This is what makes the execution of certain gymnastic routines possible.

12. When a body is free in the air, as one component moves up another moves down. In the pole vault, the feet clear the bar when the upper part of the body is still supported by the pole, but as the feet go down, the upper part of the body goes up and clears the crossbar.

"When a body is free in the air, as one component moves up another moves down." (Courtesy of the *Journal of Health, Physical Education, and Recreation.*)

13. Assuming the same angular velocity, a long lever will move faster at its end than will a short lever. Therefore, greater velocity will be obtained in the hand by swinging it from the shoulder with a straight arm than by swinging it from the elbow, keeping the upper arm stationary.

14. In some of its movements, the body demonstrates the *wheel and axle* principle. The rotation of the radius of the forearm is a good example. Closely related is the *pulley action.* The pull of the quadriceps on the patella in leg extension illustrates this concept.

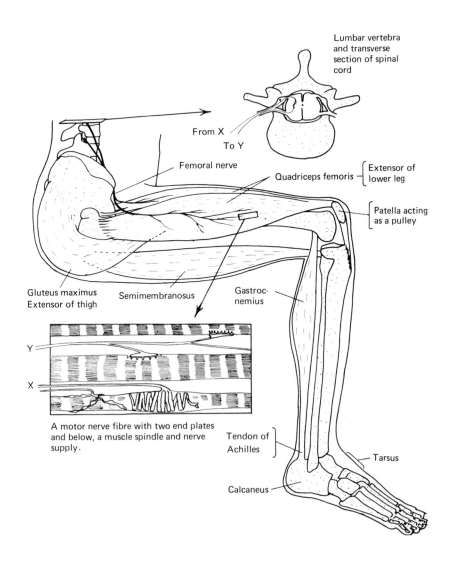

15. The moment of force about a given point is equal to the perpendicular distance from the action line of the force to the point, multiplied by the magnitude of the force applied.

16. The speed of a ball struck by an implement (bat, golf club, foot, racket, etc.) will be dependent on (a) the speed of the ball at the moment of impact, (b) the mass of the ball, (c) the mass of the striking implement, (d) the velocity of the striking implement, and (e) the coefficient of restitution of both the ball and the striking implement.

17. The force a moving ball imparts to the receiving surface (hand, glove, ground etc.) will be dependent upon (a) the area of the receiving surface, (b) the speed of the ball upon impact, and (c) the distance through which the impetus is reduced (the gradualness with which momentum is dissipated).

18. The area over which a force is absorbed must also be considered when the human body or other heavy object lands. If the shock can be absorbed over a large area, the strain will be much less. The greater the area the less force per unit area.

19. When landing after moving through the air, it is important for stability to establish as large a base of support as possible. The primary direction of the base should be in line with the direction of the horizontal movement. Jumping on skis, landing after a long vault, and completing the broad jump illustrate the application of this principle.

Figure 7.12   Completing the long jump. The greatest distance in the broad jump will be attained when, immediately before landing, the legs stretch forward slightly below the horizontal, the trunk leans slightly forward, and the arms thrust vigorously backward as the jumper jackknifes to increase his angular velocity.

◀ **Figure 7.11   Dynamics of muscle and bone.** Simplified diagram of the right leg, showing the main extensor muscles and the semimembranosus, antagonistic to the quadriceps femoris. Nerve tissues associated with one simple reflex arc are shown. Note also the patella acting as a pulley as the quadriceps femoris contracts to extend the leg. The gastrocnemius muscle, together with the soleus (not shown), pulls on the calcaneus to lift the heel of the foot off the floor. (From Tricker and Tricker, *The Science of Movement*, 1967, p. 60. By permission.)

20. Regardless of mass, bodies falling from the same height will reach the same level at the same time. The pull of gravity causes falling bodies to accelerate at the rate of 32 feet per second each second. Methods of reducing the impact as the body falls to the ground are important in ski jumping, gymnastics, dancing, and parachuting. Increasing the time and distance during which the falling body is stopped and the shock absorbed is an important principle.

21. When in the water, one should bear in mind that the body will move in the opposite direction from that in which the force is applied. Pushing downward will tend to lift the body, pushing to the right will move the body to the left, etc.

22. A body wholly or partially submerged in a liquid is buoyed by a force equal to the mass of the liquid displaced. This is known as *Archimede's Principle* and is particularly significant in all aquatic activities.

23. Water resistance is important in swimming and boating. In the propulsive phase of boating and swimming, the broadest possible surface should be presented to the water. In the *gliding phase,* the smallest possible surface should be presented.

24. The angle of rebound is important in games such as squash, handball, tennis, basketball, and golf. We have mentioned before the relationship of the angle at which a ball strikes a surface to the angle of refraction. The spin on the ball will also have considerable effect on the angle at which the ball leaves the striking surface. A basketball spinning forward on its horizontal axis as it strikes the floor will bounce low, fast, and far, while if it has a backward spin its bounce will be slow and almost straight up. Side spins on vertical axes will of course cause the ball to bounce in the direction of the spin.

Key

_ _ _ _   Direction ball moves

_____   Direction of spin

•   Center of gravity

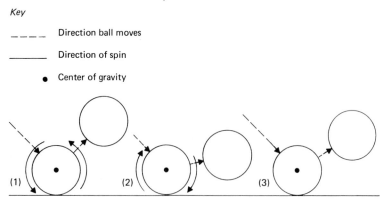

Figure 7.13(a)   Basketball being passed. (1) Reverse spin causes the ball to lose speed and bounce almost straight up. (2) Forward spin causes it to gain speed and scoot along the floor. (3) No spin—the angle of incidence = angle of refraction.

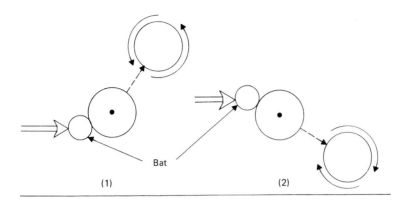

Figure 7.13(b)   Softball being hit. (1) Softball is hit by the bat below the center of gravity. This causes it to go almost straight up with a reverse spin. (2) Softball is hit by the bat above the center of gravity, causing it to go down with a forward spin.

25. *Bernoulli's Principle* is significant in sports where the spin of the ball plays an important role. This principle states that when a ball is moving at a high velocity through the air and is spinning about an axis, pressure builds up on one side and is reduced on the other. The ball moves in the direction of reduced pressure. This principle is demonstrated by the "curve" thrown by the pitcher in baseball. It also pertains to the hook or slice in golf and to the action of a tennis ball in a spinning serve.

7.11 SUMMARY
When working with students on the development of neuromuscular skills and assisting them in their efforts to reach higher levels of motor performance, there are many anatomical, physiological, and mechanical factors to be considered. Not every physical educator can be an expert in all these matters. However, it behooves all those in the profession to learn as much as possible for the particular assignments and special interests.

For those who plan to specialize in biomechanics, newer methods and new technology are proving very helpful. Computer programs for kinetic analysis [9, p. 169], cinematography, electromyography, electrogoniometry, and new techniques in physiology have added immensely to the sophistication with which human movement may now be studied. The person who wishes to make such study his life's work will find it challenging and rewarding.

SELECTED REFERENCES

1. American Association for Health, Physical Education, and Recreation, *Kinesiology Review,* Washington, D.C.: Council on Kinesiology of the Physical Education Division, 1971.
2. _____, *Kinesiology III,* Washington, D.C.: Committee on Kinesiology of the Physical Education Division, 1973.
3. Bowen, Wilbur Pardon, and Henry A. Stone, *Applied Anatomy and Kinesiology,* Philadelphia: Lea and Febiger, 1953.
4. Broer, Marion R., *Efficiency of Human Movement,* Philadelphia: W. B. Saunders Company, 1966.
5. Bunn, John W., *Scientific Principles of Coaching,* Englewood Cliffs, N.J.: Prentice-Hall, 1959.
6. Dyson, Geoffrey H. G., *The Mechanics of Athletics,* 5th edition, London: University of London Press, 1970.
7. Frost, H. M., *An Introduction to Biomechanics,* Springfield, Ill.: Charles C Thomas, 1971.
8. Hay, James B., *The Biomechanics of Sports Techniques,* Englewood Cliffs, N.J.: Prentice-Hall, 1973.
9. Jensen, Clayne R., and Gordon W. Schultz, *Applied Kinesiology,* New York: McGraw-Hill, 1970.
10. Kelley, David L., *Kinesiology: Fundamentals of Motion Description,* Englewood Cliffs, N.J.: Prentice-Hall, 1971.
11. Klafs, Carl E., and Daniel A. Arnheim, *Modern Principles of Athletic Training,* St. Louis: The C. V. Mosby Company, 1963.
12. Lee, Mabel, and Miriam M. Wagner, *Fundamentals of Body Mechanics and Conditioning,* Philadelphia: W. B. Saunders Company, 1949.
13. Morehouse, Laurence E., and John M. Cooper, *Kinesiology,* St. Louis: The C. V. Mosby Company, 1950.
14. Morehouse, Laurence E., and Philip J. Rasch, *Scientific Basis of Athletic Training,* Philadelphia: W. B. Saunders Company, 1958.
15. Plagenhoef, Stanley, *Patterns of Human Motion,* Englewood Cliffs, N.J.: Prentice-Hall, 1971.
16. Ravielli, Anthony, *Wonders of the Human Body,* New York: Scholastic Book Services, 1954.
17. Scott, M. Gladys, *Analysis of Human Motion,* New York: F. S. Crofts and Company, 1947.
18. Silvia, Charles E., *Manual and Lesson Plans for Basic Swimming, Water Stunts, Lifesaving, Springboard Diving, Skin and Scuba Diving,* Springfield, Mass.: published by the author, 1970.
19. Tricker, R. A. R., and B. J. K. Tricker, *The Science of Movement,* New York: American Elsevier Publishing Company, 1967.
20. Welford, A. T., *Fundamentals of Skill,* London: Methuen and Company, 1968.
21. Wells, Katharine F., *Kinesiology,* 5th edition, Philadelphia: W. B. Saunders Company, 1971. Reprinted by permission.
22. Whiting, H. T. A., *Acquiring Ball Skill,* London: G. Bell and Sons, 1969.
23. Williams, Marian, and Herbert R. Lissner, *Biomechanics of Human Motion,* Philadelphia: W. B. Saunders Company, 1962.

Psychological
Foundations

Chapter 8

8.1 INTRODUCTION
Teachers and coaches deal with many imponderables. They wonder why Johnny is not happy, they marvel at Mary's diligence, they groan at Bill's ineptitude, and they stare with astonishment as Susan accomplishes the seemingly impossible.

Physical education teachers are concerned about the progress and development of their students. Coaches want to know how to elicit from athletes the ultimate in achievement. Parents, teachers, and coaches all puzzle over the changing moods, individual differences, immature behavior, and disciplinary problems that confront them as they deal with children from preschool through college, from wealthy homes and poor homes, and of all degrees of intellectual and motor ability.

While there is much that still remains unanswered, psychologists have unearthed many facts and formulated numerous theories concerning personality, motivation, performance, and motor learning. They have also presented many practical and useful concepts. Those who teach people how to move, play, enjoy sport, dance and excel will be richly rewarded by a careful study and application of these theories and principles which form the psychological bases for physical education.

8.2 GROWTH AND DEVELOPMENT
Growth and development begin immediately after a human being is conceived and continue until the child reaches adulthood. The rate, extent, and nature of these phenomena are affected by both hereditary and environmental factors. The sperm joins the ovum and the journey through life begins. Cell differentiations occur and organ systems are established. Morphologic development and the establishment of vital reflexes proceed in the embryo and the regulators of breathing, circulation, digestion, and elimination are readied for their tasks in the extrauterine existence. Neurological organization and development of the perceptual apparatus continue. All this occurs before the child is born.

Assuming normal prenatal development and birth without unusual trauma, growth and maturation proceed naturally and in a given sequence. Observable behavior begins. Environmental factors and genetic tendencies exert their respective influences in determining the appearance, abilities, interests, and behavior of the becoming person.

It is difficult and somewhat futile to attempt to distinguish with any degree of accuracy what occurs during growth and maturation on the one hand, and learning and development on the other. What is more meaningful is that the child begins to move, make noise, eat, and grow. Soon its movements become more purposeful and its ability to perceive and distinguish more marked.

Figure 8.1 Development sequence in mastering locomotion. The ▶ ages listed are averages of many children. The sequence itself may be slightly different in individual cases. (From G. H. Sage, *Introduction to Motor Behavior.* Reading, Mass.: Addison-Wesley Publishing Company, 1971, p. 433.)

0 months
fetal posture

1 month
chin up

2 months
chest up

3 months
reach and miss

4 months
sit with support

5 months
sit on lap, grasp object

6 months
sit on high chair, grasp
dangling object

7 months
sit alone

8 months
stand with help

9 months
stand holding furniture

10 months
creep

11 months
walk when led

12 months
pull to stand by furniture

13 months
climb stair steps

14 months
stand alone

15 months
walk alone

"Perceptual-motor development involves both basic and high-level skills and ▶
includes all ages." (Courtesy of: *left and top right*, the *Journal of Health, Physical
Education, and Recreation; middle right*, University of Wisconsin–LaCrosse;
Bottom right, Liselott Diem, Sporthochschule, Köln, Germany.)

The child at first appears to move aimlessly on its own initiative and respond
by means of already established reflexes. Most of the initial reflexes are necessary
to adapt to the new world of the infant. A few appear to have little meaning and
soon disappear. The Moro reflex, startle reflex, palmar reflex, and rooting reflex
are among those present at birth.

Shortly after birth the child will grasp, kick, squirm, and turn his head. These
movements of the arms, legs, head, and trunk become increasingly vigorous until
he is able to roll over. Efforts to assume the upright position begin and the child
experiments with supporting movements, head-raising movements, and "pull-up"
reactions. Soon the baby is able to stand on its hands and knees and at the same
time raise its head. The next steps are to creep, crawl, to pull itself up by furniture,
and move about in the erect position.

As these processes are taking place, most of the reflexes observed in the
first few months are disappearing. Voluntary and cognitive activity take their place.
The child learns to walk, talk, run, climb, and move in a multitude of different ways.
He becomes aware of himself. He grows like the proverbial weed. Soon he is three
years old.

As the child moves through the preschool years, elementary school, secondary school, and into adulthood, growth, maturation, and development continue.
Developmental tasks are completed, challenges are overcome, and one by one
the steps to maturity are mounted. Physiological, intellectual, emotional, and social
readiness preparing the person for adult life becomes more clearly apparent. The
typical child passes through the stage of adolescence and becomes a full grown
and fully developed person eager to make his own way in the world.

8.3 PERCEPTUAL-MOTOR DEVELOPMENT
All voluntary movement must begin with a perception of the task. Perception
consists of selection, organization, and interpretation of data received through the
senses. During this process the object or event takes on meaning, is related to the
past, and is recorded in the brain.

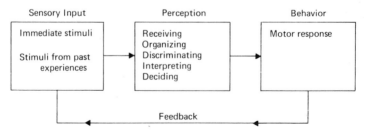

Figure 8.2 The perceptual-motor cycle.

Because nervous integration is not complete at birth, further development takes place during the first few years of life. As various kinds of movement occur, both reflex and voluntary, neurons are stimulated to grow, expand, and make new connections. As new nervous pathways become complete, increased feedback from sensory receptor organs is relayed to the central nervous system. This leads to more varied and intricate movements, which in turn stimulate the sensory receptors in the nervous system. It is in response to movement that the sensory nerves become fully developed and neurological organization is completed.

For smooth and effective movement, the perceptual processes are as important as the motor aspects. Perceptual-motor development is significant in both cognition and performance of intricate movement patterns. It usually proceeds naturally and systematically as the sensory, perceptual, and motor components function in normal fashion. Developmental tasks should be so ordered that one follows the other in the correct sequence. Gross motor movements which serve as a basis for finer, more manipulative movements should be learned first and the more complex motor patterns introduced later.

8.4 INDIVIDUAL DIFFERENCES

The concept of individual differences, while not new, has received renewed emphasis in recent years. While there are many similarities among individuals, the practice of comparing one with another at home, in school, and in the social environment is not sound. The sequence of maturational and developmental events may be much the same for most individuals but the timing, acceleration, degree, and final result may be quite different.

The chronological age of several young people may be the same and yet there are differences in physiological age, motor ability, strength, size, intellectual capacity, and emotional stability. Each child should be allowed his or her own rate of growth and development, own pace in terms of personality and ability, own tempo of living. While stimulation and motivation of an individual may at times be desirable, they should be appropriate to his or her capacity and level of advancement. The use of competition as a motivating device should be carefully analyzed in terms of its total effect on all the students. If the differences in growth, maturation, intellectual ability, motor ability, and emotional characteristics are all considered, variations in individuals will be great indeed. Patience, understanding, and wisdom are needed as students and athletes are guided in their efforts to develop and achieve.

8.5 MOTIVATION AND AROUSAL

Motivation is a psychological, sociological, and physiological phenomenon. Motives initiate, sustain, give direction to, and govern the intensity of action. They also control, inhibit, and stop certain kinds of behavior. Several categories of motivation will be considered here under the following headings:

1. Homeostasis
2. Satisfaction of needs

3. Self-concept
4. Expectations
5. Level of aspiration
6. Frustration, challenge, and self-discovery
7. Social determinants
8. Propriate striving
9. Arousal

Homeostasis
The human organism exhibits a tendency to maintain a constant internal environment. This tendency to return to a state of equilibrium is known as *homeostasis*. Any stress (e.g., trauma, heat, fright, anger, fatigue) will upset the state of homeostasis and stimulate the organism to act. Fright may cause it to flee, anger to fight, and trauma to move away from the source of danger. The need to reduce tension and return to the state of equilibrium can be, and often is, an important motivator.

Satisfaction of needs
Under conditions of danger or threat to life, the desire to survive will take precedence over most other needs. A person who is starving will have little interest in old-age pensions. The individual under threat of being run over by a car will have little thought of anything but to get out of the way.

Maslow and others have arranged a hierarchy of needs in approximately the following order: survival, security, belonging, esteem, self-realization, and self-actualization. These all serve to motivate people in certain situations. The avoidance of pain, the seeking of pleasure, and the various kinds of sexual impulses are age-old hedonistic drives. The urge to struggle when hindered, escape when confined, excel when challenged, and fight when angered are typical of people as they are stimulated to respond to treatment which restrains, humiliates, or limits their freedom.

We must not lose sight of fun and joy as motivating factors in physical education. The author has asked many children why they like "gym" and why they enjoy playing games in the backyard. Almost unanimously the spontaneous answer is, "Because it's fun!" A child's natural instinct is to play and have fun, a meaningful and important objective from the viewpoint of the child. Activity gives pleasure to the participant. Skillful performance enhances this pleasure and leads to more permanent satisfaction. Both are significant.

Self-concept
The way a person sees himself and the way he believes he is looked upon by others influence his personality and behavior. If one thinks of himself as a kind, helpful person he will try to assist another in trouble. If one perceives himself as a fighter, he will try to establish that image. If one has a concept of self as an intellectual, he will no doubt give careful, thoughtful answers to questions.

The coach and the teacher have many opportunities to influence the self-concept of athletes and students. Judicious praise, attention to the positive, and noticing little acts of kindness, thoughtfulness, or courage will exert a constructive influence on the development of a desirable self-concept. This in turn will aid the individual in his personal growth and his drive toward self-realization. Likewise, too much criticism, continual fault finding, or lack of attention to praiseworthy acts can produce an undesirable self-concept. Self-concept includes a person's level of confidence and influences his ultimate achievement.

Expectations

Closely related to the notion of self-concept is that of expectations. A person who believes others expect him to be helpful in a civic organization will probably try to be that kind of individual. Trying to live up to an established reputation can be quite motivating. The role one feels he is expected to play often determines how he acts. If a player believes his coach has high expectations of his performance, he will usually put forth every effort to meet them. When an administrator, teacher, or coach delegates responsibility in a manner which infers high expectations, the individual assuming the responsibility will try hard to please. Letting athletes, students, or other individuals know that much is expected of them can serve as an inspiration, cause them to raise their level of aspiration, and lead to high achievement.

Level of aspiration

A person's *level of aspiration* is related to the concept of expectations and involves setting goals. Aspiring to achieve a worthwhile objective, striving toward an ideal, and trying to accomplish a difficult task are marks of a highly motivated individual, generally leading to success in a particular endeavor.

Goals should be challenging but achievable. They should be worthy of intense effort and commitment. Goals which are so high that failure results generally lower one's level of aspiration and cause a drop in performance. A level of aspiration which is too low does not lead to great accomplishments. Success generally leads to a higher level of aspiration and repeated failure to a lower one.

Frustration, challenge, and self-discovery

For optimum development of the individual, tasks should be difficult enough to require effort and hard work but not so difficult that they result in frustration and a sense of failure. A gradual increase in difficulty of tasks so that the individual is constantly challenged to practice and improve will result in the greatest learning and the best performance. When the difficulty of tasks is increased so suddenly and to such an extent that a person is not ready either physiologically or psychologically, attempts to succeed will result in failure. Too many failures and the persistent blocking of goals can lead to aggression, regression, fixation, apathy, and dependency.

It has been found, in Outward Bound and similar type programs, that tasks and circumstances in which a person is asked to do something he has never tried before and which requires the calling out of hidden resources can result in the discovery of unknown abilities and capacities. True self-confidence comes when one achieves something calling for courage, intense effort, persistence, and determination and when one discovers he is capable of meeting new and greater challenges. This kind of self-discovery prepares one for facing new adventures and challenges and develops in an individual a self-confidence that has been tested.

". . . self-confidence comes when one . . . discovers he is capable of meeting new and greater challenges." (Courtesy of: *left,* the *Journal of Health, Physical Education, and Recreation; right,* Liselott Diem, Sporthochschule, Köln, Germany.)

Great athletes usually have positive self-concepts, high expectations, high levels of aspiration, and self-confidence which is tested and tried. They know from their own experience that human beings are capable of more than is normally demanded. They have found that every person has within himself wellsprings of strength, endurance, and courage that can be drawn upon in times of emergency. Of course, there must be a realistic element in all of this. Champions are usually those who believe they can perform well and can win, but are also aware that it will require serious effort and concentration on their part. It must also be emphasized that each individual has limitations and that achievements, in the final analysis, must be measured in terms of one's own capacities and talents, not against those of someone else.

Social determinants
All people are motivated to a greater or lesser degree by the opinions of their peers, the customs of the people with whom they associate, and the socioeconomic status of the group to which they belong. They may attach great importance to being elected "captain" or "president," to being invited to prestigious social functions, to belonging to the "in group." Behavior is often motivated by a desire to achieve socially, by the expectations of those to whom they look for approval, and by the cultural milieu in which they move.

Propriate striving
The proprium may be defined as that which is intimately and peculiarly ours. It is related to the "ego" and the "self" and is central to our sense of uniqueness. It includes those aspects which "make for a sense of inward unity." [24, p. 36]

Propriate striving is reaching out and upward for something greater than ourselves. It is maintaining a commitment to a goal that is high. It is the attempt to maintain a state in which there is a constant drive to action, a continual effort to reach the goal. It is resistance to the reduction of tension. In effect, it is a resistance to homeostasis until the goal is reached.

Albert Schweitzer with his lifelong commitment to the people in Africa, Roald Amundsen with his passion to become a polar explorer, and Albert Einstein with his dedication to the discovery of new truth are examples of people whose goals were not the alleviation of tension, were not the satisfaction of material desires, but were self-actualization, self-fulfillment, and ego-extension. This kind of motivation, termed *propriate striving,* is very vital for a large number of people. Students, athletes, teachers, and coaches who are motivated by a desire to be the best, the finest, and the greatest will usually contribute the most to their society and achieve the ultimate in terms of self-fulfillment.

Arousal
There are untold numbers of instances where human beings have performed unbelievable feats under the influence of strong emotion. Lifting heavy objects to free a loved one, running great distances when frightened, struggling to be free when a life is at stake, and acting more explosively under the influence of anger are examples.

Experienced athletes and coaches are well aware that individuals and teams need to be aroused in order to achieve their best performance. They also know, however, that they can become too excited, too stirred up, too aroused. There is a point of *optimal arousal* for each person in each contest, sport, and position. There is a *threshold of arousal,* the point at which one is aroused to action, for each person. The point of optimal arousal is the goal of both coaches and individual athletes. When not sufficiently stirred up, individuals react sluggishly and inadequately. When too excited, they lose their fine coordination, steadiness, and ability to concentrate and think. The more experienced the athlete, the greater will be his ability to perform in a high state of excitement and to think when aroused. The job of the coach is to determine the point of optimal arousal for each individual in each sport and in each contest.

A difference exists between arousal for performing high level athletic skills and arousal for learning motor skills. Learning takes place best when individuals are relaxed, yet attentive. Too much arousal interferes with the learning of complex motor tasks. Too little arousal causes the learner to be careless and inattentive. Again, there is an optimal state of arousal for each individual and for each set of circumstances.

8.6 PERSONALITY AND ATHLETIC PERFORMANCE

Care must be exercised not to infer cause-and-effect relationships between specific personality traits and participation in sport. Few studies have attempted to relate changes which occur during athletic experiences to changes in personality traits. Research in general has tried to identify personality traits which characterize athletes. This is difficult because of the many different kinds of sport and the individual differences among athletes. Only rather general statements can be made with any confidence. The following are typical:

1. In general, both athletes and nonathletes show a normal distribution with regard to personality traits.
2. Athletes are generally more self-confident, surgent, and dominant than non-athletes.
3. Highly successful athletes (Olympians, etc.) generally have a greater need to achieve and a higher level of aspiration than nonathletes.
4. Good athletes are able to operate efficiently and effectively under conditions of stress.
5. Inasmuch as most sports contain an element of risk, it is conjectured that athletes are more daring than nonathletes.
6. Athletes are willing to learn, work hard to achieve their goals, and generally possess a great deal of energy.
7. Athletic adolescents are more extroverted than nonathletes. However, some of the greatest "world-level" athletes are quite sensitive and introverted.

8.7 PSYCHOMOTOR PHENOMENA

There are many phenomena in sport and physical education that are both psychological and physiological in nature. The recognition of cues, the extension of peripheral vision, the increase in speed and accuracy, the improvement of reaction and performance time, and the use of sensory mechanisms in feedback are some of these. Those who teach and coach should be particularly aware of such factors and their effects on motor learning.

Cue recognition

An athlete utilizes *cues* to signal what his next movement shall be. The touch of an opponent in wrestling, the sound of a starter's gun in track, the movement of the ball as a play starts in football, and the "break" of a baserunner in baseball are cues which give the signal for action to the wrestler, the sprinter, the lineman, and the catcher, respectively.

As the student moves from the lower levels of learning to the higher levels, many movements become more automatic. The athlete needs fewer cues and less time to perceive as he responds to each situation. In activities such as gymnastics, diving, pole vaulting, and figure skating, the cues are often kinesthetic in nature as the proprioceptors indicate to the central nervous system which movement should follow which. Such movements become essentially automatic and unconscious in nature and enable the performer to give the signal for the motor pattern to begin, after which he can leave the rest to learned responses.

Practice and experience are essential to becoming a great athlete. Perception of the task itself and response to feedback from exteroceptors and proprioceptors need to be automated. Motor patterns are eventually established in the cortex and can be called out by the appropriate stimuli. As individual movements become automatized, the visual, auditory, and tactile cues are recognized more quickly and motor responses become smoother and more efficient.

Reaction time, movement time, and performance time

Reaction time is the interval between the presentation of the stimulus and the beginning of the motor response. *Movement time* is the time required for the actual task. *Performance time,* sometimes referred to as response time, is the sum of reaction time and movement time. It is generally held that both reaction time and movement time can be improved with experience and practice. In the final analysis, response time is the important element in athletic performance. An athlete needs to move quickly to ward off an opponent's blow in boxing, to field a ball in baseball, to react to an opponent's move when guarding in basketball, or to move in one direction or another to receive a hard serve in tennis.

A complex movement requiring considerable choice will require a longer time than a simple movement. There will also be a greater possibility of improvement. Greater psychological and physiological readiness will also shorten the response time. In consideration of these phenomena, it must be recognized that native endowments are important and that one cannot make a "fast" person out of one who is by nature "slow."

Feedback

Few physiological mechanisms are as important in motor learning as the phenomenon of *feedback*. Feedback includes all the sensory stimuli which keep the organism informed as to its physical condition, the position of the head, trunk, and limbs, and the movements of the body parts. Incoming information from sensory receptors is received, synthesized, interpreted, and stored. Both movement and thought processes are adjusted, corrected, and guided by means of a continual stream of nervous impulses coming from the exteroceptors and proprioceptors. External or *augmented feedback* comes from stimuli originating outside the body, while *internal feedback* comes from the receptors in the muscles, tendons, joints, inner ear, and other organs.

Kinesthetic, proprioceptive, and labyrinthine stimuli in cooperation with those from the exteroceptors maintain erect posture and body balance, coordinate movements, and provide proper orientation to the horizontal plane.

The human organism has its own *servomechanisms* which regulate, adjust, and furnish cues for action and movement. Feedback can operate at either the conscious or the unconscious level. Visual and conscious control are generally operative during the early stages of motor learning, but when basic movements and motor patterns become automatized, internal feedback, cues, and "muscle memory" are in control.

8.8 PSYCHOLOGICAL CONCEPTS AND PRINCIPLES

The physical educator needs to know some of the theoretical psychological concepts and principles relating to his field. Even more important is their application. It is with this in mind that the following are listed:

1. The principle of "wholeness" assumes that the physical educator and coach, as they teach skills, strategy, or method, will keep in mind the effect of their words and actions on all aspects of the human organism, physical, intellectual, emotional, social, and spiritual.

2. Because both hereditary and environmental factors interact to mold the individual, coaches and teachers must attempt to select for each student developmental tasks which are of appropriate difficulty. Every person should be challenged, but no one should be continually faced with insurmountable odds.

3. The adolescent growth spurt does not come at the same age for everyone. Adolescents who develop more slowly are often concerned about their lack of maturity and small size. Those who work with developing youths should be sensitive to this and govern their methods and expectations accordingly.

4. The principle of "individual differences" suggests that children and young people should not be continually competing with their peers for recognition and awards. Each person should be allowed, to the extent indicated by good judgment, to grow, learn, mature, and develop at the pace which is natural and right for him.

5. The complete development of the nervous system proceeds in response to movement. Therefore, the young child should be offered the opportunity to move in as many ways as are natural for his stage of development.

6. Readiness can be physiological, psychological, sociological, or a combination of the three. One kind of readiness will affect the others. A change in physiological readiness often has an influence on psychological and social readiness. To try to teach something to a student who is not "ready" is wasteful and inefficient.

7. Emotional involvement can be either detrimental or helpful in both motor learning and performance. Some emotional involvement will increase attentiveness and concentration on the task. It will also lead to behavior which is more explosive, powerful, and purposeful. Too much emotional involvement, on the other hand, can reduce concentration, lead to lack of muscular control, and hinder clear thinking. Too deep emotional involvement maintained for too long a period of time is exhausting and can ultimately lead to impaired mental health and psychological problems.

8. Students and athletes who are confident that they have the esteem and affection of their parents and teachers will be more relaxed and willing to take risks than those who feel insecure about their relationships. Coaches and teachers who can demonstrate their concern for the personal welfare, growth, and achievement of every student and athlete are true educators and effective leaders.

9. All those who deal with developing youth must be sensitive to the effects of failure and losing as well as success and winning. Efforts should be made when conducting classes and intramural programs to organize teams on as equal a basis as possible so that all may experience both victory and defeat.

10. Personal warmth and involvement in the activities of youth can do more to stimulate and motivate a class or group than almost any other thing a teacher can do. Care must be taken that *all* students reap the benefit of this and not just a favored few.

11. From the point of view of the participant, fun and joy may well be the most universal motivating factors in physical education and sport. There is nothing wrong with this. Playing tennis, climbing mountains, dancing, swimming, or playing soccer may appeal to different people, and to the same people under different circumstances. To participate because one "likes to" is sufficient. It is the teacher planning lessons and the supervisor formulating a curriculum who need to know and understand the biophysical, psychological, and social values involved.

12. Motor learning consists of the relatively permanent changes which accrue from experiences in physical activity. Learning a motor skill produces a decrease in the number of errors, more effective and efficient performance, and more relaxed and smoother movements.

13. Motor learning consists of (a) a clear perception of the task, (b) trial performances, (c) analyses of the performances, (d) additional trials to correct errors, and (e) repetitive performances to automatize motor patterns. A clear perception of the task can be enhanced by demonstration, moving pictures, explanation of the desired performance, and finally a kinesthetic "feel" of moving through the act. Intelligent reinforcement is important as analysis and correction are applied during repeated trials.

14. "Learning by doing," the "doctrine of self-activity," and "mental practice" are important principles in the process of motor learning. Visualizing the act, reasoning out the elements in a motor pattern, mentally applying kinesiological principles, and intellectualizing expected behavior have been found to improve performance even when there is no observable physical movement. A combination of mental practice with physical practice is the best procedure.

15. The "whole-part-whole" or the "felt need" method of teaching sports is the most effective. It is necessary for the participant to perceive the "whole," of which the fundamental skill is a part. The person who becomes aware by means of playing a game that practice on a fundamental skill is needed will be motivated to drill on that aspect. The degree of complexity of the motor task and the previous experience of the learner will influence the amount of time that should be spent practicing "parts."

16. The concept of *transfer* is basic to learning in physical education and sport. Education consists of learning something in one situation that can be applied in another. Some important principles involved in transfer are the following:

a) The more similar two situations are the greater the likelihood of transfer. Common or identical elements increase the probability that transfer will occur.

b) The common or similar elements in the two situations must be recognized by the learner.

c) The greater the extent that generalization and intellectualization occur, the more meaningful will be the education for life.

d) Transfer cannot be guaranteed—it must be taught. Teachers and coaches must assist students and athletes to recognize similarities and to generalize.

17. Motor learning is not marked by consistent, steady improvement but by periods of rapid learning, periods of almost imperceptible improvement, and a series of *plateaus* in which it appears that little or no learning occurs. It is theorized that the periods when there is generally no progress are being utilized by the individual to automatize, or overlearn, certain components of a motor pattern so that they can serve as the basis for further motor learning. It is also hypothesized that these plateaus are often caused by fatigue, staleness, or lack of motivation.

18. The opportunity for self-expression is essential to total development and encourages a favorable attitude toward physical education. Provision for spontaneous expression of "an inner feeling" through movement is an important ingredient of good physical education programs. Whenever one moves as he feels like moving, or performs a feat which he has long been eager to accomplish, he is being creative. Creativity and self-expression are self-fulfilling behavior.

19. The length and frequency of practice periods have been discussed and debated for a long time. Practice does not, in itself, guarantee improvement. However, improvement does not generally occur without practice. Practice beyond

The Relay   The Competitor

"Creativity and self-expression are self-fulfilling behavior."
These two creations of R. Tait McKenzie are now on display at the Babson
Library, Springfield College. (Courtesy of Springfield College.)

the point of fatigue is not as productive as it is when students are fresh and energetic. Distributed practice is more effective than prolonged practice on a given skill. A shorter period of intensive, concentrated effort is better than a longer period with half-hearted involvement. There is no final answer, however. The determination of the optimal length and distribution of practice periods will depend on the age and experience of the individuals, the particular sport involved, the condition of the participants, and the stage of competition.

20. Accuracy and speed are best developed together. As constructive practice proceeds and extraneous movements are eliminated, the simplified motor act will become more and more accurate. At the same time, precision develops and the learner performs with greater speed. Improvement in performance consists of an increase in both accuracy and speed.

"Each sport, each position, each event has its own special requirements of skill, stamina, and courage." (Courtesy of Springfield College.)

21. Drill is an effective way of automatizing fundamental movements. Drill should only be used for the purpose of gaining skill in individual parts of motor patterns and not for the sake of exercise or discipline.

22. The development of personality proceeds along with bodily growth, maturation, and motor learning. The outcomes of educational situations usually are much more diverse than the objectives of the lesson. As one is learning to swim, shoot baskets, play hockey, or dance, personality is formed and inner needs are satisfied.

23. An optimistic, buoyant, and cheerful attitude should be cultivated during class periods and coaching sessions. A confident spirit and a sense of humor will help make practice sessions both enjoyable and productive.

24. Physiological, psychological, and mental conditioning proceed hand in hand and one supports the other. Fatigue destroys confidence, good condition prevents fatigue, mental courage stimulates physical courage, and a confident and zestful spirit makes for positive and purposeful movements.

25. Each athlete should learn how he can best prepare himself mentally for a performance or contest. Some want to lie down and be quiet, others find they need to keep moving. One athlete feels he should concentrate on the coming event, another believes he performs best if he can take his mind off the contest before it begins.

26. A coach must consider mental preparation from several angles. He must be concerned with both individual and group preparation. He must know the amount of arousal each person requires. He also must plan his program as to long-term, intermediate, and immediate mental preparation. The great coach is concerned about the development of an athlete's personality, his physical condition, and his psychological readiness.

The field of psychology is immense. This is in keeping with the infinite complexity of man. Coaches and teachers not only deal with the pragmatic realities of day-to-day lessons and drills but are also concerned with the intangible realm of personality and spirit. They find their work both fascinating and rewarding.

SELECTED REFERENCES

1. Anderson, John E., "Growth and development today: implications for physical education." Paper presented at National Conference on Social Changes and Implications for Physical Education and Sports Recreation," Estes Park, Colorado, June 22–28, 1958.
2. Andrews, Thomas G., and Lee J. Cronbach, "Transfer of training," *The Causes of Behavior II,* 2nd edition, Judy F. Rosenblith and Wesley Allensmith (eds.) Boston: Allyn and Bacon, 1966.
3. Arnold, P. J., *Education, Physical Education and Personality Development,* New York: Atherton Press, 1968.
4. Atkinson, John W., *An Introduction to Motivation,* Princeton, N.J.: D. Van Nostrand Company, 1964.

5. Berkowitz, Leonard, "Sports, competition, and agression," *The Physical Educator,* Vol. 30, No. 2, May 1973.
6. Berkowitz, Leonard, and Bernard I. Levy, "Pride in group performance and group-task motivation," *The Journal of Abnormal and Social Psychology,* Vol. 53, November 1956, pp. 300–306.
7. Berscheid, Ellen, and Elaine H. Walster, *Interpersonal Attraction,* Reading, Mass.: Addison-Wesley Publishing Company, 1969.
8. Betz, Robert L., "A comparison between personality traits and physical fitness tests of males," unpublished master's thesis, University of Illinois, 1953.
9. Clifton, Marguerite A., "The role of perception in movement," *The Academy Papers, No. 1,* The American Academy of Physical Education, March 1968.
10. Cofer, C. N. and M. N. Appley, *Motivation: Theory and Research,* New York: John Wiley and Sons, 1964.
11. Cratty, Bryant J., *Movement Behavior and Motor Learning,* Philadelphia: Lea and Febiger, 1967.
12. _____, *Psychology and Physical Activity,* Englewood Cliffs, N.J.: Prentice-Hall, 1968.
13. Cureton, Thomas K., *The Physiological Effects of Exercise Programs on Adults,* Springfield, Ill.: Charles C Thomas, 1970.
14. Davis, James H., *Group Performance,* Reading, Mass.: Addison-Wesley Publishing Company, 1969.
15. Dinkmeyer, Don C. "Psychology in athletics and physical education," *Journal of Health, Physical Education, and Recreation,* Vol. 17, No. 7, September 1946.
16. Dollard, John, Neal Miller, Leonard Doob, et al., *Frustration and Aggression,* New Haven: The Yale University Press, 1939.
17. Easterbrook, J. A., "The effect of emotion on cue utilization and the organization of behavior," *Psychological Review,* Vol. 66, No. 3, March 1959.
18. Espenschade, Anna S., "Contributions of physical activity to growth," *Research Quarterly,* Vol. 31, May 1960, pp. 351–364.
19. _____, "Perceptual-motor development in children," *The Academy Papers, No. 1,* The American Academy of Physical Education, 1967.
20. Fleishman, Edwin A., "A relationship between incentive motivation and ability level in psychomotor performance," *Journal of Experimental Psychology,* Vol. 56, July 1958, pp. 78–81.
21. Frankl, Viktor E., *Man's Search for Meaning,* New York: Washington Square Press, 1968.
22. Friermood, Harold T., *The YMCA Guide to Adult Fitness,* New York: Association Press, 1963.
23. Friermood, Harold T., and J. Wesley McVicar, *Basic Physical Education in the YMCA,* New York: Association Press, 1962.
24. Frost, Reuben B., "Motivation and arousal," *The Winning Edge,* Washington, D.C.: American Association for Health, Physical Education, and Recreation, 1974.
25. _____, *Psychological Concepts Applied to Physical Education and Coaching,* Reading, Mass.: Addison-Wesley Publishing Company, 1971.
26. _____, "Some psychological implications for Olympic sports," Report of the Fifth Summer Session of the International Olympic Academy, Athens: Hellenic Olympic Committee, 1965.
27. Gardner, Elizabeth B., "The neuromuscular base of human movement: feedback mechanisms," *The Journal of Health, Physical Education, and Recreation,* Vol. 36, No. 8, October 1965.

28. Gordon, Chad, and Kenneth J. Gergen (eds.), *The Self in Social Interaction,* New York: John Wiley and Sons, 1968.
29. Griffith, Coleman R., *Psychology of Athletics,* New York: Charles Scribner's Sons, 1928.
30. Halverson, Lolas E., "Development of motor patterns in young children," *Quest,* National Association for Physical Education of College Women and National College Physical Education Association for Men, Monograph VI, May 1966.
31. Havighurst, Robert J., "Physical education and the tasks of the body," *American Academy of Physical Education,* Professional Contributions Number 5, Washington, D.C.: American Association for Health, Physical Education, and Recreation, 1956.
32. Henry, Franklin M., "Independence of reaction and movement times and equivalence of sensory motivators of faster response," *Research Quarterly,* Vol. 23, March 1952, pp. 43–53.
33. Hubbard, Alfred W., "Perception in sports," *Psicologia Dello Sport,* Proceedings of First International Congress of Sport Psychology, Ferrucio Antonelli (ed.) Rome, 1965.
34. Husman, Burris F., "Sport and personality dynamics," *Proceedings,* The National College Physical Education Association for Men, 1969.
35. "Individual differences, their nature, extent and significance," *Physical Fitness Research Digest,* Series 3, No. 4, October 1973.
36. Johnson, Warren, "A study of emotion revealed in the study of two types of athletic contests," *Research Quarterly,* Vol. 25, December 1964, pp. 484–485.
37. Kane, J. E., "Personality profiles of physical education students compared with others," *Psicologia Dello Sport,* Proceedings of First International Congress of Sport Psychology, Ferrucio Antonelli (ed.), Rome, 1965.
38. Knapp, B., *Skill in Sport,* London: Routledge and Kegan Paul, 1970.
39. Laban, Rudolph, *Modern Educational Dance,* 2nd edition, London: MacDonald and Evans, 1963.
40. Lawther, John D., *The Learning of Physical Skills,* Englewood Cliffs, N.J.: Prentice-Hall, 1968.
41. _____, "Motor learning at the high school level," *Psicologia Dello Sport,* Proceedings of the First International Congress of Sport Psychology, Ferrucio Antonelli (ed.), Rome, 1965.
42. _____, *Sport Psychology,* Englewood Cliffs, N.J.: Prentice-Hall, 1972.
43. Lockhart, Aileene, "Prerequisites to motor learning," *The Academy Papers, No. 1,* The American Academy of Physical Education, March 1968.
44. Maier, Norman R. F., *Frustration,* New York: McGraw-Hill, 1949.
45. Moore, J. W., *The Psychology of Athletic Coaching,* Minneapolis, Minn.: Burgess Publishing Company, 1970.
46. Moore, Roy, "An analysis of modern theoretical approaches to learning with implications for teaching gross motor skills in physical education," unpublished Ph.D. thesis, University of Iowa, 1949.
47. Morgan, William P., *Ergogenic Aids and Muscular Performance,* New York: The Academic Press, 1972.
48. _____, Contemporary Readings in Sport Psychology, Springfield, Ill.: Charles C Thomas, 1972.
49. Neal, Patsy, "Women's attainment and maintenance of championship performance," *The Winning Edge,* American Association for Health, Physical Education, and Recreation, 1974.
50. Ogilvie, Bruce C., and Thomas A. Tutko, *Problem Athletes and How to Handle Them,* London: Pelham Books, 1966.

51. Peck, Robert F. et al., *The Psychology of Character Development,* New York: John Wiley and Sons, 1960.
52. Plutchik, Robert, *The Emotions: Facts, Theories and a New Model,* New York: Random House, 1962.
53. Polidoro, J. Richard, "The affective domain: the forgotten behavioral objective of physical education," *The Physical Educator,* Vol. 30, No. 3, October 1973.
54. Radler, D. H. with Newell C. Kephart, *Success Through Play,* New York: Harper and Row, 1960.
55. Rarick, G. Lawrence, "Exercise and Growth," *Science and Medicine of Exercise and Sports,* Warren R. Johnson (ed.), New York: Harper and Row, 1960.
56. _____, *Physical Activity: Human Growth and Development,* New York: The Academic Press, 1973.
57. Robb, Margaret, "Feedback," *Quest,* The National Association for Physical Education of College Women and The National College Physical Education Association for Men, Monograph VI, May 1966.
58. Robbins, L. L., "Emotional reactions to frustration and failure," *Stress Situations,* Samuel Liebman (ed.), Philadelphia: J. B. Lippincott Company, 1954.
59. Ryan, E. Dean, "Effects of differential motive-incentive conditions on physical performance," *Research Quarterly,* Vol. 32, March 1961, pp. 83–87.
60. Ryan, F. J., "Some aspects of athletic behavior," *Track and Field Quarterly Review,* Ann Arbor, Mich.: United States Track Coaches Association, December 1968.
61. Sage, George H., *Introduction to Motor Behavior,* Reading, Mass.: Addison-Wesley Publishing Company, 1971.
62. Schendel, Jack, "Psychological differences between athletes and nonparticipants in athletics at three educational levels," *Research Quarterly,* Vol. 36, No. 1, March 1965.
63. Singer, Robert N., *Coaching, Athletics and Psychology,* New York: McGraw-Hill, 1972.
64. _____, *Motor Learning and Performance,* New York: The Macmillan Company, 1968.
65. Slusher, Howard S., "Personality and intelligence characteristics of selected high school athletes and non-athletes," *Research Quarterly,* Vol. 35, No. 4, December 1964.
66. Sweeney, Robert T., "Motor learning: implications for movement education," *Selected Readings in Movement Education,* Reading, Mass.: Addison-Wesley Publishing Company, 1971.
67. Tanner, J. M., *The Physique of the Olympic Athlete,* London: Allen and Unwin, 1964.
68. Ulrich, Celeste, and Roger K. Burke, "Effect of motivational stress upon physical performance," *Research Quarterly,* Vo.. 28, December 1957, pp. 403–412.
69. Veller, Don, "Praise or punishment," *Athletic Journal,* Vol. 48, No. 6, February 1968.
70. Walker, LeRoy, "Producing that psychological winning edge," *The Winning Edge,* Washington D.C.: American Association for Health, Physical Education, and Recreation, 1974.
71. Weiner, Melvin, "Psychological factors in physical education activities among teen age girls," *The Physical Educator,* Vol. 25, No. 1, March 1968.
72. Werner, Alfred C., and Edward Gottheil, "Personality development and participation in college athletics," *Research Quarterly,* Vol. 37, No. 1, March 1966.
73. Wilkinson, Robert E., "Effect of various motivational conditions upon boys of different age levels during muscular work," unpublished doctoral dissertation, Springfield College, 1965.

Sociological
Foundations

Chapter 9

9.1 INTRODUCTION

Sociology is the study of people. It deals with their habits and customs, their play and work, their homes and families. It also concerns itself with their interpersonal relationships, both singly and in groups. Sociology delves into culture and history, education and government, social problems and philosophies. Sociology includes a study of power and prestige, poverty and suffering. It is concerned with racial discrimination and social mobility. It studies society's agencies and institutions, the conditions that transform them, and ways of improving them. It is particularly interested in personal interaction in both formal and informal settings.

As has been stated in many different ways, the vitality and life of a people reflect, and are reflected by, the vigorous activities in which they engage and the games they play. The government of a nation and the character of its social institutions reveal much about the play habits of its people and the philosophy of its schools. Likewise, physical education and sports programs give many indications of the health and vigor of a country.

9.2 PHYSICAL EDUCATION AND CULTURE

Günter Erbach, writing about the science of sports sociology, indicates that physical culture and sport are an integral part of social culture and that they reflect the achievement of physical perfection and development of the physical prowess of mankind. Each individual's aspiration to lead a life which includes healthful cultural and sports activity is, he said, necessary for a humanistic physical culture. [15, p. 237]

Once again we see the necessity of looking at mankind as a unified and integrated entity where complete development and fulfillment can take place. Only as all human dimensions are given the freedom and opportunity to grow and mature to the limits of their potential will such development and fulfillment occur. This is the essence of the heritage which physical educators wish to transmit to future generations as part of our culture.

That physical education and sport have been elements of significance in all human cultures hardly needs any documentation. Authors and speakers attest to that fact and no one has come forth to seriously challenge it. The very nature of humanity lends emphasis to the universality of the play spirit and the urge to compete and excel.

People are both the creators and the products of their culture. Habits, customs, songs, and thoughts are transmitted from generation to generation both by accident and by intent. At the same time new rules are added to old games, new games are invented, new purposes are served by prescribed exercises, and new environments require new biological adjustments.

Social culture does influence both attitudes and behavior. Except in times of social revolution, most of the practices frowned upon by the new generation become only passing fads and the traditions of parents are, for the most part, carried on by the children. At the same time new songs and games, or new adaptations of old ones, come into being. Influences are added so that the culture of the new generation is enriched and modified as it replaces the old one.

Physical education and sport in the United States are influenced by many cultures. The *Turnverein* from Germany, the *Sokol* movement from Czechoslovakia, skiing from Norway, judo from Asia, spas from East Germany, yoga from India, and folk dances from scores of countries are cultural activities which are exerting their influences on physical education in our society. Basketball and volleyball, on the other hand, are examples of games invented here which have spread throughout the world to other cultures.

The study of the cultural milieu in which it takes place is necessary if one is to understand physical education. The same can be said for other aspects of a society. All physical educators and coaches, if they wish to be successful and productive, should examine the traditions, customs, religious beliefs, and ethnic backgrounds of the people in their communities, for without such knowledge communication may be difficult and desirable interrelationships seriously hindered.

Broom ball   Curling

"All physical educators and coaches . . . should examine the traditions, customs, religious beliefs, and ethnic backgrounds of the people in their communities, . . ." (Courtesy of the *Journal of Health, Physical Education, and Recreation.*)

9.3 PRIMARY GROUPS AND SPORT

Sociologists, in analyzing societal phenomena, speak of primary and secondary groups. *Primary groups* are those in which intimate face-to-face association occurs. It is a "kinship" group characterized by mutual identification, common purposes, a feeling of unity, and a sense of "we-ness."

A *secondary group,* on the other hand, has formal, impersonal rules and institutional characteristics. Duties are clearly prescribed, and relationships are generally impersonal, unemotional, and objective.

A collegiate basketball team is a good example of a primary group. Players have a common goal, see each other daily on a face-to-face basis, all identify with a certain school, succeed or fail together, and, if the right spirit exists, have a sense of cameraderie and personal intimacy which can only come from shared experiences and an acceptance of one another as they are.

Because sports, and particularly team sports, are primary groups in which such personal relationships exist, the probability of considerable influence is great. Not only will peer-group influences play a significant role, but there is a good possibility that players will identify with the coach or with one of their "superstars."

Teams which are comparatively stable will exhibit primary relationships to a greater extent than will those in existence for a day or even a month. Team members who practice together daily, travel together on trips, and have basically the same personnel for two years or more are most apt to display such primary interpersonal relationships. This behavior only emphasizes the importance of having the right kind of leadership and a good overall environment. It also suggests that membership on a varsity team is likely to have a greater influence on personality and character than is membership on a team that meets once a week and then dissolves at the end of the season.

9.4 THE DEVELOPMENT OF VALUES*

The entire concept of character education, i.e., the development of personal and ethical values through education, rests on the assumption that something can be learned in one situation and applied in another. This makes the concept of transfer crucial. Thomas Andrews and Lee Cronbach in 1950 summarized their thinking on this matter as follows:

> *Transfer of a previously acquired behavior-pattern to a new situation will occur whenever an individual recognizes the new situation as similar to the situation for which the behavior was learned.* We have therefore swung through a cycle, from blind assumption that transfer is widespread, through a period of skepticism when transfer was expected only in the narrowest specific knowledge and habits, to a theory which looks on transfer as common and to be expected, provided certain conditions are met. [2, p. 1483]

---

*See also Chapter 10, Section 10.4, "Educating for Values" and Chapter 16, "Human Values and Personal Ethics."

Even though a few repudiate this position, athletes and coaches who themselves have been deeply involved in sports for many years generally attest to the
positive character-building influence of sports. It is generally agreed that much
depends on leadership. If the influence is due to the primary relationships in the
group and identification with the coach, the importance of the leader's set of
values and his behavior patterns becomes crucial.

Coaches and physical educators, like any other teachers, can influence the
character of those with whom they come in contact. They can call attention to
unacceptable behavior patterns and suggest ways of changing them. They can
assist the students and athletes to identify identical or similar elements in other
situations. They can teach students how to generalize and intellectualize. They can
set examples worthy of emulation. They can try to establish personal relationships
which provide a favorable atmosphere for the inculcation of sound values.

Character development occurs largely in the first ten to twelve years of a
person's life. After that age it is more difficult to influence personality and behavior.
Personal, dramatic, and intense situations will have more impact than routine
experiences. Because sports abound with emotional and personal experiences, it
is plausible that the opportunities in sports for the development of desirable character traits and behavior patterns are numerous. Coaches and physical education
teachers should recognize these opportunities and be constantly prepared for the
"teachable moment."

Because of the informal and intimate interpersonal relationships so frequently found when coaching and teaching physical education, many students and
athletes confront their teachers and coaches with personal problems. These problems may be related to their academic achievement, boy/girl relationships, or lack
of ability to achieve physically. Occasionally students need money; sometimes
they run afoul of the law. In all such situations, opportunities exist for wise guidance
and informal counseling. The influences of coaches and teachers in such instances are manifold and provide a rich field for learning important lessons about
values.

9.5 COMPETITION AND COOPERATION

Conquering is a form of achieving and appears, in Western culture at least, to be
a natural goal. Winning is a form of conquering and is glorified, sometimes out of
proportion to its real significance. The desire to be superior to someone else can
easily be overemphasized, particularly if it does physical or psychological harm to
the opponent. The urge to surpass, surmount, and excel is characteristic of almost
everyone and is a natural form of motivation. The desire to run faster, throw farther,
jump higher and be "the best" is normal and praiseworthy.

Competition in and by itself is neither good nor bad. Actually, competition is
often dependent upon cooperation. Intragroup cooperation is necessary when
competing in team sports. Many individuals who score high on competitiveness do
likewise when tested for willingness to cooperate. Intragroup competitiveness can
act as a hindrance to team achievement. Cooperation is often called upon to serve
competition.

Competition with oneself has general approval. Both within and outside of the school environment people are encouraged to grow more, learn more, and achieve more. Many educators feel that there has been too much comparison between persons and that tests should be utilized to measure each person's improvement, not to see which individual is best or greatest.

"Cooperation is often called upon to serve competition."
(Courtesy, Scholastic Photography Awards sponsored by Eastman Kodak Company.)

In athletic situations it has become accepted practice to strive to win. This should be done by aiming for one's best possible performance and doing everything possible to excel. If all competitors do this, there will be no humiliation upon defeat and no feeling of guilt or shame when vanquished. Sportsmen generally agree that they want their opponents to do their best and resent playing against a superior opponent who does not put forth his full effort.

If there are some practices in athletics which are wrong, the answer lies not in doing away with competition but in correcting the evils. For meaningful athletic competition, opponents should be matched as evenly as possible. Rules and regulations should be strictly obeyed and no one should be permitted to win by unfair means.

One can, of course, compete with the environment. To climb a mountain, ski down a hill, swim across a lake, or run rapids in a canoe are competitive activities. One can conquer an obstacle, overcome personal fears, or discover hidden personal resources. This kind of competition, unless carried to reckless extremes, is certainly commendable. It also leads a person toward ultimate self-realization.

9.6 VICARIOUS PARTICIPATION

Not everyone can participate actively in sport. Not everyone can be on a varsity team. There are many who, even though they do participate in some sports, spend a good deal of time either attending athletic events or watching them on television. Unless overdone, this can be worthwhile expenditure of time. If one can relax, enjoy himself, and identify with individuals or teams, it can be a healthful and renewing experience. For this reason opportunities to learn fundamentals and game tactics should be afforded as many as possible so that they may appreciate the contest to the fullest extent. Vicarious participation, which takes the mind off one's troubles, can be recreative and constructive.

"Vicarious participation, which takes the mind off one's troubles, can be recreative and constructive." (Courtesy of Springfield College.)

9.7 SOCIOECONOMIC STATUS AND PHYSICAL EDUCATION
Family environment and socioeconomic status influence the choice of physical education activities and partially determine the opportunities for participation in sport. Money in considerable quantity is normally required to participate in such activities as snowmobiling, deep-sea diving, skiing, horseback riding, and golf. Other sports including tennis, mountain climbing, bowling, and sailing are also often unavailable to the poor.

Young people growing up in the crowded inner city are usually forced to play outside, making the streets their playground. In ghetto areas, large numbers of girls and boys of all ages, can be found engaged in a variety of both informal and organized games. Some are wrestling, romping, and chasing. Others are playing a version of basketball, volleyball, or football. They compete, interact, and give free vent to their feelings as they scamble, fight, laugh, and play.

Children from wealthy homes often have tennis courts, swimming pools, and pool tables in their homes. They also are members of country clubs, are sent to summer camps, and can afford to travel to ski lodges and beaches. It is not strange, therefore, that many of our best basketball and football players come from the inner city while many of the tennis and golf stars grow up in wealthy environments.

Socioeconomic status does influence the opportunities which people have to participate in certain sports. On the other hand, success in sports may also affect one's socioeconomic status. An increasing number of young people who grew up in poverty, but who have been very successful in sports, immediately find that their socioeconomic status has improved. Many are chosen to play professional football, baseball, or basketball and a few become boxers, golfers, or tennis players. In such instances, sport has increased their upward social mobility as well as their economic status.

9.8 GIRLS AND WOMEN IN SPORTS
As the furor over varsity athletics for girls and women subsides, we see such programs more and more firmly established in schools and colleges. The values which are inherent in sports for men are equally important for the full and well-rounded education of women. Girls with special aptitude and interest in this field of endeavor should have the opportunity to pursue it to the fullest extent. Furthermore, the role of women in our society is changing and competitive experiences are as meaningful to members of the female sex as they are to males. The traditional image of the tender, loving woman who tends the home and bears children has now changed considerably, particularly in Western societies. An increasing number of women are now working in positions formerly reserved for men and are sharing responsibilities for making a living, running the government, and working at some phase of community development.

It is now well agreed that healthy women will not be harmed by participation in vigorous sports. The anatomical and physiological differences between men and women (see Chapter 6) cannot be applied indiscriminately, as there are many women who possess greater physical aptitude and ability than many men.

One must be careful about assuming "causation" when dealing with personality traits for either sex. Some psychologists have stated that successful female athletes are more competitive than the average nonparticipant. This, of course, can also be said of males. Whether participation in competitive sport *develops* certain personality characteristics such as determination, courage, competitiveness, dominance, and extroversion, or whether people who already possess such traits become great athletes, is the question. It is relatively easy to test large numbers of participants and nonparticipants and compare differences or relate the presence of personality characteristics to successful performances. It will take many years of tedious, longitudinal research to determine changes which occur during participation. The best guess now is that there are latent and inherited characteristics which are brought out by challenging, vigorous, and demanding sport.

Sociologically the question seems to be whether or not girls can compete in high-level sports and still retain their "feminine image." Many parents, as well as the girls themselves, are concerned about this. Fortunately the picture in our society is changing. Observers agree that top female athletes are at least as feminine as the average nonathletic female. Some fitness proponents claim that the development of good muscle tone enhances the female figure and the image of femininity. The stereotype of the "athletic amazon" is not only unfortunate, but an actual misnomer.

It is obvious that the female and male roles are influenced greatly by the fact that it is the female who must bear and nurture the young. It is probable, as has been the case in most cultures, that the home will continue to be tended primarily by the female and that more males than females will be able to devote a great deal of time to the pursuit of sport. Cultural norms, too, have made participation in sport more meaningful to and desired by boys than girls during adolescence. This phenomenon is, at least in part, culturally induced and may change as more and more girls participate; indeed, the courts in several states have upheld girls' right to participate in such formerly all-boy activities as the Little League.

Madge Phillips concluded her presentation at a national conference on women and sport with this pertinent paragraph:

> The enthusiasm we have for sport, the belief we share that the purpose of sport is for the good of those who play, and our desire to understand the complexities of the sporting situation are all factors which should make it highly possible for the researchers to work cooperatively with the action-oriented practitioners. If the performance criteria approach invades the world of women's sports, let us make sure we do not make winning the only thing or even the most important thing. Let us stress the sociological aspect of sport. [46, p. 199]

Kathryn Johnson, speaking at The National Conference on Values Through Sports, summarized her remarks with regard to the participation of men and women, boys and girls, with and against each other in these words:

If, on the other hand, we want to encourage the appreciation of the varying contributions of individuals regardless of sex, and their cooperation with each other in reaching shared goals, such as in family life, we should perhaps consider putting them on the same teams where group loyalties, cooperation and rivalries develop in terms of interests, skills and shared goals rather than on the arbitrary basis of sex. [24, p. 52]

In any event, girls as well as boys, women as well as men, need opportunities for expressing themselves in free, vigorous movement. They also need the fun and joy that comes from playing games with and against others. The two sexes will benefit equally from hiking in the hills, canoeing in the waters, driving the golf ball, playing a hard game of tennis, and many more such sports in which the individual becomes completely involved and which he or she thoroughly enjoys.

9.9 RACE AND PHYSICAL EDUCATION

Much has been written about race and sport, but little has been said about race and physical education. Since sport is an aspect of physical education, we shall include both in our discussion. There is not much to say about race and the curricular aspects of physical education that is not just a reiteration of what can be said about education as a whole. The biological, psychological, and sociological values of physical activity are essentially the same for all races. The problems of racial discrimination are much the same in physical education as in other courses. There are, however, many opportunities for positive, constructive behavior on the part of coaches and teachers of physical education. Educational deprivation among those who have been reared in ghettos is less evident in physical education than in other classes. Care must therefore be exercised to see that all students regardless of race, color, creed, or socioeconomic status, are treated equally and that there is no legitimate cause for bringing up the issue of discrimination. A casual environment in which impartiality and equal opportunity is taken for granted should be the goal.

In George Sage's book, *Sport and American Society,* there is an article by Judith Williams and Roland Scott entitled "Growth and Development of Negro Infants." The authors hypothesize that motor development in the early stages is not a function of race but rather of the individual's early environment. They found that black infants from low socioeconomic backgrounds and environments which were more permissive and accepting showed significantly greater motor development or acceleration than did those from more affluent homes where the atmosphere was more exacting and demanding. They interpreted this to mean that early environment rather than race was the significant factor in early motor development. [37, p. 270]

It has been obvious in recent years even to the casual observer that black athletes have been unusually successful in the world of sport. In the United States, the number of black athletes who have excelled in football, basketball, baseball, boxing, and track and field has been far out of proportion to the ratio of blacks to whites in the population. Many theories have been propounded to explain this. Anatomical and physiological characteristics have been examined, measured, and analyzed. Performances have been compared. Statistical analyses have been conducted. Opinions of anthropologists, physiologists, psychologists, and sociologists have been sought. Tentative conclusions have been explored.

Harry Edwards, in his article entitled "The Myth of the Racially Superior Athlete," has written a highly intelligent and analytical treatise in which he reviews the claims for physiological, psychological, and sociological determinants. He then states:

> What then are the major factors underlying black athletic superiority? They emerge from a complex of societal conditions. These conditions instill a heightened motivation among black male youths to achieve success in sports; thus, they channel a proportionately greater number of talented black people than whites into sports participation. Our best sociological evidence indicates that capacity for physical achievement (like other common human traits such as intelligence, artistic ability, etc.) is evenly distributed throughout any population. Thus, it cuts across class, religious, and, more particularly, racial lines. For race, like class and religion, is primarily a culturally determined classification. *The simple fact of the matter is that the scientific concept of race has no proven biological or genetic validity.* As a cultural delineation, however, it does have a social and political reality. This social and political reality of race is the primary basis of stratification in this society and the key means of determining the priority of who shall have access to means and thus, valued goods and services.
>
> Blacks are relegated in this country to the lowest priority in terms of valued goods and services. This fact, however, does not negate the equal and proportionate distribution of talent across both black and white populations. Hence, a situation arises wherein whites, being the dominant group in the society, have access to *all* means toward achieving desirable valuables defined by the society. Blacks, on the other hand, are channeled into the one or two endeavors open to them—sports, and to a lesser degree—entertainment. . . .
>
> It takes just as much talent, perseverance, dedication and earnest effort to succeed in sports as to become a leading financier, business executive, attorney or doctor. Few occupations (music and art being perhaps the exceptions) demand more time and dedication than sports. A world-class athlete will usually have spent a good deal of his youth practicing the skills and techniques of his chosen sport.
>
> The competition for the few positions is extremely keen and if he is fortunate he will survive in that competition long enough to become a professional athlete or an outstanding figure in one of the amateur sports. For as he moves up through the various levels of competition, fewer and fewer slots or positions are available and the competition for these becomes increasingly intense because the rewards are greater. Since the talents of 25 million Afro-Americans have a disproportionately higher concentration in sports, the number of highly gifted whites in sports is proportionately less. Under such

circumstances, black athletes naturally predominate. Further, the white athletes who do participate in sports operate at a psychological disadvantage
because they believe blacks to be inherently superior as athletes. [14]

Carl Rowan agreed that physical characteristics do not account for the disproportionate number of blacks who are successful athletes. He concluded his
study by indicating that the factors which lead to black superiority in sports are "the
desire to succeed in the white world, the tendency to follow successful examples,
the expression of pent-up aggression, the pressure to make good, desire and more
desire, the thing called 'soul force' . . ." [18, p. 165] The author contends that in
this situation, as in so many others, there may be both genetic and environmental
factors involved and that it is impossible to ascribe, with any degree of certainty,
the causative variables.

9.10 SOCIOLOGICAL CONCEPTS AND PRINCIPLES
There are many sociological principles not mentioned above that have significant
implications for physical education and sport:

1. Sports always have, and still do, furnish a rallying point, a focus for loyalties,
and a source of institutional, community, and national pride. This can serve to unify
groups and build an inner strength sorely needed in times of stress. When a
community unites in a common cause, results can be constructive both in terms
of the objectives accomplished and in terms of improved interpersonal relationships.

2. During the excitement of closely fought contests, the audience may revert
to primitive emotions and behavior. Partisan spectators cannot view objectively the
actions and decisions of players and officials. It is important for all to recognize
this phenomenon and to realize that, even in times of strife, there must be an
adherence to rules and an appreciation for regulations.

3. Coaches and teachers must understand the influence of peers on students'
behavior. What might appear to one teacher as mean and reprehensible behavior
is often tolerated by others who are more aware of the priorities which control
students' actions, particularly during adolescence.

4. High in the hierarchy of educational objectives must be the continual improvement of interpersonal relations. This must be considered when planning
curricula, conducting classes, and counseling students.

5. Group cohesiveness is the essential ingredient of teamwork. True teamwork
consists of doing either individually or as a team that which maximizes progress
toward the goal.

6. Teachers and coaches of sports should try to provide opportunities in which
participants may identify with each other. Some of these should be in situations
other than those in which they are actually playing and competing.

7. Natural grouping will ordinarily make for more cohesiveness than forced
grouping. This is an important principle in conducting intramural programs.

8. The family environment appears to be a key factor in determining an individu-

al's attitude toward sport and physical education. This, in most instances, has been found to exert a greater influence than ethnic background or socioeconomic status.

9. An individual's view of the expectations of peers and respected authority figures, as well as the way he perceives his role under certain circumstances, has a great influence on his behavior under those circumstances. Parents, teachers, and coaches who are aware of this will be better leaders than those who disregard it.

10. Most athletes are aware of the interest and spirit of their audience. Anxious athletes may be overstimulated and perform poorly; veteran athletes usually perform better when they sense a spirited and partisan crowd. The nature of the activity and the experience of the contestants should be considered when planning mental preparation of athletes for a contest.

11. Communication does exist between athletes and the audience in most situations. The phenomenon of momentum is an example. When the crowd is excited by an exceptional athletic feat, a sudden surge on the part of a team, or a violent encounter of one sort or another, the feelings engendered are reflected in the roar of the crowd, the hush of expectation, or the cheering of the fans. There is communication, back and forth, between audience and players, crowd and team.

12. Group self-determination is one of the important tenets of a democracy. This suggests that teams have a voice in determining training rules, students be heard with regard to curriculum changes, and that interests as well as needs be considered in the formulation of programs.

13. Equalization of opportunity implies that there will be activities geared to the abilities of the physically inept, that the gifted athletes will be afforded opportunities to reach their potential, and that extensive programs will be provided for the masses whose abilities are somewhere between those of the "star" and those of the "dub."

14. Good teachers and coaches will recognize opportunities to assist those who exhibit deviant behavior. They will try to make the activities so meaningful and so worthy of complete involvement that they will supercede, in interest, the bad habits, maladjusted behavior, and aggressive tendencies that have culminated in a social and violent conduct.

15. Delbert Oberteuffer has summarized the principles of social adjustment in these meaningful words, with which we conclude this chapter:

> In summary, it should be clear that physical education programs must be responsive to the character and quality of the lives of the people for whom they are developed. Physical education programs are distinctly out of line when they teach one thing and the political or social temper of the people believes another. Wherever physical education is developed, in whatever country, the teacher should study the beliefs and customs of the people, the traditions and concepts affecting human life, and then gear the program of physical education to the perpetuation of the best and principal ones of these. [33, p. 236]

SELECTED REFERENCES

1. Anderson, Don R., "Sports and games as socio-cultural outgrowths," *The Physical Educator,* Vol. 30, No. 3, October 1973.
2. Andrews, Thomas G., and Lee J. Cronbach, "Transfer of training," *Encyclopedia of Educational Research,* W. S. Monroe (ed.), revised edition, New York: The Macmillan Company, 1950.
3. Arnold, P. J., *Physical Education and Personality Development,* New York: Atherton Press, 1968.
4. Bookwalter, Karl W., and Harold J. VanderZwaag, *Foundations and Principles of Physical Education,* Philadelphia: W. B. Saunders Company, 1969.
5. Bouet, Michel, "The function of sport in human relations," *International Review of Sport Sociology,* Vol. 1, 1966.
6. Broom, Leonard, and Philip Selznick, *Sociology,* Evanston, Ill.: Row Peterson and Company, 1958.
7. Bucher, Charles A., *Foundations of Physical Education,* 4th edition, St. Louis: The C. V. Mosby Company, 1964.
8. Cassidy, Rosalind, "The cultural definition of physical education," *Quest,* Monograph IV, April 1965.
9. Conant, James B., *Slums and Suburbs,* New York: The New American Library, 1961.
10. Cozens, F. W., and Florence Stumpf, *Sports in American Life,* Chicago: University of Chicago Press, 1953.
11. Cratty, Bryant J., *Social Dimensions of Physical Activity,* Englewood Cliffs, N.J.: Prentice-Hall, 1967.
12. *Crisis of Survival, The,* Madison, Wisc.: The Progressive, 1970.
13. Davis, Howard, "Physical education and its contribution to equality in education," *Journal of Physical Education,* Vol. 70, No. 5, May–June 1973.
14. Edwards Harry, "The myth of the racially superior athlete," *The Black Scholar.* Reprinted by permission.
15. Erbach, Günter, "The science of sport and sports sociology—questions related to development—problems of structure," *Dimensions of Physical Education,* Charles A. Bucher and Myra Goldman (eds.), St. Louis: The C. V. Mosby Company, 1969.
16. Fairs, John R., "The influence of Plato and Platonism on the development of physical education in western culture," *Quest,* Monograph XI, December 1968.
17. Frederickson, Florence S., "Sports and cultures of man," *Science and Medicine of Exercise and Sports,* Warren R. Johnson (ed.), New York: Harper and Row, 1960.
18. Frost, Reuben B., *Psychological Concepts Applied to Physical Education and Coaching,* Reading, Mass.: Addison-Wesley Publishing Company, 1971.
19. _____, "What will physical education be like in 1977?," *Journal of Health, Physical Education, and Recreation,* Vol. 39, March 1968.
20. Gallico, Paul, *Farewell to Sport,* New York: Pocket Books, 1945.
21. Hart, M. Marie, *Sport in the Socio-Cultural Process,* Dubuque, Iowa: Wm. C. Brown Company, 1972.
22. Jensen, Judy, "Sport in poetry," *Quest,* Monograph XVI, June 1971.
23. Jernigan, Sara S., *Playtime: A World Recreation Handbook,* New York: McGraw-Hill, 1972.
24. Johnson, Kathryn P., "Human values through sports, a sociological perspective," in *Development of Human Values through Sports,* Washington, D.C.: American Alliance for Health, Physical Education, and Recreation, 1974.

25. Kluckhohn, Clyde, "The American culture," *Background Readings in Physical Education,* Ann Peterson and Edmund C. Hallberg (ed.), New York: Holt, Rinehart, and Winston, 1967.
26. Kraus, Richard, *Recreation and Leisure in Modern Society,* New York: Appleton-Century-Crofts, 1971.
27. Loy, John W., Jr., and Gerald S. Kenyon (eds.), *Sport, Culture and Society,* New York: The Macmillan Company, 1969.
28. Maheu, Rene, "Sport and culture," *International Journal of Adult and Youth Education,* Vol. 14, No. 4, 1962.
29. Martens, Ranier, "A social psychology of physical activity," *Quest,* Monograph XIV, June 1970.
30. McIntosh, P. C., *Sport in Society,* London: C. A. Watts and Company, 1963.
31. Mead, Margaret, "The challenge of automation to education for human values," *Automation, Education and Human Values,* William W. Brickman and Stanley Lehrer (eds.), New York: School and Society Books, 1966.
32. Merrill, Francis E., *Society and Culture,* 4th edition, Englewood Cliffs, N.J.: Prentice-Hall, 1969.
33. Oberteuffer, Delbert, *Physical Education,* New York: Harper and Row, 1956. Reprinted by permission.
34. Reich, Charles A., *The Greening of America,* New York: Bantam Books, 1970.
35. Ridini, Leonard M., "Physical education for the inner city," *The Physical Educator,* Vol. 28, No. 4, December 1971.
36. Ross, Edward A., *Social Psychology,* New York: The Macmillan Company, 1919.
37. Sage, George H. (ed.), *Sport and American Society: Selected Readings,* Reading, Mass. Addison-Wesley Publishing Company, 1970.
38. Scott, Jack, *Athletics for Athletes,* Hayward, Calif.: Quality Printing Service, 1969.
39. Seidel, Beverly L., and Matthew C. Resick, *Physical Education: An Overview,* Reading, Mass.: Addison-Wesley Publishing Company, 1972.
40. Smith, Michael, Stanley Parker, and Cyril Smith (eds.), *Leisure and Society in Britain,* London: Allen Lane, 1973.
41. Toffler, Alvin, *Future Shock,* New York: Random House, 1970.
42. Ullman, Albert D., *Sociocultural Foundations of Personality,* Boston: Houghton Mifflin Company, 1965.
43. Ulrich, Celeste, *The Social Matrix of Physical Education,* Englewood Cliffs, N.J.: Prentice-Hall, 1968.
44. *Values in Sports,* Joint National Conference of the Division for Girls' and Women's Sports and the Division of Men's Athletics, Washington, D.C.: American Association for Health, Physical Education, and Recreation, 1962.
45. VanderZwaag, Harold J., *Toward a Philosophy of Sport,* Reading, Mass.: Addison-Wesley Publishing Company, 1972.
46. *Women and Sport: A National Research Conference,* Dorothy V. Harris (ed.), Proceedings from the National Research Conference, Pennsylvania State University, August 13–18, 1972. Reprinted by permission.
47. Woods, S. M., "The violent world of the athlete," *Quest,* Monograph XVI, June 1971.
48. *Young School Leavers,* School's Council Enquiry No. 1, London: Her Majesty's Stationery Office, 1967.
49. Young, Michael, and Peter Wilmot, *The Symmetrical Family,* London: Routledge and Kegan Paul, 1973.

Sports,
Athletics,
and Education

Chapter 10

10.1 SPORT

Sport is, in truth, a kaleidoscope. It exhibits an infinite variety of human emotions, movements, triumphs, defeats, and fantastic exploits.

Two books, *The Year in Sports** and *Man in Sport,*† contain incredible pictures of some of the experiences and achievements of sportsmen in various parts of the world. There are pictured in these two books over 400 stirring scenes depicting joy and disappointment, intensity and relaxation, beauty and violence, struggle and victory. There are also portrayed many nearly unbelievable feats of skill, daring, strength, and courage. The colorful and beautiful scene of the surfer breasting a wave at sunset, the picture of the six intense jockeys and their spirited horses bursting out of the starting gate, and the portrayal of the crew sailing the *Vim* at a precarious angle in America's Cup Trials are examples. We see also the supple body of the Olympic butterfly competitor, the cyclist winning the plaudits of the onlookers as he arrives in a snowstorm to finish the British Cross Country Championship, and the yellow kayak in the slalom race in the Colorado River rapids. There is the tragic scene in Monaco where two race cars are in flames after the crash. Three climbers rest on a flower-covered hillside looking at their ultimate goal, the crest of the Matterhorn, the boatsman executes his "counterweight to windward" in the Larchmont Spring Regatta. And there is the triumphant demonstration of Abidi Bikila and his well-wishers after he won the Olympic Marathon.

As one leafs through these pictures, one pauses to look again at the incredibly perfect and beautiful photograph of the young lady diving into a pool at Princeton, one reviews the shot of Wilma Rudolph as she finishes the anchor leg of the relay in beautiful form, and one wonders what is going on in the minds of the two competitors as Roger Bannister crosses the finish line barely ahead of John Landy in the sub-four-minute mile at Vancouver.

As one leafs further through the books, one sees Vince Lombardi speaking with intensity and conviction as he gives his Green Bay Packers final instructions. A poignant picture shows Rafer Johnson and C. K. Yang embracing in complete exhaustion and affection after the decathlon 1500-meter race. Cheerleaders are shown in tears after their high school basketball team went down in defeat in a state tournament. Raphael Pardo is caught in an unusual gyration as he completes a backward overhead kick in a Colombia-Peru soccer contest. And Bob Sauls on water skis is caught off balance heading for a big splash as he soars over a jump and his tow rope breaks.

There are pictures of baseball stars leaping for line drives, sliding into bases, and arguing intensely with umpires and opponents. Basketball is shown replete with unbelievable contortions of the human body. Players are squirming for shots, diving for loose balls, falling into crowds, exploding upward for rebounds, and piling up on the floor in their efforts to score or defend.

The Year in Sports, 1958 edition, Ted Smits (ed.), Englewood Cliffs, N. J.: Prentice-Hall, 1957.

†*Man in Sport,* Robert Riger, Director, The Baltimore Museum of Art, 1967.

Few sports provide more action or emotion than boxing. Pictures of knockouts, cuts and gashes, vicious punches, and uncontrolled spectator aggressiveness are evidence of the action and emotion involved.

There are the beauty and rhythm of the figure skaters, the"loneliness of the cross country runners," the intensity of the curlers, the skill of the fencers, the gloating of the successful fisherman, the teamwork of horse and rider, the rough-and-tumble of ice hockey, and the bruising action, teamwork, and drive found especially in American football.

Even these pictures, however, do not tell all because sport is many different things to many different people. To some it is the peace and tranquility of a hike on a secluded mountain path; to many it is the relaxation and vicarious experience of watching an athletic contest; to a number it is the challenge of jumping incredible distances on skis; to others it may be diving off the cliffs at Acapulco; to all it is absorption and personal involvement in an activity that satisfies one or more needs —biological, psychological, or spiritual. To most people it is also a step toward the realization of self as they commit themselves to such "re-creative" and self-expressive experiences. Paul Gallico, in *Farewell to Sport,* summed up his observations this way:

> I have for these past years had a ringside seat where men and women have, with their bodies, performed the greatest prodigies ever recorded. It was an incredible period, this dizzy, spinning, sports reel of athletes, events, records, personalities, drama, and speed, a geared-up, whirling, golden world in which a lifetime was lived in five years, or sometimes it seemed even overnight, as heroes and heroines, champions and challengers, burst upon the scene, shone like exploding star shells, and often vanished as quickly. [42]

Sport is a human drama of human life. Sport is deep involvement, a response to an urgent need, a challenge met, a game played. It is a struggle of people against people or people against nature. As Arnold Kaech says, ". . . in true sport the performance is not an end in itself—nor the body either—but the means of expression. Moving over the ground, thrusting through the wave, gliding over the snowy slopes, or wrestling with the rock face—these are expressions of the joy of life itself. . . ." Because sport is one thing to one person and another thing to another, it defies definition.

10.2 SPORT AS EDUCATION
Sport may or may not be education depending on the purposes to which it is put. Certainly it includes experiences which modify the human organism. Surely the media employed in physical education classes to achieve desired objectives include it. Educational outcomes do accrue, either wittingly or unwittingly, from participation in sports. A game of soccer may be simply sport to the sixth-grade child who is playing with exuberance for the sheer joy of it, but it is education to the teacher who has planned this class activity with educational goals in mind.

In the United States, England, and some other countries, sports constitute a major block of the activities included in most physical education curricula. This is especially true at the upper-elementary, junior high school, high school, and college levels. Sport does have educational outcomes. If it is vigorous in nature such as in soccer, skiing, or basketball it will lead to the development of cardiovascular endurance. If it demands daring and courage as in white-water canoeing or gymnastics, those qualities will be tested and brought out. If skill and finesse are required as in badminton, tennis, or archery, special neuromuscular skills will be developed. Where education for later life is the goal, swimming, golf, and canoeing may be chosen.

Sport can therefore be a legitimate subject, contributing toward educational goals. To those who participate purely for fun and joy, however, the thrills involved, or the opportunity to express their innermost feelings, sport is sport and they participate for sport's sake. This is not only legitimate—it is exhilarating.

Sport and society

Because people who participate in sports form a segment of any given society, obviously there is a relationship between the two. It also is reasonable that it is easier to practice competitive sports in an upright and honest manner in a climate of integrity than in an atmosphere which is grossly materialistic and corrupt. In a speech entitled "Sport and Society: At Odds or in Concert," Gerald Kenyon examined the relationship between our current society and sport. His conclusion bears repeating:

> . . . sport, as a large part of it exists today, is for the most part, "in concert" with society. It must be since it *is* society. As such, however, sport is "at odds" with an ideology with which it used to be identified—an ideology, however noble, of a different era. Thus sport can hardly be claimed as a shaper of society. Ignoring this fact is failing to recognize that as society goes, so goes sport.*

It seems, therefore, that it would be erroneous to blame the ills of society on what is happening in sports and athletics and that it would be equally wrong to place the responsibility for everything that is awry in sport on a sick society. The problem of correcting the faults and improving the practices found in athletics is part of the age-old struggle between good and evil, and everyone involved must share in the responsibilities and the outcomes. As Earle Zeigler said:

---

*Kenyon, Gerald S., "Sports and society: at odds or in concert?" in *Athletics in America,* Flath, Arnold (ed.), Corvallis, Oregon: Oregon State University Press, 1972.

◀ "Sport is deep involvement, a response to an urgent need, a challenge met, a game played." (Courtesy of (*top and bottom left*) Springfield College, and (*bottom right*) the *Journal of Health, Physical Education, and Recreation.*)

Thus, you should decide upon your own hierarchy of educational values in this pluralistic society, and then attempt to bring them to pass for yourself, for your family and friends, and most definitely for all citizens within the framework of our evolving democratic society on this continent in a rapidly changing world. [101, p. 86]

"If it is vigorous in nature . . . it will lead to the development of cardiovascular endurance." (FX2) San Francisco, California, May 20—At the start—John Farrington, from Australia (4016), takes long strides at the start of the annual Bay-to-Breakers race in San Francisco, Sunday morning. Behind Farrington, with beard and U.S. on chest, is Ken Moore, five-time previous winner of the 7.8-mile event. (AP WIREPHOTO) (dll205red) 1973.

10.3 ATHLETICS IN EDUCATIONAL SETTINGS

Athletics is a program of sports organized systematically for competitive experiences over a substantial period of time. There are intramural, extramural, interscholastic, and intercollegiate athletic programs. *Intramural* athletics is that in which teams or individuals within a given institution play against each other. *Extramural* athletics consists of games and contests between loosely organized teams and individuals of different institutions but which are not part of the highly organized interscholastic or intercollegiate structure. *Interscholastic* athletics consists of organized competition between teams or individuals representing secondary schools. *Intercollegiate* athletics consists of highly organized competition between teams and individuals from colleges and universities.

Essentially the same rationale can be used when discussing athletics and education as was employed above when dealing with sport and education. When athletics is thought of as part of the curriculum, when it occurs in an educational setting, when it is administered by educators, and when it is conducted so as to achieve educational aims and objectives, it is education. The problem is that extraneous influences, outside pressures, materialistic philosophies, and selfish motives intrude on the thinking of administrators and coaches and distort athletic practices. Only high ideals, strong and courageous coaches and administrators, and solid support from those in power can keep corruption and malpractice under control. *Athletics as education* is, however, the basic principle on which all intramural, extramural, interscholastic, and intercollegiate athletics should be based. The *welfare of the participant* is the other guiding principle that will help keep athletics in proper perspective.

When working in the highly charged atmosphere of competitive athletics, one must recognize that players, coaches, and administrators are human, subject to the same weaknesses and frailties, the same needs and desires, and the same ambitions and emotions as other people. The love of praise and adulation, the eagerness to win games and championships, the natural irritation resulting from undeserved criticism, and the frustrations which follow a succession of defeats are all present, to a greater or lesser degree, in most human beings. Likewise, the urge to identify with a successful player, coach, or team, and the anger felt toward officials or others who injure them in any way is a natural reaction. Obviously, the entire world of sport is one in which emotions must be kept under control, reason must temper frustrations and disappointments, and ethical conduct and behavior must be the concerns of everyone.

10.4 EDUCATING FOR VALUES

Values are underlying beliefs which together serve as a stabilizing foundation for the formation of attitudes and which exercise influence and control over behavior. Parents, teachers, and coaches are in especially favorable positions to assist students and athletes in the development of a value system which will survive life's many trials and temptations. A person's value system serves as the cornerstone on which his or her philosophy of life is built. The priorities which govern behavior must harmonize with this philosophy.

"When working in the highly charged atmosphere of competitive athletics, one must recognize that players, coaches, and administrators are human, subject to the same weaknesses and frailties, the same needs and desires, and the same ambitions and emotions as other people." (Courtesy of the *Journal of Health, Physical Education, and Recreation*.)

Personality and character can be influenced by experiences in athletics. Psychologists indicate that the first ten to twelve years of a person's life are the formative ones during which most values are ingrained. Character can be altered after that age, but to accomplish this, experiences must be personal and intense. Competitive sports abound with dramatic, emotional, and personal experiences. These are the teachable moments; these are the opportunities for coaches to influence behavior and attitudes.

Athletic fields, gymnasiums, and other environments where people engage in sports can and do serve as laboratories in which an athlete has experiences which relate to situations found in later life. If a person is to learn something in one situation which will affect behavior in another, the two must have some similar or identical elements. There are a number of situations in competitive athletics where athletes must control their emotions, must accept decisions of people in authority, must not whine when hurt, must subjugate self for the good of the group, and must keep trying when all seems lost. The coach in such circumstances must assist the athlete to perceive the similarities in those and later-life situations and to make the appropriate applications.

While there certainly are many athletes who do not behave as if competition in sports has had a salutary influence on their behavior, there are, in the opinion of the author, a far larger number who will attest to the favorable effect of athletic participation on their character. Within the last few years, the author has interviewed more than one hundred coaches and athletes with regard to some psychological aspect of sports. One of the questions asked concerned the effect of their participation in competitive athletics on their values. All interviewed indicated that they thought they had been favorably influenced and that they felt sports furnished a good laboratory for the learning of values which could carry over in later life.

However, a word of caution is in order. Athletics and sports per se do not build character or develop positive and constructive value systems. Character and behavior can deteriorate as well as improve as a result of experiences in the emotional and sometimes violent atmosphere of sport. The background of values with which a person enters a contest or a sports season, and the guidance and leadership which are part of the environment, will have a great influence on what happens to an athlete as a result of a given episode. Hopefully, many more coaches will be an influence for good rather than bad as athletics continues to be an important aspect of the educational program.

It is also important that coaches and physical educators resist the tendency toward chauvinism. Sports of all kinds can only make a contribution toward the improvement of a person's character and conduct. There are other educational programs which can be just as influential and have an equally significant responsibility. The building of a sound value system is the result of many influences, *one* of which may be athletics.

One more point needs emphasis. If the lessons learned through participation in athletics are to carry over into later life and have a permanent rather than transitory effect, they must become part of the participant's philosophy of life. Only in this way can there be any consistency in behavior on and off the athletic field. The many examples of inconsistencies in behavior and their dependence upon situations and circumstances rather than a commitment to accepted precepts indicate a need for more stable guidelines. If the laboratory situations are there and the leaders have the opportunity, generalization can take place. To have a permanent and positive influence, however, the experiences must be so related, so harmonized with the individual's philosophy, and so much a part of the athlete's total being that they serve as a motivating force for the rest of his or her life.*

10.5 PROGRAMS FOR GIRLS AND WOMEN
There is little question that interscholastic and intercollegiate athletics for women, which have expanded so rapidly in the past two decades, will continue to grow and flourish. The interest is obvious, support is growing, additional facilities are being built, cultural norms are changing, and administrative details are being worked out.

It is important to keep in mind the following general principles which are, from a review of the literature available, most generally agreed upon:

1. Girls and women who are highly gifted in sports should have the same opportunities to compete with others of equal ability as do boys and men.

---

*See also Chapter 16, "Human Values and Personal Ethics" and Chapter 9, Section 9.4, "The Development of Values."

"... athletics for women ... will continue to grow and
flourish." (Courtesy of (*above*) the University of
Wisconsin–LaCrosse, and (*left*) Springfield College.)

2. Where size, strength, or other special abilities make certain sports unsuitable for girls and women, only boys and men should participate. Boxing and American football are examples.

3. Where males and females are, as a whole, equally able and skillful, varsity programs should be open to both men and women. In some sports, such as volleyball, there should be special rules for mixed competition which provide both sexes an equal opportunity to handle the ball.

4. While there are many sports in which men and women, boys and girls, can participate on "mixed" teams, and some in which men can play against women, they should not be limited to this style of competition. If for some reason the women, girls, men, or boys wish to compete among themselves, suitable opportunities should be provided for the respective groups.

5. Programs for both sexes should be adequately supported by the resources necessary for high-quality instruction, good leadership, and efficient operation. Included would be budgetary support for personnel, equipment, facilities, and necessary professional travel.

6. Every effort must be made to upgrade the coaching of women's athletic teams. The past situation, in which athletics for girls and women was excluded from school programs, has resulted in a scarcity of highly qualified women in the coaching field. This void should be filled as rapidly as possible.

7. The welfare of every girl should be the prime consideration when important decisions are being made. This necessitates continual updating of the latest medical information concerning health aspects such as menstruation, child bearing,

◀ "Girls and women who are highly gifted in sports should ▲
have the same opportunities to compete . . . as do boys
and men." (Courtesy of Springfield College.)

and susceptibility to injury. It also implies leadership that is knowledgeable about growth and development, individual differences, and both biological and psychological needs.

8. Intramural and extramural athletic programs should be encouraged and fostered. All girls who wish to participate in competitive athletics should be given the opportunity.

9. All programs of interschool athletics for girls and women should be conducted in accordance with the appropriate local, state, and national regulations. At present these would be the guidelines published by the State High School Activities Associations, The National Federation, The Division of Girl's and Women's Sports of the AAHPER, and the Association of Intercollegiate Athletics for Women.

The purposes of the latter organization incorporate the philosophy now controlling girls' and women's athletics and are as follows:

1. To foster broad programs of women's intercollegiate athletics which are consistent with the educational aims and objectives of the member schools and in accordance with the philosophy and standards of the DGWS.

2. To assist member schools in extending and enriching their programs of intercollegiate athletics for women based upon the needs, interests, and capacities of the individual student.

3. To stimulate the development of quality leadership for women's intercollegiate athletic programs.

4. To foster programs which will encourage excellence in performance of participants in women's intercollegiate athletics.

5. To maintain the spirit of play within competitive sport events so that the concomitant education values of such an experience are emphasized.

6. To increase public understanding and appreciation of the importance and value of sports and athletics as they contribute to the enrichment of the life of the woman.

7. To encourage and facilitate research on the effects of intercollegiate athletic competition on women and to disseminate the findings.

8. To further the continual evaluation of standards and policies for participants and programs.

9. To produce and distribute such materials as will be of assistance to persons in the development and improvement of intercollegiate programs.

10. To hold national championships and to sponsor conferences, institutes, and meetings which will meet the needs of individuals in member schools.

11. To cooperate with other professional groups of similar interests for the ultimate development of sports programs and opportunities for women.

12. To provide direction and maintain a relationship with AIAW regional organizations.

13. To conduct such other activities as shall be approved by the governing body of the Association.*

The Division for Girls' and Women's Sports of the American Association for Health, Physical Education and Recreation published a position paper entitled *Sports Programs for Girls and Women* in which it stated:

1. Girls and women should have athletic programs equal to but separate from those for boys and men.

2. If girls are permitted to play on boys' teams, boys might request to play on girls' teams, and this might result in two teams dominated by male membership rather than a team for boys and a team for girls.

3. Research does not support the claims that girls are harmed physiologically or socially by participation in sports, and society now repudiates such ideas.

4. Sports programs in high schools and colleges should be an outgrowth of the physical education program and should provide a variety of opportunities for all students.

5. Women physical educators, coaches, and athletic directors should be involved in the planning, development, and administration of girls' and women's sports programs.

6. Adequate numbers of women coaches and officials should be prepared so that competent individuals will fill those roles.

7. Female students should be given opportunities for high-level performance and competition within the framework of girls' and women's sports.†

Dorothy McKnight and Joan Hult, in their article "Competitive Athletics for Girls—We Must Act," emphasize the need for immediate, firm action to make the dream of good programs of competitive athletics for girls come true. They call attention to the actions of the courts which emphasize equal opportunities for both sexes (Title IX of the Education Amendments Act of 1972) and opportunity for more funding for programs for girls and women. They recommend athletic encounters which emphasize the "joy of effort, the pursuit of excellence and a high level of achievement within a framework in which gate receipts, crowd appeal, and the scoreboard are not the criteria for success or the measure of individual achievement."‡ They advocate separate teams for girls and boys and insist that the girls move ahead with their own athletic philosophy and plan of operation and not model their programs after those of the men.

---

*AIAW Handbook, Washington, D.C.: American Association for Health, Physical Education and Recreation, 1973–74. By permission.

†"Sports programs for girls and women: a DGWS position paper," *Journal of Health, Physical Education and Recreation,* Vol. 45, No. 4, April 1974, p. 12. By permission.

‡"Competitive athletics for girls—we must act," *Journal of Health, Physical Education, and Recreation,* Vol. 45, No. 6, June 1974, p. 45.

Attention is called in this article to the many legal interpretations and court actions recently promulgated and the further legislation which seems to be pending.

The authors end with a call for action and the development of girls' and women's athletic programs which are consistent with educational goals and which offer female athletes opportunities for high-level achievement.*

It appears that girls' and women's athletics are rapidly being established on a sound and enduring basis. It may well be that they can avoid some of the pitfalls which have plagued programs for boys and men.

10.6 INTERSCHOOL ATHLETICS AT THE JUNIOR HIGH SCHOOL LEVEL

Junior high school students are for the most part 12 to 15 years of age. This is the age of the adolescent growth spurt, the beginning of menstruation, psychological and behavioral adjustment problems, and sexual maturation. It is characterized by a relatively wide divergence in height, weight, strength, and physiological maturity. This is an age when the urge to explore, the need for adventure, and the desire for participation in active and exciting sports are particularly strong.

While there has been and still is controversy over the issue of interschool competitive athletics at the junior high school level, the trend is definitely toward the inclusion of such programs. Because most junior high schools do sponsor interschool athletics, the treatment here will be confined mainly to a discussion of guidelines and principles for their conduct and administration. These are:

1. Junior high school athletics shall be conducted under the direction and guidance of trained and qualified leaders who know and understand the basic principles of growth and development and the psychological needs and hazards particularly prevalent at this age.

2. Physical examinations by competent physicians shall be required before permitting boys and girls to practice or compete. Those with physical impairments should be guided into activities appropriate to their physical condition and their stage of emotional and physical development.

3. Educational objectives and the welfare of the participants must receive top priority. Whenever necessary, professionally trained guidance counselors, psychiatrists, and physicians should be consulted.

4. There should be adequate provision for immediate and proper care of injuries.

5. The programs of varsity athletics at the junior high school level should not preempt the intramural or physical education programs. "The greatest good for the greatest number" is still a sound maxim.

6. Continued research with regard to both values and hazards must be encouraged and the findings applied. The evidence for and against interschool competition at the junior high school level is still far from conclusive.

---

* *Ibid.,* p. 46.

Objections to junior high level interschool competition center around the possibility of physical and psychological trauma and the likelihood that such programs will detract from physical education and intramural programs. These are potent arguments and need to be examined carefully. Long-held fears concerning the danger of physical injury have, however, not been borne out. More recent pronouncements of various educational groups have tended to support such interschool programs.

The matter of preempting intramural programs is, in some ways, more serious. There are a great many schools where all the athletic facilities are used by varsity teams at the various levels, at least after the middle of the afternoon. The reason given is that this will produce better players and stronger teams. This is, in effect, the exploitation of the many for the benefit of the few. Pressures from the community, administrators, and coaches are often enough to influence such practices. Rationalization often occurs to justify these procedures. The junior high school age is too early to single out potential high-level athletes and concentrate only on their development.

10.7 NONSCHOOL ATHLETICS FOR CHILDREN

In 1968 the American Association for Health, Physical Education, and Recreation published in one booklet two important documents concerning nonschool athletics for children. The first was *A Policy Statement on Competitive Athletics for Children of Elementary School Age*. This was approved by the American Academy of Pediatrics, the American Association for Health, Physical Education, and Recreation, the American Medical Association Committee on the Medical Aspects of Sports, and the Society of State Directors of Health, Physical Education, and Recreation. This statement emphasized the fact that children of this age are not miniature adults, that they are in the process of maturation, that the benefits from athletic participation are not automatic, and that high-quality supervision is essential. They recommended a local governing committee consisting of educational, recreational, and medical specialists and indicated that the committee should give serious consideration, among other things, to:

1. Proper physical conditioning.
2. Conduct of the sport.
   a) Competent teaching and supervision with regard for the relative hazards of each particular sport.
   b) Modification of rules, game equipment, and facilities to suit the maturity level of the participants.
   c) Qualified officials.
3. Careful grouping according to weight, size, sex, skill, and physical maturation when indicated.
4. Good protective equipment, properly fitted.
5. Well-maintained facilities suitable for the sport involved.

6. Proper delineation of the spheres of authority and responsibility for school administrators, family, sponsor, physician, coach, and athlete.
7. Adequate medical care.
   a) Periodic health appraisal of children, including a careful health history.
   b) A physician present or readily available during games and practices.
   c) Established policies, procedures, and responsibilities for first aid and referral of injuries, definitive treatment and follow-up, and evaluation and certification for return following injury or illness. [3, pp. v–vi]

The second document was entitled *The Report of the Joint Committee of the American Association for Health, Physical Education, and Recreation and the Society of State Directors of Health, Physical Education, and Recreation on Desirable Athletic Competition for Children of Elementary School Age.* In this document, past research and former statements are reviewed, facts and figures are cited, opinions of educators are presented, and problems are identified. In the final section, *"Purposes of Athletic Competition,"* the following points are made:

1. The competitive urge becomes strong in children during the upper-elementary years.
2. Team competition provides an outlet for the competitive drive in situations where personal interests must be subordinate to the good of the team.
3. The desire of youth to emulate adults and idolize great athletes is strong. There is nothing wrong with this tendency, but the need can be satisfied in intramural games. Youngsters of this age do not need to become part of adult-type, highly pressurized varsity programs.
4. The elementary years should be the time for learning basic skills and establishing fundamental movement patterns. Specialization can come later.
5. Unless there is sound guidance on the part of coaches and leaders, varsity-type experience at too early an age may give youth a distorted sense of values. Care must be exercised in the choice of coaches. The importance of the right philosophy and attitude is more important than a sophisticated knowledge of the game.

The following two paragraphs conclude the document and summarize much of the thinking:

The benefits of well-organized and well-supervised athletic programs for children and youth are many. The schools constitute the most effective structure for the management and control which such programs require. Important educational objectives can be realized through properly administered athletic programs for children and youth, and as our society now is structured, the schools offer the best medium for achieving these ends. Parents, civic leaders, and educators must work together to provide children and youth with opportunities to meet this need in ways which are healthy and educationally sound. This responsibility rests perhaps more heavily on the schools than upon community agencies.

Many questions regarding athletic competition and varsity type athletics for children still remain unanswered and are likely to remain unanswered for some time to come. It is becoming increasingly clear that what may be in the best interests of some children may not be good for all—that at a given chronological age children vary substantially in physical maturity, physique, motor development, and psychological and sociological maturity. [3, p. 26]

It is evident that the conclusions with regard to the benefits and dangers attending competitive athletics are at best quite tenuous. Subjective judgment based on experience must play a large role in decisions regarding this aspect of both education and community culture.

Arthur Esslinger, in a meeting of the American Academy of Physical Education in 1954, presented a scholarly paper entitled "Out-of-School Athletics for Children." He reviewed the pertinent literature and attempted to evaluate the programs of Little League Baseball, Biddy Basketball, Pop Warner Football, and other sports for elementary school age children. He too found conflicting evidence concerning both hazards and values. His summary statement included the following:

1. While it would be ideal if all athletic activities at this age level were under the supervision of professionally prepared teachers and coaches, there seems to be little possibility of realizing this ideal in the foreseeable future. Professionally trained leaders must therefore give guidance and assistance to these programs.

2. We must expand our efforts to improve physical education in our elementary schools. Children at this age are hungry for the opportunity to participate in sports.

3. We must undertake extensive research to determine the effects of athletic competition on children. Emphasis shall be on longitudinal studies.

4. We must increase our efforts to interpret all aspects of our recreational and physical education programs to the public. They are still woefully ignorant as to the values of play and the significance of good leadership.

5. We must upgrade the education of our physical education teachers and recreation leaders. Professional leaders must earn both respect and confidence so that the people will turn to them for advice and assistance. [33, p. 42]

In a speech entitled "Football in Grade School," child psychiatrist Henry Coppolillo said, "In considering what advice might be useful to a teacher planning to coach grade schoolers in football, the first question that arises is whether or not such a program is desirable. The issue is not a new one nor can it be definitely settled." [22]

Coppolillo goes on to mention the child's need to gratify impulses, the desire to express aggressions and curiosities, and the inhibitions that result from various reactions of authority figures. He also ventures the opinion that supervised sport at this age may involve considerably less risk than some of the unsupervised activities that groups of children might indulge in if they weren't in athletics. He also expresses concern for the inept or unskilled youngster who would like to be a star but simply lacks the capability. [22]

Once again some equivocation is necessary. There are individual differences in the nature, needs, and capacities of youngsters of the same age. There are also differences in their interests. An experience which might be psychologically damaging to one might not hurt another. The physiological readiness of two individuals of the same age and sex may differ. The knowledge and leadership styles of two coaches can be worlds apart. The ambitions which parents have for their children are very diverse. The total situation in one instance may be favorable and competition should be recommended. Under another set of circumstances it should be curtailed or prohibited entirely. The welfare of each individual must be the guide.

The only answer that can be given with any degree of certainty is that all children in the upper-elementary grades need activity and all will benefit from a well-organized and conducted program of sports. A broad exposure to a variety of activities in physical education classes supplemented by a well-conceived and administered intramural program will provide the best answer. A good summer recreation program is also necessary for complete services to the people of any community.

The whole issue of competition at the elementary level is still clouded. Many parents are concerned. They hear pronouncements to the effect that competition at this age may be harmful both physically and psychologically. They see the yearning to be an athlete in their child's whole attitude and demeanor. They feel that if the child's peers become more skillful and adept, it may dim his or her chances of making a varsity team at a later time. They believe in the values attributed to participation in sports. They can find no hard-and-fast guidelines. Educators, physicians, coaches, and others give conflicting opinions seldom substantiated by reliable evidence. Thus the dilemma continues to exist.

10.8 INTERSCHOLASTIC AND INTERCOLLEGIATE ATHLETICS

As used here, the term *interscholastic* will refer to athletics at the secondary level (grades 9–12) and *intercollegiate* will refer to athletics in the junior colleges, four-year colleges, and universities. Because so many principles and guidelines are the same for all of these programs and because a number of problems relate to all, they will be discussed together under appropriate headings.

Educational aspects

Athletics is an integral part of education and, when correctly administered, contributes to the aims and goals of education. Most educational institutions include in their official publications statements of their philosophy of athletics. In almost every instance educational objectives and purposes are stressed. In 1962 the

Division of Men's Athletics of the American Association for Health, Physical Education, and Recreation emphasized in their platform statement the relationship of athletics to education:

> Interscholastic and intercollegiate athletic programs should be regarded as integral parts of the total educational program and should be so conducted that they are worthy of such regard. [10]

It is in the implementation of policies and in everyday practices that problems arise. The problems are related in a sense to the values. Because the spirit of athletics centers around competition, because athletic performances are dramatic and fascinating, because people can become emotionally involved in competitive sport, and because the exploits of athletes are excellent subjects for the news media, the programs of interscholastic and intercollegiate athletics have attracted more than their fair share of attention. For these reasons also, athletes and athletic contests have often been exploited for selfish motives.

The human desire to identify with a winner, the urge to boast about athletic teams with which one already identifies, the commercial value of large crowds, the advertising value of well-known athletic figures, and the disproportionate emphasis placed on winning rather than excellence have all played a part in the problems related to these programs.

To win one must have good athletes, good coaches, good equipment, and good facilities. All of these are expensive. Financial inducements, both legitimate and illegitimate, are offered to outstanding athletic prospects. Occasionally parents of highly endowed players are influenced to move from one community to another by good offers of employment. Sometimes athletes themselves are attracted to a certain college by material benefits even though that college is not prepared to offer the academic program the athlete wants. Because it costs money to win consistently, large crowds are needed to bring in the necessary revenue. Occasionally even gambling and "game-fixing" are discovered.

While there have been instances where the undesirable practices mentioned above have been uncovered, the thousands of places where integrity is the rule and where educational objectives receive top priority should not go unmentioned. As in so many aspects of life, the sordid and the false attract more attention than the good and the beautiful. Those courageous and upright leaders who can administer and coach in situations which are rampant with temptation deserve the admiration and respect of everyone. The athletic program proceeds in the glare of the spotlight and the critical attitudes of the fans and alumni toward those whom they consider responsible for defeat too often are directed at an undeserving coach. It should be remembered, however, that the spotlight is focused too on those traits and performances which are admirable. As Bob Wolff said,

> How often have you heard the descriptive term, "fight and courage," applied by the broadcaster to individuals or teams? These traits can be pointed up in storybook fashion on the field of sports. I think it is important, though, for both coach and family to make the young athlete realize that the normal

routine of life, aside from sports, demands sacrifice, determination, courage, and self-control without the accompaniment of headlines or roaring crowds. The only reward may come from within. Organized sports competition, however, focuses the spotlight on fine traits, and points up their value to participants and spectators alike. [98, p. 256]

In the opinion of the author, no one should enter an athletic contest and not try to win. That is part of the game and the individual who forgets that is not true either to himself or the game. However the emphasis should be on winning by superb performance, by strenuous effort, by total involvement. When one has performed to the limits of one's capacity, victory and defeat should be put in their proper perspective both by participants and spectators. When involved in a contest and especially when representing an institution, one should put forth every effort to win. If that is done, and the play is within the rules and the code of the game, a defeat should not be cause for shame or guilt. In the same vein, the winner can justly take pride in a hard-earned victory. The winner should not, however, display arrogance or superiority toward his opponent, be it an individual or a team. The victor who intentionally tries to humiliate an opponent is demeaning both himself and the sport.

Athletics in large universities which have a tradition of striving for national leadership is subject to the greatest pressures of all. Where the athletic budgets run into millions of dollars, where the news media give an inordinate amount of attention to athletics, where the power structures of government, business, and sometimes churches feel that the successes of their athletic teams are reflections of their own accomplishments and stature, and where the coaches are swamped with letters, clippings, and statements about them and their teams, the problems of keeping their programs honest, genuine, and ethical are sometimes enormous. When honesty is accomplished, credit must be given to administrators and coaches for their moral strength and sound sense of values.

In 1955 Ray Duncan wrote an article entitled "The Contribution of School Athletics to the Growing Boy." His last paragraph summarizing his thinking is as relevant today as it was then:

> School athletics is a fast-growing giant with a tremendous potential for making a vital contribution to the physical, social, and emotional growth of every boy [and girl]* who participates. However, an athletic program is not beneficial per se. Its potential for good is matched by the possibility of bad outcomes. School authorities have the responsibility for developing a program of athletics which will make a valuable contribution to all boys [and girls]*— the parents and patrons of our schools should see to it that the responsibility is met in full. [28, p. 274]

This is sound advice and can serve as a guide to all those involved with the difficult problem of making athletic experiences educational.

---

*Author's insertions.

10.9 THE PROBLEM OF AMATEURISM

To attempt a definition of amateur is to end up somewhat confused. The tennis player competing for the Davis Cup is not under the same regulations as the runner under the jurisdiction of the Amateur Athletic Union; the boxer fighting for a purse is a different kind of professional than the person who coaches basketball for pay; the professional in one sport is permitted to compete as an amateur in certain other sports but not in all; the amateur who competes against a professional becomes ineligible for amateur competition, whereas another who receives expensive trophies and substantial expense accounts remains an amateur; and the college student who receives board, room, tuition, and books for athletic prowess remains an amateur, whereas the baseball player who signs a professional contract but receives no money has lost his amateur standing.

Sham-amateurism

The fact that "super athletes," be they classified as amateurs or professionals, have a high "market value" can hardly be denied. Since the dawn of history, winning athletes have been awarded prizes of greater or lesser value. Present manufacturers of skis, skates, track shoes, and articles of clothing are anxious to have their products used by great athletes and offer them many kinds of inducements, both overtly and covertly. Tennis players, golf stars, and baseball players are often presented gifts of rackets, clubs, bats, and gloves. Many athletes are sponsored by businesses, governments, and athletic clubs. Expense allowances in excess of actual needs, time off from normal working hours to practice, wages and salaries beyond what nonathletes would receive for the same amount of work, and sweaters, jackets, and other commodities are freely given and often just as freely received. Members of the armed forces are given time off for practice, team travel, and participation. Specific illustrations are many and varied.

It becomes obvious, then, that many who are classified as amateurs are not really amateurs at all. It becomes clear that the job of policing the numerous and varied amateur regulations with the even more diverse interpretations is well-nigh impossible. That is what has led to disillusionment on the part of many sincere sports participants and the appellation *sham-amateurism* by others.

The Olympic games

There are those, therefore, who feel that we should eliminate, particularly for the purposes of the Olympics, all attempts to distinguish between amateurs and professionals. Let the Olympics be a contest where the best are pitted against the best, be they novices or veterans, poor or rich, paid or unpaid. Furthermore, it is claimed that this would eliminate the problems of enforcement and would eventually lead to greater integrity and forthright honesty.

On the other hand, most great achievements have come about because there have been ideals which were not quite attainable but toward which athletes strove mightily. It is possible that if we relinquish the principle of amateurism, the Olympic Ideal and the inspiration received from it will suffer. When watching the Opening Ceremonies of the Olympics, one senses the tremendous impact, the inspiration, and the aura of greatness that surround both athletes and spectators. As the teams march into the stadium as the Olympic flame is lit, as the words of the Olympic Oath are recited, and the ideals of Pierre de Coubertin are proclaimed, one feels that the spirit as well as the body and mind are involved, and that all the facets of one's being are challenged to greatness. If we define amateurism in the words of Avery Brundage* as "love of the achievement rather than the reward," certainly we have no choice but to continue to support the concept and work toward the fulfillment of its truest meaning. Only in this way will athletics continue its great positive influence locally, nationally, and internationally.

There is considerable agitation for allowing both amateurs and professionals to compete in the Olympic Games. But this course has its dangers. If the negotiations and litigation which have become so prevalent in professional sports should also become characteristic of the Olympics and other high-level amateur sports, the problems pertaining to remuneration as well as the time and money involved in organization could well be astronomical. Many conflicting emotions would also surface as the rising, ambitious, highly gifted young amateur athletes began to compete with "old pros" for spots on the Olympic teams. One wonders also if Olympic contests wouldn't lose some of their spontaneity and zest if they were basically demonstrations of the prowess of athletes who were being paid to practice, perform, and compete.

Is it not "sport for sport's sake" that really distinguishes between the amateur and the professional? This sounds reasonable at first glance. The problem is that there are also many "professionals" who take part in sport for the sake of sport and they might be even more inclined to do so if there were a world championship at stake.

Captain Asbury Coward suggested classifying Olympic competitors as "independent world athletes" who would represent the Olympics and not any specific country. He suggested further that the International Olympic Committee be established as a bicameral body with greater representation for all nations. Such a plan would also allow more individuals, such as the "colored athletes in South Africa," to compete in the Olympics.[†]

This is one suggestion. Perhaps it would help. There might be better ways if people of ability and goodwill were assigned to the task of trying to improve the situation.

From sports philosophers

Paul Weiss, in his book, *Sport, a Philosophic Inquiry,* has written a thoughtful analysis of amateurs and professionals. The distinction which he draws is in terms of motivation.

---

*Avery Brundage was president of the International Olympic Committee for five successive terms (1952–1972).

†Neil Amdur, "New status for olympic athletes urged," *The New York Times,* April 25, 1968, p. 58.

An amateur, strictly speaking, is one who plays a game for no other reason than to play it. He cannot but benefit from his participation; he will undoubtedly be tested there; he will want to win; he will, more likely than not, enjoy himself even while under pressure or at the edge of exhaustion. But it will be the game with which he is concerned. A professional, strictly speaking, is one who takes some end other than the playing of the game to be his primary objective. His aim may be to win, no matter how, to entertain the spectators, to give encouragement to his government, to get publicity, or to make money. It makes no difference which of these it is. He is a professional if his play is governed by considerations which do not follow from the nature of a contest or a game. [97, p. 198]

Harold VanderZwaag generally supports Weiss' definition but emphasizes that sportsmen can be placed on a continuum, with "amateur" at one end and "professional" at the other. [95, p. 38] This makes sense, for anyone who has mingled with athletes soon discovers that there are "amateurs" who play for materialistic rewards, there are "professionals" who play because they love it, there are "semipros" who play for money but don't sign contracts, and there are athletes who do all three. But this creates a dilemma according to VanderZwaag:

What, then, can be done to assist those sponsoring or governing bodies who are concerned about delineating the amateur status? Obviously, it will be next to impossible to measure or even evaluate the motives of each would-be participant. About the best which one can hope for is that *a* governing board will make certain decisions, even though they may be somewhat arbitrary, regarding eligibility. Hopefully, these decisions will be reached with the interests of the majority in mind. [95, p. 39]

It appears likely that the problems surrounding amateurism and professionalism will be with us for a long time. There are no easy answers. The only hope is that noble rather than base motives will influence those in authority when they are called upon to make difficult decisions. The best interests of sport, the welfare of the participants, and adherence to the highest and most worthy principles should be the guides.

10.10 PROBLEMS, PROSPECTS, AND PRINCIPLES
Practices in the world of sport and athletics are replete with problems and complexities. While not offering final solutions, a number of these should be identified and thought given to prospective courses of action. A brief discussion of some of the problems follows:

1. *Recruitment.* Many rules and restrictions have been promulgated to protect promising prospective athletes from harassment by overzealous recruiters from colleges and universities. Yet with good intentions alumni and friends of educational institutions visit athletes in their schools, park on their doorsteps, and find opportunities to interview them at tournaments, summer jobs, and various other places. When they are approached in this manner by many representatives pre-

senting different arguments and various inducements, they become confused, disturbed, and occasionally hostile. Letters of intent, prior enrollment at another school, and regulations of the conferences or national organizations governing athletics do help in many instances, but there are still too many students who are hurt rather than aided by such recruiting practices. There are also a number of colleges which do not come under the jurisdiction of any governing body and are free to recruit as they see fit.

The resolution lies partly in more clearly defined rules and regulations and better communication between colleges and secondary schools. More education of athletes concerning such offers and inducements and guidance by high school staff members will also be helpful. Continual emphasis on actions which are based on the future welfare of each student is, of course, the ultimate answer.

2. *Exploitation.* The use of another person for one's own advantage is exploitation. In athletic practice, this could take the form of playing a star athlete when ill or hurt. The use of an athlete's or an outstanding team's name for the express purpose of bringing glory and fame to a school, community, or nation is another example. Exploitation might also be inducing a player to accept illegal financial aid. It would include keeping players in school longer than necessary to retain their services as team members an extra year. Teaching dishonest tactics in order to win and using drugs to artificially aid performance are other examples. Anything that is done which may hurt the athlete but work to the advantage of the school, the athletic staff, or the coach would be exploitation.

The coach and possibly the athletic director have the responsibility in such situations. Exploitation is one of the evils of athletics and has been prevalent for a long time. Like other "sins," it is difficult to control. Fortunately, most coaches and athletic directors are too scrupulous and have too much affection for those who play under their tutelage to treat them in this manner. They are concerned about the athletes' future and try to protect rather than harm them.

3. *Illegal subsidization.* Giving an athlete more financial assistance than that allowed by the rules of the conferences or other governing bodies is another practice which works to the detriment of sport and the value system of the athlete. It is difficult to devise regulations which cover all situations and to administer a policing system which will control all the forms of illegal aid. Clothes, free meals, and automobiles given as gifts to athletes, money paid by fans as rewards for superlative performances, jobs which require no labor, and envelopes containing cash slipped surreptitiously to athletes are all instances of illegal subsidization that have actually occurred. As mentioned previously, the responsibility rests in the hands of coaches, athletic directors, and other college officials. Where integrity, honesty, and courage reside, there will be no such problems. It must also be understood, however, that there are gamblers and others who have no scruples and who see athletics as an activity which may be exploited for their own selfish ends.

4. *Excessive nationalism.* Wholesome rivalries are healthy. But when the residents of a community or the citizens of a nation think only of the glory that victory can bring them, of the pride they can take in a winning team, of the opportunity

to boast, and of the ego-satisfying newspaper headlines, the values of the game or contest are completely distorted and, for many, entirely lost. To strive mightily for victory is worthy; to make winning a false idol is base. When members of two teams give every ounce of their effort to win, and yet through a stroke of fortune one team or the other emerges victorious, it is wrong for people to idolize the victor and attach shame and guilt to the loser. Or, to cite another instance, a given team may be obviously outclassed but yet it fights on to the bitter end even when victory is impossible. Such a team deserves only honor and respect.

The most obvious examples of nationalism have occurred during the Olympic Games. Here athletes of great and powerful nations exhibit their strength and abilities before the world and their feats are thought of as reflecting the strength and power of the nations they represent. To cheer for the team with which one identifies is both wholesome and natural. To want the team to demonstrate its superior strength and power for the sake of "lording it over" others is unworthy of a great people.

In a *Time Magazine* supplement entitled "The Olympics: A Summitry of Sport," the following statement appeared:

> General MacArthur's argument that Olympic results reflect a nation's achievement outside of athletics is highly debatable at best. Some measure of chauvinism is understandable, but to interpret physical feats as evidence of sociological or ideological superiority is as absurd as trying to settle a United Nations debate with a foot race up First Avenue. And the tactic can backfire. At Berlin, Hitler had to sit and squirm as an American black—the legendary Jesse Owens—clearly outshone Germany's Nordic "supermen" to win gold medals in four events. Still, rampant nationalism continues to mock the purported ideals of the Olympics. Since 1952 the focus has been mainly on whether the U.S. team, representing a free, democratic society, could beat the Russians, carrying the banner for Communism. [70]

On the other hand, when asked the question, "Are you worried about nationalism as reflected in the Olympics?," Gunter Grass, a well-known contemporary German novelist, replied:

> Fortunately, apart from the attack on the Israelis there were scarcely any examples of nationalism at the Munich Olympics. As far as the Germans are concerned, these Olympic Games have had much more the effect of reducing nationalism—even though it was the East German officials who kept on repeating that every medal won was a medal for their State. It is simply part of the fabric of all totalitarian governments that they cannot separate sport from politics, and they encourage sport because they hope for increased national prestige. The same thing happened under the Nazis, when sport was one of the main subjects taught in schools.*

Wholesome competitive athletics have much to offer our society. Chauvinism and excessive nationalism should be eliminated and good sportsmanship reemphasized as we seek better ways of expressing our national identities and group

---

*The Sunday Times, London, September 17, 1972. By permission.

loyalties. One of the fundamental principles of the Olympic Games states that *the Games are contests between individuals and not between countries.* * This principle, emphasized by Pierre de Coubertin, needs to be recalled and reinforced in the minds of all.

5. *Gambling.* Competitive sporting events lend themselves naturally to many forms of wagering and gambling. Any activity where chance plays a role in the result and where the outcome can be quantitatively measured is an invitation for gamblers. Betting on winning or losing a contest, the point spread, the scores of given individuals, and the final standing of teams tempts anyone who has the urge to gamble. Young athletes are particularly vulnerable because they are not yet completely aware of the ways of the world and are eager for the material wealth which they see others have. Coaches must inform themselves on these matters and must counsel those who play under their direction. Parents and others who might have influence on the athlete also need to be thoroughly informed as to the methods and techniques of gambling operations.

6. *Pressures on teachers and coaches.* There are situations in which the emphasis on winning puts both teachers and coaches under a great deal of pressure to do wrong. Teachers are approached by coaches, fans, and parents to do something—anything—to keep a good athlete eligible even though he clearly does not meet the required scholastic standards. Coaches are often approached by wealthy supporters of a given team and are offered money to help attract and support an athlete who cannot otherwise afford to attend that particular school. Athletic directors are pressured by their coaches to be more liberal in their interpretation of the rules and in some instances to join in attracting and retaining a good athlete.

Knowledge of the possible hazards, honesty, high-principles, and moral courage on the part of all concerned to resist such advances furnish the only answers to these problems.

7. *Disputes between governing bodies.* Only a few people in the athletic world know and understand all the ramifications of the disputes between the NCAA, the AAU, the NAIA, the Sports Federation, and (indirectly) the United States Olympic Committee. The athletic programs of our country, particularly the Olympic program, would benefit immensely from an organization with clear-cut lines of authority, providing a sense of unity and harmony. It is possible that the federal government itself will need to establish a governing body for all international competition. Only in this way can all the interested groups be brought together with more equitable representation and the necessary authority to bring order to a situation which is now somewhat chaotic.

8. *Disproportionate costs.* The budgets for athletic programs have increased tremendously. Because of the intense competition and rivalry, more and more coaches are being employed, more elaborate equipment is required, and more

---

* *The Olympic Games, Fundamental Principles, Rules, and Regulations, General Information,* Lausanne, Switzerland: The International Olympic Committee, 1962.

expensive facilities are being built. While such increases in costs are accepted with little complaint during periods of affluence, they are resisted and programs are often drastically reduced when a changing financial picture forces more austerity. When budgets are cut, the athletic and physical education departments are traditionally among the first to feel the pinch. Small colleges and high schools probably face the most severe financial problems.

It will require great ingenuity and effort to sustain the trends toward broader and more comprehensive programs. Constant vigilance against extravagance and a general commitment of the entire staff toward sound and worthwhile experiences for the student will be part of the answer.

9. *Miniature adults out of children.* It is natural for younger people to imitate those who are older than themselves. Likewise, colleges copy large universities, high schools imitate colleges, and junior high schools emulate high schools. Where there are programs for elementary children, an attempt is made to operate them like those for the older students. This suggests some very real dangers. A fifth-grade youngster does not normally tolerate the same workload as a tenth-grade student. Generally, the attention span of the junior high school student is not as long as that of the high school student. The high school athlete is usually more sensitive to harsh criticism than is the college athlete. Elementary school children generally need rest more frequently than they do when they get older. Psychological trauma from being ignored or from failing athletically can be very severe at this age.

The whole point is that those who teach and coach should understand the phenomena of growth, maturation, and motor learning and should be able to utilize methods and personal approaches which are appropriate to the age level and the nature of the students. Those who teach and coach should not merely utilize the methods and tactics which were used by their high school or college instructors, they should not think of children as miniature adults, and they should not ignore individual differences in age, sex, strength, and endurance.

This problem is accentuated by the fact that the out-of-school programs for elementary and junior high school students are increasing in both number and scope. Some of the coaches of Biddy Basketball teams, Pop Warner Football teams, Lassie Softball teams, and Little League Baseball teams are well suited and qualified for their jobs. Others are not.

Manning all teams with professionally prepared physical educators, while highly desirable, is not realistic. The alternative is to provide training for those who coach. Adult education courses in coaching, child growth and development, and the psychology of motor learning should be offered by every community which sponsors a sports program for its youth.

10. *Relationship of physical education and athletics.* Physical education may be simply defined as "education through the medium of physical activity." Sports are an important component of physical activity. Athletics is sports systematically organized for competition. Education through athletics is, therefore, physical education. Philosophically, athletics is physical education.

What, then, is the dilemma? It is essentially the fact that in most large universities and many colleges there are now two separate and distinct departments, (1) the Department of Physical Education, and (2) the Department of Athletics. The chairman of the Physical Education Department reports to the academic dean or to the dean of some other division or college. The chairman of the Department of Athletics reports to the President or to his deputy. This is the pragmatic solution to the realistic situation that exists in many places. Coaches are so engrossed with coaching their sport that they are unable to give adequate time to teaching physical education. The pressures from the students, fans, alumni, and news media to win are so great that it is very difficult to give attention to anything besides the athletic teams.

At the same time, some physical education teachers have become disenchanted with athletics and feel that not enough attention and support are being given to the important work which they are doing. They feel that they are serving a far larger proportion of the student body than are the athletic staff and that their objectives are more genuinely educational.

Besides the usual conflicts in the scheduling of facilities and the use of equipment, coaches are required to report to two individuals, one for physical education and one for athletics. In a number of institutions the Athletic Director and the Director of Physical Education are the same person and he has to report to two different superiors. Such situations can be very difficult.

There is no single solution to the dilemmas. Each set of circumstances requires a different answer. Where personnel, equipment, and facilities are shared, a combined administrative unit is usually best. Where the institution is large enough so that the coaches do not teach and the physical education teachers do not coach, separate departments may be the answer.

10.11 SUMMARY

Sports and athletics can be dramatic, exciting, exhilarating, awe-inspiring, and fun. They can on occasion be boring, frustrating, and disappointing. The same individuals or the same team can on one occasion be beautiful, intense, and flawless in their performance and in another instance be slovenly, listless, and prone to error. The greatness of athletics is related to the weaknesses. The hazards contribute to the fascination. The suspense increases the attraction. The very fallibility of the players accounts for the fact that they rise to the occasion in one set of circumstances and yet can fail miserably in another. Uncertainty is the key to the almost universal appeal of sport.

Sport can have educational outcomes. For the most part, athletics is concerned with educational objectives and takes place in schools. Self-realization, the improvement of society, and the satisfaction of human needs are among the aims. The development of a sound system of values is one of the goals of sports and athletics.

Athletic programs, correctly conducted, teach values to all ages both in and out of school.

Athletic programs for everyone should be built on the foundation of a good physical education and intramural program.

Interscholastic and intercollegiate athletics are replete with satisfying experiences and intangible rewards. The satisfaction of achieving, the sharing of fun and excitement, the feeling of friendships formed, and the spirit of camaraderie are among the most enduring values.

High-level competition also produces many problems. Unfair recruiting, exploitation, illegal subsidization, excessive nationalism, sham-amateurism, and gambling are a few. Pressures on coaches and players and the temptations they face are others. The administrative problems involved in the conduct of these complex programs are varied and not easily resolved. Roscoe Brown expressed the basic problem very well when he said:

> Nevertheless, there are many among us who have seen all types of positive values, including cooperation, respect for others, and striving against odds to accomplish noble goals, emerge from participation in sports. The question to be considered then is how do we maximize the positive outcomes from sports, while at the same time preventing the very values that we espouse through sports and physical education from being corrupted to political and excessively competitive ends. [12]

Sports and athletics, correctly administered, are educational. They also have their own intrinsic rewards. They are worthy of the best efforts of all those who make physical education their life's work.

SELECTED REFERENCES

1. *AIAW Handbook,* Mildred Barnes (ed.) Division of Girls' and Women's Sports, American Association for Health, Physical Education, and Recreation, Washington, D.C.: National Education Association, 1973.
2. Allman, Fred L., Jr., "Competitive sports for boys under fifteen—beneficial or harmful?," *Journal of the Medical Association of Georgia,* February 1967.
3. American Association for Health, Physical Education, and Recreation, *Desirable Athletic Competition for Children of Elementary School Age,* Washington, D.C.: National Education Association, 1968. By permission.
4. _____, Division of Girls' and Women's Sports, *Guidelines for Interscholastic Athletic Programs for Junior High School Girls,* revised, Washington, D.C.: National Education Association, 1973.
5. _____, *Guidelines for Interscholastic Athletic Programs for High School Girls,* revised, Washington, D.C.: National Education Association, 1973.
6. _____, *Guidelines for Intercollegiate Athletic Programs for Women,* revised, Washington, D.C.: National Education Association, 1973.
7. _____, *Division of Girls' and Women's Sports Research Reports: Women in Sports,* Washington, D.C.: National Education Association, 1971.
8. _____, *Philosophy and Standards for Girls' and Women's Sports,* Washington, D.C.: National Education Association, 1972.
9. _____, *Proceedings, First National Institute on Girls' Sports,* Washington D.C.: National Education Association, November 1963.
10. *Athletics in Education,* "A platform statement by the division of men's athletics," Washington, D.C.: American Association for Health, Physical Education, and Recreation, 1963.
11. Aydelotte, Frank, *Spectators and Sport,* reprinted from the Oxford Stamp, New York: Oxford University Press, 1917.

12. Brown, Roscoe C., "Human values through sports from the perspective of physical education," paper presented at the National Conference on the Development of Human Values through Sports, Springfield College, October 1973.
13. Baley, James A., "Physical education and athletics belong together," *The Physical Educator,* Vol. 23, No. 2, May 1966.
14. Beck, Robert H., "The Greek tradition and today's physical education," *Journal of Health, Physical Education, and Recreation,* Vol. 34, No. 6, June 1963.
15. Bouet, Michel, "The function of sport in human relations," *International Review of Sport Sociology,* Vol. 1, 1966.
16. Bucher, Charles A., and Ralph K. Dupee, Jr., *Athletics in Schools and Colleges,* New York: The Center for Applied Research in Education, 1965.
17. Bucher, Charles A. (ed.), *Administrative Dimensions of Health and Physical Education Programs, Including Athletics,* St. Louis: The C. V. Mosby Company, 1971.
18. Bucher, Charles A., and Myra Goldman (ed.), *Dimensions of Physical Education,* St. Louis, The C. V. Mosby Company, 1969.
19. Cassell, Ollan C., "Amateur athletic union—a position paper," *The Physical Educator,* Vol. 30, No. 3, October 1973.
20. Cassidy, Rosalind, "The cultural definition of physical education," *Quest,* Monograph IV, April 1965.
21. Champlin, Ellis H., "Is the program of high school athletics an integral part of physical education?," American Academy of Physical Education, Professional Contributions No. 5, November 1956.
22. Coppolillo, Henry P., *Football in Grade School: A Child Psychiatrist's Viewpoint,* December 1966.
23. Cowell, Charles C., "Status of our knowledge of effects of competition in interschool athletics," American Academy of Physical Education, Professional Contributions No. 3, November 1954.
24. Cozens, F. W., and Florence Stumpf, *Sports in American Life,* Chicago: University of Chicago Press, 1953.
25. Daughtrey, Greyson, and John B. Woods, *Physical Education Programs: Organization and Administration,* Philadelphia: W. B. Saunders Company, 1971.
26. *Declaration on Sport,* International Council of Sport and Physical Education, Paris, France: UNESCO House, 1964.
27. *Desirable Competition for Children,* Joint Committee Report, American Association for Health, Physical Education, and Recreation, 1953.
28. Duncan, Ray O., "The contribution of school athletics to the growing boy," *The Journal of Educational Sociology,* Vol. 28, No. 6, February 1955. By permission.
29. Dunning, Eric (ed.), *Sport: Readings from a Sociological Perspective,* Toronto: University of Toronto Press, 1972.
30. Eagen, Edward P. F., "Athletics—medium for international good-will," *The Journal of Educational Sociology,* Vol. 28, No. 6, February 1955.
31. Edwards, Harry, "The myth of the racially superior athlete," *Intellectual Digest,* Vol. II, No. 7, March 1972.
32. Esslinger, Arthur A., "Certification for high school coaches," *Journal of Health, Physical Education, and Recreation,* Vol. 39, No. 8, October 1968.
33. Esslinger, Arthur A., "Out of school athletics for children," *American Academy of Physical Education,* Professional Contributions No. 3, November 1954. By permission.
34. Felshin, Jan, "The social anomaly of women in sports," *The Physical Educator,* Vol. 30, No. 3, October 1973.

35. Flath, Arnold (ed.), *Athletics in America,* Corvallis, Oregon: Oregon State University Press, 1972.
36. Forsythe, Charles E., *Administration of High School Athletics,* New York: Prentice-Hall, 1954.
37. Frederickson, Florence S. "Sports and cultures of man," *Science and Medicine of Exercise and Sports,* Warren R. Johnson (ed.), New York: Harper and Row, 1960.
38. Friermood, Harold T., "Lighting the Olympic flame," *Journal of Physical Education,* Vol. 70, No. 2, November–December 1972.
39. Frost, Reuben B., *Athletics: Problems and Prospects,* Presented to Division of Boys' and Men's Athletics, Southwest District, AAHPER, Salt Lake City, April 23, 1965.
40. _____, "The director and the staff," *Administration of Athletics in Colleges and Universities,* Edward S. Steitz (ed.), Washington, D.C.: American Association for Health, Physical Education, and Recreation, 1971.
41. _____, *Some Psychological Implications for Olympic Sports,* Report of Fifth Summer Session of the International Olympic Academy, Athens, Greece: Hellenic Olympic Committee, 1965.
42. Gallico, Paul, *Farewell to Sport,* New York: Pocket Books, 1945.
43. George, Jack F., and Harry A. Lehman, *School Athletic Administration,* New York: Harper and Row, 1966.
44. Groth, John, *World of Sport,* New York: Winchester Press, 1970.
45. Harrold, Roger D., and Benjamin Lowe, "Intercollegiate athletics in the contemporary student value system," *Journal of College Student Personnel,* Vol. 14, No. 4, July 1973.
46. Hart, M. Marie (ed.), *Sport in the Socio-Cultural Process,* Dubuque, Iowa: Wm. C. Brown Company, 1972.
47. Hartman, Betty G., "Training women to coach," *Journal of Health, Physical Education, and Recreation,* Vol. 39, No. 1, January 1968.
48. Havel, Richard C., "Intercollegiate athletics an educational dilemma," *NCPEAM Annual Proceedings,* 1962.
49. Humphrey, Hubert H., "What sports means to me—and my country," *Sport Magazine,* September 1966.
50. Jackson, Nell, "Public attitude toward women in sports," *The Winning Edge,* Washington, D.C.: American Association for Health, Physical Education, and Recreation, 1974.
51. Kelly, John P., "Amateurism in sport as a viable ideal in the 1970's," *Athletics is America,* Corvallis, Oregon: Oregon State University Press, 1972.
52. Kimball, Edwin R., "Current practices in the control of intercollegiate athletics," Doctoral Dissertation, Eugene, Oregon: The University of Oregon, 1955.
53. Lämmer, Manfred, "Amateurism and the Olympics," *The German Tribune Quarterly Review,* No. 20, Hamburg, Germany, November 16, 1972.
54. Ley, Katherine, "Interscholastic athletics for girls," Paper presented at the National Conference on Secondary School Administration, Washington, D.C., 1962.
55. Loader, W. R., *Sprinter,* New York: The Macmillan Company, 1961.
56. Loy, John W., Jr., and Gerald S. Kenyon (eds.), *Sport, Culture and Society,* New York: The Macmillan Company, 1969.
57. Maheu, Rene, "Sport and culture," *International Journal of Adult and Youth Education,* Vol. 14, No. 4, 1962.
58. *Man in Sport,* The Baltimore Museum of Art, Robert Riger, Director, 1967.
59. Marshall, Stanley J., "The organizational relationship between physical education and intercollegiate athletics in American colleges and universities," Unpublished Doctoral

Dissertation, Springfield College, Springfield, Massachusetts, 1969.

60. McCloy, Charles H., *Philosophical Bases for Physical Education,* New York: F. S. Crofts and Company, 1947.

61. McIntosh, P. C., *Sport in Society,* London: C. A. Watts and Company, 1963.

62. McIntosh, Peter, "Values and competitive sport," Paper presented as Keynote Address at National Conference on the Development of Human Values through Sports, Springfield College, October 1973.

63. Means, Clarence, "Let the girls play, too," *Journal of Health, Physical Education, and Recreation,* Vol. 29, No. 5, May 1958.

64. Mohr, Dorothy R., "Dissenting reaction to position paper: should females compete with males in non-contact varsity sports?," *The Academy Papers, No. 6,* American Academy of Physical Education, September 1972.

65. "Moments in a mad Olympics," *Life,* Vol. 73, No. 12, Sept. 22, 1972.

66. Moore, J. W., *The Psychology of Athletic Coaching,* Minneapolis, Minn.: Burgess Publishing Company, 1970.

67. Morgan, William P., *Contemporary Readings in Sport Psychology,* Springfield, Ill.: Charles C Thomas, 1970.

68. Neal, Patsy, *Sport and Identity,* Philadelphia: Dorrance and Company, 1972.

69. Oberteuffer, Delbert, *Physical Education,* New York: Harper and Row, 1956.

70. "The Olympics: A Summitry of Sport." Reprinted by permission from *TIME, The Weekly Newsmagazine.* Copyright Time Inc.

71. Paterson, Ann, and Edmond C. Hallberg, *Background Readings for Physical Education,* New York: Holt, Rinehart, and Winston, 1967.

72. *Physical Education, and Athletics in Canadian Schools and Colleges,* Canadian Association for Health, Physical Education, and Recreation, Toronto, 1965.

73. Resick, Matthew C., Beverly Seidel, and James G. Mason, *Modern Administrative Practices in Physical Education and Athletics,* Reading, Mass.: Addison-Wesley Publishing Company, 1970.

74. Sage, George H. (ed.), *Sport and American Society: Selected Readings,* Reading, Mass. Addison-Wesley Publishing Company, 1970.

75. Schench, Erwin K., "Sport and politics," *The German Tribune Quarterly Review,* Hamburg, Germany, No. 20, November 16, 1972.

76. *School Athletics,* Educational Policies Commission, Washington, D.C.: National Education Association, 1954.

77. Schwertly, Donald F., "Little league can hurt kids," *Today's Education,* Vol. 59, No. 5, May 1970.

78. Scott, Harry A., *Competitive Sports in Schools and Colleges,* New York: Harper and Row, 1951.

79. Scott, Jack, *Athletics for Athletes,* Hayward, Calif.: Quality Printing Service, 1969.

80. _____, *Sport and the Radical Ethic,* Address delivered at the National Convention of the American Association for Health, Physical Education, and Recreation, March 28, 1972.

81. *Secondary School Athletic Administration: A New Look,* Report of the Second National Conference on Secondary School Athletic Administration, Washington, D.C.: American Association for Health, Physical Education, and Recreation, January 1969.

82. Shea, Edward J., and Elton E. Wieman, *Administrative Policies for Intercollegiate Athletics,* Springfield, Ill.: Charles C Thomas, 1967.

83. Sheehan, George, "Sport mirrors conflicts in American life," *Journal of Physical Education,* Vol. 70, No. 6, July–August 1973.

84. Shriver, Sargent, "The moral force of sport," *Sports Illustrated,* Vol. 18, No. 22, June 3, 1963.
85. Siedentop, Daryl, *Physical Education,* Dubuque, Iowa: Wm. C. Brown Company, 1972.
86. Singer, Robert N., *Coaching, Athletics and Psychology,* New York: McGraw-Hill, 1972.
87. Skubic, Vera, "Should females compete with males in non-contact sports?," *The Academy Papers No. 6,* American Academy of Physical Education, September 1972.
88. Slusher, Howard S., *Man, Sport and Existence,* Philadelphia: Lea and Febiger, 1967.
89. Slusher, Howard S., and Aileene S. Lockhart, *Anthology of Contemporary Readings,* Dubuque, Iowa: Wm. C. Brown Company, 1966.
90. Steitz, Edward S. (ed.), *Administration of Athletics in Colleges and Universities,* Washington, D.C.: American Association for Health, Physical Education, and Recreation, 1971.
91. Stutzman, Sandra J., Charles McCullough, and Fran Koenig, "Did DGWS Fail? Two Points of View," *Journal of Health, Physical Education, and Recreation,* Vol. 45, No. 1, January 1974.
92. Tunney, John V., "Amateur athletics act," *Swimming World,* Vol. 14, No. 9, September 1973.
93. *Values in Sports,* Report of Joint National Conference of the Division for Girls' and Women's Sports and the Division of Men's Athletics, Washington, D.C.: American Association for Health, Physical Education, and Recreation, 1962.
94. Van Dalen, Deobold D., and Bruce L. Bennett, *A World History of Physical Education,* 2nd edition, Englewood Cliffs, N.J.: Prentice-Hall, 1971.
95. VanderZwaag, Harold J., *Toward a Philosophy of Sport,* Reading, Mass.: Addison-Wesley Publishing Company, 1972.
96. Voltmer, Edward F., and Arthur A. Esslinger, *The Organization and Administration of Physical Education,* 4th edition, New York: Appleton-Century-Crofts, 1967.
97. Weiss, Paul, *Sport, A Philosophic Inquiry,* Carbondale, Ill.: Southern Illinois University Press, 1969. By permission.
98. Wolff, Bob, "Let's get the facts," *The Journal of Educational Sociology,* Vol. 28, No. 6, February 1955. By permission.
99. Woods, Sherwyn M., "The violent world of the athlete," *Quest,* Monograph XVI, June 1971.
100. *Year in Sports, The,* Ted Smits (ed.), Englewood Cliffs, N.J.: Prentice-Hall, 1958.
101. Zeigler, Earle F., "Intramurals: profession, discipline, or part thereof?," Proceedings of 76th Meeting, National College Physical Education Association for Men, January 1973.
102. Zoller, Josef O., "Sport, society and politics," *The German Tribune Quarterly Review,* No. 20, November 16, 1972.

Programs
and
Curricula

Chapter 11

11.1 PHYSICAL ACTIVITY AS THE MEDIUM

The education of children takes place by exciting, dismaying, and surprising methods. It proceeds sometimes slowly and subtly, sometimes spontaneously and explosively, but most often gradually and observably. Children learn and develop as they ride the merry-go-round, fight with their siblings, watch television, read stories, ride bicycles, and attend classes. They are also educated as they run, leap, dodge, swing, and balance. They grow and mature as they play with others, walk by themselves, build snowmen, and perform scientific experiments. The education of people consists of modifications which occur in individuals as a result of all their experiences.

Physical education takes place as children move. It occurs in their cribs as they reach out and grasp thier mothers' fingers. It almost always includes learning to roll over, creep, crawl, balance, walk, and climb. It certainly proceeds in games of tag, dodgeball, snatch-the-bacon, animal trap, or king-of-the-mountain. Rhythmic activities, gymnastics, aquatics, team games, and lifetime sports are physical education. In fact, physical education includes all of the changes that occur in individuals through the medium of physical activity.

Learning takes place not only through vigorous and extensive movement but also by studying, discussing, and contemplating movement. Physical education includes the studies of physiology, kinetics, philosophy of sport, and related behavioral sciences.

If we think of the games, sports, and dances of many lands, if we recall all the activities in which we have participated, if we review the physical activities described in our books on physical education, if we study history and anthropology in an effort to discover past modes of education, in fact, if we try to summarize all the kinds of physical education which take place in the world, we cannot but be impressed with the immense scope and infinite variety of activities.

It is estimated that more than half of all the nervous stimuli impinging upon the central nervous system come as a result of movement. Most of them emanate from the proprioceptors located in the skin, muscles, and joints. These stimuli bring about changes in the human organism. This is part of education.

While activity is generally accepted as the principle medium through which physical education takes place, the significance of the cognitive domain must not be forgotten. The acquisition of knowledge, the development of the intellect, and rational thinking are also important.

11.2 KNOWLEDGE AND UNDERSTANDING

Leonard Larsen chaired a committee that worked for several years preparing a manual entitled *Knowledge and Understanding in Physical Education.* As stated in its preface, this manual was "a pioneer effort in setting down the body of knowledge for physical education."* Particularly pertinent are the following paragraphs concerning the physical and intellectual aspects of physical education.

---

*American Association for Health, Physical Education, and Recreation, *Knowledge and Understanding in Physical Education,* Washington, D.C., AAHPER-NEA, 1969, p. iii.

"Learning takes place not only
through vigorous and extensive
movement but also by studying,
discussing, and contemplating
movement." (Courtesy of the
*Journal of Health, Physical
Education, and Recreation.*)

Physical education is primarily an activity program and many of the objectives of the program are accomplished through activity. Proof of learning will be evidenced largely in the actual performance of a skill or a game or a dance. This manual does not propose to minimize the importance of these physical performance skills and tests; rather it emphasizes the importance of basic understandings to the achievenent of all the objectives of physical education, including skill in physical activity.

Knowledge and understandings have always been considered essential elements in the teaching of physical education, but many teachers have assumed that these objectives were being achieved without seeking any direct evidence of the fact. Present-day pressures for the re-examination of curriculum and procedures demand that more attention be given the creative use of the intellect in physical education. The intellectual, the verbally expressive content of physical education is as significant as the motor content, and needs to be assessed. In appraising the student's progress in physical education, therefore, evidence should be obtained on the acquisition of knowledges and understandings in addition to the mastering of physical skills.*

The manual is intended for use by the classroom teacher and the physical education specialist, both of whom share the responsibility for the total education of children and youth. As physical education activities are taught and performed, knowledges, meanings, understandings, and appreciations should become part of what is learned. Safety practices, related scientific facts and principles, aesthetic appreciations, values and ethical considerations, and health knowledge should be acquired or developed. Self-discovery, self-esteem, self-fulfillment and self-realization should be outcomes.

Contained in the manual are factual statements relating to each skill and concept, analyses of different movement patterns, and suggestions with regard to the formulation of values and the development of appreciations. The manual is organized in three parts. Part I, Activity Performance, deals with basic movement patterns, sports skills, body mechanics, tactics and strategies, rules, and protective requirements. Part II. Effects of Activity, includes physiological principles, descriptions of effects of activity on health and fitness, and statements concerning the capacity of the human organism to move and exercise. Part III, Factors Modifying Participation and Their Effects, deals with growth and development, attitudes, nutrition, stress, and performance aids.†

The manual is intended to be utilized for an organized approach to learning knowledges and skills as part of physical education. Instructions and suggestions are also made with regard to the use of this information in evaluation. Fundamental principles of physiology, biomechanics, sociology, and psychology are included. Basic movement concepts and principles of pedagogy are listed. Above all, it is made clear that many leaders in physical education are convinced of the importance of *teaching much more in physical education than just "how to do."*

---

* *Ibid,* pp. x–xi. By permission.
† *Ibid,* p. ix.

11.3 SELECTION AND CLASSIFICATION OF ACTIVITIES

Physical education activities to be used in the classroom should be selected on the basis of the nature, needs, capacities, and interests of the students. After they have been chosen on that basis, some will need to be eliminated due to modifying factors such as (1) facilities available, (2) capabilities of the staff, (3) equipment needed, (4) time alloted for physical education, (5) climate and geographical considerations, and (6) budgetary resources.

It should be emphasized that the modifying factors listed above need not be permanent impediments. Facilities can be constructed, personnel can be trained, more teachers can be hired, equipment can be purchased and budget allotments can be increased. These take time, planning, effort, and persistence. There are, however, many examples of outstanding physical education programs which have been developed over a period of years through the intelligent, patient, and untiring efforts of dedicated teachers and/or administrators.

Nature of the student.   Age, sex, personality, ethnic and cultural background, and inherited characteristics of students should be considered when selecting activities. It is obvious that what is suitable for a six-year-old boy may not be right for a ten-year-old boy and that what seems to be the consuming passion of a girl twelve years old may not interest her in the least when she is sixteen.

While boys and girls differ in some respects, they also have many characteristics in common. The differences are more apparent at some ages than they are at others. Sometimes boys and girls group themselves by sex; at other times they seek each other's company. There are times and circumstances when the girls want to be with the boys and the boys want to be by themselves. The converse may also be true. There are some sports which they can and should play in mixed groups and some in which they should be segregated.

The ethnic and cultural backgrounds of students should be considered in the selection of activities. In a community where there are a large number of immigrants from Norway, all the children may wish to ski; in a German community gymnastics may be preferred; a group of boys from England may like cricket; Australians generally love to swim. Folk dances from the lands of their ancestors may still be the favorite activity of some children.

Personality traits also influence the reaction to certain activities. There may be groups of boys who need hockey or football in which they work off some of their aggressions through rough bodily contact. Another group may need the socialization of a class in ethnic dance. There are individuals who like activities such as cross-country running or skiing where they can be alone with their thoughts. Many desire the challenge of a mountain to climb or a wave to ride. The nature of every individual is different. This calls for a variety of physical education opportunities.

Needs of the student.   Children have physiological, psychological, and sociological needs. They require security, love, praise, and a feeling of self-worth as well as food and water. They need to develop confidence, poise, and a knowledge of how to deal with others.

The needs of people are not the same throughout life. The early years should include activities which will assist individuals to keep fit and vigorous in later years. Sports which will be absorbing at a more advanced age should be learned early.

All people do not have the same needs. Some are in need of activity which will help them lose weight, others require more strength and endurance, and a number will benefit most by learning skills and developing coordination.

Capacities and limitations. There are wide differences in the capacities of individuals. Each person's limitations and abilities change greatly as the years pass. Growth and maturity proceed in spurts, the adolescent growth spurt being particularly noticeable. This comes later for some than for others and causes anxiety for those whose physiological age lags behind their chronological age. Care should be exercised not to cause psychological or physical trauma for those who mature slowly. Attention should be given to every individual's limitations at each age.

Interests. Educators and psychologists know that children and adults learn faster when they are highly motivated. The degree of motivation is related to the individual's interest. Readiness of the students should receive consideration when selecting activities and planning lessons.

Those planning courses of study and developing curricula must be aware of the various factors which may influence and cause sudden shifts of interests. Unpleasant experiences in playing a particular game can cause a student to suddenly lose interest. Sports that attract their close friends seem most desirable to many individuals. A girl friend's or boy friend's participation in an activity will motivate many to choose the same one. What a person does well is usually satisfying and pleasureable.

Too often a student will shy away from an activity never tried. Because the student is inexperienced, he/she fears ineptness and embarrassment. There are many who originally do not like gymnastics, soccer, modern dance, or tennis, but who, after a few experiences, discover that any one of these can be both fascinating and satisfying and develop a lasting interest in it.

In planning curricula, one must be aware of the reasons for lack of interest and provide activities for which students are already highly motivated in addition to those which might capture their interest if they had the opportunity to learn.

11.4 CURRICULUM DEVELOPMENT

Educators have employed many different methods of developing curricula. When required to develop a new curriculum or to revise an old one, most physical educators will utilize one or more of the following approaches:

1. The best of current practices
2. Philosophy $\longrightarrow$ principles $\longrightarrow$ program
3. Job analysis $\longrightarrow$ functions $\longrightarrow$ competencies
4. The conceptual approach

Each of these procedures has merit. All may play a part if used judiciously and if properly organized and integrated.

The best of current practices. Visiting other schools, listening to the experiences of other physical educators, studying curricula which exist in various institutions, and selecting some elements and ideas which have proven effective and successful elsewhere may furnish inspiration for innovation, help avoid pitfalls, and stimulate creative thinking. But using this method exclusively may result in a program not adapted to the needs of a particular situation and therefore may be irrelevant and uninteresting.

Philosophy →principles →program. To begin with the study of the philosophy of the institution, an analysis of current educational philosophy, and the identification of purposes, aims, and objectives is also appropriate and salutary. It *is* important to fit the program to the educational philosophy and the goals of the specific institution and the community. Principles governing the selection of courses must be appropriate to the mission of the school for which the curriculum is being developed.

Job analysis → functions → competencies. If an institution prepares students for given trades, specific professions, or known tasks, there must be a careful analysis of the functions to be performed by the graduates and the competencies needed to perform them. An accountant needs to know how to keep financial records, a surgeon must be skillful at performing operations, and a physical educator must know how to teach. While early education is general in nature and many colleges offer liberal arts education, trade schools and professional preparation institutions must carefully diagnose the competencies needed to perform adequately in the graduate's chosen field. They must then teach those specialties as effectively as possible.

The conceptual approach. Because knowledge continues to accumulate at such a rapid pace, it is impossible, even in a given field of study, to learn everything there is to learn. This has led to what is now being called the *conceptual approach* to curriculum building. Instead of presenting chronologically every development in a field of study from its historical beginning, the question is asked, "What concepts are essential for a person studying this subject?" These concepts are then organized into a logical progression and the facts and principles supporting them are integrated into a teaching unit.

When utilizing the conceptual approach one begins with the larger concepts, the "main ideas." In physical education two such concepts might be,

1. Physical education is concerned with the overall development of man.
2. Physical education is concerned with assisting in the development of a better world.

Smaller concepts, or subconcepts, which support the larger concepts are then identified, developed, and organized. In organizing the curriculum plan, the organized body of concepts is integrated into teaching units. After this has been done the experiences, in the form of activities and courses, are fitted in.

Steps in curriculum construction
Regardless of the exact method utilized in formulating a curriculum, the steps are somewhat the same. Hilda Taba has identified the following as useful orderly steps in developing a curriculum:

1. Diagnosis of needs
2. Formulation of objectives
3. Selection of content
4. Organization of content
5. Selection of learning experiences
6. Organization of learning experiences
7. Evaluation [64, p. 12]

The curriculum is the heart of any educational program. A philosophy which includes sound planning and a careful outline of objectives is meaningless without the activities and other content necessary for implementation.

Classification of activities
There is no classification of acitivities which has universal acceptance among physical educators. There is, however, fairly general agreement on much of the terminology. The following list of activities, categorized under descriptive headings, has been drawn from many sources and is presented as a usable classification. It is not in any sense intended to be all-inclusive.

Fundamental Movements		*Team Games*
Reaching	Hanging	Baseball
Grasping	Swinging	Basketball
Kicking	Pushing	Field hockey
Rolling	Pulling	Football
Twisting	Lifting	Ice hockey
Creeping	Throwing	Lacrosse
Crawling	Running	Soccer
Standing	Jumping	Speedball
Walking	Climbing	Touch football

Games and Relays
Broom hockey
Circle games
Circle relays
Mimetics
Shuttle relays
Street games
Tag games

Self-Testing Activities
Gymnastics
Rope climbing
Rope skipping
Stunts
Track and field
Trampolining
Tumbling

Winter Sports
Bobsledding
Skating
Skiing
Snowshoeing
Tobogganing

Conditioning Activities
Calisthenics
Circuit training
Cycling
Isometric exercises
Jogging
Relaxation
Roller skating
Treadmill running

Outdoor Activities
Backpacking
Camping
Mountain climbing
Orienteering
White-water canoeing

Rhythmic Activities
Ballet
Children's rhythms
Ethnic Dance
Modern Dance
Social Dance
Square Dance

Aquatics
Boating
Canoeing
Diving
Lifesaving
Rowing
Sailing
Scuba diving
Swimming

Lifetime Sports
Archery
Badminton
Bowling
Fencing
Flycasting
Golf
Handball
Horseshoes
Horsemanship
Paddle rackets
Shuffleboard
Tennis
Tetherball

Combatives
Boxing
Judo
Karate
Wrestling

Adapted Physical Education
Body-building exercises
Body mechanics
Corrective activities
Sports for the handicapped

11.5 PROGRAMS AT THE ELEMENTARY LEVEL

The world in which today's children live may be frightening at times, but it is also tremendously exciting. Because of life changing so rapidly, and the knowledge that by the time today's youngsters are in positions of leadership the world will be so vastly different the educational process must become more flexible, more open about possibilities for innovation. [53, p. 8]

These were the words of Jimmy Nations as he spoke about "the changing elementary school." Physical education too is becoming more and more exciting for elementary-school youngsters. Physical educators are now exploring the realm of movement and accepting challenges to allow children to move in many different ways. At the same time they are satisfying many of the basic needs of young children.

Children in the lower-elementary grades need vigorous, large-muscle activity. They need to run, chase, climb, and swing. They are also ready to throw and catch beanbags and balls, climb through hoops and jump over ropes, mimic and dance, explore and create. Above all they crave active, joyous, and spontaneous play.

As children advance toward the upper-elementary level, they develop an increasing number of fine and more manipulative skills. They dribble and pass basketballs ... they swing bats and control pucks with hockey sticks ... they

throw, hit, and field baseballs . . . they dance and compose dances . . . they handle their bodies on gymnastic apparatus. They become more and more concerned about others and want to play and work in groups. They are challenged by competition and love to excel.

Victor Dauer's *continuum of program development* (Figure 11.1) indicates the range of skills which serves as the basis for elementary school programs. The child proceeds from body management competencies through various stages to high skill development.

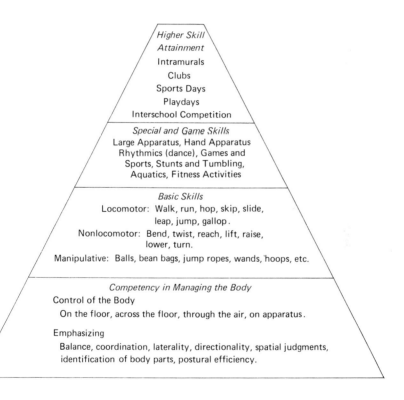

Higher Skill Attainment
Intramurals
Clubs
Sports Days
Playdays
Interschool Competition

Special and Game Skills
Large Apparatus, Hand Apparatus
Rhythmics (dance), Games and
Sports, Stunts and Tumbling,
Aquatics, Fitness Activities

Basic Skills
Locomotor: Walk, run, hop, skip, slide,
leap, jump, gallop.
Nonlocomotor: Bend, twist, reach, lift, raise,
lower, turn.
Manipulative: Balls, bean bags, jump ropes, wands, hoops, etc.

Competency in Managing the Body
Control of the Body
On the floor, across the floor, through the air, on apparatus.

Emphasizing
Balance, coordination, laterality, directionality, spatial judgments,
identification of body parts, postural efficiency.

Figure 11.1   Continuum of program development based on skill development and attainment. [14, p. 65]

◀"As children advance toward the upper-elementary level,
they develop an increasing number of fine and more
manipulative skills." (Courtesy of Springfield College.)

Margie Hanson indicates three special thrusts in elementary physical education. These are a) movement education, b) perceptual-motor development, and c) multidisciplinary approach to learning. Other trends which she identifies are:

1. Emphasis on knowledge and understanding.
2. Development of the creative process.
3. Learning how to learn.
4. Concern for education of the handicapped.
5. Increased interest in education for the very young child (preschool).
6. Learning to move *well.*
7. Self-expression through movement.
8. Cooperative learning programs with art, music, drama, and dance.

Hanson concludes her comments on curriculum by saying:

> Today, concerned leaders are looking at curriculum in a much broader way than ever before as they examine the unique and essential, yet complementary, role of physical education in total learning and child development. [29, pp. 2–3]

> Let us look further at some of these developments discussed by other leaders.

11.6 MOVEMENT EDUCATION
Movement education has now been generally accepted as an important phase of physical education. Even though the concept has been with us for some time, its reemphasis, reinterpretation, and widespread acceptance did not occur until the 1960's.

Definitions and descriptions of movement education still vary, however. Let us examine a few of these.

Kate Barrett discusses movement education in terms of four major categories, (a) body, (b) space, (c) effort, and (d) personal relationships. She indicates that while the general aspects of physical education are still games, sports, dance, and gymnastics, the difference lies in what occurs within the specific activities. The focus may be on using the total *body* or different parts of the body; it may be on the *relationship* to an opponent or teammate; in some instances it is on the *effort* required for all-out sustained or explosive movements; or it may be on directional changes added to give the idea of *space*.

In well-taught movement education, experiences are individualized, the students proceed at their own pace, the children's needs are carefully studied and considered, and decisions are made jointly by the teacher and students. In movement education physical education teachers are "committed to the goal of skill in movement, appreciation of movement, and knowledge of movement as they (the children) develop in an educational setting of decision making, independence, and self-confidence." [3, p. 5]

Evelyn Schurr says:

Movement education or movement exploration is not physical education in the elementary school but it is one approach to teaching basic skills or new skills and related aspects of movement. [62, p. 224]

Kirchner, Cunningham, and Warrell define movement education thus:

Movement education may be defined as an individualized approach or system of teaching children to become aware of their physical abilities and to use them effectively in their daily activities involving play, work, and creative expression. [43, p. 4]

"Movement education may be defined as an individualized approach or system of teaching children to become aware of their physical abilities and to use them effectively . . ."—Kirchner, Cunningham, and Warrell (Courtesy of the *Journal of Health, Physical Education, and Recreation.*)

Hollis Fait uses the term movement education synonymously with motor exploration:

> Motor exploration or movement education is a form of problem solving. It is chiefly concerned with (1) discovering the movements of which the body is capable, (2) learning the fundamental skills of movement, (3) encouraging the inherent love of movement, and (4) developing an understanding of the relationship of emotion to movement as a basis for expressing emotions through movement. It is also expected that motor exploration will foster the development of physical fitness and facilitate learning the skills of games, sports, and dance. [19, pp. 112–113]

And Joan Tillotson has this to say:

> Movement education can be defined as that phase of the total educational program which concerns the development of effective, efficient, and expressive movement responses in a thinking, feeling, and sharing human being. Its aim is to develop an awareness of the self in the physical environment, of the body and its capabilities, and of the components of movement. [67, p. 63]

Included in good programs of movement education are the following concepts: (1) using an individualized approach to teaching, (2) achieving an awareness of one's capabilities, (3) learning to move effectively and efficiently, (4) acquiring an understanding of the components of movement, (5) developing an appreciation for and a love of movement, and (6) relating one's feelings and emotions to movement.

Movement education includes the concepts and methods of movement exploration. The teacher issues a challenge, poses a question, or indicates a performance objective. The student must choose between several possible ways of achieving the objective and then must set about moving as effectively as possible toward that objective. As the student repeats the performance again and again, movements become more efficient and polished. The teacher meanwhile observes, counsels, guides, and instructs, bearing in mind that the ultimate purpose is the optimal, most effective, and most joyous movement for the given individual. The inclusion of choice and the opportunity to explore add excitement and adventure to the effort.

Using essentially the same terms as Barrett (see p. 282), Schurr has designed her own paradigm, "factors of movement study." She indicates that all basic movement is concerned with (1) qualities of movement, (2) space, (3) body actions, and (4) relationships. [61, pp. 224–225]

These four factors are analyzed each with reference to subfactors. *Qualities of movement* are dependent upon optimal adjustment to time, force, body shape, and flow. Fast reaction and response time, acceleration, quick changes of direction, and sheer speed are all related to the factor of *time.*

The control of *force* is one of the important factors determining precise movement. The basketball player leaping for the rebound, the high jumper trying to clear the bar, and the gymnast doing a walkover on the balance beam are examples of movements where force must be controlled.

Body shape plays an important role in mimetics, diving, trampolining, high jumping, and expressive dance. It is extremely important in figure skating, tumbling, and floor exercises. It is emphasized in the stance of the batter in baseball and the guard in football. Balance, equilibrium, and stability are all related to body shape.

Flow refers to the transition from one position or movement to another. A free, smooth movement with a final objective is the most common, whereas movements which accelerate and decelerate, stop, and begin again are found in a number of activities. Hurling the discus is an example of "free flow," whereas a performance of free exercise where the tempo increases and decreases is an example of "bound flow." The discus thrower is concerned about the summation of forces, the elimination of extraneous movements, acceleration, and momentum. The gymnast explodes into a somersault, slows down and does a hand stand, and whirls into a cartwheel—one change of tempo to another. [61, pp. 225–226]

When moving, adjustments must also be made to the *space* available. As Marjorie Randall indicated, one must be concerned with the direction of movement through space, whether the body moves in a straight line or a circuitous one, and whether the movement is one of curling, twisting, or stretching. [57, p. 49]

The space surrounding the body in which it can move from a stationary base is known as its *sphere of movement*. The space into which the body as a whole moves from one spot to another is termed *general* space. As a person runs, leaps, springs sideward, or crawls from one place to another, the movement is in general space. All movement of the body takes place either in its sphere of movement, in general space, or in combinations of the two. Such movements may be upward or downward, frontward or backward, and toward either the right or left side.

Awareness is an important aspect of movement education. The ability to sense one's movements, the ability to analyze one's physical actions, and the ability to recognize how each part of the body moves are important in learning correct motor patterns and in developing athletic skills. While sensory impulses from the muscles, tendons, and joints are constantly being transmitted to the central nervous system, they are not always interpreted and perceived with the same degree of clarity. Conscious efforts to understand one's own movement will improve both the perception of how one is moving and the techniques of future movement. For as Jacqueline Haslett said,

> Since human movement is fundamental in all facets of life, the child should learn his own movement capacities. He should learn the language of movement, and he should invent and create dances of his own. It is educationally sound to want the child to explore and discover, and to have the child make something *for* himself. At this level, the teacher is not interested in perfection

but in "child art" (expression), and in the "learning process" (awareness of bodily capacities and personal mastery of movement). The child must have awareness of his own instrument, the body, knowing how to use it with ease. He must gain muscular control of the body and its parts. Dance training in the child will help him to live, to move and to express himself in his *own* flow of movement. It is *how* he discovers his movement that is necessary. If the child succeeds in this, it will help him to adjust to life. [30, p. 3]

According to Godfrey and Kephart, movement education "deals with the development and training of basic movement patterns," with "psycho-motor and perceptual-motor development and behavior," and with "integration of movement performance for purposeful activity." [26, p. 19] It includes both movement exploration and motor learning. Problem solving and experimentation are emphasized. Developmental activities based on the nature, needs, and interests of the students furnish the program. As much self-direction as possible is a basic characteristic of the method.

In the United States movement exploration is utilized extensively as the approach to physical education in the primary and lower-elementary grades. As the students approach the junior high school and high school levels the traditional methods of teaching sports, gymnastics, and dance are more generally utilized. The change is gradual rather than sudden, however. It is usually agreed that the basic fundamentals, the old "racial activities," and the natural ways of moving the body need to be learned first and then the finer, more manipulative skills are added as the child becomes ready physiologically, psychologically, and sociologically.

It is interesting to note that in many instances the movement exploration approach is being employed at the high school level. Basketball players are being given increasing freedom to execute their shots in ways which they feel are most effective for them. Dancers are encouraged and assisted to create new routines. High jumpers are afforded the opportunity to explore techniques to improve their performances. In many sports one can observe increased emphasis on originality, creativity, and individual freedom in methods of achieving goals and objectives. Movement education, then, is part of physical education and athletic programs at all age levels and in many different situations.

11.7 ADOLESCENCE

The period in which an individual changes from childhood to adulthood is termed *adolescence*. It is marked by a period of rapid growth (the adolescent growth spurt) followed by deceleration of growth and solidifying of bone and muscle. Physical and biochemical changes are rapid and extensive during this period and secondary sex characteristics develop rapidly. The increase in height and weight is generally matched by greater strength, endurance, and coordination. The appetite increases, there is greater immunity to disease, and sexual maturity is attained.

Adolescents are very conscious of the image they present to others. They are particularly concerned about their development as mature men and women. It is important that they be informed about the individual differences in the exact chronological age at which puberty and sexual maturation occur. Late-maturing boys and girls often become anxious and self-conscious unless they are counseled intelligently and wisely.

Physiological age is thought to be more indicative of adolescent tolerance for stressful activity than is chronological age. Because grade level usually correlates highly with chronological age, it is not a good index of tolerance for hazardous sports such as football and hockey. Physical education teachers and administrators should be conscious of these phenomena and try to provide both appropriate activities and wise counsel.

Peer approval is particularly important to adolescents. Both parents and teachers need to understand this. Patience, tact, and understanding on the part of authority figures is essential during this trying period. But it is also important that adolescents have a firm base of support as they are changing their role from the dependence of childhood to the independence of adulthood. Dr. Martin Symonds puts it this way:

> In all the children in trouble that I've seen, one thing stands out: their parents are not providing the anchorage, the support, the guidance they need. Adolescents grow very rapidly and erratically, and need a solid point of view to push against. As parents, you must let them know what your values are —without belligerence. [33, p. 107]

11.8 JUNIOR HIGH SCHOOL EXPERIENCES
Assuming that the elementary school program has provided activities for adequate organic development, fundamental movement patterns, and an introduction to a number of rhythmic exercises, gymnastic activities, and sports, the junior high school program should stress exposure to a broad variety of physical education activities. There should be emphasis on demanding and challenging experiences because students of this age are ready and eager for action. Because students of this age should have many interpersonal experiences and need to develop social understanding, team sports should be an important part of the program. Students should be exposed to individual and dual sports because some will not continue their education beyond the age of sixteen. Camping and other outdoor experiences should be included for the same reason.

Gymnastics and other self-testing activities are also appropriate at this period. The challenge of controlling the body in many different ways is appealing and the activity lends itself to well-rounded development. Track-and-field activities can be emphasized at the junior high school level providing the distances are not too long. While opinions vary, it appears that the 880-yard run should be the longest race for students of this age.

Because the disparity between the sexes is probably more pronounced, boys and girls should be separated for contact activities at this age. Nevertheless it is important to schedule a substantial number of coeducational classes in which boys and girls can interact and maintain an informal and casual relationship with one another.

Aquatics are particularly appropriate at the junior high school level. Not only are students interested in swimming and diving at this age, but they are ready for lifesaving and other water sports as well. It is also a well-known fact that many swimmers attain their best competitive scores when in the teens.

There are practically no physical education activities for which junior high school students are not ready. They are interested in everything. They want to be "where the action is." With a little conditioning and practice, they are generally capable of almost any kind of movement. They are still flexible and pliable enough to learn gymnastic skills which require these qualities. They are eager to emulate their seniors in high school. They usually prefer being active to being quiet. Their energy seems boundless.

11.9 SENIOR HIGH SCHOOL PHYSICAL EDUCATION

The character of senior high school physical education is changing. Whereas a few short years ago it resembled an advanced junior high school program, it is now recognized that the needs of senior high school students vary from those of their junior high school years.

Assuming a reasonably sound program of movement education in the elementary school and a broad exposure to a variety of activities in the junior high school, the secondary school student is now ready for more specialization, more lifetime sports, a higher level of skill development, and more emphasis on the understanding of concepts related to physical education. The senior high school student should have more choice of activities, should be provided more opportunities for leadership, and should be presented with a number of new and challenging experiences. On the one hand he is ready and eager for adventure. On the other hand he is interested in concepts of motor learning and principles of movements. He is also concerned about his relationships with the opposite sex.

Greyson Daughtrey and John Woods discuss what they call the "pupil-choice plan" for senior high school students. It provides considerable choice of physical education courses for the students and has the following advantages:

1. It allows students to specialize and spend more time on an activity; the extra practice in turn improves the quality of the skill.
2. It provides for individual differences.
3. It provides for better staff utilization through team teaching and allows instructors to teach those activities they are best qualified to teach.
4. It eliminates most problems of discipline because students participate in the activity of their choice.
5. It minimizes organizational difficulties. [16, p. 136]

The senior high school years begin the age of emancipation for most individuals. The urge to break away from parental control, the desire to be recognized for themselves as individuals, the eagerness to determine their own lifestyles, and the need to be involved with their peers are particularly evident at this age. Rebellion against authority also surfaces in many young people about this time.

During their senior high school years many students reach their peak or near peak as far as their ability to perform is concerned. They are usually fully developed organically and for the healthy person there is almost no activity which is contraindicated.

Senior high school students generally have a strong sense of loyalty, a tendency toward hero-worship, a very competitive spirit, and a concern for the way they look particularly in the eyes of their peers.

Team sports, individual and dual sports, aquatics, gymnastics, dance, and outdoor activities have a place in the senior high school program. Some students benefit most by participation in football; for others tennis will be the most satisfying; for many swimming will provide the greatest interest and development; and for those needing the opportunity to create and express themselves, dance may have the greatest value.

The important thing is that their physical education experiences should be meaningful to them. If there is no challenge, if the activities are devoid of fun and joy, if there is no sharing of adventure and triumph, and if the program is merely a repetition of their earlier physical education, students cannot be expected to maintain their interest and enthusiasm. They must look upon their physical education as significant and important to their individual self-realization.

11.10 LIFETIME SPORTS

For students who are completing their formal education, activities which can serve them throughout their adult years are essential. Whether they are called *carryover activities, lifetime sports, individual and dual sports, outdoor activities, or winter activities,* they should provide exercise, enjoyment, and satisfaction long after school is ended. Certain team sports such as volley ball and softball also have carryover value.

The best lifetime sports are activities which can be performed either alone or with a small number of companions. It is often too difficult, in the long run, to assemble ten or more people for team sports week after week, year after year. For this reason skiing, golf, tennis, canoeing, archery, badminton, bowling, and swimming are among the most popular. Hiking, cycling, mountaineering, and sailing are also beneficial.

There are also other factors to be considered in selecting lifetime sports to be taught in physical education classes. The availability of facilities, the cost of equipment, the distance to the site, and other practical considerations must be taken into account.

For college and senior high school programs, however, lifetime sports must be given a high priority. They are often among the most significant of all physical education experiences.

11.11 COLLEGE AND UNIVERSITY PROGRAMS

College students are, almost without exception, individuals who have reached their full adulthood. They are very often at the peak of their ability to run, jump, hurl, and perform other athletic feats. This is the age when they need to discover their potentialities as well as their limitations. This is also the period of their life when

"For students who are in the terminal phases of their education, activities which can serve them throughout their adult years are essential." (Courtesy of (*top right*) Luther College, (*bottom right*) South Dakota State University, and (*left*) the *Journal of Health, Physical Education, and Recreation.*)

they are the most adventuresome and seek new experiences. They have discovered themselves as individuals and like to make their own decisions. The desire to excel is often particularly evident at this time but this competitive spirit may be channeled in a direction other than sports. For many young people of college age, coeducational activities and dance have their greatest appeal.

College and university physical education programs are complex, varied, and often quite elaborate. They may contain organizational units for the basic instruction program, the professional preparation program, the graduate program, and the intramural program. Because the professional preparation program is discussed in a later chapter (see Chapter 18) it will not be included here.

The basic instruction program
While there are a number of colleges and universities which no longer require physical education, there are still many in which all students must participate in these activities for one to two years. The vast majority of college level institutions have evaluated and revised their programs. The old plan of requiring Physical Education I, II, III, and IV without prior identification of the content is rapidly becoming obsolete. Instead we find many new offerings, innovative methods, and a great deal of choice. In a rapidly increasing number of institutions, there is also considerable student voice in planning curricular offerings.

While the goals, aims, and objectives of physical education outlined in Chapter 2 are applicable to college students as well as younger persons, there are some specific motivations which apply more directly to college students. These include:

1. Enjoyment and pleasure.
2. Personal fitness.
3. Development of a positive self-concept.
4. Learning how to play sports in which they can participate after college.
5. Satisfaction of social needs.
6. Fostering an appreciation for sports and other movement experiences which will lead to prolonged participation and a fuller and richer life.
7. Providing an opportunity for self-expression.
8. Providing a means of alleviating tensions and encouraging relaxation.

In a number of colleges, students sample each category of physical education activity and are then allowed to choose the specific activity in which they wish to participate. For example, they may register for a team sport the first semester, an individual sport the second, an aquatic activity the third, and a dance course the fourth. In some institutions they may elect to continue their enrollment in physical education after they have completed the requirement. They are then free to take any course they wish.

Joseph Oxendine reported in 1972 that 74 percent of the institutions responding to his survey indicated a requirement for all undergraduate students. An

additional 8 percent require physical education for students in certain schools or departments. Of those requiring physical education, the most common length of time was four semesters.*

To require or not to require

There is a great deal of disagreement regarding the matter of required physical education. The trend is to reduce all-college requirements in all subjects. Many institutions lack the facilities, personnel, and other resources to build a good program. In some instances an already overloaded faculty is both unwilling and unable to take on the burden of a modernized physical education program. Some student bodies are so negative toward physical education that the value of the program must be questioned. It is doubtful whether weak programs are of much benefit to either the participant or the institution.

On the other hand, when requirements are dropped, it is always those who need activity the most who fail to take physical education. The weak, the inept, the inexperienced, and the uncoordinated are generally not found in elective physical education classes. It is also true that health and fitness cannot be stored but must be maintained on a day-to-day basis. It is a fact that sedentary bookwork over an extended period increases the need for tension reduction and the catharsis that comes from a good workout. Because health and fitness are a foundation for the development of abilities and competencies leading to a richer life, everything possible should be done to maintain them at a high level. Finally, the realization of a person's potential can only come with balanced development in all his dimensions.

Innovations in college physical education

The insistence on relevance, the burgeoning student enrollments, and the reexamination of traditional programs in all areas have not left physical education unscathed. New courses, new methods, and new faculty members have brought about far-reaching and widespread changes. While a few of these may be passing fads, it appears as if most of them are here to stay, at least for some time to come. Innovations and trends which are being tried include:

1. The introduction of many new activities with carryover value. Cycling, self-defense, relaxation, paddleball, mountain climbing, kayaking, white-water canoeing, scuba diving, backpacking, yachting, orienteering, yoga, cross-country skiing,

---

*Oxendine, Joseph, "Status of general instruction programs of physical education in four year colleges and universities: 1971–1972," Washington, D.C.: American Association for Health, Physical Education, and Recreation, 1972.

◀ "College and high school students will benefit from experiences in games where there is body contact, a lack of formality, and joyous, wholesome competition." (Courtesy of (*top*) the *Journal of Health, Physical Education, and Recreation*, and (*bottom*) the University of Bridgeport.)

snowshoeing, figure skating, gymnasium hockey, and indoor soccer are among the newer courses.

2. The *core* and *subconcentration* approach is being utilized in many professional preparation programs. Subconcentrations can be elementary school physical education, secondary school physical education, coaching, perceptual-motor development, sports for the handicapped, sociology of sport, psychological aspects of physical education, exercise physiology, or administration.

3. Obtaining an academic major in physical education without any courses in education is becoming more common. Greater depth in philosophy, behavioral sciences, biomechanics, physiology, anthropology, and/or sociology is the goal.

4. Competency or proficiency examinations are being used more frequently than in the past. In some instances the passing of these examinations exempts students from taking any courses; in other cases it gives them freedom to elect different acitvities.

5. Coeducational classes have increased dramatically in recent years. Not only has there been an increase in the number of activities in which men and women participate together, but there is also a trend to combine formerly separate departments for men and women.

6. The awarding of credit for physical education is increasing. The most common basis is to award one semester hour credit for two clock hours per week during the entire semester. Some institutions require more time than this and some require less.

7. There is considerable variation in grading practices. Some use letter grades, some use pass-fail, and some give neither grades nor credit. But it is becoming more common to adhere to the same grading pattern for physical education as for other subjects.

8. An increased amount and a greater variety of field work is being tried in many places. Experiences in the inner-city schools, municipal recreation programs, sports camps, children's hospitals, institutions for the emotionally disturbed, and correctional institutions are being accepted as vital and important ingredients of the students' educational program.

9. Whereas credit for student teaching has hitherto been almost entirely confined to public schools, it is now considered desirable to give credit for physical education leadership experiences in YMCA, YWCA, boys' clubs, girls' clubs, state hospitals, retirement homes, and similar agencies.

10. Limited credit for participation in varsity sports is again being reviewed. Rather than let the "varsity-caliber" athlete set the pace and steal the limelight in physical activities where he is particularly proficient, he can earn credit for one activity course by participating on a varsity team.

11. Participating in an activity or sport for solid blocks of time is frequently considered worthy of academic credit. A week in a skiing camp, three days hiking in the mountains under competent leadership, a canoe trip into the wilderness,

sailing from one city or island to another, a hunting trip with an experienced guide, and similar experiences are being accepted as meeting physical education requirements. A written report is usually completed in such a course.

12. Independent study on a related topic is also acceptable in an increasing number of colleges. A term paper on the development of human values through sport is an example. Serving as a laboratory assistant in a physical therapy course is another. Tutoring students having difficulty in exercise physiology is a possibility. Obviously certain standards must be met in all such instances. If, however, such experiences serve to develop an appreciation and understanding of physical education, independent study could be more worthwhile than taking another course in skills and techniques.

13. The inclusion of Outward Bound activities as an element in the physical education program has accelerated in recent years. The adventure, challenge, companionship, and shared experiences of rock-climbing, rappelling, survival hiking, sailing, and canoeing demand complete involvement and usually engender deep loyalties and profound satisfactions. Testing oneself against unfamiliar obstacles and discovering hidden resources which can be called out to accomplish difficult tasks are ingredients which serve to justify this type of activity in an educational program.

14. Intensive fitness programs which place stress on the cardiorespiratory system and include scientific evaluations are meaningful and exciting to many students, particularly if they can observe their own progress. Sound testing programs increase self-awareness and provide needed motivation. Wise guidance in reading assignments often leads to the development of philosophy which includes vigorous physical activity as part of lifestyle. Among the activities in such a fitness program could be bicycle ergometry, treadmill running, circuit training, calisthenic exercises, isometrics, and jogging.

11.12 PRINCIPLES AND GUIDELINES FOR PROGRAM PLANNING
The selection of activities, the development of curricula, and the planning and organizing of programs constitute the heart of any educational enterprise. These processes must be founded on sound principles and guidelines including the following:

1. Curriculum construction should be based on (a) a study of the individuals who are to undergo the educational experiences, and (b) an examination of the situation in which the education is to take place.

2. The formulation of goals, aims, and objectives should be an early step in planning the physical education program.

3. Activities should be selected on the basis of their potential contribution to the purposes and objectives of physical education.

4. The total program should be organized with the intention of making the optimum and maximum contribution to the development of the students.

5. There should be strong emphasis on making the programs meaningful and on providing knowledges and understandings which appear to be likely to induce students to make physical activity part of their future lives.

6. The philosophy of the educational institution should be one of the guiding factors in developing a curriculum. The philosophy of the physical education department should be in harmony with that of the institution.

7. The cultural and ethnic backgrounds of the students should be considered in program planning.

8. There should be planned progression in activities. This should prevent excessive overlap and needless repetition.

9. There should be sufficient flexibility to allow for individual differences as well as changing schedules, facilities, teachers, and weather.

10. Activities should be taught long enough to provide opportunity for some degree of mastery.

11. There should be enough integration and interrelatedness among the various elements of the program so that each component will reinforce and provide support for the others.

12. Facilities should be planned to adequately support the program and should include a variety of teaching stations, each one intended for specific activities.

13. Yearly, monthly, weekly, and daily schedules and lesson plans should be formulated. There should, however, be enough flexibility for modification to meet changing conditions.

14. There should be special course offerings for those students who have physical handicaps, inadequate skill development, or other limitations which prevent unrestricted participation.

15. There should be enough testing to measure the progress of the individual students as well as to contribute to the evaluation of the entire physical education operation.

16. Classes should be planned to provide for some review of previous lessons, some learning of new activities, and some fun and enjoyment.

17. There should be provision for students who are highly skilled or advanced in any given activity to take a proficiency test and, if successful, to receive credit.

18. Adequate opportunities for students of both sexes to share experiences in a number of coeducational activities should be provided. Among these one may find dance, aquatics, golf, badminton, volleyball, skiing, tennis, judo, and softball.

19. There should be a definite and well-defined grading policy. This should be similar to the practice for other subjects and should be made known to the students in advance.

20. There should be adequate advance planning for inclement weather. Worth-while experiences should be provided during rainy-day sessions as well.

21. Curricula and methods should provide for personal relationships between teachers and students. Intense personal involvement on the part of the instructor will usually elicit a favorable response on the part of the students. Personalization of instruction should be the emphasis.

22. Faculty and students should be involved with curricular change. Committees and subcommittees should be composed of interested individuals who are committed to improvement.

23. Military drill, band, ROTC, drill squad, or cheerleading should not be accepted as substitutions for physical education. Students will not receive carry over value from these.

24. Both faculty and students should be involved with the community.

25. There should be a complete intramural sports program to complement the physical education program.

26. All activities should be selected on the basis of the nature, needs, capacities, and interests of the students.

27. All faculty members should be alert to new developments in their field of speciality. This should be shared with their colleagues on a regular basis.

28. Staff meetings should be scheduled regularly. Every effort should be exerted to make these sessions meaningful and worthwhile.

29. Students and faculty should be aware that curriculum is dynamic and ever-changing. Faculty members should be willing to experiment. At the same time,

◄ "There should be special course offerings for those students who have physical handicaps, inadequate skill development, or other limitations which prevent unrestricted participation." (Courtesy of Eastern Kentucky University.)

those activities and practices which have been used for many years should not be discarded merely because they are old. Both the old and the new should be evaluated.

30. The program can be only as good as the competence of the faculty. The employment, without bias, of the best person for every vacancy should be the aim of administration.

31. The faculty must be supported by the administration. For optimum results there must be adequate equipment, facilities, and financial resources.

SELECTED REFERENCES

1. American Association for Health, Physical Education, and Recreation, "Promising practices in elementary school physical education," Report of the Conference for Teachers and Supervisors of Elementary School Physical Education, Washington, D.C., 1968.
2. Andrews, Gladys, Jeannette Saurborn, and Elsa Schneider, *Physical Education for Today's Boys and Girls*, Boston: Allyn and Bacon, 1960.
3. Barrett, Kate R., "Physical education is movement education," *Physical Education '73*, Washington, D.C.: American Association for Health, Physical Education, and Recreation, 1973.
4. Bookwalter, Karl W., and Harold J. VanderZwaag, *Foundations and Principles of Physical Education*, Philadelphia: W. B. Saunders Company, 1969.
5. Brown, Camille, and Rosalind Cassidy, *Theory in Physical Education*, Philadelphia: Lea and Febiger, 1963.
6. Bucher, Charles A. (ed.), *Administrative Dimensions of Health and Physical Education Programs, Including Athletics*, St. Louis: The C. V. Mosby Company, 1971.
7. *Foundations of Physical Education*, 4th edition, St. Louis: The C. V. Mosby Company, 1964.
8. Burnstine, Deidre, "On considering curriculum design," *Curriculum Improvement in Secondary School Physical Education*, Washington, D.C.: American Association for Health, Physical Education, and Recreation, 1973.
9. Clarke, H. Harrison, and Franklin B. Haar, *Health and Physical Education for the Elementary Classroom Teacher*, Englewood Cliffs, N.J.: Prentice-Hall, 1964.
10. Cogan, Max, "Innovative ideas in college physical education," *Journal of Health, Physical Education and Recreation*, Vol. 44, No. 2, February 1973.
11. Collard, Roberta R., "Exploration and play in human infants," *Journal of Health, Physical Education and Recreation*, Vol. 43, No. 6, June 1972.
12. The Co-op Plan, Northeastern University, Boston, Mass., 1973.
13. Cratty, Bryant J., *Perceptual and Motor Development in Infants and Children*, New York: The Macmillan Company, 1970.
14. Dauer, Victor P., *Dynamic Physical Education for Elementary School Children*, 4th edition, Minneapolis, Minn.: Burgess Publishing Company, 1971. By permission.
15. "Elementary school physical education—a viewpoint," *Contemporary Philosophies of Physical Education and Athletics*, Robert A. Cobb and Paul M. Lepley. Columbus, Ohio: Charles E. Merrill Publishing Company, 1973.
16. Daughtrey, Greyson, and John B. Woods, *Physical Education Programs: Organization and Administration*, Philadelphia: W. B. Saunders Company, 1971.
17. Driscoll, Sandra, and Doris A. Mathison, "Goal-centered individualized learning," *Journal of Health, Physical Education, and Recreation*, September 1971.
18. *Educational gymnastics*, London: London County Council, 1964.

19. Fait, Hollis F., *Physical Education for the Elementary School Child: Experiences in Movement,* 2nd edition, Philadelphia: W. B. Saunders Company, 1971.
20. Felshin, Jan, "Rationale and purposes for physical education," *Curriculum Improvement in Secondary School Physical Education,* Washington, D.C.: American Association for Health, Physical Education, and Recreation, 1973.
21. Fox, Eugene R., and Barry L. Sysler, *Life-Time Sports for the College Student,* Dubuque, Iowa: Kendall/Hunt Publishing Company, 1972.
22. Frieschlag, Jerry, "Competency based instruction," *Journal of Health, Physical Education, and Recreation,* Volume 45, No. 1, January 1974.
23. Froelicher, Charles, "For the sake of the young," *The Johns Hopkins Magazine,* Volume XIV, No. 2, November 1962.
24. Frostig, Marianne, *Frostig MGL (Move—Grow—Learn),* Chicago: Follett Educational Corporation, 1973.
25. Furth, Hans G., *Piaget for Teachers,* Englewood Cliffs, N.J.: Prentice-Hall, 1970.
26. Godfrey, Barbara B., and Newell C. Kephart, *Movement Patterns and Motor Education,* New York: Appleton-Century-Crofts, 1969.
27. Greenberg, Herbert M., *Teaching with Feeling,* New York: The Macmillan Company, 1969.
28. Halsey, Elizabeth, *Inquiry and Invention in Physical Education,* Philadelphia: Lea and Febiger, 1964.
29. Hanson, Margie, "Directions and thrusts," *Physical Education '73,* Washington, D.C.: American Association for Health, Physical Education, and Recreation, 1973.
30. Haslett, Jaqueline G., "Concepts on movement education." From a lecture by Lisa Ullman, "Movement in Everyday Life," July 20, 1970. *Journal,* Massachusetts Association for Health, Physical Education, and Recreation, Vol. XVIII, No. 1, Fall 1972. By permission.
31. Havel, Richard C., and Emery W. Seymour, *Administration of Health, Physical Education and Recreation for Schools,* New York: The Ronald Press, 1961.
32. Hayes, Elizabeth R., *Dance Composition and Production,* New York: The Ronald Press, 1955.
33. Heilman, Joan R., "How to survive your adolescent," *Reader's Digest,* March 1973.
34. Hinderman, Lin M., et al., "Winterizing physical education," *Journal of Health, Physical Education, and Recreation,* November–December 1971.
35. Holt, John, *How Children Learn,* New York: Pitman Publishing Company, 1969.
36. Hook, Andrew J., et al., "Computer monitored physical education," *Journal of Health, Physical Education, and Recreation,* Volume 44, No. 7, September 1973.
37. *Innovation in Education: New Directions for the American School,* A Statement on Policy by the Research and Policy Committee for Economic Development, New York, 1968.
38. Insley, Gerald S., *Practical Guidelines for the Teaching of Physical Education,* Reading, Mass.: Addison-Wesley Publishing Company, 1973.
39. Jewett, Ann E., "Physical education objectives out of curricular chaos," *Curriculum Improvement in Secondary School Physical Education,* Washington, D.C.: American Association for Health, Physical Education, and Recreation, 1973.
40. Johnson, Warren R., "A humanistic dimension of physical education," *Journal of Health, Physical Education, and Recreation,* Vol. 43, No. 9, November–December 1972.
41. Jones, Emlyn H., Robert P. Nye, and Barry G. Remley, "Outward Bound at Westchester State College," *Journal of Health, Physical Education, and Recreation,* Vol. 43, No. 9, November–December 1972.

42. Kirchner, Glenn, *Physical Education for Elementary School Children,* 2nd edition, Dubuque, Iowa: Wm. C. Brown Company, 1970.
43. Kirchner, Glenn, Jean Cunningham, and Eileen Warrell, *Introduction to Movement Education,* Dubuque, Iowa: Wm. C. Brown Company, 1970.
44. Knapp, Clyde, and Patricia H. Leonard, *Teaching Physical Education in Secondary Schools,* New York: McGraw-Hill, 1968.
45. Kozman, Hilda C., Rosalind Cassidy, and Chester Jackson, *Methods in Physical Education,* Philadelphia: W. B. Saunders Company, 1952.
46. Kroll, Walter P., *Perspectives in Physical Education,* New York: The Academic Press, 1971.
47. Laban, Rudolf, *Modern Educational Dance,* 2nd edition, London: MacDonald and Evans, 1963.
48. MacKenzie, M. M., *Toward a New Curriculum in Physical Education,* New York: McGraw-Hill, 1969.
49. Moore, C. A., "Changes: relevance or irresponsibility?," *Journal of Health, Physical Education, and Recreation,* Vol. 44, No. 8, October 1973.
50. Mosston, Muska, *Developmental Movement,* Columbus, Ohio: Charles E. Merrill Publishing Company, 1965.
51. Munroe, A. D., *Physical Education,* London: G. Bell and Son, 1972.
52. *National College Physical Education Association for Men,* 75th Annual Proceedings, Minneapolis, Minn.: NCPEAM, 1972.
53. Nations, Jimmy, "The changing elementary school," *Promising Practices in Elementary School Physical Education,* Washington, D.C.: American Association for Health, Physical Education, and Recreation, 1969.
54. Nixon, John E., and Ann E. Jewett, *An Introduction to Physical Education,* 7th edition, Philadelphia: W. B. Saunders Company, 1969.
55. Oxendine, Joseph B., "Status of required physical education programs in colleges and universities," *Journal of Health, Physical Education, and Recreation,* January 1969.
56. Piaget, Jean, and Bärbel Inhelder, *The Psychology of the Child,* New York: Basic Books, 1969.
57. Randall, Marjorie, *Basic Movement,* London: G. Bell and Sons, 1961.
58. Resick, Matthew C., Beverly L. Seidel, and James G. Mason, *Modern Administrative Practices in Physical Education and Athletics,* Reading, Mass.: Addison-Wesley Publishing Company, 1970.
59. Ritchey, John M., "Coeducational mountaineering." *Journal of Health, Physical Education, and Recreation,* Vol. 43, No. 8, October 1972.
60. Rogers, Carl R., *Freedom to Learn,* Columbus, Ohio: Charles E. Merrill Publishing Company, 1969.
61. Schurr, Evelyn L., *Movement Experiences for Children: Curriculum and Methods for Elementary School Physical Education,* New York: Appleton-Century-Crofts, 1967.
62. *Secondary School Athletic Administration: A New Look,* Report of the Second National Conference on Secondary School Athletic Administration, Washington, D.C.: American Association for Health, Physical Education, and Recreation, 1969.
63. Siedentop, Daryl, *Physical Education—Introductory Analysis,* Dubuque, Iowa: Wm. C. Brown Company, 1972.
64. Taba, Hilda, *Curriculum Development: Theory and Practice,* New York: Harcourt, Brace and World, 1962, p. 12.
65. Taylor, John L., "Intramurals: a program for everyone," *Journal of Health, Physical Education, and Recreation,* Vol. 44, No. 7, September 1973.

66. Thompson, John C., *Physical Education for the 1970's,* Englewood Cliffs, N.J.: Prentice-Hall, 1971.
67. Tillotson, Joan S., "A brief theory of movement education," *Promising Practices in Elementary School Physical Education,* Washington, D.C.: American Association for Health, Physical Education, and Recreation, 1968.
68. Van Huss, Wayne, et al., *Physical Activity in Modern Living,* Englewood Cliffs, N.J.: Prentice-Hall, 1960.
69. Voltmer, Edward F., and Arthur A. Esslinger, *The Organization and Administration of Physical Education,* 4th edition, New York: Appleton-Century-Crofts, 1967.
70. Walker, June, et al., *Modern Methods in Secondary School Physical Education,* 3rd edition, Boston: Allyn and Bacon, 1973.
71. Welford, A. T., *Fundamentals of Skill,* London: Methuen and Company, 1968.
72. Welsh, Raymond, "Futurism and physical education," *Journal of Health, Physical Education, and Recreation,* Vol. 44, No. 8, October 1973.
73. Whiting, H. T. A., *Acquiring Ball Skill,* London: G. Bell and Sons, 1969.
74. "The Whole Thing," Report of the First National Conference on Secondary School Physical Education, *Journal of Health, Physical Education, and Recreation,* Vol. 44, No. 5, May 1973.
75. Zeigler, Earle F., *Philosophical Foundations for Physical, Health, and Recreation Education,* Englewood Cliffs, N.J.: Prentice-Hall, 1964.

Health Education in Our Schools

Chapter 12

12.1 HEALTH AND EDUCATION

Good health is more than simply freedom from disease. It is a dynamic condition of high-level wellness; it is manifested by a spirit of equanimity and contentment on the one hand and a vivacious zest for living on the other. As has been stated by the World Health Organization, health is a "... state of complete physical, mental, and social well-being, not merely the absence of disease or infirmity."

There are people who are able to maintain a state of reasonably good health for substantial periods in their lives without giving much conscious attention to their health. In most instances, however, their parents understood the principles of nutrition and good health habits and maintained an environment which was conducive to physical and mental well-being. For the most part, people who live long and productive lives in a state of good health have, in one way or another, accumulated a substantial amount of important health knowledge. They have also learned to live according to principles of good health gleaned from scientific investigations and/or the principles of nature's inexorable laws. As one studies health (or the lack of it), it becomes obvious that one aspect of education which is universally needed is information and understanding concerning the prevention and care of disease and the development of a state of positive well-being. It is also evident that much more is needed in the way of universal health education than has been provided in the past. While there are some excellent programs of health education in today's schools, there are many institutions in which they are woefully inadequate or entirely lacking.

12.2 THE NATURE OF HEALTH EDUCATION

In the Bronfman *School Health Education Report* is found the following descriptive paragraph:

> Health education is multidisciplinary in nature. Its *content* is largely derived from medicine, public health, and the physical, biological, and social sciences. Its scope is broad, covering such diverse areas as the nature of disease, the complexity of nutrition, effects of radiation, behavioral aspects of accident prevention, an understanding of health and medical care programs, significance of international health problems, selection of health products and services, environmental hazards in air and water, community health services, foundations of mental health, and preparation for marriage and parenthood. But, health education cannot rest on knowledge alone; it must motivate the individual toward healthful living. What is taught in the schools must be so related to the daily lives of the students that they can act intelligently in matters of health. [33, pp. 2–3]

The complexity and scope of health education as described in the above statement staggers the imagination and is challenging for educators. Add to this the recent emphasis on sex education, alcoholism, and drug abuse and there is enough significant material to justify a good program in health education throughout the average person's attendance at school. Keeping up with new health knowledge can profitably occupy a place in one's reading throughout life.

Health Education has a narrow as well as a broad definition. Traditionally and officially it encompasses a) healthful school living, b) health services, and c) health instruction. As a matter of fact, these three are often separated in schools today. The responsibility for *a healthful school environment,* a major component of healthful school living, usually rests in the hands of the custodial staff, guidance department, principal, and other school administrators. Seldom does the director of health and physical education have the administration of janitor work, counseling, and the interpersonal classroom relationships as his responsibility.

In most educational institutions of appreciable size, the health services are directed by a physician. In smaller schools the school nurse is in charge. Additional physicians, nurses, technicians, and secretaries are added as needed. Infirmaries are often provided which vary in size and degree of equipment sophistication. While physical education and athletic personnel may have certain relationships to the health services, they are seldom in charge.

In the narrower sense, health education is almost synonymous with *health instruction.* It is this phase of health education which will be the major topic of discussion in this chapter.

12.3 CONTENT OF HEALTH INSTRUCTION

The tendency in many health education programs has been to deal too superficially with the topics and to be too repetitive in subject content. This has tended to cause loss of student interest, make the subject less meaningful, and lessen the respect which other faculty members have for it. It is not surprising, then, that those responsible for furnishing financial resources as well as those formulating curricula have sometimes been hesitant to accord health instruction the place in education which it rightfully merits.

A good school program in health will be designed not only to increase the health knowledge of the students, but also to develop desirable attitudes. Such attitudes will lead to desirable health practices, habits, and skills. It requires good teaching, appropriate content, and personal involvement on the part of all concerned to achieve these objectives.

Elementary school

Included in grades K–3 should be topics such as personal cleanliness, prevention of communicable disease (elementary treatment), motor vehicle traffic hazards, school and home safety, dental hygiene, when and how to wear clothing, the role and importance of sleep, good eating habits, proper use and care of the eyes, and the relationships of patients and doctors.

In grades 4–6, some of the same topics might be included, but the more scientific and theoretical aspects treated. In addition, the role of exercise, the problem of drug abuse, the basic anatomy and physiology of the human organism, the hazards of smoking, and more advanced traffic safety should be included. Health attitudes and behavior should be the constant concern not only of those teaching health but of others who work with the students on a day-to-day basis.

Junior high school

Students in junior high school are generally 12 to 16 years old. The importance of high-quality health instruction during these years of rapid growth cannot be overemphasized. At this age students want to please their peers, desire to be considered as adults, are mobile and independent enough to be away from both school and parental authority much of the time, and are going through the stages of puberty and early adolescence. At no other age is a good health teacher more vital to the development of a boy or girl.

Junior high school students need to learn about boy/girl relationships, the wonders and hazards of reproduction, the effects of smoking, the dangers of alcoholism, and the potentially damaging effects of drugs. They should understand individual differences in the onset of menstruation, the development of secondary sex characteristics, the adolescent growth spurt, and the relationship of physiological to chronological age. Many of them need counseling and guidance with regard to their inability to cope with the problems they encounter, their lack of success in social relationships, their poor study habits, and their failure to achieve athletically, academically, or otherwise.

Junior high school students are ready to learn about community and governmental health agencies, fire prevention and aquatic safety, and scientific prevention of contagious disease. They are forming their value systems and beginning to develop a philosophy of life. They need wise guidance and assistance without undue restraint. All of this falls under the category of health instruction.

Senior high school

When students enter senior high school they are approaching adulthood. When they are seniors, many of them are, for all intents and purposes, adults. They need to know about those things which cause problems for adults and those which help them toward the goal of full, rich, and satisfying lives. Both knowledge and wisdom are involved. Health instruction for students in senior high school may need to include science, philosophy, and art.

Students in grades 10–12 need to know in great detail about the responsibilities of parenthood. They are eager to learn about reproduction and the methods of preventing it. They should be taught, in a manner which is realistic but will not cause undue anxiety, the facts about venereal disease and contraception. They are ready to learn about the basic aspects of family living.

More advanced instruction about alcoholism, human sexuality, and drugs should be furnished to students in their last years of high school. This is also the age when they learn to drive an automobile and need detailed knowledge about traffic safety. They need to know how to maintain personal fitness and how to relax and relieve tension.

Juniors and seniors in high school need exposure to the whole intangible and somewhat mysterious area of mental health. It is exceedingly important that stress be placed on attitude development and the influence of health instruction on behavior. What students have become, the way they think and feel, and the value systems they have developed by the time they finish high school will, in most cases, set the pattern for their entire lives.

Because of the terminal nature of high school education for a large number of students, they need a good background of additional information. They need a basic knowledge of both communicable and degenerative diseases, they need an understanding of depressants and stimulants, they should know something about false advertising and fraudulent health practices, and they should be aware of the legal, sociological, and religious problems surrounding abortion.

A considerable portion of time should be devoted to teaching seniors about community health programs, and state, national, and international health agencies. Particular attention should be given to the functions of the World Health Organization. With the world growing smaller through better communications and with international travel increasing at a rapid rate, the relationship of the health of the people of one country to that of the people of other countries is becoming increasingly significant.

College and university health instruction

Students in colleges and universities are ready for the most sophisticated personal and community health courses available. Such courses deal with many of the same subjects mentioned for high school students, but at a more advanced level. Research findings, physiological principles, pathological developments, and the latest medical knowledge are included in the course content for college students. Disease and mortality statistics, principles of genetics and heredity, accident data, and other scientific findings are utilized to substantiate course content.

College students study problems of obesity, malnutrition and hunger, food facts and fallacies, and desirable diets for varying physical conditions. They delve into the physiological effects of exercise, ways of coping with stress, psychosomatic illnesses, and adaptations to frustrating situations. Emotions, mental health, psychological needs, defense mechanisms, and general information about psychoses and neuroses are appropriate topics for health instruction courses at the college level. Diseases of the heart and circulatory system, cancer, diabetes, and arthritis are other meaningful subjects.

The college student in particular needs to study sexuality, marriage, and family living. The changing sexual mores, the mysteries of reproduction, deviancy in sexual behavior, and the problems of love and marriage are pertinent topics.

Marital problems and family living are relevant and meaningful subjects to most college students. They should study these in considerable depth. Sexual adjustment in marriage, testing for pregnancy, prenatal care of mother and child, complications of birth, stages of labor, and artificial insemination are topics about which college students should be informed. The relationship of desirable emotional and mental attitudes to healthy pregnancies and the welfare of the infant should be examined.

There is no end to personal health problems which provide interesting content material for college classes in health instruction. The problem is to find teachers who have the knowledge, dedication, and personal warmth to bring health instruction to life and make the students feel its importance and significance.

12.4 TEACHING HEALTH: WHO, WHERE, HOW?

Health education specialists, coaches, and teachers of biology, home economics, chemistry, and elementary school subjects are among those most commonly assigned to teach the various aspects of health. Except for the specialists, these individuals are normally assigned this task as a secondary responsibility.

Because coaches are fascinated and intensely involved with their primary responsibilities, they often have difficulty giving the time and attention to health instruction required for effective teaching. Home economics teachers generally are excellent in teaching nutrition and family living, but are often inadequately prepared to deal with other aspects of health. Biology and chemistry teachers are usually very effective when discussing theoretical and scientific background material in their fields, but can be very weak in making relevant applications and dealing with personal problems. Elementary classroom teachers may be totally unprepared by their educational experiences to teach health and fitness.

Physical education teachers may or may not have an adequate background in the sciences and in the practical application of health knowledge to daily life. Some major programs include courses in health education and others do not. Equally important is the attitude of the physical education teacher toward health education responsibilities. If a physical education teacher has prepared to teach health through the usual courses in biology, anatomy, physiology, first aid, prevention and care of injuries, and physical education for the atypical; and if, in addition, he/she has a deep interest in and commitment to health education, he/she may become an excellent health instructor. If he/she also has pursued courses in methods and materials of health education, personal and community hygiene, and nutrition, it may well be that he/she is the best choice for that responsibility. Study of current and relevant problems such as drug abuse, sexual relationships, alcoholism, smoking, and family living is, however, mandatory for today's society.

Elena Sliepcevich, in the *School Health Education Report,* summarizes her findings with regard to the educational preparation of health education teachers in these words:

> The classroom teacher alone handled the major portion of the instruction on the elementary level in over one-half to two-thirds of the small districts. A non-specialist supervisor assisted the teacher in about 20 percent of the districts. In medium districts health instruction by the classroom teacher alone and the classroom teacher with supervisory help were practices used about equally. Supervisory assistance was generally provided in large districts. A teacher with a "combined major in health and physical education" was assigned to junior high school health instruction in 65 percent of the separate health classes in the large and 80 percent in both the medium and small districts.
>
> In grades 10 to 12 a teacher with this combined major taught 90 percent of the health classes in both the large and medium and 60 percent of such classes in the small districts. In all three districts the major portion of the

remaining health instruction at the secondary level was by a teacher with a "physical education major only." [33, pp. 25–26]

Health instruction at the college level is the most complete because of the qualifications of its teachers. Most of these have earned doctorate degrees and are committed to health instruction as their life's work. They have no other primary assignments and are avid readers of current health literature. In many instances they will be assisted by well-prepared physical education teachers who also have an interest and are reasonably well prepared in the area of health education.

Correlated and integrated health instruction

Because of the close relationship of many health topics to certain disciplines, it is logical to assign them to that area of study and decrease the time allotted for independent instruction. The rationale is that alcoholism can be taught in chemistry, sex education in biology, nutrition in home economics, exercise and relaxation in physical education, and sound health habits in all classes. Where this has been tested, however, it is found that only perfunctory attention is generally given to health topics, and that most teachers feel they do not have enough time to do justice to their own subject, let alone try to teach health.

When health topics are assigned to other areas of study and the identities of both are retained, the method is referred to as *correlated.* When health topics are fused with other appropriate subjects and make their appearance incidentally in other branches of the curriculum, the term *integrated* is applied. For the most part, integrated and correlated methods have proved ineffectual. It is difficult to plan, organize, teach, and evaluate health instruction under these arrangements. Teachers who do not perceive health instruction as their primary responsibility are apt to gloss over health topics rather lightly. At higher levels of learning it is essential that teachers have a broad and deep background of knowledge and understanding of health problems. This, in itself, is challenging enough to demand the teacher's entire involvement and deep commitment.

Team teaching

In the elementary grades where a teacher is responsible for the entire range of subject matter, a "team" approach is often desirable. Either by preplanning through selective employment of teachers or by surveying the special interests and qualifications of existing teachers, an arrangement can usually be made whereby one teacher teaches health to three or four different grades or classes, another teaches art, another music, and sometimes another handles the physical education. This will enable the students to have the benefit of a teacher in each of these fields who will be interested, well prepared, and personally involved.

The utilization of health education specialists

It is almost universally agreed in educational circles that the use of health education specialists wherever possible is the best policy. The critical importance of student health as it relates to school work, attitudes, behavior, and progress toward self-realization and good citizenship should not be overlooked. While it may be difficult at present to secure specialists for all health positions, the shortage can be remedied in a few years if state departments, educational institutions, and employment agencies will make a concerted effort to do so. The trend is definitely in that direction.

The block approach
Greyson Daughtery and John Woods advocate the "block approach." Their reasons are essentially pragmatic. They point to the preponderance of situations where the physical education teacher is now assigned to teach health education, to the ease of scheduling, to the advantage of having the same teacher for both physical education and health, and to the desirability of having boys relate to a man teacher and girls to a woman teacher in both physical education and health classes. [8, pp. 281–284]

12.5 RELATIONSHIP BETWEEN HEALTH AND PHYSICAL EDUCATION
Health and physical education are not synonymous. They are, however, related. They both deal with the physical well-being of the individual. They are both concerned with exercise, growth and development, sleep and rest, relaxation and recreation, physical fitness, and with the physiological, psychological, and sociological needs of man. Many of the aims and purposes are similar.

The professional preparation of health education and physical education teachers have much in common. Both programs generally require study in anatomy, physiology, chemistry, bacteriology, therapy, and safety.

Health education and physical education are very often placed in the same unit of the institutional structure. They may be part of the same department; they are sometimes separate departments in the same division or college; they are in parallel organizational units in local, state, and national professional organizations. Many individuals find themselves assigned to teach both health education and physical education. Health education and physical education usually must share facilities, equipment, financial resources, and personnel. Close cooperation is therefore essential.

On the other hand, physical educators utilize as their media vigorous physical activities and knowledge about movement, whereas health educators have as their primary concern health knowledge, health attitudes, and healthful behavior. Classes dealing with drug abuse, sex education, or nutrition are not considered physical education. Archery, tennis and swimming are not health education courses.

There are often differences in attitudes and specific interests between physical educators and coaches on the one hand and health educators on the other. Many physical educators are coaches who are concerned with excellence of performance and the ultimate development of the talented few. Others are particularly interested in motor learning and the teaching of neuromuscular skills. Health educators are generally more interested in the alleviation of society's ills and in the normal development of all individuals.

It seems obvious that health educators and physical educators must continue to work together, their ultimate goals being quite similar. It also appears probable that there will be many individuals prepared to teach physical education who will be asked to teach health education as well. It is also the opinion of the author that both programs would benefit from a much larger number of health education specialists who could teach the more advanced courses, supervise health education at the lower levels, and conduct in-service training for those who specialize in physical education but are required to teach health education as well.

12.6 WEAKNESSES IN CURRENT PRACTICES

There are a number of flaws in current health education practices as well as misconceptions in health knowledge clearly indicated by Sliepcevich in "Highlights of the Findings." Some of the more striking misconceptions are:

1. The fluoridation of water is to make it safe to drink.
2. Chronic diseases can be transmitted.
3. The World Health Organization is part of the International Red Cross.
4. Legislation guarantees the reliability of all advertised medicines.
5. Voluntary health agencies are supported by public funds. [33, pp. 6–15]

Among the instructional problems reported were:

1. Failure of the home to encourage health habits.
2. Community resistance to certain health topics.
3. Inadequate professional staff.
4. Lack of support for health education by teachers, parents, and administrators.
5. Neglect of health education when combined with physical education. [33, p. 11]

Other weaknesses which become apparent as health education programs are observed and analyzed include the following:

1. Health instruction classes have been too completely segregated on the basis of sex. The two sexes should be together for much of their health education.
2. There has been too little emphasis on "consumer health" in most programs. People need protection against false advertising and sales psychology.
3. There has been too much emphasis on the morbid and pathological aspects of health education and not enough on the positive and joyous aspects of living.

4. In too many situations health instruction is spasmodic, being taught to a given group every two or three years. Health education should be continuous and life-long.

5. Too many health education teachers are not qualified because of temperament, education, or experience to deal objectively and unemotionally with sensitive subjects such as sex education, drug abuse, alcoholism, and smoking. Some individuals become embarrassed, tense, and ill-at-ease when dealing with these subjects.

6. A number of health education teachers fail to introduce and properly follow up the presentation of films. The effective use of all audiovisual aids requires considerable planning and preparation.

7. In many instances there is little or no interaction among the various disciplines. Many health topics, particularly at the higher levels, require a multifaceted approach.

8. Failure to utilize community resources and facilities is a fairly common fault. One of the important outcomes of health education should be knowledge of resources available.

9. The utilization of disinterested and unqualified teachers is still far too common. Regardless of the educational background, those teaching in this important field must have a commitment to the task.

10. Too many health educators assume responsibilities which belong to physicians. Those teaching health should know where to "draw the line."

11. Not enough emphasis is given to present-day health hazards such as pollution of the air, ground, and water. The hazards of these are growing more rapidly than are the remedial actions.

12. There are too many situations in which there is a tendency to feel that courses in anatomy and physiology satisfy the need for health instruction. As indicated earlier, competent health educators should teach far more than merely the rudiments of anatomy and physiology.

13. Dietary practices appear to be degenerating rather than improving. Sedentary living, the prevalence of sweet and soft foods, and the increase in dietary permissiveness must be counteracted.

14. There is too little attention given to the dramatic increase in venereal disease. According to Sliepcevich, there was an increase of 56 percent in the incidence of syphilis among teenagers between 1960 and 1961. [28, p. 39] The *Springfield Daily News* carried a story entitled "U.S. VD Cases Climb to Record Levels." This is quoted in part below:

> . . . according to the American Social Health Association . . . the incidence of gonorrhea in fiscal 1972 was the highest recorded in 53 years—ever since the U.S. Public Health Service started keeping statistics in 1919, and more

cases of infectious syphilis were reported in fiscal 1972 than in any year since 1950.*

15. There are too many states and school districts where little or no health instruction is required. In many situations where a requirement does exist, it is satisfied without any direct health instruction.

16. There are many instances where the wrong type of motivation is employed. Examples include:

   a) Competition between students.

   b) Artificial incentives and rewards.

   c) Use of morbid, abnormal, and fearful subject matter.

   d) Frequent use of individuals in classes as examples. [1, p. 275]

Rather than dwell at great length on weaknesses, let us now emphasize positives and indicate some of those things which can be done to improve school health education.

12.7 RECOMMENDATIONS FOR IMPROVEMENT

C. L. Anderson in his book, *School Health Practice, says:*

To ensure healthful living now and in the years to come, health instruction must be directed to three basic purposes:

1. Establishment of *practices* essential to health.

2. Acquisition of *knowledge* necessary for health promotion.

3. Development of *attitudes* and *ideals* which will motivate each individual to attain the highest possible level of well-being. [1, p. 272]

Let us then turn our attention to the tasks ahead in building a healthy nation composed of healthy individuals.

The following recommendations are made with the above purposes in mind:

1. Good health education programs can only be developed through better professional preparation and a more careful selection of those who teach and supervise. Employers, teacher education institutions, professional education associations, accrediting agencies, and certifying units must all be involved in this process. The people who support the government and educational agencies must be informed so as to participate intelligently and wisely.

2. Greater emphasis must be placed on health instruction in the curricula from kindergarten through college. While direct health instruction will furnish continuity and prevent the omission of important topics, correlated health instruction also has an important role.

---

*_Springfield Daily News,_ Springfield, Mass., March 19, 1973, p. 5.

3. Health is a very personal matter for every individual. Health instruction can be made fascinating if it is personalized and if the instructor becomes deeply involved in the lives of the students. A belief in the values of this kind of education is a necessary attribute of a good health teacher.

4. Positive health, joyous living, wholesome family life, and fun and friendship should be subjects of health education. Good mental health should be stressed whenever possible. The depressing aspects of poor mental health should be faced realistically but need not be dwelt upon or emphasized excessively.

5. There should be continuous and systematic evaluation of health instruction at both the local and the state level. All aspects of the program should be critically appraised. Outside consultants should be brought in every few years to evaluate what is being done and to suggest improvements.

6. The responsibility for coordinating all aspects of the health education program should be assigned to a qualified individual. A coordinating council has proven effective in many instances. The health coordinator, who would be chairman of such a council, should be thoroughly prepared by education and experience for his varied responsibilities.

7. Parents and community must be involved if health attitudes and behavior are to be permanently influenced. This involvement should not be a one-sided affair but a democratic participatory process involving students, community leaders, parents, and teachers.

8. The development of attitudes is an extremely important part of health instruction and is related to the development of an individual's value system. The home environment combines with a person's experiences in school and elsewhere to influence both attitudes and behavior. Hereditary tendencies also have their role. One's attitudes and value system exert a relatively permanent influence on his behavior and become less flexible with increasing age.

9. Whether practices precede attitudes or attitudes precede practices is similar to the proverbial question, "Which comes first, the chicken or the egg?" Perhaps Anderson answers this as well as anyone when he says,

> Health attitudes, knowledge, and practices are reciprocal and interrelated. Health attitudes grow out of knowledge and practices. Similarly, to assure that a health practice is to be most effective and lasting, it must be cemented by well-established attitudes; also, if health knowledge is to be most effective, it must be applied through proper health attitudes. Attitudes, being part of one's psychoneural organization, are the directors of life. They are developed out of and associated with the gratification of the self in the biosocial motivation of a person. They are the stick that controls the rudders of knowledge and practice.*

*From C. L. Anderson, *School Health Practice,* 5th edition. St. Louis: The C. V. Mosby Company, 1972. By permission.

10. While the acquisition of meaningful knowledge is important, it will not be attained by merely rote memory work or by piling up learned facts without relating them to the needs and interests of the students. Careful and thoughtful preparation is required, with the needs and interests of the students always uppermost in mind.

11. The health education instructor should be well versed in the facts and concepts of child growth and development. Concepts such as perceptual-motor development, the need to belong, puberty, the adolescent growth spurt, physiological versus chronological age, maturation, and individual differences are vitally important to a teacher of health. Too many instructors are employed who have inadequate knowledge of these aspects.

12. There should be mutually beneficial relationships between health instructors and those responsible for health services. School nurses and school physicians can provide health teachers with valuable insights into the health problems of students. The reverse is also true. The health services staff can be profitably utilized to teach certain technical phases of health education; their offices and laboratories are places of interest and information for students in health classes.

"Health teachers should be familiar with many methods of teaching . . ."
(Courtesy of the *Journal of Health, Physical Education, and Recreation.*)

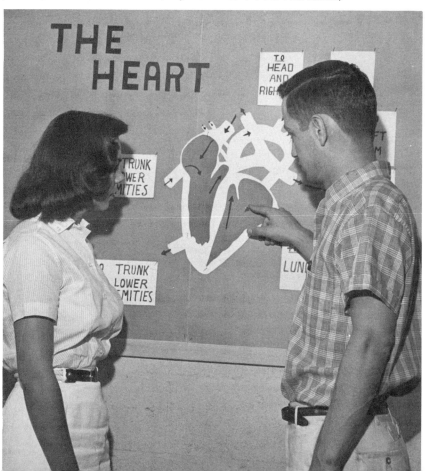

13. Health teachers should be familiar with many methods of teaching and know how to use each appropriately. Lectures, class discussions, problem solving, independent study, and audiovisual aids can all be used to increase the effectiveness of instruction. The age of the students, the nature of the subject matter, the characteristics and abilities of the teacher, the attitude of the class, and many other factors must be considered in choosing the best method for each occasion. Variety and experimentation are recommended.

14. As ecological problems continue to increase in number and significance, they must receive greater attention in health education. The disposal of wastes, purification of polluted water, control of disease, regulation of birth rate, elimination of smog, reforestation of mountains, and conservation of land are subjects with which citizens should be familiar. They are also appropriate topics for health education.

15. Health education must include more information and emphasis regarding physical fitness. At present one often finds a dichotomy between teaching health and teaching fitness. Actually, total fitness is almost synonymous with good health. The optimal functioning of all aspects of the human organism and the ultimate aim of self-fulfillment is the goal in both instances. Both knowledge and action are needed to achieve these goals. The increasing necessity for artificially planned exercise to replace the activity which formerly was fundamental to existence must be recognized.

16. There should be more liaison between health educators, law enforcement officials, and correctional agencies. The problems of drug abuse and alcoholism cannot be solved by any single approach. The legalism of enforcement groups and the overly sentimental approach of some educators should find a common meeting ground. Concerned persons can all help one another solve some difficult problems.

17. Finally, health education instructors should bear in mind that they are *educators.* The two threads running through all expressions of educational purposes and aims are (1) the self-realization of the individual, and (2) the betterment of society. With these as aims, educators need only to find the way and the means.

SELECTED REFERENCES

1. Anderson, C. L., *School Health Practice,* 5th edition, St. Louis: The C. V. Mosby Company, 1972.
2. Bookwalter, Karl W., and Harold J. VanderZwaag, *Foundations and Principles of Physical Education,* Philadelphia: W. B. Saunders Company, 1969.
3. Brightbill, Charles K., *Educating for Leisure Centered Living,* Harrisburg, Penn.: The Stackpole Company, 1966.
4. Chase, Stuart, "Are you alive?," *The Reader's Digest Twentieth Century Anthology,* Pleasantville, N.Y.: The Reader's Digest Association, 1941.
5. Clarke, H. Harrison, and Franklin B. Haar, *Health and Physical Education for the Elementary Classroom Teacher,* Englewood Cliffs, N.J.: Prentice-Hall, 1964.
6. Cowell, Charles C., and Wellman L. France, *Philosophy and Principles of Physical Education,* Englewood Cliffs, N.J.: Prentice-Hall, 1963.

7. Dalis, Gus T., and Ben B. Strasser, "The starting point for values education," *School Health Review,* Vol. 5, No. 1, January–February 1974.
8. Daughtrey, Greyson, and John B. Woods, *Physical Education Programs: Organization and Administration,* Philadelphia: W. B. Saunders Company, 1971.
9. DiGennaro, Joseph, "The exercise risk factor in coronary heart disease," *The Physical Educator,* Vol. 30, No. 4, December 1973.
10. Dunn, Halbert L., "What high-level wellness means," *Canadian Journal of Public Health,* Vol. 50, No. 11, November 1959.
11. Eichenlaub, John E., *College Health,* New York: The Macmillan Company, 1962.
12. Gothold, Stuart E., "Health education as an integral part of the curriculum," *School Health Review,* Vol. 3, No. 4, September–October 1972.
13. Grout, Ruth E., *Health Teaching in Schools,* Philadelphia: W. B. Saunders Company, 1953.
14. "A guide for development of a health education curriculum," *School Health Review,* Vol. 2, No. 3, September 1971.
15. Hagen, Kristofer, *Faith and Health,* Philadelphia: Muhlenberg Press, 1961.
16. Havel, Richard C., and Emery W. Seymour, *Administration of Health, Physical Education, and Recreation for Schools,* New York: The Ronald Press, 1961.
17. Hein, Fred V., *Not Just Exercise,* revised edition, American Medical Association, 1955.
18. Hein, Fred V., Dana L. Farnsworth, and Charles E. Richardson, *Living Health, Behavior, and Environment,* 5th edition, Glenview, Ill.: Scott, Foresman and Company, 1970.
19. Hochbaum, Godfrey M., "Behavior modification," *School Health Review,* Vol. 2, No. 3, September 1971.
20. Jenny, John H., *Physical Education, Health Education, and Recreation,* New York: The Macmillan Company, 1961.
21. Johns, Edward B., Wilfred C. Sutton, and Lloyd E. Webster, *Health for Effective Living,* New York: McGraw-Hill, 1962.
22. Kennedy, John F., "A presidential message to the schools on the physical fitness of youth," *Journal of Health, Physical Education, and Recreation,* September 1961.
23. Keyes, Lynford L., "Health education in perspective." *School Health Review,* Vol. 3, No. 4, September–October 1972.
24. Kilander, H. Frederick, *School Health Education,* New York: The Macmillan Company, 1962.
25. Kraus, Richard, *Recreation and Leisure in Modern Society,* New York: Appleton-Century-Crofts, 1971.
26. Le Bato, Loretta T., "Should tension control classes be included in the curriculum," *The Physical Educator,* Vol. 28, No. 2, May 1971.
27. Maier, Norman R. F., *Frustration,* New York: McGraw-Hill, 1949.
28. Mayshark, Cyrus, and Leslie W. Irwin, *Health Education in Secondary Schools,* 2nd edition, St. Louis: The C. V. Mosby Company, 1968.
29. Meeds, Lloyd, "Legislation as a precipitator of educational development," *School Health Review,* Vol. 4, No. 5, September–October 1973.
30. Oberteuffer, Delbert O., *School Health Education,* New York: Harper and Row, 1960.
31. *The Royal Bank of Canada, Monthly Letter of,* Vol. 39, No. 1, January 1958.
32. Saltin, Bengt, "Metabolic fundamentals in exercise," *Medicine and Science in Sports,* Vol. 5, No. 3, Fall 1973.
33. Sliepcevich, Elena M., *School Health Education Report,* Washington, D.C.: School Health Education Study, 1964. By permission.

34. Steinfeld, Jesse L., "Citizen motivation—key to health," *YMCA Today,* Summer 1973.
35. Tuck, Miriam L., and Franklin B. Haar, *Health,* New York: Harper and Row, 1969.
36. Tussing, Lyle, *Psychology for Better Living,* New York: John Wiley and Sons, 1965.
37. Voltmer, Edward F., and Arthur A. Esslinger, *The Organization and Administration of Physical Education,* 4th edition, New York: Appleton-Century-Crofts, 1967.
38. Ward, Jerry, and Francis Tracy, "A supermarket model for health education projects," *School Health Review,* Vol. 4, No. 1, January–February 1973.
39. Warren, Carrie L., "Value strategies in mental health," *School Health Review,* Vol. 5, No. 1, January–February 1974.
40. Willgoose, Carl E., *Health Education in the Elementary School,* Philadelphia: W. B. Saunders Company, 1959.
41. Wolf, Anna W. M., *Your Child's Emotional Health,* Public Affairs Pamphlet No. 264, New York: Public Affairs Committee, 1958.

Fitness
for Living

Chapter 13

13.1 TOTAL FITNESS

Total fitness is an ideal state. Just as no human being is perfect, no one is totally fit. Nevertheless, individuals should strive to reach their potential. They should seek self-realization in all their dimensions—physical as well as intellectual, social, emotional, and spiritual. Each of these strengthens and supports the others. All components of the human organism are reciprocally interrelated and each affects and is affected by the others.

A totally fit person would be free from disease and organic impairment. He would have enough endurance and stamina to do a day's work without undue fatigue, participate in wholesome and worthwhile recreation, and meet emergencies without inordinate physical or emotional trauma. Such a person would possess not only adequate strength and skill to perform daily tasks efficiently but also the zest and vitality to enjoy living and participate in vigorous activities appropriate to his/her age and interest.

If a person were totally fit he would be able to relax and find joy and contentment in the quiet hours and in repose. He would have developed, or would be in the process of developing, a philosophy of life that would enable him to meet crises without too much stress and which would provide strength in time of need. He would have a high regard for the welfare of others and would have developed optimal relationships with his fellows.

Such a person would have his emotions under control and would have developed a value system that would serve as a dependable guide and anchor for his attitudes and behavior. The discovery of the ultimate truth would be one of his goals and his beliefs and actions would be in basic accord. Reason and experience would both contribute to his living philosophy and lead to a way of life which gave testimony to what he believed. The totally fit person would be fit physically, mentally, emotionally, socially, and spiritually.

13.2 PHYSICAL FITNESS

Even as we espouse total fitness as the ultimate goal, we must also be aware that changing lifestyles and the technological revolution have eliminated much of the vigorous activity which was formerly an important component in the lives of a large segment of the population. Because the human organism needs to move in order to achieve optimal development and maintain a reasonable level of endurance, strength, and functional capability, a special effort must be made to provide exercise programs which will meet these needs. Without such activity, an individual will not be physically fit, and without physical fitness total fitness is impossible.

Physical educators must accept their special responsibility for teaching and maintaining *physical fitness*. They work with movement as their medium, assisting students in their efforts to become physically fit. Cardiovascular endurance, muscular endurance, strength, and efficient and effective movement are important qualities which can be developed through scientific programs of exercise and vigorous physical activity.

Riding bicycles in the *Little 500* at Bloomington, Indiana.
For this, a specific kind of fitness is required. (Courtesy of
the *Journal of Health, Physical Education, and Recreation.*)

13.3 FITNESS FOR LIVING

The very word "fitness" implies suitability. If a person is "fit" he must be fit for
something. Let us look for a moment at "fitness for living."

The human organism develops to meet the demands made upon it. Adaptation to stress is a basic biological concept. The kind and amount of stress must
be such that it leads to development rather than physical deterioration and mental
frustration. It must be challenging enough to call for effort and persistence; it
should not be so demanding as to be impossible to accomplish.

The person who is fit for living should possess enough energy and power to
enjoy his daily routine of planned recreation and physical exercise. This might be
in the form of vigorous games and sports, cycling, circuit training, jogging and
running, weight training and calisthenics, dancing, or any appropriate combination
of these and other activities. These should be demanding enough to stimulate the
cardiorespiratory, muscular, and other physiological systems.

The fit individual should also be reasonably well versed in fundamental skills.
Basic activities such as walking, climbing stairs, sitting, standing, lifting, and pulling
should be performed with grace, efficiency, and ease. Every person should develop enough skill in a few individual and dual sports to enjoy them and be
motivated to participate in them throughout life. People generally enjoy most what
they can do well.

To be fit for life one should have a zest for living, feel refreshed after a night's
sleep, be able to relax when given the opportunity, have the ability to function
purposefully and effectively, and have the courage and confidence to face life's
vicissitudes without being overwhelmed. Obviously this involves more than just

exercise. A sound philosophy of life, reasonable success in one's chosen vocation, a satisfactory home life, and good interpersonal relations are essential. Sound and harmonious interrelationships among the many facets of living are also important.

13.4 FITNESS AND HEALTH
Freedom from disease, adequate medical and dental care, enough good nutritious food, and careful attention to deformities and handicaps are prerequisites to fitness and health. Before any exercise program is undertaken, one should be certain that the heart and other parts of the body are free from abnormalities which might lead to harm because of inappropriate activity. Medical examinations, preventive services, immunizations, and advice from physicians should be accepted as important components of fitness programs, whether for individuals or groups. Cooperation among physical education teachers, nurses, students, and parents can do a great deal to enhance the quality and effectiveness of such activity programs.

Conditioning programs are also being utilized more and more frequently to alleviate certain types of abnormalities and pathological conditions. Under the guidance of a physician, therapeutic exercise may assist relief of low-back pain, chronic indigestion, muscular dystrophy, poor body mechanics, injured bones and joints, and certain postoperative conditions. Progressive resistance exercises are used, when prescribed by a physician, as therapeutic measures in poliomyelitis, multiple sclerosis, cerebral palsy, and osteoarthritis. Such activities are useful as one step in the prevention of heart disease, as a part of weight reduction programs, and occasionally in the treatment of Parkinson's disease.

Kraus and Raab have characterized the whole spectrum of inactivity-induced somatic and mental derangements as "hypokinetic disease" (caused by insufficient motion). They deal exhaustively with the relationship of exercise to cardiovascular fitness, obesity, emotional instability, low-back pain, and other degenerative and orthopedic disabilities. [61] One has only to read their book to realize even more fully that man is indeed intended to be an active organism.

Obviously, exercise and activity have an important role in fitness and health. It is also clear that in the hands of unknowing but well-meaning persons, exercise can be hazardous and even harmful. The importance of knowledgeable leaders and careful coordination with physicians is again emphasized.

Because each person must fit oneself for living, for participation in athletics, for a specific kind of work, for the worthy use of leisure, and for self-fulfillment, it is impossible to specify in detail programs which are beneficial for everyone or suitable for all. Rather it behooves each person to consider carefully his fitness goals and to plan his individual program accordingly.

13.5 EXERCISE AND THE CARDIOVASCULAR SYSTEM
The fact that malfunction of the cardiovascular system now accounts for more than half of all the deaths in the United States has brought about increased attention to the fitness of the heart and the blood vessels. Knowledge concerning this aspect of human health has been steadily mounting and we now have a substantial

body of knowledge on which to base our recommendations and actions.

In a leaflet distributed by the Ohio-West Virginia Area Council of YMCA's, risk factors and recommendations for reducing the hazards are identified as follows:

Coronary Risk Factors

1. Heredity
2. High cholesterol level
3. High blood pressure
4. Overweight
5. Diabetes

6. Over-nutrition
7. Too little exercise and physical activity
8. Excessive smoking
9. Excessive tension and stress

The American Heart Association recommends the following to reduce your risk of a heart attack:

1. Reduce needless tension
2. Control high blood pressure
3. Do not smoke cigarettes

4. Watch your diet
5. Keep weight normal
6. Keep physically fit
7. See your doctor regularly*

Exercise has both direct and indirect effects on the cardiovascular system. Some of the principles and concepts involved are:

1. The heart is a muscle and, like all muscle, needs some vigorous exercise to stay in the best possible condition.

2. Exercise of skeletal muscles places a demand on the heart, causing it to pump harder and faster. Thus the heart is exercised, improving the muscle tone of the cardiac fibers and increasing contractile force. The heart then develops the ability to pump more blood with fewer beats. This results in greater efficiency and less wear and tear on the heart.

3. Exercise helps to decrease hypertension. As stressful situations occur and hormones are poured into the body by the adrenal and other glands, tension is built up. Physical activity tends to rid the body of these "pressor" substances and thus lowers blood pressure.

4. During exercise, blood vessels are massaged by muscular contractions, alternately stretched and relaxed by changes in blood pressure, and twisted and bent by bodily movements. While the evidence is somewhat vague at this point, it seems reasonable to assume that such action would cause vessels to retain their tone and elasticity longer than they would if underexercised.

5. It has been maintained by some exercise physiologists that changes in blood pressure and rate of flow, which occur as a result of activity, produce an "anticlog-

---

*Ohio-West Virginia Area Council of YMCA's, 40 West Long Street, Columbus, Ohio 43215.

ging" effect, keeping fatty materials from forming on the interior walls of the arteries and veins.

6. In an exercised heart, the coronary arteries which supply it with oxygen develop and expand and are able to provide it with a richer and more adequate supply of blood.

7. As indicated in the Framingham Study [17], the risk of coronary attack is generally greater in persons whose activity index is low than it is in persons whose activity index is high.

8. William Kannel hypothesizes that exercise "promotes collateral circulation to bypass blocked vessels," thus minimizing the possibility of disastrous consequences. [17, p. 83]

9. Studies by Morris and his coworkers [41, p. 10] and by Brunner and Manelis [61, p. 102], both involving large populations, present important evidence that heart attacks occur more frequently among those who lead a sedentary life than among those whose way of life includes a good deal of exercise.

In addition to these rather direct relationships between exercise and cardiovascular condition, a few more indirect relationships are worthy of mention. These include the following:

1. Obesity is an important risk factor in diseases of the cardiovascular system. Exercise, when combined with a carefully regulated diet, is an important factor in the control of obesity. Most good reducing programs include a program of exercise as one of the procedures for obtaining desired results.

2. While the evidence is somewhat inconclusive, exercise does appear to have a role in the maintenance of a normal cholesterol level. Because the factors of obesity and nutrition are also involved, it is difficult to draw any firm conclusions. Golding, however, reviewed a number of research studies which indicate that exercise can bring about a reduction of cholesterol level. He then described the results of his own experiments at Kent State University in which the cholesterol level of adult men was significantly reduced by exercise. [41, pp. 10–11]

3. Hypertension is one of the contributing factors in the onset of cardiovascular disease. Because exercise and recreation tend to have a cathartic effect in instances of emotional arousal, and because such catharsis tends to return blood pressures to normal, it is believed that physical activity which is vigorous and which requires deep involvement has a beneficial and preventive effect.

4. The oxygen-carrying capacity of the blood is increased by exercise. More red cells per cubic centimeter of blood are found in an exercised than in a nonexercised organism. The combination of these two factors provides more oxygen to the tissues.

5. The efficiency of respiration is increased by exercise, providing more oxygen for transport to the tissues and increasing the oxidation of lactic acid. Thus the efficiency of the entire cardiorespiratory system is increased.

As more and more attention is directed toward the physiology of the cardiovascular system, it is increasingly apparent that the aerobic capacity of the human organism is central to fitness. If the respiratory apparatus moves sufficient oxygen in and out of the lungs, the oxygen enters the bloodstream quickly and easily, the blood contains an adequate amount of hemoglobin to carry the oxygen to the tissues, and the tissue cells use this oxygen effectively, the body will generally be one which can function purposefully and efficiently. Aerobic capacity, then, has become the crucial criterion of physical fitness. Programs to develop the ability to take in and utilize oxygen are increasing in number and quality. The measurement of maximum oxygen intake is becoming more common.

There are, however, some cautions which should be observed when dealing with cardiovascular fitness. Some of these are:

1. Exercising older men and women to their maximum can be hazardous. Careful physical examinations and the recommendations of physicians should serve as guides in the utilization of tests of maximum oxygen intake.

2. There are other components of physical fitness which merit consideration when testing and developing programs. Muscular strength and endurance, body flexibility, and body composition are also important.

3. A distinction must be made in the use of exercise for the development of cardiovascular fitness—*prevention* of cardiac disease on the one hand and programs for the *rehabilitation* of cardiac patients on the other. While physical educators and qualified directors of fitness programs can work with the developmental and preventive aspects with little danger to the participants, rehabilitative exercises for cardiac patients must be administered only under the direction of a physician.

13.6 GENERAL PRINCIPLES OF PHYSICAL FITNESS

While specific programs for the development of physical fitness will have their own guidelines for participation and administration, there are a number of basic principles which are applicable to all such activities. These should be understood and considered by teachers and leaders as they deal with individuals and fitness groups. They are:

1. *The principle of a sound foundation.* All exercise programs should be based on sound physiological, medical, and health precepts. This presupposes appropriate use of health services, examinations and supervision by physicians, and leadership of knowledgeable teachers and directors. It also implies the elimination of disease or other remedial handicaps under the supervision of medical specialists.

2. *The principle of reciprocal interrelationships.* Each part of the human organism affects and is affected by every other part. While exercises are directed toward the development of a given component or function of the organism, consideration shall be given to their effects on all other parts and dimensions. Total fitness is the ultimate goal and involves the development of the individual in all his aspects.

3. *The principle of Hippocrates.* That which is used develops; that which is not used deteriorates. This assumes absence of disease or deformity which would make exercise inappropriate. Development of the human organism occurs in response to appropriate stress and stimulating challenges.

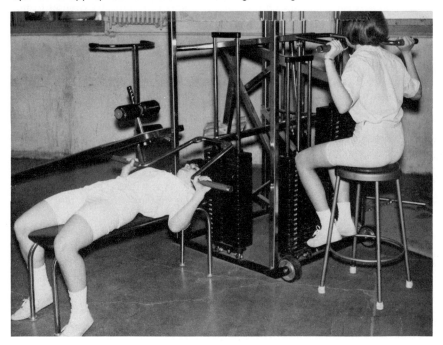

"The human organism . . . builds itself to meet the demands made upon it." (Courtesy of South Dakota State University.)

4. *The overload principle.* This refers to the systematic regulation of activity to levels beyond those usually encountered. The human organism, within limits, builds itself to meet the demands made upon it. To develop greater strength, greater endurance, and greater flexibility, one must gear the exercises to levels which challenge and demand more than usual. An increase in load can be effected by greater resistance, faster rate, greater intensity, or a combination of these.

5. *The principle of specificity.* The body responds differently to different kinds of stress. A strong biceps results from exercises which call on this muscle for strong sustained contractions; great endurance results from progressively increasing the levels of activity to that level which requires unusually demanding bodily adjustments. While there may be some development of general strength and endurance, the developmental response usually comes in the specific area where the stress occurs and in answer to a specific kind of need. One cannot become

a mile runner with great cardiorespiratory endurance by lifting weights; one cannot develop the abdominal muscles by finger-gripping exercises. Each exercise should be given to achieve a specific developmental objective.

6. *The principle of progression.* This principle is a corollary of the overload principle. As the body develops to meet the stresses of a given exercise, what was once an overload is no longer. It is therefore necessary to increase the resistance or the intensity of the exercise. In progressive resistance exercises, for example, the weights lifted and/or the number of repetitions can be increased as the individual becomes strong and enduring enough to perform the original task with ease. Likewise the person conditioning himself for distance running gradually reduces his time, and the pole vaulter gradually increases the height of his vault.

7. *The principle of motivation.* It requires effort to put the body under stress. This is the reason track and swimming coaches have emphasized the importance of being willing to "punish oneself" to become great. This is why conditioning for boxing is such a grueling procedure. This is why a strong will as well as a strong body is necessary to become a champion in sports. But motivation must come from within. Incentives and rewards may stimulate some individuals temporarily, but what must keep them going is a deep and abiding desire to make the most of their lives and to achieve such fulfillment as is possible for them. This is a significant principle of all good fitness programs.

8. *The principle of appropriateness.* The kinds of activity, the nature of the participants, the degrees of effort, and the purposes of exercise vary greatly. What is beneficial to one person is harmful to another; what is fun for one is work for another; what is good for the present may be bad for the future. Exercise and activity must then be:

a) *appropriate to the present condition of the individual.* Both physiological and psychological readiness should exist. The person who is just beginning weight training or just learning to swim should not work as long or intensely as the person who has been practicing for some time. The person who is convalescing needs different activity than the person who has not been sick. Workouts should not be the same for the highly conditioned distance runner as for the sprinter who is practicing for the first time.

b) *appropriate to the person's sex.* The nature of the female does differ in some ways from that of the male. Girls should not play *all* the games recommended for boys. Both sexes should be considered when planning activity programs. Nevertheless there are many needs satisfied more fully by coeducational activities; provision should be made for these as well. Interests, physiological development, and capacities of boys and girls, men and women should govern the selection of activities.

c) *appropriate to age.* Age as well as physical condition must be considered in any exercise program. A girl of seven should not follow the same exercise regimen as might be planned for her in her thirties. A person's strength, stamina, flexibility, and resiliency are not the same at age ten as at age twenty-five. Golf may be the best exercise for a man of sixty, while soccer was suitable for him forty years earlier.

d) *appropriate for the purpose intended.* The first and most important question with regard to exercise must be to inquire into its purpose. The doctor prescribing therapy for the postpolio patient will not give the same therapy to the person with low-back pain. The coach prescribing a training program for a potential Olympic wrestler will not prescribe it for the long-distance swimmer or the volleyball player. The convalescing heart patient will need a far different exercise program than will the football prospect. The purpose may be for fun, enjoyment, strength, therapy, endurance, confidence, conditioning, or becoming more attractive. Whatever it is, the purpose should be the determining factor in laying plans for the program.

13.7 PROGRAMS FOR PHYSICAL FITNESS
There are many ways in which the fitness of the human organism can be enhanced. There are also a large number of physical fitness programs which are both valid and viable. The purpose of this section is to introduce the reader to several programs which have proven successful and which are in operation today.

Circuit training
A circuit (see Chapter 4) refers to exercise stations located varying distances apart, each with its own prescribed set of exercises. A circuit may consist of any number of stations, but most commonly there will be ten to twenty depending upon the length of time that is desired for a complete circuit and the specific objectives of the circuit training. Circuits may be either indoors or outdoors and can be arranged in the gymnasium, on the athletic fields, or in the woods.

Golding describes an indoor circuit with nine stations, each designed to focus on a specific kind of development. For example, station 1 is designed to build strength, station 2 to develop cardiosvascular endurance, station 3 flexibility, station 4 balance and agility, etc. Three to four minutes are spent at each of the nine stations so that the circuit may be completed in about half an hour. [41, pp. 55–57]

Eleanor Gurewitsch describes the *Vita Parcours,* begun in Switzerland in 1968, which has now spread to Germany, Austria, the United States, and other countries. The Vita Parcours consists of a jogging course up to two miles long set in a wooded area. Spotted along the course are approximately twenty stations "at which participants bend, stretch, do push-ups, chin-ups and other routines." Limbering and warm-up exercises come first, strenuous and more vigorous exercises next, and finally exercises for relaxation. One trip through the twenty-station circuit is about equivalent to the exercise in a one-hour gymnastics class. [44, p. 3]

There can be an infinite number of ways of arranging circuits. They should, however, (a) be designed for a specific purpose, (b) be planned with a definite amount of time in mind, (c) provide for the possibility of substantial numbers of people on the circuit at one time, (d) be made as interesting as possible, and (e) provide for the balanced and well-rounded development of the individual.

Aerobics

"Aerobics" refers to exercises which can be sustained for an extended length of time without incurring an oxygen debt. Dr. Kenneth Cooper has developed a physical fitness program which he calls "Aerobics." Dr. Cooper defined fitness as *aerobic capacity* and worked out a scheme to quantify this quality. He then established five categories of fitness: "very poor, poor, fair, good and excellent." [10, p. 46]

Dr. Cooper then developed a point catalogue of exercises. Points are awarded for walking, running, swimming, cycling, tennis, handball, basketball, and golf. Activities are equated in terms of the amount of energy expended. This is then converted into a point system where the various activities performed a given length of time are valued at a certain number of points. Individuals who are out of condition may begin by trying to earn only ten or fifteen points per week and then gradually increase their workouts until they maintain a level of thirty points per week.

Dr. Cooper's plan allows the participant to add the values for different exercises and measure the amount of exercise in a simple and practical way. One can ski for an hour on Sunday (6 points), play four sets of tennis on Monday (6 points), run a mile in seven minutes on Wednesday (6 points), play handball for an hour on Thursday (9 points), and cycle three miles in ten minutes on Saturday (3 points), thus in one week earning the thirty points necessary to keep him fit. A person involved in this program is required to exercise at least three times per week and cannot pile up all thirty points in one weekend.

For most people, it is easier and more practical to stick with one or two activities at a time. They may, however, wish to vary their exercises according to season. Because every individual can find exercises which he can perform, this program has much to recommend it.

Isometric exercises

Muscular contractions in which the resistance is so great that there is no appreciable movement of the limb or the resisting force are termed isometric (same measurement) contractions. Isometric exercises were once known as *dynamic tension.* Some forms of isometric exercises, as when various parts of the body are pitted against each other, are termed *self-resistive* exercises.

While there has been much controversy over the value of isometric exercises and their efficacy in developing fitness, there are some situations in which they are beneficial. Isometric exercises need little or no equipment, they require little space, they are useful in developing *specific* strength, and they allow measurement of the strength of certain muscle groups.

Isometric exercises, on the other hand, do not enhance cardiovascular function, provide little or no improvement in flexibility, and are "artificial" in nature inasmuch as muscles are normally used for movement.

Isometric exercises are useful during postoperative care to develop strength in a specific set of muscles. They are economical of time as a few bouts of isometric exercises take only a few minutes. Most pertinent, however, is the fact that one can exercise isometrically when no other form of activity is possible.

There are innumerable ways in which isometric exercises can be utilized to strengthen the muscles of the body while standing, lying, or sitting. A person can sit in a chair, grasp the side edges of the seat with the right and left hands, and push hard with both hands toward the midline. He can likewise lock each foot around a leg of the chair and push toward the outside. The two feet can be pushed against each other, the two hands can alternately push and pull inward and outward against the steering wheel of a car, the fingers of the right hand and the fingers of the left can be pushed against each other. In each case, contractions of many muscle groups in the body will ensue.

While isometric exercises should never be thought of as a complete program, they can be useful as one way of keeping fit. A few contractions each day, held for a few seconds, will strengthen and maintain the tone of many muscles throughout the body. Isometrics can be useful as a supplement to other kinds of activity.

The Y's way to fitness

Clayton Myers, Lawrence Golding, and Wayne Sinning have recently edited a book entitled *The Y's Way to Fitness*. [73] It contains a complete and detailed description of the fitness program which is now being recommended for the nation's YMCA's. It contains chapters dealing with organization and administration, exercise physiology, testing, programs for various kinds of individuals and groups, leadership development, and resources such as money, facilities, and personnel.

This YMCA fitness program specifies a minimum of three periods per week, each consisting of a warm-up period, a peak-work period, and a cooling-off period. Strength-endurance muscle exercises are included in the warm-up period. These consist of a wide variety of exercises that have as their object the strengthening and stretching of all parts of the body.

The cardiac-respiratory training period is intended to "provide controlled duration exercise in order to induce cardiorespiratory training effects." [73, p. 77] Recommended activities for this period are jogging, walking, swimming, and cycling.

The cooling-off period has as its purpose the return to the nonexercising state and includes mild jogging, walking, floor exercises, and the "bicycle," all performed in a relaxed fashion.

Complete programs and schedules are outlined with weekly progressions and point values presented. Special programs for the atypical or subpar are presented and explained.

Cycling

Whereas cycling has been in existence for a long time, the purposes and nature of the activity have changed considerably, at least in the United States. A generation or two ago bicycles were used for commuting and as an economical, convenient, and fairly rapid form of transportation.

Cycling has now become one of the most accepted and beneficial ways to achieve fitness, an enjoyable and sociable form of fun and recreation, and a wholesome and pleasant way of traveling to see and enjoy the countryside. Breakfast and overnight hikes, cookouts, treasure hunts, and adventure bike hikes are some of the many forms which recreational cycling now takes. Cross-country cycling and hosteling are gaining in popularity year by year. Bike carnivals and bike derbys are now found in numerous communities. Bicycle racing is gaining in popularity and participation.

Jogging
Jogging was mentioned earlier as the principal activity in the Vita Parcours. Jogging has, however, become much more prevalent and far-reaching than that. Whereas it was unusual to see adults running along the streets fifteen years ago, few people today give it a second thought if they chance upon joggers along the highways, in the woods, or participating in the many jogging programs that have recently been sweeping the nation.

Alexander Melleby and Bill Burros, in their book entitled *Jogging Away,* emphasize the importance of jogging in the prevention of heart disease. They indicate the role of exercise in handling stress, in preventing and dealing with diabetes, in preventing obesity, and in living more abundantly. They describe the physiological and psychological effects of a good jogging program, and they present the hazards of careless preparation for such running exercises. [67]

Eugene Cantrall described a "summer family jogging program."* Total family involvement is emphasized, the suitability of such an activity for all ages and both sexes is pointed out, the sharing of experiences is mentioned, and the involvement with other community members is listed as a benefit. The flexibility of facilities is one of the advantages and the cost is minimal. Publicity and promotion are, however, necessary.

An article entitled, "We Jogged—From Sea to Shining Sea" appears in *The Jogger* (January 1973). It tells of the thousands of joggers who ran along city streets and country roads on the first National Jogging Day, October 7, 1972. Special proclamations were issued by Governor Wallace of Alabama, Governor Docking of Kansas, and Mayor Lindsay of New York City. All over America joggers were running as encouragement was given by leaders of government and by the news media. [51, p. 1]

John Friedrich of Duke University points out the following cardiorespiratory changes which result from jogging:

1. Increase in vital capacity.
2. Increase in number of functioning capillaries.
3. More potential for oxygen absorption.
4. Increase in capacity to incur oxygen debt.
5. Increase in blood hemoglobin and red cell count.
6. Increase in the stroke-volume of the heart.
7. Decrease in blood serum cholesterol.
8. Improvement in the organic efficiency of the lungs, kidneys, liver, and gastrointestinal tract.

---

*Paper presented at National YMCA Conference, St. Louis, Missouri, 1967.

In his concluding paragraph, Friedrich states:

> Besides the foregoing advantages of jogging, various other general values may be pointed out. For example, regular running improves the use the body makes of food. It improves elimination, digestion and appetite, and lessens the tendency toward constipation, kidney stones and diabetes. The individual who runs regularly will help to prevent fatty degeneration of the body, heart, lungs, blood vessels and brain which otherwise tend to occur in the sedentary individual. [36, p. 124]

Outward bound activities

Dr. Sol Rosenthal, professor of preventive medicine at The University of Illinois, stated that "risk" sports are important for a healthy life and for a complete and happy life. He indicated that men and women are more efficient, more creative, and more productive after participation in activities in which hazards are involved. Among the risk sports he names are skiing, surfing, mountain climbing, flying, and auto racing.*

"Metamorphosis of a Marshmallow" is an article in *The Healthy Life* which describes the experiences of a 220-pound obese 17-year-old at the Colorado Outward Bound School in the Rocky Mountains. It is a graphic example of what can be achieved through a combination of challenging and daring experiences, encouragement of instructors and peers, and some willpower, determination, and courage. Increased physical fitness and confidence, improved self-concept, and the discovery of hidden resources change body, spirit, and mind. This type of fitness program is also meeting with more and more favor where it is utilized as an adjunct to other programs. [45, pp. 59–63]

The Swedish training track

During the last two decades training tracks, usually one to two miles long, have been constructed in great numbers in parks and other suitable areas in Sweden. Such tracks wind across the countryside and are usually found filled with individuals of all ages walking or running at their own pace. For most adults the exercise consists of walking, jogging, sprinting, and resting, with the entire course negotiated in 20 to 50 minutes, depending on the runner's condition and the objectives of his training. Most courses have hills so that the various muscle groups are exercised at one time or another. Occasionally there is competition between individuals and groups who are conditioned for this purpose.

Ergometry† and treadmill running

Bicycle ergometers have increased in use and popularity both in homes and in the laboratory. For those who cannot find other facilities, ergometry is certainly recom-

---

* *Sunday Republican,* Springfield, Mass., April 8, 1973.

†Ergometry is the measurement and recording of work performed under controlled conditions. In this case, the work consists of riding a bicycle on which is mounted a device for measuring and recording work.

mended. While it does not have some of the exhilarating qualities of outdoor games and exercises, it is certainly one method of working out. An added advantage is the measuring device which enables individuals to scientifically plan their exercise periods and evaluate the amount of work being done.

Where treadmills are available, many feel that running on these is more natural than riding a bicycle. The measurement and control of the amount of work done can also be effected in such instances. Home treadmills are also becoming more common, practical, and economical than in the past. Ergometry and treadmill running both have their place in fitness testing and conditioning programs.

Miscellaneous fitness programs
There are almost as many fitness programs as there are leaders working with them. Each person has some exercise, game, or activity which he believes is important. There are calisthenics exercises of many descriptions. There are relaxation exercises; there is yoga. Sports which place demands on the organism have a legitimate place in fitness programs. Rehabilitative and therapeutic exercises are important where needed. Conditioning exercises for the subpar have a special function and therefore should have their own characteristics. Activities for the mentally retarded and the emotionally disturbed should be designed for their needs. Where special exercises for the perceptually handicapped are indicated, they should be provided. If individuals wish to condition themselves for proficiency in certain sports or prowess in individual contests, they should be afforded the opportunity for special training designed for their needs.

It is obviously impossible to explain or describe all the fitness programs which exist or should exist. Therefore, the remainder of this chapter will be devoted to listing general principles and guidelines for the planning, conduct, and evaluation of fitness programs.

13.8 PRINCIPLES AND GUIDELINES IN DEVELOPING FITNESS PROGRAMS
The following miscellaneous principles and guidelines have been drawn from many sources. They are intended to serve those who are planning and conducting fitness programs in schools, social agencies, homes, industries, and other places where such activities are to be found.

1. Begin exercises at the current fitness level. The lower that level is, the easier the exercises should be in the initial stages.

2. Progress from easy, to hard, to harder exercises. Improvement in fitness comes with appropriate overload.

3. Overload may be in the magnitude of resistance, speed of movement, or endurance and stamina required.

4. The best results are obtained when exercises are performed in good form. For therapeutic and rehabilitative exercises, this is particularly important.

5. Proper nutrition, adequate rest, and other general principles of good health are necessary if fitness exercises are to have their optimum effect. No exercise can cure a pathological condition, heal a wound, or mend a broken bone.

6. Provide the participant with knowledge of results. Careful periodic evaluation is important if each individual is to maintain an awareness of his own progress (or lack of it).

7. When jogging, walking, or exercising in ways which put stress on the feet, meticulous attention to footwear is especially important. Shoes must fit the foot, give adequate support, and be appropriate for the activity concerned.

8. Avoid requiring too much running on hard surfaces. Continuous pounding on hard surfaces will damage the feet and cause shin splints and other leg ailments.

9. Alternate relaxation and work is desirable in conditioning and fitness programs. The exact proportion can only be determined by the circumstances involved.

10. Even though some form of running is the principal fitness exercise, it should be interspersed with some stretching, twisting, and strength-building exercises.

11. Regularity of exercise is a cardinal principle. Three periods per week should be the minimum.

12. For competitive exercise, preconditioning is necessary.

13. Hard exercise and/or competition is contraindicated when the participant is suffering from any infectious disease.

14. Most good exercise programs will include a warm-up period, an endurance activity, and a cooling-off period. Strength-building and flexibility exercises can be included in the warm-up period.

15. Good leadership is essential for most fitness programs. Only a few individuals have the knowledge and experience to exercise wisely without proper guidance.

16. The exercise program for cardiac patients should be part of a comprehensive treatment program which would include careful examination, supervision, periodic evaluation, and attention to psychological as well as physiological adjustment problems.

17. Self-discipline is an important factor in most fitness programs. Only the disciplined person will normally continue a fitness program over a prolonged period of time.

18. The continuation and success of most fitness programs is dependent upon the inner motivation of the participant. Incentives and rewards may play a temporary role but a deep inner conviction of the value of the program will, in the long run, be the determining factor.

19. Leaders and participants should be knowledgeable with regard to responses to exercise which indicate a need for medical attention. Such responses include chest pains or referred pains, lightheadedness or dizziness, persistent or unusual fatigue, nausea, pains in joints or muscles which are increased by exercise, and irregular heart beats.

◀ "Improvement in fitness comes with appropriate overload."
(Courtesy of Topeka Public Schools, Topeka, Kansas.)

20. There is no hard-and-fast rule for amount of exercise. A knowledgeable and experienced leader will consider, for each individual, the participant's present condition, the objective of the exercise, and the facilities and time available.

21. Good posture and body mechanics not only make for efficient movement, but also provide a better environment for internal organ function. Good posture is dependent upon the tone of the skeletal muscles and the neuromuscular control of the individual.

22. Exercise programs should provide for balanced development of the various muscle groups. Agonist and antagonist should receive a balanced amount of work for best results.

23. The effect of emotional involvement on fitness has not yet been thoroughly assessed. Strong emotion, tension, and anxiety are known to affect heart rate, accumulation of cholesterol, and many other complex mechanisms of the body. Emotions resulting in secretion of hormones must receive attention in some of the fitness programs.

24. The relationship of physical fitness to self-concept and personality development cannot be disregarded. A positive body image and the self-confidence that comes with physical accomplishment will have a favorable influence on both the mental and physical health of the individual.

25. The interrelationships of mental, spiritual, emotional, and social fitness may be intangible, but they are also real. Physical fitness can only be understood as the meaning of "total fitness" becomes clearer.

SELECTED REFERENCES

1. *Adult Physical Fitness*, a program for men and women prepared by the President's Council on Physical Fitness, 1963.
2. Astrand, Per-Olaf, *Health and Fitness*, Stockholm: Skandia Insurance Company, 1972.
3. "Basic understanding of physical fitness," *Physical Fitness Research Digest*, Series 1, No. 1, July 1971.
4. Bauer, W. W., "Fitness has many facets," *Journal of Health, Physical Education, and Recreation*, September 1960.
5. Bleier, T. J., "An approach to developing physical fitness as an integral part of the physical education program," *The Physical Educator*, Vol. 25, No. 4, December 1968.
6. Boyer, John M., "Effects of chronic exercise on cardiovascular function," *Physical Fitness Research Digest*, Series 2, No. 3, July 1972.
7. Bucher, Charles, "National adult physical fitness survey," *Journal of Health, Physical Education, and Recreation*, Vol. 45, No. 1, January 1974.
8. *Cardiovascular Diseases in the U.S., Facts and Figures*, The American Heart Association, 1965.
9. Carlson, Anton J., and Victor Johnson, *The Machinery of the Body*, Chicago: University of Chicago Press, 1941.
10. Cooper, Kenneth H., *Aerobics*, New York: Bantam Books, 1968.
11. Cureton, Thomas K., "Health and fitness in the modern world and what research reveals," *Journal of Physical Education*, Vol. 70, No. 1, September–October 1972.

12. _____, *The Physiological Effects of Exercise Programs on Adults,* Springfield, Ill.: Charles C Thomas, 1969.
13. _____, *The Physiological Effects of Wheat Germ Oil on Humans in Exercise,* Springfield, Ill.: Charles C Thomas, 1972.
14. _____, "Principles of training and conditioning," *Journal of Physical Education,* Vol. 59, No. 2, November–December 1961.
15. *Cycling in the School Fitness Program,* Washington, D.C.: The American Association for Health, Physical Education, and Recreation, 1963.
16. Davis, Elwood C., and Gene A. Logan, *Biophysical Values of Muscular Activity,* Dubuque, Iowa: Wm. C. Brown Company, 1961.
17. Dawber, Thomas R., Abraham Kagan, and William B. Kannel, *The Framingham Heart Study,* The National Heart Institute, U.S. Department of Health, Education, and Welfare, Bethesda, Maryland, 1964.
18. *Design for Heart Disease Prevention Programs,* The State Education Department, Bureau of Continuing Education Curriculum Development, Albany, N.Y.: The University of the State of New York, 1970.
19. "Development of muscular strength and endurance," *Physical Fitness Research Digest,* Series 4, No. 1, January 1974.
20. Dunn, Halbert L., "What high-level wellness means," *Canadian Journal of Public Health,* Vol. 50, No. 11, November 1959.
21. Dutton, Richard E., "Physical fitness and the professor," *The Physical Educator,* Vol. 24, No. 1, March 1967.
22. *Exercise and Fitness—1969,* Proceedings of a Symposium, Chicago: The Athletic Institute, 1969.
23. "Exercise and fitness," American Association for Health, Physical Education, and Recreation, *Journal of Health, Physical Education, and Recreation,* April 1958.
24. "Exercise and fitness," *Journal of Health, Physical Education, and Recreation,* May 1964.
25. *Exercise Testing and Training of Apparently Healthy Individuals: A Handbook for Physicians,* New York: American Heart Association, 1972.
26. Falls, H. B., E. L. Wallis, and G. A. Logan, *Foundations of Conditioning,* New York: The Academic Press, 1970.
27. *Fit for College,* Report of the College Physical Education Association, Washington, D.C.: American Association for Health, Physical Education, and Recreation, 1959.
28. *Fitness Activities Handbook for Elementary Teachers,* Hartford, Conn.: The Governor's Fitness Committee.
29. *The Fitness Challenge,* The President's Council on Physical Fitness and Sports, Published by the Administration on Aging.
30. *Fitness Finders Confidential Operations Manual (YMCA),* Emmaus, Penn.: Fitness Finders, 1971.
31. *Fitness Finders Training Manual (YMCA),* Emmaus, Penn.: Fitness Finders, 1971.
32. "Fitness, health, and motor behavior," *Research News,* Ann Arbor, Mich.: Office of Research Administration, University of Michigan, Vol. XXII, No. 5, November 1971.
33. *5BX Plan for Physical Fitness,* Royal Canadian Air Force Pamphlet 30/1, June 1960.
34. Franks, B. Don (ed.), *Exercise and Fitness,* Chicago: The Athletic Institute, 1969.
35. Friedman, Meyer, "Best advice: slow down," *Reader's Digest,* October 1971.
36. Friedrich, John A., "How jogging improves body function," *Journal of Physical Education,* Vol. 67, No. 5, May–June 1970.

37. Friermood, Harold T., *The YMCA Guide to Adult Fitness*, New York: Association Press, 1963.
38. Frost, Reuben B., *Cardiovascular Fitness*, Presentation to AAHPER Fitness Council, Portland, Oregon, 1959.
39. _____, "Crossroads to fitness," *Bulletin*, Connecticut Association for Health, Physical Education, and Recreation, Vol. 7, No. 3, May 1962.
40. _____, "Physical education for the 70's—the YMCA way," *World Communique*, September–October 1970.
41. Golding, Lawrence A., and Ronald R. Bos, *Scientific Foundations of Physical Fitness Programs*, Minneapolis, Minn.: Burgess Publishing Company, 1967.
42. Gross, Nancy E., *Living with Stress*, New York: McGraw-Hill, 1958.
43. Guild, Warren R., *How to Keep Fit and Enjoy It*, New York: Harper and Row, 1962.
44. Gurewitsch, Eleanor, "How the Swiss keep fit," *Newsletter, American College of Sports Medicine*, Vol. 7, No. 2, April 1972.
45. "The Healthy Life," *Time-Life Special Report*, New York: Time, 1966.
46. Hein, Fred V., *Not Just Exercise*, revised, American Medical Association, 1955.
47. Hein, Fred V., Dana L. Farnsworth, and Charles E. Richardson, *Living Health, Behavior, and Environment*, 5th edition, Glenview, Ill.: Scott, Foresman and Company, 1970.
48. Hockey, Robert V., *Physical Fitness—The Pathway to Healthful Living*, St. Louis: The C. V. Mosby Company, 1973.
49. "In search of fitness," *The Royal Bank of Canada, Monthly Letter of*, Montreal, Canada, Vol. 39, No. 1, January 1958.
50. "Individual differences, their nature, extent and significance," *Physical Fitness Research Digest*, Series 3, No. 4, October 1973.
51. *The Jogger*, National Jogging Association, Newsletter No. 16, January 1973.
52. Johns, Edward B., Wilfred C. Sutton, and Lloyd E. Webster, *Health for Effective Living*, New York: McGraw-Hill, 1962.
53. Jokl, Ernst, *The Clinical Physiology of Physical Fitness and Rehabilitation*, Springfield, Ill.: Charles C Thomas, 1971.
54. Karpovich, Peter V., and Wayne E. Sinning, *Physiology of Muscular Activity*, Philadelphia: W. B. Saunders Company, 1971.
55. Kasch, Fred W., and John L. Boyer, *Adult Fitness—Principles and Practices*, Greeley, Colo.: All American Productions and Publications, 1968.
56. Kennedy, John F., "A presidential message to the schools on the fitness of youth," *Journal of Health, Physical Education, and Recreation*, September 1961.
57. Kilander, H. Frederick, *School Health Education*, New York: The Macmillan Company, 1962.
58. Klappholz, Lowell (ed.), *Successful Practices in Teaching Physical Fitness*, Part 1, New London, Conn.: Croft Educational Services, 1964.
59. _____, *Successful Practices in Teaching Physical Fitness*, Part II, New London, Conn.: Croft Educational Services, 1968.
60. Kraus, Hans, "Conditioning of the under exercised individual," *Journal of Physical Education*, Vol. 69, No. 15, May–June 1972.
61. Kraus, Hans, and Wilhelm Raab, *Hypokinetic Disease*, Springfield, Ill.: Charles C Thomas, 1961.
62. LeBato, Loretta T., "Should tension control classes be included in the curriculum?," *The Physical Educator*, Vol. 28, No. 2, May 1971.
63. Malmisur, M. C., "Fitness through philosophy," *The Physical Educator*, Vol. 24, No. 3, October 1967.

64. Massie, J. F., and Roy J. Shephard, "Physiological and psychological effects of training," *Medicine and Science in Sports,* Vol. 3, No. 3, Fall 1971.
65. Mathews, Donald K., and Edward L. Fox, *The Physiological Basis of Physical Education and Athletics,* Philadelphia: W. B. Saunders Company, 1971.
66. Mayshark, Cyrus, and Leslie W. Irwin, *Health Education in Secondary Schools,* 2nd edition, St. Louis: The C. V. Mosby Company, 1968.
67. Melleby, Alexander, and Bill Burrus, *Jogging Away . . . ,* New York: Volitant Publishing, 1969.
68. Milo, Mary, and Grace White, *Diet and Exercise Guide,* The Family Circle, 1966.
69. Mitchell, Curtis, "New cure for sick hearts," *True—The Man's Magazine,* Fawcett Publications, December 1962.
70. Morehouse, Laurence E., and Augustus T. Miller, Jr., *Physiology of Exercise,* St. Louis: The C. V. Mosby Company, 1971.
71. Morse, Robert L. (ed.) *Exercise and the Heart,* Springfield, Ill.: Charles C Thomas, 1972.
72. Myers, Clayton R., "Fitness is YMCA's business," *Journal of Physical Education,* Vol. 70, No. 3, January–February 1973.
73. Myers, Clayton R., Lawrence A. Golding, and Wayne E. Sinning, *The Y's Way to Physical Fitness,* Emmaus, Penn.: Rodale Press, 1973.
74. "National adult physical fitness survey," *Newsletter,* President's Council on Physical Fitness and Sports, special edition, May 1973.
75. "National workshop on exercise in the prevention, in the evaluation, in the treatment of heart disease," *The Journal of the South Carolina Medical Association,* Vol. 65, Supplement 1 to No. 12, December 1969.
76. O'Shea, John P., *Scientific Principles and Methods of Strength Fitness,* Reading, Mass.: Addison-Wesley Publishing Company, 1969.
77. *Physical Conditioning,* A F Manual 160–26, Washington, D.C.: Department of the Air Force, April 1956.
78. *Physical Fitness Elements in Recreation,* Washington, D.C.: The President's Council on Youth Fitness, 1962.
79. *Preventive Cardiology, First International Conference on,* University of Vermont, August 1964.
80. "Preventive geriatrics," *The Journal of the Michigan State Medical Society,* Vol. 56, No. 5, May 1957.
81. "Proceedings of the International Symposium on Physical Activity and Cardiovascular Health," *The Canadian Medical Association Journal,* Vol. 96, No. 12, March 25, 1967.
82. Raab, W., *Organized Prevention of Degenerative Heart Disease,* University of Vermont, 1964.
83. _____, "Prevention of ischaemic heart disease," *Medical Services Journal Canada,* Vol. XXI, No. 10, November 1965.
84. *Report of the Governor's Conference on Youth Fitness,* Robert Allerton Park, May 1957, Superintendent of Public Instruction, Springfield, Illinois.
85. Ricci, Benjamin, *Physical and Physiological Conditioning for Men,* Dubuque, Iowa: Wm. C. Brown Company, 1966.
86. Rodahl, Kaare, *Be Fit for Life,* New York: Harper and Row, 1961.
87. Rosenman, Ray H., and Meyer Friedman, "Observations on the pathogenesis of coronary heart disease," *Nutrition News,* special issue, Vol. 34, No. 3, October 1971.
88. *Seven Paths to Fitness,* Department of Health Education, American Medical Association.

89. Sills, Frank D., Laurence E. Morehouse, and Thomas L. DeLorme (eds.), *Weight Training in Sports and Physical Education,* Washington, D.C.: American Association for Health, Physical Education, and Recreation, 1962.
90. Sorich, Ted, "A functional isometric contraction program," *Journal of the Arizona Association for Health, Physical Education, and Recreation,* Vol. 13, No. 2, Spring 1970.
91. Spackman, Robert R., Jr., *Exercise in the Office,* Carbondale and Edwardsville, Ill.: Southern Illinois University Press, 1968.
92. "Special report national YMCA physical fitness consultation," *Journal of Physical Education,* March–April 1972.
93. Steinhaus, Arthur H., "Fitness beyond muscle," *The Physical Educator,* Vol. 23, No. 3, October 1966.
94. Tillman, Kenneth, *Physical Fitness Activities for Children,* Vol. 69, No. 2, November–December 1971.
95. *Tips on Athletic Training X,* Chicago: American Medical Association, 1968.
96. "The totality of man," *Physical Fitness Research Digest,* Series 1, No. 2, October 1971.
97. Tuck, Miriam L., and Franklin B. Haar, *Health,* New York: Harper and Row, 1969.
98. Wenger, Nanette K., "The role of physical activity in the prevention and treatment of coronary disease," *Journal of Physical Education,* Vol. 70, No. 5, May–June 1973.
99. White, Paul Dudley, and Curtis Mitchell (eds.), *Fitness for the Whole Family,* Garden City, N.Y.: Doubleday and Company, 1964.
100. Wilkinson, Bud, *Bud Wilkinson's Guide to Modern Physical Fitness,* New York: The Viking Press, 1967.
101. Willgoose, Carl E. *Health Education in the Elementary School,* Philadelphia: W. B. Saunders Company, 1959.
102. "Your child's health and fitness," *NEA Journal,* February 1962.
103. *Your Community, School-Community Fitness Inventory,* American Association for Health, Physical Education, and Recreation, 1959.
104. *Youth Fitness Test Manual,* American Association for Health, Physical Education, and Recreation, 1961.
105. *Youth Physical Fitness,* President's Council on Youth Fitness, Washington, D.C.: Superintendent of Documents, 1961.

Leisure
and
Recreation

Chapter 14

14.1 INTRODUCTION

If we pause in our busy lives to recall our most cherished moments, we will usually find that we remember those times when there was nothing that had to be done immediately, there was no one telling us what to do, and there were no feelings of guilt if we did nothing and accomplished nothing. Sitting by a river holding a fishing pole, lying on the grass looking up at the clouds, listening to one's favorite records, relaxing with a good book, or sitting with a group of friends and just talking are examples. Living for even short periods of time without a sense of "compulsiveness" gives one a feeling of freedom and peace which is renewing. In the past, occasional periods of this kind of living have been sufficient for most people to maintain a reasonable degree of mental health.

But if we believe the prophets of the future or if we study carefully the signs pointing out future trends, education for leisure will be more than the enjoyment of doing nothing. Most individuals will have more than a few hours of leisure each week; it is predicted that they may have days and weeks of free time. For many, most of their waking hours will be those with which they can do as they wish without accounting to anyone. If these predictions come true, it will change the very nature of leisure. Filling this time with idle pastimes will not satisfy the need to feel a sense of worth. Rather, these leisure hours must provide for creative and artistic expression, an opportunity for involvement with those who need assistance, a chance to try something new, time to do things for which individuals were previously too busy, and activities which will lead to self-fulfillment. As Richard Kraus says,

> It will be necessary for those who provide leisure services to help people deal with vast portions of free time, far beyond that existing in any previous day. They will have the task of providing services and opportunities that are so exciting and attractive that they can counter the strong attractions of antisocial forms of amusement as well as the equally strong tendency to withdraw from active involvement in a spectator-oriented age. The new recreation will have to make the fullest use of modern technology and embody the most relevant concepts of modern psychology. America's cities will need innovative planning in which recreation and parks are closely linked to transportation, housing, education, the economy, and law enforcement. [24, p. 24]

This, of course, does not mean that the leisure promised for the future should again be filled with activities which need to be completed at a specific time, or which contain the element of compulsiveness too often found in one's daily work.

14.2 LEISURE AND THE CHANGING CULTURE

Cultural changes which have been identified by sociologists include both the elements of the technological and social revolutions and the more subtle attitude changes. Michael Wilkins and Richard Ragatz identify these as changing attitudes "toward such concepts as work, transience, ownership of property, and nature." [40, p. 35]

The "protestant work ethic," with its emphasis on thrift and hard work, has been a prominent factor in the development of American society since colonial days. People laboring on farms and in factories were categorized as "good workers" and "lazy workers." The capitalistic society thrived on the importance and adulation accorded productiveness through hard work. Free enterprise was supported by the idea that one could be successful by working long and hard.

This philosophy appears to be changing rapidly. Shorter workdays, more and longer vacation periods, and increased travel are now beginning to be associated with success and status and are being sought more avidly by people at all economic levels. The young people of today support the idea of freedom to do what they wish and to travel before they settle down to work. They strive toward an increased amount of leisure even while they are earning a living.

The "working class" has also changed its habits and mores. Sabbaticals in industry, lifetime sports for the American worker, the growth of community theaters, artists among the common people, and a different philosophy of leisure are now manifest. As J. D. Hodgson says, "The American worker sees in leisure time the opportunity for a fuller life—an opportunity that his forebears were denied. [21, p. 39]

Transience can be noted in many forms and situations. People change jobs more frequently, trade in their cars more often, move from place to place at an increasing rate, change marriage partners with more freedom, use far more disposible items in the home, and rent equipment which they formerly felt compelled to own. Relationships with places, things, and people are becoming increasingly temporary. The ancient Epicurean philosophy of "eat, drink, and be merry, for tomorrow you die," appears to express the present-day philosophy of life.

The sense of transience is also intensified by the many technological advances which have necessitated adaptive changes. The acceleration of the rate of change strains the ability of people to adapt. Those who are unable to cope exhibit symptoms of withdrawal, some of which are harmful and some of which are not. Drug abuse, excessive consumption of alcohol, addiction to television—those pastimes that prevent people from being physically active—are harmful to both individuals and society as a whole. On the other hand, escape from an over-stimulating environment into nature's quiet surroundings can be both therapeutic and wholesome. Outdoor activities such as mountaineering, canoeing, backpacking, and camping are antidotes for the harassments of too much noise, too much competition, and too rapid a pace.

Richard Kraus listed five specific challenges which face the United States with respect to recreation and leisure needs in the twenty-first century. [24, pp. 465–472] These are:

1. *The need to preserve and expand the nation's outdoor recreation and park resources.* The importance of preserving the nation's natural environment cannot be overemphasized. The necessity to control off-shore oil drilling, to regulate the use of inorganic fertilizers, to curb the pollution of the air by automobiles and trucks, and to plan the size of our population are now recognized national concerns.

2. *The need for more effective urban planning.* Cities of the future must be planned and not allowed to sprawl and expand without control. Streams must be preserved; selected land areas for parks and playgrounds must be set aside;

parking areas must be constructed. Transit systems which can move thousands of people from the inner city to the recreational areas must be provided.

If the urban areas, in which approximately 90 percent of our total population live, are to contribute to good health and quality of life, there must be renewing and remodeling of present cities, carefully planned outlying suburban communities close to metropolitan areas, and development of entirely new population- and space-controlled cities, all of which must include recreational facilities and parks to serve the people in their leisure moments.

3. *The use of technology in the delivery of leisure services.* Technology has brought on opportunity for more leisure and the need for increased recreational services. It also serves to provide new forms of recreation, transportation to recreation areas, computers to calculate weather conditions, audiovisual aids for education and enjoyment, and many new and improved pieces of equipment such as snowmobiles and artificial surfing pools.

4. *Establishing national priorities for recreation and leisure.* The problem of providing worthwhile leisure must be understood and taken more seriously by all citizens if it is to be solved. It must become an important national concern. If free time is to be a constructive, rather than a destructive, factor in our society, attention must be given to its utilization to increase educational opportunities for adults and to provide an outlet for energies so as to benefit the individuals involved as well as society as a whole. Classes in art, music, dance, dramatics, woodworking, metalworking, and writing are examples. Learning and participating experiences for those who have leisure hours to spend are part of the answer. Community involvement in worthwhile projects must also be encouraged. Government support at all levels is essential.

5. *The role of the recreation and park professional.* The recreation professional of the future must be a dedicated leader. Not only must he be prepared for the many tasks which he must perform daily but he must convince the government, the public, and others working in his field of the need for the best kind of recreation. More planning, facilities, personnel, resources, understanding, and appreciation are needed. Recreation and park professionals who are sociologists, administrators, engineers, psychologists, physical educators, artists, and craftsmen must be enlisted in this effort. Forest rangers, mountaineers, canoeing experts and park managers have an important role. Leaders in industry, education, transportation, social planning, and recreation have skills and abilities which can contribute. All citizens need to be made aware of the urgency of this matter.

14.3 RELAXATION AND ACTIVITY

For those who are concerned about the quality of life, periods of relaxation are very important. Relaxation is especially meaningful to those whose duties involve meticulous, tension-producing activity such as negotiating with employees, making continuous and difficult decisions or pondering seemingly insolvable problems.

Periods of intense effort should be followed by periods of relaxation, for this is the natural cadence of life itself. Sleep follows wakefulness, muscular relaxation follows contraction, and return to equilibrium comes after energy expenditure.

Today's noisy, hurried, and often monotonous work-a-day world can be very fatiguing and can lead to nervous disorder and mental breakdown. Relaxation is essential. It can be achieved in many different ways. Conversing with family and friends, listening to a symphony concert, going to a theater, gardening, and actively playing can all be relaxing.

Josephine Rathbone emphasizes adequate sleep, tension-reducing exercises, the application of heat to tired muscles, massage, and conscious mental relaxation as methods of relaxing. [31, pp. 201–216] Others indicate fishing, swimming, walking, jogging, and vigorous, absorbing sports as beneficial activities. The "stroke-glide" principle in all of life's endeavors is urged by many. The important thing is to recognize the need for intermittent periods of relaxation and to adjust one's life accordingly.

14.4 CONTENT OF RECREATION PROGRAMS
Recreation programs are conducted in and by schools, towns, cities, parks, social agencies, youth organizations, industries, and private enterprises. They include dramatics, musical activities, art, crafts, reading, games, sports, aquatics, fishing, hunting, backpacking, orienteering, mountain climbing, and hiking. Surfing, archery, bowling, scuba diving, sailing, skating, skiing, camping, gardening, and horseback riding are other activities which are generally recreational in nature. Hobbies such as stamp collecting, woodworking, knitting, crocheting, and weaving are excellent leisure-time activities. Square dancing and folk dancing provide both the opportunity for self-expression and release from tension. Chess, checkers, bridge, and other indoor quiet games will satisfy recreational needs for many.

"Recreation programs include a great variety of activities."
(Courtesy of the *Journal of Health, Physical Education, and Recreation.*)

Cycling, hosteling, nature study, bird watching, excursions, and tours are enjoyed by others. There is no end to the specific activities which can be listed.

Many activities may or may not be recreational in nature, depending on the attitude toward them. If they are enjoyable, relaxing, satisfying, and renewing, they will be good leisure-time activities. The attitude of the participants toward them and the circumstances under which people participate will determine whether they are truly *re-creative* in nature.

Jay Shivers presented and classified recreational activities as follows [33, pp. 354–373]:

Art: Graphic art and plastic art.
Crafts: Animal, vegetable, and mineral; industrial, automotive, and natural.
Dance: Folk dance, social dance, choreographed dance, and rhythmics.
Dramatics: Manipulative performance, creative drama, forensic performance, theater.
Education: Adult education, literary activities, linguistic activities.
Motor performance: Individual, dual, team, and group.
Music: Vocal, instrumental, appreciation, and combinations of these.
Outdoor education: Biological science, physical science, natural history, outdoor living.
Service activities: Committee work, direct activity, leadership, and nonleadership work.
Social activities: Formal and informal activities.
Special projects: Exhibitions, festivals, and musicals.

Recreational programs must be comprehensive and well-balanced. They must be varied enough to appeal to both sexes, all ages, and people of different socioeconomic backgrounds. There must be programs for the inner city, the suburbs, and the rural areas. Activities for the different seasons and various geographical conditions should be provided.

At first glance, such programs seem utopian and unrealistic. If we remember, however, that recreation is partly a matter of attitude, it does not seem so completely out of reach. For those who approach an activity in a play spirit, for those who can enjoy service to others, for those to whom new places and the wonders of nature continue to be dramatic and marvelous, there are limitless recreational opportunities. The spirit of adventure, appreciation for beauty, a sincere interest in other people, and a love of the simple and natural things of life can make many activities recreational. Add to this some creative and imaginative leadership and enough financial resources to provide reasonable facilities and equipment, and a sound, comprehensive, and balanced program is assured.

14.5 COMMUNITY AGENCIES AND VOLUNTARY ORGANIZATIONS
Youth-serving agencies, community and neighborhood centers, and recreation associations have done much to foster recreational programs for certain segments of the population. The Boy Scouts of America, the Girl Scouts of America, the Campfire Girls, Boys' Clubs of America, 4-H Clubs, and the Police Athletic League

are examples of organizations whose purposes are serious, and far-reaching, but which use recreational activities as the principal program elements. Boys and girls are attracted to these organizations because they satisfy a need to belong, have fun, be involved in interesting projects, and win approval from their parents. Parents, policemen, and teachers are interested because they see in these programs a medium for developing desirable character traits and for involving youth in wholesome activities.

The Young Men's Christian Association, the Young Women's Christian Association, the Catholic Youth Organization, and the Young Men's and Young Women's Hebrew Associations are religiously oriented organizations which attempt to minister to the needs of the community. While the programs are many and varied, we note that swimming, volleyball, basketball, handball, crafts, camping, picnicking, dancing, and dramatics are on their menu of activities. Leisure needs are being served even as broader and deeper goals are emphasized.

Neighborhood centers, community centers, and association houses have similarly tried to satisfy the needs of the inner city and other localities where opportunities for people to meet and facilities for recreation were lacking. Some of these have been sponsored by churches; some are privately incorporated and operated; some are supported by government at the federal, state, and local levels.

Recently the Department of Health, Education, and Welfare, the President's Council on Physical Fitness and Sports, and the National Collegiate Athletic Association have, in cooperation with a large number of colleges and universities, sponsored and conducted summer sports programs for inner-city youth. These organizations provided facilities and made possible recreational programs far more extensive and inclusive than was possible before. In most instances, professionally prepared leadership has been available and the objectives of the program have been attained.

Voluntary and community agencies have been relatively free to experiment, have been able to focus on the needs of the community, have had considerable freedom and autonomy, and have rendered great service to the communities in which they are located. Together with the churches and schools, they have been able to meet the needs of a large number of people who otherwise might have spent their leisure time in socially undesirable activities.

14.6 THE GREAT OUTDOORS

Outdoor education, outdoor recreation, the Outward Bound movement, camping, backpacking, mountain climbing, canoeing, fishing, cross-country skiing, and nature study provide infinite variety and enjoyment. The forests and meadows, the lakes and streams, the mountains and prairies, and the rocks and deserts provide a limitless number of experiences, some essentially educational, some mostly recreational, and many which combine both characteristics.

Increasing attention is now being directed to the preservation and enhancement of our natural resources by curbing their depletion and abuse. Many depleted land areas are now being reclaimed, "green belts" are being developed around

"... cross-country skiing ..." (Courtesy of the *Journal of Health, Physical Education, and Recreation.*)

cities, and the reforestation of former timberlands is in process. Individual communities, states, and the federal government are all engaged in locating tracts of land which are suitable for parks and other recreational areas so that they may purchase them before real estate agencies can buy and develop them as residential and industrial areas.

Barry Commoner in *The Closing Circle* points out that we have relied too completely on our technological "skill" to meet the environmental crisis with which we are now faced and suggests that we must look further to the social and political aspects of our society to solve the problems of pollution and overpopulation. He states:

> Since the environmental crisis is the result of the social mismanagement of the world's resources, then it can be resolved and man can survive in a humane condition when the social organization of man is brought into harmony with the ecosphere. [8, p. 299]

Commoner speaks of the early forms of life and how the problems of ecology and overpopulation were solved. In this context he says,

◄ Bryce Canyon National Park in Utah gives visitors a chance to ride horseback in a relaxed atmosphere and amid spectacular surroundings. Wholesome recreation of this type restores man's perspective and gives him greater enjoyment and appreciation of life. (Courtesy of the U.S. Department of the Interior.)

What saved life from extinction was the invention, in the course of evolution, of a new life-form which reconverted the waste of primitive organisms into fresh, organic matter. The first photosynthetic organisms transformed the rapacious, linear course of life into the earth's first great ecological cycle. By closing the circle, they achieved what no living organism, alone, can accomplish—survival. [8, p. 299]

Surely Commoner's ideas have significance for recreation leaders. To "restore to nature the wealth that we borrow from it" [8, p. 300] is one of the larger goals of conservationists and recreationists. It is an important aspect of the total effort to solve the problems of ecology.

Conservation and recreation are closely linked in many ways. The federal government has spent large amounts of money to save and improve water and land resources and in so doing has provided new outdoor recreational facilities. The Bureau of Outdoor Recreation has attempted to control the use of recreational areas by classifying them as "high-density recreation areas," "unique natural areas," "natural environment areas," "general outdoor recreation areas," "primitive areas," and "historic and cultural sites." [24, p. 17]

The New Jersey Skyland program provides for the multiple use of some of its water resources by managing the facilities so as to permit hunting, fishing, sailing, camping, and hiking in the reservoir areas. The Sierra Club has fought to protect natural resources from commercial exploitation. It has also published many beautiful books on nature and conservation and promoted skiing and hiking in these wilderness areas. The Appalachian Mountain Club, in addition to promoting backpacking and hiking, is also now promoting mountaineering, skiing, and canoeing.

While much is being done by many people to preserve and protect our nation's land, water, and wildlife resources, the surface of this problem has been only scratched. Open spaces have been overtaken by industries, real estate dealers, and people seeking a place to live. Lakes and rivers have been polluted, rendering them useless for recreational purposes. Various pesticides used in agriculture have permeated our environment. Smog has caused serious health problems in many of our large cities.

To remedy this situation, a multifaceted program is required. Kraus summarizes much of what must be done in the following paragraph:

To increase the political effectiveness of those determined to protect and restore the natural environment, Henry Diamond, counsel for the Citizens' Advisory Committee on Recreation and Natural Beauty, has urged that five groups be assembled into a power base for political action for recreation and natural beauty. This coalition would consist of (1) the park and recreation movement, (2) the conservation movement, a diverse and far-ranging group with varied interests and causes, (3) the new urbanologists-planners, urban renewal experts, sociologists, architects, and all those who seek to rebuild the cities and make them liveable, (4) civic organizations which have an interest in the environment as an important social concern, and (5) the business community, which is often responsive to causes affecting community welfare. [24, p. 410]

Rogers Morton points out that the quality of leisure time experiences is dependent on our environment. Our parklands and some of our wilderness areas have become overcrowded. He reports on regional outdoor planning forums where it was agreed that among the urgent needs of American society were more public parks and other recreational resources, more programs to preserve our natural treasures, and more federal assistance to prevent the deterioration of existing outdoor areas and facilities. [19, p. 36]

"Charter for Leisure" in the *Journal of Health, Physical Education, and Recreation,* states:

> Every man has a right to recreational facilities open to the public, and to nature reserves by the lakes, seas, wooded areas, in the mountains and to open spaces in general. These areas, their fauna and flora, must be protected and conserved. [7, p. 48]

This really summarizes how leisure and the great outdoors are related. The sounds of lapping waves, the peace and mysteries of the woods, the majesty of the mountains and prairies, and the fascinating growth and development of animals and plants can satisfy needs and soothe ruffled spirits as nothing else can. For health and abundant living, the wonders of nature should be available to all.

14.7 MEANING THROUGH CHALLENGE AND ADVENTURE

Throughout life human beings need, both for their development and for self-realization, tasks which challenge and experiences which thrill them. The discovery of capacities to accomplish and endure, the acceptance of risks inherent in mountain climbing or white-water canoeing, the thrill of accomplishment when such tasks are completed, and the enjoyment that comes from reminiscing about such shared experiences give meaning to life and make leisure activities more worthwhile.

Many winter activities also offer excellent opportunities for adventure and challenge. Weekends at skiing resorts, winter hikes, campfires in the snow, and skating on frozen lakes are exhilarating and stimulating activities. Hockey, figure skating, curling, and recreational skating can fill many leisure hours with healthful and wholesome activity. Snowmobiling and winter orienteering induce people to seek mountaintops and hitherto unexplored areas. Snowshoeing and cross-country skiing can be combined with exploring and camping. All of these are challenging and venturesome activities.

14.8 AVOCATIONS AND HOBBIES

Although satisfied with their jobs as a way of making a living, there are many people who find little opportunity for creative expression, for involvement in the arts, for improving their minds, or for collecting interesting things. Hobbies and avocations can be at least a partial answer to these needs.

George Butler indicated that hobbies take three fundamental forms, "the acquiring of knowledge, the acquiring of things, and the creation of things." He further characterizes a true hobby as "a personal, intimate matter, capable of enjoyment by one's self, to be shared only with a few kindred souls." [6, p. 372]

Examples of such hobbies are photography and stamp collecting. They both can be enjoyed by individuals by themselves. However, the abundance of camera clubs and stamp clubs attests to the desire to share experiences with others whose interests are similar. Such hobbies are educational and can be creative as well as interesting. Exhibits and meetings add to the excitement of producing good pictures or discovering new stamps.

Hobby leagues, hobby shows, and hobby publications are other methods of increasing the pleasure and enjoyment of participation. They also increase the educational features of hobby involvement.

Hobbies are of many kinds and descriptions. Carving, embroidery, leather craft, woodworking, rug making, model building, weaving, and toymaking are examples of creative hobbies. Among artistic hobbies are drawing, painting, sculpturing, ceramics, etching, and block printing. Birdhouse building, flower arranging, gardening, nature study, and insect collecting are other exciting activities. Many people have as their special interest the collecting of such items as autographs, buttons, coins, dolls, glassware, china, medals, seashells, postcards, and clocks.

Many hobbies can become true avocations. Sports of all kinds, social activities, music, dancing, and intellectual endeavors can all be hobbies. They are separate and distinct from a person's "main business" but often consume large amounts of time, take a good deal of energy, and may even be a partial source of income.

Correctly used, avocations and hobbies can be a release from the monotony of daily living, an outlet for creative expression, and an enjoyable way of spending one's leisure hours. As the number of such hours continues to increase for more and more people, thoughtful planning for that phase of life becomes more significant. Attention must be given in schools and recreation programs to possible hobbies and avocations.

14.9 RECREATION AND EDUCATION

School and community cooperation
Recreational programs thrive on relationships with many groups and agencies, but none is more meaningful than a good, cooperative relationship with education. Many of the same people utilize the services of both education and recreation; recreation and education use similar facilities. Recreation is often educational in nature, and education for leisure is one of the goals of the schools. A large number of activities are common to both educational and recreational programs. School personnel are often employed in summer recreation programs; the converse may also be true.

Schools have operated after-school and vacation-play programs since the beginning of the twentieth century. Playgrounds have been a requirement for public schools for approximately the same length of time. One of the seven Cardinal Principles of Education issued in 1918 was education for "the worthy use of leisure." This principle has been reaffirmed time and again during the ensuing years.

School-sponsored recreation programs are spreading rapidly throughout the United States. The principle of the "lighted schoolhouse" has been generally accepted. In most communities, schools have control over many fine facilities for music, dramatics, art, physical education, and adult education. The wastefulness which would result from the duplication of such structures is generally recognized by community leaders. This plus the suitability of school facilities for almost any kind of leisure activity has brought about wide acceptance of what is often known as "The School Board Plan" for recreation.

Park boards and recreation commissions are now found working cooperatively with schools and colleges in many communities. Regardless of the specific name given to the arrangement, the advantages of such a cooperative recreation plan are obvious. Equipment, personnel, and other resources are used more efficiently and productively and both the young people and the adults benefit. Skills and knowledges are taught in schools, which may then be used to produce worthwhile goods. But more important, they fill the leisure moments with worthwhile activity.

Physical educators as recreation leaders

Many coaches and physical education teachers become recreation leaders and directors during the summer months when most schools are not in session. From one viewpoint this seems natural and good; from another some questions are raised. The field of recreation is broad and the activities many and varied. It is not the nature of a given activity alone which determines whether or not the activity can legitimately be classified as recreation; it is rather the attitude the participant brings to the experience. Nevertheless, sports still constitute a major part of most recreational programs.

From an adminstrative and practical standpoint, the combination of physical education and recreation as a full year's employment appears logical. Teachers and coaches are trained to work with young people and to teach and organize games and athletics. This combination provides a steadier income for those educational employees who might otherwise be able to work only three-fourths of the year.

To some the combination of coaching and recreation seems incongruous. The coach, it is said by some, is a highly competitive individual. It is claimed that such competitiveness is not in agreement with the philosophy of recreation which is supposed to be fun-oriented and relaxing. The physical education teacher, according to some, is often narrow-minded and not interested in important recreational activities such as art, dramatics, music, free play, and nature study.

It is evident that each situation must be carefully examined and recreation employees engaged on their own merit. There are many coaches and physical education teachers who are performing very competently as recreation leaders. It is possible to have a sound philosophy of both coaching and recreation. Some of the best students of human nature are found in the ranks of the physical educators.

The fact remains that there will be, for many years to come, opportunities for coaches and physical education teachers to assume leadership roles in some aspects of recreation. Their professional preparation should provide orientation to the philosophy and conduct of good recreation programs. The impact of this education on those boys and girls participating in the recreational programs is, of course, the significant matter.

14.10 SCHOOLS AND CAMPING

Camping is usually considered a recreational activity and it does serve many people in their leisure time. In recent years camping has also become one of the educational elements in many schools. Day camps, weekend camps, summer camps, and school camps have sprung up and are now thriving enterprises in many parts of the country.

Some colleges conduct camps both as an educational experience for the campers and as an administrative experience for students taking courses in recreation and/or physical education. In the latter case, the students, as part of their professional course in camping administration, plan the program, work out the budget, do the purchasing, conduct the camp, and evaluate the experience. The campers are often first-year students who are required to spend a week or two in a camp as part of their educational experience.

School camps have been established by some communities to give city children an experience in the mountains or the country. Some California cities have camps in the mountains as extensions of their school systems. In a certain grade, such as the sixth, all children camp for two weeks during the regular school year. Their public school teachers accompany them, help with organization and discipline, and try to make the two weeks as educational as possible. The camp staff is responsible for giving the students a good camping experience. They cook their own meals, do their own housekeeping, learn something about nature, and receive instruction in camping knowledge and skills. For many children in the inner city, this may be their only experience outside their customary habitat of brick and concrete.

14.11 GUIDELINES AND PRINCIPLES IN FORMULATING PROGRAMS FOR LEISURE

Recreational activities are so diverse and programs so varied that it is impossible to be specific about all the details. It is better to know some general guidelines and principles and apply these as they seem appropriate for a given situation. The following, drawn from many sources and from personal experience, may prove helpful to those preparing to work as recreation leaders, administer leisure time programs, or instruct in the many educational or recreational activities.

"All people should have . . . hours for rest and repose, fun
and pleasure . . ." (Courtesy of the *Journal of Health,
Physical Education, and Recreation.*)

1. Every child should be provided the opportunity, during his formative years,
to learn some activities which will make his leisure hours during adult life as
enjoyable, meaningful, beneficial, and satisfying as possible.

2. All people should have, in their busy lives, hours for rest and repose, fun and
pleasure, for reflection and contemplation, for *re-creation* and renewal.

3. Every individual should be equipped with skills, knowledges, hobbies, and
other recreational pastimes which are appropriate for small bits of leisure time.

4. People should have abilities, knowledges, and interests with which they can
fill *long periods* of leisure in a satisfying way.

5. One's recreational education should be varied and broad enough so that he
can engage in activity appropriate to sunny weather and rain, to winter and summer, and to youth and old age.

6. Every individual should have the right to decide how he will use his leisure time. Each person should, however, be exposed to enough activities so that he can make a wise choice.

7. The best leisure activities are those that not only provide rest, relaxation, and relief from tension, but also enrich life through personal involvement and fulfillment of self.

8. All people should be provided the opportunity to visit parks, enjoy the lakes and mountains, watch the animals in the zoos, and spend hours in art galleries, museums, and libraries. It is a responsibility of municipal, state, and federal governments to make such things possible.

9. Leaders should be so educated that they can assist those who are unskilled in various recreational activities to help themselves and to organize and conduct their own leisure activities.

10. Recreation must change to meet the demands of the technological and social revolutions, just as all other aspects of society must change.

11. Recreation and education for leisure must be taken seriously by all—by government, educators, city planners, professional people, and laborers. Recreation and play can no longer be dismissed as something frivolous and useless; it is a vital aspect of life in any society.

12. Recreation and the worthwhile use of leisure are dependent in large measure on the use of natural resources. Many of these are being too rapidly depleted. Attention must be given to conservation and the problems of ecology.

Surfer showing proper technique in approaching an oncoming wave.
The rider is shown "breasting" the breaking wave.
(Courtesy of the *Journal of Health, Physical Education, and Recreation.*)

"Summer or winter, water serves recreation." (Courtesy of the *Journal of Health, Physical Education, and Recreation.*)

13. Good leadership is vital to effective recreational programs, just as it is in other endeavors. Attention must be given to the best possible professional preparation in educational institutions.

14. There are individual differences in leisure needs and interests just as in other aspects of life. Some people have very little leisure, others a great deal. What interests one may have little attraction for another. Certain people are talented in one direction and others have little talent in that direction.

15. The inability to use leisure wisely is a contributing factor in the increasing problems of delinquency, crime, violence, alcoholism, and drug abuse. Because leisure hours will be filled with activity of *some* sort, worthwhile and meaningful interests must be found.

16. Compulsiveness and anxiety have been identified as national problems in the United States. Efforts must be made by individuals, educational institutions, communities, and government to develop philosophies of life where buoyancy, faith, cheerfulness, and contentment will replace pessimism, worry, and despair.

17. Materialism is the enemy of the worthy use of leisure time. While everyone should be entitled to a good standard of living, the struggle for more money, property, and material things can undo the very goals of an abundant and satisfying life.

18. Much has been done medically to assist people to live longer. If this is to be a worthwhile advancement, we must also be concerned with the quality of life. The extra years added to the life of the average American should provide additional time for creativity and usefulness if true satisfactions are to be derived from them.

19. In one's early years, there must be time for play. Play for the child is enjoyable, developmental, and educational. Charles Brightbill says the following.

To find, one must seek, search, and explore. The play world is the world of expanding experiences. Exploration is the child's road to new experiences and in uninhibited play, the child can explore to his heart's content. Play develops basic cognitions, releases somatic tensions, and develops habits of experimentation. Curiosity is one of the driving forces behind *all* learning. [4, p. 52]

20. Special effort must be made to educate the handicapped and disabled for leisure. Most of their time is what other people would describe as "enforced leisure." For the impaired, however, this may be their life's work. Leaders who understand the problems and hopes of these people must be located, trained, and employed.

21. Education for leisure is more than merely learning new skills, hobbies, and abilities. It involves the development of a value system, the attainment of a deeper understanding of leisure problems, and formulating a satisfying and helpful philosophy of life.

22. Education for leisure must involve men and women in all their dimensions. Complete organic development, attainment of physical fitness, achievement of intellectual competence, expansion and enhancement of interpersonal relationships, and deeper understandings which come through spiritual experiences are vital components in the preparation for worthwhile leisure hours.

23. Education for leisure and the recreative use of leisure is related to ecology, health education, the arts, the sciences, sociology, political science, psychology, literature, the manual arts, forestry, and almost any school subject that can be mentioned. This has two implications: (a) in the administration of large recreational programs, there should be a wide range of backgrounds among the employees selected, and (b) in the professional preparation of recreation leaders, their education should be broad rather than narrow.

24. Urbanization continues to be one of the important social trends of our time. Those living in the crowded cities and especially in the ghettos have special problems with respect to leisure. Lack of money to travel, inadequate open space, a high rate of unemployment, and too few facilities are among their handicaps. Special programs and efforts are needed to give the residents of these areas the leisure opportunities they should have.

25. Schools of tomorrow will need to concentrate more on preparation for a leisure-centered life rather than a work-centered existence. All indications are that an increasing proportion of most people's lives will be spent in leisure.

26. Family disruption is one of the social problems of our times. Recreational forms which tend to bring the family together rather than divide it should be encouraged.

27. As leisure periods increase in length from minutes to hours, from days to weeks, and from months to years, the importance of long-lasting and continually interesting activities becomes greater. Music, reading, crafts, swimming, golf, and woodworking are examples.

28. People will retain an interest in activities for longer periods of time if they have a share in planning and control. The "handing out" of ready-made programs or the foisting, on participants, of the leader's planned activities is often resented.

29. As Brightbill says, "The essence of the leisure experience is what happens to the individual as a result of it." [4, p. 150]

SELECTED REFERENCES

1. American Association for Health, Physical Education, and Recreation, *Leisure and the Quality of Life,* Washington, D.C., 1972.
2. Bannon, Joseph J., *Problem Solving in Recreation and Parks,* Englewood Cliffs, N.J.: Prentice-Hall, 1972.
3. Bowen, Wilbur P., and Elmer D. Mitchell, *The Practice of Organized Play,* New York: A. S. Barnes and Company, 1929.
4. Brightbill, Charles K., *Educating for Leisure Centered Living,* Harrisburg, Penn.: The Stackpole Company, 1966.
5. Bucher, Charles A., *Foundations of Physical Education,* 4th edition, St. Louis: The C. V. Mosby Company, 1964.
6. Butler, George D., *Community Recreation,* New York: McGraw-Hill, 1940.
7. "Charter for leisure," *Journal of Health, Physical Education, and Recreation,* Vol. 43, No. 3, March 1972.
8. Commoner, Barry, *The Closing Circle,* New York: Alfred A. Knopf, 1971.
9. Corbin, H. Dan, *Recreation Leadership,* New York: Prentice-Hall, 1953.
10. *County Parks and Recreation . . . A Basis for Action,* Washington, D.C.: National Association of Counties, and New York: National Recreation Association, 1964.
11. Curtis, Joseph E., "Heritage parks," *Journal of Health, Physical Education and Recreation,* Vol. 44, No. 9, November–December 1973.
12. Dunn, Diana R., "Dynamic programming: enabling recreational independence," *Journal of Health, Physical Education, and Recreation,* Vol. 44, No. 9, November–December 1973.
13. Daughtrey, Greyson, and John B. Woods, *Physical Education Programs: Organization and Administration,* Philadelphia: W. B. Saunders Company, 1971.
14. Fisher, Millard J., "Re-Creation or Wreck-Creation," *The Physical Educator,* Vol. 30, No. 3, October 1973.
15. Ford, H. T., Jr., "The recreation director syndrome," *Journal of Health, Physical Education, and Recreation,* Vol. 44, No. 5, May 1973.
16. Fox, Eugene R., and Barry L. Sysler, *Life-Time Sports for the College Student,* Dubuque, Iowa: Kendall/Hunt Publishing Company, 1972.
17. Gabrielson, M. Alexander, and Caswell M. Miles, *Sport and Recreation Facilities,* Englewood Cliffs, N.J.: Prentice-Hall, 1958.
18. Guggenheimer, Elinor C., *Planning for Parks and Recreation Needs in Urban Areas,* New York: Twayne Publishers, 1969.
19. Hinderman, Lin McGovern, et al., "Winterizing physical education," *Journal of Health, Physical Education, and Recreation,* November–December, 1971.
20. Hjelte, George, *The Administration of Public Recreation,* New York: A. S. Barnes and Company, 1949.
21. Hodgson, J. D., "Leisure and the American worker," *Journal of Health, Physical Education, and Recreation,* Vol. 43, No. 3, March 1972.
22. Jensen, Clayne R., *Outdoor Recreation in America,* Minneapolis, Minn.: Burgess Publishing Company, 1973.

23. Johns, Edward B., Wilfred C. Sutton, and Lloyd E. Webster, *Health for Effective Living,* New York: McGraw-Hill, 1962.

24. Kraus, Richard, *Recreation and Leisure in Modern Society,* Educational Division, Meredith Corporation, New York: Appleton-Century-Crofts, 1971. By permission.

25. _____, *Recreation Today,* New York: Appleton-Century-Crofts, 1966.

26. "Leisure today," *Journal of Health, Physical Education, and Recreation,* Vol. 44, No. 6, June 1973.

27. "Leisure today: creative programming," *Journal of Health, Physical Education, and Recreation,* Vol. 44, No. 9, November–December 1973.

28. Morton, Rogers C. B., "Leisure and the environment," *Journal of Health, Physical Education, and Recreation,* Vol. 44, No. 1, January 1973.

29. Nash, Bernard E., "Retirement as leisure," *Journal of Health, Physical Education and Recreation,* Vol. 43, No. 3, March 1972.

30. "National adult physical fitness survey," *Newsletter,* Washington, D.C.: President's Council on Physical Fitness and Sports, May 1973.

31. Rathbone, Josephine L., *Teach Yourself to Relax,* Englewood Cliffs, N.J.: Prentice-Hall, 1957.

32. Runkel, Kenneth, "Big Surf: making waves in Arizona's ocean," *Journal of Health, Physical Education, and Recreation,* Vol. 44, No. 9, November–December 1973.

33. Shivers, Jay S., *Principles and Practices of Recreational Service,* New York: The Macmillan Company, 1967.

34. Sillitoe, K. K., *Planning for Leisure,* London: Her Majesty's Stationery Office, 1969.

35. Smith, Michael, Stanley Parker, and Cyril S. Smith, *Leisure and Society in Britain,* London: Allen Lane, 1973.

36. "Sport and leisure," Second Report from the Select Committee of the House of Lords, London: Her Majesty's Stationery Office, 1973.

37. Staffo, Donald F., "A community recreation program," *Journal of Health, Physical Education and Recreation,* Vol. 44, No. 5, May 1973.

38. VanderZwaag, Harold J., *Toward a Philosophy of Sport,* Reading, Mass.: Addison-Wesley Publishing Company, 1972.

39. White, Paul Dudley, and Curtis Mitchell (eds.), *Fitness for the Whole Family,* Garden City, N.Y.: Doubleday and Company, 1964.

40. Wilkins, Michael H., and Richard L. Ragatz, "Cultural changes and leisure time," *Journal of Health, Physical Education, and Recreation,* Vol. 43, No. 3, March 1972.

41. Young, Michael, and Peter Wilmot, *The Symmetrical Family,* London: Routledge and Kegan Paul, 1973.

42. *Young School Leavers,* School Council Enquiry, No. 1, London: Her Majesty's Stationery Office, 1968.

Physical Educators and the Community

Chapter 15

15.1 COMMUNITY

The term *community* may be simply defined as a *society of people held together by a common bond.* A more comprehensive definition is the one stated by Francis Merrill as a permanent group of persons, occupying a common area, interacting in both institutional and noninstitutional roles, and having a sense of identification with the entity (the community) that arises from this interaction." [37, pp. 310–311] Most generally, a community refers to a small town, neighborhood, suburb, city, or even a metropolitan complex. Occasionally one hears mention of "a college community" or "the world community."

Sociologists, however, tend to agree that a community is more than an aggregate of dwellings, geographical area, or given group of people living in a given space. The element of interaction is necessary, regular communication is essential, and a local culture is characteristic. There should be an element of uniqueness in the cultural milieu and the institutions of the community should be varied and complete enough to provide most of the services necessary for independent and self-contained existence. Common interests, loyalties, and cultural elements characterize a community.

15.2 HEALTH, PHYSICAL EDUCATION, AND RECREATION PERSONNEL AND COMMUNITY INVOLVEMENT

Teachers, coaches, and recreation leaders not only have many opportunities for involvement in community activities, but oftentimes have difficulty avoiding too much involvement. As soon as they settle in a community, members of these professions are generally invited to be leaders of Boy Scout or Girl Scout troops, Sunday school teachers, or members of civic and fraternal groups. Not infrequently, coaches become active members of Kiwanis, Rotary, Civitan, Business and Professional Women's, and Elks Clubs; quite often they are asked to serve on community committees of many kinds; occasionally they are elected to important positions in chambers of commerce and in city government. They are welcomed as participants in community action groups espousing worthwhile causes.

Educational philosophy is changing with regard to community leadership roles for teachers. Whereas a generation ago teachers were discouraged from involvement in politics or activism of any kind, such roles are now generally accepted. Regulations and personnel policies commonly protect the teacher from loss of position or salary because of participation in these kinds of activities.

Community careers

While the community activities described above are important, they are generally only incidental to a physical education teacher's primary responsibility and are on an individual and often avocational basis. There is, however, another aspect to the role physical educators can play in community development. They may elect to pursue full-time positions such as those offered by the Peace Corps, Vista, Boys' Clubs, Girls' Clubs, YMCA's, YWCA's, YMHA's, or similar agencies seeking to improve the quality of life in the inner city, suburbs, states, developing countries, or other communities needing help. Most physical educators are interested in working with people, and the medium with which they work lends itself to the establishment of rapport, removal of barriers, ease of communication, and interpersonal involvement.

Sports and fitness
Sports and similar activities are certainly not the panacea for all the ills of the inner city or other community problems. Persons specializing in physical education must be careful not to claim too much credit. On the other hand, those who are trained to educate through the medium of physical education activities should be aware of the benefits that may accrue and the accomplishments of those who have entered upon careers in this field. Fitness programs, sports, and other community activities *do* have much to offer. Experiences shared and the interaction stimulated by such involvements create friendships and enhance understanding. Common loyalties, interests, enthusiams, and experiences are factors which make for community integrity.

Sport is also a great leveler. In sport the individual is usually judged on the basis of performance and behavior and not on the basis of race, creed, economic status, or other circumstances beyond his control.

In this era of automation, mechanization, and increased tension, we find more and more significance attached to the concept of physical fitness. Individuals have organized in groups to exercise together, fitness clubs have formed, and the concept of fitness has been recognized as important by both professionals and laymen. The physical education teacher is called upon to lead, advise, and help organize. The importance of his role in the "new world" is increasing (see also Chapter 13).

Health education
Health educators can choose a number of roles in community health development. There are far too few qualified persons in this area. Whether they participate as employees of government health agencies, as liaison persons between schools and public health agencies, as teachers of first aid, or as workers to improve health for the aging, they are in great demand. Sex education and family living are being studied by an ever increasing number of people. The problems of drug abuse and alcoholism require able and committed workers. Communities are concerned with water purification and fluoridation, immunization, sanitation, and health education to a degree never before anticipated.

The American Heart Association, the Kellogg Foundation, the American Cancer Society, and the Commonwealth Fund are only a few of the agencies which are active in many communities and which are constantly seeking qualified professional and volunteer workers. There is a constant need for individuals in the community to work with hospital committees, mental health groups, epilepsy foundations, and the many voluntary health organizations which are seeking leaders with knowledge and experience as well as general workers. These organizations usually arise in response to a community need. Leaders with vision gather friends about them, tackle a problem, raise money, and eventually start another organization to aid the unfortunate. And in our society with its modern health programs designed to prevent disease, prolong life, and improve health, there is room for everyone.

Recreation and community development

The word "community" has been attached to "recreation" to such an extent that it is difficult to even think of recreation as anything but a community activity. There are, of course, activities directed by the school, social agencies, and other specific organizations. Recreation, however, does not function independently but is intimately related to a large number of community problems and projects. Recreation makes a contribution to the elimination of delinquency, to mental and physical health, both to the prevention of disease and to therapy, to the development of character, and to the full and abundant life.

"Physical educators play a vital role in camping, aquatics, and other community activities." (Courtesy of the *Journal of Health, Physical Education, and Recreation.*)

The role of recreation personnel in the education and therapy of the physically handicapped and in the alleviation of hypertension and minor emotional disturbances is becoming increasingly significant. Mental patients, the emotionally disturbed, epileptics, mentally retarded students, those afflicted with Parkinson's disease, and others are benefitting by soundly administered therapeutic exercise and carefully designed recreational programs. Individuals who have entered the field of physical education have often assisted with such rehabilitation activities.

Recreation personnel are, by the very nature of their work, generally involved in community action. Health education specialists are commonly employed by agencies which have the welfare of the community as their primary goal. Therefore, personnel preparing to work in the areas of health, physical education, and recreation must broaden and deepen their vision of their profession. The "new world" will need closer cooperation between the community and the schools than ever before. There will also be a need for more full-time leaders in the fields of health, physical education, and recreation.

15.3 THE COMMUNITY/SCHOOL CONCEPT
The community needs the help of the schools and the schools cannot perform their mission without the cooperation and support of the community. Today's schools recognize that the world outside the walls of the schools is a meaningful and real world and that the child must learn to deal with it. The school within the walls is becoming more and more a "microcosm of the community." An increasing number of hours are also spent by students outside the confines of the school.

The "community school" uses the community as a laboratory for learning, emphasizes cooperative and coordinated action by school and community, believes in democratic and participatory methods, supports the concepts of self-help and self-direction, and uses community resources to provide educational experiences.

The community school assists the community to solve its social problems, whether they be lack of funds, drug abuse, family disruption, unemployment, or juvenile delinquency. Teachers, coaches, law enforcement officers, health officials, recreation directors, ministers, and parents meet and work together in common cause.

In a community school, facilities are shared. The school allows community agencies to use many of its facilities during evenings, weekends, and vacation periods. Likewise, the facilities of the city or town are used by the schools for athletic programs, physical education classes, and practical laboratory experiences.

Physical education teachers and coaches cannot serve all people in the same manner. If they are employed by the school, they must first of all teach and coach. While they are doing this, however, they can help students and athletes understand, appreciate, and recognize their responsibility to the community in which they live. They can also help the community understand and appreciate what goes on in the schools. Involvement in civic organizations, participation in parent-teacher meetings, membership in churches, and leadership in youth organizations will provide opportunities for a free exchange of ideas and thoughts about educational philosophies and practices. Teachers are in a position to encourage colleagues and students to be conscious of and concerned about the problems of the community. In a community school there are reciprocal relationships and constant interaction between what transpires inside and what happens outside the walls of the school.

Adult education is an important aspect of the community school. Education is a lifelong process, and in today's society constant reeducation is necessary in order to cope with changing needs and the mobility of people. Even the elderly need education if their lives are to continue to be meaningful and productive.

15.4 DEVELOPING LEADERSHIP

Of critical importance, then, is the matter of leadership. In terms of the development of the individual, it is the teacher, the coach, the playground leader, the encourager—the person who has daily and intimate contact with the people being led—who will determine whether the experiences provided will be beneficial or not to the persons involved. The kind and quality of leadership not only determines whether there will be positive or negative development on the part of individuals, but also is a vital factor in determining whether or not a program will benefit society. The leader sets the pace, indicates the tone, reflects the quality, and influences the outcome of any project.

Community action and cooperation imply voluntary democratic action for common ends. This should include self-directed activity and bringing affected groups into the planning and organization. It should involve action by the people themselves. Such action does, however, necessitate qualified and experienced leadership. Whether it be a simple thing like laying out some softball fields, a more involved operation such as planning a municipal recreation program, or attacking an involved community health problem, very little can be gained by the mere pooling of ignorance. Leaders who know what resources are available and how to tap them are necessary.

Knowledge and experience are important for the individual who is to be a leader in community development. Even more critical, however, may be the attitude and value system which serves as a guide to his/her behavior and interpersonal relations.

During the 1960's, the author was privileged to serve as the director of a Peace Corps Training Program traveling In Ecuador, Venezuela, and Colombia and observing the work of volunteers. Some of the volunteers had been trained to teach English, others recreation, others physical education, and still others construction work of various kinds. In their training program, all were exposed to the basic principles and methods of community development. Almost without fail they attested to the value of this training. Most noticeable, however, was the degree to which their success depended upon their ability to work with people. It was not always the person with the highest technical skill or knowledge who achieved the most; often that person who could communicate the most intimately and deeply and whose relationships were of mutual warmth and trust was the one who made the greatest contribution to the development of the community. Once the necessary rapport was established and an atmosphere of confidence pervaded, the processes of administration and development ran smoothly.

In his Inaugural Address, President Lyndon Johnson spoke the following words significant to those in leadership roles:

> I do not believe that the Great Society is the ordered, changeless and sterile battalion of the ants. It is the excitement of becoming, always becoming, trying, probing, falling, and trying again—but always trying and always gaining.*

Dr. Robert E. Fitch of the Pacific School of Religion in Berkeley was once asked to indicate whether there had been great societies in the past. He singled out the American Colonies at the time of the Revolution as one example, and when questioned further as to his reasons he said:

> The key word is creativity. A society is great when it is creating something significant. The American Colonies at the time of the Revolution were not marked by a high standard of living or a well-distributed level of culture and civilization. But the people were creating a political democracy of the first order. They had faith in the essential validity of what they were doing.

"Was there a driving force to spur them on?" was the next question. Dr. Fitch replied:

> There was, indeed. To achieve a great society you must have three things: Freedom. An air of adventure. And the confidence that comes from faith. By "faith" I mean a great vision of the realities of life and of the significance of what one is doing.†

Leaders, therefore, must have and induce in others creativity to initiate new programs and new ways of doing things; freedom to believe in new ideas and to try what has never before been attempted; a spirit of adventure which is not satisfied with the staid and trite but which serves as a stimulus to progress; and faith not only in the value of what is being attempted but also in the possibility of achieving it.

We are all members of some community. Often, however, the boundaries of that community are very circumscribed. We need to broaden our horizons, extend our vision, enlarge our community. For the world is shrinking and our community may soon be the universe itself.

Alexis de Toqueville, in writing of his visit to America a century and a half ago, said the following.

---

*Lyndon Baines Johnson, Inaugural Address, January 20, 1965, *Reader's Digest,* June 1965, pp. 62–66.

†"America's potential for greatness," an interview with Dr. Robert E. Fitch, *U.S. News and World Report,* March 8, 1965.

These Americans are the most peculiar people in the world. You'll not believe it when I tell you how they behave. In a local community in their country a citizen may conceive of some need which is not being met. What does he do? He goes across the street and discusses it with his neighbor. Then what happens? A committee comes into existence and then the committee begins functioning on behalf of that need, and you won't believe this but it's true. All of this is done without reference to any bureaucrat. All of this is done by the private citizens on their own initiative.*

Can this still be done? Are there tasks which can still be accomplished in this way? Should educators of all descriptions join such groups and lead efforts to rehabilitate the handicapped, encourage physical fitness activities, help prevent juvenile delinquency, and assist with wholesome recreation programs? The answer to all of these questions must be an emphatic "yes." If, however, such activity is to be a reality, and if our college graduates are to be prepared for community leadership, there must be in their educational environment teachers who believe in helping people, opportunities for student involvement, and provision for learning the right ways and means of achieving the goals.

Laboratory experiences are often part of professional preparation programs. In recent years the emphasis on more meaningful experiences in the inner city has increased greatly. It is often in the ghetto and inner-city areas that opportunities for significant community work are most prevalent and necessary. Conferences have been held and programs conducted where the emphasis has been on assisting this segment of society. Physical educators are realizing more and more fully that educators in the inner city are confronted with problems different from those found elsewhere. Educational institutions are now giving more encouragement to students interested in working in the inner city and are providing more laboratory experiences in those settings. Because it has been observed that those who grow up and are educated in the inner city are usually the most successful in the work there, greater effort is now being expended by professional preparation institutions to recruit students from these communities.

15.5 COMMUNITY DEVELOPMENT AS PROCESS
The right kind of community development involves cooperation, local initiative, and self-help. Professionals, paraprofessionals, and workers with practical abilities are needed in community action programs. While the professionals in community development ideally will have special education in the skills and methodology needed, many of the other workers will be drawn from the fields of education, social work, engineering, industrial arts, religion, and research.

The basic criterion by which success of community development projects should be judged is what happens to the people in the community. While better health practices, new buildings, and community newspapers may be among the

---

*Alexis de Tocqueville, *Democracy in America,* (translated by Henry Reeve), New York: The Colonial Press, 1900. By permission.

outcomes, they are of little value if no changes develop among the people themselves. This point is more aptly and poignantly stated in the following words of Fred Wale:

> Community development is an educational process. It is this, first, last and all the time. All else is secondary to it and must take its place as a reflection, not as the end result. Community development is not better roads, better beehives, pure water nor sanitary privies. It is something of the spirit not something material. It must reach into the deep cultural patterns of people, examining them and testing them as principles of faith. It is not a temporary physical construction. It is a building within the hearts and minds of men, not a recreation center in the middle of a playfield. It is these things because without them it relatively matters little whether the road is paved or not, whether economically you and your community are materially blessed. It is these things because with them all physical solutions follow in their proper order. [6, p. 243]

Community development, then, is a dynamic process in which its people are constantly interacting. It is a social process involving changes in the attitudes and behavior of people. It is a growth process affecting both the people themselves and the institutions in which and through which they operate. It is a constructive process whereby institutions, economic structures, physical facilities, and technological developments are constantly being improved. Biddle and Biddle define community development as "a social process by which human beings can become more competent to live with and gain some control over local aspects of a frustrating and changing world." [6, p. 78]

In their outline of the basic process of community development, Biddle and Biddle include the following:

1. *The exploratory phase.* This includes examining the history and culture of the community, securing an invitation from the community to probe a problem, arranging for an effective introduction, and establishing channels of communication and rapport through informal conversation.

2. *The organizational phase.* The organizational phase consists of formulating the problem, enlisting interested workers, focussing on first steps, adopting a structure, and drafting a plan of action. Goals and plans must be agreed upon and a statement of purpose adopted. First steps must be taken, training through discussion implemented, and record-keeping provided. Morale and a sense of loyalty must be developed.

3. *The discussional phase.* While there has already been some discussion, the discussional phase is necessary because much more is yet to be learned. Often the discussional phase will also increase the motivation and enthusiasm for the project.

In the discussional phase the problem must be more clearly defined, the scope and limitations established, and alternatives developed. All reasonable possibilities must be examined and one or more key decisions must be made.

Basic planning must be done and thorough preparations for the action phase completed.

4. *The action phase.* Activity follows planning, discussion, and decision. People are involved in the tasks which they helped to plan. They work together, talk together, evaluate in their own way, and begin planning the next steps together.

When launching a new community development, it is good practice to start with fairly simple projects which do not take long to complete. A report and an evaluation should summarize the program.

5. *The "new projects" phase.* As members of a group work on a project, they tend to think and talk about other projects. As self-confidence and skill in community development increase, interest in projects of greater complexity grows and wider community contacts occur.

The group that first begins the project, sees it through to completion, and makes it function, is referred to by many sociologists as the *nucleus.* It becomes a *primary group* when its members, through the process of working and talking together, become personally intimate and mutually supportive.

The nucleus may become aware of some conflict within the *power structure* or among those who, because of personal and selfish interests, tend to oppose the action of the community development group. In order to complete a project, it sometimes becomes necessary to exert some pressure on the bureaucrats or resisting officials. Such "pressure action" should be employed only after every effort at cooperation has been made and when the nucleus is convinced of the positive merit of the project. Pressure action may consist of newspaper editorials, political action, or peaceful demonstrations. Cooperative action by several *nuclei* engaged in their own tasks, but each with mutual interests, may be employed for greater strength and influence.

The new projects phase may develop into a more complex and far-reaching offshoot of a given task or it may turn in a different direction. The "community developer" or "encourager" may continue with the original nucleus, choose another one, or withdraw if he sees adequate leadership within the group emerging. [6, pp. 97–101]

To be truly meaningful, projects must arise out of the needs and desires of people and not from the interests of a community developer or encourager. It becomes obvious, then, that the community developer must know the people and their needs and must understand how to guide them in the desired direction.

15.6 PROGRAMS IN COMMUNITY DEVELOPMENT

Programs of community development take many forms. Public schools, colleges, and universities as institutions and faculty members and students as individuals become involved in many ways with the community. Likewise, departments of physical education, recreation, and health education conduct projects in cooperation with various segments of the community. The following are a few examples.

1. There are many recreational programs operated by joint recreation commissions or committees. Both school and municipal facilities are shared and personnel to conduct and supervise programs are furnished in part by the community and in part by the educational institutions. In such instances the respective roles of the schools and the municipal recreational agencies are carefully delineated in contractual agreements.

2. The "community school concept" has been increasingly accepted as sound and workable. A number of communities have adopted it either in its entirety or in a modified version. One of the best known and most successful examples is the Mott Program of the Flint Board of Education. Partially funded by the Mott Foundation and additionally supported by federal aid, community schools were established in more than fifteen communities in the state of Michigan. The schools have become the center of life and action for people of all ages and socioeconomic classes, and the distinct line between school and community has ceased to exist. Among other things, school physical education and health and recreational facilities are available to the entire community, and people of all ages have benefited from the programs conducted.

3. Many teacher preparation institutions have taken to heart the recommendations of the various conferences on physical education for the inner city. They are recruiting and admitting more students who have grown up in that environment; they are providing opportunities for physical education majors, even in the first two years, to observe and work with teachers in the inner-city schools; they have encouraged juniors and seniors to do their student teaching in the inner city; and more well-prepared graduates have been motivated to teach physical education and work in those communities in which the programs had previously been woefully undermanned.

4. In 1962, the Second National Conference on School Recreation was held in Washington, D.C. A major theme of this conference, chaired by Catherine Allen, was "re-engagement of school and community." Major topics included "community relations" and "municipal-school recreation." The "Pasadena, California, School and City Coordinated Recreation Plan" appears in the appendix to the report of this conference. One paragraph reads:

> Pasadena's coordinated plan makes it possible to easily schedule use of all school facilities and gear the leisure-time program to the school curriculum as well as to utilize city parks, the Civic Auditorium, and other city facilities. The director is also considered a city department head and meets regularly with the city manager in this capacity.*

5. Physical fitness is one area in which men and women trained in physical education can be particularly helpful. In 1962, the President's Council on Youth

---

* *Twentieth Century Recreation—Re-engagement of School and Community,* Report of the Second National Conference on School Recreation, Washington, D.C.: American Association for Health, Physical Education, and Recreation, November 1962, p. 62.

Fitness published a document entitled, *Physical Fitness Elements in Recreation, Suggestions for Community Programs.* A plan for organizing a community physical fitness program is described and the agencies and organizations which might be called upon to participate are indicated (see Figure 15.1).

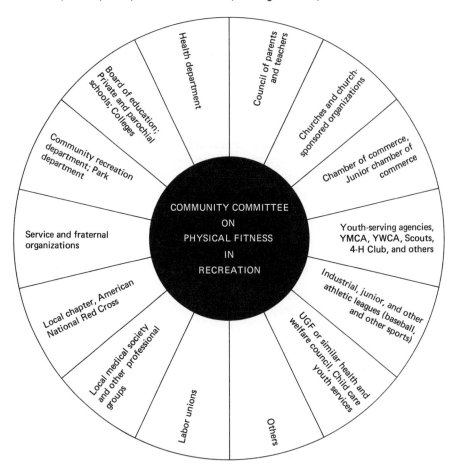

Figure 15.1 Community physical fitness organizational plan. [39, p. 4]

Other fitness activities suggested were boating, canoeing, cycling, dancing, hiking, camping, hunting, mountain climbing, roller skating, winter sports, and fishing. The emphasis throughout the plan was on school-community cooperation. Public buildings, community and school personnel, and any other governmental and community resources that might be made available should be cooperatively utilized. As many people as possible should be involved. [39, pp. 15–25]

6. Athletic programs and "walk-in" recreation for members of the entire community are a reality at Brookdale Community College, Lincroft, New Jersey. William Johnson and Richard Kleva hail this program as a progressive step and describe it with considerable enthusiasm. Any post-high school community resident is permitted to compete in the athletic program and the physical education facilities are, insofar as possible, open to community use. The fitness laboratory is likewise available to all on a drop-in basis. The philosophy behind these programs is that a community college must be dedicated to its community and regard the entire area it serves as its campus. As it accepts the responsibility for bringing post-high school educational opportunities to all who seek them, physical education must be included. [31, pp. 40–41]

7. Agencies such as the YMCA, YWCA, YMHA, Boys' Club, Girls' Club, etc. serve the community and bring together people from various parts of the city, from many different social groups, and from all walks of life. An important aspect of their work is their involvement in physical education and health and recreation programs. A review of YMCA literature reveals a long list of innovative physical education and recreation projects, all of them involving individuals from many different segments of the community. The following list illustrates the rich offerings of a good community agency:

   a) Gym Jams (Kinder Gym), for preschoolers, Berwyn, Pennsylvania
   b) Junior Volunteers in Motion (sports and other activities), brings together civilian and military communities, Dallas, Texas
   c) Iceless Hockey League for Girls, Northbrook, Illinois
   d) Water Ballet, Danvers, Massachusetts
   e) Youth Basketball League, Pasadena, California
   f) Winter Swim League, Greensboro, North Carolina
   g) Novice Swimming Championships, Evanston, Illinois

Other activities mentioned were wilderness activities, Olympic development programs, women's aerobics, Jack n' Jill gymnastics, special Olympics, YMCA aerobics, jiu jitsu–judo–karate–self-defense, and exercise testing.

Community centers, neighborhood centers, church organizations, and many other voluntary recreational and social agencies also conduct programs which include health, recreation, and physical education activities. Those who choose careers in these areas may find themselves in institutions and agencies other than schools, colleges, and universities. As we look to the future, employment in such community agencies will in all likelihood become increasingly significant.

8. Some of the best examples of community development through sports can be found in the annals of the Peace Corps as it operated in the 1960's. Sargent Shriver dramatically tells about the success of Will Prior who helped build a recreation camp out of the wilderness in Venezuela, the coaching award Joe Mullins received from the people of Ifsahan, Iran, and the young volunteer who went to Phitsanulok, Thailand and, by spearheading a fund drive for a physical education foundation, won the praise of the provincial governor who said, "The achievement

"The community can watch bobsled racing

... and participate in general self-defense."

"Physical education can be brought to the community." (Courtesy of the *Journal of Health, Physical Education, and Recreation.*)

HAZLETON AREA SCHOOL DISTRICT
ADAPTED PHYSICAL EDUCATION

has been greatly admired by me . . . for it is helpful in fostering good relations between the Thai and American people, as well as in improving physical education." [45]

Shriver continues by mentioning the accomplishments of the Peace Corps volunteers which resulted in building national pride, fostering international understanding, removing barriers to communication, and creating that inner strength and confidence so necessary to the maintenance of freedom. And, continues Shriver:

> Perhaps most important of all, organized athletics can help to build a sense of group effort and individual self-sacrifice. . . . For just as sport offers opportunities for individual self-expression, it teaches that the individual must often submerge his own desires and ambitions in the aspirations of the group. [45]

15.7 PRINCIPLES AND GUIDELINES
IN DEVELOPING COMMUNITY PROGRAMS

It is obvious that health, physical education, and recreation personnel should know something about the organization of the community, its cultural background, and its social problems. It also seems clear that those in these professions will be called upon repeatedly to serve as consultants and leaders in community projects. A number will also become involved in full-time community development. The following principles and guidelines appear valid and pertinent:

1. Educational institutions which offer professional preparation programs for health, physical education, and recreation personnel should provide instruction in the processes and principles of community development. This should include theoretical discussions, assignments in class, and laboratory experiences in the various types of communities.

2. Student-teaching experiences should be as realistic as possible and should require community involvement during the period of the teaching assignment.

3. There should be some cooperative educational programs planned jointly by the school faculty members and the community residents.

4. Meaningful participation of parents and community representatives in the operation of the schools is becoming increasingly common. This being the case, there must be provision for the education of the citizens for this task.

5. The community school plan should be seriously considered for adoption in the public schools of the United States. The advantages far outweigh the disadvantages.

6. Community authority and autonomy in the management of the schools should be supported through regulations and policies. The financial structure and budgetary organization should be appropriate to, and supportive of, this plan.

7. There should be student representatives on local school boards. They should be elected by the students and have the same powers as the other members of the board.

8. The community school should serve as a center for recreational, cultural, social, and educational activities. It should serve the young, the middle-aged, and the elderly. It should provide course offerings for children, parents, and grandparents.

9. The number of teachers trained for work in the inner-city, suburban, and rural schools of the United States should be proportional to the number of students in the respective communities. This would affect admissions procedures, course offerings, and locations for laboratory experiences.

10. Good interpersonal relationships are often the key to success in community action. Such relationships should be developed from the very beginning of community involvement.

11. A considerable number of health, recreation, and physical education personnel may find themselves working full time in community development. To learn as expeditiously as possible the basic principles of community dynamics, college students should be offered a course in community development. Practical experience would be obtained through field work.

12. In general, people respond to the way they are treated. The attitude a community worker has toward the members of the community has a great deal to do with his success in the developmental programs he espouses.

13. Instilling a positive and desirable self-concept in the members of a community is important. Through judicious praise and criticism and through sound delegation of responsibility, a good leader can develop this quality.

14. The teacher, consultant, or encourager must be constantly mindful that the objective is self-help and not control. Helping others help themselves is the aim.

15. Every individual has vast and untapped personal resources. Helping people discover these is one of the goals of the encourager. Helping people become what they are capable of becoming is the goal for which all should strive.

16. People will be motivated by altruistic and unselfish motives as well as by extrinsic rewards. Providing the proper environment and guidance to such high-level motivation is the mark of a good leader.

17. Most people will become more responsible when they are given responsibility. This is a developmental process and the responsibilities should be increased gradually.

18. As he sees leaders emerging through group interaction, an encourager should gradually withdraw. Complete self-reliance and self-direction of the group is the ultimate goal.

19. Both listening and talking are important to the community developer. It is as essential to find out what the members of the community are thinking as it is to convey the ideas of the leader.

20. Change should be achieved through a process of learning rather than be imposed through "top-down" administration.

21. The encourager or leader in community development must play a number of roles. Among such roles are those of consultant, advisor, planner, advocate, and prodder. Good judgment as to the most effective role in a given situation is necessary.

22. Lee Cary lists the basic elements of the "localized process of change" as (1) the worker who acts as encourager or change agent, (2) the people of the community, (3) the environment, (4) the resources, (5) the interpretations of reality the community members share with each other, (6) the reciprocal human relationships, and (7) the time dimension involved. Serious consideration of these seven elements should enhance a community leader's understanding and increase his effectiveness. [11, pp. 118–119]

23. Community development is a slow and unspectacular process. It involves changes in people and their assumptions of responsibility. It focuses on the development of individuals. Patience and persistence are requisites to success.

24. Community development should involve many disciplines, many professions, many processes, and many kinds of people. Because the total community is to be served, a variety of skills and knowledges are required.

SELECTED REFERENCES

1. American Association for Health, Physical Education, and Recreation, *Your Community: School Community Fitness Inventory,* Washington, D.C., 1959.
2. Arsenian, Seth (ed.), *The Humanics Philosophy of Springfield College,* Springfield, Mass.: Springfield College, 1969.
3. Bannon, Joseph J., *Problem Solving in Recreation and Parks,* Englewood Cliffs, N.J.: Prentice-Hall, 1972.
4. Batten, T. R., *Communities and Their Development,* London: The Oxford Press, 1965.
5. *Training for Community Development,* London: The Oxford Press, 1962. By permission.
6. Biddle, William W., and Loureide J. Biddle, *The Community Development Process,* New York: Holt, Rinehart, and Winston, 1965.
7. Brightbill, Charles K., *Educating for Leisure Centered Living,* Harrisburg, Penn.: The Stackpole Company, 1966.
8. Bruyn, Severyn T., *Communities in Action,* New Haven, Conn.: College and University Press, 1963.
9. Bucher, Charles, "National adult fitness survey: some implications," *Journal of Health, Physical Education, and Recreation,* Vol. 45, No. 1, January 1974.
10. Butler, George F., *Community Recreation,* New York: McGraw-Hill, 1940.
11. Cary, Lee J. (ed.), *Community Development as a Process,* Columbia, Mo.: University of Missouri Press, 1970.
12. Commoner, Barry, *The Closing Circle,* New York: Alfred A. Knopf, 1971.
13. *Co-op Plan, The,* Northeastern University, Boston, Massachusetts, 1973.
14. Corbin, H. Dan, *Recreation Leadership,* Englewood Cliffs, N.J.: Prentice-Hall, 1953.
15. *County Parks and Recreation ... A Basis for Action,* Washington, D.C.: National Association of Counties, and New York: National Recreation Association, 1964.
16. Dodson, Dan W., "Community relations," *Twentieth Century Recreation,* Report of the Second National Conference on School Recreation, Washington, D.C., November 1962.

17. Eisely, Loren, *The Invisible Pyramid,* New York: Charles Scribner's Sons, 1970.
18. Fairbanks, James N., "Y camping confronts new life styles," *YMCA Today,* Summer 1973.
19. Fantini, Mario, Marilyn Gittell, and Richard Magat, *Community Control and the Urban School,* New York: Praeger Publishers, 1970.
20. Frost, Reuben B., "Physical education for the 70's—the YMCA way," *World Communique,* September–October 1970.
21. _____, "The Role of Health, Physical Education, and Recreation Personnel in Community Development," Paper presented at the Workshop in Community Education and Community Development, Flint, Mich., November 1965.
22. Gabrielsen, M. Alexander, and Caswell M. Miles, *Sports and Recreation Facilities,* Englewood Cliffs, N.J.: Prentice-Hall, 1958.
23. Graham, Grace, *The Public School in the New Society,* New York: Harper and Row, 1969.
24. Guggenheimer, Elinor C., *Planning for Parks and Recreation Needs in Urban Areas,* New York: Twayne Publishers, 1969.
25. Hafen, William J., "Written policies to clarify a dual role," *Journal of Health, Physical Education, and Recreation,* Vol. 44, No. 1, January 1973.
26. Hals, Elaine, "A proposal to require community service," *School Health Review,* Vol. 4, No. 1, January–February 1973.
27. Hinderman, Lin McGovern, Douglas Knox, Thomas I. Meyer, and Jan Henrik Monsen, "Winterizing physical education," *Journal of Health, Physical Education, and Recreation,* November–December 1971.
28. Hjelte, George, *The Administration of Public Recreation,* New York: A. S. Barnes and Company, 1949.
29. Hodgson, J. D., "Leisure and the American worker," *Journal of Health, Physical Education, and Recreation,* March 1972.
30. *Inner City Physical Education,* Proceedings, Professional Education Section, Convention of Eastern District Association for Health, Physical Education, and Recreation, Philadelphia, April 1971.
31. Johnson, William P., and Richard P. Kleva, "The community dimension of college physical education," *Journal of Health, Physical Education, and Recreation,* Vol. 44, No. 4, April 1973.
32. Kemp, Don, "Denver runners keep it on a high level," *YMCA Today,* December 1972.
33. Kerber, August, and Barbara Bommarito, *The Schools and the Urban Crisis,* New York: Holt, Rinehart, and Winston, 1966.
34. Kramer, Ralph M., and Harry Specht (eds.), *Readings in Community Organization Practice,* Englewood Cliffs, N.J.: Prentice-Hall, 1969.
35. Kraus, Richard, *Recreation and Leisure in Modern Society,* Educational Division, Meredith Corporation, New York: Appleton-Century-Crofts, 1971.
36. _____, *Recreation Today,* New York: Appleton-Century-Crofts, 1966.
37. Merrill, Francis E., *Society and Culture,* Englewood Cliffs, N.J.: Prentice-Hall, 1969.
38. Mezirow, Jack D., *Dynamics of Community Development,* New York: The Scarecrow Press, 1963.
39. *Physical Fitness Elements in Recreation, Suggestions for Community Programs,* President's Council on Youth Fitness, 1962.
40. Poole, Roberta, "Using community resources," *Journal of Health, Physical Education, and Recreation,* Vol. 44, No. 7, September 1973.
41. Ridini, Leonard M., "Physical education for the inner city," *The Physical Educator,* Vol. 28, No. 4, December 1971.

42. *The Roles of Public Education in Recreation,* California Association for Health, Physical Education, and Recreation and California State Department of Education, San Francisco: The Trade Pressroom, 1960.
43. Shields, James J., *Education in Community Development,* New York: Frederick A. Praeger, 1967.
44. Shivers, Jay S., *Principles and Practices of Recreational Service,* New York: The Macmillan Company, 1967.
45. Shriver, Sargent, "The moral force of sport," *Sports Illustrated,* Vol. 18, No. 22, June 3, 1963.
46. Snyder, Leonard M., "Four minutes from death—do you know what to do?," *YMCA Today,* Fall 1973.
47. Weinberg, Carl, *Education and Social Problems,* New York: The Free Press, 1971.
48. Wilkins, Michael H., and Richard L. Ragatz, "Cultural changes and leisure time," *Journal of Health, Physical Education, and Recreation,* Vol. 43, No. 3, March 1972.
49. *World Communique,* World Alliance of YMCA's, 37 Quai Wilson, 1201 Geneva, Switzerland, September-October 1970.

Human Values and Personal Ethics

Chapter 16

16.1 INTRODUCTION

There are few subjects in the field of physical education which are more difficult to discuss than the one selected for this chapter. Everyone has some kind of a value system and most people live by an ethical code of one sort or another. There are, however, no two people in the world who have exactly the same set of values or who are guided by precisely the same code of ethics.

It is difficult to deal scientifically with values and behavior. Even the terms "value," "behavior," "ethics," etc. mean different things to different people. This subject is discussed in sociology, psychology, philosophy, theology, education, and many other disciplines. Research dealing with values and ethics has been conducted in these disciplines for many years. Final answers have not been found. Ultimate conclusions for each individual are usually reached on the basis of his own experience and knowledge, empirical evidence, and philosophical interpretation. It is essential that those specializing in physical education come to grips with these matters. Potential teachers and coaches must not be allowed to graduate without at least some idea of how to formulate their philosophy of life. They must also be exposed to some of the conflicting opinions held by educators and others with regard to the role of values, ethics, and character education in sports and other physical education activities.

There are those who insist that athletics are a great positive influence in the lives of the participants. There are others who hold opposing views. Banquet speeches are given and newspaper articles written which emphasize the "character-building" value of sports. In other speeches and publications this idea may be ridiculed. Some inexperienced coaches and teachers are bewildered when suddenly asked to present their views. Many finally give up and ignore the problem of developing values and formulating codes of ethics. There have also been a few who have talked glibly about value formation but who have been unable to furnish sound explanations of what "values" really are or how they develop.

This chapter is not written with the intent of indoctrinating readers. It is rather concerned with (1) assisting those in the field of physical education as they proceed to develop their own value systems, and (2) helping them as they, in turn, become involved in helping students in their struggle with these matters.

16.2 DEFINITIONS

Before we can proceed further with this discussion of values and ethics, it is necessary to clarify meanings so that reader and author will be communicating from the same, or at least a relatively similar, base. Let us, therefore, consider the definitions of the terms character education, moral development, human values, value system, personal ethics, attitudes, and behavior.

Character education. The term *character* generally refers to that combination of traits which distinguish one as an individual. It includes personality traits as well as physical characteristics, and answers the question, "What kind of person is this?" In many instances "character" is used almost synonymously with "personality."

In the context of "character education," however, it has taken on a slightly different meaning. Character education generally refers to a change from "badness" to "goodness" or a modification due to experiences in which the individual develops more desirable character traits and behavior. When speaking about "character education through physical education," the common interpretation is that, as a result of participation in physical education activities, one's value system and one's personal ethics will improve. Because of considerable disagreement with this interpretation and the disrepute into which this term seems to have fallen, we will confine ourselves largely to a discussion of the development of values or the development of value systems.

Moral development.   The term *moral* relates to right and wrong in conduct and behavior. Right social relations, right conduct, as it is dictated by one's conscience or ethical code, is moral behavior. *Moral development* is growth and maturity in the development of a conscience and in right conduct.

According to A. W. Kay, moral development proceeds in stages:

> In certain respects the moral development of children proceeds quantitatively. The attitudes of responsibility, altruism, independence and rationality, for example, emerge in childhood and slowly mature. Yet, on the other hand, the different stages of morality may not only be clearly defined and easily recognized, but also located in a fixed sequence.
>
> A young child is clearly controlled by authoritarian considerations, while an adolescent is capable of applying personal moral principles. These two moralities are not only clearly distinct but can be located one at the beginning and the other at the end of a process of moral maturation.
>
> There is an interplay between the quantitative and the qualitative elements which makes it difficult to analyze this development with complete certainty, but in general outline one may trace moral growth through a series of sequential, qualitatively different stages *and also* along a line of growth marked by quantitatively increasing stability and complexity. [42, pp. 31–32]

Human values.   Values can be of many kinds. We speak of biophysical values, monetary values, and real estate values. We value something because it has worth. It may have intrinsic or extrinsic value. If it has great worth to an individual he places it high on the priority list of things he would like to possess or be able to do. In the context of moral development and character education, an individual's values are those convictions which cause him to behave in a certain way because of what he feels is important and what he believes is right. Milton Rokeach, in his book *Beliefs, Attitudes and Values,* gives us his conception of values in the following words:

> I consider a value to be a type of belief, centrally located within one's total belief system, about how one ought or ought not to behave, or about some end-state of existence worth or not worth attaining. Values are thus abstract ideals, positive or negative, not tied to any specific attitude, object or situation,

representing a person's beliefs about ideal modes of conduct and ideal terminal goals—what Lovejoy (1950) calls generalized adjectival and terminal values. Some examples of ideal modes of conduct are to seek truth and beauty, to be clean and orderly, to behave with sincerity, justice, reason, compassion, humility, respect, honor, and loyalty. Some examples of ideal goals or end-states are security, happiness, freedom, equality, ecstasy, fame, power, and states of grace and salvation. A person's values, like all beliefs, may be consciously conceived or unconsciously held, and must be inferred from what a person says or does. [64, p. 124]

By *human values* are meant those which pertain to an individual as a thinking, communicating, expressing, and feeling, human being. Human values may be such things as concern for others, love of freedom, regard for honesty, or allegiance to truth.

Values are sometimes used in the same way as aims, goals, and purposes. The assumption is that individuals choose goals and purposes which have meaning and worth—to them at least. Values as employed here will refer to the things for which one strives. They have to do with modes of conduct and preferred end-states of existence. Values eventually become internalized and then serve as guides for action and standards upon which to judge conduct, both of oneself and of others.

Value systems.   Rokeach emphasizes the hierarchical structures into which values are organized. "Operationally speaking, the concept of value system suggests a rank-ordering of values along a continuum of importance." [64, p. 161] A value system should serve as a guide for resolving conflicts and making choices when two or more values or modes of conduct are in conflict.

Value systems are ultimately the product of all internal and external influences to which the individual has been subjected. These influences come from the home, church, school, and community. They are shaped by the culture, social system, occupation of the parents, and political orientation of a person's environment. They are modified by what a person reads, hears, and sees. They are formed, molded, and strengthened by all the person's experiences. Finally they are affected by the inherited traits, tendencies, and capabilities which go to make up the persons's personality and self-concept.

Personal ethics.   Ethics usually pertains to "goodness" and "badness." Ethics is a discipline dealing with moral duty and the ideal human character. It is a branch of philosophy that is concerned with moral problems and judgments. William Franklin divides ethical or moral judgments into (a) judgments of moral obligation, and (b) judgments of moral value. Examples of the former are, "I ought not to escape from prison now," "What he did was wrong," and "We ought to keep our agreements." Examples of the latter include, "My grandfather was a good man," "You deserve to be punished," "The ideally good man does not drink or smoke." [27, pp. 9–10]

Personal and professional ethics refer most often to standards of behavior arrived at by individuals for their own guidance or drawn up by a business for the direction of its members. While the physical education profession and various groups of coaches have, from time to time, drawn up codes of ethics for their respective groups, it still remains up to each individual to draw up his own code as a guide to his personal conduct.

Attitudes. Social behavior is influenced to a considerable degree by *attitudes.* An attitude is a disposition toward something. It is a feeling which one has toward an individual, an object, a law, an edict, a principle, or a proposition. It may be favorable, unfavorable, or neutral. Rokeach defines attitude as "a relatively enduring organization of beliefs around an object or situation predisposing one to respond in some preferential manner." [64, p. 112] For our purposes, then, an attitude will be a predisposition to react or behave one way or another in a given situation.

Behavior. The way one acts or behaves constitutes his *behavior.* His deportment, conduct, speech, posture, and responses to various situations generally reveal his attitude and often his code of ethics and value system. Behavior is observable and presents a factual base for judging a person's character and personality.

Values, ethics, attitudes, and behavior as they relate to physical education and athletics are the topics of this chapter. The aims and objectives of physical education, the development of values through sports, the problems involved in competitive athletics, and the ethics of participants and leaders are all involved.

Included in Chapter 9 is a section entitled "Educating for Values." Some of the problems relating to high-level sports presented in that chapter might well be reviewed and studied in relationship to this discussion.

We shall now discuss in turn (a) what human values might we expect to accrue from physical education and athletics, (b) the potential of physical education to contribute to the development of these values, and (c) roadblocks and barriers to such development.

16.3 WHAT VALUES?

If values are beliefs which combine to form an individual's value system and if the value system serves as a guide to behavior, it is logical to ask the question, "What are some human values which might accrue from participation in physical education activities?" Let us look at some of the human values which, it is claimed, may develop from participation in movement exploration, games, dance, competitive team sports, lifetime sports, conditioning activities, combatives, individual outdoor activities, officiating, coaching, and administering athletics.

Through movement exploration

1. Each person needs and benefits by the freedom to express himself in movement.

2. Every person is endowed with some creative ability.
3. Every person must be given his/her share of attention and space in this world.
4. It is enjoyable to play with others when all are unselfish and friendly.
5. Sharing experiences with others is satisfying.
6. People like you when you are nice to them.
7. Others look up to you when you can do things well.
8. Achievement and success are pleasant.
9. Through self-expression in movement comes a feeling of release and a lowering of tension.
10. To cooperate with the teacher is more satisfying than to be disruptive.

Through games of low organization.
1. To have a game there must be some rules.
2. Cheating spoils the game for everyone.
3. Winning is fun.
4. It's important to be kind to those who lose.
5. Losers who whine will be neither liked nor respected.
6. Arrogant braggarts are generally resented.
7. Everyone loses sometimes.
8. Acceptance of others as they are is right.
9. Controlling one's temper is a sign of maturity.
10. Your team is more apt to be successful if everyone works together.

Through dance

1. To move skillfully is pleasurable.
2. To express oneself in movement requires a knowledge of how to move.
3. Fundamentals of movement must be learned before one can dance well.
4. Moving to the rhythm of music enhances the pleasure of movement.
5. Moving with a partner can be both pleasant and exciting.
6. Moving in unison with many others is a joyous experience.
7. To become an expert at dance requires a great deal of practice.
8. Moving in your own creative way satisfies a deep-felt need.
9. To perform well requires skill, strength, endurance, and vivacity.
10. For best results, the instructor and the dancer must work as a team.

Through competitive team sports

1. A great team must be composed of highly skilled individuals.
2. A great team requires a harmonious blending of skills of all team members.
3. Championship teams must put the welfare of the team ahead of personal considerations.
4. The best teams have confidence and poise.
5. Mutual trust among players and between coaches and team members is essential.
6. The decisions of officials must be accepted (there may be rare exceptions).
7. Even the best officials make mistakes.
8. To win without boasting and lose without whimpering are characteristics of greatness.
9. To fight "to the last ditch" is an admirable trait.
10. The game is not over until the final whistle blows.
11. One leader must call the signals.
12. On a good team both work horses and stars are needed.
13. Members of truly great teams are not concerned about who gets the glory.
14. There is a price to be paid for excellence.
15. Self-discipline is the mark of a great athlete.
16. The ability to concentrate on the task at hand is a great attribute.
17. Both moral and physical courage are important to success.
18. Honesty is the best policy.

◀ "Moving to the rhythm of music enhances the pleasure of movement." (Courtesy of the *Journal of Health, Physical Education, and Recreation.*)

19. It is important to be oneself and not always do something because of peer pressure.
20. Loyalty is a desirable trait.

Through lifetime sports

1. Success comes through industriousness and a great deal of practice.
2. It is important to adhere to the rules of courtesy.
3. Honesty in calling the shots ("in or out") is a sign of good character.
4. Control of emotions is essential.
5. When things appear to be going against you it's time to concentrate more intensely on the task.
6. When one faces an adversary alone there are no alibis.
7. Respect for, but not fear of, opponents is the right attitude.
8. One should strive to win but not humiliate the opponent.
9. To refrain from profanity when things go against you is a mark of self-control.
10. It is satisfying to play a challenging opponent.

Through combative activities

1. Great fighters are aggressive.
2. Good wrestlers are always prepared.
3. A quitter never wins and a winner never quits.
4. One can learn from opponents.
5. One should never stop learning.
6. There is always someone stronger and better.
7. To help a teammate is right and good.
8. Skill and knowledge can often defeat brute strength.
9. Sacrifice is necessary to attain good condition.
10. Other things being equal, the coachable athlete is the most successful.

Through conditioning activities

1. Nature builds the organism to meet the demands made upon it.
2. It requires effort and determination to achieve and maintain physical fitness.
3. The ability to endure and overcome pain is an important asset in endurance work.
4. Regularity in exercise programs requires self-discipline.
5. When you become strong and enduring your concept of self improves and with it your personality.
6. When the concern for the appearance of the body becomes too dominant it becomes narcissism, which is not desirable.

7. Good physical condition helps one achieve in many of life's endeavors.
8. Once habits of exercise are formed it is less difficult to continue on a regular basis.

Through individual outdoor activities

1. When one is engaged in extremely challenging activities (e.g. mountain climbing), he discovers that there are hidden resources which can be called out enabling him to do what he never dreamed possible.
2. When hiking mountain trails or enjoying nature's solitude one discovers peace and develops serenity.
3. Living in the great outdoors is healthful for body, mind, and spirit.
4. An appreciation of nature is a satisfying and desirable attitude.
5. It requires good interpersonal relationships to live together in a camping situation.
6. Sharing triumphs, defeats, adventure, and living experiences generally builds lasting friendships.
7. Most adventures are enjoyed more when shared than when experienced alone.

Through officiating

1. To "call them as he sees them" without fear or favor takes courage.
2. Self-respect requires the kind of integrity that makes for good officiating.
3. One should not seek or accept an officiating assignment unless one is prepared.
4. It is how one reacts under pressure that counts.
5. When popularity becomes the criterion on which decisions are based, one's effectiveness and one's friends and admirers are soon lost.
6. When a person places himself under obligation to others, it is difficult to operate impersonally and objectively.
7. When you must make a decision where there are no rules, you should decide on the basis of what is right and fair.

Through coaching

1. Fairness and impartiality are indispensable to good coaching.
2. Acceptance of the fact that coaching is hard and demanding work is necessary for success and happiness.
3. A coach should support other segments of the school and not be selfishly concerned with only his own activity.
4. To put the welfare of the athlete above winning is the mark of a good coach.
5. A coach has a moral obligation to strive for excellence and success.

6. A loss must be placed in the proper perspective and be judged on the basis of a team's performance rather than the score.

7. A leader must set an example with regard to demeanor and attitude.

8. A coach should not expect more dedication from assistants and players than he/she is willing to give him/herself.

9. A coach should fight for the players.

10. A coach should be concerned about athletes' development in all their dimensions.

11. A coach should live so as to be worthy of emulation.

12. A coach should set an example of good sportsmanship.

"Each new experience, each new truth, . . . each new insight will contribute to a person's value system." (Courtesy of Springfield College.)

Through administering

1. Athletic directors are equally responsible for all the sports, all the coaches, all the athletes.
2. Athletic directors are also responsible to their superiors and to the community for which they work.
3. Athletic programs must be conducted within the rules of the organization governing such programs.
4. Honesty and integrity are absolutely essential in the conduct of athletic programs.
5. All staff members must be treated so that they feel that they are important members of the team.
6. There must be a feeling in the athletic department that all are working toward common goals.
7. An optimistic and buoyant, yet sincere and realistic attitude leads to good morale and ultimate success.
8. The athletic program must not be permitted to fall into the hands of non-educational interests.
9. Acceptance of personal gratuities in any form places one under obligation to the donor.
10. Competence, efficiency, and knowledge of administration are important. Good interpersonal relations are even more so.

The above list of possible values which might be stressed and accepted by those involved in physical education and athletics is not intended to be all-inclusive. These items are examples of the many subvalues which might be incorporated in the value system of an individual.

It becomes obvious that a value system is ever-changing. Each new experience, each new truth, each additional bit of evidence, each new insight will contribute to a person's value system. This will be different as an adolescent, as a participant, as a coach, as an administrator. In early life the parents and the home will play the major role in guiding a child's behavior. It is doubtful whether the child has formulated much of a value system at that time. As the individual progresses from dependence to autonomy, from a young adult to a person with heavy responsibilities and a good deal of authority, he/she will gradually formulate a more stable and complex value system which will become an important part of his/her philosophy of life. The more stable and deeply rooted this becomes and the more one believes in its truth and validity, the more it will serve to guide one's conduct.

16.4 THE POTENTIAL OF PHYSICAL EDUCATION

Assuming that a person has accepted many of the idealistic values listed above but has seen their application only to the realm of sport, will behavior in later life be affected as a result? Are these values applicable to the situations which will be encountered in business, marital relationships, legal negotiations, and interpersonal relationships? The answers to these questions are not easy. The concepts of generalization, transfer, identification, and internalization come into play here. Let us look at these briefly in hypothetical situations.

Generalization is the process of reasoning from the specific to the general. If, for instance, a participant in sports finds, time after time, that by persevering when he is overtired and ready to quit he eventually achieves success or wins a contest, he may formulate for himself the principle or value, "the person who never quits, wins." If he then applies this to an argument and wears his opponent down, thus winning the argument, he widens the application to a life situation. Assuming that he wins a great number of arguments in many different life situations by virtue of the fact that he persists longer than his opponents, he finally *internalizes* the principle of never quitting and it becomes part of his value system and *transfers* to other situations as well.

In another instance, a member of a girl's tennis team may defeat an opponent and, as they meet each other after the match, the loser says, "Congratulations. You played a fine game." Whereupon the winner replies in arrogant fashion, "Huh, it doesn't take much to beat a player like you." This is repeated and although player number one continues to win she finds that instead of receiving adulation, she becomes the object of intense dislike. When she finally loses a match it is disconcerting to her that no one sympathizes with her and everyone is happy to see her soundly beaten. She talks to the coach about this and finally comes to the realization that arrogance and boasting only lead to dislike, envy, and even hatred. This begins to change her sense of values. Meanwhile she has an opportunity to observe a world-class tennis player whom she admires greatly and whom she tries to emulate or *identify* with. She notes first that this player is tremendously popular and seems to have many friends, and second that she is very gracious and helpful to those opponents whom she defeats. She finally realizes that when one excels in anything, arrogance and boasting lead only to jealousy and anger, while good sportsmanship leads to making friends. As she becomes older she begins to apply this principle to her business dealings and, while she has to struggle with her tendency toward arrogance, she finds that she accomplishes far more by winning support through graciousness and friendship than she ever does by beating her opponents into submission. Again we see the principles of transfer, generalization, identification, and internalization at work.

There are many things we do not know about the role of the physical education teacher and coach in the building of value systems or in character education. The author, after examining a great deal of literature and evaluating personal experiences pertaining to these matters, feels that the following conclusions have merit:

1. All education consists of learning things in one situation which may be applied in another. This is true of physical education as well as other subject matter areas.

2. Young children are controlled mostly by authoritarian considerations in early life, but as they grow older they gradually begin to apply personal, ethical, and moral principles to their behavior.

3. While there are few absolutes in the realm of values accepted by everyone, there are many character traits which are generally considered worthy of careful nurture and development. A list of these would include truthfulness, unselfishness, compassion, courtesy, helpfulness, tolerance, concern for others, courage, reliability, sincerity, honesty, and self-control.

4. The more similar the elements are in two situations, the greater is the likelihood of transfer. The fact that there are many situations in sports which resemble those found in other aspects of life make such transfer probable.

5. When similar events are experienced in many different situations, the thoughtful person usually generalizes and formulates principles on which later behavior is based. Both generalization and transfer usually occur more readily if a teacher or coach assists and encourages the students to perceive the relationships. This is one of the objectives of the master teacher.

6. Experiences which are personal and intense will be remembered longer than will those more casual in nature. Such situations abound in sports. Participants are often forced to control their behavior in a tension-filled atmosphere where they are subject to various pressures. Education in values is taking place.

7. If what is learned in an exciting and emotion-packed situation is to have a positive influence on character development, sound guidance is often required. This is the role of the teacher and physical educator.

8. To have a lasting effect on conduct, the values learned must be internalized, that is, they must be made part of the value system of an individual. When this has been accomplished, the modified value system will serve as a guideline to future behavior and will enhance the stability and consistency of an individual's actions.

9. Identification or emulation play an important role in everyone's lives. This is particularly noticeable during adolescence. It may be seen in a child's imitation of a parent, in a boy's imitation of a star athlete, in a girl's imitation of an admired teacher. It is most noticeable where the child and the adult share deep involvement and exciting experiences for a prolonged length of time. It is for this reason that the responsibility for the selection of leaders and teachers for young people is so great.

10. Chauvinism, narcissism, and conceit are dangers to be avoided by all who are eminently successful in physical education and sports. It is important to recognize

a) that not all individuals are favorably influenced by participation in sports,

b) that all experiences have an influence on behavior and conduct,

c) that value systems are formulated philosophically, using as a base all previous knowledge and experience,

d) that good leadership is important if the right kinds of influences are to be effected,

e) that there must be defeat as well as victory, and that the loser may have tried as hard and fought as valiantly as the winner, and

f) that very often the person who lacks ability or has problems with coordination, obesity, or stature needs assistance and empathetic encouragement more than the individual who is endowed with all the physical characteristics of a typical great athlete.

16.5 ROADBLOCKS AND BARRIERS

If it is possible to identify the values sought through physical education and athletics and determine the potential these media have for the development of values, why is it so difficult to achieve these outcomes? As with other means through which attempts are made to influence value systems, objectives are seldom achieved in their entirety. There are a number of reasons for this. Human frailties and conflicting desires are major roadblocks. Selfishness, the need for recognition and ego-enhancement, the desire for material wealth, the drive for self-esteem, and the lack of integrity and moral fiber are other barriers.

The exploitation of athletes by those who seek to make money is not uncommon. There are unscrupulous persons who gamble on the outcome of games and attempt to secure the cooperation of athletes in fraudulent manipulation of scores. Individuals and groups often seek to identify with well-known athletes for the purpose of securing recognition. "Stretching" rules to obtain the admission of an athlete to a college, manipulating academic grades and other factual information to keep an athlete eligible, and paying illegal expenses to an athlete are among the dangers which must be avoided.

Encouragement by individuals or outside groups to break the playing rules or the eligibility rules can play havoc with an individual's developing value system. Alumni, administrators, coaches, parents, fans, and peers who put such a high priority on winning that they consider any means to that goal legitimate are coconspirators of a serious problem. A lack of moral courage or a false set of values on the part of the athletes will compound the problem.

The complexity of modern athletic programs and the influence of the behavior and mores of society as a whole pose still another problem. It is difficult to teach idealism and a sound ethical code in a corrupt society. For these reasons, all people and especially those who have influential positions must be enlisted in this cause. Teaching values is a challenging task that requires the concerted and committed attention of everyone.

16.6 PROFESSIONAL AND PERSONAL ETHICS

As mentioned previously, ethics pertain to standards of behavior. The National Education Association has established a code for the teaching profession; the medical profession has its code of ethics (the Hippocratic Oath); there is a code of ethics for lawyers; and many other groups have drawn up guidelines for behavior and practice. Such published codes usually pertain to a given group. Each individual may also have developed a code of conduct for himself. Some of these will be written and others barely formulated and stored in the brain. One's conscience may determine his code of ethics. The Ten Commandments constitute such a code for many.

The *Declaration on Sport* published by the International Council on Sport and Physical Education contains both philosophical statements and sections devoted to the conduct and attitudes of sportsmen. The following paragraphs offer a code of ethics for the sportsman and the sports leader:

Obligations of the sportsman

1. The sportsman must obey the spirit and the letter of the rules in complete loyalty.

2. The sportsman must respect his opponents and the match officials before, during and after the competition. He must in all circumstances preserve a correct attitude toward the public.

3. The sportsman must always keep his self-control, preserve his calm and dignity. He puts all his strength into winning a victory, but is capable of avoiding the discouragement which may follow failure or the vanity which may spring from success. His best reward is the feeling of well being and joy which results from effort.

Duties of the sports leader

1. The leader is faced with a mission of physical and moral education; he must show himself worthy of this responsibility. He has in particular the task of preserving the ideal of amateurism without which sport would lose one of its principal virtues.

2. The leader must be conscious of the social and cultural nature of leisure time sport and must attempt to create in the groups he leads a broad basis of solidarity which goes beyond sporting interests alone.

3. In his work, the leader must always be guided by the ideal of promoting human development through sport. He must see that fair play is respected by all, thus furthering the aim of sport to serve humanism and peace. [18, p. 10]

After the scandals in athletics which occurred in the collegiate ranks during the 1950's, the National Collegiate Athletic Association published a special report containing specific action principles dealing with gambling, bribery, eligibility rules, and illegal subsidization of athletes. This report contained specific recommendations for action in the administration of intercollegiate athletic programs. These recommendations too can be thought of as a code of ethics. Actually both the Constitution and By-Laws of the NCAA and the many other rules and regulations which are published by that organization constitute a code of ethics for players, coaches, and administrators in intercollegiate athletic programs.

The Division of Girls' and Women's Sports of the American Association for Health, Physical Education, and Recreation has published a booklet entitled *Philosophy and Standards for Girls' and Women's Sports*. This document contains an excellent exposition of values and ethics as they relate to the conduct of athletics. The section entitled "Guidelines for Intercollegiate Athletic Programs for Women" is revised yearly and contains detailed operating procedures under the categories of administration, awards, leaders, and participants. The following, from the 1973 revision of the guidelines, provides an indication of the careful thought being given to this program by professional leaders. It also presents an insight into the value systems and ethical considerations which the authors feel are important. In view of the length of the material, only those sections dealing with leaders (teachers, coaches, and officials) and participants are presented:

Leaders (teachers, coaches, and officials)

1. Good leadership is essential to a desirable sports program. The qualified leader meets the standards set by the profession through an understanding of (a) the place and purpose of sports in education, (b) the growth and development of children and youth, (c) the effects of exercise on the human organism, (d) first aid and accident prevention, (e) specific skills, and (f) sound teaching methods. It is desirable that, when possible, leaders of women's sports have personal experience in organized extramural competition. The leader should demonstrate personal integrity and a primary concern for the welfare of the participant.

2. The program should be under the direct supervision of the appropriate personnel in women's physical education. Qualified women should teach, coach, and officiate wherever and whenever possible, and in all cases the professional background and experience of the leader must meet established standards of the physical education profession.

3. It is strongly recommended that an official's rating be considered a prerequisite for coaching in order to enhance the coach's understanding of the official's role.

4. Intercollegiate events should be officiated by DGWS state or national officials. In those sports where DGWS does not rate officials, an equivalent rating is acceptable.

5. If a nonstaff member is teaching or coaching, a woman member of the physical education faculty should supervise the participants. Cooperative institutional efforts should be devoted toward preservice and in-service programs and clinics for leaders and teachers.

6. DGWS-approved rules should be used in the conduct of all intercollegiate sports events.

Participants

1. Intercollegiate participation should not interfere with primary educational objectives.

a) A girl should participate on only one competitive team during a season.

b) Participation on more than one team includes participation on an additional team within an institution or participation on an additional team outside an institution. In unusual circumstances such participation may be permitted provided it contributes to the welfare of the participant and does not place excessive demands and pressures upon her.

2. The athletic schedule should not jeopardize the student's class and study time.

a) The length of the season and the number of games should be established and agreed upon by the participating schools.

b) The length of the season will vary according to the locale and sport and should not be so long that the educational values for the student in terms of the total program are jeopardized (approximately 12–14 weeks). This season should include conditioning and instruction.

c) The season may be lengthened to include opportunities for participation in state, regional or national tournaments or meets for which individuals or teams qualify.

3. Teams for girls and women should be provided for all who desire competitive athletic experiences. While positive experiences for the exceptional girl or woman competitor may occur through participation in boys' or men's competitive groups, these instances are rare and should be judged acceptable only as an interim procedure for use until women's programs can be initiated.

4. Any woman who is presently enrolled as a full-time undergraduate student in a college, junior college, or university, and who maintains the academic average required for participation in all other major campus activities at her institution shall be eligible to participate.

5. Transfer students are immediately eligible for participation following enrollment in the institution.

6. Students may not participate in the same annual event for more than four years.

7. All participants must have amateur status. Amateur status is maintained in a sport if a player has not received and does not receive money, other than expenses, as a participant in that sport. A participant may receive money from her own school to pay for housing, meals, and transportation providing such funds do not exceed actual costs. For open or international competition governed by the respective sports governing body, a student may lose amateur status if she receives remuneration in excess of her expenses for playing, coaching, or officiating. Scholarships allowed by AIAW will not jeopardize a student's amateur status for DGWS-AIAW competition.

8. A medical examination is a prerequisite to participation in intercollegiate athletics. This examination should be given within the school year prior to the start of the sport season. Where health examinations are done by the family physician, a covering letter explaining the program of activities and an exami-

nation which would include the information needed are suggested. Written permission by the physican should be required for participation after serious illness, injury, or surgery. [2]

The Division of Men's Athletics of the American Association for Health, Physical Education, and Recreation published a brochure, *Athletics in Education, A Platform Statement,* which has been widely used and which contains the following guidelines:

To utilize fully the potential in athletics for educational experiences, interscholastic and intercollegiate athletic programs should be organized and conducted in accordance with these six basic principles.

1. Interscholastic and intercollegiate athletic programs should be regarded as integral parts of the total educational program and should be so conducted that they are worthy of such regard.
2. Interscholastic and intercollegiate athletic programs should supplement rather than serve as substitutes for basic physical education programs, physical recreation programs, and intramural athletic programs.
3. Interscholastic and intercollegiate athletic programs should be subject to the same administrative control as the total education program.
4. Interscholastic and intercollegiate athletic programs should be conducted by men with adequate training in physical education.
5. Interscholastic and intercollegiate athletic programs should be so conducted that the physical welfare and safety of the participants are protected and fostered.
6. Interscholastic and intercollegiate athletic programs should be conducted in accordance with the letter and the spirit of the rules and regulations of appropriate conference, state, and national athletic associations.[8]

The National Federation of State High School Associations publishes annually their *Official Handbook.* This contains, not only their Constitution and By-Laws, but also many excellent statements which serve as guides to the control and conduct of interscholastic programs for both boys and girls. Their "Cardinal Athletic Principles" [55, p. 23] are examples of guidelines which collectively might well serve as a code of ethics for those engaged in the administration of high school athletics.

The National Association of Intercollegiate Athletics, the Amateur Athletic Union, the Young Men's Christian Association, the United States Olympic Committee, and the International Olympic Committee are among the many other organizations which attempt to guide and control sports programs.

It becomes clear, then, that it is not for lack of rules and regulations, not because there are no ethical codes, and not because people do not know what they should do that there are so many instances of poor sportsmanship, cheating, exploitation, and other misconduct. Rather it is because of inappropriate priorities, misplaced emphasis, human greed, and selfish motives that such practices take place.

16.7 THE FUTURE OF SPORT

To predict what the future holds is, of course, impossible. The probability is that the struggle between good and evil will continue. For those who love athletics there is only one road—they must continue to seek out and fight for those things that are great, exciting, and developmental. They cannot afford to become complacent but must be continually vigilant, guarding against those influences and directions which lead to the degradation of sport. They must work for and support all efforts to make sport the wholesome and worthy endeavor that it can be.

16.8 THE PHYSICAL EDUCATION TEACHER AND ETHICS

The physical education teacher will also need to consider the many situations where athletics are not involved but where decisions with regard to right and wrong need to be made. A few suggestions for a personal code are the following:

1. Treat every person with whom you deal as someone worthy of your respect and consideration.
2. Be meticulous in fulfilling all obligations. Lean toward doing more than your "fair share."
3. Be as fair and impartial as is humanly possible.
4. Act as you believe someone representing your profession should act.
5. Treat your word and your contract as an agreement to be honored. Behave in such a way that all with whom you deal will learn that your word is to be trusted.
6. Recognize your own fallibility and admit that you do not know certain answers. Try to find the answers and bring them to class.
7. Try to establish a feeling that teacher and students work together toward mutual goals.
8. Remember that teachers, facilities, and equipment are only worthwhile when they contribute to the education of the student.
9. Try to bring some fun and joy into every class.
10. Remember that the spiritual, emotional, and intellectual dimensions as well as the physical dimension are being affected in every class.
11. Keep in mind that no one has final answers; yet the continuous search for new knowledge and new truths is a responsibility of a teacher.
12. Try to exude a love of life.
13. Maintain faith in other people, in yourself, and in the possibility of improving the world in which we live.

14. Remember that you are a teacher and that your influence will spread, like a ripple of water, to unknown destinations.

15. Keep constantly in mind not what the student is but what he can become.

16. Never forget that "Rome wasn't built in a day." Most worthy enterprises take years and even generations to accomplish.

17. The master teacher knows his subject, is deeply interested in his students, and knows how to teach.

The above principles are suggestions that might be included in a physical education teacher's code of ethics. It is urged that every teacher formulate his own. It will be developmental for him and salutary for the students.

There are many times when coaches and teachers would like nothing better than to wash their hands of the knotty problems related to values through sports. There are so many pertinent factors over which teachers and coaches have little control. It often appears as if educators cannot possibly accept responsibility for actions and behavior of students and athletes because there are too many extraneous factors which have a bearing on these matters. And yet we who have chosen education as our profession have both a contribution to make and a responsibility to the students and athletes with whom we come in contact. We also have a responsibility to our profession. As Peter MacIntosh stated so eloquently:

> The fact is, however, that we cannot opt out. We can reduce to a minimum the occasions on which we declare our position on a moral issue. We can minimize the impression that we have a concern for how people behave, but if we do this we then support the view that standards of behavior are not important or that any standards are acceptable and we have thereby adopted a moral position. It is the function of the coach and of the teacher to give social significance to a motor performance; and he will do this, either deliberately or by default. Just as a coach or teacher reinforces a good motor performance by drawing attention to it verbally, or in some other way, so he will reinforce patterns of behavior either tacitly or explicitly. [50]

SELECTED REFERENCES

1. Allman, Fred L., Jr., "Competitive sports for boys under fifteen—beneficial or harmful?," *Journal of the Medical Association of Georgia,* February 1967.

2. American Association for Health, Physical Education, and Recreation, Division of Girls' and Women's Sports, *Guidelines for Intercollegiate Athletic Programs for Women,* revised, Washington, D.C., 1973. By permission.

3. _____, Division of Girls' and Women's Sports, *Guidelines for Interscholastic Athletic Programs for Junior High School Girls,* revised, Washington, D.C., 1973.

4. _____, Division of Girls' and Women's Sports, *Guidelines for Interscholastic Athletic Programs for High School Girls,* revised, Washington, D.C., 1973.

5. Andrews, Thomas G., and Lee J. Cronbach, "Transfer of training," *The Causes of Behavior II,* 2nd edition, Judy F. Rosenblith and Wesley Allensmith (eds.), Boston: Allyn and Bacon, 1966.

6. Arnold, P. J., *Physical Education and Personality Development,* New York: Atherton Press, 1968.

7. Arsenian, Seth (ed.), *The Humanics Philosophy of Springfield College,* Springfield, Mass.: Springfield College, 1969.
8. *Athletics in Education, A Platform Statement,* Division of Men's Athletics, Washington, D.C.: The American Association for Health, Physical Education, and Recreation, 1963. By permission.
9. Baley, James A., "Physical education and athletics belong together," *The Physical Educator,* Vol. 23, No. 2, May 1966.
10. Barnes, Mildred (ed.), *AIAW Handbook of Policies and Operating Procedures, 1973– 1974,* Washington, D.C.: American Association for Health, Physical Education, and Recreation, 1973.
11. Bouet, Michel, "The function of sport in human relations," *International Review of Sport Sociology,* Vol. 1, 1966.
12. Champlin, Ellis H., "Is the program of high school athletics an integral part of physical education?," *American Academy of Physical Education,* Professional Contributions No. 5, November 1956.
13. *Contemporary Psychology of Sport,* Proceedings of the Second International Congress of Sport Psychology, Washington, D.C., 1968.
14. Coppolillo, Henry P., *Football in Grade School: A Child Psychiatrist's Viewpoint,* December 1966.
15. Crary, Ryland W., *Humanizing the School,* New York: Alfred A. Knopf, 1969.
16. Crase, Darrell, "Athletics in trouble," *Journal of Health, Physical Education, and Recreation,* Vol. 43, No. 4, April 1972.
17. Davis, Elwood C., and Gene A. Logan, *Biophysical Values of Muscular Activity,* Dubuque, Iowa: W. C. Brown Company, 1961.
18. *Declaration on Sport,* International Council of Sport and Physical Education, Place de Fontenoy, Paris, France, 1968. By permission.
19. *Desirable Competition for Children of Elementary School Age,* Joint Committee Report, American Association for Health, Physical Education, and Recreation, 1968.
20. Dollard, John, Neal Mills, Leonard Doob, et al., *Frustration and Aggression,* New Haven: The Yale University Press, 1939.
21. Duncan, Ray O., "The contribution of school athletics to the growing boy," *The Journal of Educational Sociology,* Vol. 28, No. 6, February 1955.
22. Eagan, Edward P. F., "Athletics—medium for international good-will," *The Journal of Educational Sociology,* Vol. 28, No. 6, February 1955.
23. Edwards, Harry, *The Revolt of the Black Athlete,* New York: The Free Press, 1969.
24. Ellis, M., *Why People Play,* Englewood Cliffs, N.J.: Prentice-Hall, 1973.
25. Fitts, William H., and William Hansner, *The Self Concept in Delinquency,* Nashville, Tenn.: Nashville Mental Health Center, 1968.
26. Frankl, Victor E., *Psychotherapy and Existentialism,* New York: Washington Square Press, 1967.
27. Franklin, William K., *Ethics,* Englewood Cliffs, N.J.: Prentice-Hall, 1963.
28. Frost, Reuben B., *Athletics: Problems and Prospects,* Presented to Division of Boys' and Men's Athletics, Southwest District Association for Health, Physical Education, and Recreation, Salt Lake City, April 1965.
29. _____, "Physical education and self-concept," *Journal of the Arizona Association for Health, Physical Education, and Recreation,* Vol. 15, No. 2, Spring 1972.
30. _____, *Some Psychological Implications for Olympic Sports,* Athens, Greece: Hellenic Olympic Committee, Report of Fifth Summer Session of the International Olympic Academy, 1965.
31. Gallico, Paul, *Farewell to Sport,* New York: Pocket Books, 1945.

32. Gardner, John W., *Excellence,* New York: Harper and Row, 1961.
33. Gordon, Chad, and Kenneth J. Gergen (eds.), *The Self in Social Interaction,* New York: John Wiley and Sons, 1968.
34. Harrold, Roger D., and Benjamin Lowe, "Intercollegiate athletics in the contemporary student value system," *Journal of College Student Personnel,* Vol. 14, No. 4, July 1973.
35. Hartshorne, H., and M. May, *Studies in the Nature of Character,* New York: The Macmillan Company, 1928.
36. Hullfish, H. Gordon, "Physical education and the good life," *Anthology of Contemporary Readings,* Howard S. Slusher and Aileene S. Lockhart (eds.), Dubuque, Iowa: Wm. C. Brown Company, 1966.
37. James, David (ed.), *Outward Bound,* London: Routledge and Kegan Paul, 1964.
38. Johnson, Warren R., "A humanistic dimension of physical education," *Journal of Health, Physical Education, and Recreation,* Vol. 43, No. 9, November–December 1972.
39. Johnson, Warren R., B. R. Fretz, and Julia A. Johnson, "Changes in self-concepts during a physical development program." *Research Quarterly,* Vol. 39, October 1968.
40. Kane, J. E., "Personality profiles of physical education students compared with others," *Psicologia Dello Sport,* Ferrucio Antonelli (ed.), Proceedings of the First International Congress of Sport Psychology, Rome, Italy, 1965.
41. _____, (ed.), *Psychological Aspects of Physical Education and Sport,* London: Routledge and Kegan Paul, 1972.
42. Kay, A. W., *Moral Development.* Reprinted by permission of Schocken Books Inc., from *Moral Development* by A. William Kay. Copyright © 1968 by A. W. Kay.
43. Keelor, Richard D., "The realities of drug abuse in high school athletics," *Journal of Health, Physical Education, and Recreation,* Vol. 43, No. 2, April 1972.
44. Lawther, John D., *Sport Psychology,* Englewood Cliffs, N.J.: Prentice-Hall, 1972.
45. Ley, Katherine, "Interscholastic athletics for girls," Paper presented at the National Conference on Secondary School Administration, Washington, D.C., December 1962.
46. Loy, John W., Jr., and Gerald S. Kenyon, *Sport, Culture and Society,* New York: The Macmillan Company, 1969.
47. Maheu, Rene, "Sport and culture," *International Journal of Adult and Youth Education,* Vol. 14, No. 4, 1962.
48. Maslow, Abraham H., "Peak-experiences as acute identity-experiences," Chapter 26, *The Self in Social Interaction,* Gordon, Chad, and Kenneth J. Gergen, New York: John Wiley and Sons, 1968.
49. McIntosh, P. C., *Sport in Society,* London: C. A. Watts and Company, 1963.
50. McIntosh, Peter, "Values and competitive sport," Paper presented as Keynote Address at National Conference on the Development of Human Values Through Sports, Springfield College, October 1973. By permission.
51. Mitchem, John C., and Bonnie L. Parkhouse, "Athletics—the laboratory setting for character development," *The Physical Educator,* Vol. 25, No. 1, March 1968.
52. *The National Federation's First Annual Conference of High School Directors of Athletics,* Proceedings, St. Louis, February 1971.
53. Neal, Patsy, *Sport and Identity,* Philadelphia: Dorrance and Company, 1972.
54. Oberteuffer, Delbert, *Physical Education,* New York: Harper and Row, 1956.
55. *Official Handbook,* National Federation of State High School Associations, Elgin, Ill., 1972–1973.
56. Ogilvie, Bruce, and Thomas A. Tutko, "Sport: if you want to build character, try something else," *Psychology Today,* October 1971.

57. Olson, Edward, "Intercollegiate athletics, is there no way to live with it?," *Proceedings,* Annual Meeting of the National College Physical Education Association for Men, January 1973.

58. Peck, Robert F., et al., *The Psychology of Character Development,* New York: John Wiley and Sons, 1960.

59. Pettit, Bob, *The Drive Within Me,* Englewood Cliffs, N.J.: Prentice-Hall, 1966.

60. Rado, Sandor, *Adaptational Psychodynamics: Motivation and Control,* New York: Science House, 1969.

61. Richards, Bob, *The Heart of a Champion,* Westwood, N.J.: Fleming H. Revell Company, 1959.

62. Roberts, Guy L., *Personal Growth and Adjustment,* Boston: Holbrook Press, 1968.

63. Rogers, Carl A., "A theory of therapy, personality, and interpersonal relationships, as developed in the client-centered framework," *Psychology: A Study of a Science,* Vol. III, S. Koch (ed.), New York: McGraw-Hill, 1959.

64. Rokeach, Milton, *Beliefs, Attitudes, and Values,* San Francisco: Jossey-Bass, 1969. By permission.

65. Sage, George H. (ed.), *Sport and American Society: Selected Readings,* Reading, Mass.: Addison-Wesley Publishing Company, 1970.

66. Scott, Harry A., *Competitive Sports in Schools and Colleges,* New York: Harper and Row, 1951.

67. Scott, Jack, *Athletics for Athletes,* Hayward, Calif.: Quality Printing Service, 1969.

68. _____, *Sport and the Radical Ethic,* Address delivered at the National Convention of the American Association for Health, Physical Education, and Recreation, March 28, 1972.

69. *Secondary School Athletic Administration: A New Look,* Report of the Second National Conference on Secondary School Athletic Administration, Washington, D.C.: American Association for Health, Physical Education, and Recreation, 1969.

70. Shriver, Sargent, "The moral force of sport," *Sports Illustrated,* Vol. 18, No. 22, June 3, 1963.

71. Shultz, Fredrick D., "Broadening the athletic experience," *Journal of Health, Physical Education, and Recreation,* Vol. 43, No. 4, April 1972.

72. Slusher, Howard S., *Man, Sport and Existence,* Philadelphia: Lea and Febiger, 1967.

73. Stern, Barry E., "The cultural crisis in American sports," *Journal of Health, Physical Education, and Recreation,* Vol. 43, No. 4, April 1972.

74. "Therapy in the gym," *Time Magazine,* February 15, 1971.

75. Tussing, Lyle, *Psychology for Better Living,* New York: John Wiley and Sons, 1965.

76. Tutko, Thomas A., and Jack W. Richards, *The Athletic Guide to Athletic Motivation,* Boston: Allyn and Bacon, 1972.

77. *Values in Sports,* Joint National Conference of the Division for Girls' and Women's Sports and the Division of Men's Athletics, Washington, D.C.: American Association for Health, Physical Education, and Recreation, 1962.

78. VanderZwaag, Harold J., *Toward a Philosophy of Sport,* Reading, Mass.: Addison-Wesley Publishing Company, 1972.

79. Weiss, Paul, *Sport, A Philosophic Inquiry,* Carbondale: Southern Illinois University Press, 1969.

80. Werner, Alfred C., and Edward Gottheil, "Personality development and participation in college athletics," *Research Quarterly,* Vol. 37, No. 1, March 1966.

81. Zeigler, Earle F., *Philosophical Foundations for Physical, Health, and Recreation Education,* Englewood Cliffs, N.J.: Prentice-Hall, 1964.

Pedagogical
Principles
and Practices

Chapter 17

17.1 INTRODUCTION

Pedagogy may be defined as the art and science of teaching. It includes the ability to develop a climate conducive to learning, the knack of clear communication, skill in organizing classwork, high competency in the specific material to be taught and learned, and the art of dealing with human beings. As mentioned previously, the master teacher understands the students, knows the subject matter, is an able organizer, and is familiar with many methods of presenting the subject matter. The teacher who can create an environment where students are motivated to learn, who is familiar with the processes involved in motor learning, and who has at his fingertips the many methods and devices utilized in teaching will be far superior to the one whose command of pedagogical principles and methods is limited.

This chapter will deal essentially with teaching methodology and the scientific principles on which it is based. It will be organized under the following headings:

1. Planning and preparing
2. Class management and teaching methods
3. Principles and guidelines.

17.2 PLANNING AND PREPARING

Elwood Davis and Earl Wallis relate planning to anticipation. They indicate that an important difference between the novice and the expert teacher is the ability to anticipate. They point out that the experienced teacher will be better able to anticipate questions, learning difficulties, possible discipline problems, accidents, motivational forces, future uses of activity, and equipment requirements. [22, pp. 259–260] Certainly a large part of planning is the anticipation of what might happen and what might be required. Before one can plan one must anticipate the future so as to provide a basis for planning. When lack of experience makes this difficult, one must rely on the help of others and the information provided by superiors.

Plans may be classified as long-range, medium-range, and short-range. Long-range plans would be for months and even years ahead. Medium-range plans would cover days and weeks to come. Short-range plans would be for the next lesson or the next week. Long-range plans would be more general and permanent in nature. Short-range plans would be very detailed. Medium-range plans would be appropriate to the time span involved and the type of planning considered.

When dealing with pedagogical principles and methods, long-range plans provide a yearly schedule of activities—the equipment needed, the teaching personnel necessary, the type of teaching appropriate for the grade level, activity, and kind of teaching, and the facilities available for each activity.

Medium-range plans include a fall season, winter season, or spring season. The number of periods available, the climatic conditions, the facilities and equipment on hand, and the personnel assigned to the task are carefully considered.

Lesson plans

The short-range plan or lesson plan provides a guideline for each day's lesson. It should be quite detailed and cover the following items:

1. The name or title of the class or course.
2. The date and time of day.
3. The number of students in the class.
4. The grade level.
5. The teacher or teachers assigned.
6. The nature of the activity (volleyball, fundamental movements, folk dance, etc.).
7. The specific objectives of the day's lesson.
8. The equipment needed.
9. An outline of the activities to be reviewed and presented.
10. The method to be used.
11. If more than one teacher, the responsibility of each.
12. The time planned for each part of the lesson.
13. Provision for written evaluation and progress.

Most schools will provide lesson plan forms. If not, the teacher should provide his own. They might be clipboard size or might fit into a loose-leaf notebook. Many teachers like 6 X 8-inch cards, punched for insertion into a pocket-sized notebook.

Figure 17.1 is a typical lesson plan. The objectives should be specific and worded so that the teacher knows when they are achieved. The various activities, drills, or games should be listed at the left (bottom half of plan). The time planned for each part of the lesson should be noted under "time allotted." The formations to be used, the games to be played, the drills to be employed, and the organizational details should be described on the right half of the form where indicated. If more than one teacher has a role, the exact responsibilities of each shall be specified.

Special plans and a variety of forms are necessary if there is to be sufficient flexibility and individualization of instruction. Independent study, weekend backpacking trips, white-water canoeing excursions, pack trips on horseback, and skydiving are examples of activities where the above plan would be inappropriate and where special written agreements should be required. Competent teachers will know how to deal with such situations. Individual contracts, detailed reports, oral presentations, or careful evaluations of their experiences may, in such cases, be required of the students.

A well-planned lesson is usually more successful than one for which there has been little or no planning. There is need, however, for some flexibility. No one

Name of Teacher: _____ Date: _____

Class: _____ No. of Students: _____

Time Class Begins: _____ Time Class Ends: _____

General Subject Matter _____

Objectives:

      1. _____

      2. _____

      3. _____

      4. _____

      5. _____

Equipment Needed: _____

Activity	Time Allotted	Organization and Method

Evaluation and Remarks: _____

Figure 17.1 Sample lesson plan.

can predict accurately everything that will occur in any given class. Adjustments need to be made as the need arises. There are those who say that they do not plan because of the unreliability of their forecasts. This is usually mere rationalization. Some forethought and planning for unforeseen contingencies will simplify necessary adjustments as the class proceeds.

Planning should be continuous. Even as one is carrying out the plans for a given day, there should be advance thinking with regard to coming events and future developments. Short-term planning, or the preparation of daily lesson plans, should not be done too far in advance. Current circumstances and the progress made on a given day must influence each day's plan.

The daily lesson plan should grow out of the unit plan. The unit plan should be developed as part of the yearly plan. Both long- and short-term planning should provide progression, unity, and a basic theme for the term's physical education activities. It will also make the evaluation of the class period more feasible in terms of the achievement of objectives.

Individualization

Plans must provide for many kinds of individual differences. Some students will be unfamiliar with the skills being taught; there will be those who are not ready physiologically for a given activity; handicaps of several types will prevent certain others from participating; the class will include some superb athletes and intellectual geniuses. It is important that provision for such exigencies be made in advance and not after the class begins.

In a class where the students are quite heterogeneous in capacities and needs, a good lesson plan will identify those who should have special assistance, those who are ahead of the majority of the class, and those with exceptional abilities and interests. It will also include an analysis of anticipated outcomes and ways of achieving them. Performance objectives will be listed in terms of both knowledges and activities and provision will be made for subsequent evaluation. Each child will report to the instructor who is prepared to direct the scheduled activity.

Task analysis and performance objectives

In an attempt to achieve the outcomes desired for every individual, task analyses and the formulation of performance or behavioral objectives have been accepted as enabling processes. [13, p. 4] Desired outcomes are defined, performance objectives and criteria for evaluating their achievement are spelled out, and methods for developing the necessary skills and gaining the appropriate knowledge are outlined.

It is intended that the above processes will eliminate unproductive human efforts. Major tasks and subtasks are identified and attacked in an orderly fashion. Outcomes are judged against the behavioral objectives outlined. The acquisition of related knowledge and the comprehension of relevant concepts are measured against planned objectives and original goals. Total development and cognitive growth is assessed.

The important point is that each person is considered as an individual and is not constantly compared with others. Progress is assessed in terms of the original evaluation of needs and the development of each student.

Flexible scheduling

It is becoming increasingly common to base the length of activity periods and the composition of classes on the learning requirements of the students, the subject matter selected, and the most appropriate method for the achievement of the objectives. [4, p. 6] Modules from ten to thirty minutes are joined together in various combinations so that the time-block most appropriate and effective for a given activity can be utilized.

Flexible scheduling also more adequately provides for grouping students according to their needs and interests and according to the scope and content of the lesson. Depending on how much student discussion and interaction are necessary, as well as on the nature of the activity, the classes can be divided into small or large groups.

Helen Heitman has listed the benefits of flexible scheduling:

1. Student groups of varying sizes can be scheduled within the same subject or unit.
2. A system may be developed in which classes vary in length and number of meetings each week.
3. Time can be rearranged to make maximum usage of facilities.
4. Team teaching and/or differentiated staffing can be more easily scheduled. [4, pp. 7–8]

Problems involved in flexible scheduling, according to Heitman, are the following:

1. Some teachers are neither educated in, nor experienced with, this concept, and others have been uncomfortable in the situation or unwilling to participate.
2. Some state laws and local regulations require a daily period of physical education.
3. Locker rooms and gymnasiums which have been designed and outfitted for a traditional peak student load may require revisions before the program can be completely operative.
4. If the student's schedule calls for longer, less frequent meetings, absences cause more detriment to the learning process.
5. Staffing requirements may be more than those traditionally allotted to physical education.

"... each person is considered as an individual and is not constantly compared with others." (Courtesy of (*top left*) Springfield College, and (*right and bottom*) the *Journal of Health, Physical Education, and Recreation.*)

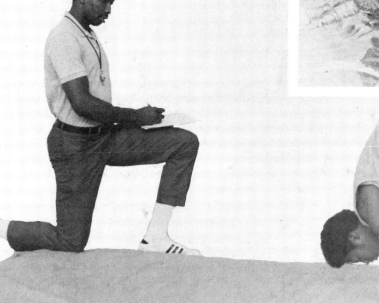

6. A period of acclimation, organization, and public relations must be undertaken before the program can be implemented successfully. This period should extend for at least two years before the program is inaugurated. Teachers, students, and parents must be fully ready for the transition.

7. Identification of various learning groups and the establishment of a differentiated learning process can take more time and effort than grouping students traditionally by year in school.

8. Not all students feel secure in, or can profit from, unscheduled class time. Special counseling and supervision of these students is needed. [4, pp. 14–15]

Variety in content and method

"Something old, something new, something fun" expresses important principles of planning for physical education. In other words, there should be in almost every class period (1) a review or use of what has been learned, (2) the introduction of a new concept or activity, and (3) some game or play element that is enjoyable and will cause class members to want to continue it.

The activities of physical education are many and varied. They call for many different approaches to teaching. The methods applied to learning basic movement fundamentals may not be appropriate to teaching advanced students working on the parallel bars. Problem solving may be an excellent method for classes in movement education but inadequate for teaching zone defense in basketball. The traditional methods of conducting a class in ballet are unsuitable for teaching mimetics. And a good teacher would not utilize the same methods for teaching scuba diving and badminton. Planning must consider the kind of activity and the level of the students.

Readiness

Complete preparation for a class includes several different kinds of readiness. The students must be adequately developed physiologically, motivated psychologically, and prepared by previous learning for the subject matter and activities scheduled. In addition, the physical arrangements must be completed. When the teacher is prepared and confident, the equipment in place, the courts or the fields marked, and the class eager to begin, the probability of an excellent learning experience is high.

Preparation for class

Preparing for a class is more than just planning. It included (1) checking to see that facilities are ready, (2) arranging for transporting needed equipment to the teaching station, and (3) assuring that the teacher is prepared intellectually and physically for his role. Boundary lines may need to be laid down, hurdles set up, nets tightened and set in place, cones arranged for relays, testing stations prepared, judges enlisted, equipment checked for safety, etc.

Student involvement

Even though the above does not preclude the involvement of students in the planning process, it does not indicate either that the teacher should come to class on a given day with no plan in mind and proceed on the "Well, class, what shall we do today" principle. *When students come to a gymnasium they want action.* Many potentially good physical education classes have been ruined by spending the first twenty or thirty minutes sitting in a corner talking. It is possible to meet as a class outside regularly scheduled periods. Such meetings can be utilized for planning purposes. Rainy days, examination weeks, and days when physical education facilities are not available can be used for group discussion and planning.

A more common method of involving class members is to have class representatives elected by the group. These representatives may or may not be the squad or team leaders. In any event they meet periodically with the teachers to help with the planning.

17.3 CLASS MANAGEMENT AND TEACHING METHODS

While each activity requires its own special methods of instruction, there are many commonalities among them. The attitude of the teacher, the atmosphere of the classroom, the interrelationships among students and teachers, and the motivational factors of the students are part of all methods. The method of presentation, the specific activity of each student, the techniques of reinforcement, the drills utilized, and the opportunities for self-expression, creativity, and spontaneity are other factors related to actual teaching methods. These and others will be discussed in the following subsections.

Perceptual-motor learning

Voluntary motor learning cannot take place without perception. For the purposes of this section, therefore, motor learning is perceptual-motor learning. It is true, however, that most nervous integration and organization occur in the early years of life and that perceptual-motor *development,* which is stimulated by movement experiences, takes place in the preschool and early elementary years.

Alan Canonico has written a cogent article entitled "Sequential Development in Early Perceptual-Motor Learnings" in which he presents his views and ideas concerning perceptual-motor programs. He outlines the skill progressions he would use to help students deficient in *gross motor skills, eye-hand coordination, form perception,* and *ocular pursuits.* He presents a suggested plan for a skill progression without equipment. He describes a sequence of activities using small equipment such as yarn balls, beanbags, hula hoops, and tires. His presentation suggests a series of perceptual-motor progressions which may be used to individualize physical education opportunities for children.*

---

*Alan Canonico, *Physical Education Perspective,* Old Saybrook, Conn.: Physical Education Publications, December 1973.

In a program such as the one identified above, the early perceptual-motor learnings would be both preventive and remedial in nature. There would be opportunities for all the children to develop perceptual-motor skills. While a rigid sequence has not always proven beneficial, there should be a logical progression, one skill leading to the next.

When teaching locomotor skills (walking, hopping, leaping, jumping, running, skipping, galloping, and sliding), teachers can use verbal cues, musical instruments, whistles, hand signals, and other means of indicating what the movement shall be. Working in pairs imitating each other, practicing in front of mirrors, mimicking figures on transparencies or film, and moving freely and creatively are all methods which stimulate and motivate.

In a program of sequential skill development using small equipment, there is limitless opportunity for creativity and ingenuity, both on the part of the children and on the part of the teacher. Progression should be from simple to complex. Emphasis should be on developing manipulative skills as well as balance, throwing and catching, eye-hand and eye-foot coordinations, and skills which can be utilized in more advanced sports and games. Methods cannot be stereotyped because there is an infinite number of ways these activities can be taught and learned. There should be considerable flexibility and freedom, with the instructor serving as guide, counselor, and helper rather than as director and commander.

Problem solving

In recent years, there has been a resurgence of interest and practice in learning through problem solving. What one learns through individual discovery is more meaningful and will be retained longer than what one learns from being told. Students are generally more highly motivated when searching for a solution to a problem than when merely completing an assignment. This of course infers that the problem is meaningful to them.

The question has been raised as to whether this method is appropriate to learning physical education. There are two answers: (1) There are many cognitive learnings in physical education which are amenable to the same methods as are other academic subjects, (2) In learning motor skills, an understanding of concepts and principles is necessary. Many of these skills may also be learned through problem solving and self-discovery.

In striving for excellence in performance, the athlete is constantly seeking to discover in what way he is doing something wrong and how he can improve. This is problem solving of the highest order. Analyzing kinesiological principles, applying physiological knowledge, and utilizing motivational concepts in an attempt to improve performance involve gathering facts, organizing data, choosing alternatives, and making decisions. Some form of problem solving is part of almost all physical education except where the command-response technique is exclusively used.

The problem solving method encourages creativity, reflective thinking, and self-direction. It permits greater individual freedom and elicits varied spontaneous

"Children in the lower elementary school need to run, chase, climb, and swing." (Courtesy of the *Journal of Health, Physical Education, and Recreation.*)

responses. It can be utilized together with other methods or by itself. It lends itself to teaching many individual sports as well as group activities.

Movement exploration (educational gymnastics)

Movement exploration is a version of problem solving (see also Chapter 10). The term is most appropriately applied to methods of teaching basic fundamentals of movement by asking the students a question or presenting a challenge and then requiring them to respond in their own way. Liselott Diem has presented her version of this method in a delightful book entitled *Who can . . . ?*. This method is used in elementary schools in Germany with a great deal of success. When the child is asked to perform a task, he is not told how to do it. [23, pp. 8–47] The following six questions are examples of how the teacher issues the challenges:

> "Squat down. Who can take big steps forward with knees bent and keep his back straight?"
> "Partial handstand with kicking. Who can keep his feet in the air for the longest time? Who can kick the most often?"
> "We run forward while skipping rope. Who can do it while running in a circle? Try running backward!"

"In a program of sequential skill development . . . there is limitless opportunity for creativity and ingenuity . . ." (Courtesy of the *Journal of Health, Physical Education, and Recreation.*)

"Bounce up and down—spring in the air. Who can spin all the way around before landing again?"

"On the horizontal ladder we travel with hands and feet. And now we swing to and fro, while swinging try to stretch out to reach for the next rung! Who can keep his feet together while swinging?"

"We roll the hoop straight forward—around in a circle—and backward. Who can run faster than the hoop, who can run around it and immediately drive it on?" [23, pp. 8–47]

Movement exploration is concerned with more than just learning fundamental movement skills. It has to do with discovering the various kinds of movement and the range of movement of which the human organism is capable. The satisfactions that come through expressing oneself freely through movement, the love of moving for the sake of moving, and the creativity that is developed by permitting the students to move in their own way are outcomes which are sought through this methodology.

The direct method

In the traditional or direct method of teaching, the teacher plans the lesson, explains the correct method of performing, demonstrates the movement (or has a skilled class member demonstrate), and then asks the students to attempt the stunt or perform the skill. Errors are identified and corrections noted. Further trials and repeated attempts generally result in improved performance. When performances become fairly satisfactory, drill continues on important fundamentals in order to automatize the movement for later recall in a game situation. Corrections and instruction in a given fundamental may continue throughout the unit and even for years depending on the complexity and degree of excellence required.

The part, the whole, and the felt-need method
If one observes a large number of physical education classes and athletic practice sessions, one will probably see students drilling over and over on movements and fundamentals which are part of a motor pattern or a highly organized game. One will also observe classes in which most of the time is spent playing soccer, touch football, softball, field hockey, water polo, and volleyball with little or no emphasis on the fundamentals or the movement parts. During one period of history in the development of physical education, one of the hotly debated issues was the *part method* of teaching versus the *whole method*. Which is right?

A synthesis of research evidence and the observations and experiences of veteran teachers and coaches lead to the following conclusions:

1. It takes a judicious mixture of both the part and the whole method to produce the greatest learning.

2. For the sake of understanding and motivation, students should know the purpose of fundamental drills, or the learning of parts, and should comprehend fully the context in which they are to be used. For this reason students should be introduced to the entire act or the complete game before they are asked to drill on the parts.

3. There are limits to what students and athletes can grasp at any given time. The amount of learning expected should not exceed what they can comprehend.

4. The performance of a given act or an individual's play in a game is limited by his greatest weakness. When a weakness is discovered special practice to correct it should be scheduled.

5. For understanding and reacting quickly in play situations, participants must spend hours practicing and scrimmaging. The whole method is indispensable for this purpose.

6. The more mature, the more experienced, and the older the students are, the greater should be the portion of practice time spent on the whole method.

7. The more intelligent, the more highly motivated, and the richer the background of the learners, the more the emphasis should be on the whole method.

8. When a movement is so complex that the learner cannot comprehend it as a whole, it must be broken down and each part practiced individually. Advanced dance and gymnastic routines are examples. On the other hand, some motor skills which require continuous movement and a special rhythm can only be practiced in their entirety (shooting free throws, fancy dives, long jump).

9. For efficient learning, students should work at the highest level of their achievement. Some "forgetting" does occur, however, and most great coaches constantly review and drill on important fundamentals.

10. There is a limit to the number of things a person can intensely concentrate on at a given time. For this reason the whole method must occasionally be abandoned.

The author has used the terms "whole" and "felt-need" method in much of his recent teaching of pedagogical principles. Common sense and good judgment suggest that in most circumstances the students should be oriented to the whole situation at the beginning of a new unit. When it becomes obvious that practice on fundamentals or parts is needed, appropriate provision shall be made in the lesson plans. The whole and the part methods will alternate as a *felt need* appears. In this way the student learns the entire activity, makes corrections, eliminates weaknesses, and is motivated to practice the parts where need is apparent.

Directed play

Children in the lower two or three grades of elementary school will enjoy and benefit by activities and procedures often described as *directed play.* This is a method which is appropriate for games of low organization or for individual and group play with simple equipment. Such equipment may be brought from home (marbles, hoops, scooters, pogo sticks, dolls, tops, etc.) or may be furnished by the school (beanbags, balls, ropes, Indian clubs, etc.). Directed play may consist of familiar games of low organization such as Beater Goes Round, Snatch the Bacon, Pom Pom Pullaway, Cross-tag, or Farmer in the Dell. Games may also be improvised by the children themselves or in group discussions guided by the teacher.

E. Benton Salt, Grace Fox, and B. K. Stevens have identified four progressive steps as a way of bringing children to the point where they are sufficiently socialized and competent to initiate the proper procedures and begin playing:

1. Children raise their hands if they have an activity they would like to play. One of the children is called upon to explain his game. He gets his equipment, finds a suitable place, and is joined by those who wish to play his game. Another child is selected to lead another game and the same procedure is repeated until all are playing.

2. This is a repetition of step one but is simplified so as to speed up the process. As soon as a child raises his hand and names his game, those who wish to play join him and they go off to get their equipment, find a place and start playing.

3. This step presents a more difficult social situation. The children (a) decide what they want to play, (b) find those who wish to play with them, and (c) form their groups at the play areas, choose their leader, get their equipment and start playing.

4. When children become able to start their play and organize without regulatory controls, they immediately form their play groups, get their equipment, and start playing. There is little or no assistance by the teacher. [71, pp. 105–107]

Obviously there needs to be some instruction at the beginning of directed play. Some safety regulations, standards of conduct, and rules concerning leaving and entering groups are necessary. Appropriate distances between groups must be established. Signals for assembling and giving the teacher attention must be understood and obeyed. The care and use of equipment must be regulated. The basic principle is to give the children as much freedom and responsibility as possible by keeping the regulations to a minimum and at the same time provide enough guidance and leadership to prevent classes from becoming too chaotic.

Teaching sports

The foundation for good performance in sports is laid when learning the basic fundamentals of movement. Walking, running, jumping, throwing, striking, dodging, tumbling, and balancing are the basic motor patterns on which manipulative movements and fine skills are built. If there are flaws in the basic locomotor and balancing skills, it is difficult to become a good performer in sports.

High skill levels go beyond the ability to run, jump, throw, and catch. Fine manipulative skills become automatized, several basic movements combine to form complex patterns, and the organism learns to react to certain cues.

Beyond automatizing motor patterns and reacting to cues, one needs to learn the tactics and strategy of the various games so that one is able to choose the most effective action in a given situation. Beyond tactics and strategy are the psychological and spiritual aspects of the game which enhance performance and assist the athlete to reach his potential.

In teaching sports to beginners, one must avoid bringing the students along too fast and extending their practice periods too long. Youngsters will expend extra energy in extraneous movements and will not be able to carry out detailed performance for great lengths of time.

Basic to learning motor skills are (1) a clear perception of the task, (2) trial performances by the learner, (3) feedback indicating the success, or lack of it, in each trial, and (4) practice on the corrected techniques.

The perception of the task may result from demonstrations, films, directions from the teacher, and written descriptions of correct performance. Feedback will come through kinesthetic responses, videotapes, analysis of the performance by the instructors, and observation of the success of the attempt.

As athletes become more mature and as they see and accept the need for improvement, there can be additional drill on fundamentals and parts of complex games. Finally there must be a great deal of practice on the complete game (e.g., soccer or field hockey) or the entire act (e.g., free exercise in gymnastics or the butterfly in swimming).

Coaches are great students of the best methods of teaching sports. Observation and study of their practices, lectures, and writings are recommended for those who wish to be successful in that aspect of the profession.

Task method

When utilizing the *task method*, the students accept a series of sequentially arranged tasks which they try to perform in the course of a season or a unit of time.

The tasks are selected so as to challenge the beginning, the ordinary, and the talented student. A task may consist of a series of tumbling stunts arranged from the easiest to the most difficult, a given number of free throws to be made out of fifty attempts, jumping a given distance or height, running a quarter mile in a certain number of seconds, attaining a certain score on a front dive, or scoring a given number of field hockey goals in ten attempts (with or without a goalie).

A task may also consist of discovering one's best technique for performing a given event or the shortest time one can negotiate a mountain trail. There could be a combination of tasks utilizing a variety of skills from gymnastics, tennis, swimming, track, and other sports. Records should be kept of practices, trials, and completions. The progress of each individual will be noted.

Circuits

The circuit method (see Chapter 4) can be utilized either indoors or outdoors and for a wide variety of activities. In physical fitness programs, it has been used extensively for testing, for movement education, and for weight-training classes.

In this method various activity stations are arranged in a circuit. These stations may be in a gymnasium, in a room, in a hallway, on a football field, on a track, or on a trail in the woods. The stations are numbered and each participant proceeds from one station to the next in a given order. Instructions may be placed at each station or a teacher posted who will have charge of the activity at a given station. In a circuit with six activity stations, a class of thirty might be divided into groups of five at each station to begin the exercise or take the test. Figure 17.2 is an example of a possible circuit for fitness development.

Weight training

Weight training was mentioned above as one of the activities where a circuit might well be used; it is also an activity in which there are some special considerations as to method. A distinction should be made between weight *training* and weight *lifting.* Weight lifting is generally thought of as a competitive sport in which the goal is to develop the technique and power to lift or "snatch" a greater weight than any other competitor. Weight training, on the other hand, has as its goal the optimal development of an individual's body both from a health and an aesthetic standpoint. Weight lifting is seldom part of a physical education program in schools; weight training is often included in a physical education program.

Weight training does not seek to build big bulging muscles but rather smooth, well-proportioned, moderately-sized muscles having considerable endurance. In weight-training classes, the number of repetitions for each event (pressing, curling, rowing, squat-lifting, etc.) is of the order of ten to fifteen, while in weight lifting it will be one to five. A program employing maximum weights with few repetitions builds strength, power, and big muscles; one employing weights about two-thirds of maximum and which can be lifted ten to fifteen times builds endurance and only moderately large muscles.

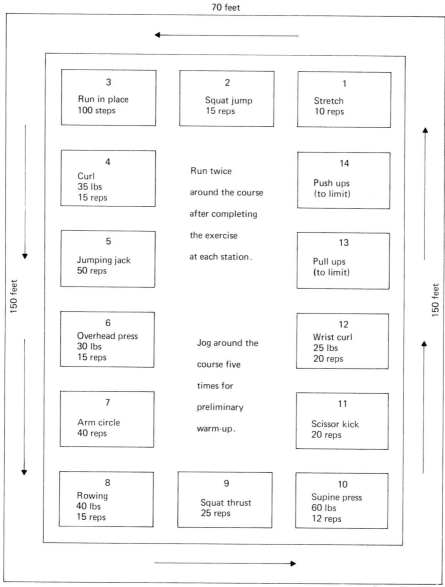

Figure 17.2 **Physical fitness circuit.** Resistance and repetitions must be adjusted for each individual.

Most weight-training classes will involve keeping individual daily records of weights lifted and the number of repetitions performed at each station. When there is enough gain in strength to lift the weight fifteen times, the weight will be increased. Weekly records of muscle girth are often kept and serve as a motivating factor.

Drill

Few people would insist that practice should be eliminated from all physical education programs. "Practice" and "drill" are almost synonymous; both terms imply repetitive performances of acts which individuals already know how to do. Drill is for overlearning, perfecting skills, and automatizing motor patterns. It is an important element in high-level skill learning. Until one can perform simple acts unconsciously and in response to certain cues, one cannot make decisions or think about what one should do in a given situation.

If drill is to be kept interesting and effective, teachers must adhere to certain principles of method:

1. Students should know why they are drilling. If they are practicing game fundamentals they should be made aware of how they fit into the total game.
2. The drills should provide for maximum participation for as many students as possible.
3. Drills should be made enjoyable. Whenever possible they should be performed in game-like situations.
4. Drills should be varied and not too long. They should, however, be continued until the students become aware that they are improving.
5. Instructors should be enthusiastic and helpful. They should move around and give individual advice and encouragement to as many as possible.
6. Drills should be followed by practical application in actual game situations.

Large group instruction

One of the major problems facing many physical educators is the fact that many classes are too large. In teaching large groups it is important that the instructor keep everyone involved. Active team games are useful for this purpose. Greyson Daughtrey and John Woods describe what they call the "Overflow Plan." This combines teaching the skills of individual sports with team games which involve many participants. While teachers work with only a few students in individual sports, the majority of the class is involved in playing volleyball, for example. By rotating groups all class members receive instruction and practice in both individual and team games. [21, p. 172] In basketball, the author has found that by utilizing baskets on the edges of the gymnasium for games of "4 on 4" or "5 on 5" and the space in the middle of the gymnasium for passing, pivoting, or defensive drilling, large groups can be kept busy.

Many of the methods outlined in this chapter can be utilized for large groups. Team teaching, using paraprofessionals and group leaders to help teach, and limited use of calisthenics are also possibilities.

The command method
While there has been considerable objection to the command method because of the military connotations, it is still widely used, often with considerable justification. An instructor can hardly tell class members what to do or ask them to practice a certain movement without giving some sort of command. Calisthenics and conditioning exercises can, however, be taught rhythmically and much less militarily than has sometimes been the case in the past.

It is still true that calisthenics provide more exercise to more people with fewer instructional personnel in less time and space than any other method. It is also true that it is necessary to give instructions to groups in many areas of life other than the military. Surgeons give commands to their assistants; the fire chief gives commands to the firemen; a quarterback gives commands to the football team; foremen give commands to their workers; and executives give commands to their employees. It is still important that people learn to accept and act upon instructions from those who are in positions of authority. A small amount of time for calisthenics, given with specific objectives in mind, often proves to be worthwhile.

Neither instruction nor command needs to be harsh, rude, or dictatorial. If students are respected as individuals and treated in the same manner, the "command method" has some advantages. June Walker and her coauthors have listed the following as advantages of this method:

1. *Ease of organization.* The teacher decides on the instruction and procedures which will lead to accomplishment of the goals.
2. *Economy of time.* The most direct route is taken to the goal. The teacher decides on and presents the "best" techniques which will lead to mastery of the skill.
3. *Clarity to students.* Students understand the expectations of the teacher as these are directly stated.
4. *Discipline and control.* If physical education classes are frequently overcrowded, this method—which is designed to control large numbers by using specific formations and drills—may be appropriate. [82, p. 119]

The command method has much in common with the direct method. It consists of instructing and explaining, demonstrating, correcting, and evaluating class activity and practice. A final critique in which the physical education period is analyzed and performances reviewed is recommended as a way to end the class period.

Programmed learning
Teaching traditional subject matter in schools through programmed learning has been long accepted as having a place in the educational scheme of things. It is just beginning to find a place in physical education. It appears to be most useful and appropriate in learning facts, principles, and theoretical material. In physical education, where the emphasis is on activity and neuromuscular skills, there is a

trend toward placing greater stress on knowledge and understanding. In view of this fact, it is time to consider seriously the use of programmed instruction in this and related subjects.

John Redd, Mildred Barnes, and Bruce Frederick list the advantages and disadvantages of programmed instruction in a booklet produced jointly by the Health Education and Physical Education Divisions of the American Association for Health, Physical Education, and Recreation. The following summarizes what they say:

Advantages

1. The immediate knowledge of success or failure serves as effective motivation.
2. Analyses of student responses tend to reduce errors.
3. Differences in learning capacities among students become less apparent.
4. Students can work at their own speed.
5. Slow learners, using programmed instruction, generally perform better than expected.
6. The immediate feedback and active responding enhances the students' retention.
7. Programmed instruction is one way of providing individualization in teaching.
8. Programmed instruction is economical in terms of learning time.

Disadvantages

1. There are too few programs available in health and physical education.
2. Programs are very expensive.
3. The time required to prepare a *good* program is enormous.
4. Too few publishers are willing to spend the money and time required to produce good materials. [2, pp. 38–41]

Programmed movement instruction is still in the experimental stage. Teaching motor skills does not lend itself readily to programming. The preparation of movement programs is tedious and expensive, and not all physical education teachers accept this method as an improvement over the traditional ones. Perhaps the most that can be said about programmed movement instruction is that advances are being made and it may become an important tool in the future.

Efforts to increase programs using factual and theoretical material should continue. Employed under appropriate circumstances, they are effective and economical of both space and personnel.

Team teaching

Harold Spears has effectively laid the foundation for an understanding of team teaching when he lists its common features.

1. A large group of students assigned to a team of teachers.
2. A curriculum block assigned as the area to be covered.
3. A block of time longer than the usual period provided for the work.
4. The provision within the program of class groups varying in size from exceedingly large to exceedingly small.
5. Freedom for the teachers to plan among themselves the flexible scheduling within the program that meets the instructional objectives of the moment.
6. The correlation of curriculum content naturally related. [77, pp. 8–9]

Team teaching is one way to improve instruction, to enable teachers to spend more time in the area of their speciality, to deal effectively with large classes, and to provide more adequately for individual differences among the students. Team teaching gives teachers the opportunity "to do for a large group those things they do best for a smaller group in a traditional class." [77, p. 31] Team teaching is equally applicable to physical education as to any other subject.

One of the best examples of team teaching is found in coaching a professional football team. The head coach (master teacher) must be a good leader and administrator and must know a good deal about the operation of the entire football team. He selects and engages a staff of specialists (end coach, defensive coach, kicking coach, quarterback coach, etc.) and gives each of them specialized teaching and supervisory responsibilities. Each specialist works in the area of greatest competency and interest. The entire staff meets, discusses, plans, organizes, and makes decisions. During the teaching periods (practices), the ends are taught by the end coach (specialist), the defensive backs by the defensive coach (specialist), and so on.

In physical education, team teaching can be considered in two ways. First, team teaching may involve four third-grade teachers, each in charge of a classroom of about twenty-five students. The four teachers are specialists in health, music, art, and physical education, respectively, each teaching his specialty to all the classes. This practice has been in vogue for many years but is not what is referred to as team teaching in the "new education."

Second, team teaching might consist of ten members of a physical education staff in a medium-sized high school. Two might be veteran teachers, one the director of physical education for boys and the other for girls. Two more might be experienced, one in dance and the other in aquatics. Because the director of the girls' program is a specialist in field hockey and tennis and the director of the boys' program is a specialist in soccer and baseball, they employ two highly qualified beginning teachers, one woman for girls' lacrosse and softball and one man for track, cross-country, wrestling, and football. Because there may not be enough money to employ two more fully qualified and certified teachers, four paraprofessionals are employed on a part-time basis. They are specialists in mountain climbing and skiing, bowling and horseback riding, canoeing and archery, and golf and camping, respectively. The staff now has the following composition.

Teachers	Specialities	Secondary skills
2 Masters		
1 Woman	Field hockey, tennis	Gymnastics
1 Man	Soccer, baseball	Paddle rackets, folk dance
2 Experienced		
1 Woman	Dance	Synchronized swimming
1 Man	Aquatics	Handball, squash
2 Inexperienced		
1 Woman	Lacrosse, softball	Basketball, volleyball
1 Man	Track, wrestling, football	Back-packing, tennis
4 Paraprofessionals		
1 Woman	Bowling, riding	Badminton
1 Woman	Canoeing, archery	Yoga
1 Man	Mountain climbing, skiing	Judo
1 Man	Golf, camping	Bike riding

Figure 17.3 Physical education staff (hypothetical).

Assuming there exists a team such as the above, modular scheduling, reasonably adequate facilities, access to lakes and mountains, and a supportive administration, the two directors could now meet and discuss preliminary plans. This should be followed by conferences with the principals and any other school personnel who would be involved. If all are cooperative, a series of staff meetings should be held to plan in detail the operation of team teaching. Needed time blocks must be established, registration procedures agreed upon, teaching assignments made, and organizational details carefully worked out.

Team teaching in physical education should employ the following general principles:

1. Large classes composed of students with diverse interests and somewhat heterogeneous abilities would assemble in one place.
2. A master teacher would explain the plan of operation, the choice of activities, and registration procedures.
3. Students would choose activities in accordance with policies established for selection.
4. Students would meet with the specialist in charge of the activity they chose.
5. Students would proceed with their instructor to the appropriate teaching station.

6. Class organization and instruction would begin as quickly and efficiently as possible.
7. There would be regular meetings of the staff to iron out details, evaluate the program, coordinate the operation, and plan for the next term or period.

Lecture

The lecture method of teaching has both opponents and proponents. It has its place and is appropriate to certain educational situations but its excessive use is fraught with a number of hazards. There is no question that a great deal of information can be presented in a given amount of time through a well-organized and thoroughly prepared lecture. But it is also true that often the information is presented too rapidly and too uninterestingly for much absorption by the class.

When students come to a gymnasium or other activity station for a physical education class they are prepared psychologically for action. A prolonged lecture by the teacher is usually self-defeating. Unless the lecture material is exceptionally interesting or is accompanied by some meaningful audiovisual materials, students soon become bored and close their minds to what is being said. It is therefore inadvisable to use the lecture method to any great extent in classes which are expected to be filled with activity.

In professional preparation and basic instruction programs where related knowledge and understanding are emphasized, some lectures are appropriate. It is important that such lectures are well prepared and organized, that they are clearly presented, and that they are related to the objectives and expectations of the students. It should also be remembered that the span of the students' attention is directly proportional to the degree of their maturity, and that there should be little lecture in the elementary school and junior high school physical education classes.

Group process

While not suitable for all situations and while it can be easily overdone, the group process is useful and effective when appropriately employed. Class involvement in setting program goals, in establishing rules for class behavior and dress, in formulating codes of sportsmanship, and in planning special events is strongly recommended. Class discussions regarding these topics can be carried on either inside or outside the regular class periods. Such group discussions serve to solidify group feeling, increase cooperation in achieving class goals, augment mutual helpfulness, and give class members a feeling of participation and involvement in the planning and conduct of the program.

If group discussions are to prove constructive and worthwhile, there should be a real problem to solve, a goal to achieve, and reasonable participation by all. The teacher will tactfully step in when necessary, but will avoid taking over the direction of the class except when absolutely necessary. A domineering or superior attitude on the part of the instructor in charge can destroy the rapport which is so necessary in the group process. The atmosphere should be friendly and casual, though not disorderly. A good class leader will usually emerge or be selected by the group. Care should be exercised so that the conversation is not monopolized by one or two people. Alternatives and their consequences should be presented. Sensitivity to individual reaction is essential. The teacher should keep in mind the direction in which the discussion should go and should tactfully interject at the appropriate moment a bit of information or the likely consequences of a decision. Input from an experienced person is particularly helpful if the discussion bogs down. The use of discussion leaders, recorders, and outside resource people is frequently very helpful.

The group discussion should end in the solution of a problem or at least advancement toward that goal. When consensus is achieved it should be understood that the class accepts this decision. Action should follow at that point.

The group discussion method is recommended for planning demonstrations, picnics and outings of all descriptions, playdays, track meets, synchronized swimming exhibitions, dance programs, and awards assemblies. It can also be used to plan events where a number of classes cooperate on any other large-scale project.

Audiovisual aids

It has been said that one picture is worth a thousand words. Educators have stated in lectures and in books that good teachers will appeal to as many senses as possible in order to stimulate their students to learn. There is no question that correctly used audiovisual aids are an important adjunct to the teacher who desires to make instruction interesting and motivating.

There are many kinds of audiovisual aids. Anything that is a planned part of a learning experience and can be seen or heard can be classified as an audiovisual aid.

Charts	Bulletin boards
Tables	Blackboards
Diagrams	Magnetic boards
Transparencies	Posters
Motion pictures	Pictures
Film strips	Models
Slides	Records
Videotapes	Opaque projectors
Television programs	Demonstrations
Loop films	Games
Audiotapes	Contests
Nature studies	Community resources

Audiovisual aids are helpful in the following ways:

1. They help the learners achieve a clear perception of the task.
2. They provide the learners with feedback or knowledge of results.
3. They assist in motivating students to learn.
4. They provide a record of performance which may be reviewed.
5. They help to clarify tactics and strategies.

6. They reinforce the instructions of a teacher or coach.
7. Often they save time.
8. They furnish a method of giving information to a large group at one time.
9. They can furnish music for classes in dance or other rhythmic activities.
10. They provide opportunities to hear and see great performances and concerts which otherwise would be unavailable to the student.
11. They provide a method of passing on pertinent information to the public.
12. They furnish a method of calling students' attention to important events and discoveries.
13. They serve as a way of emphasizing points in a lecture or class discussion.
14. They provide a constructive way of teaching physical education on days when outdoor teaching stations are not usable due to inclement weather.
15. They break the monotony of lectures and discussions.
16. They illustrate rules and interpretations of sports, contests, and games.
17. They provide a method of recording a student teacher's performance for review with the supervisor.

While audiovisual aids furnish an important tool in teaching, they can be a handicap in the hands of a lazy or negligent teacher. Teachers who use films as a way of avoiding preparing lessons, who merely show films without appropriate introduction or followup, who absent themselves from class while a film is being shown, or who use audiovisual aids for any purpose except to enhance learning are not being faithful to their educational responsibilities.

There are many excellent sources of audiovisual materials. The following are suggested:

Athletic Institute
805 Merchandise Mart
Chicago, Illinois 60654

The American Association for Health, Physical Education, and Recreation
1201 Sixteenth Street, N.W.
Washington, D.C. 20036

NEA Publication Sales
1201 Sixteenth Street, N.W.
Washington, D.C. 20036

American Association for Elementary, Kindergarten, and Nursery Education
1201 Sixteenth Street, N.W.
Washington, D.C. 20036

National Instructional Television Center
Box A
Bloomington, Indiana 47401

Educational Motion Pictures, Inc., E. Gross
550 Fifth Avenue
New York, New York 10003

U.S. Olympic Development Committee
Olympic House
57 Park Avenue
New York, New York 10016

Universal Education and Visual Arts
221 Park Avenue South
New York, New York 10003

Documentary Films
3217 Trout Gulch Road
Aptos, California 95003

Film Associates
11559 Santa Monica Blvd.
Los Angeles, California 90025

President's Council on Physical Fitness and Sports
Washington, D.C. 20201

The list of motion pictures, film strips, and other audiovisual resources contained on pages 101 to 105 of *Promising Practices in Elementary School Physical Education* is strongly recommended. This booklet is available from The American Alliance for Health, Physical Education, and Recreation at the address listed above.

There should be careful selection and evaluation of the audiovisual aids employed. The lessons in which they are used should be as carefully planned as any other. Generally speaking, these aids should be thought of as enhancing and illustrating the subject matter, not as a substitute for such subject matter.

Teachers and coaches who use audiovisual aids generally find that they work long and hard to locate materials, coordinate them with the subject matter of the course, care for them properly, and mail them back to their source. If they are used as they should be, audiovisual aids can be a tremendous help in motivating the students and enhancing their learning.

Class movement and formations
In the formalized physical education of the early part of the twentieth century, it was customary to teach marching tactics to the students. Movement from one place to another as well as forming for calisthenic exercises was accomplished by the command-response process. In today's physical education, teaching marching tactics, especially military drill maneuvers, has almost disappeared from the programs.

One of the best ways to accomplish the movement of a class and its arrangement into formations is to require class members to memorize the following formations (see Figure 17.4).

a) Group formation
b) Circle formation
c) Team (or squad) formation
d) Line formation
e) Pair formation
f) Zig-zag formation
g) Calisthenic formation
h) Game formation

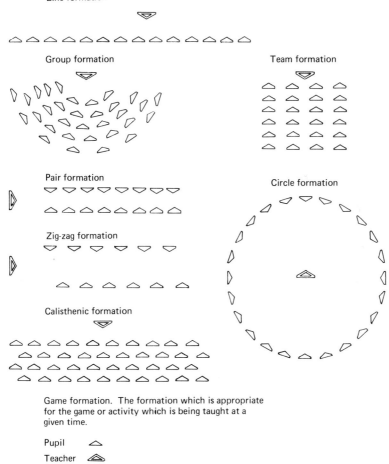

Game formation. The formation which is appropriate
for the game or activity which is being taught at a
given time.

Figure 17.4 Class formations.

Each of these formations can be by teams or by group. If the teacher calls out "pair formation by teams," each team will form in pairs facing each other. If the teacher says "group circle formation," the entire group or class will form a large circle, each student running to his respective position.

The first day of each year or term can include in its plan a little practice forming teams or groups as rapidly as possible. The tempo should be fast but not chaotic or tense. A quick, accurate response to the teacher's or team leader's call is all that is needed.

The author has found this practice efficient and one to which the students readily adapt. It is apparent that there are activities and situations where none of these formations are suitable. It is, of course, also possible to add other formations to the ones indicated in Figure 17.4.

Presentation

Assuming that a physical education teacher knows the subject matter thoroughly, is familiar with the various methods of teaching and when to apply them, and is motivated to be a good teacher, there are still some things to be learned which will be helpful. The way the teacher presents himself and the way he presents the material to be learned determine his effectiveness as a teacher. The teacher's interpersonal relationships with the students and how they feel toward him are also important factors.

It has been said that any person can draw an invisible barrier between the one who is speaking and himself as a listener. If a student perceives the teacher as an antagonist, as an insincere or hypocritical person, or as someone who has treated him unfairly, he is apt to form such a barrier. In such cases communication does not occur because both an adequate sender and an open receiver do not exist.

Each teacher is an individual personality as is each student. It is improbable that a teacher will be equally respected or liked by all. Nevertheless teachers should try to keep all the lines of communication open. It is possible for teachers to be effective if they are respected for what they have to offer even if they are not especially popular.

The author has had the opportunity to evaluate teachers at a number of institutions. In general, the following characteristics are present in the outstanding teachers:

1. The teacher is able to make every individual feel important.
2. The teacher is able and willing to give of himself without hesitation to help his students.
3. The teacher presents an aura of "we-ness," or sharing, as he works together with students in achieving their common goals.
4. The teacher is patient and obviously tries to help those who have problems. All class members appreciate this quality even if it does not affect them.
5. The teacher is willing to give his out-of-class time to help the students.

6. The teacher is buoyant, cheerful, and possesses a sense of humor. Students generally respond to this when in class.
7. The teacher is fair and impartial.
8. The teacher is warm and compassionate, yet consistent and firm.

Obviously the level and type of class will have a great deal to do with the spirit which one should try to engender. An advanced class in exercise physiology, a basketball coaching course, a class in skiing, and an elementary class in educational gymnastics would each require different kinds of presentations and a slightly different type of personality. And yet the qualities listed above are valid for each situation.

The techniques and methods used in the presentations are also important. An introductory course which has been carefully planned and is well presented can be quite motivating. The instructor's obvious interest in the subject is contagious and stimulating.

In academic subjects one is always faced with the decision as to how closely one shall follow a prescribed plan. The terms "logical method" and "psychological method" have been used to distinguish between close adherence to a sequentially planned outline of subject matter and a "let the discussion carry us where it will" procedure, respectively. The logical method is generally more efficient, better organized, and leaves fewer gaps uncovered. The psychological method often engenders livelier discussion and greater motivation. It is probably best to strike a happy medium between the two. Certainly some adherence to an orderly outline is necessary and a logical progression of subject matter is essential. On the other hand there is considerable evidence that people learn faster and better when highly motivated. The significance of this cannot be overlooked.

When presenting skills to be learned, it is essential that the learners have a clear perception of the task. All forms of communication can be used. Usually more than one is recommended—verbal explanations, physical demonstrations, audiovisual presentations, and self-activity. Individuals who themselves are able to perform a stunt easily may well have difficulty appreciating the fact that beginners need considerable help in perceiving the task clearly.

Maximum student participation is especially important in physical education. The principle of "learning by doing" is particularly applicable. "Getting the feel" of a movement is a kinesthetic reality and a significant part of motor learning.

Meaningful repetition and drill is important in high-level motor learning. The automatization which is necessary before one can become a skilled athlete necessitates drill and more drill. The individuation that may be required to eliminate extraneous movements and perfect performance of segments of complex acts is also important. Student participation is the key to good physical education classes where motor skills are to be learned.

The general rules for effective public speaking are important to all physical educators. Good voice projection, clear enunciation, careful organization, and a good command of the language are communication skills for which all physical educators should strive.

17.4 PEDAGOGICAL PRINCIPLES AND GUIDELINES

1. A good teacher will know many teaching methods as well as how and where to use them.

2. Programmed instruction is more appropriate for theory courses than for skills courses.

3. There are so many different types of subject matter in physical education that a variety of methods is needed. Methods must relate to the established objectives of the lesson.

4. The group process is suitable for discussions about problems and plans which arise in connection with physical education programs.

5. It is important that each student experiences some success. Tasks must be selected with this goal in mind.

6. Each student must be accepted for what he is, even though approval cannot be given to some of his actions.

7. Insofar as possible, a climate should be provided where there is freedom from stress, tension, threat, and fear.

8. The good teacher will respect the right of each individual to be different.

9. The outstanding teacher will try to find out as much as possible about each student's home environment.

10. Activities must have meaning in order to contribute to the overall education of the students. Teachers must help students discover these meanings.

11. Fun and joy are important in the lives of everyone. This shall be considered when plans are formulated.

12. Individual goals as well as group goals are important.

13. Physiological, psychological, and sociological readiness shall be considered when programs and lessons are being planned.

14. The more closely outcomes coincide with objectives and goals, the higher the program should be evaluated.

15. Activities in physical education should satisfy both present needs and those of later life. These goals are not mutually exclusive but can be achieved by a well-planned program.

16. Every student needs to feel that he "belongs." The teacher can work with students so that all assist in bringing this about.

17. There must be enough vigorous, sustained activity to develop physical fitness. Running, circuit training, calisthenics, and vigorous sports will accomplish this.

18. Physical education teachers must not try to make "miniature adults" out of children. Each age and grade level must be understood and treated appropriately.

19. The teacher selects activities, creates a suitable environment, and teaches the student as well as the subject matter.

20. Reinforcement of desired behavior is an effective method of teaching and learning. However, not all students are reinforced by the same treatment. What the students consider pleasurable must be ascertained.

21. Teachers must assist students using language they understand. Information or other "helps" which are beyond their comprehension are to no avail.

22. Handicapped and inept performers should be involved in the program whenever possible. Tasks which they can accomplish should be given to them.

23. Particularly in the early years, time should be provided in physical education classes to run, jump, roll, turn sommersaults, and "tear around" for the sheer joy of moving. This is a basic drive of children.

". . . in the early years, time should be provided . . . to run, jump, roll, turn somersaults, and 'tear around' for the sheer joy of moving." (Courtesy of the *Journal of Health, Physical Education, and Recreation.*)

24. When classes are divided into teams or squads, methods should be used which do not embarrass any of the students. "Choosing up"* should not be used.

25. When partners are needed all participants should be paired on some basis which does not single anyone out as being unwanted. People who are inferior in

---

*"Choosing up" refers to the time-worn practice of asking two students to choose their team members. They either flip a coin for first choice or use another method to determine who chooses first. It can be devastating for those who time after time are among the last to be chosen.

ability or otherwise handicapped are too easily embarrassed already and further emphasis on their weaknesses is defeating.

26. Activities should be varied enough so that as many as possible have the opportunity to participate in an activity in which they can perform reasonably well.

27. Explanations and directions should be explicit and clear but not too "wordy." Students who are eager for activity dislike listening to too much talk.

28. Teachers should distinguish between noise growing out of purposeful activity and that which is rowdy and disruptive. The first is healthy; the latter is un-wholesome.

29. Teachers and coaches should be positive rather than negative in their in-structions. Students should be told what they should, rather than what they should not, do.

30. All teachers should be familiar with the art of questioning. Naming the student to respond at the end of the question is often a desirable technique to keep the attention of the entire class on the question. However the entire class should normally not be permitted to answer "all at once."

31. In the early learning stages, there should be little effort to arouse or excite the performer. The atmosphere should be casual, businesslike, pleasant, and encouraging. Too much arousal leads to less control of fine movements, neuro-muscular inhibitions, muscular tension, and less concentration on the task.

32. When correcting flaws in performance, a person can concentrate on only one thing at a time. The teacher should not call attention to several faults and expect a student to try to correct all of them at once.

33. Feedback and knowledge of results are important in motor learning. Au-diovisual aids, proprioceptive feedback, and criticisms by knowledgeable people are helpful.

34. Teachers and students should understand the basic principles of the learning curve, namely that periods of improvement alternate with periods where no ob-servable improvement occurs. This may well be the time when the learner is fixated at a given point because automatization and integration of motor patterns are taking place.

35. Long lines where students waste their time are *not* recommended. There should be enough exercise stations and the program should be organized in such a fashion that all of the students are active most of the time.

36. Ability grouping is essential if a class is to learn new skills and progress in competence. When the class is composed of students who are too heterogeneous in their ability to perform, the advanced students become bored and the inept become discouraged and lost.

37. In addition to general methods of teaching, there are special methods for each activity (basketball, gymnastics, dance, aquatics, etc.). Physical education teachers are responsible for knowing both general and special methods.

38. When beginning a new unit, instruction should start at the skill level of the group and progress in the direction of greater complexity and perfection of performance.

39. Learning generally occurs more readily and permanently when students are intrinsically motivated than when extrinsic incentives are employed.

40. Failure tolerance increases as students experience success. Confidence can be shattered when poor performances are criticized too harshly or in front of others.

41. "Learning by doing" is a sound principle of education. It is particularly applicable to motor learning.

42. Where transfer seems appropriate, students should be helped to generalize.

43. The central objective of learning a skill should be emphasized. Stressing too many details of a performance at one time or too early is confusing to the learner.

44. Kinesthetic perception and interpretation while learning skills should be encouraged. Students should be asked to "get the feel" of a movement.

45. Mental practice between sessions or trials has been found to increase learning and improve performance. Before it can be effective, the learner must have formed a reasonably accurate "percept" of the desired movement.

46. Teachers should let students know the basis for grading and exactly what is expected of them.

47. Paraprofessionals and part-time professionals should be oriented to the philosophy and goals of the physical education department.

48. A standard list of instructions should be prepared for substitute teachers. Prior planning will facilitate class procedures in cases where the regular teacher is absent.

49. If student or group leaders are utilized, they should be prepared by meetings with appropriate members of the faculty. Because they are not professionally trained, they need help in carrying out their responsibilities.

50. Each teacher must be himself. He must not imitate someone else. He can draw from all available sources to formulate his teaching philosophy and methods, but eventually he must develop his own. The methods he uses must be appropriate to his personality, the students he is teaching, and the subject matter he is presenting.

51. Many physical education activities differ markedly from academic subjects in one important respect—they require physical courage. Swimming, diving, handsprings, tackling, stunts, batting, and many other activities involve the possibility of physical injury. Teachers of these activities should carefully study the psychology of fear and deal with affected students accordingly.

SELECTED REFERENCES

1. American Association for Health, Physical Education, and Recreation, *Developing Democratic Human Relations*, first yearbook, Washington, D.C., 1951.
2. _____, *Programmed Instruction in Health Education and Physical Education*, Washington, D.C., 1970. By permission.
3. _____, *Promising Practices in Elementary School Physical Education*, Report of the Conference for Teachers and Supervisors of Elementary School Physical Education, Washington, D.C., 1968.
4. _____, *Organizational Patterns for Instruction in Physical Education*, Washington, D.C., 1971. By permission.
5. _____, *Tones of Theory*, Celeste Ulrich and John E. Nixon (coinvestigators), Washington, D.C., 1972.
6. Anderson, O. Roger, *Structure in Teaching: Theory and Analysis*, New York: Teachers College Press, 1969.
7. Andrews, Gladys, Jeannette Saurborn, and Elsa Schneider, *Physical Education for Today's Boys and Girls*, Boston: Allyn and Bacon, 1960.
8. Andrews, Thomas G., and Lee J. Cronbach, "Transfer of training," *Encyclopedia of Educational Research*, W. S. Munroe (ed.), revised edition, New York: The Macmillan Company, 1950.
9. Arnold, P. J., *Education, Physical Education, and Personality Development*, New York: Atherton Press, 1968.
10. Balassi, Sylvester J., *Focus on Teaching: An Introduction to Education*, New York: Odyssey Press, 1968.
11. Beggs, David W. (ed.), *Team Teaching*, Bloomington: Indiana University Press, 1964.
12. Bookwalter, Karl W., and Harold J. VanderZwaag, *Foundations and Principles of Physical Education*, Philadelphia: W. B. Saunders Company, 1969.
13. Boston, Robert E., *How to Write and Use Performance Objectives to Individualize Instruction*, Englewood Cliffs, N.J.: Educational Technology Publications, 1972.
14. Brown, Camille, and Rosalind Cassidy, *Theory in Physical Education*, Philadelphia: Lea and Febiger, 1963.
15. Clarke, H. Harrison, and Franklin B. Haar, *Health and Physical Education for the Elementary Classroom Teacher*, Englewood Cliffs, N.J.: Prentice-Hall, 1964.
16. Cogán, Max, "Innovative ideas in college physical education," *Journal of Health, Physical Education, and Recreation*, Vol. 44, No. 2, February 1973.
17. Cowell, Charles C., and Wellman L. France, *Philosophy and Principles of Physical Education*, Englewood Cliffs, N.J.: Prentice-Hall, 1963.
18. Cratty, Bryant J., *Developmental Sequences of Perceptual Motor Tasks*, Freeport, L.I., N.Y.: Educational Activities, 1967.
19. _____, *Movement, Perception and Thought*, Palo Alto: Peek Publications, 1969.
20. Dauer, Victor P., *Dynamic Physical Education for Elementary School Children*, Minneapolis, Minn.: Burgess Publishing Company, 1971.
21. Daughtrey, Greyson, and John B. Woods, *Physical Education Programs: Organization and Administration*, Philadelphia: W. B. Saunders Company, 1971.
22. Davis, Elwood C., and Earl L. Wallis, *Toward Better Teaching in Physical Education*, Englewood Cliffs, N.J.: Prentice-Hall, 1961.
23. Diem, Liselott, *Who Can . . . ?*, Frankfort, Germany: Wilhelm Limpert, 1964. By permission.
24. Driscoll, Sandra, and Doris A. Mathieson, "Goal-centered individualized learning," *Journal of Health, Physical Education, and Recreation*, September 1971.

25. *Educational Gymnastics,* London: London County Council, 1964.
26. Ellis, M., *Why People Play,* Englewood Cliffs, N.J.: Prentice-Hall, 1973.
27. Evans, Ruth, and Leo Gans, *Supervision of Physical Education,* New York: McGraw-Hill, 1950.
28. Evans, Ruth, et al. *Physical Education for Elementary Schools,* New York: McGraw-Hill, 1958.
29. Fait, Hollis F., *Physical Education for the Elementary School Child: Experience in Movement,* 2nd edition, Philadelphia: W. B. Saunders Company, 1971.
30. Flournoy, Don M., *The New Teacher,* San Francisco: Jossey-Bass, 1972.
31. Fox, Eugene R., and Barry L. Sysler, *Life-Time Sports for the College Student,* Dubuque, Iowa: Kendall/Hunt Publishing Company, 1972.
32. Freischlag, Jerry, "Competency based instruction," *Journal of Health, Physical Education, and Recreation,* Vol. 45, No. 1, January 1974.
33. Frost, Reuben B., *Psychological Concepts Applied to Physical Education and Coaching,* Reading, Mass.: Addison-Wesley Publishing Company, 1971.
34. _____, "Trends for the '70s," Paper presented to South Dakota Association for Health, Physical Education, and Recreation, October 1969.
35. Furth, Hans G., *Piaget for Teachers,* Englewood Cliffs, N.J.: Prentice-Hall, 1970.
36. Godfrey, Barbara B., and Newell C. Kephart, *Movement Patterns and Motor Education,* New York: Appleton-Century-Crofts, 1969.
37. Greenberg, Herbert M., *Teaching With Feeling: Compassion and Self-Awareness in the Classroom Today,* New York: The Macmillan Company, 1969.
38. Haslett, Jacqueline G., "Concepts on movement education," *Journal, Massachusetts Association for Health, Physical Education, and Recreation,* Vol. XVIII, No. 1, Fall 1972.
39. Hinderman, Lin M., et al., "Winterizing physical education," *Journal of Health, Physical Education, and Recreation,* November–December 1971.
40. Holt, John, *How Children Learn,* New York: Pitman Publishing, 1969.
41. Humphrey, James H., and Dorothy D. Sullivan, *Teaching Slow Learners through Active Games,* Springfield, Ill.: Charles C Thomas, 1970.
42. *Innovation in Education: New Directions for the American School,* A Statement on National Policy by the Research and Policy Committee of the Committee for Economic Development, New York, 1968.
43. Insley, Gerald S., *Practical Guidelines for the Teaching of Physical Education,* Reading, Mass.: Addison-Wesley Publishing Company, 1973.
44. Jewett, Ann E., "Would you believe public schools 1975?," *Journal of Health, Physical Education, and Recreation,* Vol. 42, No. 3, March 1971.
45. Jewett, Ann E., and Clyde Knapp (eds.), *The Growing Years,* Washington, D.C.: American Association for Health, Physical Education, and Recreation, 1962.
46. Kaufman, David A., "Taking the guesswork out of skill instruction," *Journal of Physical Education,* Vol. 71, No. 1, September–October 1973.
47. Kirchner, Glenn, *Physical Education for Elementary School Children,* 2nd edition, Dubuque, Iowa: Wm. C. Brown Company, 1970.
48. Kirchner, Glenn, Jean Cunningham, and Eileen Warrell, *Introduction to Movement Education,* Dubuque, Iowa: Wm. C. Brown Company, 1970.
49. Klappholz, Lowell A., "Preparing and using performance objectives," *Physical Education Newsletter,* Nov. 15, 1972.
50. Knapp, Clyde, and Patricia H. Leonard, *Teaching Physical Education in Secondary Schools,* New York: McGraw-Hill, 1968.

51. Kohl, Herbert R., *The Open Classroom,* New York: The New York Review, 1969.
52. Kozman, Hilda C., Rosalind Cassidy, and Chester Jackson, *Methods in Physical Education,* Philadelphia: W. B. Saunders Company, 1952.
53. Lawther, John D., *The Learning of Physical Skills,* Englewood Cliffs, N.J.: Prentice-Hall, 1968.
54. _____, "Motor learning at the high skill level," *Psicologia Dello Sport,* Proceedings of the First International Congress on Sport Psychology, Ferrucio Antonelli, Rome, 1965.
55. Leaf, Bess, et al., "Teaching physical education K–12: a workshop," *Journal of Health, Physical Education, and Recreation,* Vol. 44, No. 7, September 1973.
56. Leonard, George B., *Education and Ecstasy,* New York: Dell Publishing Company, 1968.
57. Lindgren, Henry C., *Educational Psychology in the Classroom,* New York: John Wiley and Sons, 1967.
58. Mosston, Muska, *Teaching Physical Education,* Columbus, Ohio: Charles E. Merrill, 1966.
59. Myers, Clayton R., Lawrence A. Golding, and Wayne E. Sinning, *The Y's Way to Physical Fitness,* Emmaus, Pennsylvania: Rodall Press, 1973.
60. Nations, Jimmy, "The changing elementary school," *Promising Practices in Elementary School Physical Education,* Washington, D.C.: American Association for Health, Physical Education, and Recreation, 1969.
61. Nyberg, David, *Tough and Tender Learning,* Palo Alto: National Press Books, 1971.
62. O'Shea, John P., *Scientific Principles and Methods of Strength Fitness,* Reading, Mass.: Addison-Wesley Publishing Company, 1969.
63. "Physical Education '73," *Instructor,* January 1973.
64. Piscopo, John, "Videotape laboratory: a programmed instruction sequence," *Journal of Health, Physical Education, and Recreation,* Vol. 44, No. 3, March 1973.
65. Puckett, John R., "Videotaping in physical education," *Journal of Physical Education,* Vol. 70, No. 6, July–August 1973.
66. Randall, Marjorie, *Basic Movement,* London: G. Bell and Sons, 1961.
67. Resick, Matthew C., Beverly L. Seidel, and James G. Mason, *Modern Administrative Practices in Physical Education and Athletics,* Reading, Mass.: Addison-Wesley Publishing Company, 1970.
68. Ritchey, John M., "Coeducational mountaineering," *Journal of Health, Physical Education, and Recreation,* Vol. 43, No. 8, October 1972.
69. Robb, Margaret, "Feedback," *Quest,* National Association of Physical Education for College Women and National College Physical Education Association for Men, Monograph VI, May 1966.
70. Ryan, Kevin, and James M. Cooper, *Those Who Can Teach,* Boston: Houghton Mifflin Company, 1972.
71. Salt, E. Benton, Grace I. Fox, and B. K. Stevens, *Teaching Physical Education in the Elementary School,* 2nd edition. Copyright © 1960, The Ronald Press Company, New York. By permission.
72. Schaible, Charles H., *The Systematic Training of the Body,* London: Trübner and Company, 1878.
73. Schurr, Evelyn L., *Movement Experiences for Children: Curriculum Methods for Elementary School Physical Education,* New York: Appleton-Century-Crofts, 1967.
74. Servis, Margery, and Reuben B. Frost, "Qualities related to success in women's physical education professional preparation program," *Research Quarterly,* Vol. 38, No. 2, May 1967.

75. Shockley, Joe M., Jr., "Needed: behavioral objectives in physical education," *Journal of Health, Physical Education, and Recreation,* Vol. 44, No. 4, April 1973.
76. Silvia, Charles E., *Manual and Lesson Plans for Basic Swimming, Water Stunts, Lifesaving, Springboard Diving, Skin and Scuba Diving,* Springfield, Mass.: published by the author, 1970.
77. Spears, Harold, *Team Teaching,* Bloomington: Indiana University Press, 1964.
78. Stockner, Joseph J., "Game theory—a cold class," *Journal of Health, Physical Education, and Recreation,* Vol. 44, No. 7, September 1973.
79. Tillotson, Joan S., "A brief theory of movement education," *Promising Practices in Elementary School Physical Education,* Washington, D.C.: American Association for Health, Physical Education, and Recreation, 1968.
80. Updyke, Wynn F., and Perry B. Johnson, *Principles of Modern Physical Education, Health and Recreation,* New York: Holt, Rinehart, and Winston, 1970.
81. Van Huss, Wayne, et al., *Physical Activity in Modern Living,* Englewood Cliffs, N.J.: Prentice-Hall, 1960.
82. Walker, June, et al., *Modern Methods in Secondary School Physical Education,* Boston: Allyn and Bacon, 1973. By permission.
83. Welford, A. T., *Fundamentals of Skill,* London: Methuen and Company, 1968.
84. Whiting, H. T. A., *Acquiring Ball Skill,* London: G. Bell and Sons, 1969.
85. Wilkinson, Robert E., "Effect of various motivational conditions upon boys of different age levels during muscular work," unpublished doctoral dissertation, Springfield College, Springfield, Mass., 1965.
86. Williams, Jesse F., *The Principles of Physical Education,* 6th edition, Philadelphia: W. B. Saunders Company, 1954.
87. Wirsing, Marie E., *Teaching and Philosophy: A Synthesis,* Boston: Houghton Mifflin Company, 1972.
88. Wyrick, Waneen, "Purposes and usefulness of balls in creating rhythmic exercises," *The Physical Educator,* Vol. 23, No. 3, October 1966.

Careers in Physical Education

Chapter 18

18.1 PATHWAYS TO SERVICE

For those who have ambitions to work with people in enjoyable and interesting activities, physical education offers many opportunities. If a person completes an educational program with a major in physical education and at least a bachelor's degree, he might be employed in one of the following capacities:

1. A physical education teacher in an elementary or secondary school.
2. A director or an instructor in a camp.
3. A coach of an athletic team.
4. A playground supervisor.
5. An instructor of physical activity for the handicapped.
6. A director of physical education in a social agency.

With a master's degree, and/or a doctorate, a physical educator might obtain a position as a professor in a college program, a supervisor of a physical education program, a director of athletics, or a teacher in a specialized and advanced subject-matter area. With additional specialization in health education, many additional opportunities would become available. There is also room in part-time or full-time research for a few professors with doctorates and extensive experience.

If one wishes to be of service to the crippled, injured, or otherwise handicapped, a person can find full-time employment in veterans' hospitals, mental hospitals, and other institutions for the emotionally, mentally, or physically impaired, by taking advanced work in physical, recreational, or occupational therapy. A large number of colleges have now made such advanced programs of study available.

Some students of physical education become full-time athletic trainers. The trend, however, is toward requiring a certified physical therapist for such positions.

After a few years, many who have entered the field of coaching are appointed to positions as athletic directors. There are now several institutions which offer special educational programs to prepare coaches for these administrative duties which are becoming more specialized year by year. The administration of professional athletics is also now being acknowledged as a specialty for which a planned course of educational preparation is needed. A few institutions are offering this training as an option in their physical education program.

Physical educators who have specialized in dance may find full-time positions teaching in this field. They also coach or direct their students in performances before the public. There is still some controversy as to whether the teaching of dance in colleges and universities should be housed in the department of performing arts or in the department of physical education.

Some students of physical education establish their own health and fitness "spas" or operate business enterprises in sports such as skiing, tennis, or golf. They teach the sport as well as run a "pro shop," administer the recreational program, and schedule the facilities. As leisure time increases for many people, such business ventures will become more necessary as well as more profitable.

Employment in social agencies is also quite common. The YMCA, YWCA, YMHA, YWHA, community centers, 4-H clubs, boys' and girls' clubs, and athletic clubs are examples of enterprises where experienced physical education directors are needed. Although the work force is made up of paraprofessionals employed to instruct in sports and supplemented by volunteers, persons with adequate professional preparation are needed in the administrative positions related to the physical fitness and sports programs.

While special training is required to become a full-fledged professional in the areas of recreation and health education, an individual who has completed the requirements for a degree in physical education is frequently asked to teach in both of these fields. Most physical education programs of study include courses in both health science, and recreation. It is often administratively feasible for physical education teachers to both schedule health courses and administer school recreation programs.

It is obvious that a physical educator is not confined to a narrow spectrum of duties. The activities are numerous and varied, the professional preparation is broad and deep, the challenges are plentiful and never-ending, and the opportunities for service are ever present.

18.2 EDUCATION IS THE WAY

There are moments in the life of every physical educator when he wonders if the hours spent studying and attending school have really been worthwhile. A person often feels that a course in Latin, French, philosophy, or mathematics may have been unnecessary and impractical; the research knowledge required of most doctoral candidates may not be used after the awarding of the degree. However, one often sees a recreation leader whose formal education terminated with the high school diploma and who is doing an excellent job of coaching a YMCA basketball team.

And yet education is the way! If we remember that education is a journey, not a destination, if we recall that education is defined as the sum of all modifications in the human organism which result from experience, if we think of the fact that education is a lifelong venture, and if we think for a moment about the many times one unexpectedly finds use for something learned in an almost forgotten subject, we realize that throughout our education we continually learn more and more about students, ourselves, and teaching.

Assuming that education is the answer, one asks "How much?," "What?," and "When?" A physical education teacher needs to be respected by those of his profession. He must be able to move comfortably in the atmosphere of educated people as well as among those who have not attended college. He must, in fact, be an educated person.

A person who is certified to teach physical education is a teacher. As such he needs to know how to teach. He must be familiar with both typical patterns of growth and development and individual deviations from those patterns. He should be well-versed in the principles of educational psychology. He must be able to speak intelligently about such diverse subjects as educational trends and prac-

446

African dancing
in the United
States . . .

. . . or high jumping in
Ghana—it's all
physical education.

"It is obvious that a
physical educator is
not confined to a
narrow spectrum of
duties." (Courtesy of
the *Journal of Health,
Physical Education,
and Recreation*.)

tices, personnel policies and contractual agreements, and the budget and the community tax base. In other words he should know what all teachers are expected to know about the topic of education—and a little bit more.

An individual who is graduating from college with a degree in physical education should also be well prepared in a number of physical skills. He ought to be expert in three or four skills and have an exposure to at least twenty of those most commonly taught. He should know how to prevent and care for injuries, how to teach and evaluate, how to prepare for teaching and present material, and how to build curricula and coordinate program aspects. He must also have learned the rudiments of administration, the principles of supervision, and something about physical education for the atypical student and the handicapped. He should be able to speak intelligently and with conviction about his philosophy of physical education, his goals and purposes, and the relationship of physical education to all other aspects of the school.

It is clear that there is much to learn before one is fully prepared for a career in physical education. It is also apparent that there is more than one way in which one can acquire the knowledge that he must have. A carefully planned educational experience is, however, the prerequisite to all others.

18.3 MEANING AND RELEVANCE

Education should have practical significance for the student. If education does not serve the student, it has failed its purpose. This has been made obvious during the years of campus unrest when the battle cry was one for "relevance."

One cannot dismiss this problem, however, without asking further questions. If meaning and relevance are so important, and we must assume that they are, we need also ask "Relevance for when?," "Relevance for whom?," "Relevance for where?," and "Who is to judge?"

Educators emerge from their first year's teaching experience with hundreds of questions. They want to know how to handle disciplinary problems, manage large classes, form calisthenics groups, and deal with parents. They are eager to know more about the subject matter of their class, how to grade, and how to deal with school board members and administrators. They are anxious to obtain answers to questions which will help them solve the problems which they encountered during their first year of teaching. They wonder why they were not prepared in their college classes. They criticize the professional preparation program for lacking in relevance.

Teachers who return to college for advanced degrees after several years' experience know then how to manage a class, teach basic fundamentals, and manage their community relationships. They now want to delve more deeply into the subject matter, and to learn more about growth and development, motivation, and the way people learn. They have become interested in research and in keeping abreast of the leaders in their field. They have tried their hand at speaking and writing and wish to know more about it. They have become involved in community affairs and have talked politics with other members of the community. What they considered relevant education during their first year of teaching no longer has much meaning.

After another ten years have passed, the teacher becomes more concerned about philosophy, religion, and the development of his students. He thinks deeply about the contributions his life can make and reads about the future and its relation to the past. He now perceives the importance of some of the courses which were required and which seemed irrelevant at that time.

Relevance for where? That question must also be considered when planning a professional preparation curriculum. The teacher who plans to teach in New York or Los Angeles may need different preparation than one who is preparing to teach in South Dakota or Maine. The coach in a small town needs special training that might be unnecessary for the elementary teacher in a large city. The dance teacher in a university obviously requires different educational preparation than the athletic trainer in a high school.

It becomes more and more apparent that colleges in sparsely settled areas need curricula different from those whose graduates will work in the inner city. There is a need for different subconcentrations or "tracks" for physical education students who have differing goals in mind. It is also clear that relevance might be entirely different for one person than for another—experienced and inexperienced individuals will see different subjects and different experiences as being meaningful and significant.

18.4 PROGRAMS OF PROFESSIONAL PREPARATION

Lindley Stiles perceptively wrote the following about teacher education:

> Progress in teacher education will come with research that refines and tests theory, studies and solves specific problems, and projects deeper insights about learning and human development and their modification—rather than new orthodoxies. A need is to examine instruction itself—in terms of its artistic and scientific elements, its human and technological components, its varied impact on different kinds of students—in contrast to the concern for form (models) of the program of teacher education overall.
>
> To develop teachers for the times, present and future in all their pluralities, teacher education must learn to shun all orthodoxies and to make revolution a continuing tradition. The challenge is to live with controversy rather than try to counteract it. The persistent quest is to make teacher education relevant, to social conditions as well as to refined knowledge, and especially to the individuals who are preparing to teach. The state of the art is in its infancy. [60, p. 12]

The needs to examine instruction and its impact on students, to make teacher education relevant to social conditions and the latest knowledge, and to make professional programs relevant to those who are preparing to teach are certainly worthy of continuing emphasis.

The needs to analyze what has been accomplished in teacher preparation and to carefully select what is to be retained from past programs is equally important. One need not be an incurable optimist, but only a fair and impartial person, to recognize a number of outstanding teachers and scholars of the past who have contributed vastly to our knowledge of pedagogy and our understanding of children and adolescents.

Simply stated, the newer and better programs of teacher education will examine and reexamine what already exists in our teacher education programs and will try to retain that which is positive. They will then search the latest literature for new research findings and carefully read articles dealing with the nature of our present and future society to make the developing programs significant for teachers and their students.

Societal changes

Our society and our nation are experiencing some changes that cannot help but affect our total educational program. The technological revolution, the environmental hazards, the sociological upheavals, the complexities of personal and public finances, the exploration of space, the acceleration of change, the new life-styles, and the changes in individual philosophies, to name only a few, constitute such vast alterations that education will unquestionably be profoundly affected. Adjustments to what has happened and what is happening in society are difficult enough, but they can generally be effected. Adjustments to many of the future changes are, however, impossible, for one cannot adjust to events and trends of which one has no knowledge.

Nevertheless, "cope-ability" has become one of the bywords describing an important objective of education. There must be greater emphasis in teacher education programs on projecting our education into the future, of educating for transience, and of developing the ability to adapt.

Physical fitness and preparation for leisure

As has been noted earlier, technological advances and societal changes have produced a society in which many individuals are enjoying more hours of leisure than ever before. They are, at the same time, freed from the necessity of moving in a vigorous and sustained fashion. The tendency, therefore, is to let one's body deteriorate for lack of exercise unless some meaningful way of compensating is found.

Certainly current efforts on the part of the government, schools, and many individuals to upgrade the physical fitness of the average citizen will influence the physical education of the future. Thus education for the worthy use of leisure takes on more meaning day by day.

Athletics for women

The arrival of the 1970's marked a new activism on the part of women's liberation movements. While women were fighting discrimination in salaries, job placement, politics, and elsewhere, they also began a push for equality in the opportunity to participate in sports. Budgets were compared, participation by women in athletics was reexamined, and resources for women's sports programs were sought.

We now see a full-fledged athletic movement in the women's ranks. What has been accomplished in men's athletic programs is now being requested and fought for by the women. This development will also have a significant impact on the teacher preparation programs of the future.

Athletics versus physical education

The trend toward a separation of physical education and athletics which began in the large universities has now spread to many smaller colleges, many secondary schools, and some junior high schools. With a more careful evaluation of teacher loads, coaches are with increasing frequency being paid on an "extracurricular basis." "Extra pay for extra work" is the trend.

Whereas a generation ago almost all physical education teachers accepted the fact that they would be required to coach as an additional assignment, this is no longer true. The number of sports in the interscholastic and intercollegiate programs has risen from about five or six to anywhere from fourteen to twenty or more; the number of coaches for each sport has also increased. The coaching positions cannot be filled with only those who hold degrees in physical education, so that teachers in other fields are often recruited to coach. Many principals and superintendents feel that this is good. They like to see coaches in the classroom and academic teachers as coaches.

There is, however, increasing agitation to give those coaches who do not have a physical education background some special preparation for coaching. A number of states now require special certification for coaches. This, too, affects professional preparation programs in colleges and universities.

Physical education in the elementary school

One of the most salutary developments in recent years is the emphasis on physical education at the elementary school level. Whereas fifteen years ago most teachers were taking a general professional preparation course in which the emphasis was on teaching at the secondary level, we now find an increasing number of schools offering a program in physical education at the elementary level. Increased attention to perceptual motor development, a greater interest in and preference for teaching at the elementary level, and a more serious commitment to the goals of physical education at this level are signs of the change which is taking place.

General education

There is still general acceptance of the need for an education that is designed not only for a specific profession or vocation, but also for developing competence and knowledge in the art of communicating, the basic scientific principles and theories, the sociological milieu in which we operate, the many economic and political aspects of our lives, and the psychological and spiritual dimensions of everyday living. While no arbitrary percentage can be given for the proportion of the program to be devoted to general education, there seems to be reasonable agreement that it should comprise 40 to 60 percent of a four-year professional preparation curriculum.

General professional education

Attention must be given to that phase of the program which purports to provide educational experiences needed by all teachers. Courses such as Philosophy of

Education, Educational Psychology, Growth and Development, and General Principles of Pedagogy are examples. Student teaching is also classified as general professional education in many institutions. Regardless of how these courses are classified or where they are placed, there should be provision in the curriculum for the development of these competencies.

Preparation for international aspects of education

With communications systems improving, with the world "shrinking" in size, and with increasing numbers of people from many continents living closer together, more attention must be given to the preparation of some teachers for international work. International travel, exchange of students and professors, experiences in international service, and subject matter dealing with international education are becoming increasingly meaningful. A number of institutions are now giving courses such as Comparative Physical Education, International Relations through Recreation and Physical Education, and Physical Education in Many Lands.

Just as important as course work is the provision of an environment where the international students can meet each other, feel welcome, and sense the security of something that is theirs. Those institutions which provide opportunities for the appropriate preparation for international education are rendering a significant and worthwhile service.

The best programs of preparation for international service in physical education will combine course work in the classroom with international involvement and interracial personal experiences. The emphasis will be on motivation for service to humanity which is intercultural, international, and interreligious. The subject matter should include both theory and application, concepts, and action.

Specialized professional education

Many competencies required by physical education teachers are not needed by other academic teachers. A deeper knowledge of the structure and function of the human organism, an understanding of motor learning from the simplest to the most complex movements, a grasp of the psychological concepts involved in coaching, and an ability to perform in a variety of physical education activities are examples.

Even professional specialization must be broken down into subconcentrations in the modern programs. The coach's needs are different from those of the therapist; the dance teacher should have a somewhat different program than the aquatics director; the elementary teacher's course requirements will not be the same as those of the college instructor.

Competencies and experiences

The clearest conception and most logical presentation of a professional preparation curriculum can be obtained by indicating in general the competencies required and the experiences designed to develop such competencies. Obviously the results will be dependent on the quality of the teaching, the motivation of the individual, and the total effect of all environmental influences.

The model curriculum
The model curriculum outline presented below is not intended to be adopted exactly as it is. Each institution must assess its own situation and educational philosophy and formulate its curriculum on that basis. The author's intention is to demonstrate a workable plan whereby a student may qualify to teach a broad spectrum of physical educational activities and still teach in the area of his choice.

The following outline permits students to choose the area and level in which they would like to work and at the same time offers them an adequate foundation for beginning their career in several possible situations. The model is described under two headings, (a) competencies, and (b) experiences.

A competency is an ability, skill, understanding, or qualification which enables one to do certain things in a variety of life situations. Experience as used here refers to the learning process which assists a student to gain a certain competency.

Curriculum Leading to a Bachelor's Degree
with a Major in Physical Education

General Education (45–55 percent of total curriculum)

Competencies	*Experiences*
1. To be able to communicate clearly and intelligently both in writing and orally.	Courses in English. Public speaking experiences. Foreign languages.
2. To have a basic understanding of the principal academic disciplines needed to facilitate interaction with other faculty members and educated persons in the community.	Courses in sociology, economics, history, political science, psychology, anthropology, and the basic biological and physical sciences.
3. To possess an appreciation of good literature and the arts; to develop a love of and appreciation for nature and the natural environment.	Attend lectures and concerts. Spend time in communion with nature. Go canoeing, camping, etc. Visit galleries and museums. Take courses in literature, art, and music appreciation.
4. To be able to function as a socially competent person and as an active, contributing member of society.	Read current newspapers and magazines. Take part in extracurricular activities. Take courses in social problems and current events.

5. To be able to know oneself and through that knowledge learn to know and appreciate others.	Courses in general psychology. Experiences in introspection. Experiences studying and analyzing others.
6. To be able to develop one's own value system and ethical code.	Courses in religion, philosophy, psychology, and sociology. Intense experiences and challenges. Experiences in self-discipline. Spiritual experiences.

II General Professional Education (8–12 percent)

Competencies	Experiences
1. To have a sense of dedication to the teaching profession and a strong faith in its efficacy.	Courses in philosophy of education. Associations and personal involvement with great leaders in the field. Experience working with children and adolescents.
2. To possess a knowledge of the general concepts of pedagogy and of educational psychology.	Courses in general teaching methods and educational psychology. Teaching experiences where these concepts and methods are exemplified.
3. To understand the relationships of education to social problems and everyday living.	Courses in sociology. Experience teaching in inner-city settings. Observation of such relationships.
4. To possess a zest for continued study and research.	Experiences in research and interpretation of research.
5. To have an interest in professional organizations as they contribute to the advancement of the teaching profession.	Membership in professional educational organizations both before and after graduation. Intensive reading in professional publications. Attendance at professional meetings and conventions.

III Specialized Professional Education (33–47 percent)

1. To understand the special methods needed to teach and coach in the various activities.	Experience in skills classes taught by master teachers. Experience as group leaders and teaching assistants in skills classes. Experience on athletic squads. Courses in teaching and coaching the various activities.
2. To be able to demonstrate a number of activities.	Experience in performing a variety of activities. Reading books on techniques of performance. Observing good performers. Observing films and film loops.
3. To know how to formulate a curriculum.	Courses which include curriculum construction. Experience on a curriculum committee.
4. To know how to prepare a lesson plan.	Courses which include lesson planning. Student-teaching experience. Experience as an assistant instructor.
5. To be able to identify and interpret mechanical and physiological principles which explain movement.	Courses in kinesiology and mechanical analysis of sports skills. Practice in analyzing movements. Research in biomechanics. Courses in physics and in anatomy.
6. To be able to identify atypical human structures and functional differences.	Courses in physical education for the atypical. Laboratory work with the handicapped. Volunteer work with the retarded or emotionally disturbed.
7. To understand the principles of perceptual-motor development.	Courses in growth and development. Courses dealing with perceptual handicaps. Experiences working with the development of children through movement.

8. To possess a basic understanding of growth and development.	Courses in growth and development. Working with students at the various levels.
9. To understand what is expected of a physical educator and what the opportunities are.	Courses which provide an orientation to the profession. Conversations with teachers and coaches in the field. Attendance at professional meetings and conventions.
10. To possess a knowledge of the structure and function of the human organism.	Courses in anatomy and physiology. Experience in dissecting mammals and human cadavers. Research in exercise physiology. Reading in the biological sciences.
11. To know what to do in the prevention and treatment of injuries.	Courses in first aid. Courses in prevention and care of injuries. Experiences as assistant trainers. Experience treating one's own injuries.
12. To understand basic administrative principles.	Courses in organization and administration. Assisting the director of physical education. Summer work directing playgrounds.
13. To understand and be able to apply the basic principles of motor learning.	Courses in motor learning. Courses in psychology. Research in motor learning.
14. To understand and be able to articulate the philosophy of the physical education program.	Courses in philosophy and principles of physical education. Reading educational literature. Developing a value system. Discussing philosophical issues as they relate to sport.

The above curriculum outline represents some of the competencies and experience which should be included in the major programs of all physical educators. Over and above these, there should be experiences which would develop the special competencies needed for the subconcentration chosen. Those selecting the elementary level option would receive additional courses and more learning experiences which would contribute directly toward the development of their needed competencies. The same would be true for those choosing the secondary level, coaching, or other options.

The following curriculum (pp. 457–459), in effect at one college, has translated the above philosophy into specific courses and semester hours. It contains three parts, (a) the required academic courses by year, (b) the skills and techniques courses by year, and (c) the additional requirements for the subconcentration chosen.

The conceptual framework
The conceptual approach to curriculum development was outlined in Chapter 11, *Programs and Curricula*. Students may wish to review that section before proceeding with the following discussion.

Ann Jewett and Marie Mullan, in *A Conceptual Model for Teacher Education*, have put professional preparation for physical education teachers in a *conceptual framework*. They say that "the goals of physical education determine the selection of any conceptual framework for planning particular physical education curricula." They also indicate that "the key concepts in the field of human movement relate to the function of movement in prolonging and enriching the quality of life and to the processes of self-actualization through movement." [30, pp. 76–77]

Jewett and Mullan go on to state that the teachers of tomorrow will need more openness and creativity, will need to be able to cope with the environment through movement, and will need to be "individually oriented." They must be skilled in interpreting behavior and should have more educational experiences designed to develop their own personal teaching style. Jewett and Mullan then outline a cybernetic model for a teacher education program (Figure 18.1, page 461). Steps in their model for professional preparation are:

1. The student enters the orientation element in order to gain an understanding of the purposes, goals, and function of physical education.

2. Prospective teachers are programmed through modules describing elementary and secondary physical education.

3. Students select their professional specializations from the four modules of learning activities.

4. Students strive to clarify their values and receive guidance in the formulation of their own personal value system.

5. Prospective teachers pass through the self-assessment modules. They attempt to assess their competence and knowledge in communication, motor development, perception, motivation, attitudes, and movement analysis. They are tested for physical fitness and their appreciation of its significance.

6. The prospective teachers enter the instructional planning subelement, which includes Movement in Society, Movement Performance Skills, and Professional competencies.

GRADUATION REQUIREMENTS—PHYSICAL EDUCATION*

Name: _____   Graduation date: _____
Posted to: _____   Semester hours completed: _____

FRESHMAN YEAR	S.H.
Biol. 1: Basic Concepts	4
COR 1: Camp Counseling	2
Eng. 1-2-3: Written and Oral English	6
HE 2: Personal and Community Hygiene	2
PE 1: Introduction to Physical Education	2
Phys. 1-2-3: Survey	6
Psych. 1: Introduction to Psychology	4
Soc. Sc. 1-2: Man and Society	4
Total S.H.	30

JUNIOR YEAR	S.H.
Ed. 138 or 139: Foundations of Education	2
PE 19: Analysis of Motion	2
PE 103: Physiology of Exercise	2
PE 110: Tests and Measurements	3
PE 112: Principles and Problems of Coaching	2
COR 105: Introduction to Community Recreation	2
Expressive Arts _____	
_____	2
Physical Education Concentration	
_____	
_____	
_____	6
Free Electives _____	3
_____	
Music for Physical Education _____	
_____	2
Nonprofessional Electives _____	
_____	4
Total S.H.	30

SOPHOMORE YEAR	S.H.
Biol. 7-8-9: Anatomy and Physiology	8
Chem. 9-10-11: Survey	6
Expressive Arts _____	
_____	4
HE 3: First Aid and Safety	2
Rel. 5-6: Introduction to Bible or Religion	
8-9: Introduction to World Religion or	
Phil. 5-6: Introduction to Philosophy	4
PE 6 or 7: Elementary School Physical Education	2
PE 106: Secondary School Physical Education	2
Psych. 4: Educational Psychology	2
Total S.H.	30

SENIOR YEAR	S.H.
HE 207: Physical and Health Inspection	2
PE 154: Supervised Student Teaching	10
PE 209: Physical Education for Atypical Children	3
PE 221: Organization and Administration of Physical Education	2
PE 299: Philosophy and Principles of Physical Education	2
PE Concentration _____	
_____	
_____	6
PE 204: Motor Learning and Human Performance	2
Free Electives _____	
_____	3
Total S.H.	30

Note: In addition to the 120 semester hours listed on this page, students are required to take l6 semester hours of "skills and techniques" courses.

*Adapted from the program at Springfield College, Springfield, Massachusetts.

SKILLS AND TECHNIQUES REQUIREMENTS—PHYSICAL EDUCATION

Semester hours completed: _____

FRESHMAN YEAR	S.H.	ELECTIVES	S.H.
P 101 Football (men)	2/3	P 106 Lacrosse	2/3
P 115 Track (men)	2/3	P 164 Exhibition and Gym Activities	2/3
P 141 Swimming (men)	2/3	P 176 Modern Dance II	2/3
P 162 Gymnastics I (men)	2/3	P 181 Fundamentals of Ballet	2/3
P 160 Fundamentals of Rhythm	2/3	P 215 Track II	2/3
P 200 Basketball (men)	2/3	P 245 Advanced Diving	1/3
P 219 Wrestling (men)	2/3	P 284 Recreational Games	1/3
F 236 Handball (men)	1/3	F 019 Self Defense	1/3
F 266 Folk Dance I	2/3	F 023 Paddle Rackets	1/3
		F 024 Squash	1/3
Total S.H.	5 2/3	F 027 Street Games	1/3
		F 045 Skin and Scuba Diving	1/3
SOPHOMORE YEAR	S.H.	F 047 White-Water Sport	2/3
P 105 Soccer (men)	2/3	F 091 Relaxation	1/3
P 111 Baseball (men)	2/3	F 092 Personal Fitness	1/3
P 142 Water Stunts and Diving (men)	1/3	F 093 Jogging	1/3
P 188 Games I	1	F 131 Softball	1/3
P 221 Tennis	2/3	F 145 Boating and Canoeing	2/3
P 262 Gymnastics II (men)	2/3	F 146 Horsemanship I	1/3
Elective	2/3	F 161 Modern Gymnastics	1/3
		F 174 Bowling	1/3
Total S.H.	4 2/3	F 175 Modern Dance I	2/3
		F 177 Tap Dance	2/3
JUNIOR YEAR	S.H.	F 235 Archery	1/3
P 233 Volleyball (men)	2/3	F 237 Badminton	1/3
P 179 Children's Rhythm	2/3	F 238 Skiing I	1/3
P 263 Gymnastics III	2/3	F 239 Skiing II	1/3
P 283 Games II	2/3	F 240 Winter Alpine Activities	2/3
P 290 Conditioning Programs	2/3	F 241 Mountaineering	2/3
Elective _____	2/3	F 243 Advanced Recreational	
		Aquatics	2/3
Total S.H.	4	F 292 Fencing	1/3

SENIOR YEAR	S.H.
P 173 Golf	2/3
F 267 Square Dance	2/3
Elective _____	1/3
Total S.H.	1 2/3

P courses — Offered to physical education majors only.
F courses — Offered to all students

Note: 1 semester hour credit = 45 contact hours
       2/3 semester hour credit = 30 contact hours
       1/3 semester hour credit = 15 contact hours
       Physical education students majoring in physical education are required to take 16 semester hours of skills courses. They may elect more.

MEN'S PHYSICAL EDUCATION CONCENTRATIONS

The course requirements in the respective concentrations are as follows:

ELEMENTARY		S.H.
1.	PE 7: Elementary School Physical Education: K–3	2
2.	PE 8: Elementary School Physical Education: 4–6	2
3.	PE 9: Elementary Physical Education Program for the Exceptional Child	2
4.	PE 133: Teaching Rhythmic Activities	2
5.	Ed. 238: The Nongraded School	2
6.	Psych. 9: Psychology of Human Development *or* Ed. 250: Understanding the Behavior of Boys and Girls	2 or 3
	Total:	12 or 13

SECONDARY		
1.	Methods and Materials (Coaching Courses)	2
2.	PE 150: Practicum in Physical Education	2 or 3
3.	PE 203: Prevention and Care of Athletic Injuries	2
4.	Psych: 9: Psychology of Human Development *or* Ed. 250: Understanding the Behavior of Boys and Girls	2 or 3
5.	Socio. 132: Social Problems	3
	Total:	11 or 13

COACHING		
1.	PE 100, 101, or 102: Sports Officiating Courses	2
2.	Methods and Materials (Coaching Courses)	4
3.	PE 203: Prevention and Care of Athletic Injuries	2
4.	PE 180: Mechanical Analysis	2
5.	PE 224: Athletic Administration	2
	Total:	12

GENERAL		
1.	Methods and Materials (Coaching Courses)	2
2.	PE 203: Prevention and Care of Athletic Injuries	2
3.	PE 150: Practicum in Physical Education	2
4.	Professional Electives	6
	Total:	12

COMMUNITY		
1.	PE 105: Program of Physical Education in Social Agencies	2
2.	PE 143: Teaching and Coaching Swimming and Diving	2
3.	PE 203: Prevention and Care of Athletic Injuries	2
4.	Methods and Materials (Physical Education)	4
5.	Free Electives	2
	Total:	12

7. Students next go to the professional Physical Education Component which is organized (1) vertically into the Movement Analysis and Performance Element, the Guidance of Learning Element, and the Human Movement

Professions Element, and (2) horizontally into introductory, minimal and optimal levels (Figure 18.2). [30, pp. 78–85]

Jewett and Mullan summarize their presentation by saying that the aim is "to clarify a positive concept of the modern educator and create curricular alternatives which permit a young adult interested in the human movement professions to synthesize his unique talents into a way of working effectively with others". [30, p. 87]

The conceptual approach was utilized in the Professional Preparation Conference held in New Orleans, January 1973. Concepts were first identified, appropriate competencies were fitted to them, and experiences to effect each competency were listed. The conceptual approach is currently receiving a great deal of attention and will no doubt be the curricular model for a number of years.

Physical education as a discipline

Chapter 3 contains a fairly thorough discussion of physical education as a discipline. A number of institutions preparing physical education teachers have modified their professional preparation curricula to focus on the body of knowledge and organize it into the discipline of physical education. There are others who feel that to move too rapidly in this direction would weaken the prospective teacher's ability to actually teach. It is hoped that a middle ground can be found and made acceptable to institutional authorities so that there will be an increasing number of professional physical educators who are both competent teachers and excellent scholars.

18.5 PROBLEMS AND ISSUES

There are many issues, some of them new and some long standing, which need to be considered in developing professional preparation programs for physical education. Some of these will be briefly discussed in the following paragraphs.

Inner-city physical education

Teacher preparation institutions have received considerable criticism, some of it justified, for failing to give adequate attention to educating teachers for the inner city. This has come about inadvertently because of two factors. In the first place the selection of students for a college program has customarily been based to a large extent on grades and academic rank. Few applicants from the educationally deprived areas are chosen. In cases where admissions are competitive, most students generally come from the wealthy suburbs where the best "academic risk" students are graduating.

The second factor is related to student teaching assignments. Most student teachers, when given a choice, request that they be assigned to schools where the facilities are new and spacious, where classes are small enough to be manageable, and where equipment is ample and of high quality. They are therefore seldom assigned to the inner city.

Because this situation was recognized a few years ago, a conference of city and state directors was held in December 1969, the theme entitled "Preparing Teachers for a Changing Society." This conference made educators aware of the needs of the inner city and made many recommendations for improving the situation. Among these were the following.

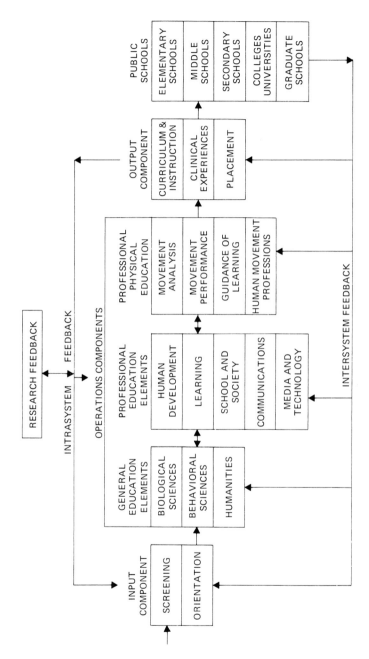

Figure 18.1 Cybernetic model for teacher education program.
[30, p. 79]

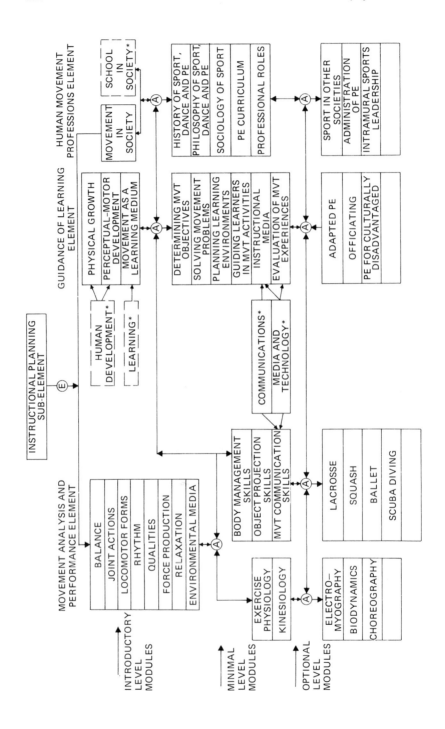

1. Reexamine the procedures for assigning student teachers.
2. Insist that more teachers in professional preparation institutions have public school experience.
3. Increase the exposure of prospective teachers to group dynamics, encounters, confrontations, and rap sessions.
4. Increase the exposure of students to the behavioral sciences.
5. Increase the cooperative efforts of the consumer (schools employing teachers) and the producer (institutions preparing teachers).
6. Provide for the interchange of faculty members between the public schools and the colleges.
7. Improve the facilities for inner-city schools.
8. Select more students for the professional preparation programs who have grown up in the inner city.
9. Make the inner-city positions more attractive.
10. Reexamine the competencies needed in the inner city and provide for them. [3, pp. 49–61]

Since the vast majority of people in the United States are now living in metropolitan areas, the above recommendations appear quite valid. However, one caution is in order. It is not only the inner city that has problems. Some attention must be given to those students attending schools in other deprived areas. Finally, there is much that can be done to improve teaching physical education in the suburbs, in exurbia, and in small towns. The fact that we must give increased attention to one segment of the population should not mean that we can forget about the rest.

Timing and scheduling
In the past it was not unusual to find the preprofessional, or general, education confined to the first two years and the professional education to the last two years. This may have some merit where more advanced theories and concepts are based on fundamental and basic learnings. But there are reasons why this should not be carried to an extreme.

When high school graduates have chosen their career, they are impatient to begin studying subjects which they feel are important in preparing them for their life's work. They do not sense the relationship of many of the general education courses to their future teaching and coaching. From a motivational standpoint, therefore, it is wise to give them some professional experiences during the first two years.

◀Figure 18.2 **Professional physical education component.** [30, p. 85] (* = modules in professional education component; E = entry point; A = assessment point.)

Many of the courses in political science, community development, and sociology have more meaning to them when they are upperclassmen. The practical application of such courses often comes after they have graduated and are established in a community. Current events studied during the freshman or sophomore years are no longer "current" when they graduate.

The present trend is to integrate the theoretical with the practical and the professional with the general. As a matter of fact there are many subjects classified as general education which may have very pragmatic value when a person begins teaching.

In summary, then, a rigid sequence may be necessary when teaching certain sciences and complex skills. Where learning or performance at a higher level is built on a foundation of prior learnings, there is sound reason for sequential curriculum planning. Where this is not true, it may be psychologically advantageous to take up subjects and topics as they seem relevant to the learner.

Activities (skills) courses versus theory courses

Skills and techniques courses are part of the subject matter of physical education. They are also an important segment of the general education which should be experienced by all people.

If performing laboratory experiments in an engineering class is "academic," if conducting research in motor learning is "academically respectable," then certainly skills and techniques courses, properly conducted and taught, can also be justified as a legitimate part of college education. Learning how to move, understanding the principles of movement, involvement in human interaction in dynamic situations, and discovering the joyous and spontaneous freedom that can come from the right kind of play are educational in the highest sense.

Truly great teachers of physical education activities teach by word, attitude, and behavior. They exude values, explain and demonstrate techniques, and teach the principles of mechanics and motor learning involved. The more deeply physical education teachers have experienced an activity, the more they can transmit both feeling and technique.

Laboratory experience

While there is considerable disagreement with regard to the details of laboratory experiences, there is now general consensus on two points: (a) laboratory experiences (observation, student teaching, field work) are among the richest and most meaningful in the entire teacher education program, and (b) laboratory experiences should begin during the freshman or sophomore year and continue, in some form or another, throughout the four or more years of college.

Laboratory experiences should be somewhat varied. It would be advantageous to one who has never taught to experience teaching at the elementary, junior high school, high school, and college levels. It would be enriching to work with the mentally retarded, the gifted, the crippled, the blind, and the otherwise

"... great teachers ... teach by word, attitude, and behavior." (Courtesy of the ▶
Journal of Health, Physical Education, and Recreation.)

handicapped. Many students majoring in physical education have never had these experiences; once they have them, they change their entire plan for the future.

Laboratory experiences should include cocurricular experiences. Assisting with administrative tasks, working with intramurals, camp counseling, coaching, and taking groups on outings in the mountains would be helpful experiences. Student teachers should become involved in the community, attempting to find out what it is like to be a teacher in each given situation and involving themselves in more than just what goes on in the classroom.

There should be as much integration and coordination as possible between laboratory experience and formalized classwork. Class excursions to observe teachers in schools, student involvement in curriculum planning, practice in the preparation of lesson plans, tutorial and elementary counseling experiences, and interviews with teachers and coaches are among the ways in which such integration can take place. Preparation for and discussion of such experiences are needed if maximum benefit is to be derived.

Graduate education

Some universities insist that their principal function is to "push back the horizons" of knowledge, to "discover new knowledge," and to disseminate knowledge.

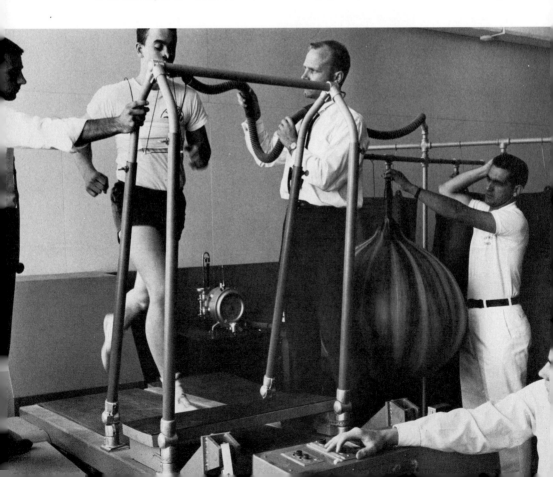

Other institutions more concerned with preparing individuals for specific professions perceive graduate study as being more practical and applied. We still find ourselves asking such questions as "Should graduate study produce the skilled specialist or the educated man?," "Should graduate study be academic or professional in nature?," and "Which is more important in graduate programs, research or practical course work?"

Graduate work should be of high quality. Some diversity among institutions makes for richer educational experiences. W. Gordon Whaley, Dean of the Graduate School of the University of Texas, said in this connection:

> The primary purpose of graduate education is one of educating the teacher-scholar-researcher who, whether he finds his life work in academic circles, the professions, industry, government, or elsewhere, necessarily will bear the hallmark of intellectual leadership. [55, p. 5]

Our effort should be to produce intellectual leaders who understand the importance of total, well-rounded, integrated development and who will seek to assist and guide their students to that end. In so doing they will use a variety of means, methods, motivations, and activities and improve both the individual and society.

18.6 CERTIFICATION AND ACCREDITATION

Individuals who wish to teach in a given state must be certified by the State Department of Education in that state. Each state has a set of regulations listing the requirements for certification in each subject offered in the public schools. These requirements consist of (a) a bachelor's or higher degree from an accredited institution, and (b) a certain number of courses or semester hour credits in the subject area to be taught. The candidate is required to submit a transcript from his college verifying all the credits earned and the fact that he/she graduated. In some instances certain colleges are registered or approved in a given state and individual examinations of transcripts are quite cursory. The college then has the responsibility for keeping the State Department of Education informed as to its program and sending to the Department a list of its students who satisfactorily complete the program.

In recent years there has been considerable reciprocity in certification. States that have somewhat similar standards and that are located in the same geographical area band together and accept teachers who have been certified in another state belonging to the consortium for employment in their state.

As standards in all states and most educational institutions are rising, and as programs are becoming increasingly standardized throughout the country, institutions are being given more autonomy and responsibility. Regulations pertaining to certification are becoming more general and programs of professional preparation, rather than individuals, are being approved. Institutions wishing to be on the approved list must file a rather lengthy application and accept visitations and careful scrutiny.

◀ "Good graduate programs must be supported by sound research." (Courtesy of Springfield College.)

Institutions offering teacher education programs normally seek accreditation from at least two sources. The Regional Accrediting Association awards accreditation to a college as an institution of higher learning. The National Council for the Accreditation of Teacher Education rules on a college as a professional preparation institution. In some instances each teacher education program in a given college is judged independently.

In the last few years there has been a movement toward *performance-based* teacher certification. The major thrust is "judging competence through demonstrated performance" as opposed to certification on the basis of the completion of a certain number of course offerings. This trend, while still in its infancy, is predicted as the wave of the future.

It appears that there will be major developments in certification and accreditation in the next decade. Included will be (a) the approved program concept, (b) reciprocal certification among the states, (c) performance-based teacher certification, (d) increasing emphasis on standardization from national professional organizations, (e) differentiated staffing, and (f) specialized certification in areas such as coaching, health education, dance, and recreation.

18.7 PROFESSIONAL ORGANIZATIONS

A large number of people with similar interests, when well-organized and united, can accomplish many things which cannot be achieved by individuals alone. They can wield a strong influence in legislative matters, can protect the rights and privileges of professional members, and can enlist the support of the public in just causes for the benefit of those students who are being educated.

Individuals who are active in their professional organizations generally reap many benefits as well. One receives inspiration from interchanging experiences and ideas with others working in the same areas and facing the same problems. The high-quality literature published by most of the organizations makes very worthwhile reading. Many members have been placed in new and better positions through contacts made in conventions and other meetings. For these and other reasons it is advisable for physical education teachers and coaches to begin serving the professional organizations of their choice while they are still young.

Organizations which have been established to serve those who work as members of the health, physical education, and recreational profession include:

1. *The American Alliance for Health, Physical Education, and Recreation.* * With its headquarters in Washington, D.C., it has over 50,000 members organized into six geographical districts and seven separate associations. These associations are:

American Association for Leisure and Recreation (AALR)

American School and Community Safety Association (ASCSA)

Association for the Advancement of Health Education (AAHE)

---

*Prior to June 1974, the American Alliance for Health, Physical Education, and Recreation was the American Association for Health, Physical Education, and Recreation, organized and operated according to a somewhat different pattern.

◄ ". . . there has been a movement toward performance-based teacher certification." (Courtesy of the *Journal of Health, Physical Education, and Recreation.*)

Association for Research, Administration and Professional Councils (ARAPC)

National Association for Girls and Women in Sport (NAGWS)

National Association for Sport and Physical Education (NASPE)

National Dance Association (NDA)

The Alliance and its subdivisions publish professional literature, organize and conduct conferences and workshops, and hold state, district, and national conventions.

2. *The American Academy of Physical Education* is an invitational group with membership limited to 125 active members. It is considered a high honor to become a member.

3. *The American College of Sports Medicine* is particularly interested in research dealing with athletic training and injuries related to sport. This is a scholarly group whose members have made many fine contributions to sport and physical fitness.

4. *The Council of City and County Directors* is a well-organized group that exerts a tremendous influence on the profession. It administers large programs, holds important conventions, exchanges ideas, and generally includes some of the most competent people in the profession.

5. *The National Association of College Directors of Athletics* is composed, as its name implies, of athletic directors in colleges and universities. This is an active group, making fine professional contributions.

6. *The National Association of Physical Education for College Women* and *The National College Physical Education Association for Men*. College staff members who are academically oriented find these organizations both enjoyable and beneficial.

7. *The National Collegiate Athletic Association,* the *National Assocation of Intercollegiate Athletics,* the *Association of Intercollegiate Athletics for Women,* and the *Amateur Athletic Union* are organizations which govern intercollegiate and amateur athletics throughout the United States. They have an important but difficult role as they try to uphold high standards of ethics and eligibility.

8. *The National Council of Secondary School Athletic Directors* is a recently formed but very active and powerful group. It has the potential for becoming a strong voice for good in high school athletics.

9. *The National Federation of High School Athletic Associations* conducts the most extensive program of competitive sports in the country. Its influence in keeping high school athletic programs wholesome and ethical is immeasurable.

10. *The National Recreation and Park Association* was formed by the merger of several smaller recreation associations. Many recreation teachers and administrators now look upon this as their principal professional organization.

11. *The Society of State Directors* of health, physical education, and recreation is a tightly knit group of persons who are employed in state departments of education with special responsibilities for the above areas. They carry on extensive professional activities, not the least of which is the formulation of curricula for the schools of their respective states.

12. *Phi Delta Pi* and *Phi Epsilon Kappa* are professional fraternal organizations for women and men, respectively. They try to maintain the standards of the profession at a high level, publish scholarly articles, and hold professional and social meetings.

13. *Presidents's Council on Physical Fitness and Sports.* Originally established by President Eisenhower as the President's Council of Youth Fitness, its responsibilities include promoting sound physical fitness and physical education programs, cooperating with community agencies in the conduct of fitness workshops, publishing brochures and bulletins, and serving as a catalyst for the improvement of the fitness of all Americans. Its office in Washington, D.C. is staffed by professional persons in administration, physiology, research, and public relations.

All of the above organizations are worthy of support from members of our profession. They each have their function and their responsibilities. A young physical education teacher or coach should examine these organizations carefully and begin working in the appropriate one as soon as possible. It is characteristic of the best members of the profession that they support the professional organizations of the type mentioned above.

18.8 CONCEPTS AND PRINCIPLES IN CAREER PLANNING
To conclude the discussion of careers and how to prepare for them, the following suggestions and principles are presented:

1. No teacher, regardless of the professional preparation obtained, can be successful if he does not enjoy working with children and young adults. There must be a dedication to teaching and a commitment to assisting with the development of students.

2. No individual is completely educated or prepared to teach by the time he has completed the four-year program leading to a bachelor's degree. The great teacher is the one who continues to search and learn.

3. A variety of experiences is more educational than repeating the same experiences over and over. A teacher will be stimulated and refreshed by exposure to new ideas.

4. Attention to possible future trends will pay good dividends. With changes taking place with ever-increasing rapidity, adaptations must also occur faster.

5. It is important to distinguish between that which is transient and that which is permanent. Some changes may pass so quickly that they are not worth becoming excited about.

6. Individualized program planning and instruction is very important. However, interaction with other people is equally significant. The effort, therefore, should be to meet the needs of the students. A balance of individual and group activities may be the best answer.

7. Physical educators must learn from many disciplines and many teachers from other fields. In the final analysis, however, they must analyze and adapt to their own students, their own subject, and their own situation.

8. Good laboratory experiences as early in the program as possible are invaluable to the prospective teacher. In fairness to the pupils of the student teacher, there must be careful supervision by a fully qualified teacher.

9. Institutions preparing physical education teachers should give high priority to teaching experience in the public schools when they employ staff members. Too many college teachers have had only college teaching experience.

10. The first professional course a prospective physical education teacher takes in college (usually Introduction to Physical Education) should be a good one. Professors who can inspire and develop in their students a commitment to their profession should be utilized.

11. Inviting teachers from the public schools to discuss their experiences and teaching methods with prospective teachers is a salutary practice. Adequate time for discussion should be provided.

12. Good advisors can be of tremendous assistance to prospective teachers. They must, however, establish contact and rapport. Freshmen and sophomores are particularly in need of sound advice and counsel.

13. Prospective teachers should be encouraged to join the American Alliance for Health, Physical Education, and Recreation and to subscribe to the *Journal of Health, Physical Education, and Recreation*. Class assignments in professional publications may lead them into a sustained interest in professional reading.

14. Sincerity and integrity are essential qualities for teachers. Students very quickly recognize the "phony"—the person who is careless with the truth. A teacher who is not honest soon destroys himself.

15. Prospective teachers should be challenged. There is little satisfaction in accomplishing tasks which are too easy. There should be an analysis of each individual's ability and some assignments which provide some "stretch."

16. There is an increasing need for co-educational classes and activities. When physical education teachers begin work in a public school, the necessity for men and women, boys and girls, to work together and share facilities and resources soon becomes evident.

17. Those who are involved in the education of physical education teachers must consider carefully the developing role of paraprofessionals. Such auxiliary personnel can do much to strengthen programs if they are intelligently utilized. Their use can damage the profession if it leads to lowering the standards for physical education teachers and coaches.

18. It is not necessary, and it may even be undesirable, for all professional preparation institutions to have similar programs. The diversity of philosophies and teaching techniques which have characterized institutions of higher education in the past have undoubtedly enriched our total educational milieu. We must exercise care, however, to make certain that the flexibility which is desired does not lead to a lowering of standards.

19. The degree to which institutions of higher education have dispensed with methods courses causes one to wonder if we no longer value the ability to teach. Learning how to teach is one of the important ingredients of a good professional preparation program.

20. Prospective physical educators and coaches should realize that they will be called upon frequently to speak in public. They should be given every opportunity to practice public speaking while they are in college.

21. All concerned with teacher preparation should realize the significance of their task.

> A teacher affects eternity; he can never tell where his influence stops . . . this minute, too, is part of eternity.
>
> —Anonymous

SELECTED REFERENCES

1. American Association for Health, Physical Education, and Recreation, *Preparing the Health Teacher,* Washington, D.C., 1961.
2. _____, *Professional Preparation in Health Education, Physical Education, Recreation Education,* Washington, D.C., 1962.
3. _____, *Preparing Teachers for a Changing Society,* Proceedings of the Seventh National Conference of City and County Directors, Washington, D.C., December 1969. By permission.
4. _____, *Professional Preparation in Health Education, Physical Education, Recreation Education*, Washington, D.C., 1962.
5. Balassi, Sylvester J., *Focus on Teaching: An Introduction to Education,* New York: Odyssey Press, 1968.
6. Bookwalter, Karl W., "Undergraduate professional physical education, its standards, status, and circumstances," *The Physical Educator,* Vol. 26, No. 3, October 1969.
7. Bowman, Garda W., and Gordon J. Klopf, *New Careers and Roles in the American School,* New York: Bank Street College of Education, 1968.
8. Conant, James B., *Education of American Teachers,* New York: McGraw-Hill, 1963.
9. *The Co-op Plan,* Northeastern University, Boston, Massachusetts, 1973.
10. Downey, Robert J., et al., *Exploring Physical Education,* Belmont, Calif.: Wadsworth Publishing Company, 1962.
11. Elam, Stanley, "Performance-based teacher education: what is the state of the art?," *Quest,* Monograph XVIII, June 1972.
12. Evans, Ruth, and Leo Gans, *Supervision of Physical Education,* New York: McGraw-Hill, 1950.
13. Esslinger, Arthur, "Improving professional preparation," *Journal of Health, Physical Education, and Recreation,* Vol. 31, No. 44, October 1960.
14. Feingold, Ronald, "The evaluation of teacher education programs in physical education," *Quest,* Monograph XVIII, June 1972.

15. Finlayson, Anne, "A consumer's position in teacher preparation," *Journal of Health, Physical Education, and Recreation*, May 1964, p. 39.
16. Flournoy, Don M., *The New Teachers*, San Francisco: Jossey-Bass, 1972.
17. Frost, Reuben B., "The professional preparation of physical educators," Robert A. Cobb and Paul M. Lepley, *Contemporary Philosophies of Physical Education and Athletics*, Columbus, Ohio: Charles E. Merrill, 1973.
18. _____, "Recent trends in certification of men physical education teachers and coaches," Proceedings of the 67th Annual Meeting of the National College Physical Education Association for Men, 1963.
19. _____, "Leaders for all," Paper presented to International Conference on Sport and Education, Mexico City, October 1968.
20. _____, "Teacher preparation in health, physical education, and recreation: directions for the 70s," Paper presented to International Conference on Health, Physical Education, and Recreation, Jamaica, August 1971.
21. Garrison, Cecil L., "A study of factors contributing to success or failure of physical education teachers and/or coaches in selected schools of Arkansas," Unpublished Master's Thesis, University of Wyoming, 1957.
22. Greenberg, Jerrold S., "How videotaping improves teaching behavior," *Journal of Health, Physical Education, and Recreation*, Vol. 44, No. 3, March 1973.
23. Graybeal, Elizabeth, "A consideration of qualities used by administrators in judging effective teachers of physical education," *Research Quarterly*, Vol. XII, December 1941.
24. Hanson, Margie R., "Professional preparation of the elementary school physical education teacher," *Quest*, Monograph XVIII, June 1972.
25. Hartman, Betty G., "Training women to coach," *Journal of Health, Physical Education, and Recreation*, Vol. 39, No. 1, January 1968.
26. Hendrix, John, Edward Coates, and Charles Mand, "The public school: a partner in teacher preparation," *Proceedings*, Annual Meeting of the National College Physical Education Association for Men, Portland, Oregon, 1971.
27. Hoffman, Ronald, "Multiple teaching experiences in the professional program," *Journal of Health, Physical Education, and Recreation*, October 1969.
28. Jenny, John H., *Physical Education, Health Education, and Recreation: Introduction to Professional Preparation for Leadership*, New York: The Macmillan Company, 1961.
29. Jensen, Gordon, "Professional preparation panel reports," *Journal of Health, Physical Education, and Recreation*, Vol. 42, No. 3, March 1971.
30. Jewett, Ann E., and Marie R. Mullan, "A conceptual model for teacher education," *Quest*, Monograph XVIII, June 1972.
31. Jones, Emlyn H., Robert P. Nye, and Barry G. Remley, "Outward Bound at Westchester State College," *Journal of Health, Physical Education, and Recreation*, Vol. 43, No. 9, November–December 1972.
32. Jordan, T. C., "Micro-teaching: a reappraisal of its value in teacher education," *Quest*, Monograph XV, January 1971.
33. Kaufman, Wayne, and Judy Pace, "Teaching internship," *Journal of Health, Physical Education, and Recreation*, Vol. 43, No. 9, November–December 1972.
34. Kroll, Walter P., *Perspectives in Physical Education*, New York: The Academic Press, 1971.
35. Larson, Leonard A., "Professional preparation for the activity sciences," Howard S. Slusher and Aileene S. Lockhart, *Anthology of Contemporary Readings*, Dubuque, Iowa: Wm. C. Brown Company, 1966, pp. 286–295.

36. Locke, L. F., "Teacher Education: One Minute to Midnight," Manuscript prepared for the National Conference on the Professional Preparation of the Elementary Specialist, 1972.

37. Lockhart, Aileene S., "The professional preparation of physical educators," *Contemporary Philosophies of Physical Education and Athletics,* Robert A. Cobb and Paul M. Lepley, Columbus, Ohio: Charles E. Merrill, 1973, pp. 200–212.

38. Love, Alice, and Patricia Barry, "The teacher education center in physical education," *Journal of Health, Physical Education, and Recreation,* Vol. 42, No. 4, April 1971.

39. McGlothlin, William J., *Patterns of Professional Education,* New York: G. P. Putnam's Sons, 1960.

40. McNeil, John D., *Toward Accountable Teachers,* New York: Holt, Rinehart, and Winston, 1971.

41. Meyers, Carleton R., "Getting to the core of professional education," *Journal of Health, Physical Education, and Recreation,* November 1962.

42. Miller, Ben, "Professional preparation for health education, physical education, and recreation," *Journal of Health, Physical Education, and Recreation,* Vol. 35, No. 5, May 1964.

43. Munch, Louis R., "Selection and retention procedures for undergraduate male physical education majors," unpublished doctoral dissertation, Springfield, Mass.: Springfield College, 1969.

44. Munroe, A. D., *Physical Education,* London: G. Bell and Son, 1972.

45. Nixon, John, and Ann E. Jewett, *An Introduction to Physical Education,* 7th edition, Philadelphia: W. B. Saunders Company, 1969.

46. Pape, Laurence A., and Louis E. Means, *A Professional Career in Physical Education.* Englewood Cliffs, N.J.: Prentice-Hall, 1963.

47. Poindexter, Hally B. W., and Carole Mushier, *Coaching Competitive Team Sports for Girls and Women,* Philadelphia: W. B. Saunders Company, 1973.

48. "Professional preparation in health education, physical education, and recreation education," Report of a National Conference, Washington, D.C.: American Association for Health, Physical Education, and Recreation, 1962.

49. "Professional preparation of the administrator of athletics," American Association for Health, Physical Education, and Recreation, Washington, D.C.: NEA, 1970.

50. Richardson, Deane E., "Minnesota modifies its major for men," *Journal of Health, Physical Education, and Recreation,* January 1969, p. 28.

51. _____, "Preparation for a career in public school athletic administration," *Journal of Health, Physical Education, and Recreation,* Vol. 42, No. 2, February 1971.

52. Russell, Frank W., "Effective personality as a factor in successful teaching," Unpublished Master's Thesis, University of Southern California at Los Angeles, 1937.

53. Salt, E. Benton, Grace I. Fox, and B. K. Stevens, *Teaching Physical Education in the Elementary School,* New York: The Ronald Press, 1960.

54. Servis, Margery, and Reuben B. Frost, "Qualities related to success in women's physical education professional preparation program," *Research Quarterly,* Vol. 38, No. 2, May 1967.

55. Seymour, Emery W., "Graduate study—search and research," unpublished paper presented at graduate dinner, Springfield College, September 1969.

56. Sherrill, Claudine, "A new approach to undergraduate professional preparation in adapted physical education," *The Physical Educator,* Vol. 30, No. 2, May 1973.

57. Snook, Chet, "The cooperating teacher: key to a successful student teaching experience," *The Physical Educator,* Vol. 30, No. 2, May 1973.

58. Snyder, Raymond A., and Harry A. Scott, *Professional Preparation in Health, Physical Education, and Recreation,* New York: McGraw-Hill, 1954.

59. *Standards for Accreditation of Teacher Education,* Washington, D.C.: National Council for Accreditation of Teacher Education, 1972.

60. Stiles, Lindley J., "State of the art of teacher education," *Quest,* Monograph XVIII, June 1972. By permission.

61. "Teacher training for physical education," International Council on Health, Physical Education, and Recreation, Questionnaire Report, Part II, revised, Washington, D.C., 1967–68.

62. Turner, Edward T., "Send the college professor back to high school," *Journal of Health, Physical Education, and Recreation,* Vol. 42, No. 8, October 1971.

63. Ulrich, Celeste, "The physical educator as teacher," *Quest,* Monograph VII, December 1966.

64. Wacker, Hazel, "The road ahead in preparing teachers of physical education," *Journal of Health, Physical Education, and Recreation,* Vol. 42, No. 2, February 1971.

65. "Washington State mini-conference on preparing teachers in a changing society," *Journal of Health, Physical Education, and Recreation,* Vol. 42, No. 9, November–December 1971.

66. Williamson, Warren, "A study of the professional preparation, coaching, and teaching experiences of coaches in 50 high schools in northeastern South Dakota," unpublished Master's Thesis, Brookings: South Dakota State College, 1954.

67. Wirsing, Marie E., *Teaching and Philosophy: A Synthesis,* Boston: Houghton Mifflin Company, 1972.

Administration: Concepts and Practices

Chapter 19

19.1 THEORETICAL CONSIDERATIONS

To manage an enterprise with skill and adroitness requires knowledge and good judgment; to lead a group effectively takes vision and courage; to both lead and manage to achieve common goals is the mark of the true administrator. As Lawrence Appley writes, "Mastery of the art of administration requires: comprehension of the forces at work; understanding of the exact nature of the responsibility; deep convictions supported by well-thought-out philosophies; competence; and skill." [54, p. xiv]

Administration in our schools and colleges exists for one purpose—to offer the students the best possible education. It is concerned with accomplishing the purposes of the institution and achieving its goals; its aim is to facilitate and improve instruction. The broad function of administration is identical to the function of the school itself. It involves examining alternatives and making sound decisions, dealing not only with the provision of facilities, equipment, personnel, and budgetary resources, but also with the establishment of an environment which will make possible the greatest development of students and faculty members. In short, administration exercises leadership and gets things done that will ensure the completion of the task.

Administration has been commonly classified into three basic types: (a) autocratic, (b) laissez-faire, and (c) democratic. A common misconception is that all administrators can be categorized specifically into one of these three types and that they then deal with all situations in that fashion. However, the majority of administrators recognize that particular situations and various individuals require different tactics and that they must manage each as a separate case. There are emergencies that call for commands and instantaneous response; there are planning sessions where wide participation and reaching a consensus of opinion are extremely important; there are instances in which able and competent leaders are in charge of a project and need very little guidance from the top administrators. The same executive may be autocratic in one situation, democratic in another, and laissez-faire in still another. The type of administration may be more a matter of attitude and philosophy than of the exact manner in which it is directed.

Autocratic administration. The administrator makes the decisions with little or no consultation with his subordinates. He then proceeds to disseminate directives and expects them to be carried out with no question. Authority and power at each step must be vested in one person and subordinates are expected to obey and see that their subordinates in turn are obedient to directions from above.

Situations in which it may be necessary to utilize at least some elements of autocratic procedures might be: (a) a surgeon and his team performing a delicate operation, (b) a military officer in charge of a company in the heat of battle, (c) a fire chief and his men fighting a blaze, and (d) a person in charge of a military base during an earthquake or hurricane. Even in these situations, however, it is possible to use democratic processes in formulating operating procedures and guidelines by participatory discussion and then training people in the emergency procedures so that little command-response activity is necessary.

The "benevolent despot," assuming he is experienced and competent, may be very effective and his organization might operate very efficiently if carefully organized and managed. The determining factors would be, however, the power and authority of the people in executive positions, the loyalty engendered, the quality of leadership, and the compensation and security of the employees.

Laissez-faire administration.   There are a number of administrators in the field of education who state that their philosophy of administration is to find and hire good people, support them with adequate resources, and then give them freedom to function. These administrators offer little in the way of guidance and leadership, almost ignore their subordinates until trouble occurs, and hold few meetings or discussions with regard to either planning or operation.

There are small educational operations in which this method has worked out quite well. In such cases, however, there is by the very nature of the school a great deal of interaction, advice, and feedback. The proximity of offices and classrooms, the common dining room, the almost universal participation in social and recreational functions, and the casual conversations in the corridors and elsewhere all make for mutual understanding and a realization of what needs to be done.

In most laissez-faire situations, however, there is a lack of serious communication, organization, and mutual understanding. The entire state of affairs sometimes becomes chaotic and eventually unmanageable.

Democratic administration.   General tenets of democracy which must be understood and applied include a belief in:

1. the dignity and personal worth of each individual.
2. shared aims and goals, accomplished through the participatory or representative process.
3. leadership as a function, not as a person. Democracy through its representative government curbs the power drives of strong men who seek to rule by autocratic methods.
4. equal opportunity for the self-realization of each individual.
5. participatory decision-making and cooperative action as the basis for administrative processes.
6. operation on the basis of fact. Research and human resources are utilized to arrive at the truth.
7. the solution of problems by reason, discussion, and face-to-face encounter.
8. freedom of speech, assembly, and publication.

Democratic administration does not relieve the executive of the responsibility to make decisions. It does not mean that all decisions are dependent on a favorable vote by the majority. The administrator is still responsible for making the decision.

It does mean, however, that before the decision is made, the director secures information and opinions from all sources and resolves the issue on the basis of all the facts, sound reasoning, full discussion, and his own best judgment. The good administrator is aware that implementation of whatever action is decided upon is crucial and that individuals usually are more enthusiastic about executing plans which they supported and helped formulate. Ordway Tead has eloquently explained democratic administration in the following paragraphs:

> Democratic administration is that direction and oversight of an organization which assures that aims are shared in the making, that working policies and methods are agreed to by those involved, that all who participate feel both free and eager to contribute their best creative effort, that stimulating personal leadership is assured, and that in consequence the total outcome maximizes the aims of the organization while also contributing to the growing selfhood of all involved in terms of clearly realized benefits. It means also that there is a periodic, orderly, shared review of control and of operating methods, that leadership in action, and that the necessary preparations of good training are all continuing as agreed and as agreeable.

> Democratic administration does not mean that the executive leadership is any less concerned than any other kind of administration with getting the job done economically and expeditiously. It means rather that it is crucially concerned with *how* this is best achieved on a long-run basis in terms of the attitudes and efforts of the participants. It is seeking to develop the kinds of attitudes and procedures which in experience prove to be those which most continuously realize the plural aims. There is no suggestion of softness, flabbiness, or vagueness in the temper of executive action pervaded by this outlook. To be sure, there are . . . real dangers to be guarded against. But what is profoundly needed for the realization of this kind of administration is the cultivation of those attitudes and practices which appealing leadership can alone provide. [54, pp. 134–135]

19.2 THE ADMINISTRATOR AT WORK

The administrator is always busy and seldom feels that he is "caught up" with his work. Correspondence, unexpected appointments, emergency meetings, and unsolved problems continue to flow into his office in a steady stream. Each day ends with a feeling that there is much unfinished business to which he must attend.

On the other hand, there is a good deal of satisfaction in feeling in the midst of important happenings, in knowing intimately what is going on, and in needing to keep the enterprise on an even keel. Whether serving as arbitrator in a personality conflict, assisting a student to decide what program to follow, discussing the personal future of a faculty member, planning a new building, or attending a meeting of the academic affairs commission to decide on a new curricular offering, the administrator is constantly dealing with interesting and significant matters. He need never feel useless. He generally senses that he is an important member of the team.

Most administrators in physical education have come up through the ranks. They have been teachers, coaches, researchers, athletic directors, or a combination of all of these. If they come from the teaching or coaching ranks, they often have a lost feeling because they no longer have much direct contact with the students and athletes. They must remember that their "team" now consists of staff members. If they keep this in mind, they will soon gain tremendous satisfaction from observing and leading their new team. Watching the program and facilities develop and true education take place can be deeply satisfying.

Ordway Tead has much to say about the work of the administrator. The following words are significant:

The administrator like any other creative artist works in and through a distinctive medium. But in his case the medium has three facets. It is a composite of the activities of the organization as such, of the human beings who compose it or relate to it, and of the total environmental setting in which both of these carry on. A going organization brings into being a real, if subjective, entity which has identifiable traits and which is at once affecting and being affected by all who are under its influence. [54, p. 7]

19.3 ADMINISTRATIVE PROCESSES
Various authors present different lists of administrative processes. In this text the following will be presented:

1. Planning
2. Organizing
3. Directing and coordinating
4. Evaluating and controlling.

Planning
Planning consists of working out a general scheme for accomplishing what needs to be done and the manner in which it must be done if the goals and purposes of the enterprise are to be achieved.

Steps in planning consist of (1) defining and clarifying the problem, (2) getting the facts, (3) analyzing the information at hand, (4) determining alternative courses of action, (5) deciding on what is to be done, and (6) arranging for implementation of the plan.

In moving through the steps outlined above, individuals doing the planning should consider previous plans, attempt to envision the consequences, establish priorities, keep the objectives and aims constantly in mind, and study the relationships of the new plan to all segments of the organization. Existing resources, calculated risks, time required, ease of control, and personnel required should be among the considerations. Possible societal changes, the cultural milieu, and the current political problems should be discussed.

Plans should be simple, yet clear and complete, they should provide for possible changes in circumstances and conditions, and there must be appropriate emphasis on the various phases of the program. Major factors must be given greater consideration than minor factors, with provision made for ease of adjustment.

Planning should be thought of as dynamic, participatory, and democratic. Where additional expertise is needed there should be no hesitation about bringing in consultants.

In a department of physical education, planning might include the following:

1. Formulating objectives, aims, and goals.
2. Developing policies governing the operation of the department.
3. Revising old curricula and planning program changes.
4. Planning new buildings and revising present facilities.
5. Estimating needs and making recommendations for new personnel.
6. Calculating financial needs and developing the budget.

Organizing

Organizing consists of analyzing the activities and functions that are necessary to accomplish the purposes of the organization, arranging them in effective and appropriate administrative units, and assigning the personnel to carry out the tasks.

In organizing a department, consideration should be given to (a) appropriate attention to each administrative unit, (b) efficiency of operation, (c) span of control, (d) economical functioning, (e) effective coordination, and (f) maximum utilization of each person's specialization.

A good organizer will clearly identify each person's responsibility and authority, indicate without confusion to whom each person reports, establish no unnecessary administrative units, and keep the spans of supervision workable. He will organize so as to take advantage of the special abilities of staff members and will study decentralization carefully.

In a sound organization, details will be delegated so as to leave each key executive with some time for planning and directing. Committees will be used when input from a number of people is needed or when important decisions must be made. Unnecessary committees are a waste of time and will not be appointed.

Organizing a division or college of health, physical education, and recreation will include drawing up an organizational chart, appointing committees, assigning duties and responsibilities to each staff member, analyzing the work load of each staff member, and giving constant attention to ways of improving the efficiency and effectiveness of the operation.

Directing and coordinating

Directing is that phase of administration which implements plans and decisions. Direction involves giving the signal to act, indicating what the action shall be, when it shall begin, and when it shall end. It begins with someone in authority, who has decided that action shall occur.

Coordinating is the interrelating of all the activities of an enterprise. It includes effective communication between staff members and particularly between the various units of the organization.

In directing and coordinating, it is important that instructions be clear and complete and that compliance is not only possible but reasonable. Instructions which are of major importance, cover a long period of time, or affect a variety of administrative units and people should always be in writing and carefully disseminated.

Standard operating procedures and guidelines clarify and simplify instructions. The rationale for issuing these should be included. They should be uniform in format and style and punched so that they can be filed in a looseleaf notebook. This facilitates revision and insertion of new instructions into the appropriate place.

When giving directions, the mission of the organization shall be kept in mind, the directions shall be given in a manner which will dignify the job to be done, and the wording shall be such as to leave no doubt as to meaning.

To provide effective coordination, modern technology should be employed, the activities of the various units should be harmonized as far as possible, and related activities should be housed as close to each other as possible. All employees should have a sense of working together as a team.

Verbal directions may be in the form of subtle suggestions, delegation of functions, assignment of a committee chairmanship, or direct commands. The individuals concerned, the task to be accomplished, and the circumstances surrounding the task must be considered in giving the most effective direction.

A director of physical education in an educational institution may ask a staff member if he would be willing to take charge of a conference. Another staff member may be directed to supervise the custodians in the gymnasium; a coach may be asked to report all injuries; special instructions may be issued as to how the budget shall be presented; a schedule for use of the gymnasium may be posted; regulations with regard to physical education uniforms may be disseminated; policies concerning student advisement may be formulated; instructions as to reporting grades may be drawn up and circulated. There are literally hundreds of ways in which directions may be given.

It becomes obvious, therefore, that definite rules with regard to issuing directions cannot be provided. The tone of voice, the attitude of the director, the wording of the message, and most of all the total atmosphere of the organization are significant. If the department is permeated by a feeling that all members are united in a common effort, if courtesy and dignity are prevalent, and if sincerity and unity of purpose prevail, directions will usually be accepted in the spirit in which they are given and democracy in administration will be evident.

Evaluating and controlling
Evaluation and control deal with the degree to which outcomes conform to aims and goals. It is the process that checks if performance is in accordance with plans. It is a continuous process consisting of many kinds of specific acts.

Evaluating may involve testing and measurement. Inasmuch as the goal of an educational institution is the education of the students, measuring their development and progress is part of evaluation. To accomplish this many kinds of tests are given, some measuring intelligence, some academic achievement, and others improvement in physical performance.

Controlling may involve reading and analyzing reports. It includes checking expenditures against budgetary allotments and occurs when progress reports are presented at faculty and committee meetings.

All staff members, particularly supervisors, are involved in evaluating and controlling. These functions are interwoven with all other administrative processes. Controlling is one of the major responsibilities of all executives. Administrators cannot relieve themselves of the responsibility for control. Every person to whom authority and responsibility are delegated serves also as a point of control in the total operation.

Control points in physical education may be the staff members responsible for instruction in different subject matter areas, the director of athletics, the director of the women's program, the person in charge of aquatics, the chairman of the curriculum committee, the department's representative on the student progress committee, or the custodian of equipment. Control must be tied to individual responsibility. The culmination of evaluation and control is corrective action.

19.4 FUNCTIONS AND DUTIES OF ADMINISTRATORS

Administrative functions and duties include:

1. Policy formulation
2. Employment and supervision of personnel
3. Program planning and conduct
4. Managing supplies and equipment
5. Budget and finance management
6. Public relations
7. Counseling and guidance
8. Reporting.

Policy formulation

A policy is a statement that serves as a guide to members of the organization. Policies are broad general statements rather than specific instructions as to procedure.

Sound administrative policies should serve as the basis for operating a physical education department. Those who try to administer such an educational unit without such policies soon find their decisions become inconsistent, time is wasted because each situation requires individual fact finding and separate consideration, and the entire operation tends to become chaotic.

Principles which should guide the formulation and administration of department policies include the following.

1. Those whom the policies will effect should have a voice in their formulation.
2. Policies should be based on all the factual information that can be gathered about that particular topic.
3. Wholehearted cooperation in the implementation of a policy is related to the degree of participation in its formulation.
4. Policies should be flexible enough to cover a reasonable range of diverse situations. They should not be so innocuous as to lose all meaning.
5. Policies should be reviewed regularly and revised when conditions indicate the need.

Policies which might be included in departments of physical education would deal with the following:

1. Scheduling the use of facilities
2. Student teaching
3. Staff travel
4. Class attire
5. Reporting accidents
6. Absences from class
7. Grading procedures
8. Athletic trips
9. Budget procedures
10. Staff ethics
11. Use of stenographic assistance
12. Personnel welfare.

Employment and supervision of personnel
When searching for and selecting a new staff member, the foremost principle should be to secure the best available person for the position. Other matters such as age, sex, ethnic background, and so on may need consideration for practical reasons, but when friendship, politics, bias, or other like considerations enter the decision, one is usually asking for trouble.

The first step should be a careful analysis of exactly what qualifications are needed for the new position. A written description of the position usually helps to clarify the situation and helps weed out unqualified candidates. Personal qualities, education, experience, and attitude toward the position are the crucial items to be examined by the screening committee and the employer. Academic achievements, extracurricular experiences, honors awarded, record of publications, and specific teaching strengths should be carefully analyzed and considered. Recommendations are very important but must be reviewed with caution. The relationship of the candidate to the one who recommends should be carefully weighed. Both written and oral communications with the candidate are urged. A screening committee is often helpful but should be guided by at least one or two experienced individuals. They should recommend two or three names to the director, who is responsible for the final choice.

After people have been hired they will benefit by careful orientation and good supervision. Supervisors play a vital role in the schools where they are employed. They can be extremely helpful to their principal or director because they orient new staff members, assist them with their problems, and evaluate their performance. Supervisors should be helpful and empathetic and not overly negative in their criticism. They should be thoroughly qualified by both education and experience for their important role.

Program planning and conduct

This is the heart of the operation of the organization and needs the careful attention of all administrators and other staff members. In Chapter 10, the development and content of the program is treated in considerable detail. It should be mentioned, however, that while much of the detail with regard to program must be left to the teachers and academic leaders, no administrator should so isolate himself from the program that he loses sight of that aspect completely. This, too, is his ultimate responsibility.

Managing supplies and equipment

The purchase, issuance, and care of supplies and equipment have become an increasingly demanding responsibility. While much of the detail involved in this aspect of administering can be delegated, the director must stay somewhat involved.

The coach usually wants and should have an important voice in the purchase of athletic equipment. The selection of archery, skiing, aquatic, and other specialized physical education equipment also requires the knowledge and experience of the specialist. Nevertheless the administrator usually has to handle the details of finalizing the purchases, storage and issue, and repair and maintenance. A few suggestions and guidelines are the following:

1. Where the school system can afford to furnish all physical education and athletic equipment, it is recommended that they do so. This provides desired uniformity, higher quality merchandise for the money expended, and a more efficient system of laundry and issue.

2. The person with the most expertise should serve as the consultant on each kind of athletic and physical education equipment. This may be the coach, the athletic director, or the teacher.

3. The purchase of good quality merchandise is usually the most economical in the long run. This assumes that an effective procedure for issuing and accounting for all the items exists and that losses through pilfering and theft are minimal.

4. Early ordering of equipment is strongly recommended. This makes possible the rectifying of mistakes and more efficient storage and issue.

5. The installation of a school laundry to wash one's own towels, T-shirts, sweat socks, and other such items is becoming a rather common practice. Both from the standpoint of economy and service, this is usually recommended.

6. Adherence to the policies governing purchasing procedures should be rigidly enforced. Requisitions, purchase orders, and other formalities required by school regulations are important and only emergency purchases should be made in any other manner.

7. An up-to-date inventory should be maintained by the equipment custodian. This is an important step in efficient equipment management.

8. It is important to deal with individuals and companies that can be trusted. Established firms and salesmen with whom one has dealt for many years are usually worthy of such confidence.

9. An honest and intelligent equipment custodian is invaluable. If such a person also has the personality and sense of humor to get along well with the students and coaches, he will be "worth his weight in gold."

Budget and financing management

There is probably no aspect of administration that requires more attention and care than the one dealing with budget and finance. Mistakes, carelessness, minor dishonesties, or inefficiency in this area can cost a person his job more quickly than in almost any other. Meticulous care and integrity in dealing with finances usually reflects favorably on the entire administrative operation.

Most educational institutions have highly qualified comptrollers who establish the basic policies for all financial management. It is strongly recommended that the director of physical education work closely with this person on all financial matters. When it comes to crucial decisions on the budget and the allocation of funds to departments, such a sound relationship will be a positive influence.

Budget administration consists essentially of four steps:

1. Gathering information
2. Preparing the budget
3. Presenting the budget
4. Expending the funds.

Each of these steps involves detailed procedures and recommended practices. Every administrator should familiarize himself thoroughly with these so as to increase his effectiveness in this role.

The budget also serves as an effective control point. The director usually has to sign all requisitions and purchase orders. In this way he can observe what is happening in the various aspects of the program. He can also control unnecessary expenditures and stop those requisitions on accounts were the funds have already been exhausted.

Public relations
The success of any program in which the public is deeply involved is enhanced
by good public relations. The public is vitally interested in its schools and generally
concerned about physical education and athletics. The community supports the
schools financially and all departments depend on the goodwill of the taxpayers.
The physical education program is often vulnerable and one of the first to suffer
in times of financial crisis. The more favorably physical education is viewed by the
community, the less likely it is to be the target of budget cuts.

Edward Voltmer and Arthur Esslinger list six principles which constitute a
sound basis for a public relations program in physical education. These are:

1. The public relations program must be based on truth.
2. The best foundation for good public relations is a sound program.
3. The public relations program should be continuous.
4. Public relations is a two-way process between the community and the
   schools.
5. A knowledge of what the public thinks about the schools is essential.
6. The effective public relations program involves all school personnel. [55, pp.
   453–456]

These six principles are a good foundation upon which to build a public
relations program. If the physical education program is good and the relationship
between the students and teachers is what it should be, there is no great need
for much else. However, in almost every school there are a few incidents which
damage the image of the program, or an ineffective teacher whose students dislike
classes in physical education. It takes a great deal of positive and constructive
work to counteract the effect of one or two such poor situations.

The public relations program does involve all school personnel. The principal, custodian, coach, school nurse, dietician, and superintendent—all have dealings with the public or with the students whose parents live in the community. Many
of these individuals do not fully realize the important part they play in keeping the
public informed and happy. The director needs to remind them of their role and
indicate how they can be of assistance.

The need for continuous public relations efforts is also stressed. The news
media, civic clubs, churches, chambers of commerce, and social agencies are vital
factors in maintaining the necessary community-school interaction and enhancing
the relationships. The involvement of teachers in community affairs and projects
is also helpful. When people in the community realize that school personnel are
interested in their community and are willing to assist in its development they, in
turn, become responsive.

Counseling and guidance
The director of physical education, whether he intends it or not, becomes an
advisor to many students and faculty members. The physical education staff takes
care of most routine matters and settles many problems. The serious ones, those

not easily solved, very often are referred to the director. The faculty member who fails to get promoted, the student who thinks he was treated unfairly, the teacher whose father passed away, the senior who wants help choosing a graduate school, the freshman who has difficulty adjusting, and the coach who is unreasonable in his demands all eventually come to the director. He in turn must listen, discuss, reason, advise, and adjudicate. Occasionally problems of dismissal or severance from the college must be handled.

There are also cases wherein faculty members or students have serious health problems, both physical and mental. The administrator's role in such instances is to make appropriate referrals. He should never assume the role of either a physician or psychiatrist. He should have enough knowledge about such things, however, to sense when referrals are necessary and to whom the individuals should be directed.

Reporting
Reports of many kinds are required of any executive who is in charge of an organizational unit or an activity. There are many institutions in which annual or biennial reports of the entire organization are required. Reports of federally funded projects, special conferences, changes in program, financial status, athletic records, enrollment figures, workloads of faculty members, and courses added and deleted are among those requested in most institutions. Placement reports, funds raised and expended, speeches given, days absent because of illness, innovative practices, and equipment purchases are others.

Besides written reports, the director should pay careful attention to the opportunity to relate progress or requirements at cabinet meetings, Board of Trustees meetings, commission meetings, committee meetings, and face-to-face conferences with superiors. There may be no formal report required but opportunities to keep high-level officials informed often constitutes the most effective kind of reporting.

19.5 MOTIVATION AND LEADERSHIP
There are administrators who know and practice good management techniques and who, on the surface, appear to be excellent executives. And yet, for some reason or other, they fail to accomplish their goals and are eventually replaced. What are the reasons?

Very often such a situation can be traced to poor morale, an apathetic spirit among the staff, and a lack of real leadership. Motivation, enthusiasm, and a concern for the accomplishment of the mission are generally to be lacking.

Esprit de corps is present when individuals take pride in the high standards of performance in their group, when there is a singleness of purpose among members, when there is enthusiastic support for the efforts of leaders, and when individuals are willing to subordinate their own selfish interests for the welfare of the group and the accomplishment of group goals.

In recent studies dealing with motivation, there has been considerable evidence supporting the idea that important things are accomplished when the members of an organization look beyond material incentives and rewards to higher motivational factors. The idea that profit making, personal wealth, and material rewards are the most important motivating factors has been repudiated to a large extent. There is no question that the drive for food when hungry, water when thirsty, and security when threatened are intense motivating factors, but they are vital factors rather than materialistic ones. Neither are there many situations in the United States where these are urgent. Most people who are employed in the educational institutions of the United States have enough to eat and drink and are reasonably secure. Other motivating factors then take precedence.

The emphasis now is rather on a feeling of personal worth, on each member of the organization perceiving himself as an important member of a team, and on a feeling that he is growing and more closely approaching his potential.

To be most effective, teachers, coaches, and other staff members should perceive the purposes and goals of the physical education department as being worthy of their best efforts and as being related to their own development and advancement. They should feel that their particular role is a contributing one and that the students and athletes in the school are benefitting from the program.

To put forth their best efforts, staff members must find their work meaningful. Their goals and ambitions should be compatible with those of the department and the school. They must feel a sense of mission in their work and must feel that their role has some significance.

The true leader can engender in a staff this sense of mission. To do so, he himself should be completely committed to the purposes and goals of the school. He should be willing to work as hard and put in as many hours as the staff. He should have the courage and determination necessary to follow things through to completion. He should have vision to see a bit farther ahead than his subordinates. He should be willing to fight for the department and the staff if necessary.

This is not to say that progressive personnel policies are unimportant. A sound retirement program, good health insurance, generous sabbatical leave regulations, competitive salaries, and other fringe benefits do much to recognize the importance of a teacher's task and the prestige of the profession. If administrators lack interest in such benefits, morale soon drops. When, however, these factors are comparable to those at similar institutions, it is inspirational leadership which increases the esprit de corps and raises achievements to new levels.

19.6 ADMINISTRATIVE RESPONSIBILITIES OF TEACHERS AND COACHES
Every teacher and coach will have some administrative responsibilities and duties which are for the purpose of assisting the director or chairman. Public relations, legal liability, committee work, selecting equipment, making arrangements for athletes to travel, and dealing with discipline problems are administrative tasks undertaken by all teachers and coaches. Not only should they have some competence in the performance of these tasks but they should have some understanding of the larger and more comprehensive responsibilites of the director. Professional preparation programs should include appropriate experiences in organization and administration for all those majoring in physical education or pursuing specialized courses in coaching. For those intending to make administration a full time career, extensive graduate work in the area is necessary.

19.7 ADMINISTRATIVE GUIDELINES AND PRINCIPLES

Administration covers such a broad spectrum of activities that the selection of pertinent principles and guidelines is difficult. Nevertheless it is believed that a list of such suggestions may be helpful to the young adminstrator and might even help the one who has spent some years at the task.

1. Try to develop pride in the organization. This kind of pride comes only with high-quality performance.

2. If you ask someone to do something, follow through to see that it gets done. Usually you get what you expect in this regard.

3. Emphasize "completed staff work." Staff members should be trained to do the necessary coordination and to follow through to see that something gets done when it is their responsibility.

4. Keep your superiors informed. Expect your staff to keep you informed.

5. Try to arrange for occasional face-to-face communications with your staff members. This keeps relationships warm and personal.

6. Use written communications to confirm details and expectations. Request written explanations sparingly.

7. When faced with an unpleasant task, get it over with. Dragging it out wastes energy and causes needless worry.

8. Prepare your budget meticulously and in detail. Time spent on this phase of administration can pay rich dividends. Be honest about your requirements.

9. Be scrupulously careful about financial records and expect the same of your staff members.

10. Don't ask for money or equipment as a personal favor. Justify a program. Do not place yourself under obligation to anyone.

11. When your department has a justifiable need, be persistent in requesting it. Use both written and verbal requests and justifications.

12. Plant ideas—sometimes they emerge as the brainchild of another person.

13. Keep doing the little things. They sometimes add up to great accomplishments.

14. Try not to bring worries home with you. Leave them in the office.

15. If you believe in a project and cannot get 100 percent of the staff to go along, don't worry. Go ahead with those who will follow.

16. All policies should be carefully interpreted to staff members so misunderstandings will be avoided.

17. It is especially important to interpret physical education to the public—it has not been completely understood in the past.

18. An administrator cannot do everything himself and so is dependent on other people. His ability to judge and appraise people is therefore vitally important.

19. A leader depends on his subordinates for success. His choice of staff members is therefore crucial.

20. Administrators seldom deal with a horde of individuals but with small, well-knit groups. The desire to stand well with "the team" is an understandable characteristic. All administrators should understand and appreciate these feelings.

21. "You cannot antagonize and influence at the same time"—J. S. Knox. [54, p. 133]

22. An administrator must know and understand people. An important function of a leader is to place the right person in the right spot. Many individuals perform excellently in one position and poorly in others.

23. It is important to be able to judge people. An executive often has to make decisions when facts are unknown or unavailable. In such instances he often has to rely on the opinions of people.

24. Accentuate the positive. Too much criticism and too much pessimism do not create a good climate for progress.

25. Be a good listener. At times it is more important for the administrator to find out what the staff thinks than for the staff to learn what the director thinks.

26. When staff members are rewarded by a promotion or a raise in salary, let them know they have earned it rather than make them feel they are receiving a favor.

27. Let your staff members know where you stand on an issue. A definite "no" is often better than a qualified "yes."

28. Make people on your staff want to accomplish things.

29. Be generous with your recognition of honors and achievement. But be consistent and impartial.

30. Expect great things from your staff. Expect great things to happen. Expectations often lead to growth and accomplishments.

31. "He who trusts men will make fewer mistakes than he who distrusts them."—Cavour.*

32. Administrators should constantly remind themselves that educational institutions exist for the benefit of the students. Their welfare and education must take precedence, in the final analysis, over all other considerations.

The following prayer written by Robert Katz is a fitting conclusion to this chapter on administrative principles. It is therefore quoted as it was found in the Harvard Business Review.

---

*Tryon Edwards, *Useful Quotations,* New York: Grosset and Dunlap, 1927, p. 661.

An Administrator's Prayer

Grant me the self-awareness to know honestly what I am, what I can do, and what I cannot;

Grant me the judgment to channel my energies into those avenues which best utilize my abilities and do not require talents which I do not possess;

Grant me the wisdom to admit error cheerfully and learn from my experiences, that I may grow and develop and avoid repetition of mistakes;

Grant me the humility to learn from others, even though they be younger, less experienced, or of humbler station than I;

Grant me the courage to make decisions whenever they are necessary and to avoid rashness when they are not;

Grant me the sensitivity to judge the reactions of others that I may modify my actions to meet the needs of those affected;

Grant me the consideration to recognize the worth of each individual, and to respect all those with whom I have contact, neither stifling their development nor exalting myself at their expense;

Grant me the perspicacity to acknowledge that I can be no more effective than my subordinates enable me to be, and to deal with them so that they can help me by helping themselves;

Grant me the tolerance to recognize mistakes as a cost of true learning and to stand behind my subordinates, accepting my responsibility for their actions;

Grant me the insight to develop a personal philosophy, that my life may have more meaning and satisfaction and that I may avoid capricious action under the pressures of expediency;

Grant me the patience to live realistically with my circumstances, striving always for the better, but recognizing the perils of too rapid or drastic change;

Grant me all these things, dear Lord, that I may live a more useful life, through serving my fellow men and, through them, serve Thee.*

SELECTED REFERENCES

1. American Association for Health, Physical Education, and Recreation, *Developing Democratic Human Relations,* first yearbook, Washington D.C., 1951.
2. Arnold, P. J., *Education, Physical Education and Personality Development,* New York: Atherton Press, 1968.
3. Bell, Wendell, Richard J. Hill, and Charles R. Wright, *Public Leadership,* San Francisco: Chandler Publishing Company, 1961.
4. Bellows, Roger, *Creative Leadership,* Englewood Cliffs, N.J.: Prentice-Hall, 1959.

*Robert L. Katz, *Harvard Business Review,* January–February 1957. By permission.

5. Bischoff, David, "Administrator," *Quest,* Monograph VII, December 1966.
6. Brown, Camille, and Rosalind Cassidy, *Theory in Physical Education,* Philadelphia: Lea and Febiger, 1963.
7. Bucher, Charles A., *Administrative Dimensions of Health and Physical Education Programs, Including Athletics,* St. Louis: The C. V. Mosby Company, 1971.
8. Butler, George D., *Community Recreation,* New York: McGraw-Hill, 1940.
9. Cary, Lee J. (ed.) *Community Development as a Process,* Columbia, Mo.: University of Missouri Press, 1970.
10. Cogan, Max, "Creative approaches to physical education," Paper presented at the 73rd Annual Meeting of the National College Physical Education Association for Men, Chicago, December 1969.
11. Conant, James B., *Slums and Suburbs,* New York: The New American Library, 1961.
12. Corbin, H. Dan, *Recreation Leadership,* Englewood Cliffs, N.J.: Prentice-Hall, 1953.
13. Dauer, Victor P., *Dynamic Physical Education for Elementary School Children,* Minneapolis, Minn.: Burgess Publishing Company, 1971.
14. Daughtrey, Greyson, and John B. Woods, *Physical Education Programs: Organization and Administration,* Philadelphia: W. B. Saunders Company, 1971.
15. Driscoll, Sandra, and Doris A. Mathieson, "Goal-centered individualized learning," *Journal of Health, Physical Education, and Recreation,* September 1971.
16. Fait, Hollis F., *Physical Education for the Elementary School Child: Experiences in Movement,* 2nd edition, Philadelphia: W. B. Saunders Company, 1971.
17. Fleishman, Edwin A., *The Structure and Measurement of Physical Fitness,* Englewood Cliffs, N.J.: Prentice-Hall, 1964.
18. Fox, Eugene R., and Barry L. Sysler, *Life-Time Sports for the College Student,* Dubuque, Iowa: Kendall/Hunt Publishing Company, 1972.
19. Friermood, Harold T., and J. Wesley McVicar, *Basic Physical Education in the YMCA,* New York: Association Press, 1962.
20. Frost, Reuben B., "The director and the staff," *Administration of Athletics in Colleges and Universities,* Edward S. Steitz (ed.), Washington, D.C.: American Association for Health, Physical Education, and Recreation, 1971.
21. _____, "The role of health, physical education and recreation personnel in community development," Paper presented at the Workshop in Community Education and Community Development, Flint, Michigan, November 1965.
22. Gardner, John W., *Excellence,* New York: Harper and Row, 1961.
23. Gellerman, Saul W., *The Uses of Psychology in Management,* London: Collier-MacMillan, 1970.
24. George, Jack F., and Harry A. Lehmann, *School Athletic Administration,* New York: Harper and Row, 1966.
25. Godfrey, Barbara B., and Newell C. Kephart, *Movement Patterns and Motor Education,* New York: Appleton-Century-Crofts, 1969.
26. Graham, Grace, *The Public School in the New Society,* New York: Harper and Row, 1969.
27. Griffiths, Daniel E., *Administrative Theory,* New York: Appleton-Century-Crofts, 1959.
28. Hall, J. Tillman, et. al., *Administration: Principles, Theory and Practice,* Pacific Palisades, Calif.: Goodyear Publishing Company, 1973.
29. Hauck, Eldon, "Evaluation of the school physical education program," *The Physical Educator,* Vol. 23, No. 3, October 1966.

30. Havel, Richard C., and Emery W. Seymour, *Health, Physical Education, and Recreation,* New York: The Ronald Press, 1961.
31. "Inner City Physical Education," *Proceedings,* Professional Education Section, Eastern District Association for Health, Physical Education, and Recreation Convention, Philadelphia, 1971.
32. Jennings, Eugene E., *An Anatomy of Leadership,* New York: Harper and Row, 1960.
33. Jewett, Ann E., "Would you believe public schools 1975?," *Journal of Health, Physical Education, and Recreation,* Vol. 42, No. 3, March 1971.
34. Kirchner, Glenn, *Physical Education for Elementary School Children,* 2nd edition, Dubuque, Iowa: Wm. C. Brown Company, 1970.
35. Kluckholn, Clyde, "The American culture," *Background Readings for Physical Education,* Ann Paterson and Edmond C. Hallberg (eds.), New York: Holt, Rinehart, and Winston, 1967.
36. Kraus, Richard, *Recreation and Leisure in Modern Society,* New York: Appleton-Century-Crofts, 1971.
37. Kustermann, Howard H., "Changes to match the times," *The YMCA World Service Reporter,* Fall 1972.
38. Likert, Rensis, *New Patterns of Management,* New York: McGraw-Hill, 1961.
39. McGregor, Douglas, *Leadership and Motivation,* Warren G. Bennis and Edgar H. Schein (eds.), Cambridge, Mass.: The MIT Press, 1966.
40. McIntyre, Martin, "A model for the 70's," *Journal of Health, Physical Education, and Recreation,* Vol. 44, No. 9, November-December 1973.
41. Meditch, Carl, "Physical educators plan facilities," *Journal of Health, Physical Education, and Recreation,* Vol. 45, No. 1, January 1974.
42. Meyers, Carleton R., and T. Erwin Blesh, *Measurement in Physical Education,* New York: The Ronald Press, 1962.
43. Munroe, A. D., *Physical Education,* London: G. Bell and Son, 1972.
44. Newman, William H., Charles E. Summer, and Warren E. Kirby, *The Process of Management,* 2nd edition, Englewood Cliffs, N.J.: Prentice-Hall, 1967.
45. Nixon, John E., and Ann E. Jewett, *An Introduction to Physical Education,* 7th edition, Philadelphia: W. B. Saunders Company, 1969.
46. Nolte, M. Chester, *An Introduction to School Administration,* New York: The Macmillan Company, 1966.
47. *Official Handbook,* National Federation of State High School Associations, Elgin, Illinois, 1972–1973.
48. Resick, Matthew C., Beverly Seidel, and James G. Mason, *Modern Administrative Practices in Physical Education and Athletics,* Reading, Mass.: Addison-Wesley Publishing Company, 1970.
49. *The Role of Public Education in Recreation,* California Association for Health, Physical Education, and Recreation and the California State Department of Education, San Francisco: The Trade Pressroom, 1960.
50. Sage, George H. (ed.), *Sport and American Society: Selected Readings,* Reading, Mass.: Addison-Wesley Publishing Company, 1970.
51. Schwank, Walter C., "The role of athletics in education," *Administration of Athletics in Colleges and Universities,* Edward S. Steitz (ed.), Washington, D.C.: American Association for Health, Physical Education, and Recreation, 1971.
52. Seidel, Beverly L., and Matthew C. Resick, *Physical Education: An Overview,* Reading, Mass.: Addison-Wesley Publishing Company, 1972.

53. Sheehan, Thomas J., *An Introduction to the Evaluation of Measurement Data in Physical Education,* Reading, Mass.: Addison-Wesley Publishing Company, 1971.
54. Tead, Ordway, *The Art of Administration,* New York: McGraw-Hill, 1951. By permission.
55. Voltmer, Edward F., and Arthur A. Esslinger, *The Organization and Administration of Physical Education,* 4th edition, New York: Appleton-Century-Crofts, 1967.
56. Webb, Ewing T., and John B. Morgan, *Strategy in Handling People,* New York: Garden City Publishing Company, 1930.

Index

Index